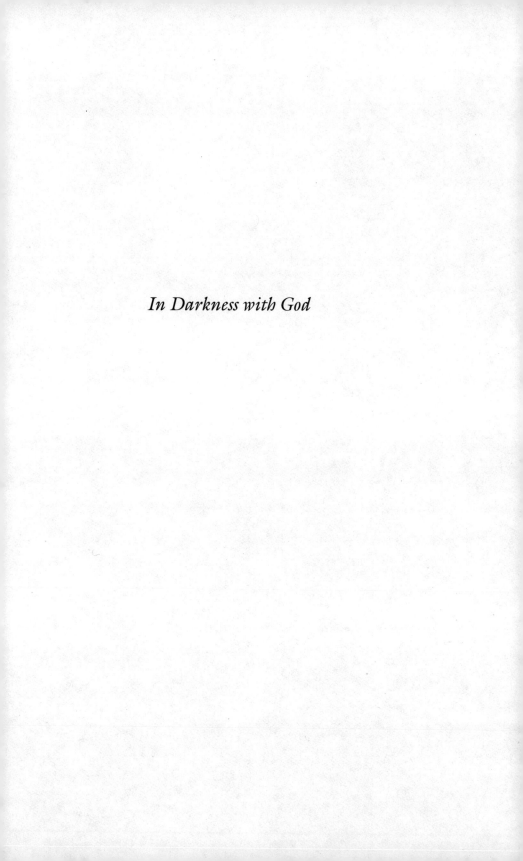

In Darkness with God

The Kent State University Press

Kent, Ohio & London

In Darkness with God ◆ ◆ ◆

The Life of Joseph Gomez, a Bishop in the African Methodist Episcopal Church

Annetta Louise Gomez-Jefferson

© 1998 by The Kent State University Press, Kent, Ohio 44242
ALL RIGHTS RESERVED
Library of Congress Catalog Card Number 98-14941
ISBN 0-87338-607-8
Manufactured in the United States of America

04 03 02 01 00 99 98   5 4 3 2 1

Library of Congress Cataloging-in-Publication Data
Gomez-Jefferson, Annetta Louise, 1927–
    In darkness with God : the life of Joseph Gomez, a bishop in the
African Methodist Episcopal Church / Annetta Louise Gomez-Jefferson.
    p.   cm.
    Includes bibliographical references and index.
    ISBN 0-87338-607-8 (hardcover : alk. paper) ∞
    1. Gomez, Joseph Antonio Guminston, 1890–1979.   2. African
Methodist Episcopal Church—Clergy—Biography.   3. Bishops—United
States—Biography.   I. Title.
BX8473.G65G65   1998
287'.8'092—dc21
[B]   98-14941

British Library Cataloging-in-Publication data are available.

Contents

◈ ◈ ◈

Foreword

by Bishop Hubert Nelson Robinson,
Eighty-fourth Bishop
African Methodist Episcopal Church

◈ They called him "The Little Giant," and that he was. The generation who knew him, his own peers and those younger, often sought what was behind the man and what made him the character he was. There was a mystery never communicated orally, but it was spelled out for all to read and see by the way this man confronted all life.

Forefather of the free-thinkers and revolutionary leaders of his day in the church he served, as a youth he proposed positions of leadership for the pastors older than he, while the younger ministers all sought the origin of his mystique. The majority of people liked the fellowship of his company. He was at his best when, in conversation, he challenged with a proposition, provoking answers and stimulating thought.

His work influenced a generation of workers and leaders, both lay and clerical. This is particularly evident in the free-thinking Laymen's Organization now found in the A.M.E. Church. As theologian, teacher, prophet of God, he thundered with telling arguments against wrongs and moral subversions of individual and corporate acts within the church.

As a little giant, a midget among those arrayed against him in proposition and political infighting, he was for many years not a favorable candidate for episcopal honors. However, as time passed and light shone in the darkness with which his adversaries had enshrouded him, he realized the height of his ambition, to be a bishop in the African Methodist Episcopal Church.

The darkness with which he wrestled during the course of his life is told in this biography, given us by his younger daughter. Herein are the aspects of the man who was known among the circles of Christendom and the African Methodist Episcopal Church, a life which spanned the decades from 1890 to 1979: Joseph Gomez, the Little Giant.

He was diminutive of physical stature small in body.
He was born on a small tiny island,
His name was short—simply Joseph Gomez.

But size is never the measure of true greatness;
For despite his size and brevity of name:

He was tall enough to bump the sky.
His arms were long enough to sweep aside the clouds.
He had imagination great enough to envision great things.
His mind big enough to conceive great ideas.
He had sagacity and wisdom to rightly divide momentous issues.
Tongue liquid enough to enunciate great principles.
Oratory sweeping enough to move great crowds;
A master both in pulpit and on the platform.

He was at home in occasional, prophetical and political forensics.
A man of integrity when involved in the Right.
A man fearless in times of opposition.

Above all he was:

a servant of his Race.
a servant of his Pastors.
a servant of his Church
a servant of his Family
a servant of his GOD.

Written and recited by Bishop Hubert N. Robinson at the Memorial Service during the General Conference of 1980.

◈ ◈ ◈

Preface

◈ *In Darkness with God* was carefully conceived and developed as a result of the efforts of several people who felt that the epic life of Joseph Gomez should be recorded as an inspiration for all who struggle for individual and collective liberation.

First, my mother, Hazel Thompson Gomez, spent most of her life collecting articles, pictures, letters, speeches, minutes, and documents about or by my father. Thank God she was the "pack rat" we jokingly and lovingly called her. It must have been with extreme difficulty that she carried this material with her as she and Joseph moved from one city to the other, in the typical Methodist tradition.

Second, my older son, Curtis Gomez, early became interested in tracing the family background. He spent a great deal of time traveling to Madeira, Portugal, and Antigua, talking to villagers, scouring through official records in government buildings, locating West Indians in New York, gathering whatever material he could that would lead him to a clear picture of his ancestors' and his grandfather's and grandmother's early years. In 1987 he paid my way to Antigua, the place of his grandfather's birth, so I could see firsthand where my father had spent his childhood. During the summers of 1993 and 1995 he took me to Madeira, where his great-great grandfather and great-great grandmother had been born and had lived before moving to Antigua. He felt that in order for the biography to depict accurately Joseph Gomez's character, it was essential that I go to the places of his roots.

Third, I have spent many years reading biographies, my favorite kind of literature, especially books about the lives of Black people. My passion for these stories seems now to have been prophetic, almost as if I had been preparing for this task all my life. For seven years I wrote series concerning

Black history and literature for WVIZ Educational Television Station in Cleveland, Ohio. During my research for the shows, it became obvious to me that so much of the history of Black Americans had not been recorded. For instance, many people, Black and white, felt that civil rights belonged exclusively to the 1960s. Except for Frederick Douglass, Harriet Tubman, Sojourner Truth, and a few others, little was known about the many Blacks who paved the way for the leaders of the 1960s. It was my desire to help correct this misconception; at the time, however, I was not sure how to go about it.

After my father died in 1979, Cecilia Appiah, a Ghanaian, helped me take care of my mother. One morning she and I decided to go down into the basement to examine my father's papers and books, which had never been unpacked. We were amazed how much material my mother had amassed about my father and the African Methodist Episcopal Church. We spent the summer putting the papers and pictures in scrapbooks and about forty picture albums, not to mention all the A.M.E. Annual and General Conference minutes we filed on shelves. Reading the material made me realize not only how much my parents meant to me but how much the African Methodist Episcopal Church has meant and continues to mean to me—how much it has meant to countless Blacks who would never have had the opportunity to develop leadership skills had it not been for this church. How important, it seems to me, that its story and my father's be told. This material also helped me to understand more vividly the contribution my father had made, not only to the field of religion but in the area of civil rights. Here then was my answer. I would write a biography about my father and the church of which he was a part. It would include the social, economic, and political events that shaped his life, the life of the A.M.E. Church, and the lives of so many other Blacks—in other words, a book that could well be called *The Life and Times of Joseph Gomez*.

I decided finally on the title *In Darkness with God*, for two reasons. First it was a part of the title of the eulogy delivered by Bishop Hubert Robinson at my father's funeral in Detroit—"Joseph Gomez, the Man Who Stood in Darkness with God." Secondly, since most people associate God with light, the idea of my father walking in darkness with God, into the light, seemed appropriate.

The question for me became when I would have the time to write such a book, since I taught a full schedule of classes in theatre at The College of Wooster and directed plays in the winters and summers. During the academic year of 1986–1987, the college awarded me a Henry Luce Grant for Distinguished Scholarship to begin to write what had become for me an all-important biography. While on leave, I spent the year researching at

Wilberforce University, near Xenia, Ohio; in Cleveland, Ohio; St. Louis, Missouri; Detroit, Michigan; New York City; and Antigua. As I visited the various libraries, it came to me how valuable the Black press was in uncovering my story. Much of the activity of Blacks in the early part of the century would have been totally lost had it not been for these newspapers. Too much criticism and not enough appreciation has been accorded these pioneer editors, who had the foresight to record Black history in the making. My sincere thanks to them.

In September 1987 I returned to the classroom. I continued to write and research when I could, but it was not until the summer of 1989 that I was able to complete the manuscript. Prior to that time I had sent rough drafts to Bishops Hubert Robinson and Frederick Talbot; Revs. Joseph Brockington and Daryl Ward; to my coworkers Carol Stewart, Ken Goings, Terry Kershaw, Steve Moore, Deborah Hilty; to Calvin Hernton, who teaches Black literature at Oberlin College; and to Casper Jordan, librarian. The comments and corrections they provided were invaluable. In 1993, Dr. James Hodges, Chairperson of the History Department at Wooster, suggested I send the manuscript to the Kent State University Press. I was gratified when it expressed an interest in the book. The director of the press, John T. Hubbell, and the second reader, Dr. Dennis C. Dickerson, Historiographer of the African Methodist Episcopal Church, made important suggestions for tightening the manuscript. Again the question became, when would I have the time to make the changes? As you can see, the biography was a long time in the making.

In May of 1995 I retired from The College of Wooster. This gave me the leisure to complete another book I was working on, a book involving the history and literature of American Blacks in theatre, and to begin the monumental task of carefully editing and rewriting sections of my father's book. The most difficult element in writing a life of eighty-nine years is the question of what to include and what to leave out. Joseph Gomez did so much, and I had found a multitude of material, all of which seemed important to me; however, it became expedient for me to make choices.

In the biography I have tried to use the language of the period. During the first part of the book, Blacks are referred to as "Negro" and "Colored," as was the custom. Personally, I prefer the term "Black," because it was a long time before most of us realized the beauty and richness of "Blackness"—so brainwashed were we by white society. Thanks to those revolutionaries who showed us the way.

Finally, this biography was written in love for a father, a teacher, a spiritual guide, a friend. With the exception of two chapters that begin with quotes from his mentor, Reverdy Cassius Ransom, and his dear friend, Bishop Hubert Robinson, each chapter starts with a quote from my father. Throughout the book I have often let him speak for himself. Being a poet, he does so with eloquence and passion. His story is a "Yes!" to life, and an acceptance of the darkness that leads inevitably to the light of understanding and wisdom which is GOD.

◈ ◈ ◈

Acknowledgments

◈ Grateful thanks to my son Curtis Gomez, of New York City, who did most of the research for the first chapter and paid my way to Antigua and Madeira; my son Joseph Jefferson, of Wooster, Ohio, who stood beside me throughout this project and gave me the time to write and research; my sister, her husband, and children—Eula, Harold, Marvin, Annetta, and Gerald Williams; my aunt, Mary Gomez, of Woodland Park, Michigan; my cousin Lorraine Richardson Harper, of New York City.

Thanks also to my faithful and devoted secretary, Jo Ann Yoder; Henry Copeland, former president of The College of Wooster, who gave me two Luce Grants to finance this project; my colleagues who offered criticism—Ken Goings, Terry Kershaw, Steve Moore, Deborah Hilty, Alphine Jefferson, Carolyn Buxton, James Hodges, James Perley, Susan Figge, and Laura and Keith James.

Wonderful friends allowed me to stay in their homes during my research: Maggie Sawyer (St. Louis), Cora and Shirley Lockhart (Detroit), Helen and Winifred Thompson (cousins from Xenia), Myrtle Teal Ransom (now deceased, of Wilberforce), Alwyn and Dorothy Talbot (Waco), Dorothy Smith (Cleveland).

I thank Arthur Bowers (New York); Cynthia Butler, Elizabeth Cornelius, John DeNully, Vincent Derrick, Daisy Pestana, Mary Thomas (now deceased, of Antigua); Bishop Hubert Robinson, Rev. Joseph Brockington, Delores Hunter, Jeanetta Woodcock, Rosa Gragg (Detroit); Casper Jordan (Atlanta); Monica Bowin (New Jersey); Geneva Clinton, Jeanette Long, Mrs. Vinton Anderson (St. Louis); Jane Lee Darr (Cleveland); Handley Hickey (Wilberforce); Annabelle Hicks (Cleveland); Bishop Fred Talbot (Little Rock); Bishop Frank Reid, Jr. (now deceased); Dr. J. W. Yancy, M. P. Harvey, Rev. and Mrs. C. C. Johnson, Rev. W. D. Johnson (Waco); Cecilia Appiah (Maryland); Daryl Ward (Dayton); Carol and Rev. Gordon Stewart (Cincinnati); Stephanie Shaw (Columbus, Ohio); Calvin Hernton

(Oberlin); Jewell Collier Richie (Altadina); Rev. Arthur Jones (Richmond); Michael Smith (Huntsville); Rev. Dwight E. Dillard, Sr. (Birmingham); Dr. Dennis C. Dickerson, historiographer of the A.M.E. Church (Williamstown).

I would also like to recognize the Schomburg Library staff (New York City); Cleveland, Detroit, St. Louis, Waco, New York public libraries; St. Louis Historical Society; Archives of Wilberforce University and Payne Theological Seminary, Wilberforce, Ohio; Archives of Paul Quinn College, Waco, Texas; Library of The College of Wooster, Wooster, Ohio; Library of Congress, Washington, D.C.

CHAPTER ONE

Dawning

Antigua, Trinidad, 1890–1908

Never given to defeat by the fell circumstances of fate or opposition, neither by the barriers of time or fortune, he was born
with an indomitable spirit and an unconquerable passion for
facing untried frontiers. . . . He was small in stature, but his
compatriots had to look up to see him, for his heights of vision
and his ideals made him lofty in stature. . . . They called him
"The Little Giant."
> —Eulogy delivered by Bishop Hubert N. Robinson at
> the funeral of Joseph Gomez, May 2, 1979, Bethel
> A.M.E. Church, Detroit, Michigan

◈ Joseph Antonio Guminston Gomes's eighty-nine-year odyssey began in
1890 in Willikies, a village on the island of Antigua in the Caribbean. He
was the first son of Rebecca Richardson, of African descent, and Manoel
Gomes, a Portuguese merchant. His arrival ensured the continuation of
unorthodox "firsts" for the Gomeses. Like his parents, he would courageously navigate trackless seas and flourish even in hostile environs.

Joseph's maternal great-grandmother was known as "Miss Providence"
(first name unknown). She lived with David Joseph, a slave who had been
born in Anquilla in 1814. As a teenager, David had come to Antigua with
his half-brother to help in the construction of a bridge. Later he worked
on the sugar estates. When emancipation came to Antigua in 1834, like
most other Blacks David chose not to continue to work for his former master, who was now offering the meager wage of six pence for a day's labor.
Some of his friends left for Trinidad soon after they were freed, but David
followed the lead of other acquaintances who moved to land outside the

estates, where they soon formed villages. Appropriately, they gave these villages such names as Freetown, Liberta, and Freeman. By 1842 there were twenty-seven such independent villages on the island.[1]

David moved his family to Willikies Village, which had received its name from Will Hickey, a wealthy "coloured" man. There David was able to amass a large amount of land, probably by availing himself of cheap "ten-acre land" originally set aside to attract new white settlers—when only a few whites took advantage of the offer, the land was sold to emancipated Blacks.[2]

As in most of the villages, the majority of people who inhabited Willikies were Black and poor. They lived in one-story, two-room "spit and fire" houses made of white clay, crowned with thatched roofs of "feeble grass." The names of the type of houses and the materials used to build them are indications of how precarious they were.[3] The villagers ate the fish they caught and the few yams, cassavas, or sweet potatoes in their gardens that managed to survive the severe droughts plaguing the island. These vegetables were complemented by mangoes, coconuts, pineapples, bananas, and other fruits found on the land.

David Joseph was one of the few villagers who fared well. A mason, he lived in a "wall house" which he built for himself. Some time in 1836 he and Miss Providence were blessed with a son, whom they named Richard Joseph; he was to become Joseph Gomes's maternal grandfather. Richard was affectionately called "Bojo" by the villagers. When he became a man, he changed his name to Joseph Richardson, because, he said, there were too many people in Antigua with the last name of "Joseph"; consequently, Rebecca (Joseph Gomes's mother) and all his other children carried the name "Richardson."[4]

Joseph Gomes's other maternal great-grandfather, a Mr. Nathaniel (first name unknown), married an octoroon, Mary Anne Gordon, the daughter of a mulatto mother and a father whose family had originated in Aberdeenshire, Scotland. Despising the fact that her birth had been the result of her mother's forced miscegenation with her white master, Mary Anne chose to marry a Black man rather than an octoroon like herself. It did not matter to her that according to white standards her Anglo-Saxon blood placed her "a cut above" her pure-Black husband. Mr. Nathaniel and Mary Anne gave birth to Sarah Nathaniel, who later became Rebecca's mother and Joseph Gomes's maternal grandmother.[5]

When Rebecca's parents met is not documented. They must have played together as children, since both lived in the same village. What is known is that some time in the 1860s Sarah Nathaniel and Joseph Richardson lived together (only approximately 30 percent of the couples on the island were legally married).[6] Sarah and Joseph had five children: Rebecca (called Zoe by the villagers), James, John, Manton, and Emma. Joseph made his living as a fisherman. In 1884, when Sarah was eight months pregnant with her last child, Joseph died in his fishing boat, apparently the victim of a heart attack. He was forty-eight, ten years older than Sarah, who suddenly found herself a widow with the responsibility of raising five children, one yet unborn.

Her greatest comfort during this period was her oldest daughter, Rebecca, who even as a child was strong willed and determined to achieve. Rebecca's favorite game was "bakery shop." Every afternoon she would slip away from the house and hide in a thick grove of trees. There in the shadows she would turn out hundreds of imaginary loaves for a crowd of invisible people waiting to taste her succulent bread. Today the older villagers refer to that spot as "Zoe's Oven."[7] It is ironic that this game became the real occupation of her future husband, and bread the means of prosperity in the early years of their relationship.

Rebecca's future baker (Joseph Gomes's father) was Manoel Gomes. He was born in the parish of Monte in Madeira, Portugal, some time during the late 1850s (because of the scarcity of records, the exact date cannot be known). He was the son of Antonio and Antonia Gomes. Antonia had had at least three children by a former marriage, Maria, Joao, and Jose.[8] The family loved their island home, encircled by the Atlantic Ocean. But the red clay–roofed houses ascending the picturesque mountains could not compensate for the poverty, illiteracy, and shortage of jobs.

Beginning in 1836, *enganhadores* ("deceivers") went through the parishes spreading propaganda about the vast opportunities to be found in the West Indies—opportunities for any family adventurous enough to come to work on the sugar estates. The British government's Sessional Papers of 1847–1848 made the venture more inviting by offering to pay the Portuguese for one year double the wages paid emancipated Blacks.[9] Before the end of the century, thirty-thousand Portuguese would go to British Guyana and thousands more to other parts of the West Indies.[10] Among the number who went to Antigua were Antonio and Antonia Gomes.

They traveled down steep, rugged mountain paths from Monte to Funchal, the capital of Madeira. There they stayed with friends while waiting for their passports and other papers to be processed. As was the custom, on the day of departure they went to the Catedral de Se to pray for a safe journey and good fortune in the New World. Finally, along with relatives, friends, and other passengers, they boarded a vessel, occupying that part of the ship designated "third class." Often these ships were little more than cattle boats, but to the passengers the crudeness of the transportation was secondary to the promise of a better existence in Antigua.

After a long, imperiled trek across the Atlantic, weakened by seasickness and hunger, they arrived at English Harbor, Antigua. They must have been a curious sight—the men in their wrinkled, soiled cotton shirts, the women in long stained skirts and wearing scarves on their heads. Going through immigration, they heard their names anglicized from Manoel to Emanuel or Mani, from Antonia to Antonetta, Jose to Joseph, Joao to John, and their last name from Gomes (pronounced "Gomesh" in Portuguese) to a flat English "Gums." This was just the beginning of their painful introduction to the British.

When they had passed through customs they were met by representatives of the various estates, who were to take them to their new homes. Some were to go to the Long Lane estate, others the Collins estate, or the Lavington estate, etc. It is not certain to which place the Gomeses were assigned; in any case, no transportation was provided, and they walked, carrying the younger children and all their belongings on their backs. Antonio carried Mani, while his cousin, Maria Rodrigues, carried a pestle and mortar she had brought from Madeira so she could grind cocoa in order to make extra money (these items are now the property of the author, in Wooster, Ohio).[11]

When the family finally arrived at their estate, they were horrified to discover they were expected to live in shacks that had once been slave quarters, the most dilapidated accommodations imaginable.[12] They soon learned not only that living and working conditions were harsh but that they were expected to endure the exploitation, arrogance, and hatred of the owners. The English needed their labor but nonetheless looked down on the Portuguese because they were illiterate for the most part, came from the laboring class, were not English, and even worse, were Roman Catholics.[13] Some Portuguese died from the Yellow Fever epidemic of 1858 in the capital city of St. John. Others returned to Madeira, disheartened by their experiences on the estates; but those who remained were able to survive because of their strong religious faith, tenacity of purpose, and loyalty to each other as members of a people.[14] Unlike the Africans, they had not been unwillingly wrested from their homeland in chains, made to endure the dehumanizing effects of slavery, the brutal attempts of their master to beat from their minds and bodies every trace of their heritage and culture.

A major disappointment for Antonio and Antonetta when they arrived in Antigua, however, was that there were only a few Catholics on the island

and no church building. With the coming of more Portuguese, there grew a pressing need for a Catholic church. Until that need could be met, they had to worship in the Anglican church or attend the few masses that were held on the Blackman Sugar estate. Occasionally during the year a priest would come from another island to rebaptize or remarry those who of necessity had had these rites performed in the Anglican church. Finally, in 1871, St. Joseph Catholic Church was built in St. John. Mani's relatives, as well as other Portuguese, played a significant role in the building of the church.[15]

Those few Portuguese who had not come to Antigua as indentured servants established themselves in businesses in St. John almost immediately. The others soon worked off their contracts and opened shops in the villages and cities. By 1900 most of the stores on the island were owned by the Portuguese, who now formed a new merchant class. In time they began to buy parcels of the old estates, which the owners had to sell because of the declining sugar cane market.[16]

A few years after Antonio arrived in Antigua, he was able by working "task" rather than "hour" jobs to save enough money to move his family to Seaton Village. Most likely he chose this location because he already had relatives living there: Impolta de Sousa, Pedro Marques, and the Trinidads and de Freitas families. As soon as he had settled his family he opened up a dry goods shop. In 1987, a 102-year-old, blind villager remembered the shop. She recalled how she and the other children used to stand outside and beg for gumdrops, the store's most popular treat. She also remembered how clean the shop was always kept. "They were clean people," she repeated over and over, "Clean—clean!"[17] In her fading memory, this image seemed to stand out more than any other.

When Mani, Antonio's and Antonetta's son, became a teenager, he worked in his father's shop so he could save enough money to go into business for himself someday, as most enterprising Portuguese sons were expected to do. He was a quiet, thoughtful young man, whose preference was to ride around the island on his favorite horse, or sit on the beach dreaming. Like other Portuguese men of his age, he enjoyed the company of women; for a time he had an African concubine, who bore him a daughter, Victoria.

Attitudes toward this kind of relationship differed among the races. To the English, it was acceptable for Portuguese or English males to have African mistresses, or to have relationships in addition to their wives, as long as their mistresses were not English "ladies." In Portugal, despite the dictates of the Catholic Church, there had frequently existed extramarital relationships; once in Antigua, however, finding themselves a minority in search of status, the Portuguese developed a stricter code of ethics, one that emulated the British. Consequently, it was all right for a Portuguese man to choose an African mistress, but never a Portuguese "lady." Equally as strict was the unwritten law that a Portuguese man must never "degrade" himself by marrying an African woman.[18]

There were many circumstances growing out of slavery that helped mold the Black woman's view of concubinage. Before emancipation she had been at the mercy of the master, who often used her at will to satisfy his sexual appetite. From this union had come mulatto children, whom the master often treated better than his other slaves. Additionally, the refusal of whites to recognize the marriages of African men and women or to consider their children to be other than chattel made such unions difficult. This was especially true because of the frequency with which masters would sell males and destroy family units, leaving the mothers to fight alone for their children's survival.

When slavery ended, an even more rigid class structure came into existence in Antigua. At the top was the English, next the Portuguese, then the sprinkling of other races on the island. Next came the "Coloureds," and at the very bottom were those of pure African descent. Some Blacks began to equate the color of their skins with their condition of poverty, illiteracy, hopelessness, and powerlessness. A common prayer heard throughout the island was, "Lord, We beseech Thee in our darkness." Frequently women would reason that a relationship with a white man, which carried promises of economic security, was a way out of darkness to light—if not for them, for their "Coloured" children. On the other hand, with few exceptions, the Black males saw such arrangements as another means of exploitation and emasculation—the deliberate destruction of their race.[19]

This background is important to any appreciation of the uniqueness of the relationship between Mani and Rebecca, Joseph's father and mother. They met probably some time around 1885, in either Seaton, where he lived at the time, or Willikies, where she lived. Both villages are in St. Phillips Parish; they are adjacent to each other. Rebecca had relatives whom she often visited in Seaton; Mani's widowed sister, Maria, ran a shop in Willikies, where she lived with her four children. How or where Mani and Rebecca got together is of less importance than the fact that they not only met but formed a love relationship. Whatever their first motives, it soon became obvious theirs would be a life partnership.

Rebecca's mother, Sarah, gave her quiet consent to the affair, believing this union with a Portuguese merchant would enable her daughter to have a better life than most Blacks had on the island. Besides, she was fond of this gentle man, who seemed from the first to worship Rebecca. Mani's parents also acquiesced, since they thought their son was just "sowing his wild oats" in a traditional Portuguese male way, as he had done with his other African mistress.

On May 23, 1887, Rebecca bore Mani a daughter, whom they named Mary Justina Gomes. Mani had insisted the baby carry his name, despite his father's strong objection. Mary was baptized by the Roman Catholic priest, even though at the time Rebecca was Anglican.[20] Rebecca had promised Mani that all her children would be baptized by a Catholic priest. Following the birth, Mani made the unorthodox decision not only to build a house for Rebecca but to live with her. This was a "first" in Antigua, and it was the final blow to Antonio, who from that day until his last never acknowledged Mani as his son and refused to allow Antonetta to visit Mani or his "Black bastards."

Undeterred by his father's extreme reaction, Mani built Rebecca what was considered at the time a spacious house in the center of Willikies. Its living room, dining room, kitchen, three bedrooms, long front porch, bakery, stable, and outhouse were the envy of the villagers. (The house later was made into a police station, and Mani's bakery outside the main house was divided into cells. In 1994 the entire compound burned to the ground.) The villagers were even more amazed when they saw the fancy carriage and thoroughbred horses Mani bought to carry Rebecca and her daughter around the island.

In the late summer of 1888, Rebecca found she was again pregnant; on December 27 another daughter was born, Amanda Indiana.[21] To assist Rebecca, Mani hired a housekeeper. Mani demanded that people treat Rebecca with the same respect they would have had she been his legal wife, but instead they politely ignored or avoided her. She was an affront to the Portuguese, and a traitor to some of the Blacks. She did have a good relationship with her mother and her favorite brother, James, but not with other family members. Mani still maintained contact with his brothers and his sister Maria, but it was taken for granted among his other relatives that the subject of Rebecca was taboo. Mani was not to mention her in their presence.

In March of 1890, Antonio became seriously ill, and Antonetta sent for Mani to come to his father's bedside. Although he knew his father would not forgive him even on his deathbed, he went. To erase any doubts as to how he felt toward his son, Antonio drew up a new will leaving Mani what amounted to about one dollar in American money. On March 17 he died of pulmonary tuberculosis without having uttered a single word to his son.[22] His death left Mani guilt ridden and filled with grief for a father he continued to love despite his rejection of his son and Rebecca.

Mani's depression was relieved in the early summer when he learned Rebecca was again with child. He hoped this time the baby would be a boy, who would carry the family name. Mani had his wish. On November 26, 1890, a son was born and was registered under the name of Antonio, after his deceased grandfather.[23] In the early spring (March 21, 1891), Antonio was baptized at St. Phillips Anglican Church, with the understanding that he would be Catholic (there was no Catholic church nearby). His first name was changed to Joseph, after his father's brother; Antonio became his second name, and his third Guminston, the middle name of Rebecca's father—Joseph Antonio Guminston Gomes.[24]

As soon as Antonetta learned of the birth of her grandson, she became reconciled with Mani. Soon all the children were visiting her with their father and calling her "Avo" (Grandmother). Rebecca never accompanied him, because Antonetta made it quite clear that to accept Rebecca in the house would be a desecration of her husband's wishes. When Joseph was old enough to understand the situation, he deeply resented this.

During the first five years following Joseph's birth, the bakery flourished. The family increased by two: Sarah Elvira (named after Rebecca's mother) was born in 1893, and a second son, James Methuselah (named after Rebecca's brother), was born October 18, 1895.[25] The household had expanded in other ways as well. In addition to the housekeeper, Mani had hired a governess for the children and a highly recommended British tutor for Joseph. He did not want his older son to go to the understaffed village schools, and to send him all the way to St. John was out of the question. In order for Joseph to thrive in a colonial society, he had to learn to be more English than the English. A well-rounded education that included the classical languages, art, literature, music, science, mathematics, and history was one way to do that.

When Rebecca was not supervising the servants or making new clothes for her family, she took the children to visit their Grandmother Sarah and their Aunt Emma. On those afternoons Sarah would see that her grandchildren had plenty of mangoes and sweet apples, as well as the pepperpot soup for which she was famous. While the children played, Sarah and Rebecca shared the latest *melee* (gossip), lapsing at times into thick West Indian patois and roaring with laughter.

Six years after the death of his father, Mani decided there were no longer any barriers to his marrying Rebecca. In his eyes she had always been his wife, but if the union had to be legalized to silence malicious tongues, then that was what he would do. He knew he would be setting a precedent as the first Portuguese man in the parish to wed a Black woman and that he would offend many people, Black and white. Nevertheless, this was something he had to do.

On September 3, 1896, Manoel Gomes and Rebecca Richardson drove their carriage through the soft rain to St. Stephen's Episcopal Church. There they were met by Rev. James McConny, who had come from All Saints Church to perform the marriage, and by David Nathaniel (a relative of Rebecca) and Randolph Abbot, who were to be witnesses.[26]

As Mani and Rebecca walked down the aisle, they were a picture in contrasts. Both were short, but where he was slight in build, she had become buxom. His skin was pale white, and his features keen; she was dark and had broad African features. He was elegantly attired, his wide mustache stiffly waxed; as usual, he carried a hand-carved cane at his side and a pipe hidden in his pocket. Rebecca was simply but tastefully dressed in a long, wide skirt; her naturally crinkly hair was carefully combed. No doubt on this day she fit the picture Joseph always painted to his children in later years: "She carried herself high like a Senegalese Queen, strong and determined."

At the close of the ceremony, Mani took Rebecca in his arms as he had so many times and again pledged his love. None of the children were present. In fact, they knew nothing about the wedding, assuming their parents had always been married. To be sure they did, Rebecca had told Joseph he had been born in Trinidad and that the family had moved to Antigua when he was still an infant, then back to Trinidad. Consequently, Joseph always claimed Trinidad as his birthplace, even though he could never find his birth certificate. Whenever he needed a passport or other papers requiring proof of his birth, his mother signed a notarized statement that he had been born in Trinidad in 1889.[27] The reason for the discrepancy in the year is still not known. It was not until 1980, after his death, that his grandson Curtis Gomez located his birth certificate in Antigua. It was dated 1890.

After the excitement of the wedding, Mani and Rebecca returned to their daily pursuits, he to his bakery and she to the children and household. Nothing had really changed. On May 1, 1897, Rebecca gave birth to another daughter, Arramenta Christophine.[28] She welcomed this child as she had all the others, but it was no secret that Joseph was her favorite and would continue to be. This did not sit well with some of his siblings, especially James, who admitted later in life that he had always been jealous of Joseph. When the children went swimming in Spencer's Bay, Rebecca would not allow Joseph to go into the water above his knees. When the others underwent the island ritual of being rowed out into the deep water and thrown overboard so they would have to swim, his mother kept him on the beach, close to her side. As a result, although Joseph loved to sail and did learn to swim, he had a fear of water and always imagined that one day he would die of drowning. The ocean remained his greatest love and his greatest fear.

Joseph was also the favorite of his grandmother Antonetta, who tried to devise ways to take him from his parents and prepare him for the Catholic priesthood. Rebecca, who was as determined as her mother-in-law, had other plans for her son: he would go to London some day and study to be a lawyer or doctor.

From the very beginning, Joseph found himself torn between two worlds, one white, the other black. His grandmothers, both of whom frequently attended St. Stephen's, vied for his affection. When he went to church with his father, he had to confront them both. They would hug him affectionately while openly avoiding one another. This was not the only conflict into which he was thrust; every day presented a paradox of some kind. He became increasingly aware that the English hated the Portuguese, his father's people; that many Portuguese considered his mother and other Blacks an inferior breed; that Afro–West Indians had little love for the English, their former masters, or for the Portuguese; and that children from mixed marriages like himself were sometimes loved, but frequently rejected, even though the general consensus was that they were a cut above their black mothers.[29] Joseph was fascinated by the West Indian *jumbi* (patois for ghost) stories about the Obeah Woman, who would catch the jumbis and put them in a bottle and bury them on the beach. On the other hand, he never tired of listening to the wistful songs of Portugal, which some of his mother's people said were lacking in rhythm, like most white folks' music. He adored his father but worshipped his mother and wanted to protect her from the ugly looks and words her presence often evoked when she walked with Mani. This fight for his mother's dignity would be the impetus for many struggles he would wage when he reached America.

Joseph's religious training was as confusing as the rest of his childhood. Mani was a devout Catholic, and in time Rebecca defied her family, who had always been Anglican, and joined the Wesleyan Methodist Church. Unlike her husband or her family, Rebecca preferred the simplicity of Methodism to the more ritualistic services of the Catholics or Anglicans. She told Joseph how Methodism in Antigua had been founded by Nathaniel Gilbert, who had been so influenced by John Wesley in England that he returned to preach Methodism to his slaves on his estate. Because of his efforts Antigua became the first island in the Caribbean to practice

Methodism. After emancipation, Zion Hill Methodist Church was built, its name later changed to Gilbert Memorial in honor of the founder.[30]

Joseph often went to Gilbert with his mother. In years to come he remembered riding through a long grove of trees to the small stone church at its end. He enjoyed the communal atmosphere as he sat beside his mother listening to her sing the old Methodist hymns. At Gilbert he did not have constantly to kneel and rise as he did in his father's church, where the service was in a language he could not understand. Laughingly, he told his daughters when they were in their teens that he had no doubt the tenderness of his knees had as much to do with his being Methodist as anything else. Nevertheless, it was in Antigua that his love for Methodism was planted.

As a young boy, Joseph resembled his father, with his short stature and mop of unruly red hair. (When he grew older, his hair turned dark brown and then silvery white.) Arthur Bowers, a New Yorker formerly from Antigua, remembered Joseph as being a loner.[31] As soon as he learned to read Joseph would spend hours poring over books of history and classical literature, his two favorite subjects. He was extremely fussy about cleanliness. If anyone sat in his chair, the housekeeper would have to scrub it thoroughly before he would sit in it again; if a fly landed in his food, he would refuse to eat it.

Joseph's parents were indulgent of some of his idiosyncrasies, but he was raised by a strict code of ethics that never left him. Rebecca was the disciplinarian in the household. Whenever some infraction of the rules occurred and no one would confess, she would line up all the children and say, "You're too nuf [gone too far]. If you can't hear, then you must feel." Then she would make them drop the flaps of their underwear and give a "good t'ump" to their bare behinds. Mani did not always escape her fiery West Indian temper, either. There was no doubt as to who ruled the roost, but Mani never seemed to mind. He was probably relieved, since he was temperamentally unsuited to inflict any kind of corporal punishment. The only time Joseph ever remembered his father striking him was once when Mani caught him smoking his pipe. Afterwards, Mani was far more shaken than Joseph, who hardly felt the blow.

Amanda was Joseph's favorite sister; she, in turn, worshipped him. He often recalled how he would climb on her back and play horsey. Her long, black braids became his reins. Sometimes he would pull them so hard that tears would fill her eyes, but she never complained.

Along with this make-believe mount, Joseph loved to ride real horses. He admired their majestic bearing and the feel of their sweaty hide against his bare legs. When he was not studying he would spend hours in the stable, helping Ezekiel Dublin, the stable boy, who talked more than he worked. Mani gave Joseph his own pony, whom he named Beauty. Joseph would hop on Beauty and ride bareback, imagining he was a knight from some Arthurian legend. On one occasion when he had gone riding, Ezekiel forgot to lift the bar in front of the stable door. Joseph rode into the yard at full speed, and, seeing the bar in front of the door, jumped from the horse to keep from being knocked off. He landed on a sharp rock, which penetrated his back. Some village women found him lying unconscious on the ground and carried him into the house. Rebecca called Aunt Polly, the folk doctor, who treated him with herbs and poultices. When the doctor from St. John came, he said Polly had saved Joseph's life.

Rebecca boxed Ezekiel's ears for his negligence, and when Mani returned home she reminded him with scathing words that she had never wanted Joseph to have a horse, and now the horse had almost killed him. Mani did not say a word, but just walked out into the backyard. Shortly the entire house rang with a deafening sound—Mani had been so upset that he shot the horse. When Joseph found out what had happened, he was inconsolable; his father later bought him other horses, but none ever meant as much to him as had Beauty.

As Joseph grew older, he helped Mani in the bakery and stable or assisted in making Mani's popular wine. Like most Portuguese, Mani grew in his backyard grapevines that had come from sprouts brought from Madeira. After Joseph helped him crush the grapes, they would put the juice in earthen jars and bury them underground until they fermented. When friends visited, Mani would offer his *vinho da casa* with pride. He was never much of a drinker himself, but he liked to take a few sips, smoke his pipe, and listen to his guests sing Portuguese songs to the accompaniment of an accordion. Joseph would sit at his feet until Rebecca hustled him off to bed.

On June 12, 1899, when Joseph was nine, Rebecca gave birth to another daughter, Violet Viviana, a noisy, spunky baby with hazel eyes that changed colors according to her moods.[32] Her arrival was not greeted with the same enthusiasm as the other children's. Mani was preoccupied with his declining business. More and more he found it impossible to play the role of the "colonial businessman." Perhaps it was because he had never forgotten the early days, when his family first arrived from Madeira, and how hard times had been for them. Or perhaps it was because of his basic decency and gentility. At any rate, he developed the habit of allowing people to buy on credit and then forgetting to collect from them at the end of the month. People took advantage of his good nature and often did not pay at all.

Ezekiel was a perfect example of the kind of ingratitude Mani experienced. The stable boy slept and ate more than he worked. His behavior was ridiculed by the village boys, who would gather outside of Mani's house and sing, "'Zekiel won't work. Nyam Satchel bread" (he eats up Satchel's bread—"Satchel" was the four-year-old James's nickname). But Mani would not fire Ezekiel, because after all "he was just a boy." Mani was not a businessman like his cousin Antonio, who lived in town and had become so wealthy Antiguans called him "Spit Gold," because they heard him say, "When I cough, I cough silver. When I spit, I spit gold."[33] Antonio had warned Mani that his unsound business practices would eventually bring him to ruin.

The failure of the family business came gradually, but to Joseph it seemed as if everything tragic was happening at once. First, Rebecca's brother James, his favorite uncle, moved to Trinidad. Then Aunt Maria moved with her children from Seaton to St. John. Finally, Rebecca dismissed the governess and tutor, and Mani let go his employees at the bakery. As Mani watched everything he had built disappear, he withdrew inside himself. He rarely had anything to say to his wife or children. He stopped hugging Joseph and asking "Como estai meu querido filho?"; he seemed not to see him at all. Rebecca was concerned about his growing depression.

Once everything began to unravel, the end came swiftly. Mani had to sell the house and his business to his cousin, Albert Pestana. He moved his family temporarily into grandmother Sarah's house until he could decide what to do. Sarah's house was too small to accommodate eight additional bodies, and everyone was in everyone else's way. Mani developed stomach trouble and refused to see anyone who came to the house, including the doctor. He felt he had failed Rebecca and his children, who had looked to him for security.

Within a few weeks the solution came in a letter from Uncle James. He urged the Gomeses to move to Trinidad, where opportunities for business were much better. Rebecca convinced Mani that they should leave Antigua for Trinidad, where they could start over again. Eventually, he agreed. There did not seem to be any alternative.

During the family's final week on the island, Sarah clung to Rebecca. She sensed that Rebecca's favorite motto—"Mountain, be thou removed into the sea"—would be sorely tested in Trinidad. Instead of her customary "Ate logo" (until later), Antonetta said to Mani the more final "Adeis, meu querido filho." Somehow Joseph sensed he would never see his grandmothers again, or any of the other people he was leaving behind. (His prediction was correct. Antonetta was to die May 31, 1902, of senile decay.[34]

There was not enough money for Joseph or Mani to attend her funeral. Sarah died January 16, 1916, at the age of seventy-two, while Joseph was living in Bermuda.[35] During his eighty-nine years, Joseph never returned to Antigua.)

Some time around the turn of the century, the Gomeses sailed the Atlantic southward past Guadeloupe, Martinique, Grenada, and Tobago, to Trinidad. Like Antigua, Trinidad was still a British colony, but its population was far more diversified. Among the whites on the island were Spanish, French, and British. Because of miscegenation and other kinds of racial mixing, "Coloureds" had some of the characteristics of these groups as well as African. Blacks born in Trinidad were referred to as "Creole"; those transported to the island during slavery were called "Africans." In addition, a few Chinese and Portuguese had been encouraged to immigrate after emancipation to work on the sugar estates, but most of them went into business for themselves. In 1845 the first shipload of East Indians, referred to as "coolies," were brought to the island as indentured servants. Those who did not return to India were encouraged by the government to buy land after finishing their period of indenture. They created small villages, as had the Blacks in Antigua. In time, the East Indians were to compete with the Portuguese in business ventures.[36]

These then were the races the Gomeses were immediately exposed to when they landed at Port of Spain, the capital, a city far more cosmopolitan than St. John. Located on the Gulf of Paria about two miles from the mouth of the Caroni River, it was marked by shaded streets, Anglican and Roman Catholic churches, public buildings, and a bustling business district. Its most famous landmarks were Woodford Square, with its large fountain, and Columbus Square, where one could see a life-size statue of the explorer.

The influence of the British could be felt and seen everywhere: in the hotels, boarding houses, shops, the library, newspaper offices, the post office; in the architecture of the governor's elaborate mansion in the exclusive St. Anne's section; and in the islanders' feverish attempt to conquer the English language, particularly the verbose and flowery phrases used by the politicians and statesmen. Having come from the small, less progressive Antigua, Joseph fell instantly in love with Trinidad; believing this was the place of his birth, he was determined to learn all he could from it. He especially wanted to learn to speak English with the precision he heard at the government buildings. If Antigua had been where he became aware of the injustices of racism and developed his love for the Methodist Church, Trinidad was where he developed a passion for rhetoric and poetic imagery.

With money he borrowed from Antonetta and Sarah and from the local banks, who considered him a good risk, Mani bought a house on Tragarete Street, in a middle-class neighborhood. Shortly afterwards he put a down payment on a bakery in Frederick Street. At first his business flourished, and again there was enough money for a housekeeper and a tutor for the boys.

On January 28, 1904, Rebecca had her eighth child, Walter Gomes.[37] With such a large family, she did not have time to brood over the racial slurs she still occasionally received because of her mixed marriage. She joined the Hanover Wesleyan Methodist Church and became involved in its functions when she could. As in Antigua, she took Joseph with her there while Mani and the other children attended the Catholic church.

Mani seemed to have regained his optimism, and the children rapidly adjusted to their new environment. Port of Spain offered many more activities than had the small village of Willikies. The boys spent the morning hours and part of the afternoon with the British tutor. Afterward they were free to pursue their own interests. Joseph used that time to explore the library or ride the horse his father had finally persuaded Rebecca to let him have.[38]

Once again Mani began to lose money, because he gave too much credit and collected too little cash. Once again the tutor had to be dismissed. Joseph and James were sent to Tranquility, the private school run by the Methodist Church on Woodbrook, which was less expensive than the private tutor. Joseph liked the school, especially most of the teachers, who encouraged his intellectual curiosity. James called him "teacher's pet" and was delighted when, as a result of a dare, Joseph put glass in the teacher's seat and was thrashed both at school and at home.

Within a few years it became necessary for Mani to sell the house on Tragarete and buy a smaller dwelling at 10 Picton, New Town. James and Joseph were removed from Tranquility and sent to Regis, a public school. There Joseph continued to excel in his studies, but not in sports.

In 1907 the family was forced to move once again, this time to a two-bedroom apartment at 40 Besson Street. Mani had to sell his bakery. As if tragedy traveled in pairs, Mary Justina, Joseph's oldest sister, died of pneumonia, and the family went into a prolonged period of mourning.[39] Joseph never forgot how at the funeral he was forced to follow the custom of kissing the corpse. He said it seemed as if her entire body had been stuffed with ice. So affected was he that he developed a dread of dead people which continued for years; for a long time he refused to sleep without a lighted lamp beside his bed.[40]

The following year Rebecca, who was in her forties, delivered her last child, Cyril Gomes. From the beginning he was "a child of sorrow," and he suffered all his life from mental disorders which no one was able to diagnose. Despite all the setbacks, Rebecca faced her change in fortune with courage and determination. Joseph would often relate how she tore up sheets to make shirts for the children and how she created thick soups from leftovers and herbs. At the Wesleyan Methodist Church she sang the old hymns with an even stronger conviction. As her religious zeal grew stronger, Mani too clung to his Catholic faith. The islanders remember him during this period walking through the streets, immaculately dressed in outdated clothes, carrying his cane with one hand and tipping his hat politely to passers-by with the other. Then he would go to a small one-room shack, remove his coat and hat, and sell coal to make a living for his family.

The older children got jobs to help with the family finances, and Mani supplemented his coal business by going to work in an East Indian bakery. Joseph was employed as a cash boy at the shop of Waterman the hatter. It was his job to take the money the salesman received from the customer to the cashier; he then waited for the change and brought it back to the salesman, who gave it to the customer. His bosses were fond of him, and when he returned to Trinidad some years later they welcomed him as a celebrity.

In November 1907 Joseph turned seventeen, the age at which he had planned to attend college; however, any thought of his studying in London was out of the question. The resourceful Rebecca had an alternate plan for his education. Her brother James, who had encouraged them to move to Trinidad, was now living in New York City. His letters home were filled with enthusiasm for America, and he urged them to come. The entire family could not afford the passage to the United States, but Mani could borrow enough money for Joseph to go. Once there, he could live with his Uncle James and work until he had sufficient funds to attend college. Mani was reluctant to let his oldest son move so far away, but realizing he could do little else for Joseph, finally gave his consent.

On July 25, 1908, Joseph Antonio Guminston Gomes boarded the *Maraval,* bound for the United States. On the ship's records he was listed as a clerk, five feet three inches tall, leaving Trinidad, Port of Spain, the residence of R. Gomes of 40 Besson Street, to stay with James Richardson. Traveling with him was a relative, George de Silva, a twenty-eight-year-old merchant of fair complexion, who was going to a Mr. Hittock at the Bowling Green Building, New York City.[41] As the two men stood on the deck waving, the *Maraval* moved slowly out onto the ocean. Joseph's family became a shadowy blur on a retreating tropical canvas.

He later remembered little about the crossing except that he slept on the lower deck with the other third-class passengers and ate stale food someone forced into his hands. He was not seasick, but there was a hollowness in his stomach that came from a different kind of malady. The vastness of the ocean and sky made him feel insignificant and alone. At one point the ship ran into a violent storm, and Joseph was swept overboard. De Silva, who had spent the entire trip drunk, did not see him thrashing about in the ocean; one of the crew members jumped into the water and rescued him. Even when Joseph was lifted back onto the deck, de Silva did not seem to understand why he was soaking wet and coughing up saltwater. The episode intensified Joseph's fear of the water and initiated his hatred of alcohol.

After days of alternating calm and turbulence, Joseph saw the Statue of Liberty and knew that this part of his odyssey had come to an end. The date was August 3, 1908.[42] He would be eighteen in November and still had not been introduced to long pants.

◈ ◈ ◈

CHAPTER TWO

The Initiation

New York City &
Reverdy Cassius Ransom, 1908–1911

For we are all strugglers, but—and herein lies the fundamental difference—we are not all prevailers. Caught in the web and twists of human passions, so many have not the will to win and are forever defeated. The glory of Reverdy Cassius Ransom is the glory of survival; the heritage he bequeaths us is that of the Prevailer. Jacob the prototype, Reverdy Cassius Ransom the modern pattern of prevailing power.

> —Joseph Gomez, eulogy for Reverdy
> Cassius Ransom, 1959

◈ After riding the ferry from Staten Island to Manhattan, Joseph and de Silva caught the streetcar that would take them to Uncle James's apartment. De Silva had promised Rebecca he would make sure Joseph had found his uncle before he left him. Joseph heard the driver calling out names; having had enough of traveling, he wondered when they would call out "James Richardson." De Silva, who had been in New York on several occasions, laughingly explained to him that the driver was calling out the names of the streets.

When they came to West 36th Street they descended to the street and climbed up the steps to the second floor of a five-story brownstone building. James, who had been anticipating Joseph's arrival, met them at the door. De Silva had kept his promise and was anxious to get on with his own affairs. He shook James's hand, wished Joseph good fortune, and left hurriedly. That was the last time Joseph ever saw him.

Uncle James's apartment was at 416 West 36th Street in the heart of the Tenderloin District, which extended from West 20th to West 60th and between 6th and 8th Avenues. It and the San Juan district (so named by the Negro veterans of the Spanish-American War) were the areas where most Blacks were forced to live. The exodus to Harlem was just beginning; only a small Negro elite lived in Brooklyn. The masses of Negroes were crowded indiscriminately in the Tenderloin and San Juan districts. Entertainers, intellectuals, criminals, professionals, blue-collar workers, prostitutes, ministers, and sports heroes all lived together, paying from 30 percent to 50 percent more rent than the Irish, Italian, or Jewish immigrants paid for comparable housing.[1]

Joseph held vivid images of his first day in New York. He recalled that after he had unpacked his few belongings in his uncle's spare bedroom he went into the kitchen. There Uncle James lifted buckets of hot water from the wood-burning stove and filled two large washtubs that stood in the center of the floor. "One is for bathing, the other for rinsing off," he said. The tubs reminded Joseph of home, and he felt decidedly less strange as he climbed in to scrub the dirt and salt from his sore limbs. Only his uncle's promise to take him for a walking tour of the area curbed his desire to luxuriate in the soothing water.

He never forgot his first walk in "the City." Women of all shades of brown and black, dressed in their bosomy box blouses and brightly colored long skirts, sauntered by. Men in frock coats and wide-bottom trousers weighted down with watch chains lingered on the sidewalks smoking Virginia Brights and eyeing the women. He heard the babble of street slang, the slow, drawling speech of Negroes newly arrived from the South, the clipped British accent of a few Africans, and the familiar musical dialect of the Caribbean. At the turn of the century approximately 60,666 Negroes lived in New York City, five thousand of whom were foreign born. James told Joseph that now there were over ninety-three thousand and that there were more foreign Blacks in New York than in any other American city. To Joseph it seemed they were all in the Tenderloin.[2]

Uncle James took him up to 53rd Street, the "main drag" of the Tenderloin. Here the talk was mostly about the upcoming presidential election, horse races, and the latest Bert Williams and George Walker musical. Joseph saw the Marshall Brothers Hotel, where famous jockeys and entertainers gathered to dine or catch up on the latest happenings. He passed the restaurants and saloons (many owned by Black prizefighters), the colored branches of the Young Men's and Women's Christian Associations, St. Mark's Methodist Episcopal Church, and a few blocks away on 40th,

Abyssinia Baptist Church, where the recently arrived Adam Clayton Powell, Sr., pastored in the midst of a red-light district.[3] Joseph was surprised by the boldness of the painted women, who openly offered their wares in front of the church on a Sunday afternoon.

As they turned onto Broadway, Joseph could see the skyscrapers that were beginning to form what would become the famous New York skyline. On the streets were a few horse-drawn carts, but most had given way to "smokeless green taxicabs" and streetcars. Joseph learned from his uncle that the Pennsylvania Railroad was being constructed and that a tunnel from New Jersey to New York had been dug under the Hudson River. They walked through areas where the sound of cable cars and elevated railroads mingled with vaudeville tunes blaring from speakeasies. Joseph was shown where the subway was being completed—that gray whale that would transport people in a sea of darkness from one end of the city and spit them out on the other. To him, New York was a teeming carnival that was never put to bed—a whirlwind in which he was easily caught up. Though his head ached, crammed full of so many impressions, he thought at the time that he would never want to live anywhere else in the world. Port of Spain seemed like a toy village compared to this vast metropolis.

Joseph soon found out, however, that America had its blemishes. He had arrived at what came to be called the nadir of Negro history, that period between Reconstruction and the Harlem Renaissance marked by lynchings, Jim-Crowism, and race riots. Between 1889 and 1908 over three thousand Negroes had been lynched in the United States.[4]

Joseph had his personal negative experience when he went to look for work a few days after his arrival. Most of the jobs in the Tenderloin were already taken; in the white neighborhoods, the employers made it clear they preferred European immigrants to Negroes. The majority of Blacks worked as unskilled laborers, and the small but growing number of professionals usually had to seek patronage in their own neighborhoods. Uncle James had been luckier than most. He could not find work as a tailor, as he had in the West Indies, but he was employed at a pharmacy. His white boss was willing to teach him all he knew about the mixing of herbs and powders, and James had dreams of opening his own pharmacy one day and sending for Amy Cornelius, the love he had had to leave behind in Antigua.[5]

After weeks of frantic searching, Joseph found a job running an elevator twelve hours a day in a hotel. His $5-a-week salary hardly seemed compensation for the racial slurs he had to endure and the sexual advances from drunken white women who tried to lure him to their rooms. He knew what the consequences would have been if he succumbed: on several occasions he was almost fired for "talkin' back to white folks." Just before he reached the point of explosion, he was hired as a busboy in a Jewish restaurant. The job paid about $10 a week, counting tips, and he only had to work ten hours a day. In addition, he was given one free meal. It took a while for him to learn how to balance the heavy trays of dirty dishes on the palm of his hand. Once while clearing a table he accidentally dumped a half-eaten dinner into the lap of an indignant lady, who wanted "the nigger-boy fired immediately." The boss paid to have the woman's dress cleaned and would not hear of firing his most conscientious worker.

Eventually Joseph had to settle for working part-time. He found that his high school diploma was not acceptable in the United States and that he would need to study for at least two years before attempting to enter college. He enrolled in the public school near his apartment and found the lessons less difficult than some he had encountered in the West Indies. The private tutors he had had most of his life and his love for reading had provided him with an excellent background, and he excelled in all of his courses. He even met a young lady named May, with whom he had a brief flirtation. The attraction disappeared as soon as she tried to kiss him—he had been told by Rebecca to beware of forward women.

After attending the Episcopal church with his uncle for several Sundays, Joseph decided to visit Bethel African Methodist Episcopal Church, on West 25th. Some time in September he put on the new long pants his uncle had helped him choose and headed for Bethel. Arriving late, he entered the large auditorium, where about two thousand Negroes were intently listening to a tall, wiry, redheaded minister who appeared to be in his late thirties. He was speaking heatedly about the presidential elections. At first Joseph, who had come to hear a gospel sermon, was disappointed, but gradually he became interested.

Reverdy Cassius Ransom was relating how W. E. B. Du Bois, founder of the Niagara Movement and professor at Atlanta University, had announced at a meeting in Columbus, Ohio, in September that Negroes should vote for William Jennings Bryan, the Democratic candidate for president. Du Bois had reminded his audience that it was Theodore Roosevelt, the incumbent Republican president, who had dismissed without honor the entire 25th Regiment of Black soldiers in Brownsville, Texas, in 1906. There had been a dispute between the soldiers and some white citizens, and the soldiers were accused of running wild and shooting up the town. Negroes all over the country had been enraged. They knew of the cruel treatment Black soldiers received in the segregated camps and surrounding towns; consequently they felt the soldiers' behavior was probably justified and the punishment by the president excessive. Du Bois had further stated that

William Howard Taft, Roosevelt's secretary of war and the current Republican candidate for the presidency, had agreed with the president's dismissal of the regiment and therefore did not deserve the Negro vote.[6]

When Ransom had finished commenting on Du Bois's position, he urged Negroes to study all the facts and not to vote blindly for any party. In the past the Negro had regarded the Democratic Party "as his traditional and hereditary foe"; by habit, Negroes continued to give their votes to the Party of Lincoln. But, pointed out Ransom, "Today there is very little difference between the two parties, so far as their attitude toward the Negro is concerned." He quoted Taft as having called Negroes "political children," incapable of maintaining their political rights. He agreed with Du Bois that such an attitude did not speak well for Taft. Ransom had not made up his mind how he would vote; after considering all the issues, he asserted, he would choose the lesser of the two evils, or perhaps even support the candidacy of Eugene V. Debs, the socialist.[7]

When the service was over, Joseph went up to shake Ransom's hand. He had always thought of a sermon in purely theological terms, concerned only with the spiritual and removed from social, political, or even racial considerations. Somehow this man had made all of these things seem important to man's spiritual well-being. Church had never held for Joseph this kind of excitement or involvement. Ransom had electrified his listeners.

Before coming to New York Joseph had taken a rather abstract interest in the history of America but had little knowledge of its politics. He said later that it was his initial encounter with Reverdy Ransom that made him realize what a significant part the political process played in the realization of Negro progress. Ransom invited him to hear ex-governor P. B. S. Pinchback speak in the church the following evening. Pinchback, a Negro, had been governor of Louisiana during Reconstruction, but with the failure of the Radical Republicans to make Reconstruction work and the compromise President Rutherford B. Hayes made with the South to gain the presidency in 1876, Pinchback had left Louisiana and was now living in New York City. The next evening Joseph listened with great interest as Pinchback talked about that short time after the Civil War when it seemed Blacks had gained some power, holding political offices in several southern states.

Joseph soon realized that Ransom's commitment to a social gospel was all-encompassing. Ransom said anyone who attempted to preach Jesus without addressing all the concerns of people was sorely lacking in an understanding of the New Testament: Jesus had been aware that in order to keep the crowd's attention on the Mount, he had to feed the people.

"Joseph," he said, "don't ever try to preach God to an empty stomach." Ransom's philosophy was to have a profound impact on Joseph's approach to the ministry.

The Sunday after Joseph visited Bethel, he joined the church. He was warmly greeted by the trustees and members. Soon there developed between Ransom and Joseph a father-son love relationship which no one was able to destroy, though through the years many would try. Their contrasting outward appearances belied the fact that inside they were alike in many ways. Both were men of immense passion. Both became righteously indignant when faced with pettiness or inhumanity. Both were dynamic preachers, effective leaders, infectious personalities, "incurable romantics," generous to a fault, loyal to their church and friends—sometimes blindly so. Ransom's tragic flaw, however, was his weakness for alcohol, which Joseph said would have destroyed a lesser man. But it was Ransom's openness and honesty, the suffering and guilt he bore because of that flaw, that helped Joseph to develop a more compassionate understanding of human nature. He became less harsh in his judgment of his own shortcomings and those of others. He and Ransom complemented each other and were formidable champions of the unchampioned. Most of all, they knew how to be friends.

Joseph was a frequent visitor to the parsonage, a four-family apartment building at 248 West 129th Street in Harlem. Ransom, his wife Emma, and their sons Harold George and Reverdy, Jr., were the only Negroes living on the block. (Seventh Avenue in Harlem was a Jewish neighborhood at the time, but 1908 marked the beginning of the influx of Negroes to Harlem.)

After many lengthy conversations with the Ransoms, Joseph was able to piece together their varied and active histories. Ransom had been born in Flushing, Ohio, to George and Hattie Ransom on January 4, 1861, a day "so cold that the streams, even the springs of water, were frozen," as Ransom described it in his autobiography.[8] As a baby he was so sickly that no one thought he would live long. In his late teens he attended Wilberforce University, an A.M.E. College in Xenia, Ohio. His tenure there was interrupted when he accepted a scholarship to Oberlin College. Later he returned to Wilberforce to enter Payne Theological Seminary, from which he graduated in June 1886. He was one of the members of the Niagara Movement (1905), organized to secure equality for Negroes and protest lynchings.[9] In his introduction to Ransom's book *The Negro* (1935), W. E. B. Du Bois would write about Ransom's contribution to the second meeting of the Niagara Movement in 1906, held at Harpers Ferry, West

Virginia. Du Bois felt Ransom's speech on John Brown had been the single most stirring event of the meeting. "It led through its eloquence to the eventual founding of the National Association for the Advancement of Colored People and twenty-five years of work for Negro equality and freedom."[10]

Ransom had come to Bethel from Charles Street A.M.E. Church in Boston, where students of all races from Harvard and Boston universities came to hear him preach. Before Boston, he had pastored in Erie, Altoona, and Pittsburgh in Pennsylvania, and in Cleveland, Chicago, and New Bedford, Massachusetts.

Ransom was a great supporter of Negro theatrical personalities. It was through him that Joseph met many of the performers of the day, including Sam Lucas, Ransom's uncle; Rosamond (composer and actor) and James Weldon Johnson (writer, educator, and civil rights leader); the comedy team Bert Williams and George Walker (Bert lived across the street from Uncle James's apartment); and the comedian Ernest Hogan. Most of the Negro entertainers belonged to Bethel, since few of the other churches would allow them to be members. Ransom had offered not only his church but his friendship. He often visited them when they were sick; he counseled, married, baptized and buried them; and he became a member of their organization, called "The Frogs." The other ministers, who had a more fundamentalist approach to religion, derisively referred to him as "the Actors' Minister."[11]

Joseph's favorite among the actors was Ernest Hogan, who had written an article in the Christmas 1908 issue of *The New York Age* entitled "The Church and the Stage." In it he had made a plea for a "more cordial relationship" between the two forces.[12] Joseph took great pleasure in Ransom's reply in the January 18, 1909, issue, expressing disdain for Christian hypocrisy when it came to the theatre. He found it "a sad commentary on . . . Christian sympathy that the stage should cry to the pulpit 'Reach forth thy hand' rather than the pulpit to the stage." He scolded clergymen whose "pulpit attitude [was] strongly in opposition to the stage" but who were known to attend the theatre when visiting other cities. He reminded the readers that most Negro entertainers had gotten their start in their churches, especially in the choirs. Many were the children of clergymen, and yet the church had turned its back on them, classifying their artistry as evil. If it were evil, why were churches always trying to put on some kind of pageant or skit?[13] Ransom's support of theatre was to have a strong influence on Joseph, his children, and his grandchildren in later years.

Ransom befriended not only actors but also the community's prostitutes, with whom he conversed on street corners and in bars and restaurants. Sometimes he took Joseph with him so he could have an understanding of street people. Ransom was convinced that these were the people to whom the Negro church should address itself most, not just the middle class, as was the custom in the more prestigious houses of worship. "The least of these" were important to the salvation of the race, he told Joseph.

Joseph also became fond of Emma Ransom, who fussed over him like a surrogate mother. Born in Virginia, she had married Reverdy in 1887 and had soon become a leader in her own right. She was an ardent church worker and was affiliated with most of the social service organizations of the city. In 1909 she was appointed chairman of the Board of Management of the Colored YWCA. Her contributions were rewarded when the colored YWCA moved to West 137th Street in Harlem and was named the Emma Ransom House in honor of her services.[14]

It was at one of Emma's Sunday dinners that Joseph was introduced to the brilliant but irascible W. E. B. Du Bois, who dominated the conversation during the meal. Joseph was fascinated by his keen mind but thought him intolerant of those less gifted than himself and given to argument for its own sake. Ransom seemed to understand Du Bois and was amused rather than annoyed by his manner. "He is one of our greatest minds," he told Joseph. Later, when he had a chance to read *The Souls of Black Folks*, Joseph envied the sheer poetry of Du Bois's language and the intensity of his message. After Du Bois gave up his teaching position at Atlanta University and became editor of *The Crisis*, the mouthpiece of the NAACP in general and Du Bois in particular, Joseph had more opportunity to become acquainted with his writings and his philosophy.

Being a member of Bethel A.M.E. Church afforded Joseph the opportunity to meet many of the church's leaders, who spoke at the Sunday morning services or the afternoon forum which dealt with more civic and political matters. Among those he heard were Bishop H. M. Turner, Historiographer of the A.M.E. Church; Bishop C. S. Smith of the Sixth Episcopal District, who was to become a close friend to Joseph; H. T. Johnson, newly elected editor of the *Christian Recorder;* Francis H. Gow of South Africa, Bishop W. J. Gaines of the First Episcopal District, which included New York; and William T. Vernon, recorder of the Treasury of the United States.

Almost from the beginning Joseph disliked Vernon, whom he described as pompous and crass. On May 20, 1909, the *New York Age* carried an article about Vernon that seemed to justify Joseph's opinion of this noted A.M.E. leader. Vernon had been ousted from the dining room of the House Office Building in Washington, D.C., by southern congressmen; instead of being indignant, he had been sorry he "had been the cause of any trouble. . . . Had he known he would have created any controversy by eating in the dining room . . . he would not have done so."[15] The following year, on September 15, 1910, Vernon was again the subject of controversy in *The Age*. This time, Vernon had said in an interview that "if he had the power he would bar all Negroes from the University of Kansas, presumably to fill up his own institution [Western University in Quintaro, Kansas, an all-Black school]."[16] It was this same Vernon who in a little over a decade, as an A.M.E. bishop, would almost cause Joseph to leave the Church.

Having met some of the bishops and officers, Joseph was anxious to learn from his mentor all he could about the history of the African Methodist Episcopal Church. He discovered that the Church had been founded by Richard Allen, who had been born a slave in Philadelphia, on February 14, 1760, was converted in 1777, and soon after began to preach. So effective had been his sermons that he converted his master, who as a result freed his slaves. In 1787 Allen and Absalom Jones had led some Negroes out of St. George Methodist Church in Philadelphia after they had been asked to take segregated seats at the rear of the balcony. This incident had convinced Allen and Jones that Negroes needed their own building in which to worship. However, before a church could be purchased, they had split over theological questions: Jones, who was more Anglican in his orientation, formed the St. Thomas Protestant Episcopal Church in 1794, and the same year Allen organized Bethel A.M.E. Church. Soon other independent Negro Methodist churches sprang up in several northern states. In 1816, sixteen of them formed a separate body, the African Methodist Episcopal Church, and elected Richard Allen as its first bishop.[17]

The fact that the A.M.E. Church had come into being as a protest against racism and religious hypocrisy impressed Joseph, and he felt a growing kinship to it that turned into a lasting love affair. The more Joseph became involved with the Ransoms and Bethel, the more he began to have second thoughts about his future career. He stopped dreaming of brilliant surgical feats and dramatic summations to juries and instead imagined himself transfixing an audience with his words as Ransom did every Sunday.

During the month of August 1909, Ransom's sermons were mostly concerned with such secular events as the city's refusal to hire Negro policemen. These sermons were the result of a week of unusual lawlessness and turmoil in the Tenderloin; Joseph had witnessed several skirmishes in front of his apartment. Between police brutality and the behavior of certain elements in the community, it was becoming dangerous on the streets after dark. Ransom noted that cities like Philadelphia and Chicago already had Negro policemen, who not only "preserv[ed] the law, but [had] very little trouble with those Negroes who insist[ed] upon breaking the law."

Along with trying to stir up people through his sermons, Ransom formed a committee of Black ministers to put pressure on Mayor John Purroy Mitchell. When they went to see him, he was at first unresponsive. This angered Ransom, who, to the amusement of the reporters present, said, "Mr. Mayor, it looks like you refuse to appoint Negroes to police duty even in the parks of the city. Is it because you are afraid they might spit on the grass and kill it?" Not long afterward, because of continual pressure and the growing support of Tammany Hall, which wanted the Negro vote, Ransom's fight was won. Several Negroes were appointed to the force.[18] Joseph was once again impressed by his mentor's ability to move what appeared to be unmovable forces in behalf of his race.

During the month of January 1910 Ransom held a series of revivals. Joseph attended all of them and afterwards said he had become converted. The experience was unlike those described in testimonies he had heard in prayer meetings; no force pulled him out of his seat or struck him dumb. He said he just felt a kind of peace he had never known before and a desire to help others find that same peace. He no longer traveled his odyssey alone. God had become his navigator.

In his letters home he was reluctant at first to reveal what he was feeling, but he spoke so enthusiastically about the Ransoms and Bethel that Rebecca sensed the direction in which he was now moving. He was going to be a minister. She found this profession as acceptable as medicine or law. The only problem facing him was acquiring enough money to attend seminary when he finished high school. He tried hard to economize, but even with the free suppers supplied by the restaurant where he worked, the generosity of his Uncle James in feeding him and allowing him to stay in the apartment, and the Sunday dinners with the Ransoms, he could not save even a fraction of the amount needed. He grew despondent.

His Uncle James told him about a cousin from Antigua who lived in Flushing, a suburb of New York City. William Benjamin Derrick was a bishop in the A.M.E. Church, lived in a mansion, and was reported to be quite well off. James suggested that Derrick might be willing to help a relative and fellow islander further his schooling; consequently, the next day Joseph had off from work he spent his last ten cents traveling to Flushing.

After walking up the long driveway of the mansion, he was greeted coldly at the door by the butler, who led him to the study and told him to wait. Joseph studied the rows of books, most of which concerned politics or history. An hour later Derrick made his appearance, ostentatiously arrayed in a silk smoking jacket. He was a handsome man in his mid-fifties, with reddish-brown skin, graying wavy hair, a firm mouth, and penetrating eyes. Not acknowledging Joseph's outstretched hand, Derrick looked skeptically at the young man before him who claimed to be his cousin. Then he sat down in the wing-back chair by the fireplace. After hearing the purpose of Joseph's visit, he began to brag with affected diction about his own background.

He had been born in Antigua, July 27, 1843, he said. His father, Thomas J. Derrick, had been a planter of some means. During the Civil War, William came to America, enlisted in the navy, served on the USS *Minnesota,* and participated in the battle between the *Monitor* and the *Merrimac.* He boasted that he had served under two flags, the British and the American. After his religious conversion in 1864 he had joined the A.M.E. Church and was licensed to preach. In 1879, he had transferred to New York, where he became prominent in politics, claiming friendship with such influential Republicans as Thomas Platt and Roscoe Conkling; he could, he said, deliver the Negro vote to the Republican party whenever he wanted to, and was, he claimed, the most powerful colored politician in New York City. He had been elected to the bishopric in 1896.[19]

Joseph later recalled that Derrick, growing tired of listing his many accomplishments, suddenly stood behind the tall chair as if in the pulpit and announced in stentorian tones something to this effect: "Young man, I fought in the Civil War . . . have been knee deep in blood during the Spanish American War . . . languished in the trenches, slept in the mud, and not once . . . not once in all my life did I ever ask anyone for help. I made [myself] Bishop William Benjamin Derrick. I suggest thou goest and do likewise." With that, he turned and walked out of the library, leaving the butler to show Joseph to the door.

By the time Joseph reached 36th Street, hitchhiking and walking, some of his anger and indignation had subsided. He vowed neither to see Derrick again nor claim his kinship, and he never did. When Joseph told Ransom about his experience, Ransom was not surprised. He had his own stories to tell about the grand bishop, who at one time had asked Ransom to leave New York because he was becoming too politically powerful. Ransom informed him that he would not leave—that Derrick had had his day in New York politics for over twenty-five years. "This is my day and I shall proceed to live my life and follow the course of thinking that would be wisest and best for the welfare of our people as a whole." Ransom asserted that "from that day forth, Bishop Derrick never again regained his political influence in the politics of New York City."[20]

On Sunday afternoon, March 20, 1910, Joseph was finally given the opportunity to meet Booker T. Washington, the founder of Tuskegee Institute and who, according to Ransom, was the white people's appointed leader of the Negro race. Many Negroes admired his accomplishments, but even more whites, North and South, championed his accommoda-tionist views on the political and social equality of Negroes. At the Atlanta Cotton Exposition in the fall of 1895 he had clearly spelled out his position: "The wisest among my race understand that the agitation of questions of social equality is the extremist folly and that progress in the enjoyment of all the privileges that will come to us must be the result of severe and con-stant struggle, rather than of artificial forcing."[21] Du Bois had eloquently denounced Washington's philosophy in his *Souls of Black Folks,* and the kindest thing Ransom had to say about Washington's stand was that he "was short sighted." Nevertheless, Emma Ransom had invited him to speak on behalf of the Colored Branch of the YWCA, and Joseph went to hear him. He was disappointed, not only by the brevity of the speech but by its underlying condescending tone.

Washington seemed to be saying that the South was the best place for the Negro, and industrial education the most important kind of learning. Joseph reasoned that Du Bois might be elitist in advocating that the tal-ented 10 percent, the brightest Negroes, should lead the rest, but at least he believed that Blacks had more potential for advancement than that found in their backs and hands. When Joseph expressed to Ransom his dis-illusionment with Washington, Ransom replied that if he examined closely Booker T.'s background, he would not judge him so harshly. Having been raised in poverty and a southern racial climate, Washington believed the only way Tuskegee could have become a reality was for him to espouse a philosophy that was not threatening to the white power structure.

Although Negroes often squabbled among themselves, they came to-gether quickly when attacked from the outside. Joseph had an opportunity to observe this firsthand when Booker T. Washington became the object of slander. According to Washington's version, on March 19, 1911, he had gone to an apartment at 111-2 West 63rd Street in New York City to keep an appointment with Daniel C. Smith, white auditor of Tuskegee Institute, but found he had the wrong address. While trying to learn the whereabouts of Smith, Washington was assaulted by Albert Ulrich, a white carpenter who alleged first that Washington was trying to burglarize the building and later that Washington had been flirting with his wife. Washington was arrested, and Ulrich brought charges of trespassing. The police released Washington when he was able to convince them who he was. Before leaving the jail, Washington brought assault charges against Ulrich.[22]

The Age for March 23 reported that Washington was in serious con-dition and under a doctor's care at the Hotel Manhattan.[23] When he was released, he went to Ransom's home in Harlem, "his face still plastered with tape and bandages from the beating he had received."[24] In late March

Joseph attended a mass meeting at Bethel which had been called to show that Negroes were united in their support of Booker T. Washington. The auditorium was filled. "Almost every speaker expressed the opinion that the brutal attack made on Booker T. Washington had done more to bring the race together than any incident in many years." Letters by President Taft and Bishop Alexander Walters of the A.M.E. Zion Church were read. Carried away by the passion of the moment, Rev. Adam Clayton Powell, Sr., asserted that Blacks had been in America before the Puritans, and that if anyone talked about sending them out of the country, he would tell them: "Let the Slavs go back to the Danube, the Russians to the Volga, the Italians to the Tiber, the Egyptians to the Nile, and the Irish to the Thames, and three months later [Blacks would] go back to the Congo to found a great state under our intrepid leader, Dr. Washington."[25]

At the court trial, which began November 6, the three judges acquitted Ulrich of assault by a two-to-one verdict.[26] Since testimonies were conflicting, even among the Washington faction, Joseph was never clear as to the real truth of the case, but he agreed with Ransom's conclusion that whether Washington was innocent or guilty, "the overwhelming majority of Americans believ[ed] that [he] was too great a man and rendered too large a service . . . to be further humiliated and challenged."[27]

By the time Joseph's years in New York ended, he had met many leaders of his race and church and had sat at the knee of his mentor, Ransom. Now he was ready to prepare himself for his life's work. Ransom had petitioned the New York Annual Conference to provide scholarship money for Joseph to attend Payne Theological Seminary at Wilberforce University. The Church was in need of courageous young ministers who were seriously committed to their calling and the A.M.E. Church; the ministers and bishop had already heard about Ransom's gifted pupil and agreed to invest in his future. It was arranged that he should begin at Payne in the fall of the next school year.

In October 1911 Joseph boarded the train for Wilberforce, Ohio. His only possession was a new leather bag, a going-away present from the Ransoms. His Uncle James pressed a few dollars in his hands and then jumped off the train just before it pulled away from the station bound for Ohio. Joseph was leaving New York with a different dream than the one with which he had come, and a different name. Having found his middle names too long, and deciding to change his surname from the Portuguese "Gomes," he now called himself simply Joseph Gomez.

◈ ◈ ◈

CHAPTER THREE

Upon This Rock

Wilberforce & Hazel T., 1911–1914

[Wilberforce has] its setting in a scene of natural beauty in one of
the richest valleys in the State of Ohio. It has highland and low-
land, woodland, mineral springs and running brooks. . . . It was,
and is, a community with an atmosphere of culture and refinement, hardly equaled elsewhere among Negroes in the United
States. That elusive thing called the "Spirit of the Founders,"
as in Harvard, Yale and Princeton Universities, is here in all its
potency, with that stamp of individuality present in the spirit of
every institution that has a soul of its own.
—Reverdy Cassius Ransom,
The Pilgrimage of Harriet Ransom's Son

◈ When Joseph arrived at Wilberforce in October 1911, there were some
new buildings, but the spirit and atmosphere had changed little since Ransom's days as a student in 1881. Joseph soon learned that the place did indeed have "a soul of its own," one that reflected the constancy and vision
of its founders.

Originally, Tawawa Springs near Xenia, Ohio, had been a health resort
because of the minerals in the water. In 1856 it had been purchased by the
white Methodist Episcopal Church for the purpose of establishing a school
for Negroes. The new institution was named Wilberforce, for William
Wilberforce, the famous English statesman and abolitionist. The creation
of a college at Wilberforce marked the initial stage of the movement to set
up institutions of higher learning specifically for Negroes in the United
States. "With this single exception, however, colleges of this type were not

established until after the abolition of slavery when the great movement began for the education of the freedman."[1]

On the property was a two-hundred-room building that could easily be transformed into a dormitory, and several small cottages suited for occupancy by the administration and faculty.[2] The Methodists were able to operate the school successfully until the outbreak of the Civil War, when slaveowners could no longer send their illegitimate mulattoes to such an institution, and the parents of free northern black children could no longer pay the tuition—all money formerly provided as scholarships by the Church had to be used for the war effort. As a result, three months before the Emancipation Proclamation was issued by President Abraham Lincoln, the college was forced to close.[3]

On June 11, 1863, Daniel Payne, a teacher and minister in the African Methodist Episcopal Church; J. G. Mitchell, principal of the Eastern District School in Cincinnati, Ohio; and Rev. J. A. Shorter, pastor of the A.M.E. Church in Zanesville, Ohio, put a down payment of $2,500 toward the purchase of the college. Soon a new board of trustees and an administrative staff were appointed. Payne was elected president of the university, J. A. Shorter treasurer, and John G. Mitchell principal.[4]

In 1888, the state of Ohio entered into an agreement with the A.M.E. Church whereby it would set up an Industrial Department at Wilberforce University to "aid Negro citizens of Ohio to equip themselves for service in the industrial society that called for skilled performances" in such areas as "carpentry, blacksmithing, brick-making, tailoring, dressmaking, cooking, etc. . . . Due to the need for public school teachers, the offering of the State was extended to include Teacher Training or a two year Normal Course."[5] Another expansion took place in 1891, when the Church organized a separate department called Payne Theological Seminary to meet the pressing need for a trained Negro ministry.[6] This, then, was the status of the university in 1911 when Joseph entered as a first-year seminary student.

He was met at the station by the ageless "Dad" Harris, as Wilberforceans affectionately called the Maintenance Supervisor. Dad provided local color and was an institution in his own right. Along with his other duties, he was the official greeter—and he took this responsibility even more seriously than he did his maintenance duties. All newcomers had to listen to Dad's formula for "how to stay at Wilberforce." It did not take freshmen long to discover that those who listened usually remained long enough to graduate; those who did not, fell by the wayside.

Dad put Joseph's bag in the "Transfer," an ancient wagon that almost always broke down before it reached the campus, twenty minutes away. As Joseph walked beside the wagon, he was moved by the Ohio countryside, which was aflame with autumn colors. There had been so much hustle and bustle in New York City that he had seldom paid attention to the autumn, except for those rare occasions when he walked through Central Park.

When they reached the campus, Dad gave Joseph the standard tour. Joseph could see through the trees Shorter Hall, built by Daniel Payne in 1878 after the original building had been destroyed by fire in 1865. It housed the main dormitory, classrooms, museum, the Ware Art Room, music rooms, and the dining hall. Next Dad pointed out the three women's dormitories: O'Neil Hall, the new Arnett Hall (1905), and Mitchell Hall for Senior Women, built only a year before. Joseph liked best Galloway Hall, with its towering belfry, large auditorium, and rooms for the trades. Dad's tour led them back to Shorter Hall, where he told Joseph that the building to the right, near the road, was Carnegie Library, built in 1907. All in all the university had ten buildings, including four halls, two farm houses, and nine frame cottages, where the professors and other university personnel lived. There were thirty-two teachers, four hundred students, and over nine thousand alumni.[7]

Joseph walked beside the Transfer up the hill, past the post office, then turned right at the corner. There on five acres of land sat Payne Theological Seminary, in a brick building which had originally been the home of J. C. Mitchell, one of the founders. Mitchell had died leaving the property to the university, and Bishop Arnett was assigned the task of remodeling and furnishing it for a seminary. It had been dedicated in the fall of 1892 and named after Daniel Payne, the university's first president.[8]

Joseph lifted his bag from the Transfer, thanked Dad for the tour, and entered the large, two-story building. On the first floor was an assembly room, a library, and several classrooms. A long hall ran the entire length of the building, ending with steep staircases on either side, leading to the upstairs dormitory.

At the top of the stairs, Joseph was greeted by a student who announced that he was A. Wayman Ward, "himself," of Denver, Colorado. Ward was tall, copper-skinned, and handsome; and Joseph was immediately attracted by his flamboyance and the authority with which he ushered Joseph down the hall to his room. Ward had already established himself as the leader.

The room that was to be Joseph's home for three years was quite compact—sparsely furnished with a bedstead, mattress, two pillows, a table, and two chairs. Already he missed the comforts of Uncle James's apartment. He unpacked his bedclothing and towels, which were marked with his full name as stipulated in the catalogue, and he began to hang up his clothes. Ward informed him there was no running water in the building; water had to be pumped from outside. However, the building did have in the basement a furnace, which Joseph would have to take his turn tending. Also in the basement were a kitchen and storage room.

Joseph soon became acquainted with the other "Theologues," or "Would Be's," as the seminary students were called because they aspired to be ministers. There was the heavily mustached A. L. Washington, nicknamed "Wash" because of his name and his cleanliness fetish; sometimes he was referred to as "the Second Rabbi Gamaliel." There was R. J. Robinson from Newport, Rhode Island, who along with Joseph was considered to be the most studious; Ezra Ousley, nicknamed "Beetle" because he was always on the ground praying; Joseph N. Carter, Latin lover from South America, "fiery in temper and hair"; stern-looking Isaiah H. Alston, called "Hubby," "solid in piety, and full of devotion"; and A. C. Casper from Salem, North Carolina, the only one not at first given a nickname. Joseph's classmates soon referred to him as "Little Joey," because of his small stature, or as "Preacher," when he changed from being mischievous to argumentative.

A. Wayman Ward was "in a class by himself." He was a "ladies' man," used a lot of slang, and liked to be thought of as suave and nonchalant. Involved in practically every organization, including all the sports teams and the college quartet, he was the most popular man on campus. He was not only extremely witty and spontaneous but also an A student in all of his courses, and he had already received one degree, from Denver University. He and Joseph became best friends and competitors.

Two other students who were not in Joseph's class but became intimate life-long friends were Russell S. Brown from Topeka, Kansas, and J. D. Smith from Bermuda. Brown came to Payne a year after Joseph and went on to become a prominent pastor and general secretary of the A.M.E. Church. J. D. was a senior when Joseph was a freshman; a staunch A.M.E. all his life, he was involved with the Church not only in Bermuda but in Connectional (Church-wide) activities as well. Joseph was often to seek his advice in both personal and church matters.

The Theologues tended to be older than the other students, some having graduated from other colleges. A few were married and lived in rented quarters in Xenia or the Wilberforce community. Unlike the other male students, they did not have to wear uniforms but dressed in dark suits, white shirts, and ties, which was considered to be attire appropriate to the sobriety of their calling. The average cost for their fees, board, light, and books ranged from $110 to $115 a year.[9] Like Joseph, most of them were on Conference Scholarships from the various Episcopal districts and had to spend at least one hour a day working in the buildings or on the grounds to maintain their scholarships. It was Joseph's job to pump and carry water for the seminary. In the yearbook of 1914 his hobby is listed as "water boy."[10]

Payne Seminary had two divisions of study, the English Theological and the Regular, both of which took three years to complete and led to a bachelor of divinity degree. The only difference between the divisions was that Greek and Latin were required in the Regular, in which Joseph was enrolled. His transcript covering his three years provides some idea as to the vigorous demands of the curriculum. Among his teachers were Williams Saunders Scarborough, president of the University and professor of philosophy and Greek literature; George Frederick Woodson, dean of Payne Seminary and professor of systematic and practical theology; Alexander Wayman Thomas, professor of Hebrew and archaeology; Pleasant S. Hill, professor of historical and pastoral theology; A. J. White, Professor of Greek; and Hallie Quinn Brown, instructor of English and elocution.

TRANSCRIPT

Joseph Gomez
Payne Theological Seminary

October 1911–February 1912			February 1912–June 1912		
Subject	Cr.	Grade	Subject	Cr.	Grade
Pastorate	3	B	Pastorate	3	A
Life of Christ	2	A	Life of Christ	2	A-
S.S. Training	3	A	Jr. English	3	A
Psychology	3	B-	Jr. Hebrew	3	B-
Jr. Hebrew	3	B-	Jr. Greek	3	A
Jr. Greek	3	B	Church Law	3	A
Logic	3	A	Ethics	3	B+
Old Test. History	3	B+	Sociology	2	B

October 1912–February 1913			February 1913–June 1913		
Systematic Theology	3	B	Systematic Theology	3	B
Homiletics	3	B+	Homiletics	3	A
Sr. Mid. Greek	2	B	Sr. Mid. Greek	2	B
Adv. English	3	A	Biblical Literature	3	A
Church History	3	A	Sr. Mid. Hebrew	2	B
Sr. Mid. Hebrew	2	B	Life of Paul	2	A
Life of Paul	2	A			
Missions	3	A			

October 1913–February 1914			February 1914–June 1914		
Systematic Theology	3	A	Systematic Theology	3	A
Archaeology	3	B	Christian Doctrine	3	A
Hermeneutics	3	B+	Hermeneutics	3	A¹
Psychology of Rel.	3	A	Philosophy of Rel.	3	A
Apologetics	3	A	Comparative Religion	3	A
			Hymnology	1	A

Number of recitation periods, 50 mins. each per week
Total Courses 31
Total Hours 112

S.S. = Sunday School   "A¹" highest average in class

Henry Howard Summers, Registrar

Although Scarborough had spoken in New York on many occasions and Joseph had heard Ransom refer admiringly to him, Joseph had not met him before. He had his first opportunity at Chapel that fall. Listening to his address, Joseph understood why so many people praised his brilliance. He had published *First Lessons in Greek* and *Birds of Aristophanes: A Theory of Interpretation,* two books which discredited the myth that Negroes could not master classical languages. After his speech to the assembly he introduced his wife, Sara C. Bierce, a white woman, who had come to Wilberforce as a professor of natural science in 1877, taught French from 1884 to 1887, and was currently the principal of the Normal Department.[11] Joseph came to admire Scarborough for his mild manner, dignity, scholarly demeanor, and impracticality—he was the prototype of the "absent-minded professor." Joseph was also fond of Sara, who had dedicated her life to the education of Negroes.

Dean Woodson was a fine scholar in his own right and an effective professor, a man who involved himself in all aspects of the campus and Church life. Joseph was stimulated by his classes and homey advice.

Hallie Q. Brown was widely known in America and England as an elocutionist and temperance lecturer. Her boundless energy made everything she did seem of crucial importance. Joseph was one of her favorite students, because, as she would tell him, "he was intelligent, did not mutilate the English language, had spunk and never accepted anything at face value."

The daily routine at Wilberforce was rigorous and left little time for frivolity. Joseph arose at 5:30 A.M. to the sound of the bell and washed himself with the water he had pumped outside the night before. If he were not already fully awake, the icy water shocked him into motion. After dressing and cleaning his room, he rushed to Shorter Hall, where breakfast was served to the male students. (The women ate in Arnett Hall.) At 8:15 he attended chapel, an everyday requirement for all students. Interrupted only by a half-hour lunch period, Joseph's schedule of classes and study hours was continuous until 3:30 P.M. From 3:30 until supper at 5 P.M. he was free to attend organizational meetings, engage in some kind of supervised recreation, or attend to his chores. From 6:30 until 10 P.M. was study hour, during which everyone had to be in his own room.

All students were expected to attend Prayer Meeting on Monday evenings and go to Sabbath School and morning services on Sunday. The rules of the university included a long list of "don'ts," such as: associate with the opposite sex without permission; have in your possession immoral books or papers; drink intoxicating beverages or use tobacco; possess firearms or other deadly weapons; absent yourself from the premises without permission; throw water, trash, litter, or anything offensive from the windows; or marry while pursuing a course of study, without permission of the faculty.[12]

The majority of students who attended Wilberforce were from poor or lower-middle-class homes and were appreciative of the opportunity to acquire a college education; consequently, they were serious about their studies. They had come from all parts of America, from Africa, Canada, South America, and the Caribbean. Serious or not, they were a lively lot and frequently found ways to get around the strict regulations. For instance, some would dance in the music room of Shorter Hall or in the assembly room of Arnett when the more pious faculty members were not in sight. During the study hour a few were known to slip into a classmate's room to play a rousing game of cards; once in a while an empty whiskey bottle, which no one seemed to know anything about, would be found in the hall wastebasket.

Joseph diligently observed the study hour, but he was occasionally known to sneak from his room to engage in a heated debate on some timely subject. Because of his tendency to exaggerate at these night sessions, his classmates jokingly said he was "known all over the world in Ohio."

To balance the vigorous routine of classes and study there were a number of extracurricular activities such as football, basketball, skating, tennis, and track; literary societies—the Sodalian and Payne for men and the Philomathean and Dobbs for women; the Alpha Phi Debating Club, which competed with schools like Howard and Fisk Universities (Joseph's work schedule prevented him from joining); the John C. Mitchell Society, a discussion and social-service group; religious societies such as the YWCA, YMCA, Preachers' Aid, Young People's Christian Endeavor League, Sunday School, and the Missionary Society; musical organizations that included the college choir, quartet, band, and orchestra; and one Greek fraternity, the Alpha Phi Alpha. The university and most of its organizations periodically sponsored guest lectures, concerts, plays, and poetry readings. A few times during the year students were allowed to travel to Xenia for special activities.[13]

Not long after coming to Wilberforce Joseph met and fell in love with Hazel Eliza Jane Thompson, a petite young woman with long, thick hair who was destined to be the most important person in his life. Her family background was as complicated as his. The family Bible lists her as having been born on May 24, 1891, in Toledo, Ohio. A cousin, Cora Lockhart, who now resides in Detroit, corroborates this;[14] however, the doctor who delivered her said she was born on May 30. Her mother told her she had been born May 29. "My mother should know," Hazel reasoned, and that was the date she always observed.

Her maternal grandfather was John Dent, a former slave born in Paducah, Kentucky. He had escaped from slavery by simply jumping on his master's horse and "riding like hell" to freedom. For a while he had settled in Ripley, Ohio, where in 1849 he married Sara Jane Grubb, a young woman of African parentage who had been born in Sterling, Kentucky. The couple moved first to Columbus, Ohio, and then to Toledo. Julia Anne, Hazel's mother, was born in March of 1858, one of their twelve children.

Hazel's paternal grandfather, George Henry Thompson, born in 1804 on the island of Madagascar, had been of Malaysian and Polynesian descent; the name given him at birth was Hari Orara. In his late teens he left his family, came to the United States, and was sold into slavery in Kentucky. Escaping from the plantation, he lived with Quakers in Philadelphia, working beside them as a blacksmith. There are different versions of what happened to him next. One is that at the age of thirty-six he settled in Philadelphia and worked as a coachman for the prestigious Ford family of Liverpool, England; shortly after he was hired, in this account, he ran off with their fourteen-year-old daughter, Eliza. The second version is that he went to Liverpool, England on a cattle boat, worked there for the Fords, and soon ran off with their young daughter. At any rate, he did marry the fourteen-year-old Eliza Elizabeth Ford in 1826 and moved with her to Amhurtsburg, Ontario. Eliza and Hari had eleven children. One of them, George Thompson, was to be Hazel's father.

When George was in his early twenties, he moved from Canada to Toledo and married a dressmaker, who died suddenly. The couple had had no children. At the age of forty-two he met Julia Anne Dent. She too had been married before, to a James Brown, who had also died, leaving her with three children. She consented to marry George, even though Julia Anne's father took an instant dislike to him because "he was a white man" (his birth certificate lists him as Eurasian)—John Dent despised all whites, because of his experiences during slavery. George and Julia Anne had one child, Hazel Eliza Jane Thompson. When George received the news of the birth of his only child, he is reported to have run down the streets of Toledo telling everyone he saw that his wife had given birth to a princess. As fate would have it, he barely had time to become acquainted with his princess, for he died when she was only a year and a half old.

Hazel described her mother's courage in her diary years later:

> I had been given a firm religious background by my mother who was a widow, and a person who helped everyone she could. She had to work hard to support the children. But when she baked (this she did often as it was one of the means of livelihood), we were sent in all directions to take bread and donuts to the sick and persons less fortunate. I often said to her, "Mama, why do you do this? You need the money for yourself." She answered, "The Lord will take care of us and maybe someday if you are in need, some one will help you."[15]

Ironically, Julia's father, John Dent, died from a concussion received when he was thrown down a flight of steps by some Polish men during a racial incident. After that, Julia Anne and her four children went to live with his widow, Sara Anne, who made life miserable for Hazel because she was of light skin. Sara had no use for "yeller niggers," and that included her granddaughter, who had "the blood of the men who killed her husband."

When Hazel was eight years old, her mother left the three older children with their grandmother and took Hazel with her to Perry Harbor, Ontario. She had been hired as a housekeeper to the wealthy Peters family. Mrs. Peters was a German Jew. The couple treated Julia Anne and Hazel as if they were family. Mr. Peters became the father Hazel had never known, and he took her with him practically everywhere he went, including to the exclusive country club. Everyone in town spoke German, and Hazel learned to speak it fluently. Because she had no contact with Negroes, when Hazel was in her late teens Julia returned to Toledo so Hazel could go to school with Negroes and regain her sense of racial identity. As soon as Hazel finished high school, Julia Anne made arrangements for her to attend Wilberforce University, where, as she told Hazel, "she could not only earn a teaching certificate and become independent, but also learn about her own heritage."

Before Hazel left for Wilberforce, Julia Anne married again, this time to a Joseph Perkins, who could neither read nor write but who had money and owned a great deal of farmland just outside the city. If Julia Anne expected him to help her finance Hazel's schooling, she was disappointed. He took good care of her but offered nothing toward Hazel's two years at Wilberforce. Julia Anne paid Hazel's tuition by selling her baked goods.

At first Hazel had a difficult time adjusting to Wilberforce. Within a week of her arrival she was so homesick that she went back to Toledo, only to be sent right back to school by her mother so she "could get an education and not have to work in somebody's kitchen all her life." When she returned she was determined to keep busy so she would have no time to think of home.

She became involved in missionary work, taking a special interest in an African student nicknamed "Klarney" [T. B. Kalene], "who had large holes in his ears and spoke no English." She and others in the missionary society at the university "had the holes filled in, gave him clothes, and taught him English. He advanced so rapidly that in a few years, he had mastered Greek, Hebrew and English; but his greatest desire was to go back to Africa and help his people."[16] Hazel kept in touch with him for a few years after he returned home and was proud of his accomplishments as a teacher.

Hazel's interest in religious work brought her in contact with the Theologues, particularly Joseph Gomez. Soon he was sending her invitations to go to "drags." The drag consisted of a promenade around the campus: couples would line up in front of Arnett Hall, the girls' dormitory; in between each third couple was a chaperone, whose job it was to see that no "spooning" took place. Joseph found a way to "outfox" the chaperone. When he was sure the woman was not looking, he would tell Hazel to look up at the moon; as she turned her head and looked up he would plant a quick kiss on her cheek. She would pretend to be shocked at this daring but later admitted she found his kisses very pleasant. Luckily he was never caught, for if he had been, he would have received a black mark. With three such marks a student had to appear before the formidable faculty discipline committee; ten marks meant being sent home in disgrace. Before he had graduated he no doubt had planted at least ten kisses on her willing cheek and gotten away with it.

Hazel was enrolled in the Normal Department, majoring in sewing, cooking, and teachers' training. In addition to her classes, she joined the basketball team. The women had petitioned the faculty at its December 1911 meeting to be allowed to form their own team and were given permission. In order to belong to the team the players had to pay an annual fee of 50 cents and practice daily in the Armory from 3:30 to 4:40 P.M., with a chaperon always in attendance, of course. According to the *Sodalian* (yearbook) of 1912, the women "played basketball hard and fast, yet always retained their womanly dignity, thus clearly demonstrating that athletic games conducted in the right spirit can safely be indulged in by young women."[17] At any rate, Joseph saw in Hazel no loss of "womanly dignity" as a result of her playing basketball, even though she was one of the best forwards on the team and was said to play "a very physical game."

Joseph said he always enjoyed watching Hazel walk across the campus headed for practice. Although he would have liked to accompany her, it was against the rules for men and women to walk together, nor could he watch her practice in the Armory or (when the weather permitted) in the rear of Arnett Hall. Professor Green, the coach, had screened off the area so the women could concentrate on what they were doing rather than on the admiring eyes that would have been watching them. Joseph was relieved in his second year when the rule about men and women walking together was changed to permit it if they were going in the same direction. After that, Joseph always found some legitimate reason to be going in Hazel's direction.

On Monday afternoons young men were permitted to call upon the lady of their choice for one hour. Joseph would present his card to the matron in charge of Arnett Hall. She, in turn, would inform Hazel that a Mr. Gomez was calling for her. Unlike the other girls, Hazel did not keep her company waiting long. She would appear promptly and lead Joseph to a couch in the sitting room farthest from the matron's view. From the beginning he would dominate the conversation, jumping from one subject to another, from literature to politics to religion and to his own lofty ambitions. He talked with his hands and eyes, and he seemed to be passionate about every subject he introduced. His penetrating look made it impossible for Hazel to feign coyness, even had she been so inclined. She was not. He loved Shakespeare, Milton, and the Brownings, especially Elizabeth Barrett; did not care for Cowper who was "too dour"; had problems with the "Virgin Birth"; liked a lady to have long hair and large ears, hastily telling Hazel she had both. Recalling these visits, Hazel would say that by the time the hour was up she was pleasantly exhausted. This impulsive Theologue held a certain fascination for her. She had never before met anyone who knew where he was going and with whom he wanted to go.

Early in his courtship he told her he was going to be a good minister, that he was going to marry her and take her around the world. She never doubted that he would.

Chapel provided another means to further the courtship and also add a bit of intrigue. The almost fool-proof method the authorities had invented to keep the students' minds on spiritual matters made the challenge even more exciting. All the young men were required to sit on one side of the room, the young women on the other. Only senior men could sit with their female classmates, and they had to sit in front, where the faculty could keep an eye on them. Joseph found the Bible useful for more than reading the scriptures—it was an excellent conveyor of love notes. Putting his message between the pages, he would start the volume passing from hand to hand until it reached a blushing Hazel.

Because Hazel was enrolled in a two-year program, she was scheduled to graduate in 1913, one year before Joseph. In her senior year she moved into Mitchell Hall with the other females in her class. Since seniors were allowed more freedom, the girls planned a festive year. The most successful activity was the coed masked Halloween Party. Joseph and some of his friends were late arriving, because the freshmen boys had tied up the upperclassmen to prevent them from attending the party. When they finally got there, they participated in a pumpkin hunt; unfortunately, no one could find the pumpkin, "because the Junior girls had hidden it and did not return it until the next morning."[18] After the unsuccessful hunt everyone returned to Mitchell for refreshments. Another activity sponsored by the senior girls that year was a Valentine party, featuring an orchestra and "colorful re-freshments."[19] Joseph managed to slip Hazel a store-bought Valentine which expressed his love in "exceedingly bad verse."

One of the most important events on campus was Founders' Day, during which there were guest speakers, a student oration, and a class fund-raising contest. At the end of the day the classes would meet in as-sembly to see which had been able to raise the most money and win the trophy. As Joseph had been elected class president his junior year, it was his job to see that the class won the Founder's Day trophy on February 25, 1913. According to the class history that appeared in the *Remembrancer,* "With 'Little Joe' at the wheel, [the class had] felt certain that he would lead [them] to victory. Nevertheless . . . the high hopes were somewhat dampened when on the fatal night [they] learned that the Seniors in a final effort had with broken pocketbooks beaten [them] by about $60." The defeat only served to make them "work harder, determined that [they] would give the Seniors a banquet in May that would make them sit up and take notice" (it was the custom for the junior class to give the graduating class a banquet at the end of the academic year).[20] Hazel did her best to cheer up the highly competitive Joseph when his class did not win the trophy.

During her time at Wilberforce Hazel conducted herself in an exemplary manner until her last semester, when the faculty discipline committee reported the "case of Misses Roberts, Thompson [Hazel], Hicks, Carnes, Mitchell, Bronell, Walker and Adams [for] leaving church before service was out."[21] Such an infraction was enough to prevent the women from enjoying senior privileges. Despite the infractions, on May 20, 1913, Hazel and her classmates sent a petition to the faculty to be allowed to have a "regular chapel service . . . known as Senior Chapel Service, at which time the President of the University may be privileged to deliver a ten minute address to [the] class." They further asked for "Senior Privileges for everyone, the opportunity to associate with each other on campus without permission and to conduct [themselves] according to the actions of [the] class organization." They pledged that if they left the campus "for a walk or ride, [they would] be under the supervision of a chaperon, matron or male member of the faculty."[22]

The faculty granted these requests for all those students who had not received a "mark against their good conduct." Evidently Hazel and the other girls who had left "church before service was out" were let off with a mild reprimand. All of them were allowed to enjoy senior privileges; consequently, even though Joseph was not in the senior class, Hazel had more liberty to see him. She also must have enjoyed his waiting on her during the banquet the juniors gave for the seniors that May.

Hazel and Joseph wanted to marry right away, but since he had one more year of seminary, they decided to wait until his graduation in 1914. Hazel would secure a teaching job for nine months and then return to the campus for his commencement.

In early April Hazel began to petition the school officials for letters of certification to accompany her job applications. On April 19, 1913, she was given two letters, one from President Scarborough, the other from Bessie V. Morris, instructor of domestic science. In his letter Scarborough noted that she was "a young lady of high character and excellent ability; that she [had] made a splendid record" since coming to Wilberforce. In his final paragraph he spoke of her as a "prominent member of the women's religious organizations of the school" and recommended her "to anyone who desir[ed] to fill a vacancy, either in Normal work" or domestic science or sewing.[23] Bessie Morris pointed to her neatness, precision, and energy, calling her a "Christian woman who is willing to do all in her power to build up greater work."[24]

A month later Hazel received word that she had been accepted as a teacher by the Industrial-Agricultural College for Negroes in Selby, Mississippi. The only description she had of the school was that printed on its official stationery.

> This school was incorporated under the laws of the State of Mississippi for the purpose of teaching the Negro children anything along the line of industry. The prime object is to teach Agriculture in a practical way, as the masses of our people will be farmers. We will operate 80 acres of land and conduct an experiment station. We have full blood pigs and chickens and are placing others as fast as we can. Will be grateful for any assistance rendered to us.[25]

Joseph expressed his reluctance for Hazel to teach at such a school, which was obviously operated in the Booker T. Washington tradition. According to the statement the children and full blood pigs seemed to be lumped together, with the pigs coming out ahead. Nevertheless, since Hazel had had no other offers, she decided to take the job despite the objections of Joseph and her mother. Julia Anne was strongly opposed to her daughter going South, particularly to a state with the reputation of Mississippi, where Negroes were known to disappear without a trace and lynching became a daily sport. Hazel was determined to try it; meanwhile, there were a few more weeks before school was over.

The senior edition of the *Sodalian* came out several days before commencement. Beneath Hazel's picture was a list of her activities: vice president of the senior class, vice president of the YWCA, Sunday School teacher, and basketball player. Hazel's class expressed their hopes for the future, in the tradition of all graduating classes, in an article with the original title "We Hope."

> That the discipline committee will not be as busy in the here-to-come as they were in the year of 1913; that socials will be given every week in order that both sexes will not seem like birds out of a cage when they are permitted to socialize; that Dad Harris will not have to load his Transfer so that it will break down; that the campus of Wilberforce University will stay this beautiful forever.[26]

Joseph had met Hazel's mother, Julia Anne, when he had gone home with Hazel during the Thanksgiving holidays, but had never formally asked for Hazel's hand in marriage. According to Hazel's notes, when Julia Anne arrived on campus for the graduation exercises "Joseph asked her to take a walk with him. . . . My mother said he nearly walked her to death before he had nerve enough to ask her consent to our marriage."[27] Julia Anne enthusiastically approved of the marriage but thought they were wise to wait until Joseph had graduated.

The commencement address was delivered by Bishop C. S. Smith, who spoke on "The Noachian Curse," using as a text the ninth chapter of Genesis, which tells of the curse put on Ham for viewing the naked body of his father, Noah. From that time forward Ham was to be a servant to his brothers. Whites had for years used this scripture to justify the enslaving of Blacks. In explaining his use of this ancient story instead of a more up-to-date topic, Smith said, "Quite recently I heard, as it were, the echo of a voice from a long past age, reminding me that I am one of the heirs of a withering curse." He disputed that the curse was ever carried out "except as it relates to a solitary and pusillanimous Canaanitish tribe known as the Hivites. With this exception, none of the Canaanitish tribes became the servant of servants either of Shem or Japeth [brothers of Ham]." After a careful historical analysis, Smith concluded that no man was responsible for from "whom he was born, where he was born, when he was born, and how he was born." Therefore, he said, if anyone does not like these things about me, "if the complexion of my skin and the texture of my hair are not according to your liking, do not quarrel with me about it, or withold from me any opportunity to which I am entitled, or deny me any right that I am capable of intelligently exercising, but wait until you get into the presence of the Great Creator and ask Him."

He advised the class, "When you depart from these classic halls to life's arena, the measure and value of the services that you may render your fellow-man will be proportionate to the quality and volume of the out-flow of the streams of your ethical and scholastic equipment. See to it, then that no deed of moral turpitude pollutes the springs of your activities."[28] Joseph was impressed by the uniqueness of this address, which was printed and distributed throughout the Connection.

Joseph gave the invocation at the literary societies' (Alpha Phi, Philo-mathean, John G. Mitchell, *Sodalian*) joint anniversary; William Grant Still, who was to become a great American composer, played a violin solo. He had enrolled at Wilberforce in the science program to please his mother; once there, however, he had directed the college band, organized a string quartet and arranged music for it, and composed and performed his own music. "He began to emulate his idol Samuel Coleridge-Taylor, even to the point of trying to grow a bushy hair style—with little success, for his hair was straight."[29] Even then it was obvious that he had exceptional musical gifts.

In mid-July, Hazel said a reluctant goodbye to her family and Joseph and crossed the Mason-Dixon Line for the first time. Mississippi was the poorest state in the Union; little attention and less money was paid for the education of Negroes, and the industrial school where Hazel was to teach was not even a glorified high school, although it called itself a college.

When she arrived in Selby she learned that she was expected not only to teach classes at the "college" but also go into the surrounding countryside and conduct classes in one-room schools a few days a week. Her pupils came from the most deprived families in the area, and few could read or write. Their parents were dirt farmers or sharecroppers, trying to eke a living from soil that had been badly depleted of nutrients by the continual growth of cotton and lack of crop rotation.

Hazel's family had not had much money as she was growing up, but she had never seen poverty on this level before. Most of the Negroes lived in wooden shacks elevated from the ground by posts. Entire families slept in one room. Cooking was done on wood stoves located in the yard, along with the water pump, outhouse, wash tub, chickens, and other half-starved domestic animals. A few Negroes who worked at the school or had been lucky enough to keep or buy land after Reconstruction lived in two-bedroom houses. Hazel boarded with a family in one of these houses. There were no cars; a neighboring farmer loaned her a mule on which to ride back and forth to school or to the outlying countryside. After being thrown on numerous occasions, Hazel finally learned how to outsmart the mule—by commanding it to do what she did not want it to do. Naturally the mule would do just the opposite, satisfying himself and Hazel. In time, Hazel became an expert rider.

Back at Wilberforce, Joseph worked on campus during the summer. When school began in the fall, he applied himself even more vigorously to his studies and was rewarded with nine As, one B, and one B+ for the year. He received the highest all-around average in hermeneutics in his last semester, surpassing even the brilliant A. Wayman Ward.

By his senior year, Joseph had been president not only of the junior class but also of the John G. Mitchell Society. He had been secretary of the Preacher's Aid, a member of the YMCA Cabinet and of the *Remembrancer* staff, and had acted in the senior class play, *The Kingdom of Heart's Content,* directed by Hallie Q. Brown. He had played Miles Alden, a Boston law student, to whom the lovely "Dixie surrenders her heart." As usual, he was second to A. Wayman Ward, who played Tom Lansing, the lead. Ward's list of accomplishments in the senior book far exceed those of Joseph's, including election as senior class president.[30] Always more outgoing than Joseph, he managed to make the conservative Theologue dark suit appear flashy by placing a colorful handkerchief in his coat pocket, raking his hat to the side, and carrying a cane. Joseph, on the other hand, preferred all his life the unadorned dark suit and tie of the clergy. But the competition between the two men was always friendly.

Another activity in which Joseph participated during his senior year was the revivals that occurred before the Christmas holidays. Classes were suspended, and ministers from a number of districts convened on the campus to win converts to Christ. The spirited sermons and rhythmic hymns were designed to bring the most recalcitrant souls into the fold. (The story goes that during the short period W. E. B. Du Bois taught at Wilberforce [1894–1896], he would become extremely agitated at what he considered these primitive practices. In his autobiography he tells how he and Charles Young, a graduate from West Point, refused to attend the revivals.[31] It was his belief that Blacks needed less Jesus and more education.)

Joseph liked the revivals when the sermons "had as much substance as passion." He learned by watching the various ministers preach. Most of all he was moved by the simple beauty of the spirituals and by the old hymns of Methodism, which reminded him of attending church with his mother in the islands.

During the year, letters traveled regularly back and forth between Mississippi and Ohio. Before Christmas the name "George" began to appear frequently in Hazel's letters. According to her, his family was quite well to do, one of the few Negro families who had managed to profit from the land. In a letter to her mother she described him as slender, with copper skin, curly hair—good looking. Of course, he was "not as good looking as Joseph."

No doubt Hazel was flattered by George's persistent attention. Julia Anne, who had a strong prejudice against Southern men, answered in strong language. Hazel should let him alone—Southern men were of a different breed. She did not trust them. Hazel would not find anyone better than Joey, and if she were not careful she would lose him. Her mother need not have concerned herself. Hazel had no intention of abandoning her Theologue no matter how rich George might be. His interest in her, however, had given her confidence. Here she was, a country girl from Toledo, Ohio, with two eligible bachelors asking for her hand. She wondered what her Grandmother Sara Anne would say to that—Sara Anne, who called her "a finicky, yellow hussy who would never catch a man."

This brief distraction was soon forgotten in light of her heavy teaching responsibilities. She was expected to be a master of all subjects: reading, writing, arithmetic, history, geography, cooking, sewing, and home making. In the spring she was sent to the cities to raise money for the school, along with a Mrs. R. J. Brady. J. M. Williamson, the principal, sent a letter introducing the two women as teachers who "know the needs of our people."[32]

For Hazel, this fund-raising lasted for only a few weeks. It was soon time for her to return to Wilberforce and Joseph's graduation. In a way, she was sorry to leave. She had come to love many of the students and to have a growing respect for their parents, who were able to survive in circumstances that would have defeated most people.

On June 18, 1914, Hazel and Julia Anne watched Joseph accept his diploma from Dean Woodson, shake the hand of President Scarborough, and ascend the platform, throwing his hat in the air with the rest of his classmates. He had graduated with honors, been ordained an elder, and assigned to his first charge all on the same day. However, the most significant event was his marriage, at the residence of Professor Hill of Payne Seminary and his wife. (The house was later used as the college post office.)

Only once had he faltered in his determination to marry Hazel. When he went to Xenia to get the license, he found that after paying for it he had only a few nickels left. He began seriously to question his right to accept Hazel's pledge of "for better or worse," when he had nothing to offer her except dreams and promises. She found him sitting alone on campus, despondent, and for the first time, quiet. When she asked him what was the matter, he said, "I can't marry you. I have no right to marry you. The only thing I have for sure is a diploma." She answered angrily, "Did I ask you to have anything?" He replied, "No." "Are you saying I was a fool to accept your proposal?" "No." "Then what is this all about?" He looked up finally and smiled, "Nothing, I guess." That had ended any further discussion on the subject.

The wedding ceremony was performed at 2 P.M. by Dean Woodson. In attendance were Julia Anne and Joseph's seminary classmates, including A. Wayman Ward. In addition there were the Ransoms, Rev. Hadley of Georgia, Russell S. Brown, and Floy Smith (whom Brown married later), the only daughter of Professor and Mrs. Charles S. Smith.

When the simple ceremony was over and Joseph had sealed his pledge by slipping a dimestore ring on Hazel's finger, he took his bride in his arms in public for the first time. He had waited none too patiently for over three years, obstructed by chapel rules, drag chaperons, and numerous other regulations. He kissed her so heartily that her hat slipped from her head and had to be rescued by the cavalier Ward, who insisted he should also get a kiss for his efforts. Joseph's senior horoscope had listed his favorite saying as, "But it is so," and it said he would be a minister.[33] As predicted, *it was so*—he had married the woman of his choice and had been ordained a minister. The only thing left for him to do was complete his naturalization papers in New York City so he could be an American citizen.

After the ceremony, the couple was taken to Xenia to stay in the home of one of the seminary students, a Rev. Massey. He zealously protected their privacy, and that night their youthful passion was finally consummated. A few days later, Uncle James sent Joseph money for his fare to New York. Since there was not enough money for Hazel, Joseph had reluctantly to leave his bride in the care of her mother, Rev. Massey, and a Rev. Becton, the pastor of the Baptist Church in Xenia, who was also studying at Payne. In a few days, with the help of his uncle and the Ransoms, Joseph was able to send for Hazel.[34] Before boarding the train, Julia Anne slipped a few dollars in Hazel's hand and kissed her goodbye. Hazel clung to her mother and cried. Too soon the train creaked out of the station like a tired old man. As she waved, Hazel never imagined this would be the last time she would see her mother alive.

When Uncle James met Hazel he liked her immediately, telling Joseph he had "done well for himself." Ransom, who went with Joseph to the station to meet her train, called her "Daughter," a title he continued to use throughout his life.

That Sunday, Hazel went with Joseph to the Church of Simon Cyrene, the mission Reverdy and Emma had opened in the worst section of the Tenderloin. It was located in a storefront on West 37th Street between 8th and 9th Avenues, four doors away from a "notorious 'gambling hall.'" To become a part of the community, the Ransoms had rented "a small apartment in the neighborhood on West 38th Street." The church was open every night of the week, and in a back room food was stored so that anyone in need could take some.[35] Hazel and Joseph were introduced to the membership, composed of derelicts, prostitutes, addicts, and others who were just down on their luck. They seemed to adore the Ransoms and trust them completely. The meals in the apartment were not as sumptuous as those in the Harlem parsonage had been, but the fellowship was even warmer. Emma and Reverdy were putting into practice to a much larger degree the social gospel in which they so deeply believed.

Joseph had only a few days to finalize his naturalization papers and squire Hazel around New York, a city she would never like. Overwhelmed by the noise and brashness of everything, she wondered where everyone was going in such a hurry. It was far too impersonal for her taste. Other than Uncle James and the Ransoms, few people seemed to her to be concerned about anybody but themselves. When it was time to leave, she was glad to exchange the congestion of the city for the expansive Atlantic, which would take them to Bermuda, their new island home, prolonged honeymoon, and first ministry . . . another step on their odyssey.

❖ ❖ ❖

CHAPTER FOUR

Early Charges

Bermuda & Hamilton, Ontario, 1914–1919

We have many a time been transported with the glories of the setting sun, viewed from our beautiful white-stone veranda that
overlooks the sea. . . . What a glorious riot of many-toned colors,
dissolving shapes and images of woodland glens, laughing mosaic
of blooms. . . . All the beauty of the landscape, the glories of the
mountain vastnesses, the calm of the lakes, the mystery of the sea
are here in glorious profusion.

—Joseph Gomez, "Sunset,"
Voice of Missions, May 1917

❖ In mid-July 1914, a few weeks after Joseph had been naturalized as an
American citizen, the newlyweds boarded a ship for Bermuda, their new
island home. Since Bermuda was a mission field, the Missionary Department of the A.M.E. Church was responsible for their transportation, but it
provided money only for second-class accommodations. This meant that
all the men slept in one part of the boat and the women in another. Joseph
suggested that Hazel pass herself off as his sister so that the other passengers would not know they were newlyweds. Later he said he had not
wanted anyone to know they were just married because the men would
have teased him about not being able to sleep with his bride. One suspects,
however, that Joseph's pride kept him from admitting he could not afford
first-class accommodations for his wife since he would not receive a salary
until he began his pastorate in Bermuda.

During the two days aboard ship, the couple learned about Bermuda
from fellow passengers. Actually it was not an island but an archipelago
of some 350 islands and reefs, only fifteen of them inhabited. Covering an

oval-shaped area of twenty square miles, the islands are joined by causeways and bridges. The largest island is Great Bermuda, on which is the capital city of Hamilton. Its flora and soft, pink, coral beaches, crystal caves, and limestone roads (composed chiefly of shells) were as yet unmarred by industrialization and the commercialism of the tourist crowd. It was an ideal spot for a first assignment and for a much-desired honeymoon.

The A.M.E. Church in Bermuda had been born at the Nova Scotia (Canada) Conference of the British Methodist Episcopal Church. Angry because of the racism in their respective churches, several Negroes who attended Anglican and Wesleyan churches petitioned Bishop William Nazrey to establish a British Methodist Episcopal Church in Bermuda. This Nazrey did in 1869, and in 1873 he organized the Bermuda Annual Conference. Eleven years later at the 1884 General Conference, the B.M.E. Church of Canada, the West Indies, and Bermuda merged with the A.M.E. Church.[1] At the time of Joseph's arrival there were ten churches in the Bermuda Conference. Among them were St. Paul's (the largest) in Hamilton and Bethel (second largest) at Shelly Bay, where Joseph had been assigned. These were the only two churches that had parsonages.

As the ship approached the Bermudas, the first island sighted was St. Davis. After the pilot from that island came aboard, the Gomezes climbed down a rope ladder to a smaller boat, which carried them to the harbor at Hamilton. There they were met by a delegation from Bethel: the Bascombes, Burgesses, Outerbridges, Darrells, and Harveys. Bethel was a family church in which sometimes more than ten members bore the same name, a name that often could be traced back two or three generations. For instance, the Outerbridge family had been noted for their skill in shipbuilding as early as 1680.[2] Hilgrove, Evan, and Esther Outerbridge, staunch members of Bethel, were descendants of this illustrious family.

In addition to the delegation from Bethel, several of the area ministers were present. Their leader introduced himself as Rev. W. E. Walker, Presiding Elder of the conference and pastor of St. Paul's, Hamilton. The ministers seemed surprised by the youthfulness of Joseph and his bride (Joseph was a mere twenty-four and Hazel a year younger), and they must have had serious doubts about this "boy minister's" ability to pastor a church most of whose members were much older than he. Joseph and Hazel sensed their reservations and were relieved to see one friendly face in the crowd. J. D. Smith, Joseph's old friend from Wilberforce, was on hand to smooth the way. After Smith had given his warm personal greetings, he introduced his wife, Charlotte, whom he had married soon after graduation, and their one-year-old son, Daniel Quinn.

As soon as the formal greetings were over, J. D. took them by carriage to the parsonage at Shelly Bay, in Hamilton Parish. They traveled some distance on the limestone road until they came to a small white cottage with a "hipped roof" and a veranda which looked out on the bay. Inside was a small living room, a kitchen with a pump and wood-burning stove, a dining room, a bedroom with "tray" ceilings, and an outhouse in the backyard. Because of the absence of streams and wells of fresh water, the islanders had to depend on rainwater. In the backyard Smith showed Hazel the cement tank in which water was preserved for domestic use. Despite this inconvenience, Hazel always later referred to their first parsonage as a doll cottage in which she and Joseph played house.

After inspecting the parsonage they went to see the church, located near the southern tip of the bay and the limestone quarry. Bethel was a small, white stone church that had been built in 1888. At the dedication George F. Woodson, Joseph's former dean at Payne Theological Seminary, had been appointed pastor.[3]

They went up the stone steps through a low roofed vestibule that led into a main sanctuary. There were pews to seat about two hundred people, though at the time the membership had dropped to sixty. The elevated pulpit, suspended over part of the altar, was similar to those found in Anglican churches. To one side was a choir loft of three rows. Hazel admired most the Gothic stained-glass windows, which could be pushed outward from the bottom so the congregation could catch the breeze from the bay. It was an attractive edifice, but Joseph noted that the outside needed to be whitewashed and the structure inside repaired. All in all, he was well pleased with his first charge and anxious to begin the elaborate program he had mapped out for the church. Hazel was just as excited as he, but being more cautious, counseled him to take one step at a time. After all, he knew nothing about Bermuda and even less about the people. Because of his youth, they might well resent his attempt to change things. She knew, however, that patience was not one of her husband's virtues.

Joseph had arrived in Bermuda just in time to attend the last day of the Annual Conference and to witness firsthand the workings of the A.M.E. Church there. As a mission field, Bermuda had only one Annual Conference.

When Bishop John Hurst read the pastoral appointments, Hazel and Joseph were saddened to learn that J. D. Smith had been moved to Barbados; but they felt a certain amount of pride to hear "Bethel, Shelly Bay, Joseph Gomez, Pastor." Polite applause followed the appointment, and after the service the bishop welcomed the couple to the district.[4]

Bishop Hurst at fifty-one was an impressive figure. He had been born at Port-au-Prince, Haiti, was a graduate of the Lycée Nationale in Haiti and of Wilberforce University, where he received his B.D. in 1886. He had been elected bishop in 1912 and assigned to the 11th District of Florida. When Bishop Derrick (Joseph's cousin from Antigua) died in April 1913, Hurst was given the supervision of the West Indies, Bermuda, and British and Dutch Guiana.⁵ He was to be Joseph's bishop until the General Conference reassigned Hurst in 1916. Having been born in Haiti, he had a keen sensitivity for the islanders and their needs. Joseph would have found it easy to accept his leadership even if Ransom had not counseled him always to try to get along with the bishop (a bit of advice Ransom sometimes forgot himself). Joseph's first test in Bermuda did not come from the bishop but from the British government.

In August 1914, war broke out in Europe. Bermudians, Negroes and whites, were required by the British government to participate. Bethel A.M.E. Church was located on land which belonged to the British, and on August 5 Joseph received a letter from the Royal Engineer Office in Prospect giving notice that the land on which the church was situated was going to be taken over "by the Military Authorities forthwith, for the erection of Defenses, etc." Attached to the letter was a map of Shelly Bay on which Bethel was circled in yellow.⁶ Joseph contacted Bishop Hurst at once and started a lengthy petition to the British government to save Bethel. There are no records to indicate exactly how they convinced the British, but Bethel was never taken over for wartime purposes or any other. (Nevertheless, military bases were built for the British elsewhere in Bermuda, and later for American naval vessels).

One of the first acts of the Bermuda government "after the declaration of war, was to appropriate £40,000 ($4,200) as a gift from the colony toward the Imperial Defense Fund. Martial law was declared, the local troops were mobilized, and steps were taken to strengthen the defenses in view of the presence of German cruisers in the North Atlantic."⁷ Negroes were not allowed in the white Bermuda Volunteer Rifle Corps, but they were asked to volunteer to serve in a segregated company under the command of four white officers.⁸

Joseph's reaction was predictable. He began to use his pulpit to protest the government's asking Negroes to serve in a segregated army. He strongly urged that the Bermuda Volunteer Rifle Corps be integrated. He stopped short of telling Negroes not to fight, but he was warned by some of the ministers and his members that if he continued to speak in this manner he would get into trouble.

In December 1914 Joseph was asked to speak at Temperance Hall in favor of prohibition. Someone told the authorities he intended to take this opportunity to discourage Negroes from joining the army. The Honorable S. S. Spurling, an admirer and friend of Joseph's, got word to him that the police had orders to arrest him if he said anything that could be interpreted as seditious. When he arrived at the hall he could see the police sprinkled throughout the audience, conspicuous in their attempt to be inconspicuous. Much to their disappointment, the major part of his speech dealt with prohibition and a strong denunciation of the liquor traffic on the island. He then spoke in general about the war—the need for a lasting peace, and about Bermuda's participation overseas. His closing words were: "If many policies in this country were changed regarding [the Negroes'] welfare as equal citizens, it would be a more inspiring thing for them to join the defense forces."[9] The police could find nothing seditious in these remarks and had to go away disappointed and empty-handed.

Joseph continued to speak out against the racial policies of the government, and his criticisms grew stronger as he became more aware of injustices. Influential friends like Spurling kept him from being incarcerated. Some of the Negroes found him too outspoken for his and their own good, and they told him so repeatedly.

The war touched Joseph in another, more personal way. He learned from his mother that his brother James had joined the British Army. At some time during the war, James stopped by Bermuda to see his brother. When Hazel went with Joseph to meet the ship she knew immediately who he was, he and Joseph looked so much alike. As they grew older, they were to favor each other even more. James's few days in Bermuda afforded Joseph the opportunity to catch up on all the family news. Papa's business was still floundering. His mother was well, and Amanda and the other brothers and sisters sent their love.

Late in 1914 and at the beginning of the new year Joseph and Hazel spent most of their time getting to know the island. Most people got around the island by horse and carriage, but the Gomezes' favorite means of transportation was by bicycle, for as Joseph was to tell the islanders in 1957 when he returned for a visit: "There were no motor vehicles at the time, and I became quite a cyclist."[10] The couple rode everywhere with abandon, like school children on holiday, stopping only to bathe in the ocean or lie on the pink beach, watching the vessels come in. His meager salary (about five American dollars a week) could not be stretched to include a horse and carriage, even though Hazel grew most of their vegetables and the church members were generous in their gifts of food and staples.

In Bermuda they also inherited their first and only cat, Snookums, a furry gray and white feline who thought of herself as a human, with all the rights and privileges thereof. She had camped on their front veranda and like the determined lady she was, refused to budge. At first Joseph would have nothing to do with her. He had hated cats "ever since one drank his milk when he was a child." Besides, "he was a dog person. Dogs were real animals." But finally Hazel persuaded him to let her bring the cat in. Every Sunday when it was time for church, Hazel would lock Snookums in the house; nonetheless, at the most intense and highly edifying part of Joseph's sermon she would walk down the center aisle of the church, climb up the steps to the choir loft, and jump into Hazel's lap, where she would sleep contentedly, unimpressed by Joseph's homily. The mystery of how Snookums escaped from the locked parsonage was never solved.

Despite his dignified demeanor, there was a part of Joseph that never grew up. This made him a favorite with the young people of his parishes and later with his daughters and grandchildren. He delighted in playing pranks, most of which were harmless. However, a prank he played on Hazel one Sunday evening after night service backfired. Hazel had lingered to talk to some of the missionary ladies about a program the church was planning. Joseph rushed home ahead of her. When he heard her turn the key in the lock, he grabbed a sheet from the bed and jumped out at her just as she entered the darkened living room. The moon cast grotesque shadows on his sheeted figure, and she was terrified. When Joseph lit the lamp, she lay unconscious at his feet. A sheepish Joseph had to call in some of the neighbors to help revive her.

It was during this period that Hazel and Joseph adopted love names for each other: she was "Tweets," and he was "Teddy." The origin of these names is unknown, but on every special-occasion card, in personal letters, and during moments of affection, these were the names they used all of their lives.

Time for frivolity, however, was limited. Joseph followed a grueling schedule: office hours from 9 A.M. to 4 P.M., Monday night board meeting, Wednesday night prayer meeting, Friday night Bible class, Sunday morning Sunday school, morning service, Allen Christian Endeavor League late Sunday afternoon, and worship service again at night. In addition there were visitations to the sick, funerals and marriages to perform, secular and interfaith church meetings to attend. When he had time, he helped with the repairing of the church and the parsonage.

A great deal of his energy was spent addressing the problems of alcoholism and racism on the island. Although slavery had been abolished in

Bermuda in 1834, as it had been in all the British colonies, British racial attitudes remained. For instance, there were no public schools because whites did not want their children to go to school with Negroes. However, most white Bermudians in 1914 outwardly held the same attitude found later in Walter B. Hayward's *Bermuda Past and Present* (1930). "The Bermuda coloured people are intelligent, well-mannered, contented, and respected by the whites. This respect is reciprocated. The colour line is drawn, the races have separate schools, but there is no race feeling, no race problem, and the political and legal rights of the coloured man are zealously guarded."[11]

Undoubtedly many whites did feel that there was no race problem and that Negroes were contented, since there was little overt resistance. It did not take Joseph long, however, to see that there was a growing dissatisfaction with many governmental policies, including the franchise. "Any man, white or coloured, [was] qualified to stand for elections to the House of Assembly if he possess[ed] a freehold rate at £240 ($1,211), the rating being the actual value of the property, and he may be a candidate in any parish. [No Negro held an office in the Assembly.] To exercise the franchise a man must receive the profits of a freehold rated at £60 ($300)."[12] That may seem like a small amount today, but at the time, like the poll tax in the United States, many Negroes found it astronomical in light of their meager incomes. In fact, of about 1,400 electors, fewer than five hundred were Negroes as late as 1918, even though there were twice as many Negroes in Bermuda as whites.[13]

During the summer of 1915 Joseph was preoccupied with planning his first Annual Conference, which was to be hosted by Bethel, July 24–27. The members were pushed to their limits to find housing and food for the bishop, nine ministerial delegates, their wives, and the visitors who would come from other districts. The choir too was busy, practicing the music it would render at the conference.

On Thursday, July 22, at 10 A.M., Bishop Hurst called the thirty-second session of the Bermuda Annual Conference to order, by lining the hymn [repeating the words before singing] "Before Jehovah's Awful Throne." Hazel and Joseph were so anxious that everything should go smoothly that they barely heard the bishop's exegesis of Corinthians or the General Confession said by the congregation before the Lord's Supper. They were somewhat relieved when the worship service ended and the conference was officially organized. This involved the calling of the roll, the election of the conference secretary, and the introduction of visitors. The bishop also announced that Rev. J. D. Smith was officially being assigned to Bermuda. In actuality he had been pastoring Allen Temple, Somerset, in Bermuda since the death of its pastor in January.[14] This would mean, however, that he would no longer be required to minister two charges and could spend all his time in Bermuda. Now Joseph would get to see more of his friend and benefit from his sage advice.

That Joseph had become a vital presence in the district was evident in the number of committees to which he was appointed by Bishop Hurst. Furthermore, the conference elected him to the prestigious Financial Committee, even though he was the youngest minister present and that honor usually went to veteran ministers.[15] In one year, his youth had ceased to be a concern; he had proved himself to be capable, resourceful, and responsible.

During the afternoon session of the first day, there was a discussion of African Methodism in Bermuda. Joseph opened it by expressing his belief that the Church should purchase a burial ground where the ministers could "perform the last rites over their deceased members." He also spoke of the "necessity of gathering in the young people . . . and laid great stress upon the fact that women are important factors in the church life," despite the opposition to both youth and women by certain groups.[16] Reading aloud the Allen Christian Endeavor League's report that night, he again emphasized the vital need for the participation of the young people in the Church's programs.[17]

The beginnings of Hazel's and Joseph's life-long involvement with youth can be traced to Bermuda and the highly successful A.C.E. League they established at Bethel, an organization where young people could discuss freely and openly their views concerning social, political, and religious questions. Furthermore, even at this early stage in his career Joseph was a supporter of the full participation of women in the Church and an advocate of their ordination. Among many ministers and male lay members, this was not a popular stand. Even some of the older women felt that females had no business in the pulpit. No doubt the influences of a forceful mother and an efficient wife were contributing factors in Joseph's strong stand on women's liberation.

Another committee report Joseph helped to draft, along with J. S. De Shields, was the report on temperance. Feeling that alcoholism had become a major problem for Negroes in Bermuda, he campaigned vigorously for prohibition. The report closed with the dramatic statement, "May the mothers and fathers whose daughters and sons are 'selling their birthright' to the Demon Drink rise as one, and under God banish from our shores all alcoholic beverages, as such."[18]

This being the last Annual Conference before the 1916 General Conference, ministerial delegates had to be elected. As Joseph had been ordained for only two years he was not eligible to run, but he promoted the election of J. D. Smith. The bishop announced the winners to be Rev. Austin Richardson, pastor of Bailey's Bay and Tucker's Town, and Rev. J. D. Smith. Almost immediately the presiding elder, Rev. Walker, rose to object to the election of J. D. on the basis of "his ineligibility." According to the Discipline, "every minister elected a delegate by an Annual Conference shall be an elder who has traveled four full years next preceding the General Conference." Smith, he said, had been "ordained an elder on the 17th day of September, 1911, and [would] not be eligible until the 17th of this coming September, 1915."[19]

Joseph replied that September was only two months away and that by the time of the General Conference Smith would have served more than four years. Walker may have felt that as Presiding Elder and pastor of the leading church in Bermuda he should have been elected—but there was no rule that said the ministers had to choose him. Walker informed Bishop Hurst that he intended to carry the matter to the General Conference. This was Joseph's first introduction to church politics, and while he enjoyed a spirited contest, he was never comfortable when differences degenerated into ugly confrontations, as this one was threatening to do. To his relief, the bishop told Walker he was at liberty to take the matter to the General Conference if he chose; he then proceeded with the election of the alternate delegates. When the votes were counted, Walker had received the highest number, but he still was not satisfied.[20]

The most important session for Joseph occurred the evening of the missionary program. He delivered the sermon on Matthew 5:13, "Ye are the salt of the Earth," using as a topic "The Value of Missionaries." He pointed out that the major obligation of the Church was to extend its message and its assistance to every part of the globe. The Church was the salt of the world, and losing its savor was equivalent to losing its soul.[21]

Although most of the local ministers had heard him preach, Bishop Hurst had not. Joseph felt as if in a way he was on trial. Having been influenced by the British, A.M.E. Bermudians seldom express their approval by saying "Amen" during the sermon, as they do in most Negro churches in the United States. The minutes, however, describe Joseph's sermon as "most edifying and instructive," and the bishop gave him a hearty handshake.[22]

On Monday, July 26, the conference passed a resolution requesting the Episcopal Committee at the next General Conference to return Bishop Hurst to Bermuda. When the bishop read the appointments at the afternoon session, no one was surprised that Joseph had been returned to Bethel for another year. Rev. Walker's presiding elder report had described him as having "worked earnestly and faithfully with unfaltering devotion," noting that "over fifty members [had] joined the church during the year." The increase in membership at Bethel was second only to St. Paul's in Hamilton, which had taken in seventy members. Walker further stated that "much needed improvements [had] been made. The blinds [had been] put on the house, the porch completed in front of the parsonage, the church white-washed. . . . All these improvements had already been paid for and the indebtedness Gomez had inherited had decreased about £700."[23]

The presiding elder also spoke of the district's loyalty to the British Empire, in that it had turned over to the Receiver General in the name of the A.M.E. Church of Bermuda the sum of £15 for the war effort. He also reported that at the Sunday School Convention held at St. Paul's in 1914 the delegates had voted to put special emphasis on the Bermuda Scholarship at Wilberforce University. So far £11 10s had been raised to assist some worthy young person in attending the university.[24]

When the last of the delegates had left Bethel, Joseph and Hazel had time to reflect on the proceedings. Bethel had done a sterling job of hosting the conference; the choir had sung well, and Joseph had acquitted himself in a manner which evoked words of praise from his members and the other delegates. These were happy times, relatively free from stress, and in years to come the Gomezes would realize how utopian the Bermuda pastorate had been.

During the next year Joseph continued his temperance activities. At the District Conference held at Richard Allen A.M.E. Church in St. George's, November 29–30, he was appointed to a committee to draft a resolution concerning the liquor traffic, dancing, and illegitimacy. Every minister in Bermuda was sent a copy and was asked to assist in raising the moral standards on the island.[25]

Joseph did not object to dancing, although he never learned how, but prohibition was more than a matter of Christian ethics with him. Throughout his life doctors could rarely get him to take pain pills, or even a simple aspirin. He was skeptical of all drugs and only used them when he was convinced they were absolutely necessary. Both he and Hazel were strong believers in "mind over matter," beginning each day by reading lessons from *Science of Mind*. For them, positive thinking was essential to a healthy mind and body, just as faith and belief in God's grace led to well-being.

Joseph was the first Negro ever to be elected executive secretary of the Interdenominational Alliance of Bermuda, and as such he was asked to address the Citizens League and the Ministerial Association at Temperance Hall, on July 25. He spoke concerning a bill before the House of Assembly that, if passed, would restrict the sale of liquor to between the hours of 9 P.M. and 9 A.M. He told the assemblage that the restrictions were "too mild" and urged them to make prohibition a platform issue in the next year's colonial elections. He said he could not understand the legislature's ability to put aside political differences when it came to war emergencies and not when it came to prohibition. "The eyes of Bermuda were on them [the legislature] as never before," he warned, and "the people would speak in no uncertain manner" during the upcoming elections.[26]

Unfortunately, none of Joseph's Bermuda sermons have survived. One can only speculate as to his style and philosophy, by reference to the few written pieces still in existence: an essay entitled "Sunset," a temperance speech given at Mechanics Hall in Hamilton, on June 25, 1917, and a speech given at the opening of the Bermuda Gymnastic Corps the same year. All three reflect youthful idealism and the ornate language of the times. "Sunset" can be classified as poetic prose, and it reflects his love of vivid imagery and archaic expressions. For example, in a passage personifying the sun, he writes: "Gladly would he grant us serene contemplation of visions of splendor and power, and more truly than 'Joshua's Son,' lingers just above the horizon . . . the master of a dying day. Then ere we are aware of it, he is gone."[27]

In his speech to the Gymnastic Corps it is obvious that he is experimenting with the ideas of Auguste Comte, Charles Darwin, and the French Naturalists. He asserts that there "are just two factors responsible for everything that is[:] . . . inheritance and environment"—even for Christian gentlemen. He then uses an example which strikes one as humorous, particularly in light of his usual command of language. "A potato is a potato because it has the potato nature. I take a potato, place it on a board. It would stay there forever and never produce potatoes, not because it had not the inheritance of potato life, but because it lacks the proper environment. I put the potato in rich soil. I cultivate it. The rain and sun fall upon it in proper season, and, behold, I get a crop."[28] One might ask how this applies to the "Christian gentleman." Is one to assume that the Christian's inheritance is his potential for spirituality, but that in order for him to realize that potential he must be brought up in an environment conducive to Christian principles? He does not say. No place in the address does he mention the function of free will and man's responsibility for his own behavior. Surely he did not believe with the Naturalists that since man had nothing to do with his heredity and often did not create the environment into which he was born, he could not be held responsible for what he became.

Recalling this period in his life, he was to say that he had been fascinated by the new social science and anxious to display his findings. At the same time he was trying to arrive at a personal philosophy that did not negate the importance of inheritance and environment on human behavior but also emphasized the power of God to manifest Himself through man's will. He believed in the mystery of faith that at times defied reason, but he also had great respect for the intellect and was convinced that both could work together for good. Very early in his ministry it became clear that he could never approach religion from a fundamentalist point of view or accept a merely literal translation of the scriptures. Forty-eight years later he still maintained that man "is greatly influenced by his environs. . . . But [, he asserted,] man is more than [that which] is claimed for him. He can, through God's grace, become whatever he wills to be."[29]

Just as Joseph was making changes in his own thinking in 1916, changes in the Bermuda Conference were also imminent, as a result of decisions made at the Centennial General Conference between May 3 and May 21. Although Joseph was not a delegate, Bethel raised money so that he could attend. He was glad that his first General Conference would be held in Mother Bethel in Philadelphia, where the African Methodist Episcopal Church had been born. A.M.E. members assert that "the real seed of religious freedom was born" at Bethel, on 6th Street, below Pine. The church was never to be moved from its site.[30]

There was a buzz of excitement as the delegates went about the church greeting one another with hugs and handshakes. Besides visitors like Joseph, the conference "was composed of 13 bishops, 12 general officers, 410 ministers, 128 laymen, 14 college presidents, and 14 deans of theological seminaries."[31] Most were dressed in dark frock coats, white shirts, and clerical collars, except for the delegates from Africa, who presented a welcome contrast in their vivid native garbs. Joseph heard the same diverse, colorful accents he had heard when he arrived in the Tenderloin in New York. The first persons who greeted him were Ransom, who was to preach Sunday evening, and President Scarborough and Dean Woodson from Wilberforce.

Joseph attended as many sessions as he could. He wanted first-hand knowledge about the workings of the Church, to hear the reports and the deliberations. Bishop Henry B. Parks delivered the Quadrennial Sermon on the subject "The Miracle of Continuance," noting that "African Methodism, the result of resistless necessity, founded upon the work of God, and the equality and brotherhood of man" had persevered for

126 years and had left its mark "in every walk of life and in every achievement of American life and history."[32]

The grand Centennial opening and public reception were held at the music academy on Broad and Locust streets the next evening, with welcoming addresses by Pennsylvania's Governor, Martin G. Brumbaugh, and Mayor Thomas B. Smith of Philadelphia. During the second week of the conference Joseph went to see "The Star of Ethiopia," a historical pageant presented by the Horizon Guild, managed by W. E. B. Du Bois. The program described it as "an encouraging recital of Negro History . . . a confidence builder . . . intended to offset the very unfortunate impression made by *Birth of a Nation* (a 1915 movie by D. W. Griffith glorifying the Ku Klux Klan and showing Blacks as savages)." Over a thousand persons from "every church denomination, civic, club and fraternal organization in the city" participated.[33]

Most exciting to Joseph was the election of the bishops. His Centennial program is filled with the careful tallies he kept of the balloting. There were 576 votes cast, with 289 necessary for election. It was not until the third ballot that the two bishops were elected, W. W. Beckett and I. N. Ross. Later, when the Episcopal Committee read the assignments of the bishops, Hurst had been transferred to the 11th District, in Florida, and Bishop C. S. Smith, of the 10th Episcopal District (Texas), was to be sent to Bermuda.[34]

Joseph had met Smith in New York at Ransom's church, had heard him deliver the commencement address at Hazel's graduation, and had read articles outlining his activities in church publications and the *New York Age*. Although to a lesser degree than Ransom, Smith was to exert his influence on Joseph's early ministry and to become a supporter and friend.

Born in Colborne, Ontario, Canada, on March 16, 1852, Charles Spencer Smith had spent his teens working at the kind of odd jobs available to Negroes at the time, such as porter in a barber shop and deckhand on a ship. During Reconstruction he taught for the Freedman's Bureau at Payne Station on the Lexington branch of the Louisville and Nashville Railroad. Soon the Ku Klux Klan broke up his school and ordered him out of town; he moved to Jackson, Mississippi. While teaching there he befriended some of the most prominent Reconstruction Negro politicians in the state, including James Lynch, secretary of state; John R. Lynch, speaker of the state House of Representatives; B. K. Bruce, sergeant of the Senate and later United States senator; and Hiram Revels, later U.S. senator. In August 1871 Smith became a preacher in the A.M.E. Church, pastored in Union Springs, and was elected to the Alabama House of Representatives.

His contributions to the A.M.E. Church had been impressive. In 1888 he founded and was appointed corresponding secretary to the A.M.E. Sunday School Union; he was elected to the bishopric in 1900; and in 1922 was to write *A History of the African Methodist Episcopal Church, 1856–1922,* one of the most complete sources for that period. His wife, Christine Shoecraft Smith, was a leader in the missionary work of the Church.[35] By the time he was appointed to the 15th District, which included Bermuda, he had made a reputation for himself as a dynamic preacher, political speaker, writer, and historian. Joseph was delighted to have him as a leader.

Smith's arrival in Bermuda, however, was delayed. The "strain of the late General Conference" had caused a recurrence of the effects of an operation that had been performed the previous winter. He was undergoing treatment and trying to regain his strength. In a letter he gave Presiding Elder Walker "full authority to do one of two things; either to hold the [Annual] conference July 20th, or postpone it to a later date."[36] Walker decided to go on with the conference as scheduled, though the ministers were disappointed that the bishop could not attend.

During the conference Joseph was again very much in evidence, making and seconding motions, reading reports, and being elected reporter to the Church publications for the island. Excerpts from his report on "The State of the Church" give valuable insight into the A.M.E. Church in general and Bermuda in particular. He divided his report into three sections, the "Church Universal," the "Church Denominational," and the "Church Local." He spoke of how the A.M.E. Church has "earned her right to belong to the world religious organizations" as the past hundred years attested. As proof he pointed to the growth of the Church: "Beginning with Richard Allen and fifteen other consecrated men of God, we have added 758,000 members to our roll." There were now 6,554 active preachers, 6,470 local preachers, 2,747 parsonages, 231,828 Sunday school pupils, and 185,804 officers and teachers. In addition there were "16 presidents of institutions of learning in America, 2 in the West Indies, 3 in West Africa, 3 in South America, 4,725 students" in A.M.E. institutions, seventy-eight Annual Conferences, eleven general officers, two publishing houses with six periodicals, and mission work in West and South Africa, Haiti, San Domingo, South America, and the West Indies.[37]

In terms of the local Church of Bermuda, he detailed the following:

The work in Bermuda, . . . and, unlike other foreign fields, is not controlled by the Missionary Board. . . . The reported membership today is about 900, with 10 points [localities or churches], 2 parsonages, 11 Sunday Schools, 168 officers and teachers, 1,248 pupils and

1,475 books. It has received the stamp of approval of the colonial government and was subsidized years ago when other denominations were so helped. It can boast of having given impetus [to], if not actually starting the educational life of our people.[38]

Among his recommendations were that the Church should develop a more positive attitude toward education, a more organized method of reaching youth, a general standardization of church work, and a systematic policy in finance.[39]

Bethel proved to be a beneficial first charge for Joseph and Hazel. The church was small enough to be manageable yet large enough to be challenging and for its influence to be felt in the community. Under Joseph's leadership the church grew from sixty to 160. The Sunday schools at Bethel and Crawl collectively had on the roll 219 members and were reported at the Sunday School Convention of September 1916 to be "the most progressive and effective ones" in Bermuda.[40] Joseph had sharpened his homiletic skills, learned to organize his pastoral duties, and become an effective counselor, especially to the parents of the two hundred or more Negro soldiers who had gone overseas. (In spite of their segregated status, these men served well as an ammunition column for heavy artillery, "taking part in the Battle of Somme, and serving also at Vimy and in the famous Ypres salient."[41] When it was all over, ten had made the supreme sacrifice, and Joseph prayed with the families in a memorial service held at Bethel.)

Hazel continued her work in the Missionary Society, helped with the young people in the A.C.E. League, sang in the choir, taught Sunday school, and did some counseling herself. She and Joseph often sang duets at the Sunday morning services, visited the sick and buried the dead, attended religious and civic meetings, rode their bicycles, and weeded and hoed their tiny garden in the back of the parsonage.

When Bishop Smith and his wife, Christine, finally arrived in Bermuda, the Gomezes got to know them well. In the evenings they would sit on the veranda of the parsonage talking about the war, Wilberforce University, local problems, or church activities. The bishop was impressed with the drive and intelligence of the young couple and soon decided they should move to a larger field. It would only be a matter of time before a charge in America would open up for Joseph.

On September 14, 1917, the *Bermuda Colonist* announced that "the Rev. Joseph Gomez, pastor of the Bethel A.M.E. Church, Shelly Bay, is about to leave Bermuda for a broader field of duty in Canada."[42] Bishop Smith had transferred Joseph to another foreign field in his diocese, St. Paul A.M.E. Church, in Hamilton, Ontario. Once again Hazel and Joseph would sail to

New York, where they would visit the Ransoms and Uncle James for a few days and then take the train to Canada.

The A.M.E. Church in Canada was over ninety-one years old; traces of A.M.E. societies had been found as early as 1826. The people involved in them had been for the most part former slaves who had escaped by the Underground Railroad, first to the northern states and then to Canada. In 1830, Rev. Richard Allen (founder of the A.M.E. Church) and four other men had called "a convention of the colored delegates from the several states, to meet on the 10th day of September, 1830 to devise plans and means for the establishment of a colony in Upper Canada . . . for runaway slaves."[43] With the efforts of these men and the money raised by abolitionists and northern philanthropists, colonies of Negroes began to spring up in various parts of Canada.

In 1832, the New York Conference of the A.M.E. Church sent Jeremiah Miller as a missionary to Canada. Within five years Negroes from St. Catharines, Ontario, had petitioned the New York Annual Conference for pastoral care. As a result, a Rev. Richard Williams set up churches at Niagara Falls (twenty-two members), St. David (twenty-nine members), St. Catharines (forty members), licensing two local preachers. By 1838 other churches had been established at Toronto, Malden, Hamilton, and Bradford, in Ontario. Two years later a Church conference was organized by Bishop Morris Brown.[44]

At its third session, July 2, 1842, in Hamilton, Ontario, Josiah Henson, Harriet Beecher Stowe's inspiration for Uncle Tom, was ordained a deacon. For a short period the Canadian churches joined the British Methodist Episcopal Church, as had the churches in Bermuda, but then they all asked for an organic union with the A.M.E. Church. The first Annual Conference after the reunion was held at St. Paul, Hamilton, June 30, 1885, with 2,909 members in attendance.[45] It was in this church that Joseph was to begin his second pastoral assignment.

Of the some forty thousand Negroes who lived in the eight provinces of Canada, ten thousand made their home in Ontario, a province twice the size of the state of Texas. The people in Hamilton seemed very British, with their emphasis on formality and correctness in their daily lives and worship. Having lived in British colonies most of his life, Joseph did not feel like a stranger, and because Hazel had spent so much time in Canada as a young girl, she too felt at home.[46]

St. Paul, Hamilton, was somewhat larger than Bethel, with a seating capacity of four hundred. The parsonage, at 116 John Street, was also roomier than the cottage home in Bermuda, but not as cozy. Hazel described

Hamilton as a relatively small city with the same scrubbed look as most towns in Ontario. The air was clean, the people friendly, and the living fairly easy.[47]

A shadow was cast on their initial feelings of well-being when Hazel received word early in 1918 that her mother, Julia Thompson Perkins, had died. She and Joseph hurried to Toledo, Ohio to attend the funeral, held at Warren Chapel A.M.E. Church though her mother had not been a Methodist. Hazel later recalled that this was the first funeral she ever attended in which cars were used to transport the deceased and the mourners to the cemetery. It seemed to her as if they were rushing her mother to the grave. She had been closer to Julia than had any of the other children, and since she had never really known her father, the loss seemed especially poignant. She had not seen her mother since 1914, when she and Joseph were married, but she had written often, detailing her many experiences in Bermuda and Hamilton.

Joseph had to take care of most of the details of the small estate; Hazel found it difficult to think of anything but her great loss. For weeks after they returned to Canada she did little more than move listlessly around the parsonage. At night she found it difficult to sleep. Some months later she received a letter from Charles A. Cottrill, a realtor, stating that Julia's house now belonged to her.[48] Julia had completed what she had set out to do: she had given Hazel an education so she would not "have to work in nobody's kitchen," and left her property so she would be independent should she ever find herself alone.

Unfortunately, little is known about the Hamilton period of Joseph's ministry. Perhaps material about this period was destroyed when his basement flooded in the 1970s and several boxes of papers and books had to be thrown out. Even the Annual Conference minutes are not among Joseph's papers. However, it can be ascertained that in Hamilton Joseph met J. C. Holland and his family; Kathleen Holland, one of the daughters, was the organist at St. Paul. Their paths were to cross again in the late 1930s, when as Kathleen Holland Forbes she would be Joseph's organist again, this time at St. James A.M.E. Church in Cleveland, Ohio.

The only recorded event during this period is that of the white Methodist General Conference in 1918, which Joseph attended. According to the Hamilton Press of August 14, in attendance at the conference was Charles Victor Roman, "a poor, untutored coloured boy" who in his youth had worked as a mill hand in the Dundas cotton mill but had since become medical inspector and lecturer for the U.S. government. A reception for Dr. Roman was given at St. Paul, where "the pastor of the church, the

Rev. J. Gomez presided at the reception, and in his introduction kept the meeting in a happy mood by his bright and witty sayings." Greetings from the church were given by J. C. Holland, and by Rev. M. Cockburn and Rev. Mr. Gillivry on behalf of the Hamilton Ministerial Association, of which Joseph was an active member. At the close of the reception Dr. Roman made a few remarks, and Joseph read a resolution extending thanks to him for his contribution as a "scholar and churchman."[49] The only other information concerning that period is that Joseph continued to be active in the temperance movement and various ministerial alliances, including the Interdenominational Alliance; and that Hazel worked with the Sunday school, Missionary Society, and Allen Christian Endeavor League.

Bishop Smith had promised Joseph that his days in the mission field would be numbered. True to his word, a little less than two years after Joseph had been appointed to St. Paul Hamilton, the bishop transferred him to Detroit, Michigan, his first American charge. There at the age of twenty-nine he was to be faced with one of the principal challenges of his young career.

CHAPTER FIVE

Baptism of Fire

Detroit, 1919–1928

No element of the American body politic is more entitled to the rights and privileges guaranteed by the constitution than the Negro. . . . Out of the travail of the world's war, the Negro has himself lifted the "Negro Problem" out of the narrow confines of American provincialism, and has taken his case before the bar of the world's tribunal. He has come to himself in a larger way. The result of this, as might be expected, is a gradual resentment on the part of the white man, which has resulted in riots, clashes and lynchings galore. The comparative statistics on lynching furnished by Tuskegee Institute is an interesting document and provides a remarkable index to the mind of the white man today. There is a corresponding note of a growing consciousness of race power.
—Joseph Gomez, address, "The New Negro Is Here!"
The Detroit Contender, October 30, 1920

◈ In August 1919, Bishop Smith wrote Joseph in Hamilton asking that he and Hazel attend the Michigan Annual Conference, which would be held in Detroit, Michigan, at Bethel A.M.E. Church, September 10–15.[1] A few days prior to the summons Bishop Smith had revealed to Joseph that he was thinking seriously of sending him to that prestigious church; but neither Joseph nor Hazel expected this to become a reality.

When the Gomezes arrived they were welcomed not only by Smith but also Ransom, now editor of the *A.M.E. Review,* who was to give the Decalogue that morning and preach at one of the sessions of the conference. Ransom pulled Joseph aside and told him he was about to enter into the most demanding task of his career to date, the pastorate of Bethel, Detroit.

{ 69 }

He warned that there would be opposition to his appointment because of his age, by now a familiar situation to the Gomezes.

Bishop Smith gave the opening sermon, which turned out to be his farewell; at the next General Conference he would not be assigned a district but would assume the position of Historiographer of the Church. He took his text from St. John 14:27—"Peace I leave you, my peace I give you not as the world giveth it unto you. Let not your heart be troubled neither let it be afraid."[2]

As was usually the case, the conference was not solely concerned with religious and church matters. There was a great deal of discussion of the aftermath of World War I. During the first evening session, in answer to ministers who were skeptical of current peace proposals, Smith gave his tacit approval to the peace treaty of Versailles and to the League of Nations. He said the League was the only constructive alternative that had any possibility of attaining its end. He warned that "national isolation is no longer possible. Henceforth no nation can live unto itself." Two days later Ransom was to agree that it was "impossible for nations to live isolated, not because of the height of civilization, but because of the selfishness of the Big Four trying to dominate the world." Consequently Ransom agreed with the U.S. senators who opposed the treaty of peace, which he found to be unfair to nations not included in the Big Four.[3]

Joseph weighed both views, but being the eternal optimist tended to agree more with Smith's position. On the other hand, he was entranced once again by Ransom's eloquence when he preached on the fifth day from the text, "If any man will come after me let him deny himself and take up his cross and follow me." He warned, "the minister who has not caught his vision of the church militant, has not caught the vision of the higher conceptions of those who strive to sit with Jesus." He appealed to the young people to see the vision and be willing to pay the price of victory.[4] These words would echo in Joseph's mind during many experiences he was to have in Detroit.

In order to introduce the Gomezes to the Michigan Conference, Smith arranged for Hazel to co-lead the devotional service the second morning and read the scriptures. On the fifth afternoon, Joseph was to deliver the sermon. He was reluctant to follow Ransom but anxious to demonstrate that he was capable of pastoring a large city church. There exists no copy of Joseph's sermon, but the minutes of the session describe it as "eloquent."[5]

In the final evening session of the conference, the bishop read the appointments. When he announced "Bethel A.M.E. Church—Rev. Joseph Gomez, Pastor," the auditorium became deadly silent. Bethel was the largest church in the Michigan Conference and had over two thousand members on the roll (between six and seven hundred attended regularly), and it paid its minister over $2,000 annually, more money than Joseph had ever earned in his life. Such an appointment was beyond his wildest fantasies, since no minister in the Connection had ever been given a church the size of Bethel at the age of twenty-nine years. "The appointment so far as the age of the incoming pastor was concerned was a shattering of all precedence [sic]."[6]

After the initial shock had passed, the silence was broken by vociferous protest from ministers who felt they should have been given this prestigious assignment. They wanted to know who this Joseph Gomez was, and what experience he had had, other than the pastorate of two mission churches that were not even in America. Members of Bethel who had come to the conference to see whether their beloved pastor, T. D. Scott, would be returned to them derisively referred to Joseph and Hazel as "the boy preacher and his baby wife." But on September 15, Joseph received a letter from the bishop containing his certificate of appointment to Detroit and an assurance that "there [would] be no serious objection" to his coming.[7]

Either the bishop had been able to convince the members of Joseph's competence or he was trying to help Joseph approach his first American charge with the kind of confidence he would need to replace the former pastor, who had been appointed as a presiding elder. Replacing Rev. T. D. Scott would be difficult. This tall, distinguished, white-haired gentleman, replete with a silky beard like that of a revered saint, was the epitome of the fatherly minister and exuded confidence and respectability. Smith believed, however, that Joseph's competence, youthfulness, and energy would be a plus. He would bring innovative programs to the church and would attract more young people, whom the church sorely needed.

The Gomezes were returning to the United States following what had been referred to as "the Red Summer," because of the more than a dozen race riots that had broken out from Texas to the nation's capital. A revived KKK had paraded in robes and hoods in more than twenty American cities (and in 1928 would march down Pennsylvania Avenue past the White House).[8] In Detroit, the Klan's membership grew from "3,000 in the autumn of 1921, to 22,000 eighteen months later."[9]

Detroit was a powder keg ready to be ignited. During World War I, Negroes had begun to migrate from the agrarian South to northern cities, seeking employment in wartime industries and also relief from Jim-Crowism. In Detroit there was the extra attraction of the automobile industry, including the Ford and Dodge companies. There had been a little over seven thousand Negroes in Detroit in 1915, most of whom lived in the St. Antoine Street district, bounded on the west by Brush, the east by

Hastings, the north by Leland and the south by Macomb streets. By 1920 the number had increased to 40,838, and the old boundaries of the St. Antoine district had to be extended eastward.[10] The most crowded lower section was referred to as "the Black Bottom," named not only for the popular dance of the period but because Negroes who lived there had indeed reached rock bottom. The housing available for the incoming Negroes was limited and substandard. In *A Study of Housing Conditions of Negroes in Detroit,* issued by the Research Bureau of Associated Charities in 1919, Forrester B. Washington, secretary of the Detroit Urban League, described the situation in this manner:

> There is not a single vacant house or tenement in the several Negro sections of this city. The majority of Negroes are living under such crowded conditions that three or four families in an apartment is the rule rather than the exception. Seventy-five percent of the Negro homes have so many lodgers that they are really hotels. Stables, garages and cellars have been converted into homes for Negroes. The pool-rooms and gambling clubs are beginning to charge for the privilege of sleeping on pool-room tables over night.[11]

Upon his arrival, Joseph soon learned that the influx of Negroes from the South posed a threat not only to the whites, who had also poured into Detroit seeking employment, but to the "original Black Detroiters" who felt that the newcomers would ruin their already precarious position. Preferring to be called "Afro-Americans," because they felt the word "Negro" had negative connotations, they shunned their "Negro" brothers and sisters from "down home." The new arrivals had to look mainly to the Urban League (largely controlled by whites), the Colored YWCA and YMCA, and most of all, to the Negro churches for help. This put a tremendous responsibility on the pastors of Ebenezer A.M.E. Church (Rev. T. J. Askew), Second Baptist Church (Rev. R. L. Bradby), St. Matthew Episcopal Church (Rev. R. Bagnall), and Bethel A.M.E. Church, the largest and most influential Negro churches in the city. "In 1914, just before the beginnings of the Great Migration, there had been only nine black religious bodies in the city, and of these, two were missions and three others very small";[12] by 1919, when Joseph came to Detroit, "more than 21,000 black people were registered as church members. The number doubled to nearly 45,000 by 1926."[13] The church became the most significant force in the Black community in terms of the religious, social, and political lives of the people.

On the third Sunday in September, Joseph delivered his first sermon as pastor of Bethel (unfortunately, again there is no copy of his sermon). He knew by the intermittent "Amens" that the reception was positive but that he still had not overcome the skepticism of many of the members, especially those who were old enough to be his parents. Soon, however, his evangelical preaching, infectious personality, and Hazel's warmth and eagerness to please prevailed. Young people, and old and new settlers from all over the city began to find their way to Bethel. By November, only a month after he had started his ministry in Detroit, Sunday morning services overflowed with so many worshippers that Joseph had to establish another service in the basement, with Isaac Baker, deacon, in charge. Soon the second service also had standing room only. It became increasingly obvious that Bethel was inadequate to meet the needs of the growing congregation. Before the year was over, Joseph began to envision a "Greater Bethel," a new church bigger and better furnished than any in the Connection. By the end of the conference year, the church had raised $34,000, part of which was allocated for the new edifice.

The 1920s was a time for visionaries, and Joseph was well equipped for this era of "Negro Renaissance." In his printed Christmas message for 1919 he warned: "The most bloody and sanguinary conflict of nations [World War I] has given place to the 'war of classes.' . . . Yet I rise to greet you, my comrades of a 'New Day,' in the spirit of cheer and goodwill; for the 'Angel's Song' is still man's hope. . . . I remind you then of the truth historical, that the steps upward have always been marked by tears and blood. This mystery of Pain is the root of Progress."[14] His message turned out to be prophetic.

One of the services Bethel rendered to the community was to provide a platform for local and national political and civil rights leaders, such as Eugene Kinckle Jones of the National Urban League, James Weldon Johnson of the NAACP, W. E .B. Du Bois (now editor of the NAACP's *The Crisis*), and the even more radical editors of *The Messenger*, Chandler Owens and A. Phillip Randolph. Their magazine dealt with such topics as "the socialist critique of capitalism, the need for solidarity among black and white workers, the Negroes' capacity to resist by violence and by boycott, and the poverty of the existing leadership among Negroes."[15]

On February 15, 1920, Joseph received a letter from Chandler Owens asking if he and Randolph could hold a meeting at Bethel.[16] The date agreed upon was March 16. The announcement of their arrival, as usual, caused a stir. Negroes and whites both criticized Joseph for allowing Owens and Randolph the use of Bethel, since the two men were alleged by many to be communists. But believing in the freedom of speech and that people had a right to express and listen to opposing ideologies, Joseph stood firm.

On the afternoon of the 16th, many in the audience had come to cause a disturbance, but when Randolph stood at the podium and filled the auditorium with his grand voice, all objections seemed to be silenced. He approached the Negro question from the standpoint of the social scientist, pointing out that the economic structure of America had to be drastically altered if poverty was to be completely eliminated and real advancement made in terms of civil and human rights. The conditions of Negroes being what they were in Detroit, few in the audience could contradict his message. Randolph also said that in order to ensure continuing employment, Negroes were either going to have to be admitted to existing white unions or unionize themselves. (In this Randolph presaged his own founding in 1925 of a union, the Brotherhood of Sleeping Car Porters.) The meeting was highly successful, and Joseph had been vindicated once again.

In addition to Joseph and Hazel's preoccupation with civic groups, they worked with the YMCA and YWCA; also, Joseph was elected president of the Detroit Alliance of A.M.E. Preachers and was a member of the Colored Interdenominational Ministers Alliance. Most of all, pastoring Bethel kept him busy. Not only did he counsel the members and supervise the church program, but he was also editor-in-chief of the weekly Bethel church bulletin. Churchgoers today would not recognize this kind of bulletin, which, like the Negro church, had to serve many functions. It carried the order of service, a schedule of weekly events, and also editorials concerned with religious and secular issues of import. On the back page appeared headlines like, "Help Us to Help Each Other, Lord—To Support Our Brothers in Business." Underneath were ads listing Negro businesses ranging from funeral parlors to taxi services and piano tuners.[17] Joseph was committed to the idea that if Negroes were to excel, it was essential that they promote Black enterprises.

Most of Joseph and Hazel's afternoons were spent in the Social Service building, which Joseph opened for business in May 1920, under the management of the Black Brotherhood and Sisterhood of Bethel. The building had a Labor and Housing Bureau which placed new southern Negroes in homes and found employment for them. On file were the names of businesses that had openings and people who owned rental property, as well as the names of real estate agents. The *Detroit Contender* called the work being done at the department "splendid." Hundreds of persons had either gone to the service for assistance or had been visited by representatives.[18] For example, when Charles Diggs, Sr., his wife, Mamie, and her brother, Wilbur, arrived in Detroit with $6.35 between them, they came to Bethel's Social Service. Joseph persuaded Dr. Rainwater, a Negro physician who owned a building on the corner of St. Antoine, to let the family stay in one of the apartments for a month, rent-free. In time, Diggs became a prominent funeral director and a Michigan state senator; his son, of the same name, became a United States congressman.

The Gomezes' involvement did not end when the church and Social Service building closed in the evening. A phone call at midnight might mean someone was sick, or had died, was having serious marital problems, or had been arrested and needed to be bailed out of jail, including young girls who had turned to prostitution because they could not find employment in the North. Joseph's excursions with Ransom in the bars and on the street corners of New York served him well in these instances. He responded to all of the calls, and most of the time Hazel accompanied him. "The boy preacher and his baby wife" were a team who could be depended on in a crisis, even if it meant they had to put someone up overnight or cook a meal in the early hours of the morning.

Despite all their activities, they still had time to feel what they considered to be their personal tragedy, the lack of children of their own. According to the family doctor, Charles Greene, it was highly unlikely Hazel could ever conceive a child, and that if she did, she would probably miscarry. After six years of a childless marriage, they decided to send for Joseph's brother, Walter, in Trinidad, so they could finish raising him. There was some difficulty getting the proper entrance papers for the seventeen-year-old, so Walter was instructed to sail to Canada instead of Ellis Island. There Hazel would meet him and bring him across the Canadian border, where few questions were ever asked. She told Walter to let her do all the talking. Evidently there was no trouble, for in March of 1920 Walter came to live upstairs in the parsonage on Napoleon Street. A few weeks later another member was added to the family. Cora Thompson, one of Hazel's relatives, came from Ypsilanti to live and work in Detroit. Now the Gomezes had a son and daughter.

What can be learned about Walter comes mostly from stories Joseph and Hazel told their daughters, and from Cora, who at this writing is in her nineties, living in Detroit in an apartment on Kingswood with her daughter Shirley. She remembers Walter as being handsome, extremely quiet, and observant. He loved to go off by himself and write poetry, which he would later read timidly to the family and Cora. When he enrolled in high school he became an honor student. Cora, who was a few years older than he, used to drag him into conversations which, before long, he would turn into a philosophical treatise of some kind. He was a favorite of the members of Bethel, especially the women, who loved to mother him.[19]

Joseph was strict with both Walter and Cora. He monitored all Cora's dates and made both of them observe a curfew. Of all the young men who came to the parsonage, the Gomezes had hopes that DeWitt Burton, a brilliant medical student, would find favor with Cora. Unfortunately, De-Witt was already engaged to a wealthy young woman named Alice from New York City. When Joseph found out about the engagement some time after Burton had disgraced himself by bringing Cora home slightly tipsy from a champagne party, he was glad that Cora was not seriously interested in Burton. Later Burton married his Alice, and the couple became lifelong friends of the Gomezes.

In spite of Joseph's strict rules, the parsonage was a lively place. Not only did Cora's and Walter's friends come and go, but the living room was a gathering place for several of the members who were especially close to the family. There were Mamie Boone, a registered nurse, and her husband, William, a clerk in the church; Hattie and Aaron Toodle, the pharmacist, and his wife; Gussie Jones, a widow who lived behind the church and who often came by to "give Hazel a hand"; and Mrs. W. T. Johnson (as she always called herself), another widow in her seventies who loved to bring fruit, canned goods, or homemade cake "to Joey and Hazel, her chillun." Joseph liked to listen to her stories about slavery, which she told in serial form, never seeming to forget where she had left off. In addition, ministers of various denominations from around the city and district would frequent the parsonage, often bringing their wives. Hazel had met most of these women at the ministers wives' club meetings.

In May 1920 Joseph left the family behind to attend the Twenty-sixth General Conference, held at the St. Louis, Missouri, Coliseum. Since he had been elected as a delegate while in Canada, he was listed as representing the Ontario Conference of the 15th District. He was a member of the all-important Episcopal Committee, which assigned the bishops and staffed the State of the Church Committee, the Educational Department Committee, and the University and Colleges Committee.[20]

As was customary, the conference opened with the Quadrennial Sermon, which this year was delivered by Bishop J. Albert Johnson, a Canadian by birth. According to Bishop Smith's *A History of the African Methodist Episcopal Church, 1856–1922*, the sermon was "a masterly effort delivered without the aid of manuscript, and with great display of spiritual energy." Johnson referred to the 1920s as the age of "dispensation of the spirit, in which God [had] communicated Himself by the highest revelation, and in the most intimate communion, of which man is capable; no longer through creation, no more as an authoritative voice from without, but as a law within; as a spirit mingling with a spirit." The sermon was followed by the Holy Sacrament, administered by Bishops Chappelle, Jones,

Conner, and Beckett, during which the entire assembly filed up to the altar to kneel and partake of the bread and wine.[21] Even though it took a long time, Joseph preferred this method to the more impersonal one in which the trustees passed out the sacrament to the audience in the pews. Listening to the organ playing the great hymns during the ceremony gave him time to reflect on his own spiritual development.

During the afternoon, after the conference had been organized, Bishop J. S. Flipper read the Episcopal Address, a lengthy dissertation on the state of the Church, country, and world, which ended with the bishops' recommendations for improvement within the Church. This particular address had twenty-four topics spread over seventy-one printed pages.[22] As did most of the delegates, after the first twenty pages Joseph became restless. He read over and over again his program and other literature that had been passed out. But he did listen attentively to what the Church had to say about mob violence. While the bishops did not condone rioting or forcible violation "of the chastity of womanhood of [any] race," the Church marshaled "every fiber of its Christian manhood, and all its moral and intellectual strength against burning, mutilating, or lynching of any human being of any race by mob violence."[23]

During the afternoon session of the second day, Bishop L. J. Coppin read the report on Organic Union, a cause Joseph would champion all his life. Since the African Methodist Episcopal Church, the African Methodist Episcopal Zion Church, and the Colored Methodist Episcopal Church had "originated in a similarity of causes, and therefore resulted in a similarity of effect as regards their respective organizations," they should "unite organically into one body, under the Denominational title of: 'The United Methodist Episcopal Church.'"[24] Although the resolution was passed by the conference, such a union was not to become a reality, mainly because no denomination really wanted to give up its autonomy and individual power.

Before the election of bishops, Ransom introduced Joseph to John A. Gregg, president of Edward Water College, who would become president of Wilberforce University following Scarborough's retirement. Joseph was impressed by this poised, highly cultured gentleman. Both Ransom and Gregg were running for the bishopric, and Joseph pledged to support their candidacies. The other leading contenders were William D. Johnson, A. J. Carey, W. A. Fountain, W. S. Brooks, and W. T. Vernon, the former Recorder of the U.S. Treasury, whom Joseph had met when he first came to America.

As the election day drew closer, the candidates made their last appeals to the delegates. There was no love lost between Ransom and Vernon, whom Ransom considered to be crude and overbearing. In his autobiography, Ransom described Vernon's antics the night before the election, which included having delegates rub his face to call attention to his dark skin.[25]

Joseph did not applaud. He had heard that Vernon had little use for light-skinned Negroes, and because Joseph had suffered a great deal as a result of his own light complexion, he could find nothing admirable in Vernon or his performance, nor could Vernon have ever endeared himself to Joseph, who despised crudeness in any form. Throughout Joseph's life he referred to "the eternal fitness of things." He would use the analogy: "Everyone makes use of the bathroom, but one never puts the toilet in the living room. It is not fit to do so." He did not find Vernon's antics appropriate or "fit" as a campaign strategy.

Joseph was elected teller from the 15th District when the voting for the bishops began on Thursday, May 13, at 10 A.M. Each delegate was required to march up to the ballot box and deposit his or her vote; it was the job of the tellers to call out the names at the end of each ballot until the five bishops had been elected. This process seemed endless. It occurred to Joseph there ought to be a more efficient means of holding an election.

After the first ballot, William D. E. Johnson of the Southwest Georgia Conference and A. J. Carey of the Chicago Conference were declared elected, and then the entire process began all over. On the second ballot, W. S. Brooks, who received 319 votes, was declared elected; W. A. Fountain was a close second. Vernon had received 278 votes, Ransom 182, and Gregg had withdrawn. The election was concluded at the end of the third ballot, when W. T. Vernon and William A. Fountain won with 400 and 311 votes, respectively.[26]

Joseph was disappointed that neither of his candidates had won, since they were the most qualified. It was a difficult lesson for him that the deserving do not always prevail. He noted that of the five bishops elected, all except Carey were from southern states; he was told this was the rule rather than the exception. Even though the A.M.E. Church had been born in Philadelphia, it was now dominated by ministers and laymen from the South. The political intrigue that had accompanied the election fascinated but also saddened him. It was hard to differentiate this election from the ones held at the national political conventions. Deals were made in closed, smoke-filled rooms; friends and foes alike were often traded when it was expedient; and in more than a few instances, money changed hands. Even he had been offered money for his vote; he had angrily refused. However, he was less appalled when he remembered Ransom's words about the churches, lodges, and societies being the only fields left in which the Negro could find "an outlet for his aspirations and ambitions. This serve[d] to account for the great flood tide of self-seeking and rivalry for office, which breaks upon us with the approach of the General Conference."[27] As if by magic, nevertheless, the atmosphere was totally altered the following Sunday, when he witnessed the moving, ritualistic consecration of bishops, superbly conducted by Bishop B. F. Lee. The charge given to these new leaders was anything but frivolous.

Before the conference closed, several resolutions were proposed. The conference petitioned the U.S. government to remove all American soldiers from Haiti. A petition in support of women's suffrage was defeated by a vote of 230 to 195, much to Joseph's disgust. The bishops' salaries were raised from $2,500 to $3,500 per annum. Bishop C. S. Smith was temporarily relieved of an Episcopal District and was made historiographer, replacing the recently deceased John T. Jenifer. Bishop J. M. Conner was sent to the 15th District in Smith's place, thus becoming Joseph's new bishop, and Reverdy Ransom was elected for the third time as editor of the *A.M.E. Review*.[28]

J. M. Conner had been elected bishop at the General Conference in Kansas City, Missouri, in 1912. Since then he had served as prelate of the 8th Episcopal District, composed of Mississippi and Louisiana, and the 12th District, covering Arkansas and Oklahoma.[29] From all reports, he was humane but not particularly strong as a leader.

When Joseph returned home from the General Conference, he and the members of Bethel decided to give the new bishop a banquet in July. Rev. Askew of Ebenezer was also making plans to entertain Bishop Conner. Neither knew of the other's plans until Askew phoned Joseph inviting him and his members to the banquet at Ebenezer. Not once did he tell Joseph that the banquet at Ebenezer was to include the entire district. Consequently, Joseph informed him that Bethel had made arrangements some time ago to entertain the Bishop and suggested that Askew and his members join in with Bethel. After hanging up the phone, Askew called the bishop and ministers of the district and told them "Joseph Gomez, pastor of Bethel, had flatly refused to cooperate or have anything to do with the banquet for the Bishop to be held at Ebenezer." When the members of Bethel were informed as to what Askew was saying about their minister, they insisted that Joseph write an open letter to the ministers and send a copy to the bishop explaining the situation. He did, stating that Bethel's reception was to have been a small affair with only "the brethren whom [he] knew could get [there] on short notice, and that had Rev. Askew told him that his banquet was to be a district affair, he would have most certainly given up his plans and joined in with Ebenezer." The letter ended with the accusation: "We see this in no other light than an attempt to discredit the pastor and members of Bethel in the eyes of the brethren and conference."[30]

As trivial as the episode may seem, it is an example of the extent to which some of the ministers would go to discredit the "Boy Wonder," as some few called him behind his back. He had been a favorite of Bishop Smith's, and they were determined that this should not be the case with Bishop Conner. According to Cora Lockhart, some ministers felt that Joseph was becoming too prominent in Church circles and in the city—and that he must be stopped.[31]

Their attempts were further thwarted at the 1920 Annual Conference, held in Fort Wayne, Indiana, when Joseph's presiding elder, C. Emery Allen, reported to the bishop that Joseph had taken in over five hundred members during his first year. He lauded the Bethel Social Service and noted that plans were being made for "a church building large enough to accommodate the people," since the overflow service organized that year had now become "itself an overflow." Finally he revealed that in excess of $32,025 had been raised, "the largest in the history of the church or conference." The membership of Bethel had now reached 2,645.[32]

During the conference, Joseph read the report he had drafted for the Committee on the State of the Country. It was considered so effective that on October 30 it was published in the *Detroit Contender.* The address was, in essence, a state of the union speech aimed primarily at Blacks but pertinent to all Americans. He mentioned the government's "frantic, almost ludicrous attempts to stem the tide" of communism by "wholesale raids." Joseph felt that instead of overreacting by accusing those who were considered to be "too Liberal," it could best attack communism by the inauguration of "a propaganda of Americanization, well-defined and comprehensive."[33]

He pointed to the "clash between Labor and Capital," which was becoming a worldwide problem. "Strikes had become the national nightmare," the problem made even more complex by "labor's internal strife." Next he discussed how the Democratic party had "dominated the affairs of the nation" for eight years. Led by Woodrow Wilson, it "essayed to speak for the nation at the Peace Table, and now to undertake a program for the task of readjustment." He noted that Wilson's cabinet had "seen more changes than that perhaps of any other administration, Mr. Colby, the present Secretary of State, being the third incumbent of that office." He reminded his audience that the national conventions would soon be coming up in Chicago and San Francisco. However, "disaffections in the ranks of both parties had led to the formation of a third party—the Liberal Party."

The addition of women voters made the outcome of the presidential election even harder to predict.[34]

He also recommended "a policy of rigid economy," since leaner days would be approaching, and rejection of the proposed amendment to the state constitution for the abolition of private grammar schools because it was unconstitutional, hostile to religious freedom, monopolistic (destroying as it would all competition in education), and economically unsound for the taxpayers. "It was not to the interest of the race to vote for any amendment that may mean the abridgement of the constitutional rights of any people," he warned. The passage of such an amendment would be devastating to Blacks in the southern states if they too decided to do away with private schools. Many of the public schools provided only "a few weeks in the entire year for the education of Negroes." Other recommendations included: "a thoughtful grappling of our churches of the problems incidental to the coming of our people in large numbers from the South. Wise investments, buying of lands and homes, and a rigid policy to support Negro business. Support [for] the Republican Party in the coming presidential election as the best instrument at hand to secure Negro rights."[35]

In his statement on Bolshevism, Joseph was undoubtedly referring to the Palmer "Red Hunts." A. Mitchell Palmer, as Wilson's attorney general, had been indirectly responsible for arresting over six thousand people, some of whom were Black, accused of being communists and engaging in espionage; however, due to a lack of evidence, most had to be released.[36] Joseph was outraged by this witch hunt.

For weeks after Joseph's address appeared in the paper, Black Detroiters were debating it in their churches and on street corners. Walter, who worshipped his older brother, memorized whole passages and repeated them for Hazel and Cora. In his naivete he believed that if his brother chose to run for president, he would surely be elected.

Between May 29 and June 6, 1921, Bethel celebrated its eightieth anniversary. Money raised during this event went into a building fund for "Greater Bethel," which was becoming less a vision and more a reality. Joseph had attempted to purchase the Presbyterian Church on the corner of Rivard and Jefferson Avenue for between $150,000 and $175,000 along with the Newberry house on Jefferson and then the lot on the northeast corner of Garfield and Beaubien. Both attempts failed. However, on May 18 Bethel successfully purchased the lot on the corner of Frederick and St. Antoine for $40,000; it was 140 feet by 145 feet, and it included a double (duplex) brick building, costing $12,000, which could be used for a parsonage.[37] Such a purchase was unprecedented for a Negro congregation, not only because of the price and size of the land but because it was located in a white neighborhood. In addition to the neighborhood's opposition to Negroes moving in, the Ku Klux Klan became involved. As soon as they learned of Bethel's plans, they sneaked during the night to the "Black Bottom" and burned crosses in front of Bethel; they followed that invasion with threatening telephone calls to Joseph and his family, giving them twenty-four hours to leave Detroit. The police were called in but seemed unable or unwilling to catch the culprits.

Cora remembers this as a time of terror for the household. Hazel was afraid when Joseph left the house that she might never see him again, and Walter found excuses to accompany his brother when he went out at night.[38] A Black policeman who was a member of Bethel came to the parsonage and showed Joseph and Hazel how to use a gun. Hazel became a markswoman ("I could aim high and shoot straight," she always claimed), but Joseph was not so adept. Once when he was demonstrating to the policeman that he had learned how to load the gun, it went off. The bullet lodged in the piano just above Hazel's head as she sat there playing. A few inches lower and it would have killed her. Joseph was daunted. He told the policeman to take the gun away. No matter what threats he might receive, he would not have a gun in the house. (The piano with the bullet hole now belongs to Eula's daughter, who resides outside Washington, D.C.)

Trouble never seemed to come in singles. On January 19, 1922, Cora eloped with Waymon Ransom, nephew to Reverdy Ransom and a minister about twenty years her senior. When Joseph found out about the elopement the next day, he was livid. Only time and Cora's happiness eventually made him accept the situation.[39] Then, early in July, Walter was helping someone paint a roof, and he slipped. He tried to cling to the ladder, but he fell to the ground several feet below. While he was in bed recuperating, he developed a severe case of pneumonia. Though Doctor Green came every day, and Mamie Boone, the nurse, seldom left his bedside, he only grew worse. Finally, on July 12th, Green told Joseph and Hazel that Walter would probably not last through the night. They sat beside him, alternately listening to his labored breathing, saying prayers, and applying cool compresses to his feverish forehead. Occasionally he would open his eyes and try to speak. At 2:30 A.M., July 13, he took his last breath.[40]

After he was officially pronounced dead, the body was removed from the house to the funeral home. He lay in state at Bethel until his funeral on July 15. A large number of people—members of the church, of the district, members of other churches and civic organizations, schoolmates, and neighborhood friends—came to pay their respects. Hazel remarked how uncanny it was that he looked so much like Joseph lying there, and she wondered if it was a premonition of things to come, given the racial trouble in the city.

The loss of Walter was the first real test of Joseph's religious faith. It had happened so unexpectedly. One day Walter was climbing a ladder; a few days later he was gone. He had filled perfectly the dual role of son and brother. He was only nineteen—still a boy. It was difficult to see the purpose in such a senseless death. When people tried to comfort Joseph by saying, "God knows best," the words became for him an empty platitude. Rebecca and Emanuel had entrusted Walter into his keeping, and he had failed them. He would have felt better if they had scolded him when he called them, but all he could hear was a deadly silence, broken only by the static coming across the wire. Gradually the pain eased, and his pastoral duties pulled life along, a little less vibrant, a little less full—but along. For Hazel it was an even more barren time, with Walter dead, Cora gone, and no hope of a child to take their places. She busied herself in her work with the young people at church.

In September, both Joseph and Hazel attended the Michigan Annual Conference, held at Quinn Chapel, in Flint. Hazel was elected to serve as secretary to the bishop during the sessions, a function she would resume later when Joseph became bishop. Joseph was again appointed to several committees, and he was recognized by the delegates for having received an honorary doctor of divinity degree from Payne Seminary at Wilberforce's June commencement.[41] When he was a student at Payne, he had never imagined that eight years later he would be honored by his old alma mater.

The highlight of the conference, however, was when Joseph had an opportunity to become better acquainted with John Gregg, now president of Wilberforce University. In an address on the second night, Gregg hoped that this generation would become dreamers—dreamers with their eyes wide open. He asserted that "no power could prevent such dreamers from obtaining their goals."[42] Joseph was impressed with this man who dignified dreams. That evening he and Gregg talked for hours about their future aspirations for the Church and for Wilberforce; they found they had ideas, and especially ideals, in common. The occasion marked the beginning of a lasting friendship. If Bishops Ransom and Smith were his mentors, Gregg became his companion.

As 1923 blustered in, it became more and more apparent that some of the ministers had not given up their campaign to discredit Joseph with Bishop Conner. In early January Joseph received an irate letter from the bishop and a clipping from a newspaper purporting to be the summary of a sermon Joseph had delivered some time ago. Whoever had written the article made it seem that Joseph was criticizing the bishopric in general, and Conner in particular. In a return letter Joseph said he viewed the clipping as an "unfortunate occurrence from one angle in that the sermon . . . [had been] distorted and misrepresented. On the other hand it gave a good chance as ever could be . . . to know of the jealousy and treachery of some people." It had been based "principally on an editorial written by Dr. R. R. Wright in the *Christian Recorder* a week previous in which he called upon the Church to raise less money but to emphasize more the winning of souls to Christ." Joseph pointed out how the sermon had been taken out of context. For instance, in responding to a suggestion by some that he would become a bishop some day, he had said: "If being a Bishop means . . . to crush and intimidate the people and the ministers, then I don't want it. If it means to carry out the promises of God and his gospel, then thank God for it." He then explained the quotation:

> Now what was said in that connection came as a result of a historical sketch [I had written] showing that the men whose names live today are those who were not too high for their fellowmen, but sought to serve humanity. . . . See how different it sounds in another connection? And so I might go on. Surely I have given too much evidence of my love for and gratitude to the Church to be forced to give labored arguments in proving it.[43]

Conner accepted his explanation, and the matter was closed; nevertheless, Joseph was growing weary of always having to defend himself.

He had given serious thought to running for the bishopric, and many of his friends were trying to persuade him to run. Perhaps this was why the article which Conner sent him had been written. It had been designed to furnish "splendid campaign propaganda [against him]. Hence the attack," Joseph concluded.[44] After some deliberation and several conversations with Hazel, he decided that at age thirty-three a bid for the bishopric would be premature. Instead, he again put all his efforts into supporting the candidacies of Ransom and Gregg. In an open letter to the delegates to the 1924 General Conference he said there was "no one more prepared to give the Church efficient service [than Ransom]. . . . For well nigh forty years this man has stood in the vanguard with those in Church and State [who have] fought to preserve inviolable things dear to us." Those seeking a conservative candidate would find in him "experience and a practical knowledge of Church." For those looking for "the young or progressive . . . 'Man of the Hour,' a scholar, an able pulpiteer and a Christian gentleman of progressive ideas, Ransom is the man they seek."[45]

In early February, 1923, while Joseph was advocating the election of Ransom because of his "experience" and "practical knowledge of Church," Bishop Charles S. Smith, another A.M.E. leader who fit that description, died. Before his demise he had made a valuable contribution to the Church by completing *A History of the African Methodist Episcopal Church, 1856–1922*. Joseph was particularly grateful to Smith for having given him the opportunity to pastor Bethel, Detroit, against the wishes of many ministers and bishops who thought he was too young. It was therefore fitting that the funeral should be held at Bethel, on Monday, February 5. Bishop J. Albert Johnson of the 2nd Episcopal District delivered the eulogy, and all the bishops and general officers were in attendance. Joseph read one of his favorite poems, "Crossing the Bar," by Alfred Lord Tennyson, presenting a copy to Christine, Bishop Smith's widow.[46] With Smith gone, it was even more important that the rich traditions of African Methodism be carried on by men, like Ransom and Gregg, who were well equipped to do so.

In March Joseph received a letter from his brother James telling him his mother was quite ill. After hastily arranging his affairs and informing Bishop Conner he would be away from his church for a time, he sailed for Trinidad in April 1923. It was his first trip home since he had come to the United States in 1908. So much had changed for him and his family since he left. Dead were his sister Arrimenta Christophine, Amanda's husband, and Walter. Joseph had never met Amanda's three sons, Josh, Junior, and Alva, who had been born after he left.

When he reached Trinidad, everything seemed smaller than he had remembered, but he was home, and that was all that mattered. Amanda reminded him of the horsey-rides she used to give him; Cyril stood shyly peeking from behind her skirt; Elvira proudly introduced her husband, and James presented May, his wife.

When Joseph was taken to his mother's bedside he was alarmed to see how aged and ill she seemed. Emanuel stood beside her, slimmer than Joseph had remembered—slimmer and somewhat defeated, but as always gentle and soft-spoken. Hidden in the corner of the room was Violet, who had had a child out of wedlock. Although Joseph had left Trinidad when she was quite small, he had always been her ideal. As soon as she was able to get her brother alone, she begged him to take her back to the United States, so she could get a fresh start. Her son, she said, would stay in Trinidad with the father. Joseph promised he would try to persuade Rebecca and Emanuel to let her come.

On Joseph's last day in Trinidad, James gave him an autograph book in which every member of the family had written a favorite verse, as was customary in the West Indies when someone was going away.[47] Joseph kept that book of simple verses all his life. Occasionally he would turn the pages and look at the familiar handwriting so that he could feel the nearness of his family. When he was to recall his visit in 1923 he would speak of the "sunset of those tropic lands . . . the glory of mountain vastnesses," the calm lakes and "majesty of the sea." Nevertheless, even in the midst of all that beauty, his most poignant memory was of his mother. "No vision that was mine," he wrote, "was to be compared with the vision of the out-stretched arms of a white-haired mother who welcomed me home, that though weak, pressed me to [her] heart with a strength born of a mother's love." No music was as sweet as the "the music of [her] voice, though cracked and faltering [, that asked], 'My boy, do you know me?'"[48]

An interesting postscript to his visit is that when he was asked by his family why he called himself "Gomez" instead of the Portuguese "Gomes," he told them that in America that was the way the name was pronounced and spelled. From that day on, the entire family called themselves "Gomez."

When Joseph returned to Detroit, he wrote Bishop Conner informing him that he was back at his "post of duty." He expressed his gratitude "to God for the opportunity granted" him to see his mother before her eyes were closed in death. Her condition was not good. He described her as "just living and that [was] all."[49]

A few weeks after his trip, Joseph became involved with the problem of a saloon, under white management, across the street from the church. Numerous times the church had petitioned the police department to close it. Since the Prohibition amendment had passed, Detroit had become one of the main stops for the illegal sale of liquor smuggled in from Canada by way of the Detroit River, thus making liquor a lucrative business for the criminal element of the city. Known members of the underworld frequented the saloon in question, and as Joseph told the police commissioner, "the place [had] become a public nuisance, a disgrace to an already bad community, and a snare to the hundreds of our people who [attended] Sunday School and [Allen Christian Endeavor] League."[50] After several petitions, letters, and editorials in the Black newspapers, the Commissioner bowed to the pressure. The cabaret was eventually closed, but not before Joseph had become a menace to the white racketeers who ran most of the illegal businesses in the "Black Bottom."

For different reasons, the Klan was also determined to get revenge. According to Cora and the Boones, there had occurred a confrontation between whites and Blacks in some part of the city, the exact cause and date unknown; however, whites, including members of the Klan, ran the Blacks back into the "Black Bottom," and a small war ensued. Cora (now Cora Ransom) received a phone call from Bethel requesting that Waymon, her husband, and any other men he could muster should come at once to help protect the church. When Waymon and his friends reached the church, they could see it was covered on three sides by armed whites. They slipped through the back door of the basement and joined Joseph and some of his trustees, who had vowed to risk their lives to protect the building. All night they could hear the rat-tat-tat and pop of rifles and handguns as the whites attempted to intimidate the residents. Although the police must have heard the noise and received numerous calls from the community, they did not come until the next morning. By that time Napoleon Street looked like a battleground of broken glass and bullet-riddled houses and businesses. Several people had been wounded, but since they were all Black there were no arrests and no mention of the incident in the white newspapers, despite testimonies from eye-witnesses.[51]

The following Sunday the trustees were forced to stand armed around the inside of the church so Joseph could conduct services. Outside could still intermittently be heard the deadly sound of gunfire. Bethelites were afraid not only of a repeat of that earlier terrifying night but that the KKK would carry out its threat to kill Joseph and his family if he continued his expansion plans to occupy the lot on Frederick and St. Antoine. The police finally cordoned off the area. Blacks were not allowed to come or go, except for some mulattoes who passed for white and got through the roadblocks by telling the police they were going to get guns to kill the "Niggers." Needless to say, these weapons eventually became the property of the Black community without the police realizing where they had come from.[52] For those Negroes who lived in Detroit during the 1920s, the Renaissance was far from utopian.

On August 9, 1923, Violet arrived in Detroit with the news that Elvira had died suddenly. James and May had decided to adopt Elvira's son, Alwyn, and raise him as their own, since they had no children and the prospect of their ever having any was slim. It seemed to Joseph that his family was disappearing rapidly. First Mary, then Arrimenta, then Walter, and now Elvira had died. There was no way of knowing how long his mother would last, or how long Papa would survive without her.

With Violet's arrival came a great deal of tension. When she met Hazel, she immediately was jealous of the attention Joseph paid his wife. Violet was a stranger in a strange place with only her brother as a connection to the past. Her need for attention was acute. Intentionally or not, she began to make trouble for Hazel; when Hazel attempted to alert Joseph as to what was happening, he brushed it off lightly, thinking in time they would adjust to one another. As a result, Violet felt she had the upper hand and became ever more caustic toward her sister-in-law.

One day Joseph came home unexpectedly from the church office. As he walked up the steps he could hear abusive language issuing from the parsonage. Violet was giving Hazel a tongue-lashing. Not realizing her brother was standing in the door listening to her in amazement, she continued to rage. Suddenly she turned and saw him. She could tell by his expression that he had heard everything. Without a word, he took her into the bedroom and locked the door. Hazel never knew what he said to Violet, but from then on things were somewhat easier, though the two women were never really comfortable with each other. Violet was impulsive, possessive, and had a quick temper, but was highly creative. Hazel, on the other hand, was methodical and thoughtful. She rarely became angry, but when she did she stayed that way for a long time. These differences between the two seemed to be irreconcilable. As long as Violet lived with them, a tension hung in the air and extended into the church. The members of Bethel never favored Violet as they had Walter, mostly because she gave them the impression they were somehow beneath her. She never let them forget that she was the pastor's light-skinned, attractive sister from the West Indies.

When the Annual Conference of September 19–24, 1923, convened at Ebenezer, Detroit, Joseph headed the election for delegates to the 1924 General Conference, with seventy-three votes. Both Reverdy Ransom and John Gregg, who were again running for the bishopric, attended the conference and addressed the ministers on the evening of September 20.[53] Listening to them speak, Joseph felt certain they were two of the most brilliant minds in the Connection. He hoped he could persuade the other delegates from Michigan to support them. Meanwhile there were other pressing matters to engage his attention.

During the year, the KKK had renewed its effort to recruit members in Detroit. They operated from a large building on Forest and Brush, where they terrorized any Black who rode those streets.[54] Racial tension had reached an all-time high, and yet the white clergy were hesitant to condemn the Klan's activities. On October 10, the *Detroit Independence* came out with an exposé, criticizing the all-white Council of Churches for its refusal to take issue with the Klan.[55] Joseph wrote a letter congratulating the editor for pointing out "the base betrayal of faith of those men of [the] city clergy who, in recent session of the Detroit Council of Churches, voted to table a resolution condemning the Ku Klux Klan." Joseph stated further that some people had forgotten this was the second time the Council had behaved in this manner. Two years ago, when he was president of the Colored Detroit Interdenominational Alliance, his group had passed a resolution "calling upon the City Council to join the ranks of other cities in condemning the Klan, and prohibiting open exhibitions within its corporate limits"; the Council had duly passed such a law. It stood to reason if the City Council was willing to take a stand, the Council of Churches should have found it a moral duty to support efforts against the Klan. Instead the Council of Churches had referred the matter to the Committee on Social Relations, and nothing was ever heard concerning the matter. Once again the "twenty-six leading white ministers of Detroit, by their refusal, were aiding the Klan." Now, instead of being merely surprised by the Council of Churches' inaction, as they had been two years ago, the Negro ministers were indignant: "for not only [had] a body of Ministers of the Gospel refused in the first instance to do what a civic body, the City Council, felt to be a righteous duty, but for the second time [had] registered their attitude in no uncertain terms. Yet they preach[ed] human brotherhood and the love of God."[56] Joseph's letter caused consternation among many of the members of the Council of Churches but was applauded by the Negro clergy, who felt it was time for someone to take on the organization for its craven stand in racial matters.

In spite of the unrest in the community, plans for Greater Bethel were completed on November 10, 1923, and a special ground-breaking ceremony was held April 27, 1924, at which the cornerstone was laid by Bishop Conner, assisted by the Grand Lodge of Michigan. Greetings were given by civic and religious leaders of the city.[57] A few days after the ceremony, the Gomezes moved from the old parsonage on Napoleon to the double brick building at 571 Frederick Street so they could be settled before it was time to leave for the General Conference in May. Mamie and William Boone occupied the other side of the duplex. To ensure the safety of the two families, Joseph bought a German shepherd, whom he named Flora. Although she was gentle with the family and the Boones, Flora became vicious when strangers invaded her territory; Hazel felt much more secure with her around. Klan members would think twice before coming on the property.

On May 5, Hazel and Joseph traveled to Louisville, Kentucky, to attend the General Conference, which was meeting at the Jefferson County Armory at 6th and Walnut Streets. At the opening session they listened as Bishop John Hurst delivered the Quadrennial Sermon, during which he espoused the cause of women's rights: "Today the progressive modern church welcomes [women] in the administration of holy things and accords her voice in the legislative assembly. Why not the African Methodist Episcopal Church?" He also spoke of the race and the Church having lost their missions:

> As a race, we have lost out almost completely in the government. Not one member of this race is in the Congress of the nation. Our status as citizens is not to the standards of the years past [referring to Reconstruction]. In the face of our helpless condition, we can't but conclude that the hope of this race is in the church, and this old church that has come through the prayers and tears of our fathers must not be allowed to be pulled down.[58]

To give substance to Hurst's stand on women's rights in the Church, on the third afternoon, during the report of the Missionary Department, the women (Hazel included) "marched through the room carrying banners with the inscriptions, 'We Want Women Suffrage and Want It Now,' 'Taxation without Representation Is Tyranny,' 'Vote for Women,' 'We Stand for Women's Suffrage!!'"[59] Joseph was among those delegates who applauded the women vigorously. It was time for the Church to join the twentieth century, he felt.

On the eighth day of the conference, Bishop Conner rose to request that the church relieve him from active duty for a year's period of rest because of his health, which had been steadily declining during the past four years. Despite the resolution of the 15th District asking that he be returned to them, the delegates granted his request.[60] This meant that another bishop would be assigned to the district, the third since Joseph had come to Michigan

The following day the election of bishops was held. Both Ransom and Gregg were hopeful they might win this time, despite the obstacles they encountered, as outlined in Ransom's autobiography. First, they were from the North in a church dominated largely by southerners. Secondly, J. H. Jones, Bishop of the 3rd District, of which they were both members, "would not permit Dr. Gregg . . . freedom to go afield and mingle with his brethren. He withheld Gregg's salary until he was almost without funds. He not only opposed his election to the bishopric but also opposed his reelection as President of Wilberforce University." Ransom also alleged that Jones prevented him from speaking at any of the Ohio Annual Conferences.[61]

On the first ballot, no candidate received a majority. On the second, A. L. Gaines from Georgia received more than the 362 votes needed to be elected; Gregg received 345, Ransom 340. After Gaines had been elected, the southerners tried to adjourn "to give them time to re-form their lines and shut out Gregg and me," Ransom wrote. Bishop William A. Chappelle, who was presiding, would not permit an adjournment, and the election proceeded. On the third ballot, with 479 and 475 votes respectively, Ransom and Gregg were both elected.[62] Joseph felt a tremendous surge of emotion as he presented Ransom to the bishops for ordination some hours later.

The assignment of the bishops was read by the Episcopal Committee on the afternoon of the fifteenth day. Ransom was sent to the 13th District (Kentucky and Tennessee), Gregg to South Africa, and Bishop William T. Vernon to the 15th District, replacing Conner.[63] Joseph was not overjoyed at the prospect of having Vernon as his bishop; however, he was determined to do what he could to cooperate with the new administration.

Joseph had his first opportunity to observe Vernon as presiding bishop at the Michigan Annual Conference in Grand Rapids, held between September 10 and 14. After Joseph preached the Annual Sermon, which the minutes described as "eloquent and forceful," the bishop addressed the conference.[64] He "expressed his appreciation for being assigned Episcopal supervisor over the . . . District" and announced "that the meritorious system [would] be the only policy he would use in making assignments and that one's ability [would] not be measured by dollar and cents only, but also by service rendered." Later that week he added that "the authority of an A.M.E. Bishop is too great to be given a man who has not a tender heart. This statement I make in light of the fact that the destinies of ministers, their families, churches and race are in the hands of the Bishops."[65] Few had ever heard the power of the bishopric described in those terms.

During the evening session of the second day, Dr. Gilbert H. Jones, son of Bishop Joshua H. Jones and the new president of Wilberforce University, replacing Gregg, addressed the conference. He "made a forceful presentation of Wilberforce's needs, emphasizing the peculiar place Negro educational institutions fill in the development of manhood and womanhood of [the] race."[66] Listening to him speak, Joseph felt reassured concerning the university's future growth and that Jones would carry on the work that Gregg had started. His optimism proved to be well founded. It was under Jones that Wilberforce became a member of the Association of American Colleges. "The same year the Board of Regents of the State of New York approved and accredited the institution, and the departments of education of North Carolina, Virginia, Florida, and Texas . . . accepted Wilberforce students on a par with students from other colleges."[67] What was left was accreditation by the North Central Association of Colleges and Secondary Schools.

It soon became obvious that women in the 15th District were not going to have an easy time under Vernon's leadership. On the third day of the conference he "highly complimented Mrs. Cornelia Young of Detroit for having served so faithfully as President of the Conference Christian Endeavor League . . . and then expressed his desire of having a young man as president . . . since a young man [could] perhaps, render more time." Before the conference ended, he had appointed his own man, a William Butler.[68]

1925 was the year of new beginnings. On June 7, Greater Bethel was dedicated. The magnificent brick building, with its large stained-glass window and towering steeple, was ready for occupancy. Early morning services were held in the old edifice on Napoleon and Hastings. In the afternoon, over three thousand proud Negroes, dressed in their Sunday best, marched through the "Black Bottom" as hundreds of others who lined the sidewalks cheered them on. The procession was led by Bishop Vernon in his rich purple ecclesiastic attire, followed by Hazel and Joseph, who walked hand in hand. Next came the trustees, deacons, deaconesses, stewards and stewardesses, robed choirs, Sunday school children, and the rest of the congregation, singing "Onward, Christian Soldiers" and "The Church Is Moving On." When they reached Frederick Street, the singing was distorted by the jeers and curses of whites. But the Old/New Negroes had arrived and, in the words of the old spiritual, were not about to let "nobody turn them around." The architect handed the key of the church to the trustee, who handed it to the bishop. He turned it easily in the lock, and the parade moved into the sanctuary, where the dedicatory services took place.

The new church, including extra work and equipment, had cost $300,000, an enormous sum for the times.[69] To those who said it could not be done Joseph had answered with youthful optimism and faith, all things are possible with God. At the age of thirty-five he had been able to accomplish what older and wiser men would have had better sense than even to contemplate.

The morning after the dedication, Joseph opened his front door to find a cross burning in the yard. Soon afterward he heard a loud thump on the front porch. Someone had thrown a rock with a note attached, which warned that this was only the beginning if he and his "Nigger" congregation did not move from the neighborhood. During the next Sunday morning service, obscene oaths could be heard outside. Once again the trustees stood in the aisles armed, as several of the stained glass windows were destroyed by bricks hurled through them. This time the police became involved, and though there were no arrests, eventually things quieted down. Inside, the service had gone on as scheduled, except that the organ and the singing swelled to a feverish pitch to drown out the drama in the church yard.

On June 17, Joseph became one of the founders, and a member of the first Board of Directors, of the Detroit Memorial Park Association. As early as his Bermuda pastorate he had been vitally interested in the establishment of a cemetery where Negroes could bury their dead with dignity. Most were barred from white cemeteries or were relegated to some dark, un-kempt corner. Joseph and twelve other prominent Negroes of Detroit decided to purchase sixty acres of land in Warren Township, in the county of Macomb. This first Board of Directors consisted of Charles C. Diggs, Douglas B. Fullwood (also first treasurer), Aaron C. Toodles (also first president), James M. Gregory, Ernest W. H. Johnson, V. A. Bristol, A. W. Womack, H. S. Dunbar, Robert L. Bradby, F. E. Dawson, M. E. Morton, and Alonzo D. Pettiford. The Articles of Incorporation listed the cost of the land as $25,000, divided into one hundred shares. Twenty subscribers held five shares each. However, in the revised Articles signed July 27, 1926, the estimated capital required for the purchase was listed as "one hundred thousand dollars divided into ten thousand (10,000) shares." Fifty sub-scribers held 125 shares each.[70]

Initially the meetings were held at the St. Antoine Street Branch of the YMCA and were presided over by Aaron Toodles. Negroes of Detroit proudly watched this association grow, knowing that its existence meant property ownership and a picturesque resting place for the race. Joseph im-mediately bought three plots, one each for Hazel and himself and one for any family member who might wish to be buried beside them. He often boasted that his investment in the Detroit Memorial Park Association was the only stock from which he received steady dividends. Though small in amount, these dividends represented far more to him than mere money: they were symbolic of the Negro's struggle to have power over his own destiny.

Joseph had additional reason to be proud when at the 1925 Annual Conference, held at Community Church in Jackson, September 16–20, Rev. T. H. Wiseman, his presiding elder, praised the work he had done at Bethel. He called the new church "the fulfillment of a dream. The reali-zation of a vision splendid." It was more than a beautiful building; it represented "the tremendous possibilities of a people who can do so great a task and do it smiling." He said that "this young man [Joseph] had out-stripped even himself," despite the "doubts, fears, criticisms from all sides." Wiseman further noted that Bethel had raised over $70,000 that year and that "the volume of business done by this church under Dr. Gomez's leadership will amount to $100,000." He also credited Hazel for her work with the young people and the inspiration she had been to her husband. "A tremendous increase in membership substantiates the fact that all roads lead to Bethel." He concluded that "there is not a greater or finer church in the United States among our people, nor is there a greater field of constructive work anywhere among our people."[71]

When it came time for Bishop Vernon to read the pastoral appointments, Joseph felt apprehensive, particularly when he prefaced the reading with: "In making these appointments, I have been perplexed more than ever before. Old men wish to reach back to other days, while young men are in too big a hurry, which I fear may prove to be injurious. Nevertheless, I have done the best I could. I have fixed appointments, prayed and refixed them."[72] Even though Joseph was sent back to Bethel, there was no doubt in anyone's mind as to whom Vernon had had in mind when he said "young men are in too big a hurry." Bethel's membership had grown to 3,520, and the church had raised its pastor's salary to $3,520, close to the total income of a bishop.[73] No wonder Vernon must have felt this particular young man was moving too rapidly.

The shadow of Vernon was diminished when in June Dr. Green told Hazel she was pregnant. For ten years she and Joseph had wanted to hear these words, and now the miraculous had come to pass. Joseph became the stereotypical expectant father, overcautious of Hazel's health, not allowing her to lift anything, making her walk every evening. Between his fussing, Violet's solicitude, and Mamie's checking in on her every day, Hazel began to feel like an invalid. But Joseph was going to make certain that nothing went wrong with the birth of his first "son."

On Sunday, February 21, 1926, while Joseph was delivering the sermon, one of the ushers handed him a note which read: "Congratulations Rev. Gomez. Beautiful perfect baby girl born 11:35 A.M. Mother and daughter doing well. Send greetings to Papa [signed C. F. Green, M.D.]."[74]

Without any explanation to the congregation, Joseph bounded out of the church to the parsonage next door to see his daughter. What difference did it make if the baby were not a boy? A few days later, the *Independent* carried the announcement of the birth of Eula Viviana. The concluding paragraph read, "While Rev. Gomez was preaching Sunday morning on the theme, 'The Tie That Binds,' the stork dropped in at his home, 571 Frederick Avenue, and left a little tie that binds."[75]

The baby had been named after Eula Smith of Bermuda, whom the Gomezes had considered adopting before Hazel discovered she was pregnant. The middle name, Viviana, came from her aunt, Violet Viviana. From birth Eula was an ideal baby, quiet and thoughtful, content to lie in her crib entertaining herself with her toys. She rarely cried, except when she was wet or hungry. Flora, the German shepherd, was highly protective of her; she would sit by the carriage in the back yard and growl and show her teeth if anyone came near the baby. Once Hazel found a scrap of cloth from a pair of man's pants in Flora's mouth, but she never learned to whom it belonged.

The shadow of Vernon towered once again in 1926, when he was asked to speak on race relations to the Detroit Council of Churches, the same group who had refused to denounce the Klan. The contents of Vernon's speech caused considerable consternation among the Negro clergy of the city. Cora Ransom remembers that her husband had come home from the Colored Ministerial Alliance livid after being informed there as to what the bishop had said to the Council.[76] At the Alliance a Negro Citizens Committee was formed, and Joseph was elected to write a letter to the press protesting the bishop's speech. Even though he knew what he would say would jeopardize his already precarious position with Vernon, Joseph wrote the letter. In it he noted that the *Detroit Free Press* had quoted Bishop Vernon as having said that one of the solutions to the Negro problem was the provision of "an area where suitable homes could be built that would satisfy the educated and well-to-do as well as the working class [Negro]." In other words, Negroes should not try to move into white neighborhoods. Vernon had also said that "his attitude toward Jim-Crowism and Separate Schools was the same as that on Housing; that he was not opposed to Jim-Crowism if in the Jim Crow cars proper accommodations were given; that he did not seek social equality."[77]

Vernon was advocating the same accommodationist philosophy as had Booker T. Washington—a philosophy highly objectionable to the "New Negro," the Black intelligentsia of the 1920s. His speech was extremely offensive to Joseph, who had long fought for integration and who was convinced that *separate* could never be *equal*.

The Negro clergy was especially rankled by Vernon's statement about housing, since there had been several incidents in which Negroes who had moved or attempted to move into white neighborhoods had been harassed and threatened, sometimes with their lives. As early as 1920, when a landlord had rented the bottom apartment of a duplex in an exclusive residential area to a Negro a riot had occurred during which five policemen were wounded.[78] In April 1925, whites had mobbed a house when Negroes moved onto Northfield Avenue.[79] On June 23, 1925, Dr. Alexander Turner, a Negro physician, had moved into a house on Spokane Avenue. Approximately 5,000 people had surrounded the house. He was visited by the Neighborhood Improvement Association, who offered to buy it back;

Turner, afraid for the lives of his family, had agreed to sell. As he was leaving the premises he was wounded when some of the crowd pelted him with rocks.[80] When Waymon and Cora Ransom had moved onto Richter the same year, the neighbors had been incensed. They had thought because her skin was so fair that she was a white woman married to a colored man. As in the other incidents, a mob had surrounded the house. To help him protect the house, Waymon had sent for Christopher Price, great-grandson of the Indian chief Pontiac, for whom the city of Pontiac was named. He also sent for Walter Ward, an employee of his, and Otis Ransom, a nephew. The police gave no assistance even when whites began shooting at the house. Only when Waymon threatened to shoot back did the police disperse the crowd.[81]

The worst of these incidents occurred in September 1925, when Dr. Ossian Sweet, whom Joseph had known in college, attempted to move into an all-white neighborhood on the corner of Garland and Charlevoix. An ugly mob gathered outside the house on the second night and started throwing rocks and threatening the family inside. Suddenly, they began to shoot into the house. Someone from inside shot back from an upstairs window, and a white man was killed. Dr. Sweet and his entire family were arrested and charged with first-degree murder.[82] Negro leaders from all over the city met and elected Joseph president of the Detroit Sweet Defense Committee. Meanwhile, the national branch of the NAACP attempted to secure the services of Clarence Darrow. Darrow asked if the Sweets had fired the shot and was told they had. He replied, "I'll take the case. If they had not had the courage to shoot back in defense of their own lives, I wouldn't think they were worth defending."[83] (It was this kind of audacity that endeared Darrow to Joseph, who offered him the full support of the Committee and the Colored Ministerial Alliance, of which he was president. The two men became friends. According to Cora, it was not unusual to come into the front room of the parsonage and see the rumpled Darrow sprawled on the couch or pacing back and forth, arguing heatedly about the case.)

If Negroes expected any great support from Mayor John Smith, they were disappointed. On September 13 he wrote to the commissioner of police, "I must say that I deprecate most strongly the moving of negroes or other persons into districts in which they know their presence may cause riots or bloodshed."[84] The Black community was incensed when Smith formed a Mayor's Committee on Race Relations and made Bishop William T. Vernon vice chairman. Some of the committee's findings reflected Vernon's views on separation. For instance, in terms of housing, the report said, "When streets in Negro district are kept in repair as they are in white districts and when equal sanitary, educational and other facilities are made available for them, there will be a more general tendency on their part to remain where they are or when they move to expand by group rather than by individual action."[85] Once again the old "separate but equal" philosophy emerged to appease the power structure and Negroes who sought crumbs from that structure.

Vernon's opinions were sanctioned by most whites in Detroit, but not by his own people. He was furious when Joseph sent a letter to the press opposing his appointment by the Mayor as vice chairman. It was no secret that Vernon was not overly fond of light-skinned Negroes, and he had said so to any number of people, including Cora, who could have easily passed for white. He was particularly antagonistic toward Joseph—the fair, young, aggressive upstart who threatened his authority and who wielded so much influence in the Negro community and among some of the bishops in the Connection.[86]

On Saturday, May 22, 1926, Joseph traveled to North Carolina to deliver the Sunday commencement address at Kitrell College and to receive another honorary doctor of divinity degree. He chose as his subject "Elements of Success," using as background the parable of the ten virgins (Matt. 25:10). He reminded the graduates that this was an hour for "retrospection, for perspective, as well as for introspection." As was the case with the ten virgins, the key to a successful life was preparation, appropriation, and exultation ("The end of the path of obedience to the primary laws of life brings exultation"). It was to the exultant life that Joseph called the graduates: "It is their 'triteness of living' that renders so many men and women impotent in the hour of struggle, and unfit for the association of an inspiring and achieving humanity." Two opposing summits, Gerizim's lofty heights and Ebal's "downward path of threatened failure . . . still sound today, across the space of years, the same unchangeable assurances of success and failure." As graduates they dared not let pass opportunities denied their enslaved fathers and mothers, who envisioned a "mighty host of free men . . . richer in things of everlasting values."[87]

Following his address Joseph rushed back to Detroit to complete plans for the Bishop's Council, which was to be held at Greater Bethel, June 24–27, the first he had ever hosted. Housing had to be found for the guests, and meals and programs planned. He was determined that this would be one of the most efficient councils ever held. News that the Ransoms would be staying at the parsonage made the meeting even more significant. This would give Hazel and Joseph an opportunity to show off their four-month-old daughter and to have her baptized with the Ransoms serving as godparents.

Although the primary function of the Bishops' Council was for the deliberations of the bishops, the Missionary Society, Allen Christian Endeavor League, and Sunday school also met while the bishops were in session. In addition, ministers and lay persons from all over the Connection attended, many in an attempt to promote their candidacy for the bishopric or some general office.

On June 24, a large number of A.M.E.s assembled in Greater Bethel for the first time to listen to Bishop W. Sampson Brooks preach the opening sermon and to partake of the sacrament.[88] Afterwards, many visitors expressed their admiration for the new building, which they said was one of the most impressive in the Connection, and they complimented Joseph effusively for having finished it and for the fine hospitality he offered during their visit.

Through the entire week Bishop Vernon went about puffing himself up as though the success of the council was entirely his doing. He avoided Joseph and the members of Bethel, and complimented only the other ministers of the city who had helped with the arrangements. This greatly angered Bethelites, who were growing more and more hostile to the bishop.

Pictures in the souvenir program show a rather stout Hazel holding Eula in her arms as she posed with the Women's Council of Bethel and the Mary F. Handy Circle of Ministers' Wives. Joseph also seems to have put on weight since his Bermuda and Canada days. As president of the Detroit Alliance of A.M.E. Preachers he is pictured with Bishop Vernon and the Alliance members. He and Hazel also appear in individual portraits at the beginning of the program. Hazel's thick, long hair is pulled back in a large bun, and Joseph's short haircut makes his boyish face seem even fuller.[89]

The Ransoms enjoyed their stay with the Gomezes and were particularly delighted with their godchild, who was growing rapidly. The two men talked for hours about the future direction of the Church. Joseph told Ransom how he, Rev. D. O. Walker of Cleveland, A. J. Wilson, and L. L. Berry felt that all of the bishops should be moved at the next General Conference, since many had been in the same districts for years and were building up little kingdoms. The group chose Joseph to write and read the resolution at the Quadrennial. He showed Ransom a draft; Ransom pledged his support and seemed certain Gregg would also but suggested that Joseph talk to him personally. Joseph did and was assured of Gregg's support as well.

When the delegates departed from Detroit, they carried with them the image of a Greater Bethel, a creative leader, a dedicated congregation, and a dangerously jealous bishop. As news of the impressive new church and the gracious reception extended to the delegates spread, those who had not heard of Joseph Gomez before came to realize that here was a young minister about whom much would be heard in the future.

Two months after the Bishops' Council, the Michigan Annual Conference opened at Olivet A.M.E. Church in South Bend, Indiana. Vernon continued to compliment the ministers and lay persons for the successful Bishops' Council but made no special mention of the work done by the host minister or his congregation. In fact, during the entire conference he never spoke Joseph's name except to ask for reports.[90]

During the evening session of the second day, Vernon announced the passing of Dr. W. S. Scarborough, former president of Wilberforce University. Joseph was sad that the Church had lost such a scholar and personality. He remembered the pleasant visits he had had as a student at the Scarborough home. The same evening, Joseph presented a leather portfolio to George F. Woodson "on behalf of the graduates, students and friends of Payne Theological Seminary . . . as a mark of appreciation of his services as Dean."[91]

Now that the church was built and the Bishops' Council and Annual Conference was over, Joseph had more time to spend at the parsonage with Hazel, Eula, and Violet. Early evenings were usually passed with the Boones, who would bring their baby daughter, Margaret, over; the two families would share a dessert of some kind. Other visitors were DeWitt and Alice Burton and their daughter, Arlyn, who was Joseph's goddaughter. Burton had gained some success as a doctor since the days when the Gomezes tried to make a match between him and Cora. Burton was not a church-going man, but he was very fond of Joseph and came often to Bethel to hear him preach. The two men were vastly different. Both were extroverts and liked to argue, but while Burton had the assurance and sophistication of the well-to-do, Joseph had the passion of a man with a cause. Burton was to amass a great deal of money; Joseph never managed to become rich. The Burtons were the first Negro family to move into Arden Park, in a huge house with a ballroom, a game room, and a breakfast nook which contained a fountain imported from Italy. Burton became the first Negro appointed to the Board of Trustees of Wayne State University, the founder and director of Burton Mercy Hospital, superintendent of Rest Haven Hospital, and chairman of the board of directors of the Beneficial Life Insurance Society of America. Often when the Burtons came to see the Gomezes their visit would be cut short by some emergency at the hospital. But the parsonage was never empty of callers for any length of time. As one group left, another would come. Cora and Waymon came by occasionally, as did the Toodles, and there were always Gussie Jones and Mrs. W. T. Johnson with their homemade breads or cakes and their colorful stories.

Sometime in April 1927, Hazel learned that miracles can repeat themselves: she was pregnant again, and the baby was due in early December. Both she and Joseph were sure it would be a boy this time. Greater Bethel was in the midst of its eighty-sixth anniversary celebration, but Hazel could not participate as she would have liked, because this pregnancy was not as easy as the first had been. Nor would Dr. Green let her attend any of the Annual Conference sessions in September, even though they were held in the city, at St. Stephen's Church. Joseph hated to be away from her to attend the lengthy meetings, but once again Mamie Boone promised to look after Hazel often.

At St. Stephen's, Vernon repeated his performance of the last Annual Conference. He ignored Joseph, whose name rarely appears in the minutes and who was not appointed to any committee. When it came time for the election of delegates to the 1928 General Conference, Vernon's influence was evident. Joseph came in fourth; this meant that although elected, he would for the first time not lead the delegation.[92] Some of the ministers admitted they had been too afraid for their futures to go against the wishes of the bishop, who had made it clear he did not want Joseph elected.

On the final evening of the conference, resolutions were made endorsing the candidacies of "Dr. Joseph Gomez and Dr. W. E. Walker for the bishopric."[93] After much persuasion from the district and from other friends in the Connection, Joseph had decided to make his first claim on the bishopric, even though he doubted he could win. At the same session, before reading the appointments, Vernon made the shocking announcement that every minister who had been at a church for five years or more would be moved. Joseph had pastored Bethel since 1919 but had been in the new Greater Bethel only a little over a year. There were debts to be paid, and he had just begun to put into operation the expanded program he had planned. The bishop had solemnly promised Joseph that he would not move him until after the baby was born, since Dr. Green had warned that any added stress might cause Hazel to lose the child. When Vernon announced that Joseph Gomez had been moved from Bethel and sent to Ebenezer, Detroit, and that E. D. Robinson (later Carl Tanner) was sent to Bethel in his place, pandemonium ensued.[94] Bethelites denounced the bishop in angry words, but he continued to read the remaining appointments unperturbed.

That evening Hazel went into false labor, and Dr. Green had to sit up with her all night. He suggested to Joseph that it might be well for Hazel to go on a vacation until the baby was born. Hazel would not hear of it.

She refused to leave Joseph's side during this crisis. Joseph tried not to show how upset and angry he was, but Hazel sensed his feelings. He wondered how much his proposal that all bishops be moved at the next General Conference had to do with Vernon's five-year ruling concerning ministers.

On September 30, 1927, the *Detroit Independent* carried the headlines: "Bethel Rejects Bishop Vernon's Appointment." The laymen, led by their president, A. C. Toodle, had voted not to accept any pastor until they had a conference with Bishop Vernon. When the bishop met with them, the various boards of the church "informed the Bishop that the church did not object to his appointment of Rev. Mr. Tanner, so much as the manner in which it was done, and also the complete ignoring of their church, and incidentally their former pastor, Rev. Mr. Gomez at the Annual Conference." They also said they refused to accept Mr. W. Wiseman as their Presiding Elder because the bishop had "passed on [approval of] his character when it had been marked. This, they charged, is a gross violation of the law of the church and an insult to the Detroit district."[95]

On October 7 the *Detroit Independent* reported that once again Bethel had rejected the bishop's appointee. Rev. Tanner had tried to attend the Sunday morning service, but he had been met at the door "by a group of about 20 women of the church who told him emphatically that the members of Bethel Church did not want him as pastor."[96] They stated as their reasons that he had been a complete failure as pastor of the largest churches in Philadelphia, Washington, Atlanta, and Chicago, and that his appointment "to Bethel had been made without consulting or conferring with the officers of the church. The Bishop not only ignored the church in the matter of a pastor, but also had not considered Bethel during the entire session of the Annual Conference." No recognition had been given to Bethel for its work during the year, and their pastor, Rev. Joseph Gomez, had not been "put on a single committee, or asked to say a single word or do anything during the conference."[97] Rev. Tanner attempted again that Sunday evening to enter the church. This time he brought plainclothes detectives and his attorney, J. P. Rodgers, Assistant City Corporation Counsel, but the entire group was refused admittance again by the women.[98]

On October 14, the *Detroit Independent* reported that Tanner had obtained an injunction enjoining the officers, members, and Rev. Joseph Gomez from further preventing him from entering the church. The trustees in turn got an injunction restraining Rev. Tanner from entering the church until the matter was settled in court. They accused him of making many false statements in his injunction, particularly as it related to Rev. Gomez.[99]

A second article in the same paper reported that "Bethel's Loss Is Ebenezer's Gain." While the fight was raging at Bethel, the Gomezes had moved into the Ebenezer parsonage, at 5459 25th Street, and had been welcomed enthusiastically by the congregation.[100] Nevertheless, Joseph's mood was one of growing gloom and frustration. For once in his life he did not know where he was going or where he wanted to go. With his usual impetuosity, he decided to prepare himself to leave the A.M.E. Church at the end of year. He enrolled in Detroit College of Law, taking the necessary courses that would enable him to pass the bar exam in June. However, it was not in his nature to neglect his immediate responsibilities. During his short time at Ebenezer he was able to pay off much of the church's indebtedness and to increase its membership and attendance.

On December 5, 1927, Joseph was once again denied a son. At exactly 11:50 P.M. Annetta Louise was born in the parsonage, with Dr. Green in attendance, assisted by Mamie Boone. Unlike Eula, she was a noisy baby, wanted a lot of attention, and shortly after being born developed three-months' colic. In later years Joseph jokingly told her he had started on several occasions to throw her out of the window. She would always start to yell in the middle of the night, just as he was deep into his law books.

Besides being occupied with the new baby, Ebenezer, and his law studies, Joseph was still involved with civic and city-wide church affairs. On January 30, 1928, he spoke at the Central Methodist Episcopal Church to a group of white Methodist ministers. He warned them of the "growing apostasy" of Negroes from the "faith of the fathers." There were, he said, "great currents of thoughts, some social, some economic, some political that are cutting the Negro loose from their old religious moorings." Many of their "overt acts" had their roots in "Religious dissatisfaction." Even though the Negro "at heart" was a Protestant, he or she was "becoming disillusioned with Protestantism because of its silent acquiescence to grievous wrongs, [and its] actual participation in the deprivation of [Negro] rights." As an example he pointed out that even though Georgia was considered the heart of the Protestant cause in the South, it now led in the number of Negroes lynched. He mentioned again the Detroit Council of Churches' refusal to pass a resolution condemning the Klan, and the fact that "the pulpits of Detroit were conspicuously and significantly silent during the Sweet Trial. If then one group seeks to curtail the full political and economic rights by overt acts, or by silent acquiescence to such curtailment on the part of the other, [the Negro] must find another alliance."

This, he reasoned, explained why the Negro had aligned with Catholics and Jews when it came to the Parochial School Amendment. In all elections, he said, the Negro was now "thinking in terms of self-preservation."

Although the large majority of Negroes were Republican at this time, they would not vote merely along party lines or according to religious preferences. He used as an example the gubernatorial election in New York, where Al Smith of Tammany Hall had received "the greater part of the Negro vote to swell his tremendous majority. . . . And mark you," he continued, "if Governor Al Smith of New York is the Democratic nominee for President, he will receive over 70% of the Negro vote in this country, even though he is a Catholic and a Democrat."[101]

As a further example of the Negro's disaffection with Protestantism Joseph referred to Marcus Garvey, Black nationalist, Back-to-Africa advocate, and president of the Universal Negro Improvement Association. White students and scholars had been for some time trying to analyze Garvey's philosophy—to "interpret the secret of his tremendous success in leadership." Most of them dissected the various groups in his organization, such as his Black Cross Nurses and Black Star Line. What they failed to realize, said Joseph, was that his religion is "the motivating force of his whole system of philosophy." He had reconstructed "all Theology to suit his needs and answer the longing hearts of the Negro race. He denominated current Theology as White Theology written by white men for the use of the white world. What Garvey did was to make articulate that which was the growing conviction of millions of his people." As a result he had developed a larger following than Booker T. Washington had "in his Palmiest days." Even though the Black clergy had to denounce his "attack on this ancient citadel of their faith" and Garvey had been finally convicted on "the technical charge of using the mail to defraud, sentenced to Federal prison and deported [and] . . . his business enterprise involving millions of dollars of his people's money collapsed," few complaints from Negroes were heard. The government accused him of robbing Negroes, but the people's answer was, "It is our money and we are satisfied." One might ask, why? Joseph's conclusion was that it was "because he still represents to them the voice crying in the wilderness pointing the way to hope."[102]

Just as Joseph had been against the colonization movement, he was opposed to Garvey's "Back to Africa" movement. Too much blood had been spilled in the struggle for freedom, too much sweat poured into the making of this country for the Negro to give up his rightful place. As other civil rights workers were to say later, the Founding Fathers had a debt to pay, and Negroes should be there to collect. Still, Joseph had a certain admiration for Garvey, even though Garvey had little regard for the "so-called Black Intelligentsia," particularly the clergy, who, he said, had sold out to the white man in the quest for integration. He specifically denounced men like Joseph who, as evidenced by their skin coloring, were not "pure

African." Nevertheless, his underlying principle, the development of Black pride and racial identity, was one with which few Negroes could quarrel; and it was this principle Joseph emphasized when he spoke of Garvey to the white Methodist ministers. So moved were they by his message that they put pressure on the Detroit Council of Churches to open its door to Negro churches. Shortly after, the Council acquiesced.

Listening to the speech, Hazel was more than ever convinced that Joseph should remain in the ministry. It was folly to let one jealous bishop drive him from the Church and profession to which he had been called. She used the best weapon she had against his stubbornness: she made it difficult for him to study at night. When Annetta cried, Hazel would feign sleep so Joseph would have to tend the baby. Still, he seemed determined to change professions. Finally, two weeks before the bar exam, she burned his books, even though she knew he would be furious. He surprised her; instead of exploding, he seemed relieved. He knew she had been right all along. If the A.M.E. Church had its faults and inequities, as did all organizations, it was up to him to fight to make it what it should be. He loved African Methodism because it had been created by his people at a time when dreams were nearly all they owned. He had never been a quitter, and it was too late for him to start being one now. He filed away his law notes and cases. One day he would take them out again and remember the crossroads they had represented in his life.

The 1928 General Conference was scheduled for May 7–23. Joseph arrived in Chicago a few days early to gain support for his resolution concerning the movement of the bishops. Most of the laymen supported him, and also at least three bishops—J. Albert Johnson, Reverdy Ransom, and John Gregg. Bishop Vernon had written articles in the *Christian Recorder* and the *A.M.E. Review* stating that he thought the bishops should all be moved, but when he learned that Joseph was behind the resolution, he was suddenly against the idea.

The atmosphere of the Armory of the 8th Regiment of the National Guard, where the conference was to be held, seemed menacing. In Ransom's autobiography he notes that the conference was "welcomed by the Mayor of Chicago and Bishop A. J. Carey, our host, who was then a Commissioner of Police at the city of Chicago." He described the police band as blasting with "horns, trumpets, and drums," followed by a multitude of police in full dress, and city detectives. "For a great national religious body, it was a most unseemly spectacle," he wrote. He attributed the spectacle to the attempt by Bishop Carey to "over-awe the General Conference and impress it with [his] power and influence." The police not only spread themselves throughout the armory but "frisked some of the delegates to see if they carried a gun. Detectives in plain clothes sat, or stood at the steps leading to the platform where the Bishops presided."[103]

Joseph was appointed to three committees: the Financial Secretary's Report, Universities and Colleges, and the Book Concern, which oversaw all the Church's publications.[104] He was very much in evidence as he made his way among the delegates, greeting old friends like A. Wayman Ward, his classmate from Wilberforce; J. D. Smith from Bermuda; of course, Bishops Reverdy C. Ransom, and John Gregg; Christine Smith, the widow of Bishop Smith; Francis Gow from South Africa; and the Hollands from Ontario. The General Conference was like a family reunion, where every four years old and new friends came together in fellowship.

Once again the Committee on Unity of the A.M.E., A.M.E. Zion, and C.M.E. churches outlined elaborate merger plans. The newly combined church would be called the United Methodist Episcopal Church. Before the resolution could be passed, Bishops Joseph S. Flipper and Ransom, and a Rev. T. Thompson, objected to the elimination of the word "African." A lengthy argument ensued. As a result the plans for a merger were sent back to committee for four more years of deliberation.[105]

In this atmosphere of controversy, on the afternoon of May 10, Joseph arose to propose his resolution to move the bishops. In a strong, clear voice he described the birth of Methodism and African Methodism as the result of "most vigorous and manly protest against intolerance, injustice and tyranny." He concluded:

> Today we face as of old, a great challenge. The time has come for us, as a Church to decentralize the districts, and connectionalize the Church. This will, in a large measure be done by a change in our present form of Episcopal supervision. Be it therefore resolved that this General Conference here assembled, do hereby instruct the Episcopal Committee to change all Bishops who have served for two or more quadrenniums in a district. Be it further resolved, that this resolution be adopted by a secret ballot.[106]

As the last words echoed through the massive hall, there was chaos. Delegates rose to their feet, some applauding, others attempting to get to a microphone. Rev. H. Y. Tookes rose to move that the Gomez resolution be tabled and that the vote to table be taken by secret ballot. Before the vote was taken, Bishop Flipper warned, "We have submitted the assignments of the Bishops to the Episcopal Committee as a matter of convenience, and the conference has no right to instruct the Episcopal Committee in reference to the assignment of a Bishop. If you do, I tell you, the Bishops will assign themselves at this General Conference." Bishop Johnson called for the vote as to whether the Gomez resolution should be tabled; the result was 263 for, 569 against. Next followed the vote on the original resolution: 642 voted to adopt the resolution, 203 voted against. The Gomez resolution was adopted. In retaliation, Bishops Carey, Flipper, Fountain, Jones, Hurst, Vernon, and a few others met and prepared a list of assignments, which they handed to the Episcopal Committee.[107]

The election of bishops occurred on Friday, May 18. Prior to coming to Chicago Joseph had withdrawn from the race, because of the large number of candidates. He would wait until the time was right. It took three ballots to elect the first bishop, R. A. Grant of Florida. On the fourth ballot there was no election; on the fifth, Rev. Sherman L. Greene, Sr., of Arkansas and Rev. George B. Young of Texas were elected. The last bishop was elected on the sixth ballot, Rev. M. H. Davis of Baltimore.[108] It was significant that not one minister from the North had been chosen.

On Tuesday, May 22, the Episcopal Committee read the assignments of the bishops. All had been moved to new districts. Johnson was assigned to the small district of Kentucky and Tennessee, and Ransom was sent to Louisiana, which was separated from Mississippi and made into a district of only two Annual Conferences. According to Ransom, this was done in order to punish Johnson and himself for supporting the Gomez resolution. Bishop Gregg, who had been less vocal in his support, was sent to the 5th District (Missouri, Kansas, Colorado, California), Vernon to the 12th (Arkansas and Oklahoma), and Carey to the 15th in place of Vernon.[109] (Actually, the General Conference minutes indicate that Carey was sent back to the 4th; nonetheless, the Michigan Annual Conference minutes for September 2, 1928, have him as Presiding Bishop.)

Carey presided for the first time over the 15th Episcopal District at the Michigan Annual Conference held in Grand Rapids that September. The minutes show that Joseph was an active participant in the proceedings and that the situation at Bethel had been resolved.[110] Two months prior to the Annual Conference, Rev. W. H. Peck had been appointed to Greater Bethel to replace Tanner, whom the members had refused to accept. Peck was well received, and peace was restored. He proved to be a valuable addition to the district and the Michigan Annual Conference.

When on the final day of the conference Bishop Carey read the appointments, Joseph had been returned to Ebenezer; as it turned out, however, the appointment was only temporary.[111] On October 6, Joseph received a telegram from Bishop Gregg: "Have just appointed you to Allen Chapel, Kansas City."[112] It was time to move again; one more step in the odyssey had been completed.

◈ ◈ ◈

CHAPTER SIX

A Broadening View

Kansas City, Missouri, 1928–1932

The world has great need of the philosophy of the aspiring soul.
Our greatest menace is not the attitude of foreign nations, or
competitive armies and navies, but the atmosphere of crass cynicism, of hopeless despair—the enemy within our gates. Let it be
known, then, in these days of economic distress, of moral and
spiritual atrophy, that men are reckoned as much by their aspirations as by their achievements.

> —Joseph Gomez, sermonette,
> "Our Aspirations," *Pittsburgh Courier*

◈ The Kansas City to which Joseph was called was second in the state
only to St. Louis; both were to figure prominently in Joseph's career. During the 1920s, these two cities had seen a tremendous growth in their Negro
populations due to migration from the South and rural areas of the state.
Between 1910 and 1925 St. Louis's Blacks grew from 43,906 to 81,214, and
Kansas City's from 23,566 to 34,226. By the time Joseph arrived, the two
cities contained "approximately 60 per cent of Missouri's 223,830 Negroes."[1]
Kansas City was expanding industrially more rapidly than ever before,
and its citizens were becoming homeowners at such a massive rate that it
had been essential for the city to add "a total of 11,000 rental units in the
four peak years to accommodate newcomers, 1923 through 1926."[2] This
sense of well-being, however, did not extend to most Negroes, who were
relegated to admiring from their ghettos the impressive park system, con-
necting boulevards, and elegant long drives. They did benefit somewhat
from the political war waged by the Democratic party machines of the
Pendergast brothers and Joe Shannon, who tried to woo them away from

the Republican party. Despite Kansas City's model city manager–type government, which included a nonpartisan council, these men found it easy to run the government by controlling the city manager and mayor.[3] They were also smart enough to know that controlling the growing Negro vote would help keep them in power.

Ironically, even though Kansas City was dominated by the Democrats in 1928, it was the site of the June Republican National Convention at which Herbert Hoover was nominated. Hoover's Democratic opponent, nominated the same month in Houston, Texas, was Alfred E. Smith, a Catholic who had grown up in the slums of East Side New York.[4] This was the same Smith who Joseph had predicted would receive 70 percent of the Negro vote if he ever ran for president.

Although Joseph still advocated Prohibition, he joined the many leaders from all over the country who were urging Negroes to bolt the Republican party and vote for Smith. If he had ever hesitated in his support of Smith, he was convinced when Ransom, at a church conference in Norfolk, Virginia, pointed out that "the Republican National Convention [had] put every Negro off the committees and put what is known as the 'lily-white' Republicans in their places in every state." He cautioned his audience that "Republicans cannot make political bed-fellows of black people and the Klan."[5]

On the day of his arrival in Kansas City, October 12, 1928, Joseph gave his first sermon at Allen Chapel, his new charge, located at 10th and Charlotte streets. After greeting the members and assuring them he would do his best to serve them spiritually and in civic matters, he urged them to vote for Smith. The *Kansas City Call,* the leading Negro newspaper in the city, called his sermon "impressive" and spoke of him as an "eloquent speaker who knew what he was talking about."[6] Because his arrival had been well publicized, the church was crowded to capacity. Many had come to see the minister who had built Greater Bethel, stood up to Bishop Vernon, and had been one of the leaders in the successful campaign to move all bishops at the past General Conference. When he finished preaching, Joseph told the congregation that within a week he would be bringing his family to Kansas City. His appointment had come so abruptly that Hazel had stayed behind to finish packing. However, within a few days she, Eula, Annetta, and Violet arrived at the parsonage at 1916 East 33rd Street—which was so deteriorated that it had to be abandoned until another could be secured.

Unlike their reaction to the first parsonage, Joseph and Hazel were attracted to Allen Chapel, a medium-sized structure with a membership of a little over six hundred. It was a far cry from Greater Bethel, with its three thousand members, but Gregg had been anxious to remove Joseph from the frustration he had experienced in Detroit. Allen Chapel would serve until a larger church in the district was available. Meanwhile, he was needed; the church had been losing members and influence steadily over the past five years. Under Joseph's leadership it soon began to prosper, and within a year over two hundred new members joined the church.

Almost all biographical sketches written about Joseph during this period emphasize his founding of the Paseo Interdenominational Bible Class, a group which met every Thursday evening to discuss and debate the literal and symbolic meanings of the scriptures and their significance for the times. Among its four hundred members, most prominent was Roy Wilkins, civil rights leader and later executive secretary of the National Association for the Advancement of Colored People. Wilkins, an active A.M.E., also served for a time as Sunday school superintendent at Allen Chapel during Joseph's pastorate.

In November of 1928 Joseph was elected chaplain of the United Ministerial Alliance.[7] His address to the group on November 11 was quoted in most Kansas City newspapers. He had emphasized that the mission of the minister was to be involved in all aspects of living in order to address the complexity of the society. He could no longer divide the "purely material from the purely spiritual," since "all life is a unit."[8] Some of the more fundamental ministers took issue with this point of view, asserting that the clergy should address only the spiritual and particularly should not be involved in politics. But Joseph knew that the future welfare of the Negro necessitated his taking an active part in the spiritual, social, economic, and political affairs of the people.

He was delighted in November to learn that Oscar De Priest from Illinois, whom he had met on several occasions, had become the first Negro elected to Congress in twenty-seven years.[9] Conversely, the nation elected Herbert Hoover as president. The "Solid South," which usually went Democratic, voted for Hoover, and he amassed an impressive victory in terms of both popular and electoral votes. In spite of the switch-over many had made to the Democratic party, in the all-Negro and nearly all-Negro wards of Kansas City the vote had gone 6,298 for Hoover and 5,230 for Smith.[10] The majority of Blacks were still wedded to the party of Lincoln and would remain so until Franklin D. Roosevelt ascended to the White House. Joseph watched with chagrin Hoover's feeble attempts to halt the Great Depression. "Hoovervilles" (cardboard shacks in which people lived), bread lines, unemployment, and mortgage failures seemed to be the only legacy the president was to leave a dying economy. Negroes suffered most from the crisis that began with the failure of the stock market on October 29, 1929, and reached its peak in 1931.

In late 1929, Bishops Gregg and Ransom advised Joseph to run for Secretary Treasurer of Missions at the 1932 General Conference, which would be held in Cleveland, Ohio. But on January 14, 1930, he received a letter from one of the newly elected bishops, M. H. Davis, who was in Paris en route to his district in Africa. He warned Joseph to be "careful of announcing for office. The old guards may defeat you."[11] In spite of Davis's warning, he decided to seek the post actively. He had plenty of time to campaign, since the conference was two years away.

On January 11, 1929, Hazel was elected to the Committee of Management of the YWCA;[12] later that month Joseph delivered the Annual Sermon to the Alpha Kappa Alpha Sorority. He warned them against class or color snobbery. If the race were to continue to progress, he said, all talents were needed; each must contribute according to her particular gifts.[13]

To complete the busy month, on the 29th he accompanied Bishop Gregg to the state capital, where Gregg had a special invitation to speak to the legislature concerning Negro education, its needs and progress. He made a passionate plea on behalf of better-quality education for the race. On the way home, Gregg remarked how ironic it was that he had been asked to speak in that particular chamber; as a boy he had often gone with his father to clean that very room. His father had worked as a janitor in the Capitol building.[14]

A singular honor came to Joseph on February 12, when he was asked by the Jackson County Negro Republican Club to speak at its Annual Lincoln-Douglass Banquet along with the governor of Missouri, Henry S. Caulfield, J. P. King (a prominent Negro principal), and other dignitaries who would bring greetings. Caulfield spoke of his pride in Lincoln as the first Republican president and promised that he would carry out the principles of Lincoln by seeing that the Negro's needs were met during his term as governor. When the governor had finished, King told of the humble beginnings of Frederick Douglass as a slave and of his rise to fame as one of the finest orators and abolitionists of his age.[15]

Then it was Joseph's turn. He had been asked to speak about Lincoln. After acknowledging Lincoln's universal mind, he addressed the criticism of many that Lincoln had not been a church-goer. Joseph asserted that "his rugged, primitive soul was far above the unholy claims of theological strife . . . his humanitarianism the very essence of Christianity." In addition, Lincoln had "taught the world the real value of education. . . . The Gettysburg Address and the Second Inaugural compare favorably with the best of literature." He asked those "who would rob him of Emancipation . . . by alluding to his desire to save the Union at any cost, even with slavery" to consider "his equally sincere declaration that the nation could not endure half free and half slave." He closed by stating that America, the "cynosure of all eyes" and the "commercial pride of the world," had diverged from Lincoln's ideals. Lynching, Jim-Crowism, "and unchecked intolerance [still existed] in the United States."[16]

Joseph did not idolize Lincoln blindly. He knew that at one time Lincoln had offered colonization of Negroes to South America or Africa as an answer to the question of emancipation; in some of his early speeches he had said that the two races could never live together. But Joseph was convinced that Lincoln had grown in understanding as he tackled the tremendous burdens of the presidency. Lincoln was "a *thought* which lives with increasing power . . . and can offer solutions to problems that confront us today." Frederick Douglass had said in 1876 that "[we as Negroes] have been fastening ourselves to a name and fame imperishable and immortal" despite the fact that Lincoln was "preeminently the white man's president."[17] Joseph concluded that this was true but that as Lincoln was essentially a gifted, decent man, the office had helped him "move beyond his provincialism into a broader world-view of mankind."[18] Later he was to believe the same of Harry S. Truman, and to a lesser degree of Lyndon B. Johnson.

After this address on Lincoln, Joseph received numerous invitations to speak around the city. He was on his way to establishing his place in the religious, social, and civic life of Kansas City, just as he had in other places where he pastored. In addition, the Gomezes were beginning to form friendships almost as dear to them as those they had left behind in Detroit. They were especially fond of the Clevelands—Fletcher, a policeman, and his wife, Pinkie—who immediately "adopted" the children since they had none of their own. On numerous occasions they would keep Eula and Annetta when their parents were at church conferences. There were Arthur and Elsie Steward, ardent church-goers, who were always bringing them pastry from their bakery near the church; Willie B. Fagan, who became a part of the family and who made the girls pastel organdy dresses; and Francis Anne Davis and her grandmother, whom the children visited on long, lazy Saturday afternoons.

Joseph and Hazel, however, spent a great deal of their free time with the Greggs. John taught Joseph how to play golf, and they became friendly competitors. Celia and Hazel had a common interest in the YWCA and its summer camp programs, and in the local and Connectional Missionary Society.

Violet developed her own set of friends. She met and fell in love with Ismael Glass, a member of the church, who often played saxophone solos during the services. He was much older than she, but his good looks, gentleness, and obvious devotion to her soon won her over. The couple eloped and moved to Los Angeles, where they remained all their lives, he working for Helena Rubenstein and she raising two daughters, Jewell and Gloria.

Joseph's sense of well-being was badly shaken on June 27, 1929, when he received word that his mother Rebecca had died. Before he could arrange to sail to Trinidad, she had been buried. Although he had known all along how ill she was and had not expected her to last this long, he was unprepared for her death. In later years he was to say that there was something final about a mother's death, like a second cutting of the umbilical cord. He wrote Papa offering him a place in his home, but he refused, preferring instead to remain close to Rebecca's grave. All Joseph could do was continue to send him money when he could and pray that his father would be able to deal with the loss of his wife and companion.

On July 21, Joseph was asked to speak at the celebration of the fourth anniversary of the Jackson County Negro Boys Home. Other speakers included Superintendent George Meicher, C. A. Franklin, and several judges, among them Harry S. Truman.[19] Joseph and Bishop Gregg were incensed when they thought Truman referred to the boys as "niggers" during his speech. When they confronted him later he said, "I didn't say 'niggers.' I said 'negras.'" They were amused to find he had difficulty pronouncing the word "Negro" and was hurt that they thought he had spoken in a derogatory manner to the boys. When Truman turned out to be one of the more liberal presidents of the United States, Joseph loved to tell that story to his family. With a twinkle in his eye he would say, "I guess somewhere along the way, Harry learned to say 'Negro.'"

Although Joseph had been at Allen Chapel for almost a year now, he had never been formally introduced to the Southwest Missouri Annual Conference. At its October 1929 meeting, which took place at New Ward Chapel in the city, Bishop Gregg presented him. When Gregg read the assignments Joseph found he was on several committees and had been appointed to the trustee boards of Western University in Quindaro, Kansas, and Douglass Hospital in Kansas City, two institutions owned and operated by the A.M.E. Church.[20]

On the second day of the conference Joseph listened with pride as his presiding elder, L. P. Bryant, read his report, which included an evaluation of Joseph's year at Allen Chapel. He noted that "the finances had increased from $35 a Sunday as high as $280 a Sunday." Many of the old debts had been paid, and the mortgage reduced. "Allen enjoys larger congregations and the spirit runs high, the result of the masterly sermons preached by the pastor," he said. Members at the last Quarterly Conference had "voted unanimously for [Joseph's] return."[21]

For Joseph the conference was a very positive experience, especially when compared to the last two Annual Conferences he had attended, under Vernon. Gregg presided with grace and dignity, and it was obvious the ministers had the highest regard for him as a Christian gentleman, a scholar, and an able administrator. It never became necessary for him to resort to histrionics to get his point across. Joseph felt honored to serve under him and to be his friend. Kansas City was proving to be a welcome respite from the frenzy of Detroit, although he would never love this city as he had Detroit.

Kansas City did not feel the real effects of America's economic crisis until the early 1930s. Being the "last hired and the first fired," Negroes were the hardest hit by the Great Depression all over the country. Joseph saw many of his members lose their meager savings and some even lose their homes. Unemployment and poverty, however, were no strangers to the Negro community. Blacks were used to surviving on little, moving from job to job as they were replaced by whites, or banding together in times of peril. Allen Chapel responded to the Depression by setting up a food kitchen in the basement and securing cots and showers for homeless people. Once again Joseph established a Social Service Bureau aimed at finding jobs and housing for those in need. None of his members or their friends had to live in "Hoovervilles." In addition, he took a reduced salary and cashed in his life insurance to make ends meet. Despite or perhaps because of these evidences of economic strain, the church continued to grow in membership and be the focal point of community concerns and activities.

Robert Weisbrot, in his *Father Divine and the Struggle for Racial Equality,* accuses Joseph of being one of those conservative, educated ministers who was "other-worldly"—who preached mainly about the rewards to be found only in heaven. Neither Joseph's religious philosophy nor his activities were other-worldly. Weisbrot ignores Joseph's continual involvement in social services and bases his conclusion on a single sermon. In that sermon, Joseph spoke of the devastation of the Depression, particularly on Negroes, and "the demand for courageous leadership," but because he was also convinced that the times demanded "meditation and prayer" Weisbrot included him in the class of ministers who disengaged themselves from the life concerns of the people.[22] Joseph believed that the practical and the spiritual were inseparable. His actions and his words exemplified his beliefs.

Just as had been the case in Detroit, the Council of Churches in Kansas City had always excluded Negro churches from its membership. Joseph felt this was a kind of hypocrisy which a so-called "Christian" organization could hardly afford, and he was determined to do something about it. His opportunity came on Monday, February 3, when he was asked to address the white Ministerial Alliance at the Locust Street YMCA. The February 7 issue of the *Kansas City Call* carried his picture under the headlines "Gomez Spoke Monday Before the City Council of Churches. Gomez Speech Lets Down Bars." Following the speech the Executive Committee voted to admit colored churches to the Kansas City Council of Churches. "The address, advertised in advance, drew the heaviest attendance the council is said to have had in the last three years."[23]

In his speech Joseph had declared that the present-day pulpit was weak as compared to that of the fathers of Protestantism. He related how the Detroit Council of Churches had refused to pass a resolution condemning the Klan and how during the Sweet trial the only white minister to say a word in support of justice for Sweet was a Catholic priest. This, in part, he said accounted for the number of Negroes who were flocking to the Catholic Church. He concluded that "either the Bible and its teachings of brotherhood [is] practicable and workable or else it [is] a lie."[24]

In an editorial entitled "Talking It Over," appearing in the same issue, Roy Wilkins wrote:

His address before the council secured the most rapt attention given a speaker at these meetings for years.

The tact, the diplomacy, the irrefutable logic, the telling persuasion, the uncompromising reasoning, the fluent citations of ecclesiastical history and the stirring plea for the practical application of Christian principles to the problems of the day, made the eloquent minister of Allen Chapel A.M.E. Church hold his listeners spellbound. . . . Mr. Gomez has performed a service to Kansas City that makes its population indebted to the A.M.E. Bishop for sending him here.[25]

The *Kansas City American* described the speech as "an acme of eloquence; a challenge to the sponsors and followers of the Master." In another editorial in *The Call*, Joseph was referred to for the first time as "the Little Giant." In later years, many people would call him by that title.[26]

Joseph sent copies of the articles to DeWitt Burton in Detroit and received Burton's reaction in a letter written February 25. Burton recalled a visit of the Gomezes of a few months before as "those brief moments . . .

the value of which you'll never be able to understand." Their friendship had proved to be "genuine and live" and had survived "even the damnable slanderous tongues which [have] been injected with the treacherous virulent toxins of jealousy and hypocrisy." He had been impressed by the accounts of Joseph's address, but not surprised, he said, because "It was my deep pleasure to hear you when you spoke before the same group here in Detroit . . . though I hardly think it was as masterful as this one." He sent love to Hazel and the babies and said he was still looking in the papers "for the announcement of the arrival of Joey Jr."[27]

Unfortunately, there was never to be a Joey Junior. Their tomboyish younger daughter would have to substitute as a son. She was as rough as Eula was gentle and ladylike. When Hazel would ask Eula why she let her sister push her around the yard, she would answer, "That's my baby sister." There was a similarity between their relationship and that of Joseph and Amanda when Joseph was a boy.

Many other complimentary letters came to the parsonage after Joseph addressed the Negro doctors of Kansas City at Allen Chapel in June, on the topic, "It Is Not Mine to Give." A letter he kept through the years came from a Dr. J. Edward Perry of 1716 East 12th Street. Joseph had told the doctors that the gift of healing was not their personal property; it had come from God and therefore belonged to all the people they served. Dr. Perry's letter stated that "many things come to us as a result of age and experience and that is true but there are exceptions to all rules and you are certainly an exception." For him, Joseph's talk seemed to come from "a man many years [his] senior." He spoke of Joseph's ability also as "a blessing from the Supreme Ruler of the Universe who [had] endowed [him] with these unusual qualities for a specific purpose." He was sure Joseph would make a "great contribution to human welfare."[28]

In 1930, Allen Chapel gave Joseph a gift of money so he could be one of the representatives of the A.M.E. Church at the World Christian Endeavor Convention, which was being held in Berlin during the first week in August. Bishop Gregg, delegate and guest speaker, would be one of his traveling companions. This would be the first of Joseph's several trips to Europe and the first time away from his family for such a lengthy period. The pictures he had seen of celebrated landmarks and the history books he had pored over in school would no longer be merely a matter of academics. As he romped with the children, he made up spirited games about the places he would visit. He wished Hazel could go along, but there was not money enough. He solemnly promised her that in the near future they would both go to Europe, as a kind of second honeymoon.

Joseph arrived in New York City on Tuesday, July 8. Two evenings later he and Gregg went to see William B. Harrison play "de Lawd" in Marc Connelly's *The Green Pastures,* a Broadway hit alleged to depict the Negro's view of heaven and interpretation of biblical lore. The play, in two acts and eighteen scenes with a cast of ninety-five, opens on a Sunday School class where a Black preacher is going through "the begats" in Genesis. From there it moves to a fish fry in heaven, where "de Lawd" performs miracles. The entire extravaganza, replete with the famous Hal Johnson choir, ended with the crucifixion. Joseph found this "Negro Miracle Play" to be "interesting [as] a white conception [of the] Negro primitive Christian."²⁹ Although the play did give employment to many otherwise unemployed Black actors, recalling the play in later years Joseph found it "essentially offensive in its ridiculous stereotyping of Blacks as a gambling, gin-drinking, loose-living, superstitious race of people." The only "great lesson" that could be distilled from *The Green Pastures,* he said, was that Blacks had been able to personalize God so that He was meaningful to them in their everyday lives, not some faraway, inaccessible white man.

The next day Joseph, Bishop Gregg, Dr. S. S. Morris, David Sims, and several other A.M.E. delegates boarded the *Ile de France,* "a floating palace."³⁰ While Joseph was examining his second-class accommodations, the steward handed him a letter from Hazel dated July 8 which had finally caught up with him. She had "felt his presence all day" and at times looked around expecting him to be there. She missed him terribly and so did the girls, but she wanted him not to worry—to enjoy his trip, because God would be watching over her and the babies. She told him Eula seemed to realize he would be gone a long time and had asked, who was going to preach while he was away, and who would drive the car? She assured him, "I love these children because they are a part of you and will see that they get every care." She thought he had looked fatigued before he left, and she had "wanted to take [him] in her arms and lay [his] head upon [her] breast so that [he] might rest." She hoped he would not be seasick and advised him to "eat, sleep, and rest" but not to bring home "a German Bay Window." She signed it "Boy Voyage, sweetheart, Tweets."³¹

Almost immediately after leaving shore the ship ran into a storm, which added to Joseph's fatigue and loneliness; but he was not seasick. On Sunday, the "usual Roman Catholic services were canceled," but the A.M.E.s held their own service in one of the cabins, despite the rolling and careening of the ship. Above the bluster of the wind, other passengers could hear faintly the singing of "A Mighty Fortress Is Our God." That evening Joseph "sent Hazel a message by moonlight" and began a journal he had promised to turn into articles for the *Kansas City Call.*³²

On July 17 at 1 P.M. Joseph's party boarded a seaplane from Le Havre, landing at Plymouth Harbor around 3 P.M., where they were met by agents from the Cook's Travel Bureau. From there they took "an exceedingly fast train to London," arriving at Paddington Station at 9 P.M.[33]

For the next few days they became typical tourists, rarely staying in their rooms at the Hotel Royal Court on Sloane Square. They took in all the traditional attractions, including Westminster Abbey, St. James and Buckingham palaces, and 10 Downing Street. At the Parliament building their guide pointed out a Mrs. Owens, the daughter of William Jennings Bryan, who was walking just ahead.[34]

On the evening of July 19 they went to see Paul Robeson, the famous Black actor and singer, in *Othello*. After the play they were taken backstage to talk to him. Despite Joseph's disagreement with some of Robeson's political views, he greatly admired his talent and his strong personality. Robeson's portrayal of "the Moor was superb," as had been the performances of Peggy Ashcroft as Desdemona and Maurice Brown as Iago.[35] It would be twelve years before Robeson would be allowed to play the role in America, with Uta Hagen as Desdemona. Although the reviews were good in 1942, Joseph always preferred the London production.

A Mr. H. G. Browning of 120 Longacre drove them to Wesley's Chapel on Sunday, July 20, to hear Rev. H. C. Foreman, a visiting clergyman from Sidney. Joseph found the service "very Episcopal." Afterwards, "piloted by a lady of the church," they saw the desk of fifty-three sermons at the museum in the old Wesley parsonage, and other artifacts that had belonged to Charles and his brother, John, including the "chintz from the bed on which John Wesley had died."[36]

Curious about the Black population in London, Joseph sought out Louis Drysdale, a renowned voice teacher, who in turn introduced him to John C. Payne, artist and singer; the Harmony Kings, which included Browning, Berry, Drayton, and Dosher; Roland Hayes, another Black American, who like Robeson, had sung before the royal family; and Layton and Johnston, singers who had made over $100,000 in a year and a half. From them he learned more about Ira Aldridge, the first Black Shakespearian tragedian, who had never been asked to perform in America, and Samuel Taylor Coleridge, the famous Negro composer. Joseph had the impression that while there was still a great deal of racism toward Blacks in England, the East Indians seemed to face an even more serious problem.[37]

England held a certain fascination for Joseph. All of his childhood had been spent in British colonies—countries which, along with their native traditions, had also adopted many English customs. Seeing the colonizing country enabled him to understand more fully the influence England had

had on his own life and those of other Blacks from the West Indies, some favorable, some not so favorable. It did partially explain his insistence on order and a certain amount of decorum in whatever he did. His passion and enthusiasm, however, came from his African mother.

On July 21 the party left from Victoria Station en route to Dover, then to Calais, and finally to Paris, where they were again met by Cook agents, who took them to the Hotel Montreal. As in London, they visited the traditional tourists sites: the Champs Elysées, the Arc de Triomphe, the Eiffel Tower, Napoleon's Tomb, and the Palace of Versailles. The following evening Joseph and John Gregg decided to be risqué and go to the Follies Bergères. One of the dancers landed in Gregg's lap, and Joseph found it hilarious to watch the dignified bishop at a total loss as to what to say or do.[38]

They left Paris July 25 via the Rome Express, on which they found the "pullman service to be especially fine." Joseph jotted down his random thoughts in his journal. From his window, he could see women ploughing the open fields. It seemed as if "everyone in Europe [was] busy." The war debt was "the nemesis that haunt[ed] these people and destroy[ed] much of the joy of living." It would take centuries for Europe to "recover from the destruction and ravage of the last war." Joseph doubted that any statesman could force the people into another war. Mussolini controlled Italy "with an iron hand"; no one knew how long that would last. Although Joseph had no love for the man, he admired somewhat his successes in remaking Italy and his insistence that the people work. "But the people [were] groaning under the heavy burden of taxation, and you [could] never count on the mob, or at any time fully interpret mob psychology." Italy, as Russia, was engaged in a "great social experiment." All the world could do was "sit back and wait."[39]

His thoughts were interrupted when the train reached Pisa, where they viewed the famous leaning tower. Then it was on to Genoa, the birthplace of Christopher Columbus, and finally Rome. There they stayed at the Minerva, a hotel one block from the ancient Pantheon. On July 28, at 1 P.M., they were received by Pope Pius XI, "a man of very kindly face and manner whom you instinctively liked," Joseph noted. "Seeing him is to understand the secret of his great success in diplomacy and his supreme triumph in the recognition recently secured from Mussolini and the Italian government through the Lateran Treaty signed February 11, 1929, virtually restoring civil power to the Pope, and ending his imprisonment of nearly 60 years."[40]

On July 29 the group traveled over the Tyrol Mountains to Innsbruck. "For hours [the] train toiled like a weary man . . . up those mountain sides, thousands of feet high." Joseph could see above him "snow-clad peaks;

below rivulets and streams, gardens and fields and little villages of the valley, with houses so arranged as though placed by an artist's hand." He found the people of Innsbruck to be so "gracious" that he was loath to leave the "little town nesting at the foot of . . . the Tyrol Mountains yet said to be 1,883 feet above sea level with a population of 70,000 and a history dating back to the 12th Century."[41]

From Innsbruck they went to Oberammergau in Bavaria, which was crowded with American tourists who had come to see the Passion Play. At first Joseph was disappointed with Oberammergau, a valley village of two thousand. After being among the citizens and sensing their simple, quiet, courteous ways, however, he began to love the village and its people.[42]

The Passion Play was put on every ten years "in solemn fulfillment of the vow they made to God," who the natives believed had taken away a terrible plague in 1622. The village council selected the characters for the play, and it was the highest ambition of a villager to be chosen as one of the players. "The earnestness, intelligence and knowledge of these people, combined with their mastery of details make of this play one that can never be forgotten," Joseph wrote.[43]

From Oberammergau they went to Munich, the center of the Bavarian government. "Even its streets [were] designed to carry out the general idea of portraying German art and culture." Joseph had heard the stories of German brutality during the war but came to believe that the "leadership [had been] . . . unworthy of the real aims of the German people" and that "under a Republican form of government, these aims [were] finding expression." He described the Germans as "kind, courteous, efficient and dignified without British reserve."[44]

On the way from Munich to Berlin they passed Gingen, at the confluence of the Rhine and the Nahe. They went through Wittenberg, birthplace of Martin Luther, and the university town of Leipzig, in Saxony. When they finally arrived in Berlin, at 10:42 P.M., they had "difficulty in being understood and finding lodging." Joseph, Sims, and Morris stayed at 20 Hardenberger Strasse, while Gregg was escorted to the Kant Hotel, Charlottenburg, where the other officials and guest speakers of the convention were housed.[45]

Berlin was still enjoying the afterglow of the "Golden '20s," during which time the Dawes Plan had regularized the payment of Germany's war debts to the allies and had brought some stability to the country. However, Germany was beginning to feel the effects of the Depression, and confidence in the Weimar Republic was fading. The communists and Nazis promised radical solutions to the economic problems facing the country, but in 1930 there was little evidence in Berlin of the political turmoil boiling underneath its surface.[46] To Joseph and the other delegates, except for an occasional nasty brawl between the Brownshirts and the communists, Berlin was still the center of the arts, the movie and theatre capital of the world—the city where nightlife flourished on the one hand, and a Christian Endeavor Convention was welcomed on the other. It would be hard for Joseph to conceive that all this would become impossible three years later, when Hitler and his followers came to power.

The convention opened August 5 with a business meeting of the German Union, at which Bishop Gregg spoke. Afterwards, he was "mobbed by the Germans in their attempt to be kind. Everywhere he went he was lionized."[47]

Friday evening, August 8, Bishop Gregg stood before a microphone in the Great Exhibition Hall at Kaiserdam in Charlottenburg in front of thirteen thousand people representing forty-two nations. He was there to deliver a "Call of Christ to Christian Brotherhood." Around him were "flags of many nations, flowers in profusion, a great white-robed choir, large orchestra in full dress, brilliantly uniformed band of musicians, people of all races."[48]

Gregg's address, which was the only one at the convention to be broadcast, began with God's query to Cain, "Where is thy brother?" In many instances, Gregg said, "the answer that selfish man has flung back to his maker" has been, "Am I my brother's keeper?" He cited this gathering as an example of how "out of one blood God hath made all nations of men to dwell on the face of the earth" as brothers. Christ was the first to teach that "there was something necessary more than the generally accepted observance of the Mosaic Law, in that one must love his neighbor as himself." In the beginning of the Christian Church, however, even the disciples "were slow to accept this new doctrine of brotherhood."[49]

"Some are asking if the Christian Message has been vital to the non-Christian world," he said. He cites the Hindu, who "misses in the Christian a receptiveness, humility, a willingness to identify . . . with the masses of India." The same is true for the Chinese, the Korean, and the American Negro—who wonders why "we are not willing to accord him simple justice"—and for the Black native in South Africa, who "called for all native people to leave the churches on the last Sunday in November, 1925 . . . to go to the hills for a return to the Gods of their people, who, it was pointed out, meant more to them in their hopes and aspirations than the God preached and practiced by Christian people." Gregg kept returning to the question, "Am I my brother's keeper?" as if to challenge the audience to ponder carefully the answer.[50]

This part of the speech angered the South Africans, "representatives of the Boer idea of the place of the Black people in world progress," and also the seven hundred white Americans, many from the South. But it brought a great deal of pride to "a group of only ten colored Americans, one [of whom] was the bearer of a message of Christian Brotherhood to the dominant and so-called superior races of mankind."[51]

On the whole, the speech was well received. "The newspapers of the German Republic added their quota of praise, and the European editions of the *New York Herald* and *Chicago Tribune* were not to be undone. Furthermore, by special request, Bishop Gregg was photographed by representatives of the *New York Times,* and interviewed both aboard ship and on arrival at New York."[52]

On Sunday, August 10, Joseph visited Heyblank Kirche, where Bishop Gregg spoke again. After church, at a dinner given by the minister, the discussion turned to conditions in Germany. The minister told them that three million Germans were unemployed, that unlike the English, Germans were poor people. He felt that Gustav Stresemann, once chancellor and now foreign minister, was too idealistic. "It is not a question of a Republic or monarchy, but of saving the Fatherland," he said. He liked Field Marshal von Hindenburg, who was "the only blessing of the revolution." He spoke of how liberalized the church was now that it had no formal connections with the government except in financial affairs. Joseph began to suspect that the peacefulness of the convention had only been a prelude to dire events in Germany. To what lengths would Germans go to save the Fatherland—even this minister of the gospel?[53]

That afternoon, Gregg met with the South Africans who had challenged the part of his speech relating to their country. He told them he would not and could not back down from what he had said. Apartheid was an abomination, anti-Christian, and should be eradicated immediately! At 3 P.M., when the American delegation met for the last time, Joseph expressed the sentiment of the colored delegates, affirming what an eye-opener the convention had been for them. An hour later, he and his party boarded the ship for home.[54] Unfortunately, there is no record of the return trip, but one can imagine the lively discussions about the convention and Europe that occurred.

When Joseph finally got off the train in Kansas City, after having been away for over a month, he was astonished to find that Hazel had driven herself to meet him. While he had been away she had persuaded one of the men from the church to teach her how to drive. It had been relatively easy compared to Joseph's attempts to teach her, during which he yelled at her at every turn. Although the ride home was relatively smooth and exceedingly slow, he was relieved when she parked the car in front of the parsonage. He spent the remainder of the day playing with the children, who followed him all around the house as he showered them and Hazel with souvenirs and stories. He tried to make them share the excitement he had felt, but there was no way he could express his elation at having at last seen parts of Europe. Hazel would understand better when she accompanied him on trips around the world some years later.

The effects of the Berlin experience were still very much in evidence at the Southwest Missouri Conference held in Sedalia in the latter part of October. Joseph read a resolution complimenting Bishop Gregg for his splendid address before the World Christian Endeavor delegates, and he asked that the conference nominate Gregg for the annual award given by the Harmon Foundation in the field of religion. The resolution was unanimously adopted.[55]

Again Joseph was pleased to hear the presiding elder's report outlining the progress he had made during the year. The report said that Allen Chapel had had another good year under Joseph's leadership. The membership had grown to 850, finances had increased, debts reduced, and a "beautiful parsonage" purchased. The members were asking for his return.[56]

The new parsonage was located at 1916 East 23rd Street. With its four bedrooms, large dining and living room areas, and well equipped kitchen, it was a vast improvement over the ones on 33rd and 23rd Streets. Most of the old furniture had been replaced by furniture Hazel had picked. The new parsonage was larger, and so too were the number of people who frequented it. As a rule, if the Gomezes were not invited out, there were at least ten people gathered around the dinner table on Sundays to taste Hazel's succulent fried chicken or chicken and dumplings. Often the guests would be young people from the orphanage around the block, one of them Lavada, who baby-sat for Hazel. In return, Eula and Annetta loved to go with Lavada to the orphanage and play with the children and sometimes stay for meals. After they had grown up, they could still recall the smell of bleach and oatmeal that seemed to hang in the air at the orphanage. At the time they envied the children who stayed there, because they always had a lot of friends to play with and they had Miss Grady, the warm-hearted director. No doubt the children likewise envied Eula and Annetta, because they had caring parents and a home of their own.

Joseph had a great deal of time to enjoy his new home during the Christmas holidays. After the candlelight Christmas 6 A.M. service, the family rushed home to open their presents together. Among the children's gifts was the large mama doll Eula had always wanted. Annetta, who was now three, appreciated most the candy and red fire engine. Hazel received a gold wristwatch, and Joseph a gold cross to hang around his neck.

With the advent of the New Year, Joseph had to fill several speaking engagements. On February 6, 1931, the headlines of the *Kansas City Call* read, "Race Relations Meeting Next Sunday." For the first time in many years the meeting, held at Grand Avenue Temple, had invited a colored speaker, Rev. Gomez. The affair was being sponsored by the Federal Council of Churches of Christ in America, through its Interracial Commission. Most cities around the country planned to have white and Negro ministers exchange pulpits.[57]

Many of the ideas expressed in Joseph's speech were echoed in an article he would write for the *A.M.E. Review* in April 1931 under the title, "Aspects of the American Race Problem." He began by referring to his recent trip to Europe and the prejudice he experienced when he came back. He said, "Here I return to the land of my love, after the privilege of Europe, a man of color, to what?" He supposed, "in a degree, we are all victims of prejudice [because] America's great problem is not that of the inadequacy of our so-called melting pot, nor the type of its amalgam." The great problem concerned the status of colored America, and the slave psychology which existed in this country. Most Americans, he said, would be happy if they could forget "our history of slavery, with all its bestiality, its inhumanity, and its blinding cause." He likened slavery to the locust in Egypt that destroyed all green things. And what was the aftermath of slavery? It was the kind of Reconstruction that supposedly freed the people, placed "within their reach a few privileges and then, when by sheer courage they [rose] from poverty and ignorance, den[ied] them the opportunities for the expression and exploitation of their abilities." The only cure was for America to "begin to think away from the master and slave idea to the brotherhood of races ideal."[58]

His thoughts on intermarriage are worth noting. He believed that the "intelligentsia of both races" has objected to laws that would prohibit intermarriage, "regarding such laws as an invasion of personal rights and liberties." Nevertheless, he firmly stated, "each race should be given fullest opportunity to develop its particular genius, and make its distinct contribution." Those cultural possibilities uniquely belonging to a race "can be best developed, if unmixed. The real history of any race is the record of its distinctive contributions," he concluded.[59]

At first glance, these opinions seem strange in light of his own mixed background and his firm commitment to integration. Many of the Black middle class did believe at the time that intermarriage might be one of the main solutions to the race problem. However, having seen how both of his parents suffered because of their marriage, Joseph had concluded that in this present world of bigotry and racism a person would be freer to grow and create if he or she married within the group. To him, integration was never synonymous with intermarriage: one involved the necessary union of all peoples for survival of the civilization; the other was the personal choice of two people.

He felt that despite the problems of race relationships in 1931, there were definite signs of progress. He cited the "growing influence and activity of the Negro in the councils of the nation," the growing number of interracial commissions, and the activities of the NAACP, Urban League, YWCA, and YMCA. His visit to Europe had convinced him that "we may never hope to escape prejudice by leaving, for in a measure, it has followed us, particularly in England, and in time, will grow worse. We must correct the evil at its source." America had to be our "field of battle."[60]

During his trip to Germany Joseph had gotten to know well David Sims, the president of Allen University in Columbia, South Carolina, and one of the candidates for the bishopric. Sims would frequently stop at the parsonage when he traveled across the country in behalf of his candidacy. Joseph and Hazel had become quite fond of him, and he was a favorite with the girls.

On January 3 the Gomezes received a letter from him (mailed at the St. Petersburg Hotel in Paris) indicating that he was on his way to South Africa to study the Church's progress there. He included a page of names Joseph should be sure to contact in his bid for the missions secretary-treasurer position. "Let's go after this to win," Sims urged. "We need you, my boy. God and the church need you." He wrote of the many who were "vulnerable, selfish, short-sighted and indifferent," who lacked "consecration and courage. May God give us some men like Joseph Gomez."[61]

Sims enclosed a letter to "My dear little friends, Arnetta [Annetta] and Eula." He thanked them for the cross and guard they had given him as a going-away present. He hoped that their "Daddy" could some time come to Africa, and ended by writing: "I'll tell your cousins in Africa you sent love. They haven't lots of things as you do."[62] The girls were thrilled to have their very own letter from Paris, France, and decided maybe they would let Daddy go to Africa some time; Joseph, on the other hand, was grateful for Sims's words of encouragement and the names he had sent. He carried them with him in February when he traveled throughout the Southwest and South seeking endorsement for the Secretary-Treasurer position. The trip took him to St. Louis, Nashville, Atlanta, and finally to Jacksonville, Florida, where the Bishops' Council was being held.

While away, he wrote Hazel letters (always addressing her as "My dar-ling Tweets") which gave some insight as to the extent of his activities. His trip from Atlanta to Jacksonville had been made in a "tremendous down-pour of rain." Sunday he was to preach at Mount Zion, the largest church there. In his party were "Noah Williams, Burnett, Barksdale, Bishop and Mrs. Gregg." That morning (February 20, 1932) he was to address an in-surance group. He missed her "so much" and assured her "beauty loses something of its real worth when [she was] not there to enjoy it with [him]." He spoke of their sacrifice now (her not being able to be with him) because of the children but promised someday they would have that second honeymoon.[63]

In another letter, dated February 22, 1932, again it was raining, but the group was planning to "motor to St. Augustine to view the places of his-toric interest in this the oldest city in America." The day before, he had preached at Mount Olive in the morning and Mount Zion in the after-noon. That same afternoon Bishop Gregg had spoken at Edward Waters College for Founders' Day. Bishop Ransom was expected to be there that evening. Tuesday evening Joseph was to lecture at Mt. Olive. He and the others, including Ransom, would leave for Tampa by motor on Wednesday. He had met many people in Florida whom he had known in Detroit, and he felt his candidacy had been "greatly helped" by the trip. He closed by describing the "wonderful moon—like Bermuda's, it [was] eloquent." He had "looked up at it last night and wondered what [she] was doing and thanked God for [her] and the most wonderful kids on earth." He won-dered if Eula had received the telegram he had sent her on her birthday and if she had had a good party. He hoped to be home by Sunday.[64]

By the time Joseph left for the General Conference he had amassed a number of letters endorsing his candidacy. One of the letters he cher-ished most was written by the Board of Managers of the Paseo YWCA, April 15, 1932, referring to him as the type of man "from the standpoint of moral fiber, social standards, Christian consistency and ambition, who so properly deserves recognition and high trust and responsibility among our people."[65]

The twenty-ninth Quadrennial Session of the A.M.E. General Confer-ence, May 2–16, in Cleveland, Ohio, turned out to be one of the stormiest in the history of the Church. The site of the meetings, the old Woodland Community Center on 46th and Woodland Avenues, did nothing to lessen the tension. Having once been a large church, it was elliptical in shape and had an auditorium that seated a thousand people, and a semicircular bal-cony, where from six to seven hundred more could sit. Despite the efforts of a large work force to prepare the center, many of the windows were still caked with dirt, and the frescoes on the walls were streaked with the grime. Because of the Depression, the Church could not afford a more suitable meeting place. Heard, the host bishop, and D. O. Walker, host pastor of St. James, had done all they could to make the eight hundred delegates comfortable despite the economic crisis.

Bishop Vernon delivered the Quadrennial Sermon. Remembering Vernon's treachery toward them, it was difficult for Hazel and Joseph to listen to him. In his usual bombastic fashion, he castigated "the Tom Paines, the Voltaires, the agnostics, the free thinkers, the transcendentalists, and kindred spirits," those "who have set the stage, have brewed the proper psychology for the ruin of the world. . . . A pistol crack resounded across the earth," he said, "and today, now—at this very hour—hungry, crazed, hopeless, we see a world-civilization discouraged, hopelessly drifting and prostrate." Then he asked, "Now where is your superman? Your man of material power only? I know one superman. I have seen him. He called himself the son of Man." He punctuated each point by long quotes from hymns, and on occasion he sang. Of the growing sectionalism he felt was becoming prevalent in the A.M.E. Church he said, "We pray that every vestige of sectionalism may be at end. . . . Some day, possibly a day farther away, all Bishops who were born in the South will preside over northern districts, and all Bishops born in the North will preside over southern districts."[66] (This part of his speech received loud "amens.") Part of his preaching style was to mix what he called intellectualism with down-home folksiness and to use symbols that ranged from baseball to Jesus Christ on the cross.

Very early in the conference it was obvious that the two issues that would predominate were the laymen's fight for equal representation on the Episcopal Committee, currently made up of ninety-eight clergymen, and an attempt to unfrock several bishops for allegedly misappropriating funds.

Joseph, who was a member of the Episcopal Committee, thought the laymen should have representation but that the committee should include one clergyman and one layman from each of the eighteen Episcopal Districts. This would reduce the unwieldy committee from ninety-eight to thirty-six members and thereby make it more manageable.[67]

The other issue, the possible unfrocking of several bishops, had to wait on the findings of the Episcopal Committee, and it would have a direct bearing on how many bishops would be elected. The delegates were divided. Some felt that the Church needed only fourteen bishops, the current number; others felt that four new bishops should be elected so that there would be one bishop for each of the eighteen Episcopal Districts. Four bishops had died during the Quadrennial.[68]

In the midst of all the controversy, Joseph was pleasantly distracted by an intriguing conversation with Rev. J. T. Sampler, an eighty-one-year-old delegate who had driven a horse and buggy from Bentonville, Texas, to Wilberforce, Ohio. It had taken him several months. From Wilberforce he had hitched a car ride to Cleveland, leaving his horse to rest for the return trip. It was impossible to leave Sampler when he started telling about all of the General Conferences he had attended and all the colorful characters he had met, never including himself as one of the characters. To Joseph, more than any other delegate, Sampler represented the real spirit of African Methodism in its purest form. He was a walking legacy.

On May 6, the Fraternal Organizations session was held in the evening. Various Methodist groups addressed the conference, pledging their support for ecumenicalism. Joseph was chosen to respond to the speech given by the representative from the Methodist Episcopal Church. He told the audience that "the history of Colored Methodism in America as a separate and individual religious entity, helped mightily in the enrichment of both Methodist and National life." Blacks had "stood at every crossroad in the history of human progress." He listed some of those crossroads as the creation of civilization "on the banks of the Nile," Jesus's Via Dolorosa, Perry's exploration to the top of the world, and World War I, where Blacks had "died with Democracy on their lips on the battlefield of France." They had "helped to mold the educational—moral—spiritual and economic policies of nations." African Methodists were doubly prepared to "render service" beside the M.E. Church, since they were "more than beneficiaries of a common heritage." He spoke of Wesley's accomplishments, which had not "gone far enough to reach Allen's [Richard Allen, founder of the A.M.E. Church] highest vantage point." He enumerated Allen's qualities, his "faith, daring and capacity . . . to thrill the hearts of all liberty loving people and provide the admiration of his early traducers." He closed by asserting, "Denominations shall endure, only as they serve the higher interests of our spiritual and moral order, serving as they must the utilitarian purposes of a modern society."[69]

The first of the charges against the bishops was laid on Friday, May 6, when Dr. John R. Hawkins, financial secretary, read his report, which accused Bishop W. D. Johnson of Plains, Georgia, of failing to report collected funds in the amount of $6,897.72. After making monthly payments on the deficit, Johnson still owed $4,147.42. It was ruled that he was to appear before the Episcopal Committee along with bishops Vernon and Joshua Jones, who also had charges against them.[70]

When the Episcopal Committee made its report, it found Bishop Vernon guilty of receiving $17,360 over and above the $4,900 allowance for salary and incidentals authorized by the Church. In light of the evidence, the committee recommended that Vernon be suspended for four years. Several of the bishops tried to have the decision set aside, but the delegates mobbed the platform. For over fifteen minutes, pandemonium ruled. The delegates were determined that the findings of the committee be upheld.[71]

Finally Bishop Vernon was allowed to speak in his own defense, his hands shaking so he could hardly hold the microphone. Joseph watched him and wondered why he had ever feared this man. In a choked voice Vernon said: "I stand on the threshold of my official death. I stand on the threshold of my financial death. . . . I know this is the end of me. I want you to remember my services in Africa, from which I still suffer from a wound in my side. I am too old. What will I do? Without salary, without home? I am 60. I throw myself upon your mercy. I am not guilty."[72]

According to the *Cleveland Press* (May 10), "This appeal had a momentary effect of calming the conference; the determined and united action of lay and clergy delegates overcame all efforts to forestall action on the motion. With head slightly bowed, Bishop Vernon left the platform."[73]

On May 11, the conference also suspended Bishop Joshua H. Jones for misappropriation of funds. Jones said that the church owed him $49,000, almost half of which he held in mortgages. He told the *Cleveland News* on May 12th that had he known the charges against him he could have come to the conference with "canceled checks and other documentary evidence to prove these contentions." He said he had "brought in the men who received these sums of money during [his] trial before the Episcopal Board." His "ability as a business man or credit risk had never been questioned" before. The reporter went on to say that "President Gilbert Jones of Wilberforce University, son of the suspended bishop, called the action of the conference a disgrace not only to his father, but to the church he has helped build for close to a quarter of a century."[74]

When Bishop Jones was allowed to speak to the conference, he said, "I am winding up my 20th year as Bishop, during which time I have given the church not only my time and effort, but money as well. . . . This will probably end my life because of the disgrace and heartbreak they are causing me."[75]

For two hours, friends sought to save him from being unfrocked. Joseph had known Jones for years and felt that the Church was making a grievous error. He may have juggled the accounts to make up deficits in certain areas, but Joseph did not believe he had taken any of the money for his personal use. But nothing could be done with the "screaming delegates," who insisted that the vote be delayed no longer. When it was finally taken, 420 delegates voted for a two-year suspension, 132 against.[76] It was obvious that the laymen and some of the ministers were out to punish the Council of Bishops, no matter what the cost might be to individual lives.

The laymen won equal representation on the Episcopal Committee, which was reduced to thirty members because the districts were cut from eighteen to fifteen. With four bishops deceased and two suspended, it was agreed that three new bishops would be elected.[77]

The election began at 11 A.M. on May 13 and ran well into the next day. In spite of Vernon's appeal for its elimination, sectionalism played a major role in the elections. R. R. Wright of Philadelphia, who was one of the top contenders during the first three ballots, was defeated on the fourth by Noah Williams of St. Louis, David Sims of South Carolina, and Henry Y. Tookes of Jacksonville, Florida. The South had prevailed once more.[78]

As Bishop Davis had predicted, Joseph lost the election for Secretary-Treasurer of Missions to the incumbent, Rev. E. H. Coit, who amassed 436 votes. Joseph had come in fourth, with a mere forty-four votes. He was disappointed by his poor showing but took consolation in the fact that his friend David Sims was now a bishop. In addition, running for an office had been good experience for when he ultimately announced his candidacy for the bishopric.[79]

Following the election, Joseph received a note saying that Bishop Vernon wanted to see him and his family. The Gomezes found him seated alone in the dark corner of a room off the hallway. For a long time he was silent. Then he lifted the two children onto his knees, looked down at Annetta, and said, "So this is the child I am accused of almost killing. I am sorry." The anger Joseph had felt for years whenever the name of Vernon was mentioned was spent, and in its place was only a deep compassion for this shrunken, broken man seated before him, his face streaming with tears. Vernon put the children down and fell to his knees. Joseph asked him to get up. Vernon did, and Joseph led his family away; he felt great relief and a sense of humility. He never forgot that scene in the darkened room, or the man who had almost caused him to leave the African Methodist Episcopal Church.

Although many progressive steps had been taken at this conference, to Joseph it was African Methodism at its worst. Perhaps, like every other organization, it was experiencing "growing pains." Joseph said later that the entire proceedings resembled a third-rate movie. He loved his Church but felt at times that it betrayed its great heritage. Once again mob rule had prevailed over more sober heads, particularly in the case of Bishop Jones, who Joseph felt had been unwise rather than criminal. Jones's untimely death two years later, which was attributed largely to heartbreak, gave many A.M.E.s cause to regret their haste and insensitivity.

Joseph, Hazel, and the girls returned to Kansas City tired and somewhat depressed but determined to expand the program at Allen Chapel, particularly in behalf of those who were suffering most from the Depression. Within a few days of their arrival, Bishop Gregg came to the parsonage on official business. He told Joseph that since Rev. Noah W. Williams had been elected bishop there was a vacancy at St. Paul Church in St. Louis and that he wanted Joseph to fill the vacancy immediately. It was a larger church and offered Joseph more challenges. After four years in Kansas City, it was time to move again.

CHAPTER SEVEN

◈ ◈ ◈

Scandalizin' My Name

St. Louis, 1932–1936

Days of great disquietude are upon us. Like the Elizabethan
mariners we have broken into untraveled seas. . . . Staggering
sorrow, losses, change of season, may serve to loosen our grip on
ourselves. These are perils that we must face courageously. When
there comes a break in the even tenor of life, and our anchor drags
unexpectedly and perilously, it is best to ride out the storm. We
cannot escape, but we can challenge then conquer.
   —Joseph Gomez, sermonette, "Thoughts for the Unsettled,"
   Pittsburgh Courier n.d.

◈ On Friday, May 27, 1932, the *St. Louis Argus,* one of the city's leading
Black newspapers, announced that on the following Sunday "Rev. Joseph
Gomez, the newly appointed minister, [would] fill his first engagement as
pastor of St. Paul A.M.E. Church." The article described Joseph as "one
of the leading ministers of the A.M.E. Church, a gospel minister, a civic
leader, and a Christian gentleman."[1]

Located on the corners of Lawton and Leffingwell Avenues, St. Paul with
its 1,600 members was closer to the size of Greater Bethel than Allen Chapel
had been. It was a large, sprawling brick building with a stately spire that
towered above the main entrance. Most unusual for a Methodist church, behind the pulpit there was a baptismal pool; members could choose whether
they wanted to be sprinkled or immersed (most Methodists preferred to
be sprinkled). Another asset of the church was its Community Center, at
3531-33 Lawton Boulevard, which fed from "75 to 150 destitute women" and
housed from "25 to 30 women and girls" until they could find permanent

quarters. This building, a "godsend" during the Depression years, had been purchased under the leadership of the former pastor, Noah Williams.[2]

More than in any other church Joseph had yet pastored, the members of St. Paul believed in "making a joyful noise unto the Lord." Long after the benediction had been pronounced on Sunday mornings, the sanctuary still reverberated with amens and hallelujahs. Most of the members had migrated from the deep South and were hard-working, warm, simple people who revered their ministers. A small percentage were professionals. An even smaller number could be described as "colorful characters." There was "Ole Miz McGregor," who like clockwork would rise from her pew the same time every Sunday, come down the center aisle to the pulpit, turn her back, and shake her rear end exactly ten times, then return to her seat. If the members had not known that she lived like a saint, they might have found her behavior toward the pastor suspect. There was also a Mrs. Peoples, a tall, massive woman who had a voice like thunder and wore all the clothes she owned on her back at one time. It was rumored that she was a man (when she died that turned out to be unfounded). Then there was Princess Wee Wee and her husband, midgets from the circus, who came to St. Paul whenever the circus was in town. On the Sunday they joined the church, Joseph picked up Princess, thinking she was a child, and planted a healthy kiss on her cheek, to the consternation of her miniature husband; Joseph was mortified when he learned that Princess was a full-grown woman. There was Mamie Caldwell, the evangelist, and her daughter, Marybelle. Mamie was hard of hearing but would not wear her hearing aid most of the time, and when she did she would not turn it up high enough to hear properly. Sometimes in her eagerness to please she became a nuisance, but she was devoted to Joseph.

The most loveable of all the members was the widowed "Ma" Eaton, whom everyone said was "older than God." She was a figure from a Victorian novel, replete with long black dress, white ruffled collar and cuffs, high-buttoned black shoes, and a bonnet decorated with tired flowers. Her second-story home on Enright Avenue was furnished with dark, heavy Victorian furniture, which she protected from the sun behind darkly draped windows. She still cooked on a wood-burning stove, read by kerosene lamp or candlelight, and slept in an antique four-poster canopied bed, above which hung an almost life-sized picture of her husband in his casket. The clock seemed to have stopped ticking for her when he died.

Her kitchen was the only room that had contact with the outside. She kept open the large window that looked out on the backyard so she could hand-feed the squirrels that jumped from the old oak tree onto her sill. When Eula and Annetta came to visit, she would let the squirrels sit on the table so the children could share their animal crackers with them while they listened to Ma's exciting stories about her childhood and idyllic marriage to the handsome Mr. Eaton. Although she lived in the past, there was enough room in that past for children, animals, and Joseph, whom she adored.

There was a friendly rivalry among the members as to who would have the minister and his family over for Sunday dinner. The girls were happy when the Newmans won, because that meant they could play with their two daughters Nello and Bessie, who were about their same age. Sometimes the family had dinner with the Sawyers, who belonged to the Baptist Church but attended St. Paul often to hear Joseph preach. Neil Sawyer (whom everyone referred to as Professor Sawyer) and Hazel had been friends in Ontario. The Gomezes had played cupid and introduced Neil to his wife Maggie, a tall, attractive registered nurse quite a bit younger than he. The Sawyers and Gomezes developed a long-lasting friendship. Other favorites of the family were Jewell Collier, a young and energetic woman in her twenties, and the twins Jeannette and Geneva Goode, whom Hazel took under her wing.

When the Gomezes first arrived in St. Louis they stayed at the Williams Apartments. Within a few months they were able to move from these confining quarters to a sizable old house at 4000 Cook Avenue. The girls were enrolled in the nearby Cole Elementary School, Annetta in kindergarten, and Eula in second grade. The new parsonage had a large living room with a wood-burning fireplace, which the family thoroughly enjoyed—except when there was a cloudburst and lightning struck nearby, causing soot to pour down the chimney onto the rug. There were four big bedrooms on the second floor, an unfinished attic, and a fenced-in backyard that offered not only unlimited opportunities for play but a home for Beauty when she was not roaming the neighborhood looking for companions. Beauty was a half-Spitz, half-Chow, red bitch with a donut tail and blue gums. Her one asset (or non-asset) was her fertility: almost every year she filled the yard with curly-tailed, blue-gummed puppies for whom the family had to find homes. One of the more handsome male pups was given to the Sawyers, who promptly named him Mike. Luckily, Mike resembled his German shepherd father more than his mother, and everyone thought he was pedigreed.

Behind the backyard was a long alley with large brick pits conveniently placed for the burning of garbage and trash. The alley provided access to the houses on the block and the adjacent street. Often Eula and Annetta would slip through the alley to the Sadlers', who lived a few houses away. Although the Sadlers had many children, the Gomezes' favorites were

Ruth, Gloria, and Tommy. Annetta especially liked to "roughhouse" with Tommy, while the other girls played "tea party."

Like most of the houses in St. Louis during that time the new parsonage was not air conditioned, and the summer of 1932 sweltered. It became necessary for the family to join other pilgrims at the riverside to seek relief from the heat. Protected only by sheets, a pillow, and some netting to keep away the mosquitoes, they would sleep all night on the grass. It was so hot that summer that Joseph would invite the men to take off their suit coats during worship service. While many of the nights were spent at the riverside, most days were spent at the Community Center, the church, or the Parish House next door, readying these facilities for the fall activities. In addition, the church roof had to be patched and the gutters cleaned.

In early autumn, all activity temporarily came to a halt when Joseph received tragic news. A telegram arrived saying simply, "Papa dead"; it was signed "Satchel" (the nickname of his brother James).[3] Once again Joseph was unable to get to Trinidad in time for the funeral, but he was told all about it in a letter dated October 1 written by Amanda. Enclosed was an announcement that Emanuel Gomez, father of James M. Gomez, had died at the Colonial Hospital on September 6, 1932.[4] Amanda described Papa as having been "just skin and bones" when he died, but she was glad that "his grief, sorrow and wants are over now." However, the death had been hardest on Cyril, Joseph's youngest brother, who had been living with Emanuel before he died and who suffered from mental disorders. When Papa became ill and was first moved to James's house, Cyril had stopped sleeping. Amanda said the day Emanuel was taken to the hospital, Cyril had run madly down the street yelling that they were killing his father and that a man with a gun wanted to shoot him. Josh, Amanda's son, finally got him back in the house and sent for a doctor, who gave him a "sleeping draught." The doctor said "had he remained a minute longer without sleep, he would of died or get a stroke," Amanda wrote. She said Papa had had a "nice funeral. James had the turn out. He had a pair of horses."[5]

In her letter Amanda accused James and May, his wife, of mistreating Papa and not spending enough money on him while he was living.[6] (James had acquired a great deal of money by this time as a meat importer.) Asked about this in 1986, May said this was not true, that both she and James had taken good care of Emanuel.[7] Amanda also accused Joseph of not sending money to Papa during the two months before his death. This was probably accurate. Joseph had been sending money home regularly since he had come to the United States, but 1931 and 1932 had seen the Depression deepen, and the church was not always able to pay his salary.

On three separate occasions in 1932–1933 he had to borrow money from his Metropolitan life insurance policy to take care of Hazel and the girls. Besides, no one had written to tell him his father was ill. Given his own financial plight, if he missed two months in sending money home, it is understandable. Had he known his father was stricken, he would have sent money somehow. Nevertheless, Amanda's words cut deeply. He already had a strong sense of guilt for not having been with either of his parents when they died; he had loved them, and in a strange way they had represented security to him. Though far away, they defined who he was.

As disastrous as the economic situation was in 1932, the Depression did have one positive effect: Americans had an extraordinary interest in the November presidential elections. The Republicans reaffirmed their confidence in Herbert Hoover, nominating him and Vice President Charles Curtis. Governor Franklin Delano Roosevelt of New York and John Nance Garner of Texas were the choices of the Democrats. Joseph read with interest a speech given by Roosevelt at St. Paul, Minnesota, on April 18, in which he outlined an unorthodox plan for overcoming the economic malaise.[8] He hoped Roosevelt would be given a chance to try it. Hoover seemed to have been in a state of paralysis during his administration, and those innovations he did try were either too late, too little, or both. Instead of a "chicken in every pot," Americans, especially Black Americans, could no longer even afford the pot. Additionally, Hoover's failed attempt to appoint Judge John J. Parker, a known racist, to the Supreme Court convinced Joseph that Hoover had little interest in Blacks.[9]

Joseph was preoccupied with not only the election that November but also his first Missouri Annual Conference. Bishop Gregg introduced him and immediately appointed him to the committees on Finance and Disbursing and on Fourth Year Studies, and made him a trustee of both Western and Wilberforce Universities.[10]

Western was experiencing a crisis involving the suspended Bishop Vernon. Like Wilberforce, the school was financed by both the A.M.E. Church and the state. In 1899 the state had opened an Industrial Department and as a result had appointed its own separate board of trustees. When Western's President King died, four new members were appointed to the state board without the knowledge of the Church. These new members were close friends of Bishop Vernon. They called a meeting on May 13, several weeks before the regular meeting was to be held, and elected Vernon superintendent of the Industrial Department. When the Church learned of this, it withdrew its support. Gregg believed that Vernon was the spearhead of the trouble at Western. Vernon had come to him saying "he was entirely destitute and begged [him] for weeks for a place." Gregg had advised him not to take any appointment but to use his suspension to lecture and write. In his usual dramatic fashion, Vernon told Gregg he did not "even have bread to eat, and that he only wanted some small place where he might prove his loyalty to his Church and thus win his way back into its good graces." Gregg had given him St. Marks in Topeka, Kansas, "hoping thereby to help a man who seemed entirely adrift find himself." As soon as Vernon received the appointment he began to petition politicians and members of other churches to appoint him head of the Industrial Department. Somehow he was able to convince these people that the A.M.E. Church had taken away his position without giving him a fair trial.[11]

It was difficult for Joseph to believe that Vernon had not learned his lesson and was up to his old tricks, particularly after the pathetic scenes at the last General Conference. As a trustee of Western on the Church side, Joseph hoped he would not have personal contact with Vernon. He was tempted to ask Bishop Gregg to relieve him from the position. As it turned out, he did become involved, voting with the other trustees to withdraw the A.M.E. Church from Western. In addition, the trustees filed a suit to prevent the state from using the name "Western," which they said belonged to the Church.

Some time in 1933 Joseph began to write weekly sermonettes for the *Pittsburgh Courier,* commentaries on world or national affairs as well as messages of inspiration. Excerpts from two sermonettes exemplify how diverse the pieces were. The first was written on the anniversary of Shakespeare's birthday, the second on the election of Franklin D. Roosevelt.

These characters of Shakespeare come trooping from the land of deep experience. They are ourselves. . . . Shylock shocks us, and we writhe under the bludgeoning of the disillusioned Brutus. The hell of avarice and ingratitude, the passions of the mob, follies of men, are all there in striking candor. He speaks of things elemental— Life, Love and Death—and we learn the ultimate truth, that life is not a Midsummer Night's Dream, nor is it Love's Labor Lost; but All's Well That Ends Well, and every man shall receive Measure for Measure.[12]

. . . .

Thousands of Negroes deserted the old faith of Party Republicanism, and dared to think for themselves. It means respect on the part of others; but infinitely more, it means conscious liberty and strength for the race. Indeed there is a new political thought in process that is destined to revolutionize our whole system of party government. So with religious beliefs. The old shibboleths of dogma must give way to a creative process which inevitable unshackles the mind and leads to freedom of spirit.[13]

Soon after these sermonettes appeared Joseph began to receive fan mail from all over the United States complimenting him for their valuable messages.

Although racism was somewhat more subtle in St. Louis than it was in the deep South, it existed. For instance, Black ministers were not welcomed in the Ministerial Alliance of Greater St. Louis. Also, they could not enroll in Eden Seminary at Webster Grove, a suburb only twelve miles from the center of St. Louis, even though the school was governed and supported by the Evangelical Synod of North America and was supposedly "open to all students of all Christian denominations."[14] Joseph was determined to change both of these organizations. First of all, he and Rev. John F. Moreland of the Metropolitan A.M.E. Zion Church decided to apply for the Graduate Program at Eden Seminary. Along with their applications they submitted the required health certificates, transcripts, and letters of recommendation from several prominent Black and white clergymen. Eden withheld its decision. The Black press ran editorials as a means of pressuring it to admit the two ministers, and letters protesting the delay poured into the seminary. Joseph and Moreland had many meetings with the Board of Directors. After several months Eden finally bowed to the inevitable and admitted them for the fall term of 1932.

As graduate student Joseph was expected to take nine courses within a year's time, write a thesis, and pass a final examination on the thesis "and its wider implications."[15] During the year he studied the New Testament: "Introduction to the New Testament," with John Biegeleisen; "The Theology of the New Testament" (the development of religious ideas of the gospels), with Samuel D. Press, the president; and a "Seminar on the Fourth Gospel" (an inquiry into the authorship, composition, background, and interpretation of the Gospel of John), with Biegeleisen. His Old Testament courses included "The Religion of the Old Testament" (origin and development of the Hebrew religion), with Biegeleisen, and "Devotional Literature of the Old Testament," with Allen G. Wehrli. In addition he took "Philosophy 1—History of Religion," with Theophil Menzel, and a religious education seminar entitled "The Curriculum of Religious Education," with Harold A. Pflug. In spite of his other numerous responsibilities, he managed to receive six A-minuses, three B-pluses, and honors on his master's thesis, which was entitled "The Significance of Negro Spirituals in a Program of Religious Education."[16]

In his thesis he sought to prove that Negro spirituals were important, first, to America, in that they "represent the only genuinely American music"; second, to the Negro himself for whom they represent not only his own vital creation but "elementary and basic truths" by which he survives; third, the world, since "the needs of America as a nation and of the Negro as a race are universal needs and the ills of [America's] body politic, are symptomatic of a world-wide disease"; and finally, to religion itself, which "is sorely in need of the spirit which dominates the spirituals." Joseph felt the Negro spirituals, like other valuable artifacts from the past, needed to be rescued from "the commercialism into which they have fallen since the Fisk Jubilee Singers introduced them to America and the world beginning in 1871." He wanted to interpret these songs in terms of their highest revelations and to support the efforts of such men as H. T. Burleigh, James Weldon Johnson, R. Nathaniel Dett, W. E. B. Du Bois, Paul Robeson, Roland Hayes, and others, who had used their talents to bring this priceless music to the attention of the world.[17]

The thesis reveals that Joseph was more interested in the chapters that dealt directly with the Negro spiritual than in those concerned with the "Genesis and Modern Trends of Religious Education." In the latter he attempted to correlate the two subjects by concluding that "no lasting program of Religious Education can ignore the composite spiritual experience, at least in its basic application. The Negro spiritual is not without significance in the modern approach to religious training, growth and development."[18]

His chapters on the "Religious Content of Negro Spirituals" contain some of his best writing. Concerning what he calls the "unmistakable trends" to be found in the spirituals, he writes:

> The genius of the Negro Spiritual is religious. Its atmosphere, tone, direction are all that the name implies—spiritual. On this basis they must rise or fall. We must therefore look for the power of Negro spirituals, not in their poetry, for most of it, judged by modern standards, is inadequate; not in their music, rhythmic as it is; but the religious appeal, the upward reach of soul, the wailing spirit, the heart throb, the questioning of life, destiny and of God himself, the triumphant notes of Faith and Hope. They are religious art.[19]

It is difficult to separate Joseph the author from Joseph the preacher. The words in his sermons and other writings rise and fall in cadences, and then gather in a final grand appeal. His romanticism reveals itself in the poetic power of his language. Add to this the distinctive clarity and richness of his voice, and it becomes clear why he excelled as a pulpiteer. At Eden he was admired as a solid student, an outstanding preacher, and an expressive writer.

In the *Keryx* (the seminary publication) of December 1933, an article of his appeared entitled "Aspects of Church Union," dealing with one of his favorite topics, ecumenicalism. The article applauds the Canadian union of Congregationalists, Methodists, and Presbyterians as the United Church of Canada (1925) and the recent Evangelical Conference in Cincinnati, Ohio, which had approved the instrument of Organic Union with the Reformed Church of the United States. He felt that these events constituted "a step toward final realization of a great ideal." He believed that as a preliminary "to a larger Union of Christian Forces" there should first be unity among those "who are nearly one in doctrine and polity, or whose differences are relatively unimportant. . . . A period of fraternizing should precede any stated attempt at Organic Union. This would make the final step infinitely easier."[20]

A few months after Joseph attended his first classes at Eden, the Missouri Annual Conference met in Cape Girardeau, Missouri. On the opening day a motion was made and passed that "the Missouri Conference concur with the other conferences of the 5th Episcopal district in re-affirming the endorsement of Dr. Gomez for election to the Bishopric in 1936." Other important business included the adoption of a special resolution applauding the actions of the Western trustees and Bishop John A. Gregg in temporarily closing the school until the matter of Vernon could be straightened out.[21]

Joseph preached on the final afternoon of the conference a sermon which, according to the minutes, was "masterful." He received many compliments from his peers and the bishop. When Presiding Elder William Burnette read his report, describing in effusive terms Joseph's first year at St. Paul, Joseph was both pleased and amused. After calling St. Paul the "Light House of our Methodism in the West . . . Mother of the Western Empire of African Methodism west of the Mississippi," Burnette spoke of how the "flocking multitudes that come to worship at her altars find it hard to obtain seats." He called Joseph a "'master builder,' [who] has led on to victory this great army of God's people until today the credit and standing of St. Paul Chapel is simply gilt-edged. Her future was never more hopeful than at the present time." During the year the membership of St. Paul had grown to 1,726, and repairs had been made, including the renovation of the Parish House. The members had voted unanimously for the return of their pastor.[22]

A few weeks following the Annual Conference, Hazel, who had only just learned she was pregnant again, had a miscarriage and was seriously ill for several days. She was nursed back to health by Maggie Sawyer and Jewell Collier, who also took care of the children. Hazel experienced not only a great deal of physical pain but deep depression. She had thought that at long last she would be able to give Joseph the son he had always wanted, but it was not to be. Joseph's assurance that she and the two girls were all he wanted now finally dispelled her feeling of insecurity.

On June 5, 1934, Joseph and Hazel gave a chicken breakfast at the parsonage for Joseph's graduating class from Eden and some of the professors. The affair was served by volunteers from the church, but Hazel had insisted on cooking the food herself. Notes the guests wrote in an autograph book at the breakfast indicate that the experience was memorable. Professor Harold Pflug, who had been Joseph's thesis advisor, wrote: "As Ohioans, friends of Reinie [theologian Reinhold] Niebuhr, interested in Negro spirituals and other such things, we began what I hope will be an ever-growing friendship. Learning to know you in the greater fellowship of the mind and spirit through classes and as you opened up to me the depth of the Negro spirituals has been a great privilege for which I am truly grateful." Others spoke not only of the friendship developed but jokingly of "the tough chicken they had had to share at the Senior Retreat" held a few weeks ago, and thanked God that Hazel was a good cook.[23]

Despite Hazel's miscarriage, the increasing responsibilities of a large church like St. Paul, and his civic duties, Joseph graduated with his class from Eden Seminary on June 7, 1934. Eula and Annetta went with their mother to see "Daddy in his preaching robe and teaching hat" receive his degree of Master of Sacred Theology. The commencement address was delivered by Rev. Louis Goebel, followed by a second speech, by President Samuel D. Press.[24] Years later Hazel would tease Joseph about the big grin and devilish wink he gave her and the children as he descended the platform with diploma in hand. For the many Blacks who came to see him and Moreland graduate, it meant far more than merely the attainment of a master's degree; it meant one more step toward being recognized as a people capable of meeting any challenge white America proposed, including success in their educational institutions.

Following the graduation, a group of citizens gave a banquet in honor of Moreland and Gomez at the Pine Street YMCA. The *St. Louis Argus* of June 15 noted that "many felicitations and congratulations were given these two ministers, it being said that they were the only members of the race to receive such degrees from Eden Seminary." When asked to say a few words, Joseph told the audience, "I am sick and tired of the way in which we [Blacks] as a group, are divided. If we are to get things to which we are justly entitled, we must find some way to unite our forces." He and Moreland were examples of what could happen when an A.M.E. Zionist and an A.M.E. decided to tackle a problem together.[25] The uniting of the denominations is one example of what unity among Blacks could produce.

The year 1934 proved to be extremely busy. Months before the graduation Joseph had led St. Paul in an observance of Richard Allen Day, during which Carter G. Woodson, founder of the Association for the Study of Negro Life and History, and editor of the *Journal of Negro History,* gave an insightful address on the importance of the church in the Negro community, not only as a place of worship but as a training ground for political awareness and community living.[26] On April 9, along with other prominent Blacks of St. Louis, including Mitchell, editor of the *Argus,* Joseph spoke at a mass meeting on economics and the social welfare of Negroes. The same month he gave the opening address for the YMCA membership campaign and spoke at the Kewpie anniversary ceremonies.

In July, Bishop W. Sampson Brooks died, and funeral services were held at St. Paul, where Brooks had pastored at one time. Although saddened by the untimely death of the popular bishop, Joseph was blessed with the opportunity to converse with Bishop Ransom, who stayed at the parsonage and delivered the eulogy. After the funeral they caught up on personal and church business. Joseph told Ransom of his desire to run for the bishopric, and Ransom promised to do all he could to assist, even though he was not sure this was the time for him to run. Joseph was sorry to hear from Ransom that Bishop Sims was being called home from Africa by the Bishops' Council to answer charges of desertion brought against him by his wife, Annie Mae.

The remainder of the summer was uneventful except for the Educational Chautauqua held at Paul Quinn College, Waco, Texas, July 17–20; Joseph attended with Bishop Gregg, who preached at the opening session. During the afternoon Joseph gave a lecture centered on the question, "Is the Influence of Nordic Christianity Threatened in the World Crisis? If so, What Are the Chief Causes?"[27] This was Joseph's first visit to Texas and to Paul Quinn College. He had no way of knowing how important this school would become to him in later years.

On September 9, at 7:15 A.M., Rollin R. Dent, Hazel's half brother, died in Chicago. He was fifty-five years old and had worked for the Post Office since 1907. Starting from the lowest rank, he had been promoted from special clerk to foreman in charge of equipment and the supply section, an enviable position for a Negro at the time. Hazel, Joseph, and one of Hazel's friends, Maggie Morant, attended the funeral at Grace Presbyterian Church, September 12, in Chicago.[28] Even though Carrie Dent's sister, Mamie Shivers-Range, was there to comfort her, Hazel was reluctant to leave Carrie, who went into an excessive period of mourning from which she never recovered. Hazel had to hide her own grief. She had been very fond of Rollin, who had had the talent to have become a professional singer had the opportunity presented itself. Through the years she and Rollin had kept in touch, though they had seen each other only every two or three years when she had taken the girls to Chicago to visit their aunt and uncle.

Back in St. Louis the following month, Joseph received a letter from Bishop Sims postmarked October 19, Cape Town, South Africa. He had been concerned about his friend ever since his talk with Ransom after Bishop Brooks's funeral. Sims wrote enthusiastically about his work there: he had received 4,673 members into the A.M.E. Church in less than two years. He said he and a Rev. Gow (an A.M.E. minister and a native of South Africa) had been appointed to the mayor's Unemployment Relief Committee and were "included in the twenty who were the Mayor's guests at dinner for Prince Geo[rge] of England." In addition, he was one of the two Negroes to have become a member of the Continuation Committee for Federated Missionary Enterprise for the Union of South Africa. He hoped "Mrs. Gomez and the girls [were] well" and assured Joseph that he had a "jewel in Mrs. Gomez."[29]

At the end of his letter he spoke of his domestic affairs. He said he had "lived in hell for ten years" in his home. "I grinned and bore it for decency's sake. It grew unbearable," he confided. Sims had not mentioned his troubles when he had visited the Gomezes last, because he was "embarrassed to discuss the matter." He promised he would explain everything in detail when he returned to America, and he solicited Joseph's help. Finally he gave his "unqualified endorsement" to Joseph in his bid for the bishopric at the next General Conference.[30]

Sims had indeed divorced his wife and had taken another, who was with him in South Africa. When all aspects of the case had been examined he was exonerated by the Council of Bishops, and the courts decreed that his divorce was legal. Joseph, who felt that divorce should be avoided in most cases, sympathized with his friend and stood by him through all the turmoil that followed the announcement of his having taken another wife.

Meanwhile, in addition to Connectional backers like Sims, Joseph's candidacy for the bishopric gained local support. According to the *St. Louis Argus* of October 4, 1934, "seventy-five representative citizens . . . civic leaders of all professions and religious leaders of all denominations, [had] gathered at a banquet in the Pine Street YMCA" the preceding Friday night to "pledge their support for the candidacy of the Reverend Joseph Gomez . . . for the office of Bishop." W. G. Mosely, assistant principal of

Vashon High School and a member of St. Paul, was chosen chairman of a permanent committee of a thousand to promote Gomez's candidacy.[31]

At the Missouri Annual Conference held in St. Louis from October 31 through November 4, Joseph was again assured of the conference's endorsement. Several church leaders who attended also pledged their support: Dr. George A. Singleton of Springfield, Illinois, who was to become one of his most ardent friends; Rev. R. R. Wright, editor of the *Christian Recorder* and president of Wilberforce University; Rev. S. S. Morris, general secretary of the Allen Christian Endeavor League, who had traveled with him and Bishop Gregg to Berlin; and Dr. L. L. Berry, general secretary of the Missionary Department.[32]

Now that both girls were in school all day, Hazel had more time for church activities. As in Kansas City, she was a tireless worker in the Missionary Society, was the sponsor of the Young People's Choir, and the sponsor of the Allen Christian Endeavor League. Early in November 1934 she surprised Joseph and the board of trustees of the church by asking to meet with them and read a paper she had prepared. In it she made a plea for the creation of a Vacation Bible School during the summer. She felt that "St. Paul [had] a rare opportunity to further the teachings of the principles of Christian Living." Such a school could "reach many boys and girls in [the] community, who never attend Sunday School or church; who do nothing during the summer but roam the streets and get into all sorts of trouble." So earnestly and practically did she make her request that she was assured she would receive a budget to operate the school the following summer. Joseph was proud of the way in which she handled the more penny-pinching board members, and when he came across her paper that evening lying on the dining room table, he wrote across the top of it, "An Excellent Paper. Success to you in your school."[33] In time the Vacation Bible School became a vital part of St. Paul's yearly program and the best attended of its kind in the city.

Joseph spent most of November visiting other Annual Conferences, including the Columbia Annual Conference in the 7th Episcopal District, where Bishop Noah Williams was presiding. On December 12, when he finally returned home, his frenetic activity caught up with him. While conducting a funeral service for one of his members he suddenly became ill and had to be "conveyed home."[34] The doctor attributed his collapse to fatigue and high blood pressure and suggested that he remain in bed for at least a week. Hazel found it impossible to keep him in bed. He was constantly playing games with the children, making phone calls, dictating letters to his secretary, Mrs. Ross, and threatening to leave the house. By Christmas he had recovered enough to join in the family festivities and to sing (out of tune) the traditional carols, which were always sung around the fireplace on Christmas Eve.

On January 4, the *Memphis World* carried excerpts from an emancipation speech he had given at St. Andrews A.M.E. Church during its "Freedom Celebration." After being presented by the master of ceremonies as the next A.M.E. bishop, Joseph had introduced his subject: "A New Commandment." He began by outlining the growth of the Black man in America. Despite the progress that had been made, he was chagrined by how some "young Negroes scoff at the past and the old methods employed by their grandfathers." He warned about the discrimination within the race itself, using as an example how Negroes would often go to white professionals rather than support their own. "Let a black doctor make a mistake or a Negro lawyer lose a case, and he is branded a scamp, but should a white doctor butcher a Colored patient, nothing is said of it. We are being made fools of by white men because we are a light-hearted people." He was again pointing out that some Negroes were themselves still caught up in the slave psychology, that "white is right."[35]

All his life Joseph had a Black family doctor, and only when sent by his doctor to a specialist or to seek a second opinion did he ever go to a white physician. The majority of the lawyers he used were also Black, as were his accountants. He was a great admirer of the Jewish race, who, he felt, supported their own; he wanted Blacks to do likewise.

In April, at an affair sponsored by the St. Louis alumni chapter of the Kappa Alpha Psi Fraternity at St. Paul, he had an opportunity to speak about another issue on which he had deep convictions. His emphasis this time was on commitment. "Those who go into a certain field should have a passion for it. They should be ever alert and willing to do more than just what is demanded of them. . . . There is a great danger of professionalism, that is, just doing what is asked of the profession or trade." He spoke of many people who went through college with an "attitude of aloofness," believing that if they understood most of the material in the book, they needed not concern themselves with its practical aspects. Nor did they think they had any obligation to contribute to the progress of mankind. He said it was the responsibility of organizations like the Kappa Alpha Psi Fraternity to bring young people back to the commitment of their forefathers, who used as their guide the teachings of Jesus Christ.[36]

Until this time in his ministry, Joseph had avoided the kind of scandal which most public figures experience sometime in their career. But on August 16, 1935, William A. Morant, Constable of the 4th District, filed charges in the Circuit Court accusing Joseph of alienating the affections of his wife, Maggie W. Morant, and asking for "$25,000 actual damages and

$25,000 punitive or exemplary damages." The specific charges were that on September 11, 12, and 13 the year before, in the city of Chicago, the minister had had improper relations with his wife.[37]

Morant and his wife were members of St. Paul and lived right around the corner from the church. The highly attractive Maggie and Hazel were apparently good friends, and Maggie had accompanied the Gomezes when in September 1934 they attended the funeral of Rollin Dent, Hazel's half brother. Shortly after their return Morant had gone to the trustees board of St. Paul with complaints that Joseph had alienated his wife's affections. After examining the charges carefully the Board had voted unanimously to dismiss the charges as unfounded. It was reported in the *St. Louis Argus* that William Morant divorced his wife in April 1935 but that before filing charges with the court against Joseph they had remarried.[38]

After notifiing Mr. Morant that it had dismissed the charges, the Board had heard nothing further from him and assumed the matter had been dropped. Consequently, everyone was surprised when the petition was filed. Now Joseph welcomed the opportunity to have this aired in a court of law, because "so many wild rumors about the whole thing, and so many malicious lies [had been] told that it would be a relief to have it heard before a forum where everybody [could] be pinned down to definite statements and the truth [could] be established."[39] The *Argus* carried in its August 23 issue Joseph's statement, in which he denied "emphatically each and every charge made by Mr. Morant in his petition. Neither on the occasions he alleges nor at any other time have I ever been guilty of any wrong doing with Mrs. Morant." When Joseph had learned that Morant had filed a suit, he and his attorney had gone to the sheriff and asked to be served with the petition. In it Morant had for the first time named a time and place when the affair was supposed to have taken place. He firmly believed that the suit had been filed to hinder his preparations to entertain the Missouri Annual Conference and to defeat his effort to be elected bishop. He wondered who had put Morant up to this treachery.

According to the *Argus* in 1935 and the people interviewed by this writer in 1986, the congregation of St. Paul and the general public for the most part backed Joseph. They found it highly suspect that Morant would wait almost a year to petition the court.[40] Knowing how closely Hazel and Joseph worked together and that were in each other's company most of the time, it was inconceivable to many that Joseph could have had an affair with Mrs. Morant while in Chicago, especially since he had come to attend his wife's brother's funeral and stayed at the widow's house with Hazel. Others felt that it would have been wholly out of character for him to have been intimate with another woman while his wife was grieving for her brother. Maggie Sawyer, who still lives in St. Louis, has said that no one believed the story but that it did give people something to talk about. "Even if Joseph had had no integrity at all (which believe me he had plenty of), he was too intelligent to become entangled in a situation which had the potential to ruin his career."[41] Jewell Collier, who in her eighties resides in California, remembers the incident well. She recalls that Joseph had never been known as a womanizer and that she, as well as the other young women in the church, always felt perfectly comfortable in his presence. "I recall once he had gone to visit a sick lady who answered the door in a scant negligée. From then on, he always took Hazel with him when he visited sick females," she laughed.[42]

Knowing of Joseph's inordinate pride and the importance he placed on character, it is easy to imagine how this incident affected him. Hazel too was deeply hurt. She never once doubted Joseph, but she had difficulty understanding why anyone would go to such lengths to soil her husband's reputation. Papers in other cities had carried the story, as well as the St. Louis papers. No doubt the many letters the Gomezes received reaffirming the esteem in which Joseph was held were of some comfort. The Paseo Bible Class of Kansas City sent a resolution signed by its 567 members. They did not extend their sympathy, "because [he] didn't need it," but heartily congratulated him "that it took that damnable lie so long to get dressed up and get on the tongues of its worshipers" and that he had so "indelibly stamped [his] Christian Life into the hearts of the real men and women of this country that it could not harm [him]."[43]

Another letter came all the way from Athens, Georgia, from an A. E. Berry. Joseph had helped him when Berry was a student at Wilberforce by allowing him to preach at Bethel, Detroit, and by taking up an offering for him. Berry said he was pained to hear Joseph was being sued. "You are a perfect Christian Gentleman. It is a trick of the devil to halt your progress. For it is my prayer that in '36 you will be elected as one of the Bishops of our Church." He hoped that Joseph's faith would not fail.[44]

The real motive behind Morant's charges can only be surmised. Perhaps, as Joseph guessed, they were politically inspired. They may have been motivated by jealously; many women found Joseph attractive. Some even alleged that Vernon might have been behind the entire plot. Morant evidently dropped the charges, or the court threw the case out; at any rate, nothing else can be found about the case. Like so many rumors, it died as other news took over the headlines—but not before the harm had been done.

The Missouri Annual Conference was held at St. Paul, November 6–10, 1935 with Joseph acting as host pastor, as scheduled. On the second day the election of ministerial delegates to the 1936 General Conference were held, with the following results: Gomez sixty-one votes, Burnette (presiding elder) fifty-two, Jonathan A. Dames (pastor of St. James) forty-nine, R. L. Phillips (pastor of Wayman Temple) forty-nine, and S. R. Stanley, forty-one. Bishop Ransom assisted Bishop Gregg during the conference and preached the ordination sermon for the new elders. Joseph was glad to greet again his classmate, the still-stylish A. Wayman Ward, who brought greetings from the Chicago Conference.[45]

Burnette's presiding elder's report was, as usual, highly complimentary of the work Joseph had done at St. Paul during the year. Burnette recognized Joseph as "a great civic leader and high churchman, who justly deserv[ed] to be elevated as one of the Bishops." On the last day of the conference a motion was made and unanimously passed to "give a vote of confidence to Dr. Gomez, and reaffirm [the conference's] faith in his integrity."[46] This was the ministers' way of letting Joseph know they did not believe Morant's charges and that he still had their support.

During December and January Joseph had two important speaking engagements. On December 31, he was the guest speaker for the Kappa Alpha Psi Fraternity's twenty-fifth (silver) anniversary, in St. Louis. He spoke on the subject "Unsafe Deliverance," emphasizing faith as defined by the writer of Hebrews as "the substance of things hoped for, the evidence of things not seen." He said that in this day the world needed "the kind of leadership that, when necessary, will refuse deliverance." He deplored the ease with which individuals "put themselves beyond the sphere of community service; choose the path of quick money, popular favor, fakish maneuvers and ungodly manipulations in an effort to gain success."[47]

On January 12, 1936, he was the guest speaker at Fisk University in Nashville, Tennessee. This time, speaking on the topic "The Menace of Cynicism," he stated he was ready to declare war on cynicism. "We can never hope to cure depression and to have peace, until we have, in a measure, stilled the cynic. This fellow is not to be confused with the intellectual skeptic, nor with the infidel as such. These admit of some discussion, research and analysis. The skeptic has a closed mind, disdains man, knows all, sees all and is all." He repeated much of this address the next day, to the students of Tennessee Agricultural and Industrial College. To him it was important that these young people start out with the attitude that all things are possible. Even if they did not reach nirvana they would at least have made an attempt, and that in essence was what life was all about—the striving. "To look forward to nothing, dream of nothing, hope for nothing, is death of the spirit," he declared. "Civilization cannot be advanced on the backs of dead spirits."[48] The fight against cynicism, then, was a fight for life itself. If Joseph had become bitter as a result of the Morant incident, none of it is reflected in his sermons or speeches through the winter and spring of 1936.

The thirtieth Quadrennial Session of the General Conference was held at Rockland Palace in New York City between May 6 and 18. At the opening session, the delegates gathered to hear Bishop Reverdy C. Ransom deliver the Quadrennial Address, on the subject "The Church That Shall Survive," based on Exodus 14:15—"Speak unto the children of Israel that they go forward." One of the questions he posed was, "How may the Negro Church survive as a thing apart?" If it continued to copy the programs and practices of the white Christians, it had little chance of surviving: "The Church that shall survive must know neither race, color, nor nationality; or recognize distinctions of wealth, class or station, but only the dignity and sacredness of our common humanity."[49]

One of the more contentious episodes of the conference involved Ira T. Bryant, secretary-treasurer of the A.M.E. Sunday School Union. A General Officer, he had also been elected a delegate from an electoral college in one of the Tennessee conferences. This gave him two votes at the conference; one of the ministers pointed out that by law only one vote was permitted each delegate. Bryant's troubles did not end there. During a presentation by the Committee on the Sunday School Union, a minority report was read by Rev. P. E. Womack of Texas accusing Bryant of mismanaging funds, in that he had loaned money to other departments instead of using the money for the efficient running of the Sunday School Union. When it came time to vote for the Secretary of the Sunday School Union, Bryant was replaced by E. C. Selby, who received 436 votes to his own 363. For years to come the Church would be forced to fight legal battles with Bryant, who refused to give up his office and his records.[50]

Other important legislation under consideration was the question of whether or not laymen on the Episcopal Committee could be appointed to the Judiciary Committee, which tried cases involving bishops. The Discipline (that is, Church regulations) made it clear that bishops could be tried only by elders. It was finally decided that laymen could not serve on the Judiciary Committee but could vote on the recommendations of the Judiciary Committee. Women did not fare as well: the conference voted that the ordination of women be tabled. On the other hand, Bishop Sims, whose character had been questioned by some ministers because of his recent divorce, was exonerated.[51] Joseph voted for most of the legislation passed, except that which denied women the right of ordination.

On May 14, at the afternoon session, Joseph listened attentively as Bishop Ransom read a letter from President Roosevelt, who wrote that he was familiar with the A.M.E. Church, comparing its progress with "the long stride forward . . . being made by the African Negro community." He was especially interested in the democracy and devotion to education of the Church, as exemplified by the numerous schools and by the book concern that had been established. The 945 delegates in attendance at the General Conference made this "the largest delegated Negro assembly in the world," he noted, and the eleven million dollars raised in the last twenty-four years indicated that the Church was on sound financial grounds. Roosevelt had sent as his representative the Honorable Daniel C. Roper, secretary of commerce.[52]

The election of bishops took place on May 15; two bishops were to be elected. The number of votes to be cast on the first ballot was 940; 463 were needed for election. R. R. Wright, president of Wilberforce University, received 285 votes, E. J. Howard 136, J. L. Butler 128, and Joseph Gomez 88. These were the leading contenders of the over forty people who ran. The pattern continued on the second ballot: Wright 367 votes, Howard 192, Butler 134, and Gomez 107. Still no one had been elected. On the third ballot, Wright received 524 votes and was finally elected; Howard received 371, Butler 199, Gomez 133, and Reid 129. At this point Gomez and Reid withdrew from the race, because it seemed certain they could not beat Howard. On the fourth ballot, E. J. Howard was elected with 619 votes.[53] Ransom consoled Joseph by pointing out how well he had run, given the number of candidates, and assuring him that his time would come. Even though he had fought hard, Joseph was not very disappointed, in light of the controversies in which he had been involved the past four years. He was, however, determined to try again at the next General Conference.

Joseph hurriedly left the General Conference to attend the annual meeting of the St. Louis Ministerial Alliance, held at Eden Theological Seminary. There, much to his surprise, he was elected the first Black vice president for the ensuing year. According to the *Argus,* "the selection of Rev. Gomez [was] regarded with a deal of significance due to the fact that Negro ministers have only been members of the alliance about a year. The Federation of Churches, a separate body whose membership is based on denominational representation, has not seen fit to admit Negro churches."[54]

As it turned out, Joseph was only to serve as vice president for a few months. Sometime in June, Bishop Ransom asked Joseph if he would consider an assignment in the Third Episcopal District, at St. James A.M.E. Church, Cleveland, since the former pastor, D. O. Walker, had been elected president of Wilberforce University at the last Trustee Board meeting. He and Hazel gave a great deal of consideration to the offer; their decision was published in the *Argus* on September 25, 1936: "After weeks of serious study of the situation relative to my candidacy for the bishopric in my Church, and after intense consultation with friends and advisers both here and at large, I have decided to accept the invitation of Bishop R. C. Ransom." Joseph would be reporting for duty in Cleveland the following week. "I go to serve under one who has been through the years my father in the ministry, and has made the largest single contribution to my success," he explained. He assured the people of St. Louis that he had no other motive "than that which center[ed] around the question of the advantage of [his] candidacy" for the bishopric, and that while in St. Louis he had pastored "one of the finest congregations . . . and found the people of St. Louis [to be] among the most responsive." He invited all the members to attend church next Sunday so he could say goodbye.[55]

The *Argus* listed Joseph's accomplishments in St. Louis. They included his being one of the first Blacks to receive a master's from Eden Seminary; being one of the leaders in a movement that resulted in recognition of Negro ministers by the Ministerial Alliance of Greater St. Louis; his election as first vice president of the organization; service on all the interracial commissions of the city; activity in the YMCA; and service as vice president and then as member of the Executive Board of Peoples' Hospital. The reporter also noted that Hazel had been active in work among the young people of St. Paul, a member of the Missionary Society and YWCA, and a member of the Board of Management of the Phillis Wheatley Association and chairman of its Camp Committee.[56]

Armed with numerous gifts, best wishes, and resolutions from the church and from city organizations, the Gomezes left on September 28 for the Buckeye State, where Joseph at long last would be working under his mentor and friend, Bishop Reverdy Cassius Ransom, and where they would be united again with Emma Ransom and with the place where it had all started for them, Wilberforce University.

◈ ◈ ◈

CHAPTER EIGHT

Incendiary Specters

Cleveland, 1936–1944

We [must] have mutual respect and affection. We can build a
common line of defense to meet the onslaught of the sworn enemies of religions who, under the guise of racialism and nationalism, would destroy not only the democracy we know and love,
but the religious impulse upon which the democracy was built and
upon which it now rests. As the light fades in Europe, may there
be a growing vision for a larger and more comprehensive definition of our common heritage.

—Joseph Gomez, Conference on Judaism,
January 14, 1940

◈ On October 4, 1936, the last day of the North Ohio Annual Conference,
Bishop Ransom officially appointed Joseph to St. James A.M.E. Church,
Cleveland, Ohio.[1] Located at 8401 Cedar Avenue in the all-Negro Cedar-
Central area of the city, St. James was the second-largest church in the
district. From 55th to 105th streets, Cedar was lined with churches, bars,
funeral parlors, restaurants, drugstores, gas stations and other small businesses; the numbered side streets were largely residential. People who lived
on these streets looked upon St. James as more than a place of worship. It
was a community center where they praised God, worked, played, engaged
in the arts and in political and social debates, were married and buried. Its
membership included the little old deaconess seated on the front row who
could barely read or write, and the Ph.D. who thought it fashionable to sit
in the rear of the sanctuary or in the balcony on Sunday mornings. Unlike
at St. Paul, the congregation's "joyful noise unto the Lord" was confined
to an occasional hearty "Amen."

The building had been bought from Trinity Congregational Church in 1926, when whites were fleeing the inner city.[2] At the time it was considered to be one of the finest structures of its kind. Its stone walls were thickly covered with ivy, and in front was a multicolored stained glass window of "the Good Shepherd." At the feet of the Good Shepherd children of different nationalities frolicked with young lambs. To the community the window symbolized hope and the kind of peace that was sure to accompany integration when it was fully realized. Inside, the main sanctuary was spacious and could be made even larger by opening the doors that led to the Sunday school assembly room. The extra space was always needed on Easter, Thanksgiving, Christmas, and conference days. Above the choir loft, the golden pipes of the organ vibrated on Sunday mornings to the touch of Kathleen Holland Forbes, Joseph's former organist from Ontario, who had moved to Cleveland some years before with her husband, Louie.

Much of St. James's prestige in the larger community was the result of the Literary Forum, founded by Rev. D. Ormande Walker, the former pastor. Every Sunday at 4 P.M. prominent local, state, and national figures of all races, creeds, and political persuasions spoke there, addressing themselves to the burning issues of the day.[3] Anyone arriving a few minutes after four might well have to stand, even if the Sunday school assembly doors were open.

Walker, also a West Indian, was a personality Joseph would have difficulty replacing. He was bright, handsome, highly political, controversial, and a dynamic speaker, qualities which endeared him to the members of St. James and now qualified him for his new position as president of Wilberforce University.

The parsonage was just around the corner from the church, at 2184 East 85th Street. The Gomezes' first impression was that everything, including the front porch, was sinking sideways. The carpet had more holes than carpet should, the kitchen was obsolete, the basement leaked, and the furniture was barely functional. The girls discovered that by jumping through a hole in the attic they could land in a bedroom closet; they thought this great fun until Hazel made them stop—she could see no humor in the situation. She wondered why it was always their luck to inherit the most rundown parsonages. At least they did not have to move in right away; while the trustees were trying one more time to fix it up, the Gomezes would be living with the Forbeses. Eula and Annetta would take piano lessons from Kathleen Forbes.

A few days after their arrival in Cleveland, the girls were enrolled in Bolton Elementary School. The grayness of the Ohio fall matched their mood. They had not wanted to leave St. Louis and were finding it increasingly difficult to be uprooted as they grew older. The ten-year-old Eula was placed in the sixth grade, the eight-year-old Annetta in the third. Bolton Elementary was located on 89th Street across from Antioch Baptist Church, where the prominent Rev. Wade Hampton McKinney pastored one of the largest Black congregations in the city. (His sons, Hampton and Samuel, were to become good friends of the Gomez girls.) As soon as the children were settled, Hazel became active in the PTA, where through the years she held positions of leadership. She also immediately became involved with the young people's programs at the church, the Missionary Society, the Ministers' Wives Organization, and the YWCA. Her most prized involvement was with her young men's Sunday school class, which at one time numbered one hundred students between the ages of twenty-one and thirty-five.

For Joseph, pastoring St. James entailed heavy involvement in civic affairs. For example, he was called upon to assist in getting paroles for deserving men and women and to find jobs for them after they were released from prison. In addition, he worked with the neighborhood groups who were trying to secure public housing for the homeless and were petitioning the Cleveland Board of Education to improve and integrate inner-city schools. Prior to World War I most schools in Cleveland had been integrated, but by the early 1930s, the Board of Education [began] to enforce segregation by "artificial means." One of the schools affected had been Central High School.[4]

In March of 1937, Joseph joined the fight to change conditions at now all-black Central High School. As early as 1933 parents had complained that most Negro children on the East Side were being forced to attend Central, while white students who lived in that district were given special transfers.[5] They were concerned about the inadequate education their children were receiving and noted that the emphasis was gradually being shifted from liberal arts to vocational training. Equipment was scant, and books scarce. Test scores were down. Many students read below their grade level.[6]

As a means of appeasement, the board superintendent asked the principal, P. M. Watson, a white man, to select and head a committee to evaluate the program and make suggestions for changes in the school. When the subject of the committee was raised at one of the St. James Literary Forum meetings, Joseph openly criticized the committee, which he said was evaluating itself. Watson was furious when told what Joseph had said, and he demanded an explanation.

Joseph sent his explanation in the form of an open letter. In it he asked how a committee organized by Watson, "meeting always at the Central High School building" and always subject to his presence, personality, and approach to the problems, could make an objective evaluation of the school. He reminded Watson that "the Board of Education [had] absolute power to change" the prevailing conditions if it chose to. Watson, as principal, was a "paid servant of that board and [was] responsible to it in the carrying out of its policies." How then could he be effective in his research and recommendations? He did not question Watson's honesty or earnestness; it was just that the way the committee had been set up made a thorough investigation impossible. Joseph regarded the "Central High School problem and the school system generally as it affects Negroes, [to be] one of the three major problems of the race in Cleveland." There seemed to be a definite shift toward segregation, which could only be solved by redistricting the entire system. "Experience has taught us," he said, "that a school inevitably suffers *in most vital considerations* where the students are all Negroes or predominantly so."[7]

He pointed out that redistricting was not new to the board, since it had already done this in the case of vocational schools.[8] In principle, Joseph was not against an all-Negro school, but in America anything whites provided separately for Blacks was always vastly unequal; seemingly, therefore, the only way to ensure equality of education in the public schools was to integrate them. (In 1954 the U.S. Supreme Court unanimously accepted this view in its decision *Brown vs. the Board of Education of Topeka.*) On the other hand, universities like Wilberforce, which had been *created by Negroes,* provided an opportunity for higher education which many Negroes would have been denied due to segregation or the high cost of tuition in many white institutions. They gave Negroes a knowledge of their heritage, developed in them a sense of self, and urged them to return to the Black community the knowledge they had been fortunate enough to gain.

Joseph heard these same ideas expressed by D. O. Walker when he was officially installed as president of Wilberforce on March 18, 1937. In his address Walker admitted that Wilberforce may not have had an "extensive array of costly buildings . . . [or] expensive laboratory equipment," but he declared that it more than compensated for these physical limitations by the quality of its graduates and the service they "render to society." That Wilberforce "is owned and controlled by black men gives a measure of pride that perhaps cannot be felt on any other campus in the world. Here black men have prayed to build a heritage for the race," he told his audience.[9] It is interesting to note that Walker frequently used the word "Black," as early as 1937.

When Walker had finished speaking, Bishop Gregg announced another honor that had come to a Wilberforcean. Bishop Ransom had been appointed to the Ohio Parole Board for a three-and-a-half year term by Governor Martin L. Davey. As the *Cleveland Call and Post*, the leading Negro newspaper in the city, put it, Ransom, "the Dean of the Negro Democrats in the State," had received the most prestigious appointment of any Black in Ohio.[10] (On behalf of the St. James Literary Forum, Joseph would send a letter to the governor commending him for appointing Ransom.)[11]

Throughout the spring and summer of 1937 Joseph was in demand as a speaker, making appearances at the Old Stone Church in Cleveland, the YMCA in Toledo, and the Sesquicentennial Festival of Negro Methodism in Memphis.[12]

In August, Charles S. Spivey, who had been appointed dean of Payne Seminary at Wilberforce, asked Joseph if he would consider teaching courses at the seminary. Joseph replied that both he and Hazel felt he should "help in this [Spivey's] first year of service." However, a full schedule of speeches and conferences meant he could teach only on Mondays the first semester, and on Tuesdays the second.[13] During the years he lectured at Payne (1937–39) and later at Oberlin Seminary (1940–42), he found that he was at home in the classroom, especially with young ministers. He often said if he had not gone into the ministry he would have enjoyed being a teacher. The trips back and forth to Wilberforce were tedious, especially during the winter months, but to him they were worth it. In addition they gave him more opportunity to visit Ransom, who lived at Tawawa Chimney Corner on the campus, a large rambling house considered to be one of the landmarks of Wilberforce.

In September 1937 Ransom returned from a World Conference of Churches in England in time to hold the North Ohio Annual Conference in Akron, Ohio. Following the opening worship service he told the conference that Governor Davey had received much criticism for appointing him, a Negro, to the Parole Board. This made Ransom's sense of responsibility even greater. "I want to so conduct myself that I shall make a place for some young man to assume the position in the future," he said. He reiterated a familiar theme of his by reminding the elders, "You cannot help out people by just standing in the pulpit; you must reach out in various lines of activities. I know some of you think everything I do is motivated by politics." Some of the ministers, he scolded, had even accused him of appointing Joseph Gomez to St. James as a political move. To this accusation he replied that he had looked for the best man he could find to succeed D. O. Walker, one who could also be elected to the bishopric. He reminded them that Joseph had been fourth in the race for bishop at the last General

Conference. "What kind of leadership do you want?" he asked. "You know what some of the Bishops on the bench are like now."[14] With Joseph, he believed, the Church would have excellent leadership.

On October 25, at Tawawa Chimney Corner, the district gave a celebration in honor of Bishop and Mrs. Ransom's fiftieth wedding anniversary. In addition to A.M.E.s from all over the district and Connection, Ransom's children and grandchildren were in attendance.[15] Joseph and Hazel watched as Reverdy in a conservative black suit and Emma in a gold lace gown marched toward an altar lighted with fifty golden candles and decorated with white roses and white and yellow chrysanthemums. As they processed down the aisle, a harp played the "Wedding March." Ransom responded to the ceremony's testimonial speeches by reading an original poem he had written for the occasion.[16] Hazel and Joseph were to remember this experience when they celebrated their own golden anniversary years later.

In addition to the many activities in which the Gomezes were involved in 1937, there was an increase in their family's size. Some time in the fall Frankie Crawford, a classmate of Hazel's, and her granddaughter (Evy) Dolly Gordon came to live in the parsonage. Dolly's mother had been confined in a tuberculosis sanitarium, and Dolly was being raised by her grandmother until her mother could be released. Eula and Annetta found Frankie amusing, especially when she clicked her false teeth in an attempt to be proper; Dolly, however, they learned to love as a younger sister. She resembled her nickname in that she had long curls that fell almost to her waist, like a mama doll in the toy store window, and she was tiny and shy. At first she cried a lot, perhaps because she missed her mother; by the time the Christmas holidays came around, however, she had become an integral part of the family and no longer seemed sad. Dolly and Frankie were to live with the Gomezes for about three years.

A little after 2 A.M. on January 2 of the new year (1938), the entire household was awakened by an insistent pounding on the front door. Hazel put on her robe and went downstairs. By the time Joseph reached the landing she was standing at the foot of the stairs with a strange expression on her face. "The church is on fire," she said, too shocked to show any emotion. Frankie and the children had reached the landing, and when they heard what Hazel said they scrambled to their rooms to dress.

When Joseph reached the corner of 85th Street he could see angry red flames coming from the roof of the church. Cedar Avenue was a grotesque painting, replete with red, contorted faces, spectators, ominous smoke clouds, and firemen with snakelike hoses that uncoiled on the sidewalk and kept springing leaks. It was a full thirty minutes after the arrival of the firemen that they were able to put their hoses into operation. Meanwhile the roof collapsed, but luckily no one was injured. Somebody said everything would be all right as long as the stained-glass window held; at these words, what sounded like a blast of wind hit the window. Sharp fragments of glass spattered in every direction, leaving a dark hole where "The Good Shepherd" had stood. The sight of the jagged shreds of colored glass was too much for most of the people, and they turned and went home, leaving only the firemen, the Gomezes, and a few members and reporters at the scene.

Joseph told the reporter from the *Cleveland Plain Dealer* that he believed "the roof and much of the structure would have been saved if the hose had been put into action sooner and if there had been better equipment on hand. This certainly is an argument for better equipment for the Cleveland Fire Department."[17] The fire had been discovered by Jessie Charlotte Hill of 2123 East 83rd Street, a choir member, who was returning from visiting friends when she saw smoke coming from the church. She had immediately called the fire department, which had sent out three alarms that were answered almost at once by ten fire departments. "That many firemen should have been able to control the fire," Joseph reasoned.[18]

He stayed until the last of the smoldering fire had been extinguished and then returned to the parsonage to ascertain where the Sunday morning services could be held. News of the fire had spread rapidly by word of mouth and by radio. The telephone in the parsonage rang continuously with people wanting to help. Before Joseph had time to make plans, the Phyllis Wheatley Association called and offered him the use of its auditorium.

Some hours later, Joseph started out of the parsonage door, his face still streaked with soot and tears. Upstairs, Hazel was crying in her room. Eula and Dolly were huddled together in a corner; Frankie was nowhere to be seen. Annetta took Joseph's hand, and they returned to the ruins together. She was frightened. Never before had she seen her father like this. He was the strong one who always told them what to do—always made a joke when things went wrong. Now he said nothing. They walked through what had been the sanctuary, carefully stepping over the organ keys, scattered like so many false teeth. When they reached the Sunday School Assembly Room, only one beam was left standing; around it hung a banner left by the Primary Department. As they moved closer, they were able to make out the words "He Will Not Forsake Thee." Joseph stood for a long time staring at the sign, then took it down and moved on. Here and there they found hymnals that were still useable despite the water damage. They gathered as many as they could carry and took them home along with the banner.

Later that morning, when the Gomezes arrived at the Phyllis Wheatley Association on 44th and Cedar Avenue, the auditorium was filled with expectant and confused people who wanted to know what was to be done now that their church was gone. Joseph described as best he could the events of the early morning. The more he talked, the gloomier seemed the faces in front of him, until he came to the part about finding the banner. "Sometimes in the midst of destruction, God manifests himself most clearly. It's when we have tried all of our own devices and are up against the wall—when we have to be still and listen, that we hear the reassuring voice that lets us know that He is there. He will not forsake us. We are going to rebuild St. James—a new, modern structure—better than the old. Offers are coming from all sections and from all people. . . . Ministers in the city have offered their assistance. We are not alone."[19]

During the following week the Cultural Arts Studio across the street from St. James offered space for a church office; the Angelus Funeral Home next door expressed its willingness to let the church use some of its facilities for meeting rooms; and the Seventh-Day Adventist Church on 79th and Cedar invited the congregation to worship there on Sundays until St. James was rebuilt.[20] Promises of support came from Mayor Harold H. Burton and Governor Davey. City leaders formed a Citizens Committee to initiate a building campaign. Daily contributions came from organizations and individuals. President D. O. Walker of Wilberforce sent a personal check for $500, and Glenn T. Settles, director of the popular Wings over Jordan choir, offered to give a benefit concert at Antioch Baptist Church for the building fund.[21]

The Citizens Committee had its first meeting on February 11. Leaders of civic, religious, and political groups headed fifty teams of four hundred members each to raise $100,000, $60,000 of it to be collected between February 21 and March 7. Dr. Franklin D. Butchart, associate secretary of the Cleveland Church Federation, pledged to make the campaign a Federation priority. Other speakers were Professor Charles Devitt Ryan of John Carroll University; Sheriff Martin L. O'Donnell; William R. Connors, executive secretary of the Negro Welfare Association; Daniel E. Morgan, honorary chairman of the Citizens Committee; and the acting chairman, Perry B. Jackson, an attorney who was also a devoted member of St. James.[22]

As their contribution to the campaign over 75 percent of the members of St. James promised to tithe, and the leading newspapers ran editorials soliciting donations, by reminding Clevelanders how important St. James was to the greater community. The *Cleveland News* of February 24 referred to the church as the "center of spiritual activity and civic ferment in Cleveland" and said that the "St. James Forum had served for 11 years as a sounding board for the continuous discussion of public affairs by some of the ablest men in this city and in the nation, both white and Negro."[23]

Taking time from the building campaign to observe the lenten season, once again Joseph preached at the Old Stone Church. This time his text was the Third Last Word of Christ: "Woman! Behold thy son. Son! Behold thy mother." He told the audience, "Here may be discovered the deepest meanings of the Kingdom which [Christ] came to establish. . . . The Kingdom of Christ was and still is the Kingdom of the inner life. . . . Sonship meant more than ties of blood or proximity of domicile. Motherhood meant more than the claims of nature." Thinking about his own mother, he assured his audience that "two may be separated by lands and oceans and yet be connected by a cable of love upon which may come constant messages of trust and affection, undisturbed by distance or fate." The "understanding genius of motherhood" could also belong to the childless. "World motherhood and sonship rest their cause in deeper roots of spiritual understanding." Though Joseph had had so little time to spend with his mother and seldom spoke of her now, still he missed her greatly and always felt her presence, especially during the crises of his life.[24]

Prior to the July 3 cornerstone-laying ceremonies for the new building, Joseph and some of the trustees removed the old stone and, much to their surprise, found some papers carefully concealed behind it: the *Scholar's Quarterly* for April–May–June 1926; minutes of the fifty-second annual session of the Northern Ohio Sunday School Institute, July 21–15, 1925; and a copy of the *Cleveland Call,* predecessor of the *Call and Post,* dated May 16, 1926. Its headlines read, "Dr. Sweet Is Acquitted."[25] The article concerning Sweet reminded Joseph of his turbulent days in Detroit building Greater Bethel, and of the faithfulness of the members who helped him realize his dreams. Part of that drama was being replayed in Cleveland.

When the cornerstone laying took place a week later, the *Pittsburgh Courier* called it "a colorful scene." The carpenters had built a platform in front of the church for the occasion. Those seated on it "could see a sea of faces that ran for blocks." On hand were the Salvation Army Band with its marches and religious songs, the Masons, Elks, and the Boy Scouts, all sporting their crisp uniforms.[26]

The procession had begun at East 55th and Central and continued until it reached St. James at 85th and Cedar. All traffic in the area had been rerouted, and WGAR, a radio station, was on hand to broadcast the first half hour, which began with the singing of "O God, Our Help in Ages Past," followed by an address by Mayor Burton. Joseph C. Bowman, Black candidate for the Ohio Supreme Court, brought greetings from Governor

Davey.[27] President D. O. Walker of Wilberforce delivered the keynote address, and Councilman Harold T. Gassaway read a resolution from the City Council which "hailed St. James and its leadership as a great community value, and [called] upon the citizens of Cleveland for financial assistance in the rebuilding program."[28] The new cornerstone was then ceremoniously put in place by the Masons.

Up to this point the building program had been moving along smoothly, but in July a committee from the predominantly Black Association of Building Trades Craftsmen met and "urged that the citizenry cease to pay for and support discrimination." They charged Joseph with failing to include in the rebuilding contract a clause that would guarantee the employment of skilled Negro mechanics. Joseph had tried to find a Negro contractor able to finance the rebuilding or to raise sufficient money to superintend the rebuilding, but had been unable to do so. Anxious to get started, the trustees had accepted the best bid they could get. None of the companies who had bid were willing to put such a clause in their contract, because it would make them responsible for all subcontractors. However, the company finally chosen promised to hire a large percentage of Blacks, skilled and unskilled. At first this was not satisfactory to the craftsmen, who insisted on the clause. Arguments pro and con, accusations and denials were aired in meetings and the newspapers for several weeks before the church and the Association were satisfied.[29]

Months later Joseph was able to say with pride that the entire job had been done by Negroes. But at the time of the controversy he was terribly upset at being accused of discrimination against his own people. Wrongly or not, he had accepted the word of the construction company that many Blacks would be hired, even though the company refused to include a clause to that effect in the contract. The injustice of the accusations stung Joseph for a long time. In fact the only positive news that July was his appointment to the Wilberforce State Board of Trustees for a term that was to begin at once and end June 30, 1943.

Joseph preached the annual sermon at the North Ohio Annual Conference held that year in Piqua, Ohio, September 28 through October 2. The conference minutes describe the sermon as "doctrinal, philosophical and evangelical." Dr. Archie Nichols, pastor of the First Methodist Episcopal Church of Piqua, who welcomed the conference to the city on behalf of the Ministerial Association, invited Joseph to give the same sermon in his church the following Sunday morning. Additionally, the pastor of the First United Brethren Church asked him to preach to his congregation that same Sunday evening.[30]

Among the many guests introduced to the conference were Dr. Gilbert H. Jones, vice president of Wilberforce University, and Mrs. Mills Jackson, mother of the famous Mills Brothers singers. After the delegates expressed their pleasure at having such distinguished guests, Joseph read a resolution once again asking for the organic union of the A.M.E., A.M.E. Zion, and Colored Methodist Episcopal churches. Bishop Ransom urged him to send a copy of the resolution to the *Pittsburgh Courier*. Other important business of the conference was the endorsement of Revs. A. J. Allen and Joseph Gomez for the bishopric at the 1940 General Conference.[31]

Progress had been made so rapidly on the construction of the new building that in December Joseph announced the congregation would move back to St. James on Christmas Day. There they would worship in the unfinished sanctuary until the Sunday school auditorium was available, when they would move into the Sunday school room until the sanctuary was completely finished. It seemed symbolically important to him that not quite one year after the church had burned to the ground, the congregation would return to its site.

One of Joseph's closest friends during the rebuilding period and his several bids for the bishopric was Rev. George T. Singleton, editor of the *Christian Recorder*, a leading Church publication. He was a short, ebony man with remarkable energy; Eula and Annetta had liked him immediately. They loved to hear him sing to them, "I love my doggie, my doggie loves me. I carry my doggie on a rainbow tree," even though they had no idea what the words meant. When Singleton visited it was fun time for the entire household. Even Frankie would stop clicking her teeth and join in the games.

The two men shared their joys and their problems. Singleton was having trouble keeping the *Christian Recorder* afloat on an extremely limited budget and with little help. Joseph for his part found it difficult to keep the building funds coming in and also maintain some kind of campaign for the bishopric. On February 1, 1939, having talked to Singleton by telephone a few days before, Joseph wrote, "I can well appreciate some of the problems you have had this past year. But you must be comforted by the same thought that has comforted me, to wit: that this may be one of the means of fashioning us for the greater task ahead." He spoke of his travels through the South in his campaign for the bishopric, realizing that without southern support, he could not be elected. "During the next 12 months, I must build and build fast."[32] Despite all the activities associated with the building program, the General Conference was never far from his thoughts.

In many ways the Cleveland years were family years. There Eula and Annetta developed from childhood to teen age to womanhood. Joseph did not have a great deal of time to spend with his daughters, but when he was with them they cherished his company. Joseph continued to manifest his wonderful sense of humor, to the horror of Hazel, by playing pranks. He was generous to a fault with his money, and his daughters knew where to go when they needed some extra change. He was warm and outgoing, dramatic and passionate, and thrived on outward shows of affection. This suited Annetta, who was in many ways like her father. Eula, on the other hand, was more private and often found it difficult to communicate her affection to this father she loved. Instead of kissing and hugging she tried to please him by always being the best in what she did, but she often felt that this was not enough. When she was in the seventh grade he took away her privileges for bringing home a C in mathematics. Feeling she had somehow failed her father, Eula became so distraught that the doctor had to put her in bed for two weeks. The incident so frightened Joseph that that was the last time he ever reprimanded her about her grades. Eula was more comfortable with Hazel, who understood her far more than she did her younger, demonstrative daughter, who was always in defiance of some rule.

In many ways Joseph was strict, in others excessively liberal. The girls could not date until they were seniors in high school, and then they had to be home by midnight. Drinking and smoking were out of the question. Only through the intervention of Hazel were they allowed to dance in the parsonage at their birthday parties. On the other hand, Joseph could never bring himself to spank his daughters, regardless of the infraction. Physical punishment was always left to Hazel, just as Emanuel had left it to Rebecca, his mother. Eula, now a senior at Fairmount Junior High School and an honor student, rarely needed scolding. She loved the old school building and her favorite teachers, Mrs. Potee and Mrs. Folee. She studied hard and practiced her cello and singing without prompting. Annetta was totally undisciplined when it came to her homework or practicing the violin. (She had begged for the violin so that she would no longer have to practice the piano. Another incentive was the handsome Everett Lee, her violin teacher, who she said looked like the actor Tyrone Power; Everett later became director of the Sweden Symphony Orchestra and the New World Symphony in New York.)

It was not easy being P.K.s (preacher's kids). The church members expected them always to exemplify the most proper behavior and were quick to tattle if they did not. In spite of such problems the girls were basically happy, because of the love and support they found in their home. Birthdays and holidays were not only times for family togetherness but also when friends were invited to share the festivities. Whenever the girls appeared on any kind of program, Joseph and Hazel were in evidence in the front row, cheering them on no matter how amateurish the performance. But there was a great deal of unspoken pressure to succeed. Both parents made it clear that their daughters had had more advantages than most Negroes and therefore had an obligation to give something back—to make a contribution, to be somebody. Eula and Annetta and their own children found this later on to be both a blessing and curse. It is the blessing and burden of the Negro middle class: that nobody feels that it is enough to be average; if a person is average, she or he has to endure the guilt of not living up to expectations—of letting down their relatives, themselves, and the race.

Both girls inherited their parents' affection for the arts. There was always a much-used piano in the house; there were records of all sorts, volumes of poetry from which Joseph liked to read to the family, and frequent trips to concerts and plays. It was discovered early that Eula loved to sing and had a beautiful voice. She was enrolled in the Cleveland Music School Settlement and later the Cleveland Institute of Music. Annetta loved to paint in oils and to act. She was always on stage, real or imagined.

The girls had acquired many close friends since coming to Cleveland. Some belonged to the church, others they had met at school. Eula's best friend was Jane Lee Darr; as a baby she had been given by her mother to Miss Bertha Blue, an unmarried elementary school teacher whose fiancee had died on the day they were to be married. (After placing Jane in the care of Miss Blue [known as Aunt Bee], Jane's mother had moved to New York and passed for white.) Jane was a loyal friend, warm, and so idealistic that she often seemed to be living in another world. To the Gomezes, she was family. Eula's other girlfriends included Erylene Poindexter, whose mother was superintendent of the Primary Sunday School Department; Helen Vance, whose mother had gone to school with Hazel; the brilliant Doris Brown; and the cheerful Beatrice Phillips.

Gwendolyn Poindexter (Erylene's sister), Fanny Pierce, Elaine and Ethylene Patton (who lived down the street from the parsonage), and Patricia Marshall, a gifted pianist, were Annetta's close friends. Patricia was even more tomboyish than Annetta, and both were more comfortable with boys and boys' games than with girls and playing house. Patricia even went around in her brothers' shoes. She and Annetta pulled such tricks as picketing the Sunday school because they found it "boring," and hiding the shoes of the choir so they would have to march down the church aisles in stocking feet.

As long as the girls could remember, there had always been someone from the church who helped Hazel take care of them, since she was often as busy as Joseph with church work. The person they remembered most was Mae Basey, who lived down the street. Mae was full of life, loved to sing and tell riddles. She entertained the girls when Hazel was off with the Missionary Society, planning some activity for her young men's Sunday school class, or gone to a conference with Joseph. Hazel had also organized a children's choir and an orchestra, to which Eula, Annetta, Dolly, Jane, and Patricia belonged. As did most of the church members, the Gomezes spent more time at St. James than anywhere else, especially on Sundays, when there was some activity going on until around 10 P.M.

Sometimes the girls even went to the Literary Forum with their parents—as they did on Sunday, April 23, when people from all over the city came to observe Wilberforce Day and to celebrate the fact that Walker had been able to get the university accredited by the North Central Association of Secondary Schools and Colleges.[33] This was especially good news since it was expected that Eula and Annetta would attend Wilberforce when they completed high school.

Two months later, on June 4, the family went to hear Joseph deliver the Baccalaureate Sermon at Wilberforce. Standing in the same auditorium from which he had graduated twenty-five years ago, had been "ordained a minister, and took a life partner in marriage, he compared modern society to the historic message of Babel."[34] After acknowledging the accomplishments of contemporary civilization, he pointed out how just as people were about to translate these accomplishments into a moral and useful society, we had allowed pride to take over. With the impending war we had become "side-tracked, confused, destructive, and the 'Frankenstein' of our brain became an instrument of death to its creation." However, despite the "hell of a world that crucified righteousness, Daniel saw the vision of a better day, and John strolled the golden streets of a new world. This was not fancy, but vision." Thus he challenged the graduates to "dedicate heart and mind to the realization of the dream of ages for which others have yearned, sacrificed and died through the centuries, and toward which we have made progress despite our 'Babel.'"[35] When he finished, the graduates stood and applauded enthusiastically for several minutes.

June 18, 1939, marked the twenty-fifth year of Hazel and Joseph's marriage. The members of St. James gave them a wedding anniversary celebration in the church parlor. Congratulations from around the country were read, including a telegram from the Ransoms, who could not be present because the bishop was ill. A photograph shows Hazel in a lace gown and matching hat standing beside a plump Joseph, dressed in his traditional dark suit and tie. Both daughters wear large picture hats and heavily starched organdy dresses. Eula is taller than either of her parents.[36]

Sometime that summer the family moved from the parsonage on Cedar Avenue to 10925 Pasadena Avenue. Realizing the old house could not be patched up any longer, the trustees had taken out a mortgage on a new parsonage in the Glenville area, which was largely Jewish with a sprinkling of Black professionals. Glenville was in the middle stages of a familiar transition—from Jewish to Black.[37] In a few years it would be all Black and the expansive synagogues converted into Baptist and Methodist churches. The greatest attraction in the neighborhood was Glenville High School, which was rated second in the country academically. Eula, at fourteen, would attend there in the fall. Annetta would transfer from Fairmont Junior High School, which was being torn down, to Patrick Henry, a cold, fortress-like building which she came to hate.

The house on Pasadena was a vast improvement. The rooms were large; there was a sizeable front porch, back and front yards, and to Hazel's delight, a dry basement. Both schools were in walking distance. Most of Eula's friends transferred to Glenville with her; Annetta had to make new friends. She met Alice Hickman, Jackie and Maxine Lee, and Louise and Jean Curtis. Her best girlfriend was Cora Perry, an attractive young woman whom she nicknamed Candy. Cora was older than Annetta; by the time they were ready to attend Glenville High School she drove a Nash convertible, which kept slipping out of gear. She was the only person who ever dared to call Joseph "Pops" and get away with it. Eula and her friends organized a singing group, the Sepianitas; for a time Annetta belonged to the Wyonetes, a social club. Although the neighborhood took some getting used to—the chants on Saturdays from the nearby synagogues, the delicatessens with their pungent smell of kosher foods, the rabbis with their long robes, little round caps, and heavy accents—in time the family came to adjust. They did so despite the elitism of some of the Negroes, who, with their light skin and "good" hair, felt "they had arrived." Hazel and Joseph had warned the girls about such intraracial snobbery and discrimination, which they had not experienced in the old neighborhood.

Joseph had barely settled his family in the new house when it was time to attend the 1939 North Ohio Conference, which luckily was held at St. John, Cleveland. On the first day, Bishop Ransom recalled a time "when [he] was aspiring to be a Bishop, right in [that] very church." He then turned to the conference and affirmed that he was for Gomez and Alexander J. Allen, head of the American Bible Society, for the bishopric in 1940 and that he was going to vote for both men.[38]

When the election for ministerial delegates to the 1940 General Conference was held that afternoon, Joseph was elected with fifty-nine votes, J. Otis Haithcox of St. John with fifty-eight, and R. C. Ransom, Jr., with thirty-six. After the election, Eula delighted the delegates by singing "My Desire." The conference ended on Sunday with the bishop's sermon and the reading of the appointments. As expected, Joseph was returned to St. James.[39]

On November 8, Frank Steward, church editor of the *Cleveland Press,* attended the Sunday morning service at St. James; he wrote a feature article the following day. What he had seen as he sat in the unfinished auditorium were "bare rafters—uncovered steel girders—mortar—specked brick walls—rough, uneven floors—exposed plumbing—temporary pews." Then he told about the January 2, 1938, fire and the progress made in the rebuilding since. He mentioned the over one thousand members and described the various organizations of the church, commenting on their effectiveness. Joseph's sermon that morning, based on Jesus' temptations and entitled "Bread from Stones," had impressed him. Also, he noted, after the sermon there had been an announcement that candidates for mayor would be speaking at the afternoon forum. Steward concluded, "The 'comeback' of St. James almost places a dent in the idea that the age of miracles is past"; he advised his readers, "If you want to see friendliness in a church—just go visiting at St. James."[40]

During most of November and the first part of December, Joseph traveled to cities in the South on behalf of his candidacy. He returned in time to spend the holidays with the family in the new house. The peace of the Yuletide was broken in early January by a letter from Singleton stating that the *Christian Recorder* was in dire financial straits. Joseph suggested that he write a personal letter to "200 men whom [Singleton] and the Recorder [had] helped." He would send money, he said, "after the third Sunday when these good folks attempt to give me some salary after a lapse of six weeks during which time we [the church] have paid off some pressing bills."[41]

These were difficult times for both men. On many occasions Joseph had refused to accept a salary because some "pressing bill" at the church had to be paid. Hazel, who was attempting to put aside money for the girls' college tuition, found it impossible to do so under the circumstances. She had never met anyone who cared as little as Joseph about money. She also worried about him, because he had not been sleeping lately, his blood pressure was up, and he seemed to be exhausted all the time. Building the church was a full-time job in and of itself, and trying to run a campaign at the same time was impossible. Nevertheless, there was little she could do.

He had his heart set on accomplishing both. Given the prejudice against him by some ministers because of his West Indian background, his light skin, and northern orientation, she wondered if he would be elected and how another defeat would affect him.

On January 14, 1940, Josephy, as a representative of the Ministerial Association of Greater Cleveland, had an opportunity once again to strike a blow for ecumenism. The occasion was the Fifth Seminar of Judaism, a banquet held at the Euclid Avenue Temple in Cleveland in an attempt to bring about beter understanding among different religious groups. After acknowledging the contributions Judaism had made to the world throughout history, Joseph went directly to the core of his message. He said, "Perhaps for a long time to come, at least until mankind becomes more spiritually adult, we shall have a need for labels of distinctions, but these days demand that a basic religion shall have a common and compelling channel of expression." Such an examination, he said, "may lead to an abandonment of much of our smugness, and reveal our sectarian insularity." What would come to light is "some common religious connotations, the essential morality of religion," since throughout the ages religions have borrowed from one another. His final hope was that "as the light fades in Europe, there may be a growing vision for a larger and more comprehensive definition of our common heritage."[42]

Joseph often used the symbol of "the light fading in Europe" to describe what he believed was the inevitability of the growing European conflict that would decide once and for all whether the concept of equality or "Aryan superiority" would prevail. Meanwhile, there was the matter of the upcoming General Conference.

In February 1940 Joseph sent a letter to all of the delegates stating his philosophy concerning the episcopacy and asserting his qualification as a result of twenty-six years of active ministry. He saw the bishopric "not as an escape, but as an imprisonment such as was defined by Paul when he declared himself to be a prisoner of Jesus." The position would allow him to give greater service in the "direction of unifying the forces that shall help to make meaningful and workable the religion we preach."[43]

When Joseph attended the Bishops' Council the same month, he was alarmed to hear that the election for bishops might be fixed. A letter to George Singleton reflects his feelings at the time:

My dear George:
    What seems to be pretty good evidence has come to me that there is a well-laid scheme for that party about whom you wrote in your letter to buy the Bishopric. [No copy of Singleton's letter can be

found.] I cannot exactly say what that evidence is, but to me, it is fairly convincing. It is said that there are two of the leaders who are involved; the plan is to get Alabama and Georgia tied up, then to get [a] scattering [of] votes around different sections, and though they may fall short of the necessary amount to elect him, the rest can be easily gotten, the right man presiding. The thing is so diabolical that I could hardly believe it. It is difficult for me to believe it now, despite what I call evidence. . . . . It is unbelievable that such a thing could happen in our church. The same forces are to work, it is claimed, for other elections running down even to the general officers.[44]

In all likelihood, Joseph was referring to Rev. George Edward Curry, who reportedly told others after the 1940 General Conference that he had bought the election. Curry's underhandedness caught up with him finally. He was brought to trial in Tulsa, Oklahoma, in 1945 and suspended for mishandling Church funds. Restored by the Bishops' Council in June 1946, he was expelled again from the bishopric at an extra session of the General Conference in November of that year.

Prior to the General Conference there was also a dispute between Bishop Ransom and Rev. O. Haithcox of St. John, Cleveland. Ransom wanted the 3rd District to be united, first behind Gomez and secondly behind Alexander J. Allen of the American Bible Society. At first Haithcox wanted to run for bishop himself. Realizing he lacked sufficient support from the ministers and the bishop, and having a personal dislike for Gomez, he began a campaign for Allen in which he excluded Gomez from all consideration. More than likely Haithcox was jealous of the attention Joseph and St. James were receiving, particularly since St. John had been the city's first Black church (1830) and at one time its leading A.M.E. church. This was the climate prior to the Quadrennial.

Despite a freakish rain and snowstorm, the General Conference opened in Detroit on May 1 at Ebenezer A.M.E. Church. The delegates were welcomed by Governor Lauren D. Dickinson of Michigan. During the early sessions Ira T. Bryant, the deposed secretary-treasurer of the Sunday School Union, continually attempted to get the microphone; but the bishops refused to recognize him either as a delegate or an officer, since legally he was neither and therefore had no voice. He still had refused to turn over his books and his office, and had taken his case to the Nashville courts, where he was awaiting trial.[45]

Other controversial issues to be decided included Bishop Vernon's attempt to be reinstated and the struggle by a number of ministers and bishops to create a new episcopal district that would include Cuba, South

America, and nearby islands. Since there were no A.M.E. churches in the area, it would be the task of the bishop assigned there to establish some. Vernon's request was voted down, but the conference did vote to create another district, thereby raising the number of bishops to be elected from three to four.[46]

The balloting began Friday at 9 A.M. and was not concluded until Saturday at 5 A.M., twenty hours later. At the beginning Joseph ran a strong sixth. Ransom was campaigning hard for him, and Haithcox was doing the same for Allen. On the first ballot none of the candidates had a majority, but on the second D. Ward Nichols of New York was elected with 369 votes. There was a possibility that those who had voted for Nichols would now switch to Gomez. However, on the third ballot George E. Curry from Philadelphia, the minister referred to in Joseph's letter to Singleton, became the second bishop elected. Since Allen was running slightly ahead of him, Joseph withdrew from the race and threw his support to Allen so that at least one person from the 3rd District would have a chance. On the fifth ballot Frank Madison Reid was elected with 336 votes, and finally on the sixth, Allen with 345 votes.[47]

No doubt Joseph felt disappointment at having lost, but he took comfort in the fact that though his campaign had been limited by time and finances, he had done exceptionally well. He thanked all who had supported him, especially Ransom and the ministers of the 3rd District, and promised he would run again at the 1944 General Conference. With the building of St. James completed, he would have more time to campaign then.

Some important legislation was passed at the conference, including equal representation for laymen at the Annual Conferences, regular auditing of all books and the bonding of anyone handling Connectional money, and a resolution commending President D. O. Walker for the improvements he had made at Wilberforce and for getting the university accredited.[48]

According to the May 16 *Call and Post*, the "most eloquent speech of the conference" was made by Gomez, in response to the greetings from a representative of the C.M.E. Church. "Many of the delegates expressed the opinion that had the Cleveland minister delivered the speech before the balloting, he would most likely have been elected to one of the bishopric positions."[49] On such a thread seemed to hang the election or non-election of some of the bishops.

For Joseph, the remainder of 1940 was an anticlimax. The one exciting event was the presidential election. D. O. Walker, in his annual appearance at the Literary Forum on October 15, had predicted a victory for Roosevelt.

The editor of the *Call and Post,* William O. Walker—a Republican who liked neither Ransom, Roosevelt, Gomez, nor Walker—began a satirical article on the speech with the headline "Non-Political Speech at St. James Forum Advocates FDR's Re-Election."[50] Among the criticisms against President Walker by the editor and other Republicans were that he was too political and that his open support of the Democrats might cause the Republican-dominated Ohio legislature to withdraw its support from Wilberforce University.

Of all the U.S. presidents during Joseph's lifetime, he most admired Franklin Roosevelt. When Walker's prediction came true and Roosevelt was elected for a third term, Joseph noted with pride that the majority of Blacks had supported him. It was always a mystery to Joseph how any Negro could belong to the Republican Party during or after Roosevelt's administration.

As 1941 approached, the subject of war was becoming all too real to Americans. On September 16 Roosevelt had signed the Selective Service Act, which called for the first peacetime draft.[51] Black leaders, including Joseph, wanted the act amended to prohibit discrimination in the armed forces. This, however, did not happen.

Members of Hazel's Sunday school class were among the first group of Blacks drafted from Ohio, and put into the 25th Infantry, and sent to Fort Huachuca, Arizona. In March 1941 more left for Fort Dix with the 372nd Infantry, after a rousing send-off at the Coliseum.[52] The patriotism felt by the draftees and those who waved goodbye was soon dampened by reports of the discriminatory practices in the various army camps, particularly, but not exclusively, those located in the South. For instance, Negro soldiers at Fort Knox, Kentucky, were Jim-Crowed when they went to the movies, and they lived in the worst barracks on the base. Hazel read these reports with misgivings as more and more of her class left for the service.

The impending war, however, did not halt the progress of the building program at St. James. On Easter Sunday, 1941, the new auditorium was ready except for the installation of pews and some minor details, but the congregation decided to postpone the dedication until May, when everything would be complete. On May 4, right on schedule, the formal dedication service began, with the bishops, clergy, choirs, and congregation marching into the auditorium as soon as trustee W. R. Ricks had handed the keys to Bishop Ransom.

"Nature conspired to grant a perfect day. . . .The new church was an architectural expression of unusual beauty," wrote Alma Polk in the *Christian Recorder:*

The massive wall of light buff color is set off by a ceiling of lighter color composition block, beneath an insulated roof. . . . The entrance is 8-inch oak tile blocks. The main floor, solid oak covered by a maroon carpet. The pews are walnut. Unique is the arch behind and above the choir loft and pulpit. The lighting is created by new indirect reflectors. During the service a life-sized portrait of Rev. Gomez was presented as a gift of the church.[53]

The newly elected bishop, Frank Madison Reid, delivered the dedicatory sermon, during which he said "to future generations this church will show forth its greatness, not only in its grandeur and beauty, but also in its towering faith."[54] The *Cleveland Plain Dealer* saw another reason for celebration. "At a time when the leaders of the race have been trying, with active cooperation of many others in all walks of life, to break down the notion that the Negro lacks ability in the more skilled crafts, this church has been built entirely by Negro artisans." Joseph called the building "a permanent monument to the mechanical skill of our race."[55]

The following Sunday, D. O. Walker preached and, along with Louis B. Seltzer of the *Cleveland Press,* spoke at 4 P.M. at a mass meeting designed to honor friends of both races who had helped in the building program. Ironically, as St. James was having its Dedication Week, Greater Bethel was celebrating its one hundredth year as a congregation.[56] Joseph managed to get away for one day to participate in the celebration and to greet once more his old friends who had struggled so faithfully with him during the turbulent 1920s in Detroit.

Joseph had planned to take a group in June 1941 from St. James to Washington so they could participate in A. Phillip Randolph's March on Washington to protest discrimination in war industries. Before the march could take place, Roosevelt asked Randolph and Walter White (chief executive of NAACP, 1929–55) to meet with him, the assistant secretary of war, the secretary of the navy, and a representative of the Social Security Board. The result was Executive Order 8802 of June 25, which stated that "no discrimination in the employment of workers in defense industries" should exist and that it was the duty of employers and labor organizations "to provide for the full and equitable participation of all workers." In addition, a Fair Employment Practice Commission was established.[57] Although Joseph had looked forward to the march, he was delighted by Randolph's success and sent telegrams of congratulations to him and the president.

While progress was being made in one area, there were setbacks in others. At its July meeting the University Board of Wilberforce, led by

Bishop Ransom, fired Walker from the presidency.[58] The Ohio legislature and the Republican-dominated State Board had put pressure on the university to let Walker go or risk a withdrawal of funds. The state had been attempting to get more control of the university by giving the governor power to appoint more members to the State Board, and Walker had been vehement in his opposition. Consequently he had made many enemies, including Chester K. Gillespie, a powerful Black Republican from Cleveland, who had been determined to remove Walker. The Church had given into the pressure by the state. In time it was to discover that Walker had been right. The firing of Walker turned out to be one of the most grievous errors made by the Church, the university, and Ransom.

On July 5 an angry Walker told a *Call and Post* reporter, "There were no charges against me except the statement of an empty-headed lawyer in Columbus who possesses more zeal than knowledge, who stated that I am 'temperamentally unfit,' and therefore he could not work with me." Walker referred to the State Board as the "most politically minded ever to be appointed by any governor" and accused it of taking orders from the administration no matter what effect it might have on the students of Wilberforce. He threatened to "expose [the governor's] hypocrisy on every platform available" and to do everything he could to "retire him from public office," since it was obvious he did not have the interest of Negroes at heart and "resent[ed] any Negro speaking to him on the basis of equality."[59]

Joseph, who had personally always liked Walker despite his lack of diplomacy at times, wondered if Ransom had not been hasty in his decision to let Walker go. On the other hand, Walker's outspokeness had made enemies, some unnecessarily, Joseph reasoned. Nevertheless, like Ransom, Joseph came to realize that Walker had been right in his zealous fight to prevent the state from getting control of the university through its board.

Just as it seemed the month could not be gloomier, Joseph received a telegram from Bishop Gregg stating that Celia, his wife, had died; the funeral would be held at the First Church in Kansas City, Kansas.[60] Joseph and Hazel gave what comfort they could over the telephone and then drove to Kansas to be with their friend and pay their last respects to Celia. Gregg's quiet grief was for more than the loss of a wife—it was also for a friend and companion who had been by his side most of his adult life. The funeral exemplified her life: dignified, tasteful, quiescent.

On December 7, 1941, the United States could no longer debate the issue of war. The Japanese attacked the U.S. naval base at Pearl Harbor and within two hours destroyed eighteen ships and nearly two hundred airplanes, and killed 2,335 American soldiers and sailors and 68 civilians. As

Roosevelt put it in his address to the joint session of Congress, "Yesterday, December 7, 1941—a date which will live in infamy—the United States of America was suddenly and deliberately attacked by naval and air forces of the Empire of Japan."[61]

Even though a Black man, Dorie Miller, had been the first to be wounded at Pearl Harbor and was awarded the Navy Cross for downing four Japanese fighters, the Red Cross refused to accept Negro blood in its blood banks. Black soldiers' blood was good enough to be spilled in the name of democracy but not good enough to be used for saving lives, particularly if those lives were white—even though biologically there was no justification for such a decision. On December 30, Sloan Colt, director of the Red Cross Drive, said in its defense, "The Red Cross is now about to obtain from white donors enough blood to keep all the processing plants fully occupied so that the total amount of blood plasma available to the armed forces is not lessened by our inability to accept Negro donors."[62]

The Cleveland Methodist Ministers' Union, of which Joseph had recently been elected president, and the Interdenominational Ministers' Alliance, of which he was a member, met at St. James on January 8, 1942, to draw up a formal complaint to the Red Cross. In it they called the policy of the Red Cross "unjustifiable and unscientific . . . an unwarranted assault upon racial as well as national morale" and asked that the policy be altered so that the Red Cross would accept "any and all human blood."[63]

Joseph's sermons reflected his anger against the Red Cross and the discrimination against servicemen which had already resulted in thirty people being wounded in a Los Angeles race riot, and twenty-eight Black soldiers wounded in a similar riot in Alexandria, Louisiana. Nevertheless, he agreed with Bishop Ransom that Negroes should participate fully in the national defense. Fascism had to be fought abroad at the same time Negroes were fighting for justice in their own country. This was to be the paradox for Blacks throughout the war. Meanwhile, so much pressure was put on the government concerning the Red Cross policy that the Red Cross finally announced in February that blood would be accepted from Negroes—but would be stored separately. This compromise was totally unacceptable to Joseph, as it was to all Blacks, who continued to be outraged.

They were just as angry in March 1942. In that month one of the worst of a series of riots broke out in Detroit, Michigan, when Blacks attempted to occupy the Sojourner Truth Federal Housing Project, which had been built for them on the borders between a Negro and white neighborhood. Encouraged by the police, a mob of whites, including members of the Klan, prevented them from moving in, and a riot ensued. Later in the month another riot broke out in Houston, Texas, as the result of the lynching of a Black man.[64] Seemingly the war was not confined to Europe; it was as real for Blacks on American soil.

On April 10, Joseph became the first Black to address the North-East District Congress of the Parent-Teachers Association, held in Cleveland. He told the congress that much of the trouble in the country was caused by the lack of religious principles in the home, church, and daily life. He made it clear that he was not advocating any special creed but rather the practical application of the humaneness that is a part of most religions. "In this new world, man will no longer be interested in religion of creedal statements or theological distinctions, but the workable formula of living." Quoting Micah—that the Lord required man to "do justly, love mercy, walk humbly before your God"—Joseph pleaded for "mercy, not the superficial passing out of charity as giving a bone to a dog, but mercy that has in it the essence of fellowship." Walking humbly did not include "the arrogance of race . . . the theory of Nordic supremacy," or the exploitation of other countries. It did, however, include the recognition of the "oneness of the human family, and the philosophy of human brotherhood."[65]

Two months later Joseph attended a Board of Trustees meeting at Wilberforce assembled to appoint a permanent president of the university. Dean Charles Wesley of the Graduate School of Howard University became "the first President to be selected through joint action of Church and State trustees."[66] Wesley, from all appearances, was the consummate choice—extraordinarily handsome, well educated, and intelligent. His copper skin, dark wavy hair, and penetrating eyes made him an idol of the students. He had received his M.A. from Yale in 1913, studied at the Guide Internationale in Paris, and received his Ph.D. from Harvard in 1925.[67] He, his attractive wife Louise, and his two daughters were the epitome of Negro high society and fashion.

On June 11, two days after Wesley's appointment, Wilberforce observed its seventy-ninth commencement, and the faculty and student body got a chance to see their new president. Probably as a means of mending political fences, the university awarded Governor John A. Bricker an honorary degree. In addition, Bishop Lorenzo H. King of the Methodist Church of Atlanta, A. E. Perkins, principal of Dannell High School in New Orleans, and Joseph also received doctor of law degrees.[68]

The St. James Literary Forum opened its sixteenth season on October 11. Joseph spoke generally about present-day events which affected the Negro. His main concern was how America could carry "a good neighbor policy to South America when right here at home she [was] denying the Negroes the right of being human beings even though they were dying in Europe in her defense."[69] His growing impatience with American hypocrisy was even more obvious in December, when he addressed the Oberlin Graduate School of Theology, warning the predominantly white student body "that the new Negro . . . will not tolerate many of the injustices suffered by his forefathers. Rather than beg for what he wants, the new Negro will take that which he deems to be rightfully his own."[70] He had been rereading Alain Locke's 1920 essay "The New Negro" and reinterpreting it in terms of the war years.

In January 1943, two special honors were afforded Joseph: an Award of Merit from the Church Civic League of Greater Cleveland for "meritorious service to the Kingdom of God . . . [and] service in support of interracial goodwill and understanding";[71] and an appointment by the governor to the chairmanship of War Price Rationing Board 18-11, which served a major portion of the Black community in Cleveland. When asked by the *Call and Post* how he felt about these distinctions, he "registered less pride in the honors accorded him than he did in the revelation that his wife [Hazel] last week [had been] appointed as a member of the Board of Trustees of the Cleveland YWCA—the first Negro woman ever to hold that position."[72] The appointment had been made at the Annual Meeting held at the Hotel Statler on Saturday, January 23.[73]

Joseph's annual Good Friday sermon at the Old Stone Church reflected his growing concern with the way the news media was perpetuating hate for the Japanese, Germans, and Italians by caricaturing them as subhuman, especially the Japanese, whom they depicted as yellow, slant-eyed devils. In California and some other western states, loyal American citizens of Japanese extraction were being taken from their homes and incarcerated in camps until the end of the war. Joseph sensed that hate was growing like a cancer in America. "We can buy war bonds and give our all to our nation without hatred for Japanese or Germans or Italians. We shall win, not because we hate more, but because we love more, not because of numerical or economic superiority [but because our cause is right]." He spoke of hate as "a bad investment," a "double-edged sword" which becomes a "dangerous habit. When we find no one afar to hate, we turn on those at home," he warned. Here again was the clear command that as Christians everyone was called upon "to love those who despitefully use you," lest hate beget hate, as had already become a reality in some cities in America. White hatred for Blacks was making a mockery of the fight against fascism.[74]

The members of St. James, under the leadership of Mae Basey, gave a Ceremony of Appreciation for Hazel and Joseph on May 10; Ransom and his wife attended.[75] Among the hundreds of telegrams and letters which came to the parsonage was one from Rev. Peck of Greater Bethel, Detroit, who wrote, "We feel that we can join with you in spirit on this occasion for our church was built under the leadership of Dr. Gomez, and much that we have now in property and in spiritual leadership in this city is due to his years of unselfish service here." He also acknowledged "the unselfish companionship of [Joseph's] fine wife, Mrs. Hazel Gomez . . . [who] equally shares at Bethel Church Detroit any honor that is given her husband."[76]

The ceremony was a great success, but its aftermath was marked by tragedy. The next morning when Bishop Ransom woke up in the parsonage guest room he found that his wife could neither move nor speak. Only her eyes seemed to be trying to express some terrible frustration. Ransom summoned Hazel and Joseph, who stayed at her bedside until Joseph Brown, the family doctor, arrived. There was nothing to be done for Emma. An ambulance was secured to take her back to her home in Wilberforce, where she died on May 15 at the age of seventy-nine after fifty-five years of marriage. Ransom was inconsolable. In his autobiography, he described his feelings:

> We were each a part of the other. When she went away and left me solitary in the agony of my heartbroken loneliness and pain, the light of life burned low and all the stars were dead. In my grief I prayed in my bed; I prayed beside her grave, until in the darkness, by faith, I touched the right hand of God, who lifted me up and gave me strength to stand and walk the few shortening steps that lead into the eternal silence beyond which the day dawns and the shadows flee away.[77]

Emma's funeral was held on the campus in Shorter Hall's Jones Memorial Chapel on May 18 at 11 A.M.[78] After the funeral Joseph and Hazel lingered at Tawawa Chimney Corner with Ransom until they felt his anguish had lessened somewhat. They tried not to let him see their own grief for the woman who had been a mother to them throughout the years.

The Gomezes were back in Cleveland in time to see Eula graduate from Glenville High School. The exercises were held at the Masonic Temple, June 10, 1943. As a member of the National Honor Society Eula had been chosen to discuss "Democracy—What Does It Mean to Us?"[79] She performed with a sophistication beyond her seventeen years, and her parents were proud. Graduating with Eula were Jane Darr, Doris Brown, Helen Vance, Winston Richie, and Leon Yancy, her Black classmates, who made up less than 1 percent of the class. Jane would be rooming with Eula at Wilberforce in the fall. Eula had wanted to attend Oberlin Conservatory of Music, but because of her parents' commitment to Wilberforce and the high cost of tuition at Oberlin, she would go to their alma mater. Meanwhile, Annetta would be in the tenth grade at Glenville High School.

During the latter part of June Joseph read with great interest that following a conference with President Roosevelt at the White House on Tuesday, June 15, "eight prominent clergymen announced that Bishop John A. Gregg . . . had been selected to represent the Fraternal Council of Churches in America on a tour of training camps and various war fronts where Negro troops [were] stationed." Gregg left immediately for the South Pacific. For security reasons he could not give his exact locations, but he was able to report that although the soldiers he was visiting were a bit homesick "they [were] doing fine and [were] determined to give their best endeavor for the winning of the war. That they are loyal Americans goes without saying."[80]

While Black soldiers in the South Pacific were being "loyal Americans," six people were killed in New York in a riot caused by a police officer shooting a Black military policeman. Joseph noted with amazement that the optimistic reader of Sunday comics over the radio, Mayor Fiorello La Guardia, naively reported that it was not a race riot.[81] Alarmed by the disturbances in New York and other northern cities, Mayor Frank Lausche called together fifty whites and Blacks to form "The Mayor's Committee on Democratic Practices." Joseph was one of the fifty. At the second meeting, on October 7, the mayor said that the second generation of foreign-born residents were often the cause of racial upheaval, and he asked the newspapers to use their editorial pages to create good will.[82]

Mayor Lausche came to the Pasadena parsonage to ask Joseph for other suggestions. As usual his hair was wind blown and his tie rumpled; not knowing who he was, Annetta was not sure she should let him in. She left him standing on the porch while she went to call Joseph, who was appalled that she had not invited the mayor in. During their conversation, Joseph told Lausche that he hoped this committee was not going to turn out like so many other committees and commissions—merely a lot of talk and promises during a crisis. When the crisis disappeared, often the committees ceased to function. He also shared with the mayor his conversations with soldiers (from Hazel's Sunday school class) on leave, and with other young people from the church who felt that Cleveland was ripe for racial upheaval. The Murray Hill area, largely Italian, was off-limits for Blacks, many of whom had been assaulted when merely riding through the neighborhood on the way to somewhere else. Lausche was aware of the hostilities between Italians and Negroes in Cleveland and promised to focus on bringing about better relations between the two groups. He assured Joseph the committee would be an active one. The Committee on

Democratic Practices did continue to operate throughout the war, and if it did little else, it kept Clevelanders aware of immediate problems like Murray Hill and demonstrated Lausche's sincerity in addressing racial unrest.

At the North Ohio Conference held in Lima, Ohio, in October 1943, Joseph was once again endorsed for the bishopric and elected to head the 3rd District's delegation to the General Conference: his colleagues were R. C. Ransom, Jr., R. E. Hutchingson, D. D. Irving, H. H. Hughey and John Bright. As soon as the conference closed Joseph headed south to campaign once again.[83]

Finding it increasingly difficult to run St. James, his campaign, and the Ration Board, in February 1944 Joseph gave up his post at the Ration Board. Arthur C. Spath, District Board Operations Executive, regretted Joseph's decision but appreciated that he was leaving the board "functioning splendidly."[84] Joseph would miss his coworkers, but he knew he had made the right decision in light of his other responsibilities and also of the pressure of people who tried to get more than their allotted rations simply because they were his friends. They became angry when he refused, but he would not betray the governor's trust in his fairness.

On April 16, 1944, St. James celebrated the burning of its mortgage. After a preliminary speech by Joseph, which was broadcast over WGAR, Bishop Ransom preached at the official ceremony.[85] When he had concluded, the trustees handed him the mortgage. The bishop reminded the congregation of their splendid accomplishments: eleven months after the fire they had moved back into the building; on Easter Sunday 1941 they had dedicated the new auditorium; and by Easter 1943 every penny of building indebtedness had been paid. Now, in April 1944, they were burning the mortgage. With these words he set the document afire. The congregation stood watching, awed by the small pile of ashes which represented so many months of sacrifice.

◈ ◈ ◈

CHAPTER NINE

On Ma' Journey Now

Cleveland, 1944–1948

The dawn is clear and the new day inevitable. This does not
say that the vision is fulfilled completely; but we are definitely on
the way. And I have come to tell you not to be dismayed by the
awesome spectacles that greet your eyes. "The vision is for an appointed time. Though it tarry, it will come. It will surely come."
                        —Joseph Gomez, "The New Society of God,"
                    May 21, 1968

◈ The General Conference of 1944 met from May 3 to 14 in Philadelphia.
With more than usual anticipation, the Gomezes waited for it to open.
They felt certain that when it was over Joseph would emerge a bishop, an
honor for which he had long worked. Most of the meetings were held at
the Arena on 4530 Market Street, but for the opening session the delegates
assembled in the newly constructed St. Matthews A.M.E. Church to listen
to Bishop George B. Young deliver the Quadrennial Sermon.[1]
    The highlight of the conference occurred the next day, when Eleanor
Roosevelt delivered "a stirring and widely humanitarian address that lifted
high the hopes of her vast audience." Bishop Gregg, who had recently
returned from the European front, greeted Mrs. Roosevelt as a "short
snorter air traveler" (a person who travels so much she only gets to take
short naps while in flight). Fellow world travelers, they exchanged signatures on their "short snorter membership cards," to the amusement of the
conference. Then Careve Sims, daughter of Bishop and Mrs. Sims, presented her with a huge basket of American beauty roses. After expressing
her appreciation, Mrs. Roosevelt had her picture taken with the bishops.[2]
Even more than her husband, she was a favorite among the majority of

Blacks, who felt that much of the progress made toward equality was largely due to her promptings. If Franklin was the consummate politician, Eleanor was his consummate conscience.

Among some of the important legislation passed at the conference was the repeal of the law that dealt with the retirement age for bishops; this meant that neither Ransom, Young, nor Williams, though well up in age, would have to retire. There was also the creation of a second Episcopal District in South Africa. Despite the effort of some delegates to have three new bishops elected, it was decided that there would only be two;[3] nevertheless, Joseph was fairly confident that he would be one of the two. His mood was one of cautious optimism.

The long-awaited election of bishops began on Monday, May 8, when the delegates went through the outdated ritual of casting their ballots one by one until everyone had voted. Then came the calling out of names by the tellers, a process which made the waiting even more painful. In the first ballot 1,476 ballots were cast; five were thrown out; 736 were needed for election. George Baber received 427 votes, Gomez 287, Hemingway 233, and Clayborn 210. These were the top contenders, as had been expected. The trend continued. On the second ballot, Baber received 671 votes, Gomez 443, Clayborn 368, and Hemingway 316.[4] Still no one had been elected, but Joseph was not discouraged. After all, he had the second-largest number of votes. Throughout the long wait, he and Hazel drank coffee, chatted with the delegates around them, and encouraged each other.

On May 9, at 8:15 A.M., the delegates voted again. In the middle of the third ballot, some of the delegates charged that the ballot box had been stuffed. Bishop G. E. Curry requested a recess for thirty minutes, which was extended to one hour. It was decided that voters would hand their ballots to the teller rather than cast them in the box, and on the suggestion of Bishops Curry and Nichols relief tellers were appointed, one from each of the sixteen districts.[5]

As soon as the new tellers were in place, Bishop M. H. Davis, who was now presiding, ordered the roll call to begin. Since Baber had been leading all evening, no one was surprised when he was elected at 7:45 P.M., with 915 votes. What was surprising was the decrease of votes for Gomez and the increase for Clayborn, a southerner. It was obvious to everyone that something had happened during the hour recess. Conflicting theories circulated around the convention floor. Some felt the ballot box had deliberately been stuffed after the second ballot so the election could be halted and the southern delegates could regroup. Other said the tellers had been changed so that new ones could be selected who were opposed to two northerners being elected; these new tellers then could call out whatever name they chose once the vote had been handed to them and passed down the line of tellers. The one thing that everyone agreed upon was that there had been foul play. On the fourth ballot, Clayborn of Arkansas became the second new bishop, with 962 votes.[6] In reporting the election results the *Call and Post* noted, "It took extremely sharp trading to turn the tide of southern delegates against [Gomez] and in favor of Dr. Clayborn after the North had succeeded in assuring the election of Baber."[7]

Joseph was profoundly hurt. It was one thing to lose, but another thing to be robbed of the election. Nevertheless, he concealed his feelings well, except to those who could read his eyes and the firm set of his chin. He thanked all who had supported him, most of whom, like Bishop Gregg and Singleton, were now angry and bitter. He congratulated Baber, who he felt brought great dignity to the position. Clayborn was another matter. Ransom put his arms around Joseph and said, "This is one of the lowest points in African Methodism. This Church would be too ashamed not to elect you Bishop at the next General Conference. You will see."

The Gomezes headed back to Cleveland to try to explain to the congregation what had happened. Joseph doubted that he would ever run for the bishopric again. When he revealed his thoughts to Hazel, she listened in silent disbelief.

The 1944 North Ohio Annual Conference met in September at Community Church in Cleveland. It was there that Bishop Ransom introduced his new wife, Georgia Myrtle Teal Ransom, to the district.[8] The marriage had come as a shock to many people, because although not a young woman, Georgia was considerably younger than the eighty-three-year-old bishop. Joseph and Hazel, however, were pleased that Ransom would have someone to take care of him in his twilight years. Because of their mutual esteem and concern for Ransom, Georgia and the Gomezes became confidants. She was not Emma, the mother figure they had adored, but she proved to be a dear friend. Born in South Carolina, she had received her college training at Allen University, State Teachers College at Cheyney, Pennsylvania, Cornell University (A.B.), and Columbia University (A.M.).[9] Ironically, she had been the director of the Emma Ransom House in Harlem before her appointment as Dean of Women at Wilberforce (1934–43). Because of her very fair skin and silky white hair which she wore in a bob or a bun at the back of her head when she let it grow long, she was often taken for a Caucasian. She was an astute businesswoman, possessed the culture and refinement of a southern lady of her generation, and had a slight drawl that was pleasant to the ear. Writing in his autobiography of his marriage to Georgia, Ransom said that "life always has its compensations. It was not romance but reality that brought light, comfort and love into my days. It was not a flash of light that blinded, but the light of a gentle personality that brought comfort to my life and made it luminous in the lengthening days."[10]

In addition to the marriage of Ransom, another topic of interest at the Annual Conference was the state and national elections. Ransom advised that if the ministers believed the campaign promises of Thomas E. Dewey, the Republican candidate for president, they should vote for him; on the other hand, if Roosevelt had kept his promises, he was entitled to a fourth term, since the war had not ended and a change would be disastrous for the country and the Allies.[11] It was no secret that both he and Joseph would support Roosevelt as long as he wanted and was able to run.

On the state level, Frank Lausche, mayor of Cleveland, was running for governor of Ohio. Ransom compared the kind of left-handed politics being waged against Lausche to what had occurred at the last General Conference. "The voters are saying [Lausche] is a foreigner, just as some . . . said of Dr. Gomez. Is a man responsible for his place of birth? It is only around election time when a man is running for public office that many false propaganda and lies are said of him." He told the conference how Joseph's West Indian birth had been used against him in Philadelphia. Joseph knew that what Ransom was saying was true.[12]

Joseph passed the rest of the year attending to his pastoral duties at St. James, spending time with his family, helping Annetta with her homework, and trying to assess his future plans. The annual Christmas message he sent to his friends reflected the somberness of his mood in 1944: "It is for us in the face of the greatest human tragedies to re-examine all attitudes and actions that create suspicion and that result in any form of enslavement and of unhumbled hate that separates man from man."[13]

As disappointed as he was to have been cheated of obtaining his most cherished goal, the bishopric, he knew that he would always love the African Methodist Episcopal Church. On several occasions in the past he had been asked to join other denominations—white-dominated churches which had more national and international prestige and which were financially more lucrative—but he always turned them down. The A.M.E. Church was made up of people and was therefore subject to human strengths and human weaknesses and excesses, but it was more than that. Its ideals were based on dignity and pride in one's race and in love of God and man. Whether or not he ever became bishop, he was certain of one thing: he would not abandon his Church, as some had suggested after the election. In the years ahead he would have ample opportunity to prove his faithfulness. Meanwhile, he had a church to pastor and other issues to address.

A. Phillip Randolph, now international president of the Brotherhood of Sleeping Car Porters, was invited to address the St. James Literary Forum in March 1945. His topic was "What the Negro Expects in the Post-War World." In his smooth, deep baritone, he enumerated "the elimination of segregation in the armed forces, a voice at the peace table, a federal education law, a national commission on race relations and a permanent Fair Employment Practices Commission" as what the Negro expected. The audience "was completely thrilled with his masterful presentation."[14] Afterward Randolph and Joseph had the opportunity to reminisce about the times Randolph had come to Bethel, Detroit, and the problems Randolph had had with Judge Parker in the judge's "Red-baiting" days.

Another prominent Negro who spoke at the St. James Literary Forum was Langston Hughes, who on April 2 gave a reading of his poems. At the close of his presentation he described his visit to Russia, which had led him to believe that Russia was a land free of racial discrimination. He contrasted the cordiality he experienced in Russia with his reception on a cross-country tour of America, when he had been confronted by the Ku Klux Klan.[15] In years to come Joseph found that Hughes was less enthusiastic about the Soviet Union than he had been in 1945.

On April 12, 1945, President Franklin Delano Roosevelt died of a stroke at Warm Springs, Georgia, and the nation was plunged into mourning.[16] In the Black community people could be seen standing around the streets in a state of shock or reduced to tears. They had lost more than a commander in chief; they had lost a friend. As long as he was in the White House they had had hope that they would at long last become first-class citizens. Now Harry Truman, basically a southerner, would be president. Only God knew whether or not he would assist or deter Blacks in their struggle for full equality. Joseph remembered when he and Bishop Gregg had spoken to Truman about his allegedly referring to Blacks as "Niggers" at the Boys Home in Kansas City, only to find out he had not said "Niggers" but "Negras," because he could not pronounce "Negroes." Whenever Joseph had told that story he had always rolled with laughter. But the prospect of this man heading the country was no laughing matter.

Almost a month after Roosevelt's death, Germany surrendered; when Japan refused to cease hostilities, Truman ordered that the atomic bomb be dropped on Hiroshima. Russia declared war on Japan on August 8; the next day, America dropped another atomic bomb, this time on Nagasaki. To most Americans, these acts meant merely that the war was finally over and their men would be coming home. Only later did they begin to assess the significance of the bombings. In the pulpit and at civic meetings Joseph expressed his revulsion that the government had chosen this means to bring Japan to its knees—the indiscriminate slaughter of thousands of civilians, children included. As he had told the graduates at Wilberforce in his 1939 Baccalaureate Sermon, the "Frankenstein of our brain" had now been loosed. He was never convinced that dropping the atomic bomb had been the only way to end the war.

In July 1945 Joseph was alarmed to learn that his friend Bishop David Sims had been charged with maladministration of his district. Ransom told Joseph that at the June 23 Bishops' Council meeting in Kansas City, Bishop R. R. Wright had been appointed to help Sims with the supervision of the 1st District (which included New York) until matters could be straightened out. Apparently Sims had agreed with this arrangement; however, before long he and some of his followers took out a temporary injunction restraining Wright from any official action in the New York Conference.

Joseph called Sims and pleaded with him to allow the Church to settle the matter through its judicial structure; dragging the case through the civil courts would only cause embarrassment to both Sims and the Church. But Sims was determined, and Joseph could not dissuade him. An argument ensued during which Sims accused Joseph of betraying their past friendship and Joseph accused him of disloyalty to the Church he had sworn to serve. Joseph warned him that the bishops would not allow him to subject the Church to ridicule and scandal, and he was right: before long, a majority of the bishops would decide Sims should be brought to trial before his peers. But that was in the future.

In December, the Young People's Department of St. James gave a banquet for the returning servicemen of the church and for college students home for the Christmas holidays. From Wilberforce Eula brought home Betty Lou Allen, who along with Leontyne Price was one of the lead soloists of the Wilberforce Singers. The Gomezes fell in love with this warm, good-natured young woman, who had been orphaned at an early age and was glad to be in a close family atmosphere for the Yuletide. At the crowded dinner table, which included the usual guests, she and Eula talked constantly about their college experiences, their boyfriends, the strict dormitory rules, required chapel, nosey house mothers, their voice lessons, and the Delta Sorority, which Eula had joined. They teased Jane about being homesick during her first year and having to go home. There was much music and laughter, opening of presents, stuffing down of food, and general festivity, of which Annetta was also very much a part. Joseph and Hazel were glad for the diversion from their own troubled thoughts, and to have such an energetic house guest. No one was surprised when Betty Lou became a successful opera singer, performing all over the world.

On February 16, 1946, Hazel gave a dinner at the parsonage for the members of her Sunday school class who had returned from the war. She invited Sidney Williams, executive secretary of the Urban League, to make a few remarks. Among other things, he observed how miraculous it was that not one member of the class had been killed or wounded. At the conclusion of the dinner, the class presented Hazel with a token of their appreciation for her prayers and the care packages she had continually sent them overseas. Every Sunday while they had been away, she and another class member, who had been classified 4-F (not physically qualified), had sat in the pews preparing the packages, sharing their letters, and praying for the soldiers.

As predicted, during the latter part of February the bishops attempted to try Bishop Sims and also W. A. Fountain (the senior bishop who was allegedly conspiring with Sims), at the Brooklyn Bridge Street A.M.E. Church in New York. Bishop Ransom was chosen to act as presiding judge. In the middle of the proceedings, Bishops Sims and Monroe H. Davis and several ministers marched into the session and disrupted the trial with shouts, prayers, and songs. When the dissidents ignored Ransom's plea for order, the trial was moved to Union Bethel Church at Schenectady and Dean avenues. Before reconvening, Ransom told the audience that he had nothing "in the world against Bishop Sims or any other Bishop," that the bishops were not there "to railroad or condemn anybody out of hand." All they wanted to do was to "put the Church back in order so that it [could] continue to function." As things stood, Sims had brought charges against all the bishops not only to the civil courts but also to the Church's Episcopal Committee. Unless things could be settled that day, the Church would be impotent. Once again the trial was interrupted, by the same parties. Finally, after caucusing with the other bishops, Ransom announced that they had decided to call an extra session of the General Conference to be held in Little Rock, Arkansas. The date was to be set later.[17]

Meanwhile, in June 1946, Hazel, Joseph, and Annetta (now a freshman at Wilberforce) attended Eula's senior recital given jointly with Irma L. Clark, another music major. They listened with pride as Eula sang pieces from Mozart, Verdi, Puccini, and Delibes.[18] A few weeks later they returned to the campus to see her graduate magna cum laude after three years and two summers of study. The commencement program listed her as a member of the Alpha Kappa Mu National Honor Society and the Delta Sigma Theta Sorority, which awarded her with further honors for having the highest scholastic average of all the Deltas that year. Bishop John A. Gregg delivered the commencement address, and among others, Mary Church

Terrell (teacher, author, civil rights leader) and Colonel Benjamin O. Davis, Jr. (later the first Black general in the U.S. Air Force), received honorary degrees.[19]

Eula hoped to attend UCLA in September to pursue graduate work in music, and Annetta wanted to accompany her so she could study drama. Reluctantly, Joseph's sister Violet, who was living with Ismael and her two daughters, Gloria and Jewell, in Los Angeles, agreed that her nieces could come stay with her while attending the university. Joseph was uneasy about the arrangement; he would have preferred Annetta to finish her studies at Wilberforce. This would be the first time his daughters would be so far from home, and he was not sure how reliable Violet would be when it came to supervising the girls, especially since she had her own young daughters to care for. He also remembered her fierce temper. After much discussion, he and Hazel decided to take a chance and let them go. Around mid-August they put their daughters on the plane and hoped they had not made a mistake. As it turned out, they had cause to be worried.

Joseph led the Ohio delegation to the special session of the General Conference in Little Rock, Arkansas, November 20–24.[20] It was not an easy time for him. Torn between his friendship for Sims and his love for the A.M.E. Church, he sat through the proceedings tight lipped and solemn.

Sims was charged with rebellion in that he had "flagrantly and openly" disregarded and criticized the action of more than a majority of his colleagues. Bishops Fountain and Davis were charged with conspiring with Sims, betraying and misrepresenting the action taken at the regularly called session of the Bishops' Council in Kansas City in June when Bishop Wright had been appointed to preside with Sims over the 1st District. Bishop Curry was charged with maladministration and misappropriation of Church monies. Both Sims and Davis refused to put on their robes and take their seats on the platform with the other bishops at the conference.[21] In fact, it was rumored that Sims left Little Rock soon after the conference opened.

Following the Episcopal Committee's reading of its report, in which it found both Sims and Curry guilty, the delegates voted 999 to 35 to expel Sims and 812 to 94 to expel Curry. Davis was suspended until the Bishops' Council meeting in February 1947, when a final decision would be made. Fountain was exonerated. All the charges brought against the other bishops by the Sims's faction were dismissed for lack of evidence.[22]

Important legislative action was taken to prevent similar incidents in the future. The presiding officer of the Bishops' Council would no longer automatically be the senior bishop; instead, there would be an annual election of a president and vice president of the Council. The president could preside for only four years. In the future, all bishops would be required to make a full and complete financial report to the Bishops' Council. These reports were to be printed and sent back to the districts for examination.[23] This would prevent bishops like Curry from misappropriating funds.

With removal of the dissident bishops and the passage of the new legislation, the Church had once again set herself on an even keel and proven indisputably that she was greater than any one faction or any individual. Still Sims's pride would not let him accept the verdict of the General Conference.

In a last-ditch effort, he called a meeting of some one thousand members of the 1st District in December to establish an Independent A.M.E. Church, headed by himself and Curry. It was also expected that his brother, George Sims, who had been removed as secretary of the General Conference, would join the group.[24] That same month, however, Justice Samuel Dickstein of the New York Supreme Court ruled that the unfrocking of Bishop Sims was legal and in accordance with the A.M.E. Discipline, and Bishop Wright was granted the right to bar Sims from administering the business of the 1st District.[25] Sims's attempt to fight through the courts and to establish his own church had ended in failure. He became a bitter, vindictive man, who felt he had been wronged by the Church and deserted by his friends, especially Joseph.

Joseph had always prized friendship above most other things, but when the choice was Sims or the African Methodist Episcopal Church, he chose the Church. Even so, he had received heavy criticism for refusal to join in the verbal abuse leveled at Sims. Those close to him said his greatest asset and greatest detriment was his loyalty to those to whom he had given his friendship. Sometimes that loyalty would nearly cause his own downfall. Joseph tried on several occasions to talk to Sims and explain further why he could not support him in his battle with the Church, but Sims would not receive his calls. Joseph found it difficult to accept the fact that their friendship could not be repaired.

The new year brought new problems at home. In February 1947 the Cleveland Detective Bureau released a report to the newspapers that stated Negroes had been responsible for 63 percent of the crimes in Cleveland. "Of the 53 Criminal Court convictions for first and second degree murder, and first degree manslaughter, 70% of the guilty verdicts were returned against Negroes." Most of these murders had taken place in the Central area, one of the poorest Black ghettos of the city.[26] The Interdenominational Ministers' Alliance met in emergency session to discuss the significance of this report. The result was a statement, presented by Joseph, to the city and its administration.

Joseph expressed the Alliance's concern over the "alleged abnormal crime rate among Negroes" and "an abiding concern with the total problem of law and order." Having said that, he continued, "These figures of crime, true or otherwise, do not tell the whole story." Such figures of necessity had to take into consideration the "unfortunate people victimized by . . . racket, graft and greed—of men, women, boys and girls made gullible by the pressure of a poor economic status, poor education, poor housing and inadequate law enforcement." Sometimes law enforcers themselves were guilty of connivance, and the "so called better people . . . grow rich and fatten at the expense of these unfortunates."[27]

The Alliance and other religious leaders proposed that they be "empowered to prepare immediately a program of approach to this" problem; that this committee ask the mayor, safety director, and police commissioner to appoint an "impartial fact finding committee with the authority" to find out the truth and make remedial recommendations; that each church appoint a social action committee to assist in the work of the investigators; that a mass meeting be called to "give stimulus to the movement"; that during Lent emphasis should be placed on the meaning of better social order and of the present crisis, through sermons, the Sunday School, and other young people's organizations; and that the aid of all religious, civic, and social agencies in the city be enlisted.[28]

The Alliance was well aware of the neglect of law enforcement in the inner city, of the slow police response to calls, of a seeming uninterest when the crime was "Black on Black," and of the poor quality of education and social services in these areas. Joseph hoped that such a committee would focus on the problem, which for so many years had been swept under the rug. The bare statistics of crimes committed by Negroes gave a twisted picture and placed the blame solely on the victims—often the effect, not the cause. Since no one group within the race had the power to correct conditions by itself, a bringing together of the forces of religious and other social agencies might not only create an awareness of the real problems but provide some remedies. Only time would tell.

Trouble was also fermenting at Wilberforce University. The root of the problem went back to the decision made in 1887 that the state of Ohio would set up a Combined Normal and Industrial Department (two-year program) at Wilberforce.[29] Since that time, as has been seen, there had been constant friction between the university (later referred to as the College of Liberal Arts) and the state, each of whom had its own board of trustees.[30]

The university board always viewed the Combined Normal and Industrial Department as an integral part of the overall school; the state board viewed it as a separate entity. Those who sided with the state referred to the words in the original agreement, "A Combined Normal and Industrial Department *at* Wilberforce" rather than *of* Wilberforce.[31] Those who sided with the Church pointed to the equal representation on the first state board of trustees as an indication that the state had wanted to be a part of the university.[32]

Through the years the level of cooperation between the two boards had depended on the governor, who appointed the state board trustees; the superintendent, who headed the Normal and Industrial Department; the president of the University; the A.M.E. bishop of the district, who headed the University Trustee Board; and the members of both boards. National, state, and church politics played a significant role in the deliberations of all factions; the result was disharmony and frustration.

When Charles Wesley became president in 1942, the majority of A.M.E.'s believed he was the panacea who would solve all the difficulties facing the school. He had successfully served as the dean of Howard's Graduate School and was respected as a scholar and educator. He had sworn not to become involved in partisan politics, which he felt had split the school into factions in the past. Among the new programs he instituted were a student self-governing council, a summer school, replacement of the semester system with the quarter system, and he changed departments into divisions (three in the College of Liberal Arts and four in the College of Education).[33] For the first two years, his record seemed impressive.

Despite these innovations, however, Wesley's presidency had many detractors. Bishop Ransom charged him with "collaborating with other school officials to gain control and rule the hitherto Church-controlled College of Liberal Arts." In other words, Ransom accused him of systematically selling out to the state.[34] Others said Wesley had been effective in terms of public relations and highly regarded by the students but had much difficulty with some of the faculty members and the university (Church) board, because of his educational practices, many of which were considered to be unsound, and because of his constant courting of the governor's appointees on the state board. In addition, he was accused of not being firm in his policies, of yielding readily to pressure, of allowing students to register for an excessive number of credit hours against faculty rulings, of giving special permission through the Admissions Committee to enroll students who were not qualified for admission, and of spending excessive time off campus in pursuit of his own interests.[35]

In March 1947 the school had lost its accreditation, under Wesley's administration—a loss which, he said, was caused largely by the policies of the university board. The state agreed with him;[36] consequently, the Church felt betrayed by one of its own. (Wesley was an A.M.E. minister and a long-standing member who had on occasion been mentioned for the bishopric.)

The same year Wesley allegedly supported a bill before the Ohio legislature which would increase the number of the governor's appointees on the state board to eight, leaving only one member to represent the university.[37] After talking to Ransom, Joseph went to Columbus to oppose the bill and represent the Church faction, which considered the legislation a slap in the face.

In the *Call and Post* Joseph quoted Senator Albert L. Daniels of Greene County, Ohio, as saying "We shall pass this bill, and if this does not do, the State of Ohio will come down there and run Wilberforce." With those words Daniels "moved to send Bill 258 to the Ohio Senate with the approval of the Educational Committee." This drew the curtain on the "dramatic battle which . . . lasted for three consecutive committee hearings, and in which opponents of the bill sought to show the great danger that inhered in such legislation." To Joseph, Senator Daniels's words represented the thinking of many whites, who believed that there should be a separate state school for Negroes in Ohio. At the end of the article Joseph warned, "Let [Daniels] know now and all others who think alike, that the State of Ohio will never, no never, operate a college apart and separate for Negroes, not while free men shall live and speak."[38] If the bill passed, Joseph said, once again there would be a Black school set up by whites, inherently separate and unequal.

More and more it was becoming clear to Joseph and Ransom that D.O. Walker had been right to fight to keep the state from gaining more control of the school. The initial mistake had been in not realizing that if the state invested money in the university, it would eventually want and demand power. The school should have been supported and run by the A.M.E. Church, even though it could not hope to compete financially with the state. What it lacked in money it would have more than made up for in integrity.

On April 27, when Walker addressed the St. James Literary Forum on the subject "The Struggle for Control of Wilberforce University," not even standing room could be found in the auditorium.[39] He reviewed the history of the state's participation at Wilberforce, reminded his audience that the university had been accredited by the North Central Association under his administration and had lost its accreditation in March 1947 under Wesley's. In order for Wilberforce to regain its accreditation, the university had to "cure administration inefficiencies by removing an inefficient president and not by reducing the power and prerogative of the presidency." There would have to be "a complete change in the boards of control." Instead of "wasting time" with the present bill before the legislature, another bill should be introduced in which the office of superintendent, appointed by the state, should be abolished and the president of the university become "the chief fiscal officer. The present board of the State Department of Wilberforce should be dismissed because the board came into existence in payment for political services."[40]

Despite the objections of the Church, the strong appeal by Joseph, and the powerful speech of Walker, which was printed and distributed to all concerned, the Ohio Senate passed the Wilberforce Reorganization Act. Senators Charles C. Davies of Fulton County and Harry E. Davis of Cuyahoga spearheaded the final passage of the bill. Davies said that "passage was necessary to insure the continued control of the State of Ohio over that part of the university for which it provides funds," and that in terms of the arguments he had heard against the bill, the Church representatives "had great oratory, filled with much heat but little light."[41] Joseph left Columbus in a fury.

On June 11, 1947, one day before graduation, the university board met and by a vote of sixteen to five dismissed Charles Wesley from the presidency.[42] At an open meeting after the announcement, Bishop Ransom dramatically read the charges against Dr. Wesley from a long scroll which hung all the way to the ground. He accused Wesley of being "out of harmony with the ideals and spirit on which Wilberforce was founded," of being "incapable of maintaining the ideals of student morality and of religious education." Instead of "defending and protecting the interests of an integrated educational policy," he had shown sympathy for the State Board of Education, which was against such a policy. He further accused Wesley of hiring teachers who were immature and "out of sympathy with the purposes and spirit of Wilberforce." In dealing with the North Central Association, Wesley had "created the impression that the blame for all weaknesses of the university belong[ed] to the University Board of Trustees. He therefore was not a spokesman and defender before the accrediting agency but a critic and antagonist." He had sold himself but not the university to the public. As a result the university board was convinced "that his continued leadership would result in great damage."[43]

Walker best summed up the church's position when he told the *Call and Post* after commencement, "The Church has yielded throughout the years, but now it has reached the place where it can yield no further, and has reasserted its right to have control over the life and leadership of Wilberforce."[44]

The university board immediately appointed Charles Leander Hill to replace Wesley. Hill was considered to be a brilliant scholar. He had been educated at Hammon School of Divinity at Wittenberg College, Ohio State University, from which he had received his Ph.D., and had done further graduate study in philosophy and theology at the University of Berlin. At Zurich he had sat in on the lectures of Emil Brunner while researching original Latin and Old German documents. He had served as dean of Turner Theological Seminary at Morris Brown College in Atlanta and had pastored Bethel A.M.E. Church in Columbia, South Carolina.[45]

After his dismissal, instead of leaving the campus Wesley set up a summer school, and the state hired him as president of the College of Education and Industrial Arts at Wilberforce.[46] Joseph was chosen by a citizens committee as one of the six church dignitaries to approach Governor Herbert in July with a request that the state release its holdings at Wilberforce, Ohio, to the Church.[47] The governor, Thomas J. Herbert, listened politely and said he would consider the matter. Instead, in September Herbert reappointed all of the former state trustees, including Joseph. Given the position he had taken concerning the State's continual interference in the affairs of the university, Joseph was appalled by the governor's audacity.

How strongly Joseph felt was revealed in a letter he wrote Herbert on September 8, 1947, refusing the appointment. He reminded the governor of the "violation of the original intent and meaning of the arrangement of Wilberforce between the A.M.E. Church and the State of Ohio . . . [and of] the vicious pattern of separate and segregated educational policy which such a bill would create." To him the act was arbitrary, since the Church "as one of the parties to the original agreement that brought the State to Wilberforce, was not consulted in the writing of that bill." In light of all this, for him to accept the position on the board would at the least be "illogical and hypocritical, and contrary to the best interest of the people." Furthermore, to serve on a board where "no dissent, or challenge, or an objection" could be heard would mean a loss of his self-respect.[48]

All his life Joseph was to believe, as did Ransom and many other Blacks, that Wesley had been used by the state. They reasoned that by dangling before him the possibility of becoming president of a state-controlled Wilberforce University, with considerable more prestige and salary, the governor had been able to get him to betray his church. As it turned out, Joseph had been overly optimistic about the people of Ohio not allowing a "separate college for Negroes supported by the public treasury." Judge Frank L. Johnson Greene of the Common Pleas Court of Greene County ruled that no school could have the name "Wilberforce" except the Church school then in existence;[49] the state simply set up another liberal arts college at Wilberforce, made Wesley its president, and in 1951, after Wesley had resigned, renamed the school Central State University.[50]

At the North Ohio Conference held at Warren A.M.E. Church in Toledo, October 7–12, 1947, Bishop Ransom told the members that the Church had just passed through "a more crucial stage than any Church, black or white, in lawsuits, in suspension and unfrockings of bishops." He assured them that the Church had withstood the storm and was still standing tall. "Wilberforce . . . is the oldest Negro University in the world, organized, controlled and operated by Negroes in America, and is not to be sold or bought by the politicians of the State."[51] On October 8, Charles E. Loeb, associate editor of the *Call and Post*, continued the focus of the conference on the situation at Wilberforce. Unlike his editor, W. O. Walker, he had supported the Church throughout the controversy. Shaking with emotion, he said, "We cannot allow cheap political men to take over Wilberforce. . . . The A.M.E. Church of which I am a member is the greatest Church in the world."[52]

Loeb's words prompted Joseph to say, "I am one hundred per cent A.M.E. All I have, all that I have achieved was given me by the Church, and I will die for its rights." He then read a resolution asking that November 23 be set aside for prayer, fasting, and raising of money for Wilberforce University.[53]

The high emotional mood of the conference seemed to affect everyone. For instance, after a Dr. Cooan, who had spent nine years in South Africa, gave a speech about apartheid, Bishop Ransom waxed philosophical and poetic:

Young men shall see visions; old men shall dream dreams. I am dreamy tonight. Listen! Listen! I hear the pattering footsteps of thirty million unborn dusky children coming down through the corridors of time, battering at the doors of the United States. What kind of America shall they find? These generations of African descent with aspirations, with ambition, with zeal? Shall they find a door of opportunity opened to them? God deliver them from the compromise, from the weak and fearful and from the selling of heritage, and from those who seek to barter for money. God help them![54]

When he ended the conference sang "Amazing Grace," with emphasis on the verse that begins, "Through many dangers, toils, and snares, I have already come." Charles Leander Hill, the new president of Wilberforce, then outlined his plans for the university.[55] Appropriately, at the Sunday morning worship service Bishop Frank Madison Reid preached on the topic "Choose Ye This Day Whom Ye Will Serve: A Choice of Heritage." The conference ended with the reading of appointments by Bishop

Ransom, the shaking of hands, and pledging of loyalty to the African Methodist Episcopal Church and Wilberforce.[56]

Joseph and Hazel spent the early months of 1948 trying to locate a drama school in the East where Annetta could study. After only a few months with Violet, the sisters had found living with their aunt an ordeal and had moved. Annetta returned to Cleveland, while Eula remained in California to continue her studies at UCLA and to marry Tory Butler, a law student. Annetta tried taking classes at Fenn College (now Cleveland State) to please her parents, but she was finally able to persuade them that she really wanted to go to a school designed exclusively for the study of drama.

As a teenager, Annetta had taken acting lessons at Karamu House and later at the Cleveland Playhouse on Saturday mornings from a Mrs. Mullins. As the lone Negro in the group, the only role in which she was cast was Topsy in *Uncle Tom's Cabin*. Hazel and Joseph tried to persuade her not to take such a demeaning role, but she was determined to be on the stage regardless of the part. When she came out on stage in black face, black stocking, pigtails all over her head, and dressed in a burlap sack, the audience had howled. She ran off the stage in tears and could not be consoled. It was then that she decided she would be a great actress some day: no one would laugh at her then. Now her parents were examining the various theatre schools. They had almost decided that in September 1948 she could attend Erwin Piscator's Dramatic Workshop in New York City.

Besides looking at drama schools, Joseph spent a great deal of time traveling to parts of the country where he felt he was least known. As Hazel had anticipated, after recovering from the initial shock of the last General Conference he had reconsidered his determination not to run for bishop. He would give it one last try.

The Thirty-third Session of the General Conference was scheduled to begin on Wednesday, May 5, 1948, but by the Sunday before the opening, delegates from all over the United States and from the foreign districts were already forming long queues in hotel lobbies throughout Kansas City.

On Wednesday morning, when Joseph, Hazel, and William Hodge (Joseph's campaign manager) left their hotel by taxi to attend the opening services at First A.M.E. Church, at 8th and Nebraska avenues, the sky was overcast with a misty rain. Reaching the church they saw an impatient crowd attempting to get into the already packed sanctuary. Someone told them that Bishop Gregg was trying to get the service transferred to Soldier and Sailor Memorial Hall, where the rest of the meetings were to be held. Evidently Gregg was successful, for soon the hugh crowd "emptied the church and walked in the soft falling rain to the regular seat of the General Conference."[57]

Years later Joseph was to remember the prayer delivered by Bishop Ransom which followed the singing of the hymn, "And are we yet alive." Although he was now eighty-seven years old, Ransom's voice was clear and forceful, much as it had been when Joseph first heard him preach in New York in 1909.[58] "The Grand Old Man of African Methodism," "The Sage of Tawawa," as he was affectionately called, was about to be retired along with Bishops Williams and Young, or so it was rumored.

Most of the early sessions were devoted to organizing the conference and seating the delegates. Soldier Hall soon resembled a political convention: the delegates were seated behind banners that indicated their district and their choice of candidates for the bishopric and general offices. When proceedings became tedious people could be seen milling from one delegation to the other, greeting old friends, pushing their candidates, or just simply talking, much to the consternation of the fire marshall, whose job it was to keep the aisles clear. Outside the main auditorium the halls were lined with refreshments stands, tables where books and other literature were given out or sold, and booths that served as campaign headquarters for aspirants not lucky enough to find a room for that purpose. A diversity of color was to be found not only in the clothes worn by the delegates but also in skin tones, ranging from mulatto to rich black, and in speech—from the thick, chocolatey dialect of the South to ice-blue, clipped accents that reminded one of Oxford.

As Joseph met with numerous delegates to promote his candidacy, his support seemed to be strongest among the northern, western, and foreign districts, particularly within the lay delegations. Among the bishops, he was receiving strong support from Ransom, Gregg, Reid, Nichols, Baber, and Allen. In addition, he knew he could count on friends like Hubert Robinson, Frank Veal, George Singleton, F. W. Grant, John Bright, Wallace Wright, J. D. Smith, John Hunter, who had always supported him.

When the question of the retirement of bishops was brought before the convention, it was obvious that there were two strong factions. One group sought the retirement at half-salary of Williams, Young, and Ransom. The other group, of which Joseph was a part, felt that Ransom should be retained. The dilemma was resolved by Ransom himself. On May 13 he rose from his seat and asked that he not be given a district but be appointed Historiographer of the newly formed Department of History and Research.

White-haired, erect, proud, still eloquent [he] delivered a simple moving farewell that evoked tears, then cheers. . . . He stood tall and stiff while scores of lay and ministerial leaders showered him with their praises; revering his long and useful career. Later he told admirers "This is the way I have always prayed it would be. That the time would come was inescapable. I'm happy to 'bow out' with sustaining warmth of a 'well done, good and faithful servant' ringing in my ears."[59]

Bishop Gregg read a resolution to the conference that whereas Reverdy C. Ransom knew more about the history of the Church than anyone else, he was "eminently qualified to conduct a department of research." Therefore, he should remain active "with special assignments" in the Department of History and Research.[60]

Many seconding speeches followed, among them one by Rev. Lutrelle Long, representing the 3rd District. He said, "The greatest connection in the A.M.E. Church is stepping down today. Between us and Richard Allen is Reverdy C. Ransom[,] . . . who organized the regiment that walked up San Juan Hill. And W. E. B. Du Bois in his book acknowledges that the one who organized the NAACP was R. C. Ransom." After the seconding speeches Bishop Gregg led the conference in singing the Wilberforce alma mater, which he had written when he was president.[61] The last chord seemed to finalize the passing of a grand era.

During the same session, Paul Robeson appeared. The delegates were rapt as he entertained them with songs that had made him famous: the spiritual "Mount Zion," the folk ballad "Water Boy," and a selection from *Showboat,* "Old Man River." When he came to the part, "Get a little drunk and land in jail," to the delight of the audience he changed the words: "Get a little *spunk* and land in jail." He urged the A.M.E.'s to join with all other minorities the world over to fight for justice and self-determination.[62]

On Friday, May 14, the Episcopal Committee recommended that all the Episcopal Districts remain the same in terms of area and that the salaries of the bishops be raised from $4,200 to $8,500. It further recommended that Bishops Young and Williams be supernumerated (discharged from duty) with full pay and that six new bishops be elected. The conference emended the recommendation concerning Young and Williams to supernumerate them with half pay. Bishop Ransom was to become the historiographer and director of the Department of History and Research with full pay and maintain his headquarters at his home, Tawawa Chimney, at Wilberforce. The conference agreed that the salaries should be raised to $8,500 and directed the Financial Department to pay the entire amount. It approved the election of six bishops and set the election for 3:30 P.M. of the same day.[63]

Promptly at 3:30 "delegates and officers filed past the ballot box to personally deposit their ballots." After all the districts had voted, "the tellers and clerks settled down to an all-night grind of tallying the votes."[64] Those who had a personal interest in the election tried to make themselves comfortable in the drafty Memorial Hall. They stretched out on hard benches, dozed off, woke up long enough to get coffee or cocoa to warm their chilled bodies. In the background one could hear the chief teller calling out the votes: "Gomez, tally, Walker, two, Bonner, three." On and on droned the count.

Joseph tried to persuade Hazel to go back to the hotel and rest, but she refused to leave his side. She wanted to be there when the results were announced, regardless of the outcome. From time to time William Hodge would lean over to show Joseph the current tally: he was doing well, but D. O. Walker was ahead. Joseph wondered whether, if he lost this time, he would have the heart to run again. Maybe the Lord had called him to be a pastor all of his life. "Gomez, two, Walker, three, Hemingway, tally." It seemed as though the tellers would never finish counting the first ballot. At 2 A.M. Walker and Gomez were ahead, but Hemingway was gaining rapidly. At 4 A.M. it was "Gomez, tally, Walker three, Hemingway, two"— and still the teller read on. Someone bought sandwiches, which Hazel gratefully accepted but Joseph could not bring himself to eat. To the outside observer, he was calm, but he had always been plagued by a spastic stomach that flared up whenever he was experiencing great tension, as he was now.

Rumor was going around the hall that Hemingway had spent thousands of dollars buying votes, and tempers were on the verge of exploding. It was also rumored that the conference would never elect two West Indians. If this were true, would it be Walker or Gomez? At this point, Walker was still ahead.

Near sunrise, Fannie K. Smith of West Palm Beach, Florida, an election clerk who had worked all night counting votes, collapsed. Some of the tellers rushed to her side and tried to lift her; they found that she had no pulse and had stopped breathing. Someone applied cardio-pulmonary resuscitation, while another went to call the emergency room. For three-quarters of an hour the election was halted, and the attention of the delegates was focused on the comings and goings of medics and stretcher bearers who carried her body from the hall. Later it was announced that Fannie had died of a heart attack brought on by extreme fatigue and tension.[65]

Before the conference learned of her fate, the hypnotic voices of the tellers resumed: morning, noon, afternoon, until 4:40 P.M. Saturday. The first ballot had taken twenty-one hours and forty-five minutes, eighteen hours and forty minutes of which were consumed by the tallying. Each name appearing on the ballot had to be read first by the chief teller and then repeated by the chief clerk; in other words, 23,926 names had been read aloud by the two clerks. By the end of the counting, three of the six bishops had been elected: L. H. Hemingway with 981 votes, D. O. Walker with 958 votes, and Joseph Gomez with 942 votes. For election, 924 votes had been necessary.[66]

Charles Loeb described the scene as the three new bishops were called to the platform to be congratulated by Nichols, the Presiding Bishop, and the rest of the College of Bishops. Walker approached the platform first, with tears streaming down his face; he said, "God is good." Next came "Dr. Joseph Gomez, whose quiet dignity and poise has stood out like a sore thumb in this riotous conference." He stepped to the microphone and said, "God give me the strength to serve His church with honor and unselfishness." Bishop Hemingway, "the last to reach the platform was tight-lipped and noncommittal. He was still smarting under widespread rumor that he had expended large sums of money [to] insure his election."[67]

After the presentation of the new bishops, Joseph and Hazel left the auditorium to look for Eula, who had arrived from Los Angeles on Friday, and to call Annetta in Cleveland and tell her the news. As they moved toward the hall, people pushed to get to them and offer personal congratulations. The mixture of fatigue and excitement lent an unreality to the scene, and Joseph's stomach was rioting.

Back in Memorial Hall, the second balloting had begun. The process took much less time, because many of the delegates, too exhausted to endure any more, had left for their hotels. By 1 A.M. the tally was completed, and two more bishops had been elected, Isaiah H. Bonner and William R. Wilkes. At this point the fire chief declared that the hall had to be vacated so it could be cleaned for the Sunday service. The election was shifted to First A.M.E. Church, and the balloting and tallying continued. To prevent the necessity of a fourth ballot or a heated debate concerning a plurality, Jordan, who was second in votes to Rev. C. A. Gibbs, withdrew— to the applause of the exhausted delegates, who assured him that because of his unselfish gesture he would surely be elected in 1952. Gibbs became the sixth bishop.[68]

On Sunday afternoon, May 16, the new bishops were consecrated. Just before the formal ritual, Eula sang "O Divine Redeemer" in honor of her father's election. As if by divine decree, the atmosphere was metamorphosed from the hawking and bartering of election night to an afternoon of reverence. When it was Joseph's turn to be consecrated, he was presented to the bishops by J. D. Smith of Bermuda, William Hodge of Ohio, M. R. Dixon of Illinois, Henry Murphy of Georgia, F. W. Grant of Texas, and Wallace Wright of Ohio. The service was read by Bishops Ransom, Gregg, and Reid, Joseph's most loyal supporters through the years. Ransom's hands shook and his voice quavered with emotion during the reading, but he held his head erect as he laid his hands on "his son in the Gospel." After the consecration, old and new bishops and prominent elders celebrated Holy Communion.[69] This was Joseph's first experience of administering communion as a bishop, and he was sobered by the sudden realization of his new mission—his new odyssey.

The delegates waited most of the next day for the report of the Episcopal Committee, whose job it was to assign bishops. Their patience exhausted, the delegates sent an ultimatum to the committee, demanding a report immediately. It was rumored that the committee was deadlocked as a result of pressure by bishops requesting certain districts, and by the Texas delegation, led by F. W. Grant, who was insisting that Joseph be assigned to the 10th Episcopal District. Meanwhile the election of General Officers went on. Bishops Walker and Gomez were given the chance to preside. According to the minutes "their baptisms were not made pleasant by irritated delegates . . . but both conducted themselves with poise and confidence."[70]

Finally the Episcopal Committee was ready to make its report. Among the new bishops, Hemingway was sent to the 2nd District (Baltimore, Washington, Virginia, North Carolina), Walker to the 5th (Missouri, Kansas, Colorado, Nebraska, California, and Puget Sound), Gomez to the 15th (South Africa), Wilkes to the 16th (Cuba and South American islands), Gibbs to the 14th (Liberia, Sierra Leone, Nigeria, and the Gold Coast), and Bonner to the 17th (Transvaal, Zambezi, Central Africa, the Belgian Congo). Despite the repeated requests of the Texas delegation that Gomez be sent to the 10th, that assignment went to Bishop Henry Y. Tookes.[71]

When Joseph's appointment was read there was excitement among the South African delegates, who had asked for him, but disappointment among those from the 10th. Joseph would have preferred to go to Texas, but did not doubt that South Africa would present a challenge. Besides, he would get to work with his friend Francis Gow, a native who had been fighting apartheid most of his adult life. The problem would be, as it had been with other bishops, getting into South Africa in the first place: the government did not welcome Black Americans, who they felt would "stir up the natives."

After the appointments had been read, the conference listened to the third reading of the report of the committee on the revision of the Discipline. Joseph paid special attention to Part XIV, pertaining to bishops assigned to a foreign district.

A Bishop assigned to a foreign district who fails to enter upon his duties in the district to which he is assigned within ninety days after his assignment shall cease to receive the salary of a Bishop until he arrives in the district to which he is assigned . . . .

In the event of a vacancy in a Home District, the Bishops' council shall not assign any Bishop assigned by the Episcopal Committee to a foreign field to fill such a vacancy.[72]

Part XIV was adopted by the conference.

At the close of the conference the Council of Bishops met to elect chairmen for the various committees.[73] As soon as the meeting adjourned, Joseph and Hazel left for Cleveland to prepare for their departure for South Africa. When they reached the parsonage they were greeted by hundreds of telegrams, cards, and phone messages. Most of them congratulated Joseph for his elevation, "which had been long overdue." Attorney Sadie Alexander wrote that she and her husband knew that he would "add dignity to the bench of Bishops and . . . maintain a standard of intellectual and moral honesty." Frank J. Lausche felt sure that "the expanded field in which [Gomez] will be permitted to do [his] religious work will inure greatly to the benefit of the people." Clevelanders expressed their regret that he would be leaving the city "but were happy that he and Mrs. Gomez had realized [their] life-long ambition." Joseph also found a message from a Rev. S. N. T'ladi, one of the South African delegates, requesting that he meet with the South Africans in New York before they departed for home.[74] He agreed to come in mid-June, when he would accompany Annetta to New York to audition for Piscator's Dramatic Workshop.

Bishop Tookes had left the General Conference at once for his new district in Texas; however, after only a few days in Dallas he had to be flown back to New York because of a serious illness. A specialist labored over him for several days, but on Tuesday morning, June 9, at 1 P.M., two weeks after the close of the General Conference, he died in his New York apartment. Funeral services were held on June 15 in Jacksonville, Florida, at Grant Memorial A.M.E. Church.[75]

Following the funeral, Bishop Gregg called an emergency session of the Bishops' Council for the purpose of filling the vacancy in the 10th Episcopal District. Outside of the meeting place were a number of representatives from Texas who had come to petition for Bishop Gomez to be sent there. Joseph was not surprised. Before leaving for the funeral he had received a telegram from Eric E. L. Hercules of Dallas asking him to "consider seriously the wishes of Texas" that he become their bishop and informing him that Rev. Grant and Dr. Jenkins had prepared a petition to be presented to the Council of Bishops. The telegram was followed by phone calls from Texas, one of them from Rev. Grant himself.

As soon as the Council meeting began, Bishop Reid moved that the vote for the replacement of Bishop Tookes be taken by ballot. At this point, Bishop Fountain rose to ask whether or not bishops assigned to foreign fields were eligible for consideration, in light of Part XIV of the revision of the Discipline passed at the General Conference. Bishop Williams observed that he was himself a supernumerary and therefore available to be called to a district in case of emergency. A heated argument ensued, during which Joseph asked for the floor. He told the bishops that he did not want his tenure in the bishopric to begin under a cloud; he proposed that since the Council would hold its regular meeting the next week in Atlantic City, filling the vacancy should be deferred until then. Bishop Nichols then moved that Bishop Gregg, as chairman of the Council, should oversee the 10th District until the Council meeting, when an appointment would be made.[76] The motion was passed, and the Texas delegation was informed as to what had taken place. They vowed they would be in attendance at Atlantic City with the same petition.

Although preparation time was short, Bishop Nichols, the host bishop, entertained the Council in grand style in Atlantic City, beginning June 23. The weather cooperated; it was warm enough to walk on the boardwalk or to splash about in the salty Atlantic. Most of those present, including the group from Texas, took advantage of the setting.

After the opening worship service, the bishops met to settle the matter of the 10th District. Hours of discussion followed before the Council decided to assign Joseph Gomez to Texas; however, the vote was not unanimous. Four votes were cast against his appointment, supposedly because of the new ruling concerning bishops assigned to foreign districts. The factors that convinced the majority he should be sent to the 10th were the petition signed by seventy-five prominent laymen and clergy from outside the Texas district, the tremendous appeal made by the representatives from Texas, and the report that conditions in Texas were so acute that strong leadership was needed immediately. Following the appointment there was talk of establishing an office of Bishop Co-Adjunctor of the 15th District (South Africa) and naming Francis Gow to the post, but no agreement could be reached. In the end, Bishop Bonner was assigned to the 15th in place of Gomez.[77]

A.M.E.'s in Texas were delighted to learn that at last their petition had been granted. Telegrams poured into Cleveland welcoming Joseph and Hazel to Texas. Rev. F. W. Grant was ecstatic. There were others, however, who felt the Council had acted illegally, and they expressed their objections. Hoping to settle the controversy once and for all, Vincent Townsend wrote an article in the *Southern Christian Recorder* for July 10, arguing that there should never be a law which prevented the removal of anyone or the filling of a vacancy when the interest of the Church demanded such action. "Let the interest of the Church always predominate, not the man, but the Church have first consideration," he concluded.[78]

On Saturday, June 12, Dr. Hubert N. Robinson, affectionately called "Hubie," arrived in Cleveland to assume his new pastorate at St. James. He was a native of Springfield, Ohio, a graduate of Ohio State University and of Hammon Divinity School of Wittenberg College, and the former pastor of St. James, Pittsburgh.[79] He had a reputation for strong administrative skills and an ability to develop active youth programs wherever he pastored. His wife, Mamie, was a tiny, attractive, energetic woman. The couple were greeted by the Gomezes and members of St. James, who felt that if they had to lose their pastor, they were glad to gain a man of Robinson's stature. The Robinsons were to share the parsonage until the Gomezes left for Texas.

Sunday morning, Robinson and Joseph conducted a Children's Day Program, at which the members also gathered to say goodbye to Hazel, Joseph, and Annetta (Eula was still in Los Angeles). Before the benediction was pronounced, the congregation formed a large circle around the auditorium and sang "God Be with You Till We Meet Again." It was a moving scene—the unbroken chain of tightly held hands and the plaintive chorus, "Till we me-e-t, till we me-e-t. Till we meet at Jesus' feet. Till we me-e-t, till we me-e-t. God be with you till we meet again." Then followed a moment of silent meditation while Kathleen Forbes, the organist, repeated the refrain on the chimes. It was difficult for the congregation to say farewell to their pastor and his family after twelve years. For some of the young people, Joseph was the only pastor they had ever known. After a great deal of weeping and hugging, the Gomezes stood in the empty auditorium, quietly remembering; then, hand in hand they left the church, reluctantly closing the door behind them.

When asked in later years what they remembered most about their father's pastorate at St. James, Eula and Annetta agreed: the Christmas morning 6 A.M. candlelight services, the peace they felt when the lights in the church were darkened and everyone lifted their candles and sang "Silent Night, Holy Night." Then the family would return home to open presents and prepare for the massive Christmas dinner. There was the "Hallelujah Chorus," sung by the joint choirs on Easter Sunday. There was the New Year's Eve Watch Night Service, which began at 10:30 P.M. with only a few people in attendance; by 11:30 the houses in the neighborhoods and the bars on Cedar Avenue would be empty, and hundreds of people, members and non-members, would pour into the sanctuary to spend the last few minutes of the old year on their knees as Joseph counted away the seconds. "It is eleven fifty-five, and the old year is passing. It is eleven fifty-nine and the old year is passing fast." When it was twelve, the entire congregation would stand and sing "What a Happy New Year," and everyone would hug and shake hands. After a brief fellowship and snacks in the church dining room, people would return to their homes, their bars, or their parties, with renewed strength to face the coming months. Most of all, Eula and Annetta would remember the warmth and love poured out to them by the faithful members of St. James as they went through their "growing pains."

Joseph gave his farewell appearance in Cleveland at Lakewood Methodist Church, on Sunday, August 1. Describing the service, Louis Gale, church editor of the *Cleveland Plain Dealer*, said, "It's called Brotherhood, and it stood out bold and clear from the pulpit and every filled pew in Lakewood Methodist." He pointed out that few visiting ministers could have filled such a large church on a perfect August Sunday, just right for a picnic, especially when the pastor of Lakewood, Dr. Harold F. Carr, was nationally known for his superb preaching skills. But "it was a time when people who believed in God listened to a man tell them of a Divine Spirit that can fill the lives of people . . . all people whether they are black, white, red, or yellow."[80]

Joseph chose for his topic "Faith of Our Times." He spoke of it being a time when there was need to believe again in the "sacredness of [Jesus'] personality . . . [a time] to cultivate the love of all people." He cautioned the congregation that as great as the Methodist Church was, it was still "weak, puerile and infantile" in its attempts to help people with their contemporary problems. He spoke of the danger in "Palestine, Germany or other centers of tension [where] at any time some fool may do an act that will precipitate a war [and] wipe civilization off the earth. . . . Human hate had a strange way of multiplying itself," he said. "You have to isolate it. Hate must be destroyed. The intelligence that can deflect this destruction is a reaffirmation of our faith in God."[81]

When the service was over the huge crowd formed "a long line in front of the pulpit to grasp the hands of Bishop and Mrs. Gomez. . . . It was a heart tingling scene in which sincere affection and regard for two fellow townsmen was demonstrated through the medium of hearty handshakes and cordial good wishes for the Bishop and his wife in their new Texas home."[82]

◈ ◈ ◈

CHAPTER TEN

Yellow Roses and Thorns

Texas, 1948–1951

The right of the Bishops of the African Methodist Episcopal Church to "assign" is a fundamental right. It has the sanction of history, polity and practice. . . . We are not "Congregational" but "Episcopal" in Church government. In all the history of the "Episcopus" governed churches, there has always been recognized this basic question of continuing authority. Thus, the General Conference wisely legalized the Bishops' Council to act "ad interim" and to govern the entire Church. . . . Under fundamental Methodist practices, it has that right.

—Joseph Gomez, notes, 1948

◈ Texas was no place for the fainthearted. Joseph would find this out as bishop of this vast, unwieldy district, and also as chancellor of Paul Quinn College in Waco (see appendix A).

On August 7 Hazel, Joseph, and Annetta arrived on the campus, which was to be their home for the next eight years (Eula was still in California). The sun beat down as they descended from the car that had brought them from Houston. It was not humid, as it had been in Ohio; instead, it was dry and dusty. Tall, coarse grasses almost obscured the tiny administration building in the center of the campus facing Elm, one of the two streets that bordered the college. To the right, near Garrison Avenue, was a fortress-like three-story brick building, Johnson Hall. A men's dormitory, it also served as a library and classroom facility. To the left of the administration building and parallel to Johnson was another ancient bastion, Grant Hall, which housed the Home Economics Department and the women students.

Other buildings included the George B. Young Auditorium, a long, barn-like building with a row of doors on two sides that could be opened to catch any stray breeze that might be stirring; a two-story apartment building for faculty housing; a small house for the nursery; and two other houses, which would soon become the Episcopal Residence and the president's home. To the rear of the campus was a mechanics shop, and behind it a large stretch of uncultivated land where the football team practiced.

The college had been founded in Austin, Texas, in 1872 by a small group of A.M.E. circuit-riding ministers who felt it imperative to educate Blacks following the Civil War. In 1881 the school had been moved to Waco, where it occupied twenty-two acres of the old Garrison plantation. It was named after William Paul Quinn, a missionary, who had been born in the East Indies in 1788 and had become the fourth bishop of the A.M.E. Church in 1844.[1] The college had had its fat and lean years. When Joseph arrived, it was obviously in a lean state.

The catalogue listed Paul Quinn as being a "liberal arts, manual arts, science, and teacher training college" that offered degrees in "the arts and sciences, general education, elementary education, primary education, secondary education, rural education, administration and supervision." In addition students could earn a bachelor of divinity degree and a doctorate of divinity in theology, despite the fact that the school had no seminary. There were courses listed that had not been taught for years. The faculty was small, and only a few teachers had advanced degrees; some did not even have a bachelor's degree.[2] In actuality, Paul Quinn was little more than a high school in terms of quality and the scope of its offerings. In no way could it compare with Wilberforce University.

The Gomezes were met on the campus by retired Bishop George B. Young, several presiding elders, including Joseph's friend Thomas R. Clemons, and by the college president, Nannie Belle Aycox—a medium-height, copper-colored woman with Indian features who wore her jet black hair pulled tightly to the back of her head. The group moved to the auditorium, where a crowd had gathered to greet formally the new bishop and his family.

After the welcoming program, the Gomezes inspected the Episcopal Residence, which had been a dormitory and was being redecorated and furnished by the district. Most of their personal things had already arrived from Cleveland but were still packed in boxes in the middle of the living room floor. On the first floor of the two-story white frame building, in addition to the living room, was a guest bedroom and bath, a spacious dining room, and kitchen. Around the left side of the house was a screened-in porch where meals could also be served. In months to come one could view from the porch the varicolored rose bushes Hazel planted in the yard and the tiny hummingbirds that swarmed around them.

The second floor was reached by a long staircase off a foyer near the front door. Facing the campus was a sunroom, a master bedroom, and one other bedroom. At the rear of the house was a study, a bath, and a third bedroom. The house was not to be ready for occupancy for several weeks, and the Gomezes were to live with the Aycoxes in the meantime.

When they finally moved into the Episcopal Residence, they were introduced to Jessie Dickerson, the housekeeper, who soon became a permanent fixture. Anyone who wanted to see the bishop when he was in his study had to go through her. Jessie was in her fifties, dark-skinned and plump, wore her hair in a severe bun at the back, and had an air of "no nonsense." Eventually the college assigned several work-study students to help her with the heavy work in the house and yard.

Everyone's favorite student, except Jessie's, was Sonny (Willford Gowens)—whose disposition was "sunny." Although Hazel did not find him the most efficient helper, he was the most entertaining. He had a head full of yarns that he just "had to tell," especially when there was work to be done.

To complete the family unit, Louella Hinton, a former member of St. James, Cleveland, came to work temporarily as a secretary for the bishop; she became so attached to Texas that she stayed on as college bookstore manager, post office clerk, and chapel organist. Later, Dorothy Williams, the registrar, came to live for a while in the Episcopal Residence. She was a young, attractive, fair-skinned woman, with hair that hung down to her ankles when she unpinned it. Most of her life she had been crippled as a result of polio; however, she had learned to move swiftly on crutches and had a great deal of energy. The "Bishop and Mother Gomez" became her adopted parents.

Another member of the unofficial family was Rev. A. S. B. Jones, a six-foot, five-inch mountain, who volunteered to be the bishop's driver. Like Sonny, he was good natured and devoted, but he was also mischievous, and he liked to pester Jessie. Joseph was always having to get him out of some minor difficulty. He was married to a New Orleans woman named Myra, who kept him in line by making him believe she knew how to cast spells on people. Later, when Jones moved to another conference, Rev. Herman F. Dodson became Joseph's driver. Both men knew how to get the bishop where he needed to go in a hurry—too much of a hurry for Hazel.

In many ways, the Gomezes found Waco to be like a typical town in the deep South, even though Texas was considered to be in the West. The train station had separate waiting rooms, drinking fountains, and toilet facilities. In the larger waiting room marked "For Whites Only" the doors to the toilets read "Ladies" and "Gentlemen"; the toilet doors in the smaller "For Colored" waiting room read "Men" and "Women." Blacks could not eat in restaurants, at the counters in drug or ten cent stores, or try on certain clothes in the department stores. They had to sit in the back of buses and in segregated bleachers at Katy Park or at Baylor University Stadium. Baylor was the Baptist college, and Blacks could not attend.

In terms of housing, Blacks were relegated to a few neighborhoods near the railroad tracks in the most undesirable sections of town. Public schools were segregated, and those "for Colored" were poorly equipped and often had the least trained teachers. The schools let out early or began late in the year so the children could pick or chop cotton. From his study window Joseph could see them leaving for the fields early in the morning with their burlap sacks slung across their shoulders, and return in the evening exhausted but a few pennies richer. If they picked extra-fast, there might be a few coins left for the "Colored" movie house, owned and operated by the Pryors, a Black family; or they might go to Walker's Auditorium, where on occasion they could hear visiting artists such as Ray Charles and Duke Ellington for fifty cents; or they might feast on barbecue, collard greens, corn bread, and pinto beans at Frye's Restaurant.

There were a few Black professionals in Waco: Dr. G. H. Radford, a dentist; Dr. Alfred T. Braithwaite, a general practitioner; Dr. J. W. Yancy, former president of Paul Quinn (1939–42) and journalist, and his wife, a musician and teacher; and several ministers and teachers. For the most part, however, Blacks worked in menial jobs. If they wanted to be reminded of their limited social lives, they could buy the *Waco Messenger*. There was little communication between the races. Segregation was an established way of life which everyone, including most Negroes, seemed to take for granted. This was the Waco that Hazel and Joseph faced in 1948. Already there were stumbling blocks—which, surprisingly, at first came largely from outside Texas.

On July 1 an article had appeared in the *Christian Recorder* titled "Poor Bleeding Africa," by Bishop John H. Clayborn, who had voted against Joseph's reassignment to Texas. In it he severely criticized the Bishops' Council for its decision not to send Joseph to South Africa. He stated that Africa always seemed to get the short straw, especially when home districts became vacant as a result of the illness or death of the presiding bishop; hence, the article's melodramatic title. In light of the legislature passed at the last General Conference, he asserted, the Council had acted not only in bad faith but illegally.[3]

On July 10th, another article had appeared, this time written by J. P. Q. Wallace, who wrote that despite the confusion at the General Conference in 1948, three laws that had been passed were indisputably clear: the law relating to the reassignment of all bishops, the law raising the salary of bishops, and "the law that related to the assignment of a Bishop to a foreign district."[4] After that a series of articles appeared in the *Recorder*, including another by Bishop Clayborn entitled "Haven't You Had Enough Broken Laws?"[5] Within a few months of his election Joseph found himself already embroiled in a controversy that was hotly debated throughout the Connection.

The new law relating to bishops assigned to foreign districts seemed clear enough by itself, but it became less clear when put beside a revision to the Discipline passed at the same General Conference, which read, "The Bishops' Council shall have authority to administer all affairs, and have the supervision over the entire Church during the interim of the General Conference."[6] Joseph had accepted the ruling of the Bishops' Council. His reasons were clearly outlined in an article dated November 1948 found among his papers. It concluded, "The General Conference is supreme, only subject to limitations imposed upon it by the very nature of the organization. One of these limitations to be found in all books of law is that it cannot do away with the General Superintendency or Episcopacy."[7] Nonetheless, Clayborn brought charges against Joseph, which led to his salary being held up until a hearing could be convened. This was an inconvenience Joseph could ill afford, with both daughters needing financial assistance, but he had little time to dwell on his financial state. There were many other things confronting him.

One of the most important events for Texas African Methodists is the Annual Ministerial Institute, Missionary, and Youth Congress which convenes on the campus of Paul Quinn College during the latter part of the summer. In 1948 it opened August 24 and ran through the 29th. More than seven thousand people from all over the state and from other districts assembled to attend the sessions and to greet the new bishop. Among those in attendance were Bishop C. A. Gibbs of the 14th Episcopal District, who delivered the opening sermon; Wallace M. Wright of Cincinnati, Joseph's campaign manager during his run for the bishopric, who preached the following evening; and Francis H. Gow, pastor of Bethel A.M.E. Church in Cape Town, South Africa, who was the guest speaker during Missionary Night.[8]

The most significant business of the Congress was the unanimous passage of a resolution "commending the Bishops' Council for its action in assigning Bishop Gomez to preside over Texas . . . [and] declaring its displeasure respecting attempts of persons outside of Texas to meddle and create confusion." With such leadership the district was sure it would take its place "among the leading Episcopal Districts of the African Methodist Church."[9]

On the Saturday before the Congress closed, Joseph met with the college trustees. He recommended that several additions be made to the faculty and administration, including a dean, business manager, and maintenance supervisor. His top priority before his Annual Conferences convened in the fall was to initiate a reorganization plan. The financial books of the college were a disaster; the permanent records of the students were filed in no particular order and were not up to date (many were on the floor of the Administration Building in boxes); there was no new catalogue for 1948. Most important, all the buildings needed major repairs before school opened September 13 and about four hundred students arrived.[10]

The Congress closed on Sunday, August 29, with a worship service. A hundred-voice choir shook the rafters with its syncopated gospel beat, and Joseph delivered a sermon based on the story of the Prodigal Son. His emphasis was on the older brother, who, he concluded, had "a cold, calculating heart and had lost his ability to love. If you want love, you must love; it you want mercy, you must be merciful." The *Southern Christian Recorder* compared the service to an "old camp meeting."[11] The fervor of the congregation reminded Joseph of the Sunday morning services at St. Paul, St. Louis, where the shouting had continued long after the meeting closed. At St. James, Cleveland, the members had said an occasional "amen," but anyone who became too demonstrative received looks of displeasure. But here in the George B. Young Auditorium the building rocked with cries of praise and hallelujahs. Joseph would have to reaccustom himself to this more vocal and physical kind of worship. In a way, he found it satisfying to have an immediate and spontaneous response to his sermon.

In late September Joseph and Hazel put Annetta on the train for New York City, where she would be attending Piscator's Dramatic Workshop and living at the Emma Ransom House. Soon after, they left Waco for a series of nine Annual Conferences, beginning with the Mexico–Rio Grande Valley Conference in Corpus Christi (September 30–October 4), and ending with the North Texas Conference in Fort Worth (November 24–28). The schedule was grueling, because of the vastness of the territory to be covered and because Joseph would have to return to Waco between conferences to supervise the work being done at Paul Quinn.

The Mexico and Rio Grande Valley Conference opened with a welcoming program, followed by a banquet. Clergy and laymen had come from all over to see that Joseph was given a proper start as he began his conferences. On the following day the delegates elected Hazel as accountant to the bishop, with Rev. Lionel C. Young, Bishop Young's nephew from Wichita Falls, as auditor.[12] Hazel's careful bookkeeping was to prove invaluable to Joseph in some of the troubled days to come.

During the Mexico–Rio Grande Conference Joseph pleaded with the elders to devote more time to the work there. He knew that in the eyes of many to be sent to "the Valley," as the conference was disparagingly called, was to be sent to the wilderness. Joseph, however, envisioned a vast expansion of African Methodism in "the Valley" and considered it to be a rich challenge for any enterprising pastor.[13]

The conferences varied little from each other or from other Annual Conferences of which Joseph had been a part; only this time, he was the presiding prelate. Nevertheless, despite the similarity in form, the personalities were different. In some the atmosphere was spirited and cooperative; in a few others there could be felt an undercurrent of resentment or apathy. For instance, at the Texas Conference, when it came time for the bishop "to pass" on the character of the ministers, several were absent. This was an important event, since a pastor could not be assigned to a church until his moral behavior had been judged acceptable. Joseph, who had always regarded tardiness or absenteeism as "two of the seven deadly sins," would not "pass" on the characters of the absent ministers until they appeared before the conference and gave valid excuses for missing the session. At this point, Dr. C. W. Abington, editor of the *Sunday School Union* and an old friend of Joseph's, asked for the floor. He pleaded with the bishop not to deal drastically with the absent or late ministers, as "this was the first real up-to-date and business-like conference that [they] had had in Texas in many years."[14]

In most of the conferences Joseph found it necessary to emphasize what he referred to as "ministerial efficiency." He was appalled to learn how many ministers did not live in their parsonages or how many of their wives had jobs elsewhere and lived in other cities. This practice left the minister open to all kinds of negative speculation by the members and general public. Joseph was old-fashioned enough to believe that the ministry was a special calling which demanded full participation by the minister and support from his wife. He should be available to his congregation at all times, and his wife could not be very supportive if she lived miles away. This belief led some to spread the rumor that the bishop did not approve of women working. He categorically denied this. Many pastors' wives lived in the parsonages with their husbands and successfully held jobs outside of the home; it was not the job that bothered him, but the separation. He was also disturbed to learn that many of the congregations were better educated than their pastors. He encouraged these ministers to enroll in college and further their studies as soon as possible.

Despite some of the problems encountered, Joseph was able to say generally that the people seemed anxious for leadership. He was inspired by the warmth of his reception and the willingness of the ministers and laity to accept the innovations he suggested, including a new budget plan. In this plan, each minister was to be given a yearly assessment for his church at the same time he received his appointment. Instead of going along in the old haphazard fashion of waiting for needs to develop and then trying to raise money, the bishop, presiding elders, pastors, and lay persons together would determine the financial needs for carrying on the work in the coming year. Knowing the assessment ahead of time would enable the ministers to budget carefully and allow them more time to pastor their congregations. All nine conferences voted unanimously to accept the new plan, and also to raise $250,000 for the expansion of Paul Quinn College before the next Quadrennial. At each Annual Conference, one night was set aside as Paul Quinn Night; the college choir, directed by Wilhelm Sykes, would sing, and the president of the college would speak concerning its progress and needs.

The sessions were not all devoted to the reporting of money and planning for expansion. A good deal of time was spent in worship. African Methodists have always been noted for their congregational singing of the old Methodist hymns, and Texas A.M.E.s were no exception. They soon learned that "Amazing Grace," "Pass Me Not O Gentle Savior," "Softly and Tenderly, Jesus Is Calling," and "Oh, for a Thousand Tongues to Sing My Great Redeemer's Praise" were the Bishop's favorites, and he would sing them lustily over and over again along with other familiar hymns, spirituals, and gospel songs. A.M.E.s were also noted for the stirring sermons of their clergy; though they were considered not as emotional as a good Baptist sermon, they held their own. As Joseph told them in one of his sermons, "Spirituality must be made a fundamental part of our living in order to enjoy a close fellowship with God," and that spirituality was often expressed with "joyful noise."[15]

The committee reports were also an interesting part of each conference, particularly those given by the Committee on the State of the Country. These documents varied in sophistication: in some conferences they were four printed pages long, in others only a half-page. In spite of the difference in length, there was a commonality in subject matter—Church concerns and politics as it affected civil rights.

Thanksgiving 1948 and Joseph's fifty-eighth birthday came on the same day. At the time, he was holding his last conference at Baker Chapel in Fort

Worth. The *Waco Messenger* reported, "A parade of distinguished notables of the Church were presented and lauded Bishop Gomez as the best prepared and the most outstanding leader in the entire Church Connection. . . . Gomez was presented with many gifts."[16]

In terms of Christian fellowship, receptiveness of new ideas, and money raised for the Connection and the college, Hazel and Joseph had reason to be well pleased with their first Annual Conferences in Texas. Further evidence of their success was expressed in a letter sent to Joseph from the Pension Department, November 15, 1948, complimenting him for his "fine reports." It further stated, "It is providential that a man like you was sent to that district to bring those people out of the chaotic conditions under which they have labored." It was signed, L. Nerissa Mance, secretary to Rev. Beard, Pension Department.[17]

When Joseph returned home from his last Annual Conference, he found a letter from attorney Herbert L. Dudley forwarding an enclosure from a letter sent to him by Bishop S. L. Green, current president of the Council of Bishops. Dudley had been advising Joseph to seek an injunction against the Department of Finance in regard to the release of his salary. Joseph, who had refused to take the matter to civil court, had asked Dudley, a leader of the laymen's organization, to find out what other steps within the jurisdiction of the Church could be taken. Bishop Greene agreed that something had to be done quickly "by some tribunal, individual or individuals to settle out of court if possible this most unfortunate affair." He suggested that Joseph wait until the regular winter meeting of the Bishops' Council when the matter could be resolved he was sure.[18] Although Joseph was experiencing financial difficulties, especially with Annetta in school in New York, he decided to take Bishop Greene's advice and wait until the winter council meeting.

Meanwhile, between December 1 and 3 the Gomezes attended the Federated Council of Churches in America, held in Cincinnati. Joseph preached in San Antonio on December 12, after which he and Hazel left for Los Angeles to spend Christmas with Eula, who had given birth to a twelve-pound baby boy on December 3. Marvin Dewitt Butler was Eula and Tory's first son and Hazel and Joseph's first grandchild. Joseph already had elaborate plans for the baby to attend Harvard and be a lawyer when he grew up; Eula was just glad he was healthy and normal.

While in Los Angeles, the Gomezes visited Violet, Ismael, and their daughters, Jewell and Gloria. They listened skeptically to Violet's side of the story as to why Eula and Annetta had moved from her home. Joseph became a great favorite of his nieces, especially Gloria, who liked to call him "Moony" because of his round face. He was also fond of Ismael, who reminded him of his father. He was by no means a match for Violet's fiery temper, which flared up at the least provocation, any more than Mani had been a match for Rebecca's.

In January 1949, Hazel and Joseph went to Washington, D.C., to attend the 1949 inauguration ceremonies of President Truman. Joseph hoped that Truman would expand Roosevelt's domestic program, especially in the area of civil rights. He was impressed by Truman's attack on "that false philosophy, Communism," and his determination "to win the victory of the Cold War," as expressed in his January 20 inaugural address. Before he left Washington, along with others of his delegation from Texas, Joseph had an opportunity to speak briefly with Truman, who assured them he was in favor of strong civil rights legislation.

When Joseph returned to Waco on February 3, he learned that Bishop George B. Young had died the night before and that his funeral would be held on February 9 in the auditorium named after him. Hundreds of people from throughout the Connection were in attendance. The congregation sang "Abide with Me," after which Joseph approached the podium to deliver the eulogy. He began, "George Benjamin Young, pioneer, preacher, missionary, bishop, now triumphs in rest eternal." He recalled Young's southern background. His parents had been slaves, but he had "determined early . . . that neither lowliness of birth nor the inhibitions of circumstances would rob him of the achievements possible to those who will and dare." Joseph closed by hailing Young as "friend and counselor."[19]

Before leaving for Washington to attend the winter session of the Bishops' Council, Joseph received a letter from George Singleton concerning Bishop Clayborn, the main instigator of the attempt to deny Joseph his salary unless he went to South Africa. Seemingly, Clayborn was having his own problems: charges had been brought against him, and he was to be tried before the Judiciary Committee on Thursday of that week. Clayborn was expected to feign illness. Singleton thought that if the verdict was guilty, the Council would give Clayborn's 13th District (Kentucky and Tennessee) to Bishop Williams. If he were exonerated, Singleton said, "it would be a fine thing to send him to 'Poor, Bleeding Africa.'" With Clayborn silenced, he did not expect Joseph would have any trouble getting the Council to release his salary. He hoped to see Joseph at the Council so they could discuss problems of Paul Quinn. Having once been president of the college, Singleton was vitally interested in its progress.[20]

Just as Singleton had predicted, at the Bishops' Council in Washington a few days later Joseph's appointment to Texas was reaffirmed and his salary finally released.[21] After the meeting, Joseph told Singleton of his growing misgivings concerning Mrs. Aycox's ability to run the college.

The records were still in disarray, and he was sure that when the State Department of Education released the evaluation it had made of the educational program at the college in January, the findings would not be favorable. On a brighter note, he told Singleton of his plans for a dining and student union building and a new administration building, which would replace the inadequate facility currently being used. He also spoke of his bid to the federal government for the purchase of a surplus army gymnasium and chapel now located at Fort Hood. To ensure expansion, he had also gained permission from the owners and the college trustees to purchase the property adjacent to the campus. Now that the question of the legality of his appointment had been settled, he could execute his plans without having to worry about being moved.

On April 28, Joseph spoke to the Waco Commission on Interracial Cooperation at its second yearly public meeting. Before the address, Eula, who had been invited to Waco to give a concert, sang. Then Rev. Karl Kluge of Robinson, Texas, a former classmate of Joseph's at Eden Seminary, introduced him.[22] Joseph tackled the problem of racism without restraint. He said, "The cause of segregation in America is not money. It is not the Negro's lack of ability, talent, and education. The problem is purely psychological—the mind." Prejudice is irrational, based on false preconceived notions and the imagination. "People are always afraid when they lack knowledge about something, and it is ignorance which keeps the races apart." He spoke of the resentment the Negro felt "because he had been robbed of a part of the freedom he has fought for, and because he has been made half citizen." In his conclusion he declared, "Racial discrimination in the South will be wiped out. It may be slow, but we shall win despite resentment of the South to pressure without. And it will come not from forces outside the South, but from pressures within the South. The solution is to be found in youth movements and interracial committees, and the determination of Negroes to be free."[23] He had presaged the sit-ins and nonviolent tactics that would originate among young Blacks in the South in the 1960s.

The *Waco Messenger* of May 6, 1949, reported the mixed audience's enthusiastic response. "The entire audience, amidst thunderous ovation, rose from the seats and stood erect in honor and reverence to the episcopal leader who thought through the problem of race with his audience. And this happened in the South—deep in the heart of Texas."[24]

On May 17, Eula sang to a packed college auditorium. She received accolades in many forms, including bouquets of flowers. The concert had been sponsored by Rev. E. C. Gibson and the St. Luke A.M.E. Church of Waco.[25] After the reception that followed, she boarded the plane back to

Los Angeles. Hazel and Joseph had been excited to see her but thought she seemed thin and troubled. The day she left they also received information about Annetta, in a letter from Susie Pardon, the girls' former St. Louis piano teacher, who was now living in New York. She said she had visited Annetta at the Emma Ransom House, and that Annetta seemed happy. "From my own experience, I believe New York suits Annetta's temperament admirably, and it may be that she will not be satisfied living anywhere else." She promised to visit Annetta frequently but realized she had to "be tactful" so as not to seem meddlesome. Sensing that Hazel and Joseph did not really approve of Eula's husband, she wrote: "Glad to have news of Eula. You know my father did not approve of my second marriage, yet before the end, he came to see that Mr. Pardon had a wonderfully constructive influence in my life. He approved of the first, and you know how that turned out. It is all in the lap of the Gods, isn't it?"[26]

On May 26, Paul Quinn College awarded Joseph a doctorate of letters.[27] Immediately after the commencement exercises he and Hazel caught a plane from Dallas to Miami, where they boarded the S.S. *Alcoa Clipper* for Trinidad. The *Alcoa* was a modern ship some 455 feet long, and unlike when they had gone to Bermuda twenty-five years ago, the Gomezes had first-class accommodations. Cabin A9, which was to be their home for several days, was furnished with a sitting-room area, large bedroom, and a shower; it was an ideal setting for some much-needed rest. Hazel recorded the highlights of the trip in her diary.

On May 30, Hazel wrote: "Today's my birthday. Daddy gave me a beautiful brooch of emeralds and rhinestones. Spent the day on deck. Saw Haiti at a distance. . . . Had many nice visits with the passengers. At dinner, the steward bought a beautiful cake with one candle, and a group of passengers sang 'Happy Birthday.' . . . Will go to bed early as we reach Ciudad Trujillo in San Domingo tomorrow."[28]

When they docked at Ciudad Trujillo at 7 A.M., they were met by a Rev. Boyce, who took them to breakfast at "a quaint cafe ashore." Then they taxied to one of the new A.M.E. churches under construction. The most exciting experience of the day for Hazel was when she was taken to see how her favorite cashew nuts and mangoes were grown.

Two days later, after a rough Wednesday at sea, the ship docked at La Guaira, Venezuela. They "went 5 miles up the seashore to an Italian hotel called Palmer where they bathed in the sea and had lunch which cost $11 a piece." Unlike her husband, Hazel was extremely practical and was always aware of the cost of things. Her assessment of the places they visited was that "everyone was out to fleece Americans." That evening they went to see *Knock On Any Door*, with John Derek as "Pretty-Boy" Nick Romano and Humphrey Bogart as a crusading lawyer. The movie was taken from the novel by Willard Motley, a Negro. Few people realized he was Black, since the movie did not deal with Black characters.

The next morning at Puerto Cabello they saw the Andes Mountains. In the afternoon they sailed for Guanta, where Hazel commented that the shoreline "looked like all the other South American shores." On Sunday, June 5, Joseph conducted the religious service, preaching on the subject "Reflex Glory." A widow of an Episcopalian clergyman, Carol E. Veazie of New York, played the piano. On the trips to and from Trinidad, Joseph was asked to conduct all of the Sunday services.

As they sailed into the harbor of Trinidad, Hazel saw James at a distance and commented, as she had in Bermuda, that "James looked so much like Daddy." The entire Gomez family and Rev. and Mrs. Mayhew (the pastor and his wife of the A.M.E. church in Trinidad) had come to meet them. Joseph was especially glad to see his favorite sister, Amanda.

They drove to Santa Cruz, to one of James's homes, where there was a formal reception. Joseph was presented a scroll that had been written by the family; in it they said that his being "elected Bishop was the greatest boast and happiness of [their] lives." They hoped that "each succeeding anniversary" of his election would "find him happier than the last." They also congratulated Hazel, "for without her co-operation, coupled with sincere devotion, [Joseph] would not have reached the summit of [his] ambition." The scroll was signed Aldwyn R. Gomez, Ruby Gomez (that is, James's adopted son and his wife), Audrey Cecilia Thomas, Alva H. Thomas (Amanda's son and his wife), Oscar Thomas (Amanda's other son), Amanda Thomas, and James and Mary Gomez.

Friends of the family came to greet Hazel and Joseph throughout the day. In the evening, everyone rode out to James's farm, where he had prepared an outdoor feast. The yard was filled with long wooden tables and chairs. On each table was a succulent roasted pig with an apple in its mouth, and platters of colorful tropical fruits and vegetables. The conversations of the guests were syncopated by the intermittent pop of champagne corks. Bars were set up outside the gates so those not invited to the party could partake of the wine.

The governor of the island arrived in a black limousine escorted by police on motorcycles. James had pulled out all the stops for his brother. Money was not a consideration, since he had a lucrative import business, a farm, a house in Santa Cruz, and a house in Port of Spain, all maintained by indoor and outdoor servants. After having lived in New York for a time in 1920, he had returned to Trinidad and begun immediately to build a small empire. He had succeeded in business where his father, Emanuel, had failed. His rise in station more than made up for the impoverished years of his late childhood, and it gave him great satisfaction to show Joseph, his mother's favorite, that he too had done well for himself. Joseph and Hazel were gratified to see that he had accomplished so much, but they were concerned about his health. He seemed always to be troubled by stomach cramps, obviously caused by his love for spicy cuisines, which he prepared himself, and fine wines. In addition, he seldom got enough sleep. Like so many of his parties, this one lasted well into the night. Not used to such festivities, Hazel and Joseph spent the following day back in Santa Cruz recuperating.

The *Trinidad Guardian* reported on June 8 that "Bishop Gomez, back in the Colony after an absence of 25 years, will be given a public welcome at the A.M.E. Church this evening. . . . Bishop Gomez says he is glad to be back in Trinidad after twenty-five years away. He is impressed by the apparent economic improvement of the people, and thinks that 'Trinidadians should work together for the advancement of the country,'"[29]

On the morning of the 8th, the entire family visited Emanuel's and Rebecca's graves, laid wreaths, and had family pictures made at the site. In the evening they attended the reception at Metropolitan A.M.E. Church, where they were presented to Mayor Norman Tang.

The next day was a holiday in celebration of the king's birthday. The family arose too late to attend the annual parade; instead, they drove to Maracas Bay. There was a fierce wind and rainstorm on the way to the bay. Evidently the storm soon abated, because they were able to visit the nursery of Mayor W. Kagge, where they saw all kinds of birds which Hazel said were "the most beautiful [she] had ever seen." She also saw a Saman tree that was two hundred years old. On the return home, they "had to detour . . . as the storm had blown down a number of trees on the road." Nevertheless to Hazel it had been a "wonderful day."

On Sunday, June 12, the Gomezes went to Wesleyan Methodist Church, Hanover, where Joseph's mother had taken him every Sunday when he was a boy. Time moved backward, and Joseph could hear his mother singing above the voices of the congregation, "A Charge to Keep I Have." That evening he preached at Metropolitan on the timely subject, "Back to Bethel."

In the evening of Wednesday, June 15, they had dinner at the home of Aldwyn and Ruby, and then went to Metropolitan Church again, where Joseph spoke this time on "Forty Years in America." The meeting was chaired by the Honorable Deputy Mayor Thompson, the oldest member of the church. He presented Joseph with a handmade cane, which he proudly displayed for the rest of his life.

Corpus Christi Day, June 16, James took his brother and sister-in-law to Blandaro Bay, "the best bathing place on the island." After an invigorating swim they went to the Copra House and saw how men climbed the coconut trees, and how coconut oil was made. Later they witnessed "pineapples growing 40 miles from Port of Spain, and saw the thatched houses of the workers who were mostly Indian; they passed through Waller . . . the American Air Field." Before the "traditional English tea" at 4 P.M., they watched charcoal being made, saw groves of rubber trees and also brilliantly colored wild parrots flying above.

On Sunday, June 19th, Joseph conducted a worship service at James's home for the entire family. Later he and Hazel went to tea at the home of His Lordship, Bishop Fabien Jackson. Hazel was asked to pour the tea (considered to be a high privilege). That evening Joseph preached at Tranquility Wesleyan Church, on the topic, "The Language of the Years." The church was packed with islanders who had come to hear the American bishop.

The next day they went to town to see about their tickets since they were to leave that afternoon. After visiting Joseph's parents' graves one last time and taking more pictures, they "went back home and spent a quiet time until 3:30 P.M. Most of the family was with us," Hazel wrote. "Then [we] left for Aldwyn's house where we had tea. James gave a farewell speech which was answered by Daddy. Many tears fell as there was a feeling we would not meet again. . . . I hated to leave." Joseph noted that Cyril was the only member of the family who did not come to see them depart. The others explained that he had been morose and very difficult since "Papa" had died: he rarely cut his hair, had to be made to bathe, and declared that he was gifted in witchcraft. The only person with whom he communicated was Amanda.

Joseph and Hazel left Trinidad on Monday. Two days later the ship anchored at Curacao, "a picturesque, clean little country which had yellow, red, and beige houses with red and green roofs." The population was "a mixture of Dutch, Spanish, and Negro. Another place where there was no prejudice," Hazel noted.

They arrived in Jamaica about 8 A.M. the next morning and were met by two A.M.E. ministers, Rev. Haynes and Rev. Spencer, the presiding elder, a Mrs. Winston, who was the niece of Septimus Craig (Frankie Crawford's old Cleveland boyfriend), and attorney Parkinson. They drove to Gains A.M.E. Church at St. Anne, where an Annual Conference was in session. The ministers and laymen gave many welcoming speeches, and they appealed to the Gomezes to ask the churches in the United States to send financial aid to Jamaica. Joseph and Hazel were appalled by the poverty on the island. When the ship left the port at 2 P.M., they were pleasantly surprised to see that the pilot was a Negro. Hazel's last diary entry was dated Sunday, June 26.

When Joseph talked about his trip to Trinidad in later years, he was not certain how he felt about it. His mother and father's absence caused an emptiness. It had seemed strangely sad to stand at their graves mouthing platitudes and taking pictures. He thought about the intense love they had felt for each other and of how fitting it was that they were buried side by side. Amanda was still grieving for her husband, "Mr. Thomas," as she called him, even though he had been dead for many years. She refused to wear any color except black, and she would eventually take to her bed and remain there until her death. Aldwyn and Alva both seemed to be happily married, but Cyril had been like a shadow, appearing and disappearing at will, and never talking much when he was around. Of all the children, he seemed most like "Papa," too sensitive and fragile for this life. James was prosperous and proud, but not in the best of health. Perhaps going back home had helped Joseph define himself better, but he knew he would never want to live there again. "You can never go home again" was not merely a cliché.

In late July, Joseph met with the trustees of Paul Quinn to plan the August Congress. The emphasis this year would be on training workshops for ministers, which was part of Joseph's expansion program for the district. He had found that many men had gone into the ministry because they believed they were "called" to do so; they had not felt, however, that this calling involved seminary training. Others who had had formal studies now needed refresher courses. The Congress workshops would be a beginning. They would deal with pastoral and Bible studies, church music, church management, missionary work, the art of preaching, English, the Junior Church, Sunday school, and the Allen Christian Endeavor League. Experts in each of these areas would be invited to conduct the workshops. Near the end of the Congress, Joseph would lead the delegates in a groundbreaking ceremony for the new administration building.[30]

After the planning session the trustees elected M. P. Harvey as business manager of Paul Quinn, J. W. Yancy as trustee (in place of Professor Hardin, who had resigned), S. J. Matthews as treasurer; Nannie Belle Aycox was reelected president despite Joseph's growing skepticism about her ability to handle the job. Approval was given for several new teachers to be hired for the fall and for the appointment of departmental chairpersons.[31]

On August 22, over ten thousand people gathered on the campus for the Congress. Some stayed in homes throughout the city or in surrounding towns, others in the dormitories. After the opening worship service the presiding elders submitted their financial reports, which represented 20 percent of the yearly budget. Many of the ministers had paid more than the required 20 percent, and some had paid their entire yearly assessment. Joseph's new budget plan was working even better than he had anticipated.[32]

The Episcopal Residence was crowded with guests: Hubie and Mamie Robinson; Dr. and Mrs. V. C. Hodges, of the American Bible Society; Dr. H. M. Micken, dean of the R. R. Wright School of Religion in Nashville; Vince Townsend, from Arkansas; and McCoy Ransom and Fred Jordan from Los Angeles. There were so many visitors for meals that Jessie Dickerson had to employ several students—including her nemesis, Sonny—to assist with the cooking and serving.

On Sunday, August 28, all A.M.E. churches in the state were closed for the joint service held in George B. Young Auditorium. Prior to the service, the president, bishop and his wife, presiding elders, ministers, and laymen marched in a long procession to the site of the proposed new administration building, where the short groundbreaking ceremonies were held. In front of the site was a large architectural drawing of the 132-by-62-foot, two-story stone building, which the trustees had decided to name the Joseph Gomez Administration Building. Joseph turned the first spade of dirt.[33]

Following the ceremony, the procession moved to the auditorium for the worship service. During his sermon, Joseph reminded the audience how important religious schools had been in the lives of the Negro and warned that "the life of Christian Educational Institutions is being threatened more vigorously than ever before. . . . People stress the need for large appropriations to state schools, [but] little is said about the great need for funds in the church institutions. . . . Both are needed to educate the young people as they should be." He knew that without low-tuition church schools, many Negro youth would never receive a higher education.[34]

The Congress ended on a note of optimism for the tenth Episcopal District and for Paul Quinn College. There was no doubt in anyone's mind that the work was moving forward under the leadership of the new bishop, not only in terms of the church and school, but also of race relations. A year had passed since Joseph had come to Texas. It had been a whirlwind with little time for evaluation. He had had to move rapidly from one day to the next, and the entire year had seemed like one long day. Despite the dispute over the Bishops' Council sending him to Texas, things had not gone badly. At any rate, here he was—in Texas, where he planned to stay for his allotted eight years.

More and more, Joseph's doubts about Nannie Belle Aycox's ability to manage the affairs of the college were proving to be true. The most damaging evidence came in the form of two evaluations, one from the State Approval Agency for Veterans Education under Public Law 349, and the other from the Veterans Administration Center. Joseph had found out there were many discrepancies in the college's billing practices for veterans studying under the G.I. Bill, and he asked the two agencies to come to the campus and evaluate the program and the veterans' records so he could know where the college stood.

The report from the State Approval Agency of Austin, Texas, dated October 26, was addressed to the president, with a copy to the bishop. The most damaging deficiencies listed were: no catalogue for 1949–1950; poor record keeping for finances, student transcripts, and class attendance; forged grades for courses not taken, and double credit for the same course taken more than once; excessive college-level credit given for vocational courses; lack of adequate definition of the duties of the registrar, business manager, and dean, and insufficient clerical help. The report warned that "continued approval of academic courses [would be] dependent upon continued approval by the State Department of Education and the school's ability to publish a satisfactory catalogue and correct the records and administrative inefficiencies" that existed in the school.[35]

The report of John C. Horn, chief of the Texas Vocational Rehabilitation and Education Division of the Veterans Administration, was even more damaging. He cited specific cases where veterans had never attended classes and yet the Veterans Administration had been billed and the students given credit. Some were even given credit for classes not offered during the semester. In terms of individual veteran files, it was found that Mrs. Aycox "handled all matters relative to veterans' affairs, and [did] not permit the Dean, Mr. F. R. Tillman, to have access to veterans' records in [her] office. . . . And further, it was found that [Mrs. Aycox was] unable to determine exactly the number of veteran students currently enrolled." In conclusion, he wrote, "Further payments to your school will remain in suspended status pending your compliance with our recommendations and the findings of the audit of your school which is in the process of being made now."[36] (This was in reference to A. C. Upleger and Company, certified public accountants whom Joseph had hired to audit the college books.)

When the letters and reports reached Joseph's office at Paul Quinn, he was in Houston conducting the Texas Annual Conference. His secretary, Della Johnson, reached him in Houston and told him the reports had arrived. As soon as the conference closed he returned to Waco to meet with President Aycox, M. P. Harvey, the business manager, and Dorothy Williams, registrar. He pointed out to them that the college could very well have been taken to court but that the Veterans Administration was willing to give them an opportunity to set things in order. He made it quite clear that straightening out the veterans' records was top priority. Since Tillman had resigned as dean, Joseph appointed Henry Burks, a professor he had brought from Cleveland originally to head the Social Science Department. Burks was a hard taskmaster, highly organized, thorough, dedicated, and not to be intimidated. When Joseph left to attend the West Texas Conference in Smithville, the administration building was buzzing with activity, with Henry Burks trying diplomatically to work around a recalcitrant president.

After Joseph reached Smithville, he ran into problems of another nature. When the Brenham District made its report, it was short by $2,001.63 because only five pastors had paid their total assessment. With the pressures of the college weighing on him and the realization that if the ministers did not meet their assessments the expansion of the district and college might well come to a standstill, he became highly agitated and spoke impetuously of asking to be transferred to another district at the next General Conference. His friend Grant was able to calm him down by assuring him that "Texas was solidly behind the Bishop's program and hoped that . . . he would never think of leaving." Luckily Joseph's temper never lasted beyond a few minutes, and when it had passed he was again filled with enthusiasm and optimism. All his life he had to make a concerted effort to curb his temper and develop patience. This did not come easily to a man of his spontaneity.[37]

Joseph had a respite from the pressures when he returned to Waco on November 8 to address the students of Baylor University for World Community Week, sponsored by the United Council of Church Women. This was the first time he had been asked to speak at the university; few if any Blacks had ever been asked. He told the students, "It is now or never that we must translate ideals into practice; and the Christian forces of the church, home and school must lead the way in this action. . . . We must have a world community or shambles. . . . A politically controlled world community without the moral suasions and convictions of deepest spiritual meanings can only delay the day of judgment." He urged the students to "meet the challenge of the world by utilizing every effort to establish a world community that will unconditionally and uncompromisingly recognize God as our Father, Jesus as our elder brother, and all mankind as brothers."[38] Joseph was frequently interrupted by applause, and the students "gave the prelate a great ovation at the conclusion of the speech."[39] After his Baylor engagement, Joseph had to return to his remaining Annual Conferences.

The Northeast Texas Conference (November 9–13) had its own set of problems, involving largely Rev. P. E. Womack, who was to continue to cause serious disruption throughout Joseph's tenure in the tenth Episcopal District. When the report for the Farris and Palmer Circuit, where Womack pastored, was called for, he did not answer; consequently his report had to be read by the Presiding Elder of the district. It was noted that Womack was "indebted to the conference in the sum of one hundred dollars by reason of a bad check given . . . in payment of certain Connectional Claims in the month of February, 1949." Because of these discrepancies he had to go before the Judiciary Committee, which reported that "after the said Rev. P. E. Womack found these charges were legal according to the *A.M.E. Discipline,* he . . . gave . . . a written excuse for being absent." The committee recommended that he be given one year to redeem himself of all charges.[40] In all Joseph's dealings with him, Womack always wanted to know what the Discipline said, and then interpreted it as he saw fit.

Bishop and Mrs. Ransom visited Joseph's last conference, the North Texas Conference, which was held November 23–27 in Fort Worth. If any of the ministers had doubts of Ransom's mental faculties at the age of eighty-eight, these doubts were dispelled as they listened to him deliver the closing Sunday sermon from the text, "What think ye of Christ? Whose son is He?" Ransom emphasized that humanity has always tried to measure Christ by "human and carnal standards." He vividly declared "that carnal standards of ideology fall and crumble with each generation. . . . The only hope of mankind is full acceptance of God as Spirit. . . . When the surrender of the heart is made, the hope of Eternal Life becomes reality."[41]

Following the close of the conference, the Gomezes gave a reception for the Ransoms in Waco before putting them on the train for Wilberforce. On December 5, Joseph received a letter of thanks from him.

Dear Bishop and Mrs. Gomez:

There are so many superlatives connected with my visit to you, I scarcely know how, or where to begin. It was one of the most satisfying and heartwarming visits I have ever paid to anyone. You have achieved fulfillment; by that I mean aspiration, preparation, and the slow and toilsome steps of your career, unfolding through the years of toil and struggle to reach the goal, armed and prepared for the duties and responsibilities that confront you. I do not know of anything that gives me more pleasure than to witness your capacity and grasp of the situation with which you have to deal. Sister Hazel shares equally with you in all of this. Never did a man have a more perfect helpmate than is she. We shall be looking for you about Christmas time, or any time you find it convenient to come and visit with us.[42]

In conclusion, he noted that "all the papers concerning search of title, and all other matters connected with property at Bitely, Michigan," were ready for Joseph's examination.[43]

The property in question was Ransom's cottage at Woodland Park, which had been deeded to him for one dollar by Hallie Q. Brown some years ago. He was now in the process of deeding it to Joseph. Woodland Park had been settled by Blacks who had migrated from the South in the early part of the century. Unable or unwilling to adjust to big-city life in the North, they had found Woodland more suitable to their lifestyles. Here they could fish, hunt for deer, and raise enough food to sustain themselves. They preferred Woodland to the more resort-like atmosphere at Idlewild, fourteen miles away, which had become the summer playground for middle and upper middle-class Blacks. Hallie Q. Brown was one of a few middle-class Negroes who had preferred the more rustic life at Woodland, and she had bought the cottage around the turn of the century.

Ransom's cottage looked out on a lake of diamonds, or so it seemed when the sun settled on the water in the early morning. He had been going to Woodland every summer since 1941, and he had often invited Hazel and Joseph to visit him there. They had fallen instantly in love with the site and were delighted when Ransom offered them the property. In his declining years Ransom found it more and more difficult to make the trip, and he knew that his friends needed some restorative place to reside during the summers before the Annual Conferences began each fall.

The Gomezes spent the Christmas holidays at Tawawa Chimney with the Ransoms and then left for Cleveland to meet Annetta, who had damaged her knee in ballet class at the Dramatic Workshop. She was admitted to the Cleveland Clinic for a cartilage removal. Joseph had to leave a few days after the operation, but Hazel stayed until the doctor let her bring Annetta home to Texas. He had assured Hazel that Annetta should be able to return to New York after a month and a half of therapy.

On January 3, 1950, Annetta Louise Butler, Eula's second child, was born in Los Angeles. Eula brought her new daughter and her son, Marvin, to visit their grandparents in Waco the next month. For the first time in a while, the entire family was together. Joseph and Hazel thoroughly enjoyed watching the playful antics of their grandchildren, especially Marvin, who insisted on trying to take care of his sister. Annetta was proud that Eula had named her daughter "Annetta Louise."

Other family matters occupied Joseph that month. On February 13, he received a letter from his brother James in regard to a house Joseph planned to buy for Amanda. James wrote that he had found "a wooden tenement on a lot of City Council land which cannot be acquired."[44] In other words, Joseph could purchase the house but not the land. Most people in Trinidad did not own the land on which their houses sat.

James was happy to report that Amanda, who had been ill, was much better. "The doctor [was] satisfied with the way she [had] responded to treatment" and would be sending Joseph a bill when the treatment was completed. He said that he had suggested to Amanda that she let Cyril live in the "room in the yard so that he [could] be nearer to her, and she might be able to use her influence which may bring about a change in his life." She had gladly agreed to this arrangement.[45] He wrote further:

> We cannot all turn our backs upon Cyril. There must be someone to take care of him. I spoke to him about his behavior to you when you were down and told him to write you a letter of apology. Letter attached. Although it is not the best nor what I desire, nevertheless it shows some redeeming features. Please give him some kind consideration and make mention of him sometimes in your letters to me. Christ came not to call the righteous but sinners to repentance.[46]

He also noted that Joseph never mentioned Violet in his letters, and wondered why.

Joseph was glad to have heard from James but disliked the patronizing tone of the letter. He had always been called upon to give financial assistance to the family and was glad to be able to do so; but this did not prevent him from wondering why James, with all his wealth, had not provided for Amanda or Cyril, and why he had not been told before his visit to Trinidad of the full extent of Cyril's problems. He put aside James's letter and turned to Cyril's.

Cyril apologized for not being present when Hazel and Joseph had departed from Trinidad. He had been happy to see his brother for the first time. He could not recall what his father thought of Joseph, but he could "remember that he used to tell us of you and so many miles across the sea from us." He signed it, "Your loving brother."[47] Joseph wondered how much of the letter James had dictated and how much was Cyril's own expression. Joseph bought the house for Amanda, and Cyril moved in with her. For the rest of their lives Joseph continued to assist them by sending money, taking care of medical expenses, and paying for all repairs, taxes and insurance on the house.

He was never able to accumulate the money his brother had, mainly because he was "generous to a fault" and because he felt that money was not to be coveted, but shared. His friends and enemies alike found him to be a "soft touch." In later years, his grandchildren would go to him when their parents had forbidden them something they wanted but did not really need. It was different with Hazel; memories of the lean days made her practical. She did not mind sharing what she had if a person was in need, but she did not believe in indulging her children or grandchildren. Nor would she spend any money on herself until Joseph was able to convince her that one of the pleasures of his earning more money was to be able to buy things for her. After that she began to take an interest in clothes. Ironically, Joseph rarely spent money on himself. He continued to wear a conservative black suit, a clerical collar or black tie, socks, and shoes until some of the ministers of Texas got together and bought him a dark blue suit and insisted that he wear it with an attractive blue or gray tie. They also traded in his Pontiac for a Cadillac, which Joseph reluctantly accepted; nevertheless, he insisted that it also be black.

Joseph received a troubled phone call from Hubie Robinson in March. St. James had been reduced to rubble by a five-alarm fire. Later he read in the *Cleveland News* that "the blaze which was of mysterious origin was discovered at 5 A.M. A smoke explosion blew out the rear wall. Twenty minutes after the fire started, the roof fell in."[48] Joseph thought about all the work that had gone into building the church back in 1938. He promised Robinson he would do as much as he could to help him rebuild St. James.

In April the Gomezes left for Washington, D.C., to attend the Bishops' Council's winter session and for Joseph to fulfill a speaking engagement at Howard University's Andrew Rankin Memorial Chapel. His appearance on April 23 was part of a guest lecture series which also included George D. Kelsey of the Federal Council of Churches and Benjamin E. Mays, president of Morehouse College in Atlanta, Georgia.[49]

While in Washington, Joseph received word that his close friend, and the person most responsible for his being in Texas, F. W. Grant, had died suddenly. He rushed back to Texas to preach the eulogy at Bethel A.M.E. Church in Dallas, on April 27. Ministers and laymen from throughout the district and country came to pay their tribute to this faithful A.M.E., who in all likelihood would have been elected bishop at the next General Conference. Joseph said that Grant "had mastered the 'Art of living.'" Though he had been betrayed on occasion, he bore calumnies with dignity. He was not a man of "heritage, prestige, and superior training, nor the outward circumstance of a great fortune of the favored, yet he sat in the councils of men and lent weight, dignity, and directions in deliberations." Most of all, Joseph spoke of him as a friend who "gave friendship without guile" and who never exploited it.[50]

Grant's death was a profound loss to Joseph. He had been one of Joseph's staunchest supporters. The two men had had the kind of relationship where they "could disagree without being disagreeable." Grant had that special ability to bank the flames of Joseph's anger and to bring him to reason when his pride overruled his judgment. As outgoing as Joseph seemed, in many ways he was a private person—but he had opened himself to Grant. He would miss his counsel and friendship, especially in the turbulent days ahead.

Early in May Joseph received a letter from Ransom which seemed to reflect his own melancholy mood. Ransom wrote of his recent visits to Boston and New Bedford, where the "personalities, the social, economic and political issues and the men and women, whose voices were most influential were nearly all gone. . . . [Left were] a few gnarled old oaks, and melancholy reminders of the vanished past." In reference to the death of Grant he thought it "rather sad to see one cut down in the prime of his life when there was so much hope and promise before him." He trusted that God would give Joseph "wisdom and light in adjusting [his] work caused by the passing of Dr. Grant."[51]

Ransom told Joseph that he planned to go "to Woodland Park about the middle of May for a day or so to clear the way" for Joseph's visit in June, when he would "pass over to [him] the care of [his] property." Near the close of the letter he spoke of Hazel. Again he said that "the wife of no Bishop on the bench begins to stand as high in appreciation and personal regard as she does." When he had known her as a girl he had "little dreamed of her efficiency and capacity as the wife of a high servant of the Church." He considered Hazel and Joseph to be his "ideal of fatherhood and motherhood." He advised that they "let Annetta continue to follow the beckoning hand of her aspirations." He called "the gentle Eula . . . a heaven-kissed personality. She could not be bad if she wanted to be; if she has made serious mistakes, it is because of her trustful spirit and goodness of heart."[52]

Obviously, Hazel and Joseph had shared with Ransom their growing concern about Eula's marriage, which both believed to be a mistake. On the few occasions they had seen Eula, it was clear to them that she was not happy; however, what to do about the situation had to be up to her. They never doubted that she would make the correct decision when the time came, and they would be there for her.

Before Joseph and Hazel could leave for Woodland in June, Joseph had to attend a Board of Trustees meeting and the commencement exercises at Paul Quinn. On April 3, he had sent out a letter to the ministers, laymen, and friends of Paul Quinn, attaching a copy of the report of the Expansion Fund to date and a report of the auditing committee. He spoke of the need to call for a final report of the Expansion Fund during Commencement Week so that the student union building and chapel could be completed. The architects were now ready to "submit plans and specifications for the new Administration Building," which meant money was needed to begin the erection of the building. The attached audit revealed that the total cash received so far was $33,601.23. The report showed that all withdrawals had been signed by the president, treasurer, and bishop, and that the Expansion Fund had been put in an account separate from the regular college bank account. At the end of the audit report, the committee commended "most heartily the Bishop for the care with which he [had] guarded the fund, and the secretary for the clear and correct report."[53]

Joseph and some of the trustees felt that the Expansion Fund had run its course; consequently, it was changed to the "Century Club." One thousand persons were asked to give a hundred dollars each year, with the understanding they could withdraw their membership at any time. This club would ensure the college of an annual income of at least $100,000 for expansion. Soon hundreds of people had joined the club, from inside and outside the district.[54]

On May 21, Joseph addressed the graduating class of Paul Quinn, which included the first class of practical nurses. In addition to the further development of the school, he voiced concerns relating to Providence Hospital, a Catholic institution that relegated Negroes to its basement. He urged that every citizen of Waco exert influence to have this evil practice ended. He recalled when he visited Bishop George B. Young at Providence, he had found him in the basement. "Basements of hospitals are not fit places for human beings," he asserted. He would build a clinic and convalescent home on the campus if Providence continued to segregate its Negro patients.[55]

Having completed her two-year course at the Dramatic Workshop in New York, Annetta came home. Immediately after school closed she had gone to casting offices seeking roles in the plays to be produced on Broadway in the fall. In most cases she had been told she was "too light for Negro roles, and too dark for white roles." Although she was discouraged, she was determined to try again in September, much to the disapproval of her parents, who wanted her to go back to college and get a degree. They had hoped this drama business was merely a passing fancy. They need not have been concerned, for within a few weeks of being home she met, fell in love with, and married Curtis Field Jefferson, a native Wacoan, a student at the college, and star end on the football team. At first, Hazel and Joseph were opposed to the hasty marriage; after all, they knew nothing about Curtis. However, his parents seemed to be good, hard-working people, particularly Curtis's mother, Berdie, whom Annetta loved immediately. She was highly intelligent, creative, and had she had the advantage of an education, no doubt would have assumed a leadership position.

Initially, Annetta and Curtis lived in the Episcopal Residence. This proved to be an awkward situation, particularly since Joseph insisted on bringing them blankets throughout the night, every night, after they had gone to bed. The problem was solved to everyone's satisfaction when Joseph bought them a small house on East Walnut, only a few blocks from the college.

The Annual Ministerial Institute, Missionary, and Youth Congress of August 1950 was the largest yet. There were representatives from four hundred churches and seven bishops in attendance, and numerous general officers and candidates for the bishopric. At the Thursday afternoon Interracial Cooperation Session, the speakers included Caso March, former Baylor law professor and recent candidate for the state governorship; Rev. Carl Kluge, president of the Waco chapter of the Commission on Interracial Cooperation; Septimus Craig, former Cleveland city councilman and present official in the Cleveland branch of the Department of Internal Revenue, soon to become the college's comptroller; and Mack Hannah, prominent Port Arthur business and civic leader. The ministerial workshops had been expanded to include many pertinent topics, and attendance was mandatory for the clergy of the 10th Episcopal District. In return, they could receive fractional credit toward graduation.[56]

Sunday morning worship service was so crowded that loudspeakers had to be placed around the campus so that those who could not get into the auditorium could at least hear the service. People had arrived in a cavalcade of chartered buses and cars from all over the state. As reported by the *Southern Christian Recorder,* "There is nothing remotely resembling the Sunday morning mammoth procession of colorfully robed church dignitaries, officers, clergy, laymen, combined choir, choruses, stewardesses, ushers, evangelists and missionaries in picturesque beauty and dignity" who had come for fellowship and to hear the sermon of their bishop.[57] This service marked the closing of a fruitful week. On August 21 the student union and dining room had been dedicated, and on August 26 the chapel. Joseph's old classmate Wayman Ward had delivered the chapel dedication sermon.[58]

An additive to the optimism that permeated the Congress was the audit report of the college books by the A. C. Upleger firm, which was pleased to note vast improvement in record keeping. The auditors concluded their report, "We must state that the records were in better condition than they had been at any time in several years."[59]

In September Joseph appeared before the Waco Appeals Review Board to ask for $200,000 for the expansion of Paul Quinn. His appeal was based on the fact that Paul Quinn spent approximately a million dollars a year in Waco in operating expenses, money spent by visitors who come to the college, and money spent in stores by the administration, faculty, and student body. He pointed to the many improvements already evident on campus, including the upgrading of the faculty, of whom there was now no member without at least a master's degree, most holding or near completion of a Ph.D. The Board agreed to consider seriously the request.[60]

That same month, Maggie Sawyer came from St. Louis to visit the Gomezes and accompany them to their Annual Conference held in Corpus Christi. This was her first opportunity to see Joseph function as a bishop, and she was immensely impressed, not only by the manner in which he presided but also by Hazel's quiet participation in the proceedings. On the first day Hazel was elected accountant to work with Rev. W. E. Green, the new auditor.[61] Why L. C. Young no longer functioned in that position is speculative; however, it became increasingly evident that the relationship between him and the bishop had deteriorated. Perhaps Young felt that some of the statements Joseph made concerning conditions at Paul Quinn were veiled criticisms of the administration of his uncle, Bishop Young. For whatever reason, Young became one of Joseph's severest critics. He joined a group of dissidents who were determined to destroy the bishop; leaders of the group included L. C. Graves and P. E. Womack. Unlike Young, however, Graves and Womack continued to shower the bishop with compliments while undermining his program.

There were undertones at this conference that portended what was to happen later. For instance, when the bishop asked if anyone had objections to being transferred to another conference, Revs. Young and U. S. Washington did. This was the first time that had ever happened at any of the conferences. During Paul Quinn night, Mrs. Aycox brought her family, who listened while friends spoke of her contributions to the Church and college. A Mrs. Lucy T. Wadley called her "a living example of the Christian principles that had been instilled into her life and character by

[her] sainted father, the late A. R. Jenkins, and [her] charming mother, Mrs. H. M. Jenkins, present in the audience."[62] It was almost as if the Aycox faction was building up a defense in case she should be dismissed from the college.

All the conferences endorsed Joseph as their choice for bishop of the 10th Episcopal District for the four years following the 1952 General Conference. At the West Texas Conference (November 1–5), Rev. Womack, who would later take Joseph before the Judiciary Council, stated "that he was happy for Bishop Gomez's leadership in Texas" and that he hoped the bishop would "make the next Quadrennium the crowning point in his life."[63]

Most of the Committees on the State of the Country voiced the concerns of their respective conference about the controversy in the United Nations on the seating of Communist China, and the Russian walkout. They praised the Supreme Court for opening the doors of the University of Texas so that now, in addition to Heman Sweatt, fifteen other Black students were enrolled. They also voiced their approval of Ralph Bunche's appointment to the faculty of Harvard University.

Appropriately, Joseph closed the North Texas Conference, his last for the year 1950, with a sermon based on Judges 11:40: "For I have opened my mouth unto the Lord and I cannot go back."[64] It was apparent that the honeymoon with Texas had come to an end and that progress would only come as a result of continual struggle.

Following the close of the Annual Conferences, Joseph and Hazel returned to Waco to spend Christmas with their family. Eula was home with her two children, Marvin and Annetta (Sissy). Big Annetta, as the family now called her, was expecting a child sometime in June. Although Joseph enjoyed having his children home, he was preoccupied by the enormous amount of work yet to be done on the campus and in the district. The Christmas message he mailed to his friends seemed somewhat dark, despite the promise of the light at the end, a light that shone across the "Stygian darkness," assuring the world once more of the reality of peace as embodied in the Christ Child.[65]

Since the evaluations from the State Approval Agency and the Veterans Administration Center, President Aycox had been moving rather slowly to rectify the deficiencies listed. Despite the tireless efforts of Burks, she still controlled some of the veterans' files and refused to release them. Even more discrepancies were uncovered. Burks, supported by other administrators, faculty, and trustees, advised the bishop to fire her. Along with this recommendation came another report from John C. Horn of the Vocational Rehabilitation and Education Division on February 20, 1951; in it he "noted that discrepancies which [had] been previously found" had not been corrected. "As a result, a large overpayment of tuition and subsistence [had] been made by the Veterans Administration." The VA would bill the school for the overpayments made to eighty-seven veterans "through failure of the school to notify the Veterans Administration of a reduction in training load, or regular attendance."[66]

It was obvious that Paul Quinn would be bankrupt if it continued to keep Mrs. Aycox as its president. Throughout the year Joseph had warned her to turn over all the veterans' files and that if the affairs of the school did not improve drastically, he would more than likely ask for her resignation. Evidently she had not taken the warning seriously or felt that her friends in the district would prevent her dismissal.

During Commencement Week of 1951, at the regular Board of Trustees meeting, the faculty committee and the bishop brought documented charges against Mrs. Aycox, who was in attendance. She seemed to have very little defense against the charges. The following day the trustees met again to act upon the faculty committee's and bishop's recommendation that Aycox be relieved of her duties. Before the recommendation could be voted on, several of the trustees asked questions. Some had been told that Aycox had had no prior warning that her performance had been unsatisfactory. Joseph assured them this was not true; he had spoken to her privately and in the presence of the dean on numerous occasions. He also reminded them that at the previous day's meeting she had been given ample opportunity to answer the charges but had addressed only one of them.[67]

At this point, L. C. Young rose to express his opposition to the dismissal of the president, stating that Aycox had come to the college when it was badly in need of leadership and within a few years had increased the enrollment and improved the educational program. Joseph answered that the facts did not coincide with Young's statement. Then Aaron Jefferson, a plain-spoken layman, arose to announce that he had originally been in favor of retaining Mrs. Aycox but after hearing all the evidence, wished to change his vote. Rev. A. R. Nelson expressed his concern that the decision to fire the president might turn into an ugly affair; he hoped the announcement and transfer would be done in a fair way. After all the pros and cons had been weighed, the trustees voted thirty-five to two for dismissal. Before the meeting adjourned, Dr. Prince F. Jackson, secretary of the Board, moved that the Board thank Aycox for "her past service[s] rendered as president and [extend] best wishes for the future."[68]

For most of the trustees, the decision had not been an easy one. After all, Aycox and her family were admired in the Black community and in the A.M.E. Church in Texas; her husband was an A.M.E. clergyman. The trustees had found her to be personable and had had no indication until recently that she was having difficulty running the college; however, they could not refute the overwhelming evidence of incompetence and had to vote their consciences.

On May 26, 1951, the following letter was sent to Aycox by Prince Jackson: "As secretary of the Trustee Board of Paul Quinn College, Waco, Texas, I am officially informing you that by vote of the Board of Trustees on Thursday night, May 24, a change in the presidency of the college was decided, and Rev. S. L. Greene, Jr. was elected."[69]

Although Aycox had been informed verbally about the change in presidents, the letter was abrupt and cold. Joseph regretted that he had not read it before it was sent. In days to come, it was used as proof that the bishop and the Board of Trustees were inhumane.

On Saturday, June 2, 1951, a rather slanted article written by C. W. Cubia appeared in the *Informer* concerning the dismissal. The first part of the article merely reported factual material, that Mrs. Aycox had been fired and Sherman Greene, former president of Campbell College in Jackson, Mississippi, was to take her place. It quoted the bishop as saying "the action of the board was based upon a desire not just to build a first-class Negro college, but a first-class American college," and that the college needed stronger faculty members and administrative personnel.[70]

In the second part of the article, Cubia defended Aycox. He criticized the Board of Trustees for dismissing her "summarily" and without "any provision for her to have time with pay to make adjustments in finding another job and protecting herself." He said that all over the state it had been known that Gomez and Aycox had been having trouble getting along. Some people alleged that departments and faculty at the college "bypassed President Aycox and went directly to Bishop Gomez with problems and with complaints" and that the bishop had objected to the removal of five faculty members whom Aycox wanted fired simply because they were friends of his. Despite all the charges against her, Aycox was said to stand well "with the white business people and educators in Waco, and with many of the white educators throughout the State" including the "State Education Department in Austin, under whom she worked before coming to Paul Quinn."[71]

That same month the *Informer* carried another article, in which the bishop defended his actions. He had been stunned by Cubia's article and said he "would gladly welcome any unbiased organization, individual or individuals to come to Waco to get the true facts of the case." He denied that Aycox had been "summarily dismissed." She had been "contacted by him as early as eight months ago and told then that because of her inability to deal efficiently with administrative problems that were brought to her attention in numerous conferences during the past two or three years . . . she would not be recommended for reelection by him to the Board of Trustees." He reminded the reporter that all teachers recommended to be dismissed by Mrs. Aycox had been dismissed, except one. Although six or seven serious complaints had been filed against Mrs. Aycox with the Committee on Faculty by the chancellor, she had attempted to answer only one of them.[72]

The article quoted T. R. Clemons, presiding elder of the Waco District, who had supported Aycox until he was "convinced that she couldn't do her job." The bishop had been "long-suffering with her hoping that she would improve." Clemons, Rev. E. M. Bracy, and Rev. S. J. Matthews (presiding elders of the South Houston and Austin districts, respectively), had gone to her and asked her to resign at the end of her term. She had refused.[73]

Joseph knew that there would be a faction of ministers and laymen who would never accept the dismissal, but even so he was to be surprised at the lengths to which they would go in the future to destroy his reputation. There had been some criminal acts committed prior to his coming to Texas. He did not know who was responsible, but, he had been told, a great deal of money supposedly raised for the college was never used for that purpose. For instance, when the new administration building was opened, people wanted to know why their names were not on the windows; they said money had been collected for that purpose years before the bishop had come to the 10th District. Others wondered why it was necessary to raise so much money now for the college, when every summer at the Congress thousands of dollars was collected for Paul Quinn. What had happened to that money? No one seemed to know. Texas was a paradox. There were men who were scrupulously honest and loyal—men like Clemons, Grant, Matthews, Johnson, Carter, and Nelson; on the other hand, there were others who were treacherous and deceitful. Just how treacherous and deceitful, Joseph was soon to find out.

On June 25, Annetta was on her way to work in the administration building when she began to have labor pains. She cut across the campus to the Episcopal Residence so Hazel could drive her to the hospital. At Providence Hospital they put her in the basement, where all the Black patients were relegated. They immediately gave her shots to bring on hard labor and broke her water, but the baby did not come. When Joseph arrived at the hospital and saw where his daughter was being kept, he was infuriated. Next to Annetta was a dying pregnant woman whose husband had stabbed her in the stomach; another person had already died and had been carried out on a stretcher in view of all the other patients. Regardless of the nature of their illnesses, the Black patients were lumped together in a ward that was overcrowded and impersonal.

Joseph stormed into the office of the hospital head. He reminded him that Providence was a Catholic hospital—supposedly a Christian institution. How could they justify segregating the sick? He told them this was not the last they would hear from him. Having been apprised of the bishop's reputation as a fighter and knowing that he was well thought of in Waco, the administrator quickly moved Annetta into a private room upstairs. Although he had won a small victory, Joseph warned that this did not solve the problem of a segregated Catholic hospital, only his daughter's immediate problem.

By Tuesday night, June 26, Annetta had gone into convulsions and could not recognize her parents, husband, or mother-in-law, who never left her side. The next morning, after taking X-rays, the doctor performed a caesarean section. At about 10 A.M., June 27, 1951, at six pounds eleven ounces, Curtis Field Jefferson, Jr., was born.

On July 22, the last of Eula's children was born, Gerald Seone Butler. A few months later, Eula arrived in Waco with her three children. She had left her husband and come home. Once more, the family was together.

CHAPTER ELEVEN

◈ ◈ ◈

Conquering Hebron

Texas, 1951–1956

We are taught that difficulties are to be welcomed, not shunned. To possess such powers and not use them is to impoverish our strength. As Philip Brook says: "Every day the power that we will not use is falling from us." And when we accept difficult situations in the less crowded ways of men, we nourish and strengthen ourselves for the larger issues. Caleb conquered Hebron because he had been conquering Hebrons all his life.

—Joseph Gomez,
"Conquering and Possessing Hebron," n.d.

◈ The new president of Paul Quinn College was Sherman L. Greene, Jr., son of Bishop S. L. Greene of the Georgia Diocese and recently the president of Campbell College in Jackson, Mississippi. He arrived in Waco on June 4 and was greeted at the train station by the Gomezes and a delegation from the college and town, who escorted him to the new student union building for a formal welcome reception. Green's wife Zadie, his son Sherman L. Greene III, his daughter Velma, and her daughter Gwendolyn would be joining him soon. Most Wacoans had their first opportunity to hear him on Sunday, June 10, when he spoke over the radio on radio station WACO. He told his listeners that he hoped to make the priorities of his administration "spiritual enrichment and intellectual excellence."[1]

His first challenge came in the form of a letter from L. P. Sturgeon, Associate Commissioner of the Texas Education Agency in Austin. Sturgeon pointed out discrepancies in the credits of several students who were taking courses toward their teaching certificates. He concluded, "Until a satisfactory clarification of these matters has been made available, we feel that it is our responsibility to hold in abeyance any further applications for certification which are based upon credentials from your institution." This meant students from Paul Quinn who were applying for teaching certificates would be unable to get them until Sturgeon received a full explanation from the president.[2]

Joseph had told Greene before he came that there were also gross discrepancies in the veterans' records. In the past, it had been impossible to tell how many records had been falsified or were defective, because either Aycox hid them in her office or took them home with her. In fact, after her dismissal Burks, the acting dean, had to climb over the transom to get into her office, because she had taken the key with her. When he got into the office he found that she had taken some of the records. After finally securing many of the missing records, Greene and Burks went to Austin to see what could be done to restore the college's credibility with the Department of Education.

Joseph was impressed by Greene's ability to communicate to the faculty and students his confidence that the situation could be straightened out. Almost immediately the atmosphere on the campus was altered. Instead of lethargy and despair, there was hopeful activity and growing trust in the administration. Burks returned to his post as chairman of the Social Science Department, and Dorothy Williams, the registrar, resigned to accept another job. Green appointed Dr. Amos J. White as dean/registrar. White held degrees from Wilberforce and Harvard universities, and he had done advanced study at Middlesboro College in Vermont and at Witwatersrand University in Johannesburg, South Africa. He had been the president of Wilberforce Institute in Evaton, South Africa, and of Edward Waters College in Jacksonville, Florida.[3]

Many of the changes on campus had been effected by the time the A.M.I.M. & Y.C. was held in August. This time the city of Waco became more involved. Since his arrival in 1948, Joseph had been chipping away at the prejudice and lack of communication between the races. The mayor of Waco proclaimed the week of the Congress as "Paul Quinn Week." As its contribution, the Waco Transit Company named the downtown loop bus after the college and abandoned its practice of segregated seating. Blacks found all manner of reasons to go downtown so they could ride in the front of the bus for the first time. Further recognition of change came when Thursday evening was designated as "Interracial Night." Speakers included A. M. Goldstein of Goldstein Migel Department Store, Dr. W. R. White of Baylor University, and other business and civic leaders.[4]

As soon as the Congress had ended, Joseph and Hazel left for Oxford, England, where Joseph was to be a delegate to the Eighth Ecumenical Conference of Methodists. In a three-part log of his trip published in the *Houston Informer*, Joseph seems to be as concerned with postwar Europe as he is with the conference; however, the record of his personal experiences are more interesting than his political generalities, which tend to be colored by his natural optimism.

The Gomezes boarded the Texas Special for New York City the same Sunday the Congress closed. Hazel was smartly dressed in a picture hat and three-piece suit; Joseph's usual conservative look was softened by a straw hat turned down at the brim and the knowledge that he had kept his promise to take Hazel to Europe. After attending the conference in Oxford they planned to visit London, Paris, and Rome and to return by way of Le Havre in time for the Texas Annual Conferences, which would begin early in October.

At 8:30 A.M., August 22, the *Queen Mary* sailed, "towering far above the other ships in the New York Harbor and far above the water line like a floating sky-scraper." Traveling with Hazel and Joseph were Dr. Arthur S. Jackson, financial secretary of the A.M.E. Church; Louise Routt, his daughter and also a home economics instructor at Paul Quinn; and Bishop Womack of the C.M.E. Church, and several representatives of his church. They all stood on deck waving to relatives and friends as the vessel pushed farther and farther away from shore. Despite its obvious beauty Joseph found the *Queen Mary* to be "a rather impersonal set-up." Although the officers and attendants were courteous, "as in all big organizations, be they cities, colleges, or ships, you miss the personal touch without which man loses his most satisfying and enduring experiences." He recalled his trip to the Caribbean two years ago when he had traveled on a ship of only sixty-five persons and had "experienced a fellowship in many respects like a large family." On the *Queen Mary* most of the passengers seemed "aloof and preoccupied."[5]

On Sunday, August 26, the ship ran into a storm and "tossed like a toy on the bosom of the angry waves," so that worship services had to be canceled. Several passengers were hurt, a few seriously. Joseph learned that this kind of weather usually occurred only during January and February.

They arrived in Southampton, England, in the evening of August 27. On the train to London they were unable to see the English countryside because outside their "quaint, un-American compartments . . . it was both dark and rainy." They occupied their time talking to a young man from the University of California who had received a scholarship to Oxford.

"These trains are divided into classes, viz: first, second and third," Joseph wrote. "The sharpness of lines of class distinction, so true of English life, are on many levels disappearing; but some are still . . . as rigid as ever . . . and will continue for generations to come." However, the conversations they had with the people they had met so far convinced them "that a great social upheaval as a result of two world wars [had] made deep cuts into the traditional practices of the people."

When they reached London, they stayed at the Picadilly Hotel overnight and left in the morning for Oxford. Joseph was delighted to be in Oxford, particularly since he had not had an opportunity to visit it twenty years ago. He found it to be a city of about a hundred thousand people, completely dominated by the university. Most of the delegates were housed in the dormitories, where "one [could] see the strict discipline and austerity to which British youth of the middle class and rich are subjected." On the walls hung "pictures of kings, prime ministers, jurists, educators, statesmen, financiers." Joseph noted that one could spend days "reading the names and brief biographies of some of the makers of history."

The emphasis of all the programs was "a return to the fundamental faith of Methodism: the recapturing of the Evangelistic note that made Methodism so loved by the common people and feared by the exploiters of society, particularly of the Eighteenth Century; the working for an ultimate union of all Methodism and eventually toward a union of all churches in a World Communion."

At a function held at Cecil Rhodes's house, Joseph and Hazel stood looking at the bust of the man who was responsible for the Rhodes Scholarships, which benefited students from all over the world. Suddenly a man from Michigan came up to them, introduced himself, and said, "I cannot quite enjoy the bountiful gift of Rhodes when I recall at what misery all this was procured." The same thoughts had been running through Joseph's mind. Rhodes, the acclaimed "great benefactor and statesman, [had] maimed, [and] killed natives of South Africa to enrich both himself and his people with the diamonds found in the black man's native soil." This house represented to Joseph a "substitution, poor indeed," and he said to Hazel, "God has an answer for this."

Hazel had developed a new hobby, that of taking motion pictures. Throughout the trip she recorded on camera most of what she saw. She was especially impressed by the ride up the Thames River, where she filmed "the ancient town of Abingdon," and the castle where Queen Victoria spent her honeymoon. On Saturday, when the party toured the usual tourist attractions of London she took pictures of Buckingham and St. James palaces, the Admiralty, Westminster Abbey, the Houses of Parliament, Lambeth Palace (home of the Archbishop of Canterbury), Scotland Yard, the Temple (for British barristers), Victoria Embankment, Waterloo Bridge, and St. Paul's Cathedral, "the crowning achievement of Sir Christopher Wren."

They traveled to East London, which had "suffered the greatest damage of any section" during the past war. They had tea with the Rev. Mr. Spivey, minister of Wesley Chapel. Joseph was fascinated by the story Spivey told them about the "miracle of salvation" experienced at this Shrine of Methodism which Wesley had built and where he spent the last years of his life. During the bombing of East London the flames twice destroyed everything on both sides of the church. On each occasion, the wind shifted at the last moment to the opposite direction, leaving the church untouched. Joseph, who had read extensively in biographies of and writings by Wesley, said that often during the trip he felt this spiritual pioneer's presence, especially when he stood in the room where John Wesley studied and labored at Lincoln College in Oxford.

Both he and Hazel were moved by the scars of war still so evident in all parts of London. Both Westminster Abbey and the Houses of Parliament had experienced serious damage. "Yet in many areas the scars of war were skillfully removed." Reconstruction of the city was a continuous goal, but it was often "hampered by lack of money and materials, and by labor demands for higher pay and better working conditions."

On Sunday, September 9, they joined hundreds who poured into the massive Central Hall of Westminster Methodist Church to listen to Dr. W. E. Sangster, "one of England's most beloved preachers," who spoke from the text, "Ye are the salt of the earth." Joseph expressed his reaction to the total experience in these words: "Great singing; Great fellowship!"

On Tuesday, September 18, they boarded the R.M.S. *Mauritania* for the six-day trip home. Hazel used this time to arrange all the film she had taken and to reflect on what she had seen; Joseph spent his time summarizing his thoughts for the newspaper. He concluded that in terms of economics, England was facing some difficult times, "but with the same courage [with which] she fought the Germans during World War II." In France, prices were soaring each day, "and the American tourist [was] made the 'goat of the situation.'" He felt that the Marshall Plan had been "the saving grace" of most of Europe, but he believed that there should be "constant and diligent inquiry [into] the administration of this fund."

News came to the ship that Prime Minister Clement Atlee had decided on a national election for England. Joseph believed this to be wise, because "the margin of votes by which the Labour Government [had] exercised authority was far too slim." In Italy, the De Gasperi government seemed to be popular, and "with the aid of Allied Parties" was doing a creditable job. As for France, Joseph felt that she had always been "an enigma. . . . The constant friction between the Communist and De Gaulist caused confusion." He could not see how France could be "an effective instrument in the organization of Western Europe with the uncertain and chaotic political situations that embroil her."

Racism was still a problem for much of the world. It had been a problem at Oxford, not openly in terms of the hosts, "but raised . . . at least covertly by the American Methodists who themselves were guests." This was evident by "certain avoidances and by the distributions on the programme." Little recognition was given to Black clergymen. The uprisings in Africa and the West Indies were pointing up the problem of racism and causing people all over the world to reexamine their stands, Joseph believed. Some things had improved. He recalled how twenty years ago many of the London hotels "would adroitly fail to accommodate a person of color." By the time the Gomezes landed in New York on September 24, they had concluded that despite her problems, America remained "the best home."

When they arrived in Waco they found that although there were still rumblings about the bishop having looked outside Texas for the new president, progress was being made. Besides increasing and upgrading the faculty, Green was arranging a statewide fund-raising campaign. He also told Joseph that the State Education Department had agreed to give him time to straighten out the discrepancies in the students' permanent records and in the Education Department as a whole.

Following the 1951 Annual Conferences, on December 16, Joseph returned to baptize his grandson, Curtis Field Jefferson, Jr., in the new chapel and to spend the holidays in Waco. This Christmas was a particularly happy one, with the entire family together. There was the traditional sitting around the tree amidst all the packages and poinsettias while Joseph distributed the presents. Next came the picture-postcard turkey and stuffing, a variety of fresh vegetables, salads and breads, and best of all, the chocolate cake—made from a special recipe that belonged to Hazel's mother and which Hazel mysteriously guarded from everyone.

After dinner, the grandchildren played with their toys as visitors from all over Texas came and went, and friends from around the United States and other countries called to express Yuletide greetings. In the midst of the chaos, Eula sat at the piano and led everyone in singing carols, her own beautifully cultivated voice carrying the monotones and no-tones of some of the others. When the last grandchild, who had curled upon the couch and fallen asleep, was carried upstairs, Joseph retired to finish his Annual

New Year's message, which would be delivered over the radio. Hazel, lit only by the Christmas tree lights, sipped her eggnog and looked at the mound of paper boxes, colored ribbons, and shredded paper wrappings and wondered what on earth "Daddy" would do with all the briefcases, ties, tie clips, cuff links, shirts, and handkerchiefs he had received again this Christmas. Laughing at her own cleverness, she pulled out the several boxes of ornate, sweet-smelling soap she had hidden from Joseph behind the couch. "Daddy" thought it was in bad taste for anyone to give soap as a gift, but she loved the fragrance and the flowery shapes of the tiny bars. It had been a good Christmas.

The New Year started with a family emergency. Early in January James, Joseph's brother, was rushed from Trinidad to the United States for stomach surgery at the Cleveland Clinic. James took an instant dislike to the nurses there and transferred himself to Mount Sinai. Joseph and Hazel met him and his wife, May, in Cleveland and remained with them until he was out of danger. In February he was well enough to fly to Waco for a few weeks of recuperation. Within a short time his unorthodox behavior had made him a favorite among the students and faculty. Once, after everyone had spent several hours looking for him he was found sitting behind the chapel hidden by the high grass, writing poetry. Another time he went into town and was discovered bidding on hogs at an animal auction, though he did not have a cent in his pocket.

His greatest prank was to go into the segregated restaurants and drugstores downtown and order food. When the waitresses heard his mixed British and West Indian accent, they had to serve him, because they could not be sure of his nationality. On one occasion the entire family was invited to Professor George and Margery Morrison's house on the campus. Mrs. Morrison went to the back porch to get some onions from a basket and returned to the front room screaming—she had seen some kind of animal in the basket with dangerous-looking eyes. Like one of the gallant Three Musketeers, James grabbed a saber hanging on the wall, stalked onto the porch, and proceeded to chop up the creature. It turned out to be a timid opossum who had jumped from one of the trees near the porch and landed in the onions. Needless to say, after so much carnage nobody had much appetite, especially not for onions—that is nobody except James, who washed them off and ate them raw.

James boasted to his two nieces that he could preach better than their father. To prove his point, one Sunday when he was visiting Annetta's house on East Walnut he preached a sermon on the Prodigal Son. So dramatic was his presentation in the description of the Prodigal Son wallowing with the pigs that everyone was choked with tears. Hazel would shake her head after his antics and say, "I often wondered where Annetta came from. Now I know."

Not everyone was amused by his behavior. Eula found his old-fashioned strictness and chauvinism to be rather tiring at times. There could be no doubt that to Uncle James, God had created the world, and especially women, for the pleasure of men. Men might drink and smoke, but not ladies. He constantly nagged Annetta about her smoking while he and Curtis enjoyed a good cigar. No decent woman stayed out after midnight even if she were accompanied by her brother-in-law. (Curtis, Sr., frequently walked Eula back to the Episcopal Residence after she had spent the evening visiting her sister.) He also had a fierce temper and seldom forgave anyone with whom he had a serious disagreement. His wife May, on the other hand, was as gentle as he was rough. She was an ardent Seventh-Day Adventist who tried hard to live by the tenets of her faith, while James seemed to be scornful of organized religion. The time spent with the two of them was anything but dull.

The pleasure of having James and May visit was tainted by growing tension in the district. It had its roots in the firing of Mrs. Aycox and climaxed during the elections of ministerial delegates to the General Conference. At the North West Annual Conference, for the first time in many years Lionel Young had not been elected as a delegate, and neither had been some of his friends.[6] This seemed to fuel the anger of the small group of ministers who were fighting the bishop and who believed he had used his influence to defeat them.

Soon after the close of the Annual Conferences on December 9, Womack had written an article in the *Informer* entitled "Womack Supports Bishop Gomez." As was soon to be discovered, Womack, a perennial troublemaker, was pretending to support the bishop so that Joseph would use his influence to help him in his bid for the bishopric. In the article he alleged that the unrest among the dissident ministers could be attributed to the fact that they had not been elected delegates to the General Conference. He also stated that many of these ministers were angry because the bishop had changed the manner in which money was handled so that it was no longer possible to steal from the various funds; consequently, these ministers were trying to destroy the Expansion Drive.[7]

In the Sunday, January 12 *Informer* Young replied to Womack's article. He stated that it was no secret that he had fought the administration, but he had not fought the Expansion Program for Paul Quinn. "I have differed, yes, and am still differing and objecting to some things, but I did not get behind anybody's back to do it," he wrote. He denied that the election of delegates had started "the unrest in Texas," but on the other hand, it had done nothing to help the situation. As for money being stolen in the past from the college, he said that if Womack knew who was guilty he should name the individuals; he, Lionel, as a trustee, would certainly ask for the names of those individuals at the next trustee meeting. He concluded that despite the many improvements made at Paul Quinn, "it remains a stubborn fact that the Texas ministry is more divided . . . more friendships broken than have existed over the years . . . more distrust . . . more lie mongering . . . more pimps than Texas has ever known in her history."[8]

Womack enclosed all of these articles in a letter he wrote to Joseph. He said he did not understand why his original article had provoked Young, since no one else had taken the article personally. The remainder of his letter was concerned with the upcoming General Conference. He said he had decided "to accept a place on the Episcopal Committee if other of *our* friends feel that my service is needed to accomplish *our* purpose." As a member of the Episcopal Committee he would take care of the District's interests while "God, [Joseph] and others could look after the interest of [his] election" to the bishopric.[9]

Joseph resented the confidential tone of Womack's letter, particularly the references to "our friends" and "our interest." He never had and never would consider Womack to be a personal friend, nor did they have friends or interests in common. At least he knew where Young stood, and he appreciated Young's willingness to express his convictions, no matter how erroneous; but Womack bore watching closely. As for his becoming bishop, there was no danger of that. He was not a popular choice in the Connection, nor was he qualified to lead.

In March 1952, Joseph was informed that a group of ministers had filed a petition with Judge R. B. Stanton in the 19th District Court of McLennan Country against him, the president, treasurer, president of the trustee board, and the business manager of Paul Quinn College. They had asked the judge to prevent Gomez and the others mentioned from spending any of the college's money or destroying any records until charges of mismanagement and misappropriation had been cleared in a court of law. The original petition accused Gomez of having received large sums of money for the Expansion Fund and using that money for his personal benefit, of keeping confused records of the money received and spent, of not having an annual audit of the books, of mixing the money for the running of the college with that of the Expansion Fund, of not having all checks properly signed by the bursar (Lionel Young's sister, Ceola) and the treasurer of the trustee board, and countersigned by the president of the college. It further accused him of forcing the secretary of the trustee Board at its last meeting in Houston to sign falsified minutes. It alleged that the original minutes recorded that the trustees had approved of the bishop borrowing from $50,000 to $55,000 from the Citizens National Bank of Waco for the college, but that the bishop had changed the figures so that he was able to borrow $81,000. He, therefore, should be made to pay from his personal account the excess $26,000 he had actually borrowed. The petitioners accused the bishop of setting up a separate Expansion Fund without authorization from the trustee board and that he had never reported to the board how much money he had spent and for what.[10] In regard to others mentioned in the petition, the plaintiffs said:

> T. R. Clemons, S. L. Greene, S. J. Matthews, M. P. Harvey are dominated and controlled by the said defendant Bishop Gomez and . . . they have conspired with, agreed to, and followed the orders and commands of the said Bishop Gomez and that as a result the manner in which they have handled funds and accounts belonging to Paul Quinn, the said funds are confusing, incorrect, ambiguous, padded, irregular. Plaintiff should further show to the court that the said defendant Bishop Gomez will upon service and citation herein and upon the knowledge of this suit, immediately begin to undermine and destroy and to question the reputation of these plaintiffs and will attempt to destroy their official standing in the A.M.E. Church and that he has and will continue to forge false and untrue reports with reference to these plaintiffs. . . . He should be restrained from doing this [in an either] orally or written [fashion].[11]

These charges were supposedly brought by G. E. Browne, F. D. Crenshaw, L. C. Young, W. N. McGrew, J. C. Oliphant, P. F. Jackson, R. N. Reed, L. C. Browning, L. S. Godley, John Walker, T. F. Smith, and S. J. Curry. Of this group, three resided in Waco, and eight were members of the Paul Quinn trustee board (Browne, Reed, Crenshaw, Young, McGrew, Browning, Oliphant, and Jackson). They were to be represented in court by E. O'Dowd of O'Dowd and O'Dowd, a local white law firm. Strangely enough, McGrew, Jackson, Reed, and Godley's signatures did not appear on the original petition; only Oliphant's, Walker's, Godley's, Browne's, and Curry's signatures were on the original amended petition, dated March 24, 1952.[12]

When Joseph first read this petition, he was outraged. This was the first time in his life anyone had accused him of misappropriation of funds, a sophisticated way of saying "stealing!" He was known throughout the Connection for his punctilious honesty; consequently, the petition did not reflect on his character as much as it did on that of the 10th Episcopal District. Even those who did not like him found these charges ludicrous. Hundreds of people had visited the campus and had seen the prodigious job he was doing there, and they wanted to know what was wrong with Texas. Letters came from everywhere voicing confidence in his integrity. Hazel, Eula, and Annetta kept reminding him that only people who accomplish little escape criticism. Nevertheless, they too were angered by the viciousness of the attack.

Joseph hired R. L. H. Rice, a Black lawyer and minister in the District, and Hilton E. Howell of the prestigious Naman, Howell, and Boswell firm to defend him. Their answer to the plaintiff's petition emphasized the fact that the plaintiffs had no authority to represent the college or the A.M.E. Church, as they claimed they were doing in their petition. They further denied any "mishandling or misapplication or misappropriation of funds . . . and specifically den[ied] that Joseph Gomez" had taken any of the money for his personal use. The college's business affairs had been "fully audited . . . and all business transactions [had] been duly approved by the properly constituted authorities and officials of said respective institutions."[13]

Waco buzzed with excitement as the trial began at 9 A.M. on Wednesday, March 25, in the 19th District Court. From the beginning it had all the aspects of an *Amos and Andy* episode, written by whites for the purpose of caricaturing Blacks. The plaintiffs arrived in court replete with wide-brimmed Texas hats and cigars and, shaking hands with as many spectators as they could reach, strutted to their seats. For three and a half days the courtroom was crowded with Blacks who had taken time off from work to watch the spectacle. Most carried their lunches in brown paper bags. O'Dowd, lawyer for the plaintiffs, became so carried away at one point in his attack against the bishop that he slipped and called his own clients "poor unfortunate Nig—." Before he could get the entire word out the spectators began to boo.

One of the most effective and humorous testimonies for the defense was given by Aaron Jefferson, who knew how to trick "massa" by pretending to be ignorant. When in cross-examination O'Dowd asked Jefferson if he did not think the bishop had put some of the money in his pocket, Jefferson scratched his head and, speaking very slowly, asked something to the effect of: "Do you see the new gymnasium on the campus? Do you see the new dining hall and student union building? Do you see the new chapel? Do you see the construction going up for the new administration building?" O'Dowd answered, "Yes." Jefferson scratched his head again and said, "Well, after all that, if the bishop has stolen any money, he can have it." This provoked prolonged laughter from the onlookers, and O'Dowd's face turned red.

Several of the plaintiffs, including Young, complained that the bishop insisted that his signature be on every check that left the campus. The attorney for the defense, Howell, asked some of them if they were not on the Board of Trustees. They answered, "Yes." He then reminded them that most of the banks would not honor the checks if Gomez's name was not on them and that the Board of Trustees had voted unanimously that the bishop's signature should be on the checks. Young told him that they had had to vote that way, because the bishop would have found some way to get revenge—possibly by assigning them to a smaller church. It was soon established that none of the plaintiffs had been sent to smaller churches. Young then said the bishop could talk men into doing anything he wanted them to do. To this Howell replied, "Well then, I would say he's a pretty powerful bishop, wouldn't you? Step down!"

At one point O'Dowd, who had torn several pages from the auditor's report, tried to show that there were discrepancies in the report. Unfortunately for him there were over fifty copies in the court room and Howell handed him a complete copy. In addition, the auditors, Upleger and Upleger, announced that the books of the college were in better shape than they had ever been before. That seemed to end the matter. The judge ruled on Friday, March 28, that he found "no proof of dishonesty or mismanagement on the part of the defendant" and that other matters involved were "ecclesiastical [and] beyond the jurisdiction of this court." He dismissed the case and billed the plaintiffs for court costs.[14] When the judge had read his decision the spectators applauded, shook the judge's hand, and began to sing one of the old Methodist hymns.

James had attended the first day's session. He had become so upset by the lack of decorum of the plaintiffs and their lawyer that Joseph and May would not let him attend any more sessions. He, of course, had been used to British court procedures and was highly embarrassed by what he called "the circus" before him.

Even after the trial, however, the plaintiffs were by no means finished. Someone among them called the Internal Revenue Service suggesting that it should audit Joseph's last year's tax returns. The I.R.S. did, and when nothing was turned up as a result, they prepared to embarrass the bishop at the General Conference to be held in May.

Outwardly, Joseph was humble and gracious in victory. The Waco papers had carried hardly any news of the trial, in deference to the bishop whom they had come to love and respect. All of them, however, carried an article of his vindication. Only his family and closest friends knew how badly scarred he was. For days after the trial, when he thought no one was around, he would sit in his office looking out on the campus. Much of the joy of his accomplishments had turned acrid. The indignity—the mockery—of the three days' proceedings sickened him. It was as if all the respect Blacks had earned for themselves in the past four years in Waco had been reduced to ten-gallon hats and ten-cent cigars like "De Lawd" in *The Green Pastures.*

He pulled himself together enough to give a bon voyage party for James and May, who were leaving for Trinidad on April 3, and to help in the preparations for Sherman Greene's formal inauguration ceremonies on May 2.[15] A few days later Joseph and Hazel left for Chicago, where the General Conference was being held.

Before going to the conference, several of the Texas ministers who had been involved in the trial against Joseph brought the same charges against him to the Episcopal Committee. They were determined to embarrass the bishop, if nothing else. In addition to the charges, they put fliers on the chairs of all the delegates accusing Joseph of being a crook and a tyrant. Most of the delegates threw them in the trash, but others gave them to Joseph, urging him to sue the perpetrators for libel. As angry as Joseph was, he decided to ignore the fliers, thinking this would end the matter. However, at the Thursday morning session, when the secretary read the names of the delegates assigned to the Episcopal Committee from the various districts, W. A. Carr of Texas challenged the method that had been used in the selection of the committee members from Texas. At this point, Joseph rose and stated that the members had been chosen properly. Bishop Ransom, who chaired the session, "ruled that this was not the time nor place to consider this matter, and suggested that it be worked out, if possible, by the Bishop and members of the district. To this, Bishop Gomez and the members of his district, agreed."[16]

It became obvious at the Friday morning session that the dissident ministers from Texas were determined to keep up the confusion. When Ransom asked the secretary to read the minutes of the previous session, Rev. L. C. Graves of Texas "objected to the adoption of that part of the minutes which referred to Appointment of Committees," especially as it related to those delegates from Texas alleged to have been elected to the Episcopal Committee. After much discussion, Gomez was recognized by the chair. He said the initial election had been fair, but he was willing to call the members of the delegation together and have another election by secret ballot. The conference agreed to this, and the amended minutes were adopted.[17] Joseph was able to announce at the afternoon session that the delegates from Texas had confirmed the election of the original members. Once more the dissidents had been defeated.[18]

One of the most important actions of the conference was the forming of a Judicial Council composed of seventeen members, nine elders and eight laymen, all of whom had to be at least thirty-five years of age. The duties of this council were to "determine on appeal, the constitutionality of any act of the General Conference, and to exercise other judicial functions as hereinafter designated, provided, however, that the Judicial Council is amenable to the General Conference; and any ruling or decision of the Judicial Council may be modified or reversed by majority vote of the General Conference."[19]

On Friday, May 16, the Episcopal Committee again reported to the conference. It recommended the location for four years of Bishop M. H. Davis, the retirement of Bishops Ransom and W. A. Fountain, and the election of three new bishops. The report was approved by the delegates.[20]

The ninety-one-year-old Ransom thanked the Church for the honors he had received in his sixty-six years as pastor, editor, and bishop. He asked to continue in his position as historiographer, because he wanted to bring the history of the Church up to date while he still had time. Ransom was followed by Joseph, who paid tribute to "a great man, a great mind." He credited Ransom as having contributed greatly to any success he, Gomez, had had, and urged the delegates to reappoint Ransom as Historiographer. In conclusion he said "that when shadows fall and the book of Ransom is closed, his tombstone shall read 'He was a maker of men.'"[21]

There were tears in Joseph's eyes as he spoke. He knew full well the conference would retire Ransom this time, but he wanted Ransom to know what he had meant in Joseph's life. As was expected, despite Ransom's request the conference reaffirmed its adoption of the Episcopal Committee's recommendations.[22]

On Monday, May 19, Bishop D. O. Walker moved that the election of bishops begin at 11 A.M. It was not until 6 A.M. the next morning after the third ballot had been counted that the three new bishops were elected: Howard Thomas Primm of Louisiana, Fred D. Jordan of California (as promised at the 1948 conference), and Eugene C. Hatcher, former editor of the *Southern Christian Recorder*. The four men from Texas who ran had done poorly: Womack received one vote on the first and second ballots and then withdrew; L. C. Graves received twenty-four votes on the first ballot and eighteen on the second before he withdrew; E. M. Bracy received sixty-nine votes on the first and withdrew before the second; L. C. Browning received three votes on the first and withdrew before the second.[23] Had he not died, the man from Texas who most likely would have been elected was F. W. Grant.

When the appointments were read Joseph was reassigned to the 10th Episcopal District. The majority of the delegates from Texas led a noisy demonstration in support of the appointment;[24] those who had tried to destroy his credibility sat in sullen silence. They had been sure the Episcopal Committee would not send Gomez back to Texas, but they had made two mistakes: taking their grievance to a civil court before bringing it before the Church, and underestimating Gomez's unblemished record of honesty and integrity throughout the Connection. No doubt as they watched the demonstration they wondered if the bishop would retaliate against them during the next four years.

The Gomezes returned to Waco to help Eula make plans to move to Cleveland so she could complete her master's degree and teach in the public schools there. In a few weeks they boarded a plane for Cleveland, and soon after Eula settled in the large three-story brick house her parents had bought on Wade Park Avenue. (It had always been Joseph's plan to retire in Cleveland some day.) In the fall she would register in the Graduate School at Western Reserve University. It had been arranged that Marvin, Sissy (Annetta), and Gerald were to stay in Waco with their grandparents and Mrs. Dickerson until Eula was better situated.

The Gomezes then traveled to Wilberforce to pick up Bishop Ransom, and the three of them headed for Woodland Park, Michigan. On September 4 Joseph wrote a tribute to Ransom in the *Christian Recorder*, describing their time together at the cottage. He spoke of Ransom as "pioneer and statesman, Bishop and Sage of Tawawa . . . master of the language . . . philosopher and friend . . . [who] from his vast reservoir of knowledge . . . drew great truths gathered through three generations of a life, lived in active, heroic sacrificial service." With the "world [as] his text, the moral order his theme, he discussed life's issues with a vigor of mind that an aging body [had] left unfettered and therefore, unafraid." Joseph found him, though often "misinterpreted, maligned and pilloried," to be tranquil of spirit. Ransom had "a morale that [kept] march with progress, and a faith that chuckl[ed] at disaster and treat[ed] with disdain the malice of the world of small men, of small souls." The setting that surrounded the cottage, particularly the lake, "lent charm to his words and . . . matched the artistry of his eloquence."[25]

Ransom's presence and words were a healing balm to Joseph's bruised spirit. When they first arrived Joseph told Ransom of his fear that he would not be able to continue his work in Texas. Ransom reminded him that he had wanted to be bishop and that along with the office went the scorn of small minds. "You, Joseph, are made of stronger stuff than to succumb to depression and faintness of heart," he chided. Ransom's confidence and the incredible beauty of Woodland ministered to Joseph's needs, and every day he felt stronger. Near the end of September he was ready to return to Waco.

On September 28, 1952, thousands of people from around the state gathered at Paul Quinn for the dedication of the Joseph Gomez Administration Building, the fourth new structure to be added to the college in four years. President Greene was applauded loudly when he said, "This building is much more than stone and chimes. It is a symbol of Paul Quinn's attitude [toward] tomorrow, for it is within this building [that] we shall organize our staff and plan the strategy of our approach to tomorrow so that we shall not lose the gains we made today."[26]

Shortly after the dedication and before the Annual Conferences began, Joseph announced that if the ministers who had disgraced the district in civil court and at the General Conference apologized for their actions to the A.M.E. Church and the 10th Episcopal District, the matter would be closed, as far as he was concerned. No apology to him was needed. The minutes of all the conferences are filled with apologies from various ministers, among them L. E. Browning (Presiding Elder), L. W. Jenkins, L. C. Young, F. D. Crenshaw, L. C. Browning, and G. E. Browne. All of the apologies were made behind the pulpit in the presence of the full conference. It was hard for Joseph to believe that any of them would stand in the pulpit and lie; consequently, he believed all of the apologies had been made in good faith, and some of them were. But the more hard-core dissidents pretended to be repentant while in private they continued to demean the administration. Why they were so determined to cause havoc was best analyzed by C. W. Abington, a native Texan, in an article he distributed to all the church papers; it was entitled, "The Whole Truth about African Methodism in Texas."

He said that "for practically three Quadrenniums, Texas was without that rugged, aggressive, planned leadership that a great district like this must have to get best results." Prior to the administration of Bishop Young, Bishop W. Sampson Brooks had provided that kind of leadership. Bishop Young had felt that Brooks had been too exacting, and as a result, "in his zeal to introduce a more liberal policy and to be brotherly with men with whom, for the most part, he had grown up, he allowed the reins of government to slip from between his fingers, to the extent it might be said of Texas, as it was said of Ancient Israel at a time, 'In those days there was no king of Israel; every man did that which was right in his own eyes.' The whole truth is, any Bishop assigned to the 10th would have had the same difficulties, or worse."[27]

Abington then outlined the reasons for the opposition to Gomez, who had followed Young. First of all, Gomez had insisted that the wives of ministers should live in the parsonages. Secondly, he had created a new, systematic budget which those who liked the old "hit and miss" arrangement objected to. Thirdly, Gomez followed the General Conference law that "ministers serving a district or a charge eight or more consecutive years should be moved." Gomez had moved all the ministers who fell under that law—even his closest friends.

Abington then reviewed the entire trial episode and the "vicious" fliers that had been passed out during the General Conference. He rejected the claim that the dissidents had gone to court in the interest of Paul Quinn. If they had been so interested in the college, why had they tried to get the authorities in the Department of Education at Austin to take away the college's accreditation?

Although he thought of himself as a Christian, Abington did not see how Gomez could have said to the dissidents, "I hold no ill will toward you, but your offense has been against the African Methodist Episcopal Church." Nevertheless, he noted, those who had apologized remained in good standing in the district. Abington also noted the changes made in the way money was handled: the time when money raised for the college never got there was over. With the system set up by the bishop, the presiding elders reported the money "directly to the treasurer of the college." This accounted in a large measure for the progress made at Paul Quinn.

There were many people who held that a major reason for the dissent was indeed money. Certainly, it is difficult to believe that anyone would go to the lengths these men did to unseat the bishop unless some kind of profit was involved, in terms of money, power, or both.

On December 19, 1953, the Waco Chamber of Commerce's Board of Directors made known its confidence in the bishop and his program by endorsing unanimously a fund campaign to raise $150,000 for Paul Quinn College. Gordon Rountree, a prominent Waco citizen and car dealer, moved the endorsement and was seconded by A. M. Goldstein, owner of Goldstein Migel department store.[28]

Goldstein did not fit the stereotype of the southern store owner. Although he followed the customs of the region when he felt it was expedient to do so, there were times when his principles caused him to rebel. For example, Hazel once went to his store to buy a present for Maggie Sawyer; she took her package to the packing department to be wrapped and addressed. The clerk asked to whom the package should be made out. Hazel said, "To Mrs. Maggie Sawyer," whereupon the clerk wrote "Maggie Sawyer." Then the clerk asked for the address, but Hazel told her she did not have the name written correctly yet. By this time the clerk was running out of patience. "You said 'Maggie Sawyer,' and that's what I have written," she yelled. Hazel informed her she had not said "Maggie Sawyer," but "*Mrs.* Maggie Sawyer." "I ain't gonna put no *Mrs.* in front of no Nigra's name," the clerk retorted. By this time, unknown to the clerk, Mr. Goldstein, who had heard the commotion, was standing behind her. When she quieted down, he told her that Mrs. Gomez was one of the store's best customers and a fine citizen. "You will treat her as such. You will write on the package what she has asked you to write and then report to me." The flustered clerk did as she was told. Hazel learned later that she was fired that day. Goldstein was representative of the kind of men who would head the funding campaign for Paul Quinn and would see that it reached its goal.

A few days after the Waco Chamber of Commerce made its announcement, Joseph, Hazel, Annetta, and Curtis (Senior and Junior) left for Cleveland to spend the holidays with Eula and her children. This would be the first of many Christmases celebrated at what came to be known as the family home. Eula was doing well in her studies at Western Reserve. She was an active member at St. James A.M.E. Church, where Hubie Robinson was still pastor, and she was now the organizer and director of the chancel choir.

The family house was located on the corner of Wade Park and Magnolia Drive, around the corner from the Cleveland Music School Settlement. It had a huge living room, dining room, and kitchen, and a small solarium and powder room on the first floor. On the second floor were three bedrooms, two baths, and a sitting room, which led to a porch overlooking the backyard. Joseph eventually built a large library, bath, and bedroom on the third floor, which became his hideaway. This house was important; it was the first he had ever owned. All the other houses where he and his family had lived belonged to the A.M.E. Church, designated as parsonages. He loved this house best of all; consequently, this Christmas was special for him—as he sat at the head of the long table passing out the turkey and stuffing, admiring his wife, daughters, lively grandchildren, and friends. Texas was his assigned district, but Cleveland was his home.

Earlier that year, following the Southwest Annual Conference, October 14–18, Rev. L. C. Graves had left the A.M.E. Church and established what he called the Independent A.M.E. Church and appointed himself bishop. Reportedly he was discouraged by having made such a poor showing in his bid for the bishopric, by seeing his case against Bishop Gomez dismissed by the Judicial Committee, and at having been demoted by the bishop from presiding elder to pastor of a small charge. (Graves had not been one of the ministers who apologized to the district.) The other ministers who had decided to join Graves's Independent Church were Rev. G. E. Browne, whose name had appeared on the civil suit against the bishop; I. S. Aycox, husband of the former president of Paul Quinn; Reverends E. A. Thomas, L. S. Godley, John D. Walker, U. S. Washington, S. E. Sims, and M. C. Collins. Noticeably missing from this list was Lionel Young, who despite his differences with the bishop remained faithful to the A.M.E. Church, as did his entire family.

On January 6, 1953, Revs. E. L. Burton, C. H. Sanders, and J. Bennett Brown brought charges to the district against the breakaway ministers. The charge was that they had not reported to their assigned churches at the close of their respective Annual Conferences: "That each and all of them [had] absented themselves from the A.M.E. Church, and [had] failed and refused to be governed by the rules and regulations" of the Church. They therefore had violated the Discipline of the A.M.E. Church.[29] A special trial committee reviewed these charges and on January 23 recommended that the men be suspended until the Annual Conferences in the fall of 1953.[30]

According to the *Houston Informer* (February 2), Rev. I. S. Aycox, pastor of Allen Chapel, had held a church meeting at which the members had voted twenty-seven to one to transfer their chapel to the Independent A.M.E. Church. They notified their presiding elder, E. M. Bracy, of their decision; when he arrived the following Sunday for Quarterly Conference, Aycox "dismissed the service when he finished the 11 o'clock preaching, and Rev. Bracy had no congregation for his Quarterly Conference." Bracy immediately sought an injunction to prevent the pastor from transferring the congregation to the Independent A.M.E. Church. A jury found that Allen Chapel A.M.E. Church at Huntsville was the property of the Mother (or original) Conference and could not be taken by the departing members to the Independent A.M.E. Church.[31]

The month of February was a melancholy one for Joseph. Two of his dear friends died, Rev. Thomas R. Clemons and Bishop John A. Gregg. Clemons, along with Grant, had been one of the first ministers to befriend Joseph when he came to Texas. He was a colorful character, with a down-to-earth approach to life and a homespun sense of humor. On Monday, February 2, he died at Providence Hospital (not in the basement but in a private room), at the age of seventy-one. His last concerns were for Mary, the wife he adored, and the A.M.E. Church in Texas. Clemons died saddened by the infractions of some of the Texas ministers over the previous two years; he told Joseph that in all of his fifty years in the ministry he had never seen the A.M.E. Church held up to so much ridicule.

At the funeral on the campus, Joseph said that "Rev. Clemons's defense of men and measures was lofty and overwhelming. Opponents thought twice before engaging T. R. Clemons [in a controversy]. [But] once he gave his pledge of friendship, it stood unwavering to the end." Joseph admitted that sometimes they had disagreed but declared that he had always found Clemons unselfish, honest, and true, to love Paul Quinn, and to be solicitous of his wife Mary of forty-seven years, to whom he always thought about coming home no matter where he went. He had not had an opportunity to attend school, but he had learned from books gathered by his wife and daughter. "The world was his book learning. College training might have unfitted the man who knew only the grace of God," Joseph concluded.[32]

Bishop John A. Gregg died in a Jacksonville, Florida, hospital on Tuesday, February 17, following a month's hospitalization. The funeral was held in Kansas City, Kansas, and again Joseph delivered the eulogy. It must have been a difficult task in light of the deep friendship the two men had shared through the years. Looking out at an audience of ministers, bishops and laymen to whom Gregg had meant so much, Joseph compared him to another John—John the Baptist. Gregg had watched the rise of industrialism and the ebb and flow of racism. "He was a part of this struggle. . . . What he accomplished—from Eureka to Africa, then Florida—establishes a record, arresting and dominant, and places him far beyond the level of ordinary men," Joseph said.[33]

He reminded the mourners that many had thought Gregg too "easy and tolerant . . . [and] mistook a genuine kindness of heart and a burning desire not to hurt people as appeasement and surrender." But Joseph had seen him righteously indignant. "Often you were made to know that the 'velvet scabbard held a sword of metal.'" Joseph spoke of Gregg's contribution at the World Conference of Christian Endeavor in Berlin in 1930, when he "flayed the South African Government for its unjust treatment of Colored and Native peoples, in plain uncompromising language." He praised Gregg for being a "man of deep religious convictions." He felt sure that Gregg would always be present when "the Church needs to be reminded of its mission; when men get 'too big' for their jobs and the ministry is tempted to forsake its ancient moorings; when the Holy Fathers and leaders lose the vision of the Divine Purpose of the Church of God. . . . In those days will come John."[34]

Gregg would have been proud of the accolade that came to Joseph in the spring of 1953. When the newly organized Texas Council of Churches was formed, with representatives from eleven different denominations, Dr. M. E. Sadler of the Christian Church was elected president, and Joseph was elected First Vice President. This seemed incredible.[35] After all, this was Texas, and it was the early 1950s. The telegram that came to the Episcopal Residence on May 5 from Rev. C. C. Davis was typical of the hundreds of congratulations received: "We think that the A.M.E.'s in general and those of Texas in particular should feel proud of you and your Texas leadership."[36]

Changes seemed to be in the making that May. At the A.M.E. Church Annual Board of Education Meeting on May 7 at Nashville, Tennessee, Sherman L. Greene, Jr., was appointed the new secretary-treasurer of the Division of Educational Institutions, in place of W. A. Fountain, who had died in April.[37] This meant that he would have to relinquish his position as president of Paul Quinn, and a replacement would have to be found immediately. The Board of Trustees appointed Frank Veal, pastor of Emanuel A.M.E. Church of Charleston, South Carolina, a graduate of Boston University, and a former teacher at Allen University in Charleston.[38] Veal and Greene had contrasting personalities: where Greene was noted for his dignity and quiet efficiency, Veal was exuberant, flamboyant, and always in a hurry to get things done. He never walked; he bounded. Because he was so outgoing he made an instant hit with the faculty, student body, and the people of Waco. The month of Veal's arrival on campus, Hazel flew to Cleveland to get her grandson, Gerald. The doctors had discovered he had a heart murmur and needed a good deal of rest; Hazel would keep him until he was better. Finding Eula exhausted from studying and trying to keep up with the children at the same time, Hazel hired a housekeeper to help her with Marvin and Sissy.

A few days after Hazel's return to Waco, tragedy struck the city. On Monday, May 11, at 4:36 P.M., a half hour before most of the people in the college administration building would have left for the day, Joseph heard a terrifying noise like large stones hitting the sides of the building, accompanied by rushing water. Suddenly all the power went off, and people huddled together in the hallways, not knowing what to do. The impossible had happened. Notwithstanding the tradition that Indians had settled the site of Waco because it was too low to be hit by tornadoes, a twister had struck, and with deadly accuracy. Downtown, "brick and steel buildings crumpled like pasteboard houses; tons of shattered plate glass flew through the storm to cut and slash even the people who took refuge indoors." The twister went through "two square miles of retail business houses in the center of the high valued district, through manufacturing plants, churches and homes. Hardest hit was the R. T. Dennis Furniture, a five-story build-ing[,] where many people were buried alive."[39]

(Within fifteen minutes the tornado killed over 150 people and injured some three hundred. Every ambulance was called into service, and people were asked to volunteer their private cars to transport the wounded, first to Providence and then to the nearby James Connally Air Force Base when Providence became too crowded. Blacks and whites lay indiscriminately in the beds, on the floors of private rooms, wards, and halls of Providence, and no one seemed to be concerned. Complicating matters further was the rain; between Monday and Wednesday, 8.21 inches fell. Allen Shivers, governor of Texas, appealed to President Dwight D. Eisenhower for emer-gency funds.)[40]

Once the immediate danger was over, Joseph stepped out onto the campus to see the results. Every building had been damaged except the ad-ministration building and the chapel. The roof of the new gym was partly ripped. Joseph hurried to the Episcopal Residence, where Hazel, Curtis Jr., Gerald, and the housekeeper were. To his relief, they were safe. (Luckily, Annetta, who was pregnant with her second child, had been in the ad-ministration building running the switchboard when the storm hit.) His son-in-law, Curtis Sr., had been helping to make repairs on the Home Eco-nomics building; he had climbed down from the ladder and laid on the open floor until the twister passed.

Moving from building to building, Joseph learned that none of the stu-dents had been hurt. Then he walked over to Taylor Elementary School, where the nearest aid station had been set up. He saw about fifty people lying or sitting on cots provided by the Red Cross. Many had lost every-thing they had. Everywhere there was confusion—people incoherently telling of their experiences during the tornado—Red Cross workers trying to administer to immediate needs—children playing games and yelling as if at a Sunday school picnic—some old people just staring blankly, in a state of shock. Alwyn Talbot, a West Indian English teacher at the college, had come to offer his services and was working beside a young woman named Dorothy, who was later to become his wife. Joseph talked to as many people as he could and then returned to the campus to make plans for giving aid to the victims and repairing the damage.

A few days later he addressed the citizens of Waco over the radio. He offered condolences on behalf of the college, the district, and the A.M.E. Church. He noted that one of the only two buildings that had not been hit at Paul Quinn was the chapel. It stood as a "a symbol of our faith and a challenge to our courage. We [citizens of Waco] have suffered damage—

material and physical—of over 50 million dollars, but like that chapel, our faith, our courage remains undamaged by the storm and stands amid the physical chaos as the indestructible element of our society. . . . If then, during this crisis, we have discovered the soul of Waco, we shall not have suffered in vain."[41]

Joseph received personal encouragement in the form of a letter of June 4 from Bishop Ransom. It said:

> You are being tested and tried in a succession of events of administrative experience that you have gloriously survived. I think of you and pray for you every day. . . . In the case of Paul Quinn College and the disaster that visited Waco, both Paul Quinn and Waco shall arise from the ruins to put on a larger and better program than they have known.
>
> Things most always happen after this pattern. Both you and our people there should greatly profit by the new and more intimate contacts of black and white citizens in their effort at social, moral and cultural contacts. . . . Please be assured I shall try to visit you for a few days at Woodland Park. I want to say more to you than I am writing. May God preserve us both until we meet again.[42]

Joseph was again cheered when Mayor Edgar Dean of Fort Worth issued a proclamation making June 16 "Paul Quinn College Disaster Fund Drive Day." He called for all citizens to attend a mass meeting at Allen Chapel, or if they could not attend, to find some "other manner as may be appropriate to assist those in making the most laudable appeal in behalf of Paul Quinn."[43]

Unfortunately, not all of Joseph's efforts in 1953 could be directed to the repair of the campus. On September 23 he went before federal Judge Ben C. Connally asking that an injunction be issued against Bishop L. C. Graves and the Independent African Methodist Episcopal Church to prevent them from using the name "African Methodist Episcopal Church." The judge ruled "that the use of the name by the new group infringed on the privileges of the A.M.E. Church," and he issued a temporary injunction against it.[44]

Soon after this court decision, Joseph's 1953 Annual Conferences commenced. They too were largely concerned with the Independent Church and its attempt to take A.M.E. Church property. At the Northwest Texas Conference, a special judiciary committee found that "Reverend U. S. Washington, Rev. W. E. Sims and Rev. M. C. Collins were guilty of changing the titles of their church properties and deeding them to the Independent Church without the knowledge of the Quarterly Conference and the Annual Conference." The committee therefore recommended that they be expelled from the A.M.E. Church.[45] At the Southwest Texas Annual Conference at San Antonio, the judiciary committee recommended that E. A. Thomas, L. C. Graves, L. S. Godley, and John D. Walker also be expelled from the A.M.E. Church.[46]

During the West Texas Conference in Somerville, news came to Joseph that Rev. L. C. Browning, pastor of Wayman Chapel, Temple, and his congregation had drawn up a resolution stating that Wayman Chapel "had severed its relationship with the A.M.E. Connection," and that they had sold the chapel to the Independent Church for the sum of ten dollars. The A.M.E. Church had valued this property at $100,000.[47]

On November 10, the district judge in Belton, Texas, issued a restraining order against the Independent Church, stating that Rev. Browning should vacate the parsonage and church property immediately and turn the keys over to the A.M.E. Church. Relating this incident to the Central Texas Conference in mid-November, Joseph vowed that as long as he was bishop of Texas "no property [would] be lost to the Connection, so help [him] God";[48] none ever was.

The Central Texas Conference was not without its own drama. Rev. Womack claimed that he could not turn in his conference claims, because he had been robbed. He assured the bishop that a proper investigation had been made by the sheriff of Travis County. A judiciary committee asked that papers with the signature of the sheriff be turned in and ordered Womack to appear before it by Friday morning, November 29. The same committee found Browning guilty of "improper ministerial conduct" in that he had made a "fraudulent attempt to convey the real property owned by Wayman Chapel Church and to misapply funds belonging to the church in the sum of $490." They recommended that he be expelled and that his name be dropped from the roll of the conference.[49]

At the Northeast Texas Conference (November 11–15) in Corsicana, Joseph "challenged the defiance of the ministers who walked away from churches that were paying them lucrative salaries, to attempt the organization of another religious body." Why did these men leave the A.M.E. Church? "Not because they were poorly paid; not because they were not honored, but because of what the A.M.E. Church stands for." In their selfishness and desire for personal aggrandizement, they did not want to abide by the rules of African Methodism. "They wanted to make their own rules to suit their own purpose." Nevertheless, he said, "a miracle [had] been wrought, despite opinionated opposition of those who would destroy the Church." Titles and abstracts to property that no one knew the Church owned had been reclaimed; other property thought lost had been recovered. He said he was not criticizing Bishop Young, who had "been weakened by the weight of years, physically and mentally." But he *was* criticizing, and sharply, those "low-down scoundrels who took advantage of Bishop Young to abuse the opportunity they enjoyed as leaders [in order to] aggrandize themselves—even to the destruction, if it were possible, of the A.M.E. Church." To him, these men were "cheaters and vindictive pastors."[50] He uttered no curse words, but the ministers had never heard the bishop use such strong language before. This was the "righteous indignation" they had heard about. The fiery West Indian temper he had inherited from his mother would emerge full blown whenever anyone threatened the Church he loved, or questioned his personal integrity.

It became obvious to everyone that Joseph was losing his patience with the ministers. He chided them for not attending the School of Religion at Paul Quinn College, which he had established to help them become better prepared; from this time on, attendance would be mandatory. He became angry when ministers or presiding elders continued to turn in personal checks to the conferences after he specifically asked them not to. He had had his fill of bad checks from ministers. At the Northeast Texas Conference, Rev. A. S. B. Jones, whom he had treated like a son and who was now Presiding Elder of the Denison District, tendered a check for $112. In addition, when Jones read his report, several serious discrepancies emerged. Joseph appointed a finance committee to investigate the predicament in the Denison District. The committee found that Jones had reported more than he turned in in order to cover up the fact that his district had not met its budget. He was charged with "official negligence, [and] improper conduct in the handling of the finances." The committee recommended that he be "marked," or given a bad assessment, by the conference. One of the ministers made a substitute motion, "that he be reproved by the Bishop and that the conference exonerate him." This motion was passed unanimously.[51]

Everyone knew that Jones had driven for the bishop when he first came to Texas and that Joseph was fond of him. They waited to see if he would play favorites; they did not have to wait long. When the appointments were read, Jones was transferred to the Northwest Texas Conference and given a church at Brownwood Station, a charge which carried considerably less prestige than being a presiding elder.[52] Jones did not consider this move vindictiveness on the part of the bishop. He knew that time and time again Joseph had gotten him out of difficulty and that the bishop was saying, in essence, "It's time for you to be responsible for yourself." Jones knew that he had only himself to blame, and said so to Joseph.

During the latter part of November Joseph won his litigation against the Independent Church in the U.S. District Court at Houston, Texas. The judge permanently banned the new organization from using the name "African Methodist Episcopal." Graves told the court that he had pulled away from the regular church because of what he termed "dictatorial, arbitrary and capricious policies and inordinate assessments levied by Bishop Gomez." Joseph countered by saying that "Graves rebelled mainly because of his unsuccessful efforts to be elected Bishop at the 1952 General Conference." Of the 1,056 votes cast on the first ballot, he had received twenty-nine, on the second, eighteen; now he had made himself bishop of a small following—many of whom within a few months would drift back to the African Methodist Episcopal Church.[53]

Surprisingly enough, Rev. L. C. Young had attended many of the conferences and was a positive influence. He preached, sang, and was willing to cooperate whenever his assistance was needed. Also, Rev. L. E. Browning, presiding elder of the Brenham District (and one of the original rebels), had done such an excellent job with his district during the year that the bishop complimented him on several occasions.

On November 24, the day before the North Texas Conference convened, Joseph hurried back to Waco to witness the birth of what would be his last grandson. Joseph Jefferson was born at Providence Hospital at 10 A.M. Not wanting to take the risk of losing the baby as he almost had Curtis Jr., the doctor performed a caesarean section right away. After being assured the operation had been successful and both mother and six-pound, seven-ounce son were all right, Joseph drove back to Dallas to close his last conference for the year and to attend a birthday celebration the district had planned for him.

He returned to the campus exhausted. This series of conferences had been most difficult, as a result of the various trials needed to retain the Church's property and name. But there was no time for relaxation. The tornado had delayed the Paul Quinn College Expansion Drive that was to have been conducted by the city of Waco in May of 1953. At the December meeting of the Waco Appeals Review Board the drive was rescheduled for March 1954, only three months away. The board complimented Bishop Gomez and President Veal for the "amazing progress" shown by the college in the past year, as evidenced by the annual audit report. It showed that the college now had no bank indebtedness or mortgages and would pay off the last of its tornado-related repair bills by February 15. It was decided that in March two hundred volunteers would comb Waco streets to solicit $200,000 in cash or subscriptions, payable over a two-year period. The campaign was to be headed by Chester D. Harris, the sales manager of

Dr. Pepper. The collection and disbursement of the fund would be supervised by a board of trustees made up of Waco civic and business leaders, headed by Russell A. Cox; A. M. Goldstein would serve as treasurer.[54]

Between January 6 and 8, Joseph and Hazel attended the first Annual Meeting of the Texas Council of Churches, which was held at the First Methodist Church in Austin. As first vice president, Joseph was chosen unanimously by the delegates to preside over the council in the absence of the president, Dr. M. E. Sadler, who was ill.[55]

In his introductory remarks Joseph called upon the Protestant Church to "exert itself before it [lost] possession of its soul as a leader in the affairs of the nation. We must prove our detractors are wrong when they say our church has no constructive function in our society." The Church could not stand by and "let [this] generation groom the world for a suicide plunge." It must continue to lead in "education, and morality, justice and civic secularism." Joining the churches of Texas together through this Council is a "great advance . . . a forward move and a giant step." He warned, however, that in order to succeed in all its endeavors the Council must "disregard the false standards of race, color or creed." He predicted that Texas would "lead the way in showing Protestant Unity."[56]

In the afternoon there was a panel discussion, "The Church and Public Education," led by Dr. Matthew S. Davage, president of Houston-Tillotson College; Dr. J. D. Miller of the Texas Military Institute, San Antonio, Texas; and Dr. Kenneth Pope of the First Church of Houston. In regard to the case of school segregation then pending in the Supreme Court, Dr. Davage said, "Should the Supreme Court rule against segregation in education, Christians will go along because they are Christians. I believe in the fundamental sense of justice and fair play and the Christian attitude of people. It could bring glee to the Kremlin if there should be a violent reaction to such a rule."[57]

Joseph was given a standing ovation for the excellent way in which he presided over the conference, and he was urged by many to accept the presidency for the coming year.[58] The weakness of the resolution on the desegregation of schools, however, was a clear indication to him that many of the member churches were not ready to accept a Black man as president yet; he declined the invitation. He had made a profound statement by presiding over this assembly, particularly since its members for the most part, had grown up accepting segregation as a way of life and found no incompatibility between that practice and Christianity. In addition, his innumerable responsibilities in the district and at the college had to have priority. He did, however, accept positions as executive committee member at large and as a member of the Board of Directors, and he continued to be involved as long as he remained in Texas. He had paved the way for other Black ministers to assume leadership positions in the Council.

On January 28, 1954, he received a letter from Harold Kilpatrick, executive secretary of the Council, acknowledging the valuable service he had rendered and noting that because of Joseph's "leadership and the wide participation of [his] constituents, [the Council was] able to begin as a genuine inter-racial organization."[59]

Bishop Ransom also made mention of Joseph's accomplishments with the Texas Council of Churches, in a letter written January 8, 1954:

My dear Bishop and Daughter Hazel,

You feel to me as my children after the flesh. You certainly have acted as my son in the Gospel. For me, my fondness grows more tender with the flight of time.

As you know, I celebrated my ninety-third birthday this week and I hope to live to celebrate my thirtieth anniversary as a Bishop sometime this year. The things you have accomplished in Texas testify to your success and achievement in the state of Texas. It is almost unbelievable that such a thing could happen in our day.

I pray for you many times each day and for your children who are dear to my heart. Please be assured that I am always your devoted father and friend.[60]

The Waco Drive for the Expansion of Paul Quinn began on Monday, March 23. Campaign workers, whose slogan became "Match Their Faith," were provided with brochures presenting the college's expansion outlook and how the Waco Building Fund fit into the total picture. One hundred and ninety-six business and professional leaders began solicitations after a kick-off meeting.[61]

At noon, however, before the campaign began, speeches were made at the Kiwanis, Optimist, and Exchange clubs. Speaking at the Kiwanis luncheon at the Raleigh Hotel, A. M. Goldstein philosophized, "America is not a melting pot, but a symphony orchestra. Human beings are not metals thrown into a melting pot to produce an alloy—each drop of which becomes exactly like each other drop—but in a symphony orchestra, the more varied the instruments, the better the orchestra. Whatever our present differences in faith, race, color, or creed," he reminded his listener, "let us never forget that we are all children of one Father, and are all created in His image and likeness."[62]

Alf Skognes, a white philosophy professor and pastor of Hillcrest Baptist Church, told the Optimist Club that Waco should be proud of being the home of the oldest college for Negroes in Texas and therefore should contribute generously to its expansion. At the same time, Chester Harris, the drive's chairman, was telling the Exchange Club, "The people connected with Paul Quinn are doing their part and now it's up to Waco to do its part."[63] By March 31 the *Waco News-Tribune* was able to report that the Paul Quinn Fund Drive had collected $70,315 toward its goal.[64]

In May, to Joseph and Hazel's delight, the Supreme Court, with Chief Justice Earl Warren as its spokesman, decreed: "We conclude that in the field of public education the doctrine of 'separate but equal' has no place. Separate educational facilities are inherently unequal." Thus it struck down the 1896 *Plessy vs. Ferguson* decision that had sanctioned segregated schools. Winning the *Brown vs. Board of Education of Topeka* case on May 17, 1954, was a monumental step forward for Black Americans. The Gomezes also noted that President Eisenhower never said whether he approved of the Supreme Court's decision but merely pledged as the chief executive of the country to support the Court's authority. Joseph was appointed by the governor to serve on the State Board for School Desegregation.

Joseph recognized the challenge this decision presented to Black colleges and other organizations, to help Blacks prepare for the change. Because of the crippling effects of past segregation, many Black teachers might lose their jobs if there was no opportunity for them to get further training. In addition, some affirmative-action legislation would have to be effected in terms of hiring practices and scholarships. Black children who had attended scantily equipped and poorly staffed schools in the past should not be made to feel alienated and consequently develop negative self-images in the newly integrated schools. All Americans, North and South, would have to be committed to creating programs that would help undo past injustices which had kept Blacks from reaching their full potentials.

In June, Curtis Sr. graduated from Paul Quinn College with honors. It was announced that he had received a National Science Foundation grant to work toward a master's degree in mathematics at the University of Denver. He decided to leave shortly after graduation. Annetta and the babies were to stay in Waco. In September he decided to send for them; Annetta was glad to go. When Ransom heard that Curtis was in Denver and she in Waco, he had advised, "Annetta, go to your husband! Young people need to be together. It is not good to be apart." Consequently, sometime in early fall, Hazel and Joseph put their daughter and grandsons on the plane for Denver. A year and a summer would pass before they would return to Waco.

The most important issue discussed during the Annual Conferences in 1954 was the upcoming Bishops' Council, which would be held on the campus of Paul Quinn in February 1955. Each of the conferences pledged money for the housing and boarding of the Connectional leaders and members who were expected to attend. It would be the first time the Council had ever met in Waco, and Joseph wanted the district to "pull out all the stops" in terms of hospitality.

Other important legislation passed at the conferences was the approval of the coming year's budget, and the writing of a petition asking for the repeal of the eight-year law so that Joseph could be returned to Texas at the 1956 General Conference. Most of the Committees on the State of the Country were concerned that (as an NAACP report of September 4 had stated) only five southern states had announced public school integration, and that legislatures of Mississippi and Georgia were meeting to enact laws to abolish public schools and set up all-white private ones. On the positive side, the reports noted that Tennessee, Arkansas, Texas, Washington, D.C., West Virginia, and Missouri had integrated many of their colleges and universities.[65]

In October, while Joseph was attending the Southwest Texas Conference, he received word that his Uncle James in New York had died, leaving behind Amy, his wife, and a daughter, Lorraine. Sitting at the funeral a few days later, a rush of memories of his first coming to the United States, returned. He recalled how James had taken him in, an awkward young man fresh from the West Indies, without even a pair of long pants to call his own. He would always think of his uncle with warmth and gratitude. Immediately after the funeral he had to return to Texas to attend the remainder of his conferences, but he promised Amy that he would keep in touch.

On Friday, November 26, Joseph's birthday, the new girls' dormitory, Grant Hall, was officially opened. (Old Grant Hall had burned down two Christmases ago while the Gomezes were in Cleveland.) Shortly after the opening, Joseph and Hazel left for Denver with Annetta and her family. The Jeffersons were living in a housing project while Curtis was in school. Money was especially tight, and they were highly appreciative of the gifts the grandparents bought for the babies. Hazel insisted on buying Annetta a washer and dryer when she saw how the clothes froze on the lines outside during the bitter Colorado winter; when they thawed out, the clothes were dirty and had to be washed again. Since there was no roasting pan large enough to accommodate the Christmas turkey Joseph bought, Hazel improvised with tin foil and a large cookie sheet. Despite the lack of proper utensils, the Christmas dinner was succulent, as evidenced by the empty plates, full bellies, and yawns when it was completed. Annetta was sorry to see her parents leave a little after New Year's. Denver was cold and dreary; Curtis was gone most of the time to classes or to work, and she was homesick.

On Sunday, January 30, 1955, Joseph was a convocation speaker in Atlanta, Georgia. The event was sponsored by six schools: Atlanta University, Clark College, Gammon Theological Seminary, and Morehouse, Morris Brown and Spellman colleges. Joseph spoke on the topic "What Is Freedom?" "Freedom," he said, "has always been sought after. . . . Most times those who sought for it knew little about its meaning or why they sought it because it was difficult to define or achieve. . . . Freedom is not wishful thinking or a gift of the Gods—It involves blood, sweat, tears and death. It is not a commodity to be bought—nor is it rhetoric." It is something one must live through. He pointed out that the enactment of laws alone could not make Blacks free—rather, their labor, gifts, and creativity would give them the self-assurance "that marks the free individual." This meant that Blacks would have to hold on to their recent victories in civil rights, so that these gains would not be short lived, as they had been during Reconstruction—which, in some ways, had been more devastating than slavery. The Jim Crow era following Reconstruction had represented the South's vengeance and the apathy of the North toward its Black citizens once it had saved the union.[66] Joseph's message was well received by the students and faculties crowded into Sister Chapel to hear the renowned bishop from Texas who had achieved so much, in the building up of a college and in the area of civil rights, in the past seven years.

The Bishops' and Connectional Council convened in Waco from February 12 to 15. Three thousand people from all over the United States assembled on the campus. Joseph petitioned the city government to encourage the owners of hotels, inns, motels (all of which had been segregated) to open their places of business so the guests could be accommodated. In deference to the bishop, the city obliged. For the first time in the history of Waco, Blacks were able to get first-class accommodations throughout the city, particularly in the downtown area, where they received courteous, efficient service.[67]

At the opening session, Bishop Frank Madison Reid delivered the Annual Sermon, after which Holy Communion was celebrated. All of the bishops were in attendance except Fred Jordan, who could not get back from his district in South Africa. Allen Shivers, governor of Texas, Sam Rayburn, speaker of the U.S. House of Representatives, and Lyndon B. Johnson of the U.S. Senate sent letters of greetings.[68] Rayburn followed up his letter with a personal call to Joseph. They had become good friends and frequently corresponded with each other. Whenever Joseph visited Washington, D.C., and Rayburn was in town, he sent a limousine to pick up Joseph. Rayburn also tried to attend at least one of the Texas Annual Conferences when his busy schedule allowed.

The platform meeting was held on Thursday evening. H. I. Bearden of Atlanta, Georgia, president of the Connectional Council, reported three major projects which the Council would recommend to the General Conference in Miami, Florida, in 1956:

1. The establishment of a minimum salary standard for all pastors, with the recommendation that the general church organization supplement salaries of pastors whose churches were unable to meet the standards.
2. The establishment of a Connectional Budget for the entire Church.
3. The development of an educational plan for full support of Church schools.[69]

During the three days of meetings, the city of Waco was alive with activity, and for the first time Blacks moved freely all over the city. The Episcopal Residence was filled to capacity with friends of the Gomezes, including the Ransoms, Robinsons, and Rev. and Mrs. V. C. Hodges from the American Bible Society.[70] Many of the bishops would gather in the front room or on the side porch to chat informally after the more tedious business meetings. Others who enjoyed the cuisine of Jessie Dickerson were George Singleton, Rev. and Mrs. S. S. Morris, and attorney Herbert Dudley, president of the Laymen's Organization. There were so many people in the residence that when Annetta (whose house had been rented out for the year) came home unexpectedly to surprise her parents, she had to stay with a neighbor on East Walnut.

Most of the delegates expressed their surprise at the vast improvements made on the campus in such a short time. They also found it hard to believe how much the racial climate in Waco had been altered for the better. The city extended the delegates every courtesy, and in appreciation Joseph published an open letter in the *Waco Tribune Herald* on March 6, expressing the sincere thanks of the bishops and other visitors.

In every city, particularly in the South, with its complex racial situations, there are those—and the number increases daily—who are convinced that we must have more demonstrable expressions of tolerance and understanding. But in Waco, the significant fact is that your newspaper has given voice and meaning to those feelings in editorials, in news matters, and in general attitudes of journalistic responsibility. May God continue to bless Waco and to prosper her in every effort.[71]

On June 28, 1955, in Kansas City, Missouri, seven years after his election to the bishopric in the same city, Bishop D. O. Walker (former president of Wilberforce) died, ending an illustrious career in the ministry. Following the funeral, the Bishops' Council met in special session to make provisions to cover the work of the 5th District, over which he had presided. The Council decided that for the interim until the General Conference it would be best to split the district into three sections; in this way, no one bishop would be encumbered with two complete districts—the entire 5th plus his own. Accordingly, Thomas H. Primm of the 8th District took over Colorado, Kansas, and Nebraska; Fred Jordan of the 15th and 17th overseas districts picked up the Missouri Conference; Joseph was asked to supervise the work in the Puget Sound, California, and southern California.[72] Prior to these assignments, the Council had been flooded with telegrams asking that Gomez be given California. One congregation said their pastor was "a mere boy and [did not] know what it [was] all about. Have the Bishops' Council assign Bishop Gomez to the West Coast in that real men will be encouraged and supported and placed . . . and goodwill shall prevail."[73] Joseph must have smiled at this telegram, considering his own age and the congregation's initial reaction when he was assigned to Bethel, Detroit, in 1919.

With the assistance of Yvonne Walker, Bishop Walker's daughter, Joseph conducted all three of the California Annual Conferences during July and August. At each the ministers expressed their desire to have him assigned to the 5th at the 1956 General Conference. While in Los Angeles for his last conference, he tried to find his sister, Violet. He had been told that she still lived there, but no one knew her address; he had to leave without seeing her. Someone told him she was passing for white and had cut off all contacts with her Black friends. Later he found this to be true.

As soon as they left Los Angeles the Gomezes flew to Cleveland to attend Eula's wedding on August 13, 1955. The groom-to-be was Harold B. Williams, an administrative assistant for the Community Chest, who would soon become the executive secretary of the Cleveland Chapter of the NAACP. He was originally from Montgomery, Alabama, where his mother, Bertha W. Williams, still lived and worked as an elementary school principal. His father was deceased. All three of Eula's children adored him, and he them. (Gerald had recovered and was back in Cleveland.) Harold's wife of only a few years had died of heart trouble, and they had had no children. Harold looked forward to Eula's children becoming his own.

Attired in a yellow dotted swiss dress, matching yellow slippers, and a large picture hat, and carrying a white orchid, Eula stood beside her groom. The simple service was performed by Hubie Robinson, Eula's pastor. James Gomez had flown in from Trinidad to attend the wedding and had brought with him rare anthuriums, tropical lilies, which he had grown. After the wedding the guests moved from the church to the Wade Park home for a reception, which extended into the early evening.[74]

The Jeffersons were unable to come from Denver to attend the ceremony. Annetta had just returned from the hospital after an ectopic pregnancy, and baby Joseph had had a bad case of the chicken pox. She did talk to her sister long-distance, remarking later that she had never heard Eula sound happier. The Gomezes could return to Texas with the assurance that the future of their older daughter looked considerably brighter. Harold was a stable, responsible, gentle man, who was obviously deeply in love with Eula. Time would prove she had chosen wisely.

The Annual Conferences that began in the fall of 1955 went relatively smoothly until the Central Texas Conference (November 23–27) in Austin. When Joseph called for the reports of the Temple District, everyone turned one in except Rev. P. E. Womack, who said he would read his because the report forms given to him by the bishop were not in accordance with the A.M.E. Discipline. After much discussion, Womack said he would appeal to the Judicial Council (Connectional) that he had not been allowed to read his report, in accordance with the Discipline. Joseph told him "he would gladly let him, or any minister read his report according to or per Discipline," the implication being that the way Womack wanted to read his report was not in accordance with it. The next day Womack decided to withdraw "his appeal and protest . . . after prayerful consideration." He then made his report.[75] However, Joseph had not heard the last of him.

A few weeks later, Womack came to the Episcopal Residence to tell the bishop he had changed his mind again but if the bishop would give him a sum of money, he would not take him before the Connectional Judicial Council. Joseph said he was not afraid to go before the Council, since the report forms were legal. Then Womack told him that whether the bishop's actions were upheld or not, after all that had happened in Texas it would be an embarrassment for him to be called before the Council again. At this affront Joseph's anger turned to blind fury. He hustled Womack down the steps and out the front door, calling after him, "Nobody blackmails me—nobody!" Moving quickly away, Womack mumbled over his shoulders that before it was all over the bishop would be sorry he had not given him the money. At this point Hazel, who had witnessed the scene, pulled Joseph back into the house and tried to calm him down.

On March 17, 1956, the *Houston Informer* noted that Bishop Joseph Gomez had received official notice from the Judicial Council requesting his appearance at a hearing concerning a decision he had made at the Central Texas Conference in reference to Reverend P. E. Womack. Since Womack had no clear charges, he accused the bishop of "levying of un-authorized assessments on the laity and ministry of the A.M.E. Church in Texas in direct defiance of 'positive law' in the A.M.E. Discipline." The hearing was to be held at the Hotel Hollenden in Cleveland on April 6, 7, 8, 1956.[76]

Womack based his appeal on the fact that the 10th Episcopal District's Pastor's Report Sheets asked for such financial items as pastor's contingent, Annual Conference sustentation, Sunday school offering, and scholarships. Since these additional assessments had been voted on and approved by each Annual Conference in the 10th District, as well as other districts in the past, Womack really had no case.[77]

Joseph denied that he refused to allow Womack the right to report as set out in the Discipline. He reminded the council that Womack had eventually turned in his report on the sheet. Joseph then handed over "a photostatic copy of the minutes of the conference, signed and sworn to before a Notary Public," stating so.[78]

The Council ruled that the Pastor's Report included "all that is set forth in the Discipline and more in as much as the additional assessments were authorized by the Annual Conference." True, there was no provision in the Discipline for a bishop, presiding elder, or pastor to place additional assessments unless those assessments had been approved by a majority vote; since all the Annual Conferences of the 10th District had voted for additions, there was no violation. However, it suggested that the legislative branch of the Church, the General Conference, needed in the future to set forth specifically and in detail the extent of assessments and new projects and the method whereby they could be put into effect. Womack had failed to support his claim "that he was denied a substantial right . . . and the appeal was therefore denied."[79]

Womack had lost, as he had known he would, but he had caused Joseph the inconvenience and expense of having to appear before the Council; however, the embarrassment Womack anticipated for Gomez was not forthcoming. It was his reputation that suffered, not the bishop's. Members of the Council knew what Joseph was trying to do in Texas. They also were aware that putting the district back on its feet would call for extra financial sacrifices by everyone connected and that those sacrifices were paying off.

On March 29, the Executive Committee of the Board of Trustees of Paul Quinn College received a letter from Reid E. Jackson, administrative assistant to President Veal, who announced that on March 25 the Association of Texas Colleges had voted Paul Quinn College the "status of an affiliated institution." The next step, he explained, "is that of associate member, and the final step is to be elected a full member in the group." He further stated that Paul Quinn's affiliation with the association was the result of a year of self-study by the college faculty, which had resulted in "a thorough reorganization of the college's educational program."[80]

Jackson also reported that before the March meeting a six-man committee from the Association of Texas Colleges had inspected the college and commended it for its improvement of faculty, reorganization of curricula, development of an effective general education program, an alert and progressive spirit on the part of the acting registrar, and the accuracy of the records maintained by the business manager. Weaknesses cited were the sparsity of science facilities and equipment, and low faculty salaries—which had improved but needed further upgrading.[81]

On September 15, 1956, the State Board of Education would meet to receive recommendations from the State Commissioner of Education for a categorical decision as to the college's ability to prepare teachers under the revised teaching standards that had resulted from the Supreme Court school-desegregation ruling. Jackson felt sure Paul Quinn would receive an affirmative vote. It seemed the college was on its way to becoming a creditable institution of higher learning; it no longer resembled the disorganized, educationally unsound institution Joseph had found when he arrived in 1948.[82]

That same September, the bishops of the A.M.E. Church went to Montgomery, Alabama, to kneel in prayer at the Capitol for the end of segregation in the state. Later they planned to appeal to Eisenhower to end the "tragic persecution of the Montgomery, Alabama Negro Bus Boycott leaders."[83] Joseph had learned with pride of the refusal of Rosa Parks, an A.M.E., to give up her seat on a Montgomery city bus to a white man, and of her incarceration. This had set off the Montgomery bus boycott of December 1955 and had brought Dr. Martin Luther King, Jr., to national prominence. On January 26 King had been jailed for allegedly driving thirty miles an hour in a twenty-five-mile-an-hour zone; later his home was bombed and his family harassed by threatening phone calls. Many of the

Blacks who participated in the boycott lost their jobs and were also subjected to threats of violence. Eisenhower had remained silent. He refused to take a leadership role in seeing that Black Americans received the justice that was long overdue. Joseph recalled later how as he kneeled on those steps in the cradle of the Confederacy, he felt an assurance from God that the strong back of segregation would be broken by millions of Blacks who were not "gonna let nobody turn them around." This small symbolic gesture by the Fathers of African Methodism would perhaps encourage the people of Montgomery, many of whom were A.M.E.'s, to continue the boycott until the courts ruled in their favor.

When Joseph returned to Waco he found a delegation from the Texas Conference meeting on the campus. They had written a resolution branding Womack's recent "irresponsible attack on Bishop Gomez as base and unwarranted." They called for the return of the bishop for another four-year term: "His intrepid leadership [had] brought the A.M.E. Church in Texas a growth and progress unprecedented and [had] strengthened the moral and spiritual fiber of the entire membership throughout the entire state."[84]

Several prominent citizens of Texas also wrote letters of support to be presented at the General Conference. W. R. White, president of Baylor, called him "one of the outstanding citizens and personalities in Waco . . . a Christian gentleman, and incisive thinker and a masterful leader." While acknowledging his loyalty to his people, he described Gomez as "very effective in promoting goodwill among the races and various beliefs." He commended Gomez to the General Conference "as one of the strong Christian statesmen of our day."[85]

Another letter came from Harold Kilpatrick, executive secretary of the Texas Council of Churches, who "considered it a real privilege to be permitted to add [his] word of testimony to the courageous and prophetic leadership that Bishop Gomez [had] given to this Episcopal District."[86] Sidney Dobbins, manager of the Waco Chamber of Commerce, addressed his letter personally to Joseph. He stated that in his lifetime in Waco he had known "no other person that the city of Waco has been so willing to work with for the betterment of Paul Quinn"; he felt "obliged to say that if the A.M.E. Church does not see fit to reassign you to your present job, both Paul Quinn and the city will suffer."[87]

The three letters quoted also appeared in the *Texas Record,* a pamphlet put out by the district that listed all the improvements over the last eight years, explained the three-point expansion program and its progress: the education program; the new campus buildings, churches, and parsonages; and the growth of A.M.E. membership in Texas by 25 percent.[88]

Rebecca Richardson-Gomes, Joseph's mother, in April 1923. She was born in Willikies Village, Antigua, June 8, 1865, and died in Port of Spain, Trinidad, on June 27, 1929.

Manoel Antonio Gomes, Joseph's father, in April 1923. He was born in Monte, Madiera, Portugal, ca. 1858 and died in Port of Spain, Trinidad, September 6, 1932.

Julia Anne Thompson, Hazel Thompson Gomez's mother, in 1910. She was born in Ontario, Canada, March 12, 1858, and died in Toledo, Ohio, in 1918.

George Thompson, Hazel Thompson Gomez's father, in 1889. He was born in Amhurtsburg, Ontario, in 1848 and died in February 1893.

Amanda Indiana Gomes, Joseph's favorite sister, in 1923. She was born in Willikies Village, Antigua, December 27, 1888, and died in Port of Spain, Trinidad, May 1976.

Cyril Gomes, Joseph's youngest brother, in 1923. He was born in Port of Spain, Trinidad, in 1908, and he died ca. 1966.

Walter Gomez in 1920. He was born January 28, 1904,
in Port of Spain, Trinidad, and died July 13, 1922,
in Detroit, Michigan.

The Reverend Reverdy Cassius Ransom in 1910.
Born in Flushing, Ohio, January 4, 1861,
Ransom was the pastor of Bethel A.M.E. Church,
New York City, and Joseph's mentor.

(Opposite) James Methusalah and Mary (May) Gomes in 1920. James was born
October 18, 1895, in Willikies Village, Antigua, and died November 2, 1965. His
wife, Mary, was born March 11, 1901, in Port of Spain and now, at ninety-seven,
lives in Michigan.

Joseph Gomez in his first pair of long pants, New York City, 1908.

William S. Scarborough, president of Wilberforce University (1902–35)
when Joseph was a student there (1911–14).

George F. Woodson, dean of
Payne Theological Seminary
(1902–35).

Hallie Q. Brown, professor of
English and Elocution,
directed Joseph in his senior
class play in 1914.

(Above) Joseph *(third row from front, at far right)* with faculty members and other students of Payne Theological Seminary, 1914.

(Left) Joseph Gomez, "The Theologue," in a serious mood, 1913.

(Right) Hazel E. Thompson, a student from Toledo, Ohio—the future Mrs. Joseph Gomez, 1912.

(Below) Hazel, Joseph, Helen "Sadie" Carter, and other friends in front of Arnett Hall, Wilberforce University, 1913.

(Left) Hazel taught in Selby, Mississippi, in 1913 while Joseph finished his studies at Payne Theological Seminary.

(Below left) June 1914, Joseph's graduation from Payne Theological Seminary.

(Below right) A. Wayman Ward, self-titled "Himself," was the most popular male student at Wilberforce, 1914.

Joseph with some of the area ministers and members of his first pastorate, Bethel A.M.E. Church in Shelly Bay, Bermuda, 1915. Joseph is seated in the front row at the far right.

Hazel (*third from the left*) poses with her Sunday school class at Bethel A.M.E. Church in Bermuda, 1915.

Joseph Gomez, "Baby Pastor" of Bethel A.M.E. Church, Detroit, his first
American pastorate, 1919.

The Bethel Social Services Department, which Joseph started in 1920 to
find housing and jobs for Blacks migrating from the South.

Joseph *(front row, third from the right)* with the Bethel tennis team, July 4, 1922.

The Gomez family in Detroit, Michigan, 1928: Eula (born February 21, 1926), Hazel, and Joseph, holding Annetta (born December 5, 1927).

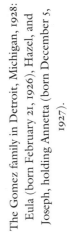

Joseph and Hazel in 1926, standing in front of their first car, a Ford.

Violet Gomez, Joseph's sister, holding baby Annetta on the parsonage steps in 1928.

(*Opposite*) Joseph with the Bethel Junior Choir, Detroit, September 25, 1921.

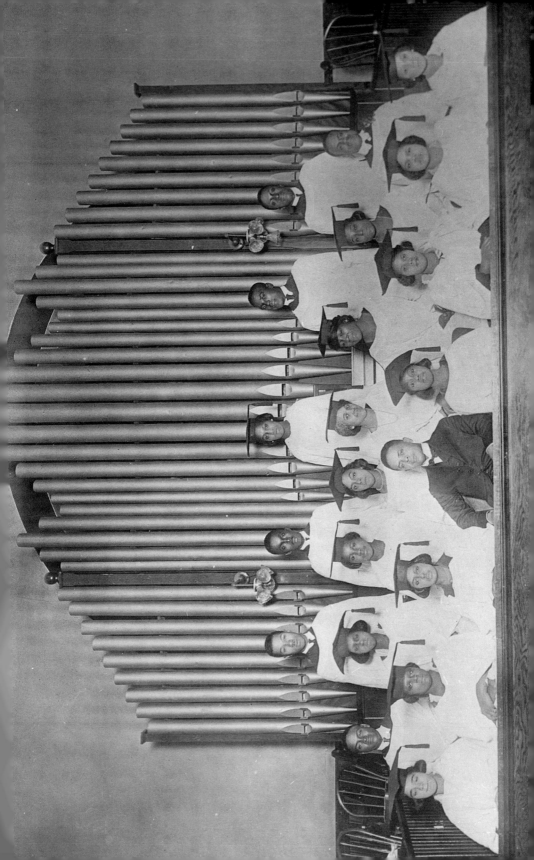

Celia Gregg, John's wife, 1930.
She and Hazel were active in the Missionary Society
in Kansas City.

Bishop John A. Gregg of Kansas City,
Missouri, 1930. He was Joseph's bishop,
friend, and golf partner.

(Below) Joseph dreaming at the river's edge, Kansas City, 1929.

(Right) Annetta and Eula playing in the yard of the parsonage (Allen Chapel), Kansas City, 1931.

(Opposite) Hazel, Joseph, Eula, and Annetta in 1935 in St. Louis, where Joseph was the pastor of St. Paul A.M.E. Church.

(Left) The fiftieth wedding anniversary of Bishop Reverdy C. and Emma Ransom, October 25, 1937, Tawawa Chimney Corner, Wilberforce, Ohio.

The twenty-fifth wedding anniversary of Rev. Joseph and Mrs. Hazel Gomez, St. James, Cleveland, 1939. Pictured: Berdie Perkins, Celia and Bishop John Gregg, Eula, Hazel, Joseph, Annetta, Mamie Boone, Kathleen and Louis Forbes, and Evy "Dolly" Gordon.

(*Opposite*) Worshiping at Christmastime in the Sunday school room after the 1938 fire that destroyed the St. James Auditorium, Cleveland. In the upper right corner, from the far right, are Hazel, Earlynne Poindexter, Joseph, Gwendolyn Poindexter, Jane Lee Darr, and Eula.

The rebuilt St. James A.M.E. Church, 1941.

(*Opposite*) In front of St. James following the Annual Conference of 1943: (*from left*) Reverdy Ransom, Jr., R. E. Hutchingson, J. Otis Haithcock, Bishops Frank M. Reid and Reverdy C. Ransom, the Reverends Singleton and Joseph Gomez.

Bishop Reverdy C. Ransom introduces his new wife, Georgia Myrtle Teal Ransom, to the North Ohio Annual Conference, Community A.M.E. Church, Cleveland, September 1944.

(*Opposite*) A 1944 reunion of one of Hazel's St. James Sunday school classes. The students had all returned from fighting in World War II. Among those pictured are Superintendent Ernest B. Escoe (*front row, fourth from the left*) and the Reverend John H. Hunter, Joseph's assistant pastor and later a bishop in the A.M.E. Church (*front row, third from the right*). Hazel and Joseph are seated in the center of the front row.

(Opposite) Eula poses with President Charles Wesley and her father at her graduation from Wilberforce University, June 1946.

Joseph is ordained as a bishop in the A.M.E. Church, General Conference, Kansas City, May 16, 1948. Bishop Frank M. Reid is to his left, and Bishop John A. Gregg is to his right. Kneeling behind Gregg is Bishop Reverdy C. Ransom. At the far left Bishop D. O. Walker is also being ordained.

Bishops George B. Young, Joseph Gomez, and John A. Gregg at the A.M.E. East Texas Annual Conference, Mexia, Texas, October 1948.

(*Opposite*) The family standing in front of Manoel's (Mani) and Rebecca's graves, Trinidad, 1949: Alva Thomas, Amanda Thomas, Joseph Gomez, Hazel Gomez, Aldwyn Gomez, James Gomez, Audrey Thomas, Mary Gomez, Ruby Gomez.

The Episcopal Residence, Paul Quinn College, Waco, Texas, 1949. *Standing:*
Bishop D. Ward Nichols, Georgia Myrtle Teal Ransom, Hazel, and Joseph; *seated:*
Bishop Reverdy C. Ransom.

(Opposite) The Reverend F. W. Grant with Joseph in front of the Episcopal
Residence (Paul Quinn College) during the Annual Ministerial Institute Missionary and Youth Congress, Waco, Texas, August 1949.

(Overleaf) Joseph and Hazel with a group of young church members at the Texas
Annual Conference. The Reverend A. S. B. Jones stands at the far right.

Dedication of the Joseph Gomez Administration Building, Paul Quinn College, Waco, September 28, 1952.

Bishop Reverdy C. Ransom in his nineties, 1952.

The family in their Wade Park home, Cleveland, 1955. *Standing:* Curtis F. Jefferson, Annetta Gomez-Jefferson, Eula Williams, and Harold B. Williams; *seated:* Joseph, holding Joseph Jefferson, and Hazel, holding Gerald Williams; *on the floor:* Annetta Williams, Curtis Jefferson, and Marvin Williams.

(*Opposite*) A.M.E. bishops met with President John F. Kennedy at the White House on January 21, 1961, concerning civil rights. Joseph is standing in the back row in front of the right column.

During the World Council of Churches Conference, New Delhi, India, Joseph wrote in his journal on November 18, 1961, of the visit to Ghandi's grave: "We were not ashamed to take off our shoes to tread on . . . Holy Ground."

(*Above*) The 38th Session of the
A.M.E. General Conference,
Philadelphia, May 2, 1968. After
Vice President Hubert Humphrey addressed the conference,
he shook hands with Joseph, the
presiding bishop; between them
stands Mayor James H. Tate of
Philadelphia.

(*Right*) August 1962, Awards
Banquet, National Association of
Colored Women's Clubs, Sher-
aton Park Hotel, Washington,
D.C. Rosa Gragg (president)
stands with Robert Kennedy and
Bishop Joseph Gomez.

(Right) "Some day I'll take you around the world," Joseph told his bride, Hazel. Here they are in Israel, December 5, 1961.

(Below) The Gomezes celebrate their fiftieth wedding anniversary and fifty years of Joseph's ministry in the A.M.E. Church. The celebration was held in the Sherman House Grand Ballroom, Chicago, November 13, 1964. *From left:* Mayor Ralph Locher of Cleveland, Mayor Richard Daley of Chicago, Joseph, Hazel, Pearl L. Washington of *Ebony* Magazine, Lucille Thomas, and the Reverend Arctic S. Harris.

James Gomez presenting his brother with the Golden Jubilee Medal from the mayor of Trinidad at James and Hazel's fiftieth anniversary celebration in Chicago, 1964.

(*Above*) The grandchildren in 1964 at Joseph and Hazel's fiftieth anniversary celebration in Chicago: Joseph, Toni Jo (Jane Darr-Dawson's daughter), Curtis, Marvin, Annetta, and Gerald.

(*Opposite*) A.M.E. Church bishops sometime in the 1960s. *Front row*: Bishops Gomez, Wright, Gibbs, Green, Baber, and Bonner; *middle row*: Bishops Sims, Sherman, Primm, Jordan, Hatcher, and Wilkes; *back row*: Bishops Bright, Collins, Hickman, and Ball.

Joseph remembering the past
at his home on Wade Park Avenue, Cleveland, 1970.

Joseph went to the thirty-fifth session of the General Conference with documents and letters to support an impressive record. The conference was held in Key Auditorium in Miami, Florida, from May 2 through 16. Curtis Sr. and Annetta, who had accompanied the Gomezes, shared a suite with them in one of the oceanfront hotels. Since they were not delegates, they and the other ministers' sons and daughters had plenty of time to explore the beaches and bask in the hot sun. Hazel and Joseph, on the other hand, were seldom free from meetings and therefore rarely could be found at the hotel.

At the opening session, Bishop George W. Baber delivered the Quadrennial Sermon, in which he called that juncture of the A.M.E. Church "The Golden Age of Our Zion." In reference to the participation of Alabama A.M.E.'s in the Montgomery bus boycott, he declared, "Richard Allen's spirit walked out at Philadelphia, and more recently he walked out in Montgomery." The spirit which led Allen to walk away from St. George Methodist Episcopal Church in Philadelphia in 1787 was the same spirit that had led Rosa Parks to remain in her bus seat in Montgomery. Following the sermon the bishops administered the Holy Communion to over three thousand celebrants, who kneeled in front of a railing arranged in the form of a cross.[89]

Among the most significant legislation passed was a resolution by Dr. Charles S. Spivey to move all bishops, and a motion by Ralph Jackson, seconded by Joseph, to develop a budget that would cover all Connectional monies. There had been much opposition to both resolutions from some of the old-timers who wanted things to remain as they had in the past. Following the passage of the budget on the afternoon of May 10 there was a huge demonstration led by the Brotherhood (a group of activists who had formed to bring about significant changes in the Church) and other supporters of the budget. "The rousing acclaim . . . prevailed for an hour. A band marched down the aisles. Brotherhood members followed, and hundreds joined the procession. Banners of victory were carried and songs of victory filled the house. . . . Bishop Gomez compared the hour with the one in Chicago in 1928 in which he participated where laymen in [the] A.M.E. Church were given equal representation."[90]

Womack had come to the General Conference to plead further his case against Bishop Gomez, this time with the Episcopal Committee. When he tried to address the delegates on May 8, he was denied access to the microphone because, as Joseph pointed out, he was not a delegate and therefore had no voice. He then went before the Episcopal Committee charging Bishop Gomez with "persecution and immorality." The Episcopal Committee turned Womack's charges over to the Judiciary Council, which again found that "on the merits of the appeal, it is the considered opinion of the Judicial Council that the appellant has failed to support his claim"; Womack's appeal was therefore denied.[91]

On Sunday, May 6, Joseph delivered the morning sermon, on the subject "Divine Leadership for the Time." He spoke about Saul as a leader and of how Israel changed from "the Theocratic to the Monarchical form of government against God's will." After assessing the strengths and weaknesses of past leaders (historical and contemporary), Joseph referred to the Black race as now the spiritual leader of America. "No torture, suffering, no interposition shall keep us from the place of destiny for our race—Our destiny is spiritual—We are to be the Disturbers of the Conscience of America." Then he chastised the A.M.E. Church for its loss of leadership in contemporary times, stating that "too often African Methodism has failed God. Too often our leaders have not inquired of God." Saul had not followed God's will, and his kingdom had been given to David. "Formerly, we were leaders—now we follow!" If the A.M.E. Church did not assume its former position, other organizations would move to the forefront, for "God is determined that He shall provide continuity for His Kingdom."[92] Once again his words were prophetic. Already the Baptists were at the forefront of the civil rights movement; soon secular organizations would also assume leadership.

Throughout the two-week session, a great deal of attention was paid to the growing civil rights movement. At the evening session of May 7, Dr. H. D. Gregg, president of Daniel Payne College in Birmingham, spoke on the "Effects of the Supreme Court Decision on Negro Educational Institutions." The following evening, Thurgood Marshall, head of the NAACP Legal Division (later the first Black Supreme Court justice), gave a "factual discourse on the problems of desegregation and discrimination." At another session, Dr. R. W. Hilson related the experiences of Rosa Parks; Nathanial Howard of Tuscaloosa then recounted his experiences when he had rescued Autherine Lucy, a young Black woman, from danger as she attempted to attend the University of Alabama.[93]

On May 11 the conference turned its attention to the election of five bishops, as recommended by the Episcopal Committee. It was agreed that at least one should be from a foreign field; consequently, on the first ballot, and to Joseph's delight, his friend Francis Gow of South Africa was elected with 1,355 votes. Rev. E. L. Hickman of Kentucky was elected on the third ballot, with S. C. Higgins of South Carolina, S. F. Ball of Florida, and Odie L. Sherman on the fourth. The election had taken from Friday until Monday afternoon, May 14. The delegates, outraged by the time-consuming inefficiency of the old voting methods, passed legislation that future General Conferences would use voting machines.[94] Joseph thought the change was well overdue.

During the business session on Thursday Ralph Jackson read a resolution that Bishop David Sims, who had been expelled from the A.M.E. Church ten years before, should now be restored to the office of bishop in "located" status—without assignment, salary, or vote in the Council of Bishops. A special committee appointed to consider Jackson's resolution drew up an agreement, duly signed, in which Sims undertook "on behalf of himself and his heirs, and assignees to give up any and all claims, actions, causes of actions arising from the beginning of time until the present" and to "dismiss without prejudice any and all actions pending in any court of the land against" the A.M.E. Church. Jackson's resolution was passed, and Sims was once again "Bishop Sims."[95] Joseph welcomed his friend back into the Church.

When the Episcopal Committee read the assignments of bishops, Joseph found he had been sent to the 13th Episcopal District, which comprised Kentucky and Tennessee. Bishop H. Thomas Primm had been sent to Texas in his place.[96] Joseph would have liked to have finished his work at Paul Quinn, but, ironically, he was now subjected to the same kind of resolution he had introduced himself back in 1928—the removal of all bishops who had spent eight or more years in one district. He would miss Texas and the many close friends of both races he had made. On the other hand, the 10th District had tried his faith as no other assignment had. He had been maligned in private and public. The constant fight to raise funds for the expansion of Paul Quinn had taken its toll on him, physically and spiritually, and he had aged considerably—as evidenced by his hair, which was now totally white. Hazel, too, was weary. She had never left his side, and luckily for his biographer, had kept careful records of all reports, letters, finances, and lawsuits. It had been a grueling eight years for them both. The 13th District was much smaller and would not call for so much exertion. In spite of it all, however, the Gomezes would always remember Texas with warmth and excitement. It represented the highs and lows in Joseph's career, and he and Hazel had survived it all.

When they returned to Waco from the General Conference, they found thousands of letters and telegrams wishing them well in their new assignment but bemoaning the fact that they would be leaving Texas. After all the farewell banquets in Dallas, Houston, Fort Worth, and Waco were over, Joseph gave his final speech to the people of Texas over Waco. He said, "As we go we shall carry vividly pleasant memories of those periods of stress and strain in the new Expansion Program of the college when only faith in a leader and the cause produced the kind of sacrificial giving that was demonstrated." He gave special thanks to the people of Waco for the privilege of serving on "many boards, committees and . . . organizations in the public interest." He warned that some cities in Texas were ahead of Waco in terms of "interracial cooperation. We who love Waco must insist that she shall lead, not follow in the new and challenging venture of our American society." He closed by recommending Bishop Primm to the district and to the people of Waco as a man "of training, experience and one who understands our problems."[97]

A few days after Joseph and Hazel left Waco, an editorial appeared in the *Waco News Tribune*. It observed that the new assignment of Bishop Gomez would "take from the community a remarkable leader. Bishop Gomez can go into history books as the savior of Paul Quinn College, for the old Negro school was near extinction when he came here in 1948." The editorialist called Joseph the "principal architect" of all that had been accomplished in Waco in terms of the college and racial cooperation, and a man of "rare qualities of leadership, of eloquence, of understanding."[98]

CHAPTER TWELVE

Back to Bethel

From Tennessee & Kentucky to Michigan, 1956–1964

Every segment of human endeavor is now caught up by relentless forces, and the changes taking place in the world are the most significant and decisive in world history. New nations, and institutions are emerging and many old ones that hitherto survived changes, are being destroyed. Survival is the test. The Church is affected by this modern pressure. The problem to be met is . . . shall the Church set about to analyze these forces and move forward, not in surrender, but in understanding, interpretation and in leadership?

 —Bishop Joseph Gomez, President, statement,
  February Council of Bishops, Louisville, Kentucky, 1961

◈ Joseph and Hazel returned to their home in Cleveland until the 13th District could provide them with an Episcopal Residence. (Eula and her family had moved to their own home on Throckley, and Harold was now executive secretary of the Cleveland Branch of the NAACP.) Joseph had conflicting emotions about presiding over Tennessee and Kentucky. He knew that many of the bishops felt he had started his episcopacy with a large district, rather than working his way up as most of them had; therefore, it was only fair that he should now supervise a smaller area. They were correct, of course; but he had always had a nagging desire to be assigned to the 3rd District, so he could be near Ransom and assume some of the responsibilities for Wilberforce University. Many of the ministers of Ohio had asked for him; Ransom himself had expressed such a hope in a letter to

Joseph dated January 20, 1956, some three months before the General Conference in Miami. Because of the importance of the information found in the letter, it is quoted here at almost full length:

> You have been much in my mind since I last saw you. It chiefly revolves about your coming to the Third Episcopal District, and setting up your Episcopal Residence here at Wilberforce. From the establishment of the institution here, almost everything of importance has revolved around the Bishop of the District, who has always been the President of the Trustee Board of Wilberforce University. At present, so far as relates to the college, we are, as you know, in very bad condition. The chief reason for this is that most of them who are put here to administer the school, seem to be chiefly concerned with their own personal and financial welfare, and not with order, discipline and tradition as relates to the school. From almost every standpoint, you are made to order for the needs and opportunities for which Wilberforce is crying loud. You are not a novice. You know its history, and tradition, and you have breathed the atmosphere of the spirit of its founders.
>
> Besides all this, you have a home of your own in Cleveland, and you have here the house in which I live, which seems to be built and designed to be the home of the officiating Bishop, and to possess the dreams and aspirations and cultural future of Wilberforce. You may live here at Tawawa Chimney Corner where I now make my home before Georgia Myrtle and I move up the road to occupy her little cottage; for Tawawa Chimney Corner was not built for the home of a "retired Bishop." . . . Both you and your wife seem like children of my own, and perhaps unconsciously, I am trying to establish a little parental direction over your public service and activities.[1]

Joseph was profoundly moved by Ransom's offer of his residence, particularly since it was more than just a house; it was a monument to all that Wilberforce stood for.

He had an opportunity to discuss his feelings with Ransom when he went to Wilberforce to deliver the June Commencement Address. Although Ransom was disappointed that Joseph would not be coming to the 3rd, he was able to assure him that he would find the experiences in the 13th rewarding; Ransom had been bishop of that district at one time.

The *Christian Recorder* called Joseph's commencement speech, "Things That Remaineth," the "most dynamic and challenging address ever delivered in the one-hundred-year history of Wilberforce University." In it Joseph stressed changes for the better as Black people everywhere were "asserting their place of leadership and a voice in the affairs of the world."[2]

Once again fate altered the course of Joseph and Hazel's odyssey. On Wednesday, November 21, 1956, Bishop Alexander Joseph Allen of the 4th Episcopal District died.[3] At a special session of the Bishops' Council following the funeral (which was held at St. Johns, Cleveland, on November 27), the Council voted to send Joseph to the 4th, a district that included Indiana, Illinois, Michigan, and Ontario.[4] He had been in Tennessee and Kentucky only long enough to hold one series of highly successful Annual Conferences. Nevertheless, the 4th was considered to be one of the most illustrious in the Connection, and its ministers were some of the best prepared. To Hazel and Joseph, it would be like going home again. They would be working with such friends as A. Wayman Ward, Joseph's classmate at Wilberforce, now a presiding elder in the Chicago Conference; Hubie Robinson, who had left St. James, Cleveland, and was pastoring Ebenezer, Detroit; attorney Herbert Dudley of Detroit, a strong layman who had assisted Joseph in legal matters his first year in Texas, when his salary was in question; Charles S. Spivey, of St. Stephens, Detroit, who had been dean of Payne Seminary when Joseph lectured there; Harvey E. Walden, an old friend and the pastor of Grant Memorial in Chicago; Russell S. Brown, a Wilberforce classmate who had attended Hazel and Joseph's wedding and was now general secretary of the Church; Rev. John Hunter of First Church in Gary, Indiana, who had been Joseph's assistant pastor at St. James for a few years; and other ministers whom Joseph had taught at Payne Seminary.

In January, before assuming his duties in the 4th, Joseph and Hazel traveled to Tawawa Chimney Corner to celebrate Bishop Ransom's ninety-sixth birthday. Ransom received birthday greetings from all over the nation—including his two sons, eleven grandchildren, and thirty great-grandchildren.[5] He was feebler than Joseph had ever seen him, and his thoughts had begun to wander slightly, but one could still sense the keen mind underneath. Joseph felt a tinge of sadness when he realized there could not be many more birthdays.

Joseph's first official function as bishop of the 4th District occurred on February 10, 1957, in Chicago at the 170th anniversary of the founding of the A.M.E. Church. On that Sunday afternoon he was the principal speaker at Grant Memorial.[6] Speaking from the subject "What We Believe and Why," he traced the history of the Church from its founding. Finally he spoke of his fervent faith in the "Negro race—children of sorrow but children of destiny; moral lever of the human conscience," who were facing a new day with courage and were "confident that they cannot fail now."[7]

A few days later, Richard Daley, mayor of Chicago, along with other dignitaries, brought greeting to the Gomezes at a welcome banquet held at Chicago's Parkway.[8] Then on March 1, Detroit, not to be overshadowed by the way Chicago had welcomed the bishop and his wife, held its own welcome banquet. The list of greeters was even longer and more impressive than in Chicago. G. Mennen Williams, governor of Michigan, whom Joseph had always admired for his strong stand on civil rights, brought greetings from the state.[9]

As Joseph observed in his acknowledgements, he had come home again; he was not being treated "as a stranger in his own land." The entire 4th District had put out the welcome mat, but Detroit's welcome was most special to Hazel and him. It held so many poignant memories. This was where he had really got his start in the ministry in America, and it was here that his daughters had been born.

In the latter part of May, Joseph and Hazel sailed to Bermuda. Joseph had been invited to preach at his first pastorate, Bethel, Shelly Bay, and then to speak at Allen Temple in Somerset, where Hazel, who had been elected first vice president of the Connectional Missionary Branch, was to be honored at a special missionary service on May 26.[10] They were surprised to see how much the island had changed since 1914. Some of the natural beauty was being replaced by commercial businesses, and the simplicity in which they had reveled was being exploited to attract the tourist trade. The people, however, greeted them warmly and were lavish with hospitality; but the Gomezes still found time to stroll the pink beaches and reminisce about the early days of their partnership, when life had been less complicated. As idyllic as it had been, however, they had no desire to go back. The years had bought fullness and deeper devotion; as they were well aware, each age had its own compensation.

Joseph returned in time to hold a three-day Ministers' Retreat at Camp Baber in Cassopolis, Michigan, a facility owned by the District. (The camp had been founded and named after Bishop George W. Baber, who had been prelate of the 4th before Allen and Gomez.) So successful was the retreat that the ministers requested Joseph to make this an annual affair. In time, it was to become one of the most important experiences of his episcopacy.

After spending July and the first part of August at their cottage in Woodland Park, the Gomezes began their six Annual Conferences (the Canadian, Michigan, Northwestern, Chicago, Indiana, and Illinois), which ran from August 22 to the end of the first week in October.

The tone of all the conferences was one of cooperation and enthusiasm. They were well organized, well attended, and lacked the backbiting Joseph had often experienced in Texas. The Gomezes were able to relax among old friends, revel in the spirit of the young ministers who were anxious to be led, and applaud the strong lay members, for whom Joseph had fought most of his ministry.

The Committees on State of the Country were concerned about Arkansas Governor Oval Faubus's recalcitrant attitude toward the integration of the high school at Little Rock, and President Eisenhower's reluctance to intervene. They recognized the first civil rights act passed by Congress since 1875 but lamented that it had been so watered down that many important items had been omitted.[11]

After the close of the last conference in October, Joseph and Hazel returned to their home on Wade Park with a feeling of accomplishment and well-being. Although Cleveland was to remain their home base throughout Joseph's supervision of the 4th District, the Wade Park home was frequented by the clergy and laity of the district. At different times the ministers offered to buy an episcopal residence in Detroit or Chicago, but for some reason, Joseph preferred to stay in Cleveland during the limited times he was not involved with the district. Perhaps this was because the whole family was there now. Curtis had received his M.S. from Denver, taught for two years at Paul Quinn, then moved his family to Cleveland and was teaching mathematics at Kennard Junior High. Annetta had earned a B.A. from Paul Quinn and was teaching English and drama at Addison Junior High in the Hough area, and Curtis Jr. was enrolled in kindergarten.

For Christmas 1957 Joseph gave "Tweets" a framed original poem entitled "Sonnet to Hazel T." It was not a sonnet in the literary sense, exceeding as it did the traditional fourteen iambic pentameter lines, but it expressed in lavish language Joseph's love and gratitude. Hazel kept it by her bed.

The year 1958 was filled with speaking engagements and other district duties, but on January 12, 1959, as a member of the Inaugural Committee from Ohio, Joseph traveled to Columbus to witness the inauguration of Michael V. DiSalle as governor. He was anxious to see what stand the governor would take in relation to the fair employment practices legislation pending before the Senate. Joseph was one of four religious leaders who spoke before the General Assembly in favor of the bill. He said (as paraphrased by a newspaper) that "he had appeared on behalf of FEPC legislation before the last four sessions of the Legislature and hoped that this would be his last visit," and that Ohio would "take its place among those states that have accepted the fact that the protection of civil rights is a fundamental part of our ever-present drive to protect and extend human rights under the Constitution." It was ironic that Ohio, "which once boasted of an underground railroad to expedite the freedom of slaves" and which had "established the first college for Negroes and women" should now be behind other states in the area of civil rights.[12]

On April 19 Joseph received a call from Georgia Myrtle Ransom informing him that Bishop Ransom had had a stroke and that he and Hazel had better come at once if they wished to see Reverdy for the last time. The doctors were certain the end was near. Joseph and Hazel left immediately for Wilberforce and Tawawa Chimney Corner, where Ransom lay in a coma. Georgia had done everything she could to make him comfortable, and for the next few days she sat with the Gomezes by his bed.

When not at Ransom's side, Joseph walked aimlessly through the historic old house, looking at the books, trophies, and awards, vainly trying to find the essence of the man somewhere among his possessions. The house had so many memories for him—the long dining table crowded with young ministers who had come to be fed spiritually by the seer; the library's overburdened shelves of material on every conceivable subject; the front room with its heavy furniture, made to accommodate the midnight visitors who came so often with their emergencies and their problems. When Joseph's mind could no longer contain his thoughts, he went back upstairs and sat again beside the bed with the others.

At 4 P.M. Wednesday, April 22, 1959, while Hazel held his head in her arms, Reverdy Cassius Ransom took his last breath. That evening and the next morning newspapers all over the country carried the story of his passing and attempted to encapsulate his long, extraordinary life. The *Sun* in Springfield, Ohio, remembered how in 1903 "he had single-handedly led an attack on a Chicago policy syndicate." As a result his church had been bombed, but he had been instrumental in 110 policy men being indicted.[13] The *Journal Herald* of Dayton and the *Chicago Defender* recalled his seventy-six years as a minister, twelve years as editor of the *A.M.E. Church Review*, thirty-five years as a bishop, sixteen years as president of the Board of Trustees at Wilberforce, his founding of Institutional A.M.E. Church in Chicago and St. James A.M.E. Church in Cleveland, his assistance in organizing the Niagara Movement along with W. E. B. Du Bois, his knighting by President William S. V. Tubman of Liberia, and his friendships with Frederick Douglass, Paul Laurence Dunbar, Sojourner Truth, Henry Wadsworth Longfellow, Henry Ward Beecher, Elijah McCoy, Andrew Carnegie, B. K. Bruce, John M. Langston, and Franklin D. Roosevelt.[14]

At Ransom's funeral on April 28, 1959, in the Chapel of the Living Savior at Payne Theological Seminary, Joseph gave an eloquent eulogy in honor of his spiritual mentor and father. He titled his tribute "Reverdy Cassius Ransom, Prevailer Extraordinary." Among those things over which Ransom had prevailed were his "overwhelming physical odds." Born "a frail child," he never weighed over 170 pounds though he was over six feet in height. He had also prevailed in "intellectual combat . . . in the social and civil struggles of his day. He was fitted by experience to understand human frailties. . . . The gnawing devastating appetites that maim and kill so many men of weaker stuff" caused him to know both "self-abasement and glorious personal triumph." His other superb qualities were "his spiritual sensitivity . . . [and] his candor and disarming frankness" about his own frailties. But he was ever sure of God and His redeeming presence. As a preacher and orator, he could "combine solid profound content with eloquence, rhetorical flavor, chaste language, delivery, and the passion of the Evangel." Last of all, Joseph said, Ransom had "prevailed over the beast and over the dragon and finally conquered death." Therefore, he concluded, "Hesitate not, Ransom the Ransomed. Thou hast found favor with God and Man and hast prevailed."[15]

All the way back to Cleveland, Joseph and Hazel talked about Ransom's life, rather than his death. They felt exceedingly blessed to have had his friendship and guidance for so long. Although the death certificate listed him as having died at ninety-eight, most people believed he had reached the century mark, the records of the births of Blacks being what they had been when he was born.

With a heavy feeling of loss, Joseph began his series of Annual Conferences. Since this was the year prior to the General Conference, there was much to be done. Ministerial delegates and alternates had to be elected, endorsements made, resolutions passed to take to the Quadrennial, and money to be raised for Payne Seminary, which was badly in need of funds. All of the conferences endorsed Rev. James Aiken, presiding elder of Michigan, and Hubert Robinson of Ebenezer, Detroit, as their candidates for the bishopric. For secretary-treasurer of Pensions, they chose Rev. Roy L. Miller.

When all the committee reports had been read and debated, all the sermons preached, hymns sung, and delegates elected, it was time for Hazel and Joseph to return to Cleveland, where they read with excitement of the sit-ins by four students from North Carolina A & T College. They had taken seats at a "whites only" Woolworth lunch counter in Greensboro,

North Carolina, and would not leave when refused service. Stimulated by their courage, hundreds of college students, Black and white, followed their example. A few weeks later, some students formed their own organization and called it the Student Nonviolent Coordinating Committee. This activity by young people had been predicted by Joseph in Texas in the '50s, when he said that Black youth from the South would lead the way in fighting for their own liberation.

On March 31, 1960, Rev. John Hunter asked the ministers and laity of the district to contribute letters to a Book of Tributes, which was to be presented to Bishop and Mrs. Gomez at an appreciation banquet on April 19. The banquet at Coppin Chapel celebrated the past three years of the Gomezes' superintendency.[16] So overwhelming was the response that it was impossible to read all of the letters the night of the affair. The letter which probably meant the most to them was that written by Hubie and Mamie Robinson:

> The love and fidelity shared with each other as husband and wife, the concern you always showed your own family and children, you now transfer to the families of your pastors. . . . Your holding on to an unfaltering trust in the providence of God and His will and purpose through years of disappointment have been discipline enabling you to deal with the disappointments you see in human nature. . . . Your generous nature, almost to the point of fault, to friends and situations is a matter of loyalty which so many know. Friendship to you is not fragile nor thin, neither stepping stones for the sake of self gain.[17]

The month after the banquet, Joseph turned his attention to the General Conference. He was concerned about the trouble that had been brewing for several years in the form of civil and Church suits against Bishop D. Ward Nichols, alleging that he had mishandled church money. A grand jury had indicted him on forty-two counts of embezzlement and fraudulent conversion. Joseph found this impossible to believe, since Nichols was a wealthy man in his own right. He had known Nichols for years as a close family friend and felt obliged to defend him. Many of Joseph's associates warned him that he was allowing his loyalty to blind him and that if he were not careful, he would be pulled down with Nichols. As in the Sims case, Joseph found himself torn. Nichols had assured him that none of the accusations were true and that those bringing charges against him were waging a personal vendetta. However, a special Church trial committee had found Nichols guilty and had sent its findings to the Judicial Council, which would make recommendations at the Quadrennial.

The thirty-sixth Quadrennial Session of the General Conference opened May 4, 1960. After a sunrise service at the Rose Bowl in Pasadena, California, the delegates assembled at the Shrine Auditorium in Los Angeles for the official opening, which began with a colorful procession of the bishops and dignitaries as the choir sang "All Hail the Power of Jesus' Name."[18] Bishop S. L. Greene, Sr., delivered the Quadrennial Sermon on the subject, "Show Thyself a Man."[19]

On Thursday morning the auditorium was packed as the delegates listened to the Judicial Council's thirty-two-page report. Of most interest were dockets 6, 7, 8, and 9, which were involved with Bishop Nichols. In every case the Judicial Council had reversed the decision of the Trial Committee. However, a minority report was read; it argued that the evidence brought before the Committee had proven incontrovertibly that Bishop Nichols was guilty, that his acts had been "fraudulent, illegal and in extreme violation of the A.M.E. Discipline." A motion was made to adopt the minority report, at which there was so much noise and confusion in the hall that the chair called for a vote by secret ballot. When the votes were counted, the conference had accepted the minority report, 401 for, 359 against. Nichols was suspended for four years.[20] Joseph had followed his convictions to the end, but now the General Conference had spoken.

On Friday morning, May 6, Joseph read the lengthy Episcopal Address. He listed materialism, secularism, socialism, communism, and pseudo-science as some of the enemies of the Church, which had first to purge itself and then act to arouse the people from moral lethargy. Near the end he warned the delegates, "We know, because of our past, that if we are to succeed, our great emphasis must be the Presence and Power of the Holy spirit. . . . Legislation without it is cold, calculating, discordant; legalism leaves us dissatisfied; Rules of Order become secondary; parliamentary skill is unavailing. Ultimate authority is God and of God."[21]

According to the conference minutes, Joseph's address "brought the bishops and congregation to their feet. . . . Bishop Frank Reid moved that the General Conference express its appreciation for one of the best Episcopal Addresses ever delivered to a General Conference." Then a "host of persons rose to second the motion. The Bishops and others all but lifted Bishop Gomez from his feet."[22] Afterwards Joseph remarked to Hazel how empty the conference seemed without Ransom. Even when he was too old to participate, his presence had been a calming influence, a reminder of the most important reason for the Quadrennial—spiritual regeneration.

On the following afternoon, Bishop David H. Sims was restored to full status, assuring the conference that he would accept a junior relationship to the other bishops.[23] Sims had waged a long, bitter, lonely fight; in the end he had come back to the Church and friends he loved, and was received in love.

The election of bishops took place on Saturday afternoon, May 14. Two bishops were to be elected, and voting machines were used for the first time. It took three ballots before John Douglas Bright of the 1st Episcopal District was elected; on the fourth ballot, George Napoleon Collins of the 8th District became the second bishop elected. Hubie Robinson, Joseph's favored candidate, had withdrawn his name after the second ballot.[24]

When the assignments of the bishops were read by the Chairman of the Episcopal Committee, Rev. Harvey Walden, Joseph had been returned to the 4th for another Quadrennial; the new bishops were assigned to the 17th and 18th districts (Africa) respectively; Bishop R. R. Wright was made Historiographer, as he had requested; and Bishop Baber presented Joseph as the new president of the Council of Bishops.[25]

The 1960 reports of the Committees on the State of the Country at the 4th District Annual Conferences reflected a decade of change. Most reported on the progress of the sit-ins South and North, the activities of Ralph Bunche as undersecretary of the United Nations, voter registration drives, and the coming presidential elections. Both political parties had avoided adopting stronger civil rights platforms at their national conventions. Commenting on the nomination of John F. Kennedy, the committee at the Chicago Conference said that for the second time in American history a party had "selected a man whose religion is one that does not in policy represent the basic concept of our Constitution." The question was, should a man because of his religion be prevented from making his contribution "when and if he measures up to all the other requirements necessitated by our day and time?" They concluded that religion should not be a factor.[26]

At the Illinois Conference in Champaign, Joseph made known his concerns regarding the November election. He strongly advised that no man had "a right to campaign against segregation, discrimination and bigotry in Alabama and come to Champaign and the cities of the North and not register to vote." That was the highest form of hypocrisy. He added that he had joined the Crusade for Freedom Movement headed by Dr. Martin Luther King, Roy Wilkins of the NAACP, and A. Phillip Randolph, an organization aimed at registering an additional million Negro voters. "No minister could justifiably call himself a 'spiritual leader' without being registered and actively participating in elections," he admonished.[27] It was no secret that he and Hazel were going to cast their votes for the young John F. Kennedy, who, in a close election, defeated Richard Nixon and became the first Catholic president of the United States.

During the early part of December, Hazel and Joseph flew to San Francisco to attend the National Session of the Council of Churches of Christ in the United States. The main controversy at the conference centered on a proposal by Dr. Eugene Carson Blake and Dean James Pike that the United Presbyterian, the Protestant Episcopal, the Methodist, and the United Church of Christ should merge.[28] Joseph admired the boldness of the proposal; however, he also understood that some denominations would rather keep their autonomy than unite. It would be a heated battle.

At the Thursday session, Joseph gave the closing prayer. He asked God to "save [the conference] from the peril of 'bigness' and of priority, that we may not be deceived, thereby reducing the efficacy of our Christian testimony, our witness of the spirit and the triumph of our fellowship." Undoubtedly these words were aimed at those who opposed the Pike/Blake proposal. Reacting to the bombings of several civil rights workers' homes and churches in the South, he said, "In those centers where violence abounds and conflict deepens, threatening . . . peace and the very existence of . . . Christian and democratic standards, lessening our moral leadership, may the Church not fail . . . in her demonstrable testimony of love, goodwill and understanding."[29]

The Council of Churches was very much on his mind as he presided over the first of many summit meetings of the 4th District he was to call. In Chicago in January, he told five hundred minsters and lay persons that the Church would lose its effectiveness if it did not gear its preaching and its activities to the social and economic needs of the community as well as its spiritual needs.[30] On the final day of the meeting, Joseph delivered a special address devoted to Christian social action, entitled "To the Summit with Christ." He made it clear he expected the members of his district to create programs in their churches which gave financial, physical, and spiritual aid to the Black Community. He reminded them that "freedom will not be won by abstract theorizing or beautiful words. It will only be won by day to day pressure on the opponent. As it has so often been said," he warned, "freedom has never been *given* to the oppressed—never in the history of the world."[31]

While in the process of catching up on the correspondence he had neglected during the Annual Conferences, Joseph remembered to send Sam Rayburn greetings on his birthday. Rayburn's response was warm, and Joseph looked forward to visiting him when he attended Kennedy's

Inauguration on Friday, January 20, 1961.[32] Along with the other A.M.E. bishops, he had been invited to meet with the new president.

At the White House on January 21 the bishops found Kennedy to be gracious but somewhat evasive when it came to his commitment to civil rights; nevertheless, like the rest of the country, they were caught up in his youthful energy and believed that he would lead America into a new, more progressive era. Kennedy had done his homework and seemed to know a great deal about the A.M.E. Church. He complimented the bishops on the accomplishments of the Church, and before they left, he posed with them for a picture on the steps of the White House.[33] Joseph had a short visit with Rayburn, who assured him the new president would indeed make a positive difference in the country. Then Joseph headed for home and Hazel.

As president of the Council of Bishops, and on its behalf, Joseph extended an invitation to Bishop J. W. Walls of the A.M.E. Zion Church and Bishop Luther Steward of the C.M.E. Church to meet with representatives of the A.M.E. Church to discuss the feasibility of a merger. He stated that such a merger would aid the progress of Negroes, "both in America and in the new nations of Africa," particularly since the Christian Church was "moving toward ecumenicity on all fronts." The merger would include 1,200,000 A.M.E.s, 780,000 C.M.E.s, and 400,000 A.M.E. Zions, and would bring to bear power on all issues involving Blacks.[34] Responses to the invitation came not only from the churches mentioned but from secular organizations pledging their support. It was Joseph's hope that this would be the first step to a World Methodist Church, and that the merger would be completed before all the Methodists met in conference in Oslo in August.

In his Presidential Statement at the February Bishop's Council meeting in Louisville, Joseph spoke about the embarrassing positions of Bishops Gow, Gibbs, Bright, and Collins in Africa due to the lack of adequate financial support from the Church. It was especially crucial that the Church give concrete evidence of its concern if it was to be a factor in the "religious guidance of these new nations at the very beginning of their nationhood." With regard to America, now that the Church had established a new Department of Social Action it were up to all of its members to concern themselves with "population shifts, with the migrant movement, the critical situations of our rural and urban work, job opportunities, houses and the probable effects of the recession on the morals of the people, not to mention its effect on the budget of the Church." Most of all what was needed was a ministry that was "prepared and dedicated, sanctified, not bullies . . . men of God, shepherds of the people." Now more than in any time in history, Negroes needed heroic leadership.[35]

During March and April, Joseph traveled widely and spoke often. So much activity caused the seventy-one-year-old Joseph to suffer from sleeplessness, high blood pressure, and fatigue. In a letter to James he mentioned that he had lost forty pounds. James replied that he was worried about the extensive travel Joseph planned to do during the year and was glad that Hazel would accompany him. In the same letter, after saying he had received $331.18 for the taxes on the house Joseph had bought Amanda, James asked that he send more money for repairs.[36] Joseph sent $3,000 that May, but James found the amount to be insufficient. It seemed that Joseph now was the sole support of his sister and her sons.

The Bishops' Council endorsed the Freedom Rides at its June meeting, and it strongly protested the "inhuman violence perpetrated against groups that [were] using non-violent methods in their pursuit of equal justice and public travel accommodations." From the pastors of the A.M.E. Church the Council asked for financial aid for the Freedom Riders through voluntary offerings to be taken during the month of July. In addition, it sent a message to Attorney-General Robert Kennedy asking him to see that the riders were protected by the federal government and that the administration consider qualified men regardless of race in filling some seventy judgeships recently created by Congress.[37]

The next month the Ministers' Annual Retreat at Camp Baber convened, using as its theme "The Sacrament of the Lord's Supper in African Methodism." During the last day, at a time set aside as the "Bishop's Hour," Joseph chatted informally with his ministers, repeating points he had made during his keynote address. He stressed that the new crisis facing the ecumenical Church was to rescue the "real apostolic Christianity from imprisonment." What his contemporaries called "Christianity [was] a mild form of 'Churchianity,'" he affirmed.[38] Once again, this camp on Stone Lake and the ministers who gathered to debate the issues facing them as spiritual leaders restored Joseph's sense of well-being, despite the turbulence in the world.

Curtis Sr. received another National Science Foundation Grant, this time to earn a master of science degree in mathematics from Notre Dame. Annetta, who had been able to complete her master of arts in English from Western Reserve University, resigned from Addison Junior High where she was teaching, packed the children, their clothes, tricycles, and little Curtis's piano in a U-Haul, and went with her husband to Indiana. Since Curtis Jr. had shown a great deal of promise in music, she was determined he should not lose valuable practice time while they were away.

Joseph and Hazel waved as the Jeffersons slowly backed out of their driveway on 138th Street, where they had lived since their arrival in Cleveland.

Big Curtis had never pulled a U-Haul before, and he was none too confident. The heavy upright piano did not make the task any easier. Although the children were used to moving from place to place, they looked back anxiously at their grandparents. Curtis Jr. would miss his grandfather most. He had delighted in following him around the house on Wade Park and listening to his fascinating stories.

Not long after that departure Joseph and Hazel sailed on the *Queen Elizabeth* to attend the tenth World Methodist Conference in Oslo. The highlight of the conference for them was the speech by Archibald J. Carey, a minister from Joseph's district, on the topic "The Negro Methodist Churches in America." He mentioned several Negro Methodists who had played major roles in the civil rights struggle: Oliver L. Brown of the *Brown vs. Board of Education of Topeka* case, which had led to the desegregation of schools; Rosa Parks of the Montgomery bus boycott; James L. Farmer, national director of the Congress of Racial Equality; Roy Wilkins, executive director of the NAACP; and lesser-known ministers and lay persons who had been a vital part of the protest marches. All of these personalities were the "spiritual heirs of the fathers whose yearning for freedom and independence first bought the Negro Methodist Churches into being."[39]

The Gomezes returned in time to conduct the Annual Conferences, which began in Toronto, September 14, and ended in Peoria, Illinois, October 29. The conferences proved to be fruitful in all respects, especially in terms of worship and concern for national and international issues. Appeals were sent to the United Nations: not to accept the Soviet *troika* system in filling the post of the late Dag Hammarskjöld as secretary-general; for total disarmament and an end to nuclear testing. They lauded the president for extending the Civil Rights Commission, for the appointments of George L. Weaver as assistant secretary of labor, Thurgood Marshall as a judge on the United Circuit Court of Appeals, Andrew Hatcher as the president's assistant press secretary. Attorney-General Kennedy was also commended for prosecuting election officials in the South who prevented Blacks from voting, protecting the Freedom Riders, and for desegregating interstate buses.[40] The conferences unanimously voted to support the Blake/Pike proposal for the merger of the Methodist, Presbyterian, the United Church of Christ and the Protestant Episcopal Churches. On the other hand, they noted with alarm the number of individuals and groups who were advocating racial separatist policies, even to the point of demanding a separate state for Blacks with its own separate black economy.[41]

The conferences reflected Joseph's concern over the growth of the Black Muslims, a religious, separatist organization who preached the superiority of Blacks over the "white devils." Nevertheless, he had to admire their advocacy of Black entrepreneurship, respect for Black women and the family, and their emphasis on the purity of the body and mind. In time, Joseph came to admire Malcolm X, who was gaining prominence as the leading spokesman for the Black Muslims. He was fascinated by the quickness of Malcolm's mind, his ability to challenge some of the most astute white leaders in debate, and his deep insights concerning race in America, particularly in the North. Where Dr. Martin Luther King's strategies were highly effective in the South, Malcolm understood better the complexities of northern prejudice. Joseph later told Annetta that in time historians would reevaluate the contributions of Marcus Garvey and Malcolm X and find them to be two of not only the most controversial but also most original and important leaders in the liberation struggle. This belief seemed all the more strange coming from a man who had been an integrationist all of his life, but it was not so strange when one understood that as a young man he was often an iconoclast. Malcolm and Marcus were provocative, candid, and outspoken. Being a passionate man himself, Joseph identified with the depth of their passion.

When the last assignments had been read at the Illinois Annual Conference in late October, Joseph and Hazel anxiously returned to Wade Park to prepare for a trip around the world, which included a visit to New Delhi for a World Council of Churches meeting. They hoped their travels would give them a global perspective on the '60s. How had the protests in America, the emerging independent nations in Africa, and the establishment of a Jewish homeland in Israel affected other countries? These were questions they hoped to address.

On November 5, the Gomezes left Cleveland for San Francisco, where at 3 P.M. they would board Japan Airlines for Tokyo. Joseph carried with him a letter of introduction from Mayor Anthony J. Celebreeze of Cleveland;[42] there were also boxes of pencils and paper to be used in the writing of articles he had promised the *Cleveland News, Cleveland Call and Post,* and the Church papers. As always, Hazel carried her movie and still cameras and boxes of film.

After a journey that was "relatively calm and uneventful," at 9:30 P.M., "having crossed the International Date Line, losing a whole day in progress, they landed in Tokyo." The Cook Travel Agency's representatives took them to the new wing of the Hotel Imperial, where they would stay for two days.[43]

The next day they toured Tokyo. Joseph was amazed at not only the vastness of the city, with its nine million people, but at the traffic problem, which was "the most acute to be found anywhere, the average number of traffic casualties [being] 20 per day." Hazel's camera was kept busy filming the Imperial Palace plaza, the exotic Yasukuni shrine, the Diet, the American Embassy (where they chatted with many of the officials), Meini Park, the Happeen Garden (for a Japanese tea service), Tokyo University, a Kabuki theatre (which was of particular interest to Hazel, who wished Annetta could have seen the highly stylized performance), and an excursion by rail to Nikko to see Kegon waterfall and Lake Chunzenji.

All of these sights impressed them, but Joseph's main concern was with "the economic, social and spiritual life of the people." He found the changes in them to be "revolutionary." As was true in many cities of Asia and Africa, there was "a definite conflict going on between East and West," seen mainly in the clashing of the cultures. Joseph felt it would be in the interest of the West to assist these people in developing their own cultures rather than imposing Western culture on them.

He was amazed how much Japan had recovered from World War II. Trade had increased to the point that "Made in Japan" was "fast gaining the prominence it once had." Traveling through the rural areas, he and Hazel found much "distress and poverty," but they felt the government was addressing these problems.

They arrived on November 11 in Hong Kong, where they were impressed by the business district and the amazing panorama of the harbor, mainland and islands from Victoria Peak." As they toured the city, they found "a strange mixture of wealth and poverty, of British efficiency and the sense of ease and fatalism." One of the main problems facing the government was that of the refugees. "Despite all precautions on the part of Red China, [the people] cross into Hong Kong by the thousands." In one section of the city, they saw over eighty-six thousand immigrants huddled miserably together; standing on a hill overlooking the line that divides British Hong Kong and China, Hazel and Joseph were sobered by the sight below. In that moment they were more than ever grateful for the freedom they enjoyed in America, however limited.

On the afternoon of November 14 the Gomezes, Babers, and Bonners arrived in Bangkok, "the city of Temples and the reclining Buddha." They were awed by the Temple of Dawn, "a magnificent work of art 248 feet high." Joseph found the people to be "fanatically religious" and "devoutly monarchistic."[44]

Having read about the floating market, they were anxious to see it firsthand. It was even more remarkable than they had anticipated. "For

14 miles we traveled in a boat along the Klong River and saw the people as they sold and bought from boats and stores situated on the river or anchored there," Joseph wrote. At one time they "ran into as tight a traffic jam" on the river, as one would "experience in [the streets of] New York or Chicago."

On November 16 they flew to New Delhi and were soon settled in their suites at the Hotel Ashoka. These were to be their quarters during the World Council of Churches Conference.

Prior to the opening of the conference they had the opportunity to explore the city and found New Delhi to be full of "beautiful and costly homes, broad avenues and squares, well-kept gardens and a general air of modern living and culture." In contrast, "Old Delhi [was filled with] noise, poverty, dirt and strange smells," an unpleasant combination of curry, human excrement, and unwashed bodies. Delhi was "typical of the enormous gap between the rich and poor, learned and illiterate," just as the plush suburbs in the United States were the antithesis of the ghettos in the inner cities, except that Old Delhi was more extreme and there were many more people. Both examples epitomized the neglect and unconcern for the masses by the "haves."

In terms of politics, India's future was "not as secure as one would wish." Prime Minister Jawaharlal Nehru was having difficulties, and there was a "slowly rising tide of opposition to his leadership. The young, progressive leaders who still rever[ed] Mahatma Gandhi [were] nevertheless giving a new interpretation to the principles of non-violence." They were critical of the government's conduct "in relation to the Portuguese encroachment at Goa and that of the Chinese on their border."

Early the second morning the party went to see the famous Taj Mahal. The discrepancies between the opulence of the temple and the poverty and dirt they saw on their drive to the site spoiled the occasion for them. In addition, they were often delayed by "the ever present Cow," which they certainly would not have hit even aside from its religious significance.

The most meaningful experience for the Gomezes was their trip to the tomb of "Mahatma" Gandhi, "the World Saint and Holy One of India." In keeping with the simplicity of the man himself, a plain slab of concrete marked his monument. Along with the Ethiopians, Malayans, and others gathered there, the American Negroes laid wreaths on Gandhi's monument. "We were not ashamed to take off our shoes to tread on what we believe was Holy Ground," Joseph wrote. As long as he could remember, Joseph had been awed by this man whose influence was paramount in America's civil rights movement. Even a "thousand years from today" he would be "greater and his voice clearer in the interest of morality and peace," Joseph believed.

The World Council of Churches Conference, the first of three to be held in a non-Christian country, was full of pageantry and color, impressive in outward appearance. It opened with a procession from the Vigyan Bhavan to the Indian Shamiana. Top religious leaders from all over the world were in attendance, dressed in their native garbs. Even the Roman Catholic Church had sent observers for the first time. Nevertheless, in terms of what the conference achieved, Joseph had reservations: the "endless discussion on creedal differences and the hair-splitting distinctions of theological terms, and the almost total absence of emphasis on the place of the Holy Spirit as the directing agency of Church unity." On the credit side, despite the opposition of many delegates the organization admitted the Russian Orthodox Church and the "twenty-two Asian and African Churches." The Russians, Asians, and Africans had center stage throughout the conference, but the American Negroes "were almost forgotten. They did not have a single place on the program of the council." Joseph wondered how much the delegates from the American South had to do with this neglect.

Ironically, racial equality was emphasized. The Council condemned anti-Semitism and, after much discussion, the Portuguese brutality in Angola. Some felt that the Portuguese "should not be singled out for condemnation when so many others were equally as guilty." After all, South Africa had "many able advocates in the Council and . . . the Southern U.S.A. was ably represented." Although the United States accounted for only 30 percent of the membership, it paid 70 percent of the budget and was in a position to dictate policy. Joseph reiterated the feelings of the American Negro delegates when he wrote he had hoped "that in a day fraught with danger as this, the World Council would have spoken in clearer tones to the millions of the earth who are in utter despair and have neither knowledge of or interest in abstract theological discussions," especially people in Third World countries.

For Joseph the most enjoyable events of the conference included his conversations with Vice President Sarvepalli Radhakrishnan of India, who hosted a gathering in the Gardens of the Presidential Palace (Radhakrishnan represented the president, who was ill); and his meeting at the home of Bishop Shot K. Mondol of the Delhi area, who entertained all the Methodists.[45]

On December 3 they left New Delhi for Tel Aviv, arriving the next morning at 2:25 A.M. and going by private car to the Hotel Dan. They rested until noon and then viewed the Cultural Center and the Habimah

Theatre. Continuing on to the ancient city of Jaffa, the Fort Area, Bat Yam, and Holong, they saw the innumerable projects for the housing of new settlers. From there they traveled to Haifa, and thence to Tiberias on the Sea of Galilee. They saw the tombs of Maimonides and Rabbi Meir Baal Haness, the Hot Springs, and Degania, the first collective settlement established in the country. Hazel and Joseph were elated when they finally reached Nazareth, the place where Jesus lived as a child.

Then, on December 8, they went by private car to Jerusalem, passing through the Valley of Zerek, Martyrs' Forest, and Abu Gosh (biblical Kiryat Yearim). They ascended Mount Zion, visited the tomb of King David, the Church of Dormition (site of the Last Supper), and then went to the National Institution.[46] The impression Joseph carried with him of this thirteen-year-old nation was one of hallowedness. At times it almost seemed as it he were back in biblical times, walking and talking with the prophets. After climbing the hills of that rough terrain, he was convinced that the effeminate, pale Jesus pictured on the Sunday school cards was far from accurate: Jesus had been strong and dark.

As the Bible had predicted, the Jews had indeed "made the desert bloom." Joseph noted that "in the realm of education and business, in social progress, in resettlement of refugees, in the arts and sciences and trade, Israel pushes on relentlessly." Although the land was small and could provide for only about three million people, the Jews planned "to make that nation, barring the accident of war, the greatest of its size, and the best in social progress."[47]

The last stop on their tour was Cairo, where on December 10 they took an excursion to the pyramids of Cheops and Khephren and visited the Sphinx.[48] The entire party traveled by camel, and Hazel could not help but remark that this trip was even more challenging than her rides on the donkey when she taught in Mississippi in 1913. Joseph was not amused; he only wanted to feel the firm ground under his feet again.

Joseph found Egypt under Gamal Abdel Nassar's leadership was still a "land of charm, history and wonderment," but as in all dictatorships, the country had not progressed as rapidly as it could have under a more liberal form of government. "American capital continues to flow there," he wrote. "The Hilton Nile is one of the most beautiful and adequate of its kind in the world." Very much in evidence were many other American enterprises.[49]

By December 12 the Gomezes were ready for the flight home. The trip, though highly educational and mostly enjoyable, had been tiring, and the World Council meeting somewhat disappointing. They wanted to be back in Cleveland in time to spend Christmas with the family. The Jeffersons would fly in from Indiana, Eula and her children would be on holiday from school, and Harold would steal a few hours from his busy schedule at the NAACP office. The evenings would resound with violin solos by Marvin, piano solos by Curtis Jr., trumpet solos by Joseph, and skits by Gerald, Sissy, and Toni (Jane's daughter). Hazel had enough slides to fill numerous pleasurable hours of family viewing, and Joseph had written enough for a dozen or more articles.

On February 25, 1962, at Soldiers and Sailors Memorial Hall in Pittsburgh, the *Pittsburgh Courier* sponsored its first "Appreciation Day." The two guest speakers were to be "Dr. James Nabrit, erudite and forceful president of Howard University and one of the great legal minds of the generation, and Bishop Joseph Gomez, prelate of the A.M.E. Church and one of the most gifted and learned orators of the day."[50]

The occasion was auspicious. Thirty-one achievement awards were given to prominent Blacks in a variety of fields. In addition, several young people were granted educational scholarships. This was the first of many Annual Achievement Awards Programs sponsored by the *Courier.*[51] Joseph felt honored to have been a part of the first and to have had the opportunity to share the platform with Dr. Nabrit.

In August, the National Association of Colored Women's Clubs, led by their president, Dr. Rosa Gragg, met at the Sheraton Park Hotel in Washington, D.C., to give awards to prominent Americans who had made significant contributions in their various fields. Among those honored were Robert Kennedy, Arthur Goldberg, Walter Reuther, Dr. Jonas Salk, Henry Ford, Isabelle Lindsy, Louis Blound, A. G. Gaston, A. Phillip Randolph, Senator Phil Hart, Charles Fisher, Harvey Russell, and Bishop Joseph Gomez—"for his outstanding contributions in the field of Religion."[52] Joseph felt extremely fortunate to have been included in such an august group of national figures and expressed his gratitude to Rosa Gragg and her organization. Hazel never tired of telling her daughters and grandchildren about the occasion and how proud she was of "Daddy."

Later that summer Joseph held his 1962 Annual Conferences. Topics of interest were the past World Council of Churches in India (made clearer by Hazel's slide presentations), the condition of Black churches in general and of the A.M.E. Church in particular, and the stepped-up progress of the civil rights movement.

Since urban renewal and the beginning of open housing were gradually changing neighborhood patterns, some of the more progressive white churches were actively seeking Blacks to join their congregations. At the Michigan Annual Conference, the Committee on the Condition of the Church observed that in the past because of segregation the nation had "left to the 'Negro church,' principally Methodist and Baptist, an almost exclusive right to the patronage and allegiance of the Negro Community and people." As a result "we developed a 'Negro Church' philosophy and developed 'Negro Church patterns.' While our avowed principle has always been one of total brotherhood, our performance has been limited to 'Negro Brotherhood.'" The Church could not ignore changes in circumstances. Were the losses of rural churches being balanced by the increase in urban churches? Were the quality and quantity of ministers keeping pace with the educational and cultural advances of the membership? Did the A.M.E. Church command the respect and influence it once had, and could it effect realistic reforms of parochial structure, programs, and practices? Trained personnel, better facilities and program content, and financial support through an established, realistic budget were essential, reported the committee, if the A.M.E. Church were not to lose more members to white churches.[53]

At the Chicago Conference, the Committee on the Condition of the Church found it to be "somewhat inconsistent that we are now waging a relentless fight for full freedom of Negro Americans and for integration in all areas of citizenship" while still maintaining divisions in the various Negro denominations, "principally Baptist and Methodists." Even though Blacks were united in the fight for civil rights, they were still "hopelessly divided in matters of church affiliation."[54]

A paradox was becoming obvious to Joseph. On the one hand, he believed firmly in ecumenism, integration, and unity. On the other hand, he had a "love affair" with the A.M.E. Church, with all its strengths and weaknesses. It was because of the A.M.E. Church that he had become what he was. Would integration mean the elimination of that rich uniqueness which was the African Methodist Episcopal Church—that moving singularity which was the Black church? The thought was too painful to contemplate. He could not envision a time when the A.M.E. Church would not be there for him, for his children and children's children. It was their rightful heritage. But then perhaps so was integration—unless, as Malcolm X had said, the goals of the Negro civil rights movement were wrong, that Blacks should be concentrating instead on ownership of businesses and land, that Blacks should be about the building of a strong race rather than integrating with white people, who would never really be willing to give up their power. What then? Separation? Unthinkable. Privately, Joseph would struggle to answer these questions for the remainder of his life. Outwardly, he continued to be an integrationist, because he could not find a justifiable alternative—one that would be compatible with his Christian belief in sisterhood and brotherhood.

At the Indiana Conference, the Committee on the Condition of the Church noted that clergymen, white and black, "from the Metropolitan New York and Chicago areas [had] responded to the call of the Rev. Martin Luther King to converge on Albany, Georgia to give moral support in the struggle for human rights." Many had been jailed. The committee concluded that the Negro Church was finally awakening from its "lethargy" and facing its challenge courageously and in turn commanding world attention and respect.[55]

All of the conferences noted the activities of A.M.E.s in organizations such as the Congress of Racial Equality (CORE) and the NAACP, in sit-ins, kneel-ins, and other forms of non-violent action. The Indiana Conference praised Rev. John Hunter, chairman of the Committee on Education of the Gary, Indiana, branch of the NAACP, for spearheading a drive to achieve school integration in the Gary school system. As a result of that drive a suit was pending in the federal district court of Northern Indiana.[56]

Several ministers and lay persons of the 4th were disturbed because the Baptists had taken the limelight in the area of civil rights—that the A.M.E. Church as an organization had done very little. Joseph acknowledged that the Church could have done much more but argued that rather than waste time being envious of the achievements of the Baptists and King's Southern Christian Leadership Congress, members of the A.M.E. Church should assist in any and all meaningful ways they could. He reminded them of the thousands of individual A.M.E.s who were making significant contributions in terms of voter registration, finances, boycotts, and protest marches. Those who had only the kind of criticism for the A.M.E. Church they had for the NAACP should look at the record: the NAACP continued to use litigation as its main tool; in addition, it was often called upon to bail the protesters out of jail, because the other civil rights organizations were short of funds. The A.M.E. Church used pressure in the form of resolutions, petitions, boycotts, telegrams, and letters; it provided legal and organizational funds; and it made group visits to politicians who had the power to effect change. Although these tactics might not be as dramatic as other kinds of direct action, they too were necessary. As Joseph often said, "Every method is essential. No one method represented a panacea. Instead of Blacks making comparisons, and casting blame, they should use every available strategy. That is what it would take to win the war, and make no mistake, that is what Blacks are in—a war!"[57]

As if to confirm Joseph's statement about war, at the final conference in Illinois, the Committee on the Condition of the Country reported that three hard-core states in the deep South still had a completely segregated school system, namely Alabama, Mississippi, and South Carolina. The federal courts that same week had ruled that James Meredith should be admitted to the University of Mississippi. He had been barred from entering by state officials, but Attorney General Robert Kennedy had promised to take whatever steps necessary for his safe admittance. The Committee informed the conference that Rev. Blaine Ramsey, pastor of Ward Chapel A.M.E. Church in Cairo, Illinois, had led several protest marches against segregation there and had been arrested. (Joseph had been in constant touch with Ramsey and watched the activities in Cairo closely, making sure funds were made available to the protestors.) Additionally, the committee reported that several Negro churches had been burned and homes fired upon around Albany, Georgia.[58]

The conference sent a telegram to Illinois governor Otto Kerner protesting the infringement of the rights of citizens to peacefully protest against any injustice" and the police harassment of demonstrators now filling the jails in Cairo.[59] The delegates went on record as pledging "moral, spiritual and financial support" to Rev. Ramsey and "the non-violent movement in the stride toward freedom." All of the conferences ended with the members pledging to continue the fight in their own neighborhoods.

Meanwhile on April 9, 1963, Joseph received a letter from the new president of Eden Theological Seminary in Wester Grove, Robert T. Fauth.

> Since coming to Eden Seminary last fall, I have been delighted to learn that among our alumni we have a bishop of the A.M.E. Church. As far as I know you are the only bishop who is a graduate of Eden Seminary. . . .
>
> We are delighted to have Van Covington as one of our students at the present time. He tells me that it is because of you that he has come to Eden Seminary. If you have any more students of his caliber, we would be happy to have you send them along to us.[60]

Remembering how he had had to fight for admission to Eden back in 1933, Joseph felt a certain satisfaction to hear the president of the Seminary ask for his help in securing more Negro students. Things had a way of coming full circle.

Joseph delivered the Baccalaureate Sermon for the Agricultural Mechanical and Normal College at Pine Bluff, Arkansas, on May 26, 1963.[61] In June he attended the regular session of the Council of Bishops at Ebenezer A.M.E. Church in Detroit. The bishops sponsored an Allen Anvil Awards Banquet on June 19 as an expression of gratitude to A.M.E.s and others who had "wrought so nobly and courageously for the realization of the highest hopes and aspirations of all mankind in the area of human rights and dignity of persons." Among the seven honored were Rosa Parks, who had been the inspiration for the Montgomery bus boycott; Daisy Bates, who had helped to desegregate Central High School in Little Rock, Arkansas; and G. Mennen Williams, now Assistant Secretary of State for African Affairs. Joseph introduced Williams, who said that "the existence of open discrimination in the South and illegal but de facto discrimination in the North are but two sides of the same coin. . . . The time in which we have to work grows increasingly short," he warned. "The challenge to Christianity is to grasp the leadership."[62]

During the summer of 1963, the Jeffersons returned to Cleveland. Curtis had successfully finished his work at Notre Dame and was to begin teaching at East High School in the fall. Annetta would teach at Glenville High, her old alma mater, which was now all Black, as was the area. Most of the synagogues had been taken over by Black congregations. The chanting of the rabbis had been replaced by the gospel beat, the rich simplicity of the spirituals, the anthems, and old Protestant hymns. The Jeffersons had enjoyed the time away but were glad to be in Cleveland with the family. Marvin, Sissy, and Gerald had grown so much that they seemed like strangers to their cousins at first, but soon the five children were plotting mischief together as if they had never been apart.

The Cleveland to which they returned had undergone many changes. The Cleveland branch of the NAACP had sought to bring together over fifty civil rights organizations, including the more militant ones, into what became known as the United Freedom Movement. "Its integrated membership included inner-city ministers, leaders of the Jewish community, traditional Negro leaders, and some of Cleveland's new breed of angry young men." Its first fight was over the hiring practices of contractors who were building a convention center; despite marches and boycotts, the U.F.M. gained little ground.[63] It would have better success when it attacked the segregated school system during the fall months. Since Eula, Annetta, and Curtis Sr. taught in the public schools, they would find themselves very much involved.

Chicago was becoming another of the focal points for civil rights demonstrations in the North. During the first part of July the NAACP held its national convention there, and on July 4 sponsored a march. Harold and Joseph were two of the eighteen thousand people who paraded down State Street through the Loop to Grant Park, where speeches were to be given.[64] In light of the jailing of Martin Luther King, Jr., in Birmingham during the spring, followed by Bull Connor's use of police dogs and high-powered water hoses on children during their protest march, and then the assassination in June of Medgar Evers, Field Secretary of the NAACP in Jacksonville, Mississippi, the crowd was in no mood to listen to talk about "good will."

Mayor Richard Daley walked in front of the procession carrying an American flag; he encountered some signs which read, "Mayor Daley, what the hell are you doing here?" Many Blacks were still angered by his declaring at one of the convention sessions that "Chicago had no such thing as a ghetto." When he got up to speak at the park he was booed for twenty minutes. Many in the crowd jeered and heckled him, shouting "'Daley must go!' Flustered, red-faced and angry, Daley gave up after several starts and thundered, 'I recognize a contingent of the Republican Party here.'" Then he stormed off the platform, disappearing amid the incensed crowd.[65]

Rev. J. H. Jackson, head of the National Baptist Convention, met a similar fate. At an earlier session he had told the delegates, "Negroes ought to have a quiet period of two months and stop demonstrating." He was greeted with, "Uncle Tom! Uncle Tom!" The jeers became so loud he too had to leave the platform. Even Roy Wilkins experienced minor heckling, from some who were beginning to feel he and the NAACP were too conservative and needed to alter their tactics. Despite the reception of Daley, Jackson, and Wilkins, Joseph "was very graciously received and given a rounded ovation upon completion of his speech." He warned the crowd, "These are times when men must show courage as well as the understanding necessary to properly guide the millions of people who don't quite [comprehend] the urgency of our times." He told them how the history of the A.M.E. Church and its beginnings reflected "the very mood of the present day struggle for freedom." Senator Paul Douglas of Illinois was also "enthusiastically cheered before and after his speech . . . though he . . . advised a policy of moderation and non-violence, such as that of the late Mohandas K. Gandhi in India."[66]

In addition to civil rights, Joseph was preoccupied with the general role of the A.M.E. Church. He was weary of the constant criticism of the laity against the leaders and the absence of positive suggestions for change. The diminishing power of the Church could not be laid at the feet of any one person or group; the responsibility was collective.

At the Connectional Laymen's Convention August 5–10, he had an opportunity to voice his concerns, in a sermon entitled "Corporate Guilt and Responsibility in the Church." He spoke of the achievements of the A.M.E. Church in the past, and in the present. The entire Church, however, had to take the blame for the loss of power it was now experiencing. He reminded them that in addition to the bishops, presiding elders, and pastors, there were over a million lay persons. "What have you done with or without a pastor's direction to engage the Church in the social 'good' of your community? How much involved are you in the people's total welfare?" he asked. Then he turned to the ministers and said that the Church would only recover its glory "when at its leadership are men, not sycophants; men who speak not only against tyranny, but are not tyrants themselves, who love truth for truth's sake." He recalled a time when Detroit had ten "'Giants of the Word' [who] filled the homiletical and evangelistic sky." He had known the A.M.E. Church "in days when tall and sun-crowned men walked across its pulpits and there was power." He called for "Repentance—Conversion—Reconciliation—Peace!"[67]

In the days that followed, he received many letters and phone calls telling him how timely his message had been, one which everyone needed to hear; consequently it was printed in a pamphlet and sent to people throughout the Connection.

The 1963 4th District Annual Conferences were concerned with what turned out in retrospect to be the apex of the civil rights movement, and with the ministerial delegates and endorsements to be sent to the General Conference in 1964.

At the Canadian Annual Conference, the focuses were Dr. Martin Luther King, Jr.'s, visit to Windsor, Ontario, to speak at the Council of Christians and Jews; intensified discussions concerning the protests in Birmingham; and President Kennedy's long-awaited statement to the nation that "the time [had] come for America to remove the blight of racial discrimination and fulfill her brilliant promise" of justice, and that he was sending a civil rights bill to Congress. Most of all under discussion was the August 28 March on Washington, led by Dr. King.[68]

Delegates to the Michigan Conference in Detroit passed resolutions endorsing the March on Washington, and they urged members of the A.M.E. Church to take part in the march and to write letters to their congressmen asking them to support the civil rights legislation now before Congress. The delegates recognized the "moral emphasis of this march . . . as an opportunity for people of good will to demonstrate their concern for the welfare of large segments of the population of our great nation."[69]

A.M.E.'s made up a significant portion of the mass who crowded in front of the Lincoln Memorial on August 28 to sing freedom songs, listen to great orations, and share the dreams as expressed so profoundly by "The King," spiritual leader of the march. Most of the churches hired buses to carry their members to Washington. Ironically, just before the procession began the leaders got word that the "Grandfather of the Movement," W. E. B. Du Bois, had died in Ghana, where he had been self-exiled for years because he no longer believed in America's promises of freedom.

In light of Joseph's increasingly high blood pressure, Dr. Joseph Brown forbade him from attending the march, and Hazel supported him. Joseph had to content himself with watching the proceedings on television, from 1:30 P.M., when Camilla Williams sang her moving rendition of "The Star Spangled Banner," to the late afternoon, when King proclaimed the words of the old Negro spiritual, "Free at last! Free at last! Thank God Almighty, I'm free at last!" Joseph had never thought he would live to witness such a dramatic spectacle—thousands of beautiful rich-toned Negroes pushing their way to the Lincoln Memorial and cooling their tired feet in the reflecting pool beside the determined whites who had joined them.

On Sunday afternoon, September 15, Rev. C. E. Thomas, pastor of St. John A.M.E. Church in Birmingham, who was visiting the Chicago Conference, told of a telephone call he had just received. The 16th Street Baptist Church in his city, "a meeting place for many civil rights efforts," had been bombed. It was later learned that four little Negro girls attending Sunday School had been killed. The delegates were enraged.[70] Was this the South's answer to the March on Washington? Joseph asked for several moments of silent prayer for the children's families and for the people of Birmingham, who had had more than their share of violence.

The Illinois Conference sent a strong resolution to the Attorney General, the president, and the Congress deploring Alabama governor George Wallace's open defiance of federal authority, his "making himself a symbol of lawlessness, disregard and disrespect for the orderly processes of law." The resolution asked for federal intervention in this state where "all seeming law and order have broken down, and more lives snuffed out and more property destroyed."[71]

Feeling that the district should make some concrete expression of grief, the Indiana Conference resolved that the churches in the district should go immediately into mourning "by draping black upon altars, pulpits and over entrances, with signs reading: 'Till Freedom Rings!'" It was also the unanimous wish of the conference that Governor Matthew E. Welsh, "the first governor in the United States to issue an executive order (June 4, 1963) banning such discrimination in places supervised or licensed by agencies of the Indiana state Government," should be given the Richard Allen Award at the General Conference in May 1964.[72]

When the last conference was over on September 29, Hazel and Joseph, completely spent emotionally and physically, returned to Cleveland, only to be confronted by another crisis facing their daughters. The United Freedom Movement, having failed to get more minorities hired by contractors building the convention center, had decided to attack segregation in the Cleveland public schools.[73]

The United Freedom Movement had presented the Board of Education with a list of demands and threatened to picket the Board if they were not met. The Board's response was to call a public meeting on September 30, at which it promised to move toward "fullest possible integration consistent with sound educational practices" and to create a Citizens Council on Human Relations.[74] Harold felt the U.F.M. had, at least for the time being, won this particular battle. The pressure on him and his family was heavy; there had been hate phonecalls, obscene notes, and threats on their lives. Hazel and Joseph were concerned for their safety but could not in all honesty ask them to curb their activities any more than they had themselves when confronted with threats from the KKK in Detroit during the 1920s.

Tragedy seemed to come in legions, relentlessly eclipsing progress. On November 22, 1963, while riding in a motorcade through Dallas, President John F. Kennedy was shot. With him in the car was his wife and John Connally, the governor of Texas, who was also wounded. Joseph was working on his Christmas message when Annetta called him and told him what had happened. He and Hazel, like so many Americans, were hypnotized by the drama as it unfolded on television. They tried to make sense of the death of this young president, who seemed to have everything in front of him. Something was radically wrong with a country that murdered little children, civil rights workers, and now presidents. Only a few months ago, June 12 to be exact, Medgar Evers had been assassinated. Although there were two suspects, no one had been brought to justice; and now Kennedy. Where was God in all of this? Joseph watched the faces of Jacqueline and her children, whose expressions, like those of mannequins, remained the same throughout the proceedings. Their shock, fear, and pain mirrored the emotions of a nation, just as did the lone, riderless horse in the funeral cortege.

Gradually the pain began to dull, and like the rest of the country Joseph accepted the reality of the situation. Kennedy was dead. The question now became, what kind of president would Lyndon Baines Johnson make—a Southerner, a Texan? Would this mean the end of the civil rights legislation? Everyone would have to wait and see.

In January 1964, more trouble was brewing in Cleveland. Believing that the school board had not lived up to its promises, the United Freedom Movement picketed several white schools that it felt had continued to segregate the incoming Black students. The picketers were met by mobs of angry white parents, who threw rocks, spit on the students, and uttered racial slurs. One such school was Collingwood High.[75] The authorities there had locked the Black students in the cafeteria, supposedly to keep them from being hurt by the crowd outside. Somehow they got out, marched to Glenville High School, where Annetta was teaching, and called to the students inside to join them in disbanding the mob outside Collingwood. In spite of the attempts of the principal and teachers to keep the Glenville students inside, they climbed out of windows or found unguarded doors and joined the Black students from Collingwood. The police finally arrived and sent the young people home. Shakily, Annetta drove to her parents' home on Wade Park to ask their advice. She had watched from her classroom window, which faced the street, the seething crowd of Black students descend on Glenville, and she had tried to keep her class calm. As a teacher it had been her duty to restrain the students, but as a Black woman she had understood their frustrations. When she arrived at her parents' house Joseph put his arms around her and said, "I understand your anger. You must follow your own mind. What do you think was the best thing for the students? That is the question you have to ask yourself." He would give no further advice, but she understood that he was trusting her to follow the dictates of her own conscience. This was one of the qualities she loved best about her father.

Blacks and whites were growing farther and farther apart, as an incident at Murray Hill School exemplified. The United Freedom Movement had prepared to picket Murray Hill, which was in an Italian neighborhood known to be especially hostile to Blacks. When the U.F.M. got word that an unruly crowd had gathered, it postponed the action. Sensing victory, the whites stood on the street corners stoning cars with Black passengers and randomly beating Negroes and cameramen. On February 3 the U.F.M. staged a sit-in at the Board of Education and was removed forcibly by the police the next day. The mayor, the school board, and even the media now felt that the protestors had gone too far.[76] The militants in the group were demanding stronger action, but Harold and the NAACP thought it was time to assess the situation and plan their strategy carefully.

Although in February the school board promised to diffuse bused students "on a level designed to induce integration," it began to construct more schools in the Black areas, which would give an excuse to contain Black students in their own neighborhood schools. In one construction site in the Glenville area, where the U.F.M. joined parents in picketing, Rev. Bruce Klunder, a white minister, lay down behind a bulldozer to prevent it from moving; he was run over and killed. Pandemonium erupted in the community, as enraged Blacks roamed the area throwing bottles at policemen and looting stores. It was several days before the confrontation died down. When the school board secured an injunction preventing the blockage of any school construction, the U.F.M. decided to boycott the schools on Monday, April 20. Eighty-five percent of Black students stayed home from school. Eula, Curtis Sr., and Annetta went to work, but their children stayed home.

The boycott was successful in terms of the number of children who did not attend school, but it did little to change the pattern of segregated schools in Cleveland. A new superintendent was hired, Dr. Paul Briggs, whose emphasis was on quality education for all the schools in every neighborhood.[77] This idea pleased both whites and Black Power advocates, who believed Blacks should stay in their own neighborhoods and control them. This brief respite from conflict allowed the A.M.E. Churches in the city to prepare for the General Conference.

Bishop W. R. Wilkes, who was to write the Episcopal Address for the 1994 General Conference, asked all the bishops for their input, since the speech was to represent the collective thinking of the Council. On January 8 Joseph had sent Wilkes his suggestions, which summarized his thoughts at the beginning of this new year. In pondering the Black man's struggle for freedom, he wrote:

> It is important . . . to note that the struggle has now assumed global meaning. It is identifiable with the fight for freedom of the emerged and emerging nations of Africa, Asia and the world. There is more than sympathy here for the Negro struggle; there is identification of suffering and fellowship. The problem is therefore not isolated but cosmic.
>
> The situation has now developed to the point of "no return" for both the Negro and the world. Theorizing is no longer appreciated and gradualism has lost the war. Direct action, even where personally costly for individuals and institutions, is the order of the day. No organization today can earn respect, belief or leadership except on the basis of its own involvement and direct intervention.[78]

Joseph was also ever aware of the African nations that had attained their independence since 1956. Wherever the A.M.E. Church was in Africa, it must support the liberation movements and the governments that came into being. In terms of America, the A.M.E. Church must urge President Johnson to move forward in civil rights, even more rapidly than Kennedy had. Time was running out, and the patience of Blacks was growing exceedingly thin. Those advocating separation and even violence were being listened to. He ended with the hope that his observations would be included in the Episcopal Address.[79]

In preparation for the Quadrennial, the 4th District printed a pamphlet outlining the improvements that had been made during the administration of Bishop Gomez between December 1956 and May 1964. Over some $2,750,000 had been raised and spent in development. For instance, at Camp Baber there was a new Handy Memorial Dormitory and a new chapel. New churches had been constructed in Flint, Windsor, Champaign, Robbins, Madison, Michigan City, Waukegan, and Pontiac, among others. Following a fire that destroyed Ebenezer in Detroit, Rev. Hubert Robinson had purchased a plant at Willis and Brush Streets with forty classrooms, a sanctuary, chapel, gymnasium, social room with stage and lighting, parking lot, and offices. On March 2, 1962, Greater Institutional A.M.E. Church (Rev. Roy Miller, pastor) had organized the first licensed school for exceptional children.[80]

In a section headed "The Bishop Speaks" at the front of the pamphlet, Joseph wrote of this period of his leadership as having been his happiest and most productive.[81] Certainly his record was impressive, not only in physical improvements and acquisitions, but mostly because of his spiritual leadership and civic involvement. The years he spent in the 4th were indeed the mountaintop of his ministry. He hoped the General Conference would see fit to let him remain for at least four more years.

The thirty-seventh Session of the General Conference opened at the Cincinnati Gardens in Cincinnati, Ohio, May 6th, at 10:00 A.M., with the traditional worship service, during which the Quadrennial Sermon was delivered by Bishop Carey Gibbs.[82]

One of the most impressive sessions took place on May 7, designated as Missionary Night. After being entranced by the African singers, the delegates heard a ringing speech delivered by Bishop Frederick D. Jordan, who told the foreign delegates they must demand more money and attention from the Church and must make sure their ideas were seriously regarded. He then introduced Bishop Gow, who reminded the audience of the inhumane treatment Blacks were experiencing in South Africa while many other African nations were being granted independence. Irene Knight, a Liberian attending graduate school in the United States, then sang the Lord's Prayer in Golah, evoking "amens" and "hallelujahs." In closing, Joseph thanked those who had attended and said, "We should know that when we talk about the islands and Africa, we are not talking about the least of our Church but the best."[83]

Dr. Martin Luther King, Jr., addressed the conference on Friday evening, May 6. He applauded the contribution of Richard Allen as a pioneer in civil rights and expressed appreciation for the role the A.M.E. Church was still playing in the struggle; however, he hoped there would be even greater involvement between North and South.[84] Joseph had heard King speak on many occasions, and as usual he was impressed by his dedication to Gandhian principles and his ability to sway people with his oratory.

On May 11, at the Civil Rights Night Session, Walter Reuther of the United Auto Workers; A. Phillip Randolph, president of the Sleeping Car Porters' Union; Roy Wilkins (in absentia), the National Executive Secretary of NAACP; and other civil rights leaders from each of the eighteen districts were honored. Later, further acknowledgements and tributes were given to Bishop Price Taylor, the first Negro appointed as president of the Council of Bishops of the Methodist Church; attorney Herbert Dudley, who was stepping down as president of the A.M.E. Laymen's Organization; and S. L. Weaver, assistant secretary of Labor for International Affairs, who addressed the convention on the evening of May 12, stressing the effect racial incidents in America and Africa would have on the world.[85]

Prior to the election of bishops and general officers, the Episcopal Committee made its final report on May 15th. It recommended the assignment of Bishops Greene, Wright, and Sims to write the Polity of the Church at half salary (plus an additional two thousand dollars) and the election of four new bishops. Joseph had worked untiringly for the election of Hubert Robinson, as had most of the delegates from the 4th. With four new bishops to be elected, they felt that Robinson had a good chance. Their feelings were justified when on the next afternoon Reverends G. Wayman Blakely from St. Louis, H. T. Bearden from Atlanta, Harrison J. Bryant from Baltimore, and Hubert N. Robinson of Detroit became the eighty-first, eighty-second, eighty-third, and eighty-fourth bishops of the African Methodist Episcopal Church. Just as Ransom had conducted the consecration of Joseph, Joseph was now able to present one of his "Sons in the Gospel," Hubert Robinson, to be consecrated to the episcopacy. Assisting were Bishops Bright, Hickman, and Bonner.[86] Joseph's remaining dreams now were to see John Hunter and S. S. Morris elected to the bishopric.

On the final day of the conference, the Episcopal Committee recommended that "the suspension of Bishop D. Ward Nichols be continued for another four years and dealt with by the next General Conference," and that all bishops be required to submit their birth certificates for retirement purposes. When the assignments of the bishops were read, Joseph had been returned to the 4th; Robinson had been sent to the 18th District, in South Central Africa.[87]

Resolutions concerning civil rights had played a major part in the conference. On Friday evening, May 15, Donald Jacobs, now pastor of St. James, Cleveland, rose to resolve that "the African Methodist Episcopal

Church . . . heartily endorse all properly sponsored and well-planned, non-violent demonstrations against racial prejudice and segregation . . . [and that] all the members of the Church including Bishops, ministers, and laity be encouraged to participate in the planning and the direction of such demonstrations," and to support selective buying campaigns. The resolution was unanimously passed. Other resolutions were sent to Congress, urging that Civil Rights Bill, H.R. 7152, be passed and that the "undemocratic device of filibuster" be ended.[88]

On the afternoon of May 18, the General Conference came to an end,

with the delegates and friends from all over the world greeting their Bishops and enjoying the relaxation from two weeks of strenuous actions. . . . The litter and hand bills and surplus reports, many of which could not be considered from press of time, left the Cincinnati Gardens with tons of debris to be consigned to the heap of "What might have been."[89]

CHAPTER THIRTEEN

◈ ◈ ◈

The Golden Years

1964–1968

The shifting patterns of life are always sources of fruitful study
and understanding of men and things. Looking across this half
century of public life and sifting gold from dross, I come up with
buoyant faith in the Providence of God and the worthwhileness
of life. The shadows which I experienced were so many opportunities to probe for light and the deeper meanings of the universe,
to discover good and choose that good as against evil.
        —Bishop Joseph Gomez, 50th Anniversary Remarks,
        November 13, 1964

◈ Joseph's first official function after returning from the General Conference took place in Indianapolis, where he and Hazel were to attend the
Pontifical Low Mass and Testimonial Banquet of the Most Reverend John
Kodwo Amissah, archbishop of Cape Coast, Ghana, West Africa. Amissah
had once been a pupil of Dr. Kwame Nkrumah, president of Ghana. Being
a Black man, his rise in the Catholic Church was singular. He had been ordained for the priesthood on December 11, 1949, at Elmina, his birthplace,
eight miles from Cape Coast. He had been awarded a doctor of canon law
degree by the Urban College in Rome; named Auxiliary Bishop to Rev.
William T. Porter, the Archbishop of Cape Coast, the day after Ghana proclaimed its independence; and appointed archbishop for the Metropolitan See of Cape Coast upon the resignation of Porter, and had been en-
throned in June 1960.[1] Joseph was elated when Father Bernard L. Strange
of St. Rita's Church in Indianapolis asked him to be the principal speaker at
a testimonial banquet given in Amissah's honor.[2]

After getting settled at St. Rita's Rectory, where they and the Archbishop would be staying, the Gomezes attended the Low Mass. The combined choirs of St. Rita's, Holy Angels, and St. Phillip Neri churches set the stage for the sermon delivered by the Reverend Clarence Rivers, a Black priest from Catholic University in Washington, D.C. (Joseph and Hazel had met him on the flight into Indianapolis.) Rivers expanded on the ancient question, "Am I my brother's keeper?" by asserting, "The question is not who is my neighbor, but rather how can we get together. Brothers and Sisters, it is as simple as this: We must love one another, or we will perish."[3]

At the testimonial banquet, Joseph told the 350 assembled guests that the civil rights movement was a "fight to save America from herself. We must win for the sake of the Negro, to be sure," he said, "but also for the sake of America, whose image remains blurred and distorted by the injustices perpetrated in America." He spoke of the significance of the Archbishop's visit to America in terms of the civil rights battle. "It points to the great courage exhibited and the suffering borne by the people of which he is a part." Both remain as "symbols of the eternal vigilance which is the price of liberty," he affirmed. Amissah spoke not only for "his land and his people, but for all in bondage and for all Christians."[4]

Joseph would not easily forget Amissah, with his keen intelligence and dignified bearing, or the words he had written on the back of Joseph's program: "May the good God bless Your Lordship's effort in the Lord's vineyard. God bless the whole family."[5]

On June 5, Joseph became the first Black to deliver the commencement address at Eden Seminary and to be given an honorary doctorate of divinity, just as he had been one of the first Blacks to graduate from Eden.[6] Speaking from the subject, "Dynamics of the Christian Ministry," he offered a challenge to the young seminarians before him. "We must have the conviction before we can convince others that ours is a particular and peculiar calling, ordained of God, commissioned for a special task, subject to the Will of God, with the continuing incitement and inspiration of the Holy Spirit." He reminded them that no other profession could make those claims. In reference to the civil rights bill before Congress, his admonition was that the Christian ministers must lead, because "by nature of our heritage and commitment, we are best fitted to bring to bear moral and spiritual resources to the solution. . . . History fully supports our view."[7]

When Joseph left Webster Grove, he went to Wilberforce to participate in the commencement exercises there, and then on June 12 flew to Washington, D.C., to speak to the thirty-ninth Session of the Church Assembly on Civil Rights, on Capitol Hill. Here once again he emphasized the role the Church must play in the struggle to correct injustices toward Blacks. Although some argued that the pace of the movement was too fast, Joseph urged alacrity, because "the life of the nation and the world is at stake." Even with a victory in the Senate, there was the problem of "the implementation of that victory by the acceptance of the American people in the true spirit of democracy. Complacency may still defeat the final victory." He pointed to the number of churches whose ministers were reluctant to make a strong stand for civil rights for fear they might offend some of their most influential members. These ministers would make the task even more difficult, because "indeed for a while the struggle will grow even more desperate as we witness the death of a mighty giant, old in practice and even wearing the cover of law or respectability, whose habitat is both North and South."[8]

August found the Gomezes again attending the 4th District Annual Conferences. The Canadian Conference was only the first to announce that the district was planning an immense anniversary celebration for the Gomezes' fifty years of marriage and Christian ministry. This event was to take place in Chicago on November 13, 1964. Hazel and Joseph had their own quiet celebration on June 18, the actual day of their wedding, but were looking forward to the district's affair.[9]

There were many important issues discussed and acted upon at the conferences. One was the 1964 presidential election. Although no particular candidate was endorsed, most of the delegates were satisfied with the performance of Lyndon Johnson. He had seen to it that the Civil Rights Act was passed, along with a program to relieve poverty and illiteracy, and a Medicare bill, and he promised to "use the full power of his office in the implementation of these laws." To ensure that this would be done he had formed a citizens committee headed by former Governor Leroy Collins of Florida. One of the members appointed to that committee was Bishop Baber. The Republican candidate, on the other hand, did not support "any of the legislation that would relieve much of the burden of segregation and deprivation of the nation's largest minority." Joseph made sure that all the facts were brought out so members of the conferences could make intelligent decisions in November.[10]

There was great concern among the delegates about the riots that had occurred that summer in New York, New Jersey, Chicago, and Philadelphia, and about the murders of James E. Cheney, Michael Schwerner, and Andrew Goodman, three civil rights workers, following a protest march in Philadelphia, Mississippi.[11] Joseph said he was relieved that Malcolm X had separated from the Black Muslims and was forming the Organization of Afro-American Unity; now perhaps he would add his brilliance to the other civil rights organizations. What an impact he and Martin Luther King would make if they worked together.

In fulfillment of the 4th District's elaborate plans, on Friday, November 13, more than three thousand people jammed into the ballroom of the Sherman House in Chicago to celebrate the Gomezes' marriage and ministry. The entire ballroom was decorated in gold and white, and a large banner inscribed "50th Anniversary" spanned the platform where the speakers were to sit.[12] Eula and Harold; their children, Marvin, Sissy (Little Annetta), and Gerald; Annetta and Curtis; and their two sons, Curtis Jr. and Joseph had flown in from Cleveland for the event.

The daughters commented on how young and radiant their parents looked. Hazel was dressed in a full-length white gown with a white fox fur draped around her shoulders. Joseph had on his customary black suit, white shirt with a clerical collar, and black shoes, except they were "brand spanking new," as Sissy observed.

Soon it was time for the couple to parade into the ballroom behind the twenty-five ministers' wives, dressed in white and gold gowns, who were serving as hostesses. Hazel put her arm through Joseph's as they left the corridor. When they had reached the ballroom the crowd burst into applause. It was some time before the clapping ceased, the guests were seated, and the program could begin.[13]

Finally Bishop Robinson, the master of ceremonies, gave the signal for the singing of the National Anthem by a special ministers' chorus, and then the invocation by Rev. G. W. Brewer. After the choir had sung "How Great Thou Art" (one of Joseph's favorites), greetings were given by Judge Perry B. Jackson, president of the A.M.E. Judicial Council, on behalf of the laymen; John Hunter for the ministers; J. L. Roberts for the Detroit Metropolitan Council of Churches and the Connectional Council of the A.M.E. Church; Russell S. Brown, A.M.E. General Secretary, for the general officers; H. Howard Primm for the bishops; and Dr. Edgar H. S. Chandler for the Church Federation of Chicago.[14]

The grandchildren grew restless and were glad when Eula came forward to sing "Through the Years" for her mother and father. Although she always sang with a great deal of expression, this "sweet and melodic" rendition had special meaning for her and for her parents.[15]

When she ended, the second series of greetings began. Father Bernard L. Strange spoke for the Catholic Church, Sylvester Williams for the Church Civic League of Cleveland, Jean Ferguson for the National

Conference of Christians and Jews, J. H. Jackson for the National Baptist Convention, and J. Quinter Miller of New York for the National Council of Churches.[16]

Bishop Robinson read a letter from Senator Frank L. Lausche, a telegram from Archbishop John K. Amissah, and an editorial which had appeared in the *Cleveland Press*. Then Mayor Richard Daley, who had left his daughter's wedding reception to be present, and Mayor Ralph S. Locher, who had flown in from Cleveland, brought greetings from their cities.[17]

James Gomez had come all the way from Trinidad to present his brother with the Golden Jubilee Medal on behalf of Mayor Edward Taylor. The medal, designated for "outstanding natives and citizens," was being awarded for the first time to someone from outside of Trinidad. The brothers were "deeply moved when Gomez pinned the medal on the Bishop's coat lapel," as he brought the mayor's words of commendation for "this citizen who had, by his leadership, brought honor to Trinidad."[18] James spoke with his usual aplomb, but his hands shook, betraying his feeling of pride for his "big brother" who had come to America and—despite his color, his origin, and the destitution into which his family had fallen before he left Trinidad—had succeeded.

After James had taken his seat, the daughters, their husbands, and children were introduced, along with Lorraine and Alfred Harper, cousins from New York.[19] Lorraine was Amy and Uncle James's daughter, the Uncle James with whom Joseph had lived when he first came to New York in 1908. Throughout the program Hazel and Joseph must have wished their parents and Uncle James had lived long enough to experience this tribute to "Little Joey" from Trinidad, and, as her grandmother Sara used to call Hazel, "that little yellow hussy" from Toledo. How proud they would have been.

The last part of the formal program was taken up with presentations, a golden album of memoirs filled with clippings, programs and pictures, and a book of letters and gifts from the bishops. Joseph Brockington, nattily dressed in a gold dinner jacket, gave Joseph a gold plaque from the Michigan Annual Conference. Hazel received two huge bouquets of roses, which everyone knew were her favorite flowers, one from the Johnson Publishing Company (publishers of *Ebony* and *Jet*), and the other from the Young People's Missionary Department of the 4th District. Then, with a great flourish, Harvey Walden presented the couple with a golden treasure chest of cash gifts from the District. "It was not easy for either Mrs. Gomez or the Bishop to respond to such a copious outpouring of felicitations in such a regal setting, but with brevity, charm and calmness,

Mrs. Hazel Thompson Gomez expressed sincere thanks for all that had been done to make this the most colorful event in her life."[20]

Joseph stood behind the dais looking out at faces so familiar to him. Many he had known since he had first started out in the ministry, an abrupt, sometimes arrogant, young man. Now they expected some profound utterance from him, which he felt inadequate to give. Whatever he would say could not express what he felt at this moment, but he began to speak, slowly at first.

He told how overwhelmed he and Hazel were at "this manifold outpouring of regard and love." This audience had come from all over the country and from abroad "to greet and congratulate two people, who [had] neither sought nor cherished greatness, but [had] tried, sometimes desperately, but at all times honestly, to perform the responsibilities of home, church and society." For him this was not a time to boast but a time for humility. Throughout these years he had learned "increasingly to forget and forgive the wily, ugly persons and circumstances that crossed [his] path, and to cherish and honor the friends and loved ones who [had given] solace and succor to [him]." He thanked God for a "good and wise mother and father, for a devoted family," for his brother who had crossed the ocean to honor him, for "two unusual daughters and families," for the A.M.E. Church which had given him a chance, and for the ecumenical movement that was beginning to bear fruit. He thanked God for his "beloved Father in the Gospel, Reverdy Cassius Ransom . . . for a Son in the Gospel Bonds, Bishop Hubert N. Robinson," for the entire Church, cousins, friends of "all races and faiths who give such unstinted expressions of support and confidence."[21]

Finally, he turned to Hazel, and with tears streaming down his face said, "What more can I say of this woman—my Hazel T.—who for fifty years wrought wonders, who breasted the storms, crossed oceans, endured hardships, cheered my successes, gave wings to my dreams, allayed my fears, turned darkness to light?—Companion, friend, critic, team-mate, mother, wife."[22]

When the formal program had ended, the crowd followed Hazel and Joseph to the rear of the hall, where the couple stopped before a multi-tiered gold and white anniversary cake, and looked up at the tiny bride and groom on top. Joseph placed his hands over Hazel's, and together they cut the first piece of cake. Years later, hidden in the back of their dresser drawer, Annetta found the wedding dolls and several white napkins inscribed in gold.

The *Cleveland Plain Dealer* devoted a half-page to the celebration in its November 14 issue, noting that "the Bishop, who will be 75 on

Thanksgiving day, has been a part of all of Cleveland's civic and religious betterment programs during his 28 year residence. But race relations and church unity are his prime interest."[23]

In the December issue of *Missionary Magazine,* J. W. Yancy of Texas commemorated the anniversary and recalled the many triumphs the Gomezes had had in Texas, especially in race relations. He said, "The benefits of integration in Texas and the beginning of the whole picture was initiated in a large way by Bishop Gomez and his wife. Speaking from nearly every platform in Texas, he launched a program of human equal treatment, the dignity of every race and the role Christians should play in fair play and justice to all men."[24]

The Gomezes' Christmas message for 1964 was a poetic expression of thanks for a year of fulfillment:

> Friend, with grateful hearts we greet you; great
> Joy in contemplation,
> That in this day,
> Of measured time, of changes swift, of sure decay
> And quickened hours,
> We pause to reminisce; and in the process hear
> Kind friends
> In tenderest tones, say:
> "God bless you both. We give you now in
> Rarest form
> Our choicest flowers."
>
> The fragrance of the flowers make captive,
> And fashions into power
> The greetings we outpour.
> To befit this Anniversary span, that like accolades
> From bells that peal
> An endless thanks to God for Church, Family and
> Friends,
> Who gave so much and more
> To make this an unforgettable year.
> Eureka! Fifty years of ministry and connubial weal.[25]

Back in Cleveland, resting and watching television, Joseph saw his regular program interrupted for the announcement that Malcolm X had been assassinated by Black Muslims while speaking at the Audubon Ballroom in New York City. The first thought that came to him was that someone high up in government had ordered Malcolm killed. When he denounced Elijah Muhammad and started his own organization, many powerful people had become afraid of the influence Malcolm might have on the civil rights movement.

By chance Joseph turned on the television Saturday morning and saw Malcolm's funeral; there had been no publicity about its being televised. He heard Ossie Davis's masterful eulogy, in which he said that Malcolm had symbolized "our manhood, our living Black manhood."[26] Joseph turned to Hazel and Annetta, who were watching with him, and said that there was great truth in what Ossie had said. Malcolm had refused to be silenced, even though it cost him his life. In a sense, that was what the entire struggle was all about—immense courage.

On March 31, 1965, Joseph was a part of the Union Meeting of bishops of the A.M.E., A.M.E. Zion, and C.M.E. Churches. The purpose of the meeting was to create an atmosphere that would ultimately lead to the unification of the three great branches of Negro Methodism in America. It was agreed that conversations between the three denominations should continue, "with the hope of consummation by 1972." The ultimate goal should be "an inclusive non-racial Methodism." The Commissions on Church of these denominations should find "pilot union projects, such as the exchange of presiding officers in general meetings, annual conferences, presiding elder districts and episcopal district meetings."[27]

Before adjourning, the organization sent a telegram to President Johnson thanking him for using the sources of the federal government to protect the protest marchers from Selma to Montgomery, for his address to Congress asking for laws that would ensure voting rights for every citizen, and for his pronouncements against the Ku Klux Klan. The meeting informed him that they represented three denominations that had over two and a half million members, all loyal citizens of the United States.[28]

During the Lenten season, Joseph and Dr. Ralph W. Sockman, emeritus pastor of New York's Christ Methodist Church, filled the pulpit at the Old Stone Church on Cleveland's Public Square. At the Monday services, Joseph spoke on the subject, "Conscience and the Cross"; he emphasized the transformation of the penitent thief who hung on the cross next to Jesus. "For the first time he saw his life for what it was, empty and meaningless . . . and had a look into the realities of the new kingdom Christ had come to establish." Joseph summarized his message by assuring the audience that there "is one language the human heart understands, and that is the language of love, tolerance, and courage." This is what the thief had experienced in those last moments with Jesus.[29]

For his Tuesday sermon, Joseph preached from the topic "When Sight Becomes Vision." He used the story of the blind man whose sight Jesus was about to restore. At first the blind man looked up and said, "I see men, as trees walking." Then Jesus put his hands again upon his eyes and his sight was restored; he saw every man clearly. "When at first he saw men as trees, this was only partial vision, a blurred sense of truth." Joseph used the analogy of the world being shackled by blind people or by those whose sight is partially restored. He spoke of this generation as suffering "from a moral and spiritual astigmatism, a lack of symmetry in focus." But sight alone was not enough to cure today's ills. To understand truly and effect change, one must have vision, the ability to see beyond what is, to what can be.[30]

For several months Joseph had been promising Rev. Fred Talbot he would visit the Guyana Annual Conference. A visit in April would correspond with his plans to go to Trinidad to see his family. On April 18, the Gomezes departed from the United States, carrying with them a letter of greetings to Mayor Edward C. Taylor from Mayor Locher of Cleveland.[31]

In Trinidad Joseph embraced Amanda, who was now completely bedridden but comfortably situated in the home he had bought for her. Cyril still seemed unfocused, but he, Oscar, and Junior, Amanda's sons, greeted Hazel and Joseph warmly.

When Joseph went to City Hall to see the mayor, he was presented with a key ring bearing the coat of arms of the city. Afterwards James took him to his house on Rosalino Street. He had had to sell his farm and other properties because of financial reverses that had occurred when he had had his stomach operation in Cleveland. The more James tried to keep up a cheerful front, the more it became obvious to Joseph that James's joy of life had disappeared with his fortune. People who saw him during these last months of his life said he looked much older than Joseph. Joseph had a premonition that this was the last time he would see his brother.

Both the *Trinidad Daily Mirror* and the *Guardian* wrote articles about the visit of the Gomezes and about the racial situation in the United States. Joseph told the *Guardian* reporter that the leaders of the civil rights movement "needed now to determine whether demonstrations are to be continued and to what extent, or whether they should adopt a new technique of protest." He was not sure the Negro "could win complete independence by the methods now being used." More and more Joseph was beginning to think the marches had served their purpose. They had brought about the end of segregation in most public facilities, but Negroes needed more than that: they needed economic and political power.[32]

Instead of resting when he got home, Joseph filled several speaking engagements. He ignored the advice of Drs. Brown and LeFevre of the Cleveland Clinic, who warned that he was overweight and that his blood pressure and blood sugar were high. A few days after delivering the baccalaureate sermon at Morris Brown College in Atlanta, he collapsed on the bathroom floor.[33] Strange noises came from his throat, and his eyes seemed unable to focus. Hazel immediately called for an ambulance, which took him to the Cleveland Clinic, where Dr. Royston C. Lewis, a heart specialist, told her he had suffered a mild heart attack.

When news of his illness became known, flowers, cards, and telegrams filled the hospital room, so many that Hazel had several of the floral arrangements sent to other patients on the floor. On June 21, Joseph was pleasantly surprised to receive a letter from his sister Violet in California, and one from his brother in Trinidad asking about his health. Violet indicated that both she and her daughters had been quite ill. She did not put a return address on the letter, although she did sign it, "Lovingly."[34]

After about three weeks in the hospital, Joseph was released with strict orders that he was to rest for at least another month. Hazel and the daughters did their best to keep him quiet, but he was not a cooperative patient. He insisted on dictating letters to Annetta, writing sermons, calling on the telephone, and preparing for the Annual Conferences, which would begin mid-August. When he received word that his presiding elder and former classmate A. Wayman Ward had died, only a stern warning from Dr. Lewis prevented him from going to the funeral at Greater Bethel, Detroit. Bishop G. Wayman Blakely delivered the eulogy, and several of the bishops offered words of tribute, among them Bishop Robinson, who had returned recently from Africa.[35] Having learned of Joseph's illness, Robinson assured Joseph he would take over or assist with the 4th District Annual Conferences. True to his word, he was at Joseph's side at every one of them.

Prior to the conferences, Joseph attended the ministerial retreat at Camp Baber (August 1–7), where he delivered a series of sermonettes under the title "With Christ in the Outdoors." In the sermonette on Sunday, August 1, he said, "There is great danger that in our mass movements so indicative of our mass psychology and so prevalent in our religion, that each may lose his identity with God and thus become one of the crowd in our worship, devotion and service."[36]

On August 2 he dealt mainly with prayer and how Christ had gone to the open spaces when he sought "rest and spiritual renewal." In the third sermonette he spoke of the orderliness of nature—of how "symmetry and profound intelligence are written everywhere." Nature was a grand symphony, but God's greatest creation was man. Knowledge of this both exults us and shames us—shames us in the realization that we "fall pitiably short in the portrayal of what God is." One of the most interesting sermonettes dealt with man and his environment. What man sees "is largely the reflex of his own mind. The outside scene remains, but the interpretation is man's. In this sense—and a true one—'the pure in heart shall see God.'"[37]

Hazel and Joseph left Camp Baber and traveled to their cottage at Woodland Park for a few days. They spent most of the afternoons riding around the lake on their neighbors' pontoon. (The Bogesses were old friends from Cleveland and former members of St. James.) In the evenings, after a light supper, they read and then went to bed early. Their health and their appetites improved as a result of the country air and the fresh vegetables people brought in profusion from their gardens.

Though still somewhat weak from his heart attack, Joseph flew to Windsor for the first conference during the later part of the second week in August. He found it necessary at times to turn the session over to Bishop Robinson, but at other times it was difficult for anyone to imagine he had ever been sick.[38]

All of the conferences discussed the new Annual Conference Commission on Expansion, which had been appointed to raise emergency money for those churches in need, and funds for the building of new churches. The commission presented its many proposals to the delegates, among them the creation of a pilot group of lay persons whose job would be to develop new church organizations in selected areas. The delegates were filled with anticipation that the success of the commission would lead to the growth of the district and the entire Connection.[39]

The State of the Country reports reflected the aftermath of the Watts Riots, which had dominated the news between August 11 and 16, 1965. Many believed that this was just the beginning of "long, hot summers." The committees recognized the importance of Johnson's having signed the Voting Rights Act on August 6, which "insured a wider franchise at the polls," but they were highly critical of America's involvement in Vietnam. They praised Dr. Martin Luther King for having received the Nobel Peace Prize the previous December and for his efforts to bring his civil rights fight to the North.[40]

In September, between conferences, Hazel received what was to be the last letter from James, in which he asked about Joseph's condition and said that his wife May was looking forward to coming to the United States if nothing happened to disturb her plans. Something did happen. On Monday, November 1, James went to his office as usual but suddenly experienced severe pains in his stomach. He was rushed to the Seventh-Day Adventist Hospital but did not receive attention immediately, because there were so many patients ahead of him. At 4:30 P.M. the doctors operated on him and said the surgery had been successful. The next morning he collapsed and was in a coma until 9:35 in the evening, when he died at the age of sixty-four; he was eleven years younger than Joseph.[41]

Joseph received the news of his death in a letter from Amanda on November 8. In it she said that Violet had cabled May.[42] Joseph was glad, since Violet and James had not been on friendly terms for years. Hazel was afraid that the news of James's death would cause Joseph to have a relapse. Somehow he was able to get through the next days, but he was quieter than usual, and his eyes revealed the depth of his sadness.

On New Year's Day Annetta and Eula were able to offer him some humor when they showed him an article in the *Christian Recorder* by J. W. Yancy, who had visited the Chicago Annual Conference. After lauding Joseph for the success of the conference, he recalled how at one session Joseph had introduced a long line of female visitors. "One good sister of about 50 years handed Bishop Gomez a note. The note read . . . 'Bishop, I think every conference should furnish its own women.'" Yancy recalled how amused the bishop had been. But after "he [told] the church sister that the context of her note could mean many things," he said he understood that she was trying to say the women of the district should attend their own conferences more often so they could have more say in the running of the district.[43]

Annetta then began to talk about other amusing incidents. One Sunday in Texas when her father was preaching, a rather heavy-set, elderly, unattractive woman got happy and began to shout. In her religious zeal she shouted out, "Oh, Bishop! Oh, Bishop! You so good I believe you could sleep in the bed with me and never touch me." Some disgusted brother at the back of the auditorium grunted sarcastically, "Amen!" Annetta had become so tickled that Hazel made her leave the auditorium. Then she reminded her father of the time he was preaching and his new false teeth began to fall out; he put his hand to his mouth and started to moan, like the "Holy Roller" preachers did. Not knowing the cause for his behavior, everyone wondered what had happened to the bishop. Had the Holy Ghost gotten a hold of him? Was he speaking in tongues? This time Annetta had risen from her seat quietly and left before her mother had a chance to ask her to go. She could always send her father into gales of laughter with her stories. And when he laughed, he threw his head back and roared until the tears rolled down his cheeks. Hazel would pretend to be shocked, but Joseph's laughter was so contagious that she was soon holding her sides from laughter. Eula would take in the scene with quiet amusement. She was used to her sister's and father's antics and had heard these stories over and over again.

Joseph began his church activities in the New Year by delivering an address at the Annual Meeting of the Evanston, Illinois, Council of Churches on January 25, 1966. During his speech, "The Ecumenical Outlook," he listed the enemies of church union as ideology; materialism; the scoffers, doubters and iconoclasts; human ambition; exclusiveness; racism; and bigness. He defined union as denominations having the same organic structure, and unity as sameness in plan, program, basic beliefs, and spirit. He was not sure we could ever have "organic union on a practical level without unity of spirit and purpose." Whenever the churches had tried to force union it had resulted "in the creation of further disunity, splinter groups, division more serious and bitter than those existing before." He saw racism as being the greatest enemy of union and unity, and he felt that Christianity itself might "rise and fall on this very issue." What ecumenism should mean is the act of "seeking the mind of Christ and the guidance of the Holy Spirit into advances of mutual respect, trust and brotherly love." No lasting movement could be drawn except "from the heart dictated by Christian love."[44]

At the end of March, Harold, Eula's husband, resigned after ten years from his post as executive secretary of the Cleveland Branch of the NAACP to work as a consultant to David Seeley, acting assistant commissioner in the U.S. Office of Education in the Office of Equal Educational Opportunity. The OEEO was "charged with administering the two parts of the Civil Rights Act dealing with nondiscrimination in school districts." This new job would put him in line for "the newly created job of deputy commissioner for OEEO."[45]

When asked by the reporter of the Cleveland Press what he thought had been the biggest problem during his tenure as executive secretary, Harold said, "I would have to say it was de facto segregation in the schools." This to him was the major defeat of the decade. He noted, however, that when he had first come to Cleveland, "there was no race relations readiness—Negro demands made the back pages; the community was not ready." A large portion of his time had been spent "removing 'white only' signs . . . right here in the northern city of Cleveland." Some of the signs were visible; other were not. But they had been there. He felt his greatest success had come in the "advance of Negro employment in places like banks, the airport, insurance companies, utilities."[46]

At a farewell party for Harold and Eula, over two hundred people crowded into Leo's Casino. Harold told the group he hoped the NAACP would pay more attention to politics and poverty. "Our first job was to establish the security of the individual. Now we must begin to become involved with the problems of the poor and to develop leadership among the people who live in these neighborhoods."[47]

Joseph and Hazel would miss their daughter, son-in-law, and three grandchildren, especially during the holidays and many weekends, when the whole family gathered at the house on Wade Park. Although excited about moving to Washington, Marvin, Annetta, and Gerald hated leaving their grandparents, cousins, and friends, and changing high schools. They had enjoyed their activities and studies at Lutheran East High School, and their home and neighbors on Throckley. (Because of the inadequacy of the Cleveland public schools, both Eula and Annetta had sent their children to Lutheran East.) When they moved, Eula would be the only Black teacher in an elementary school in Arlington, Virginia, where many of the children of members of Congress attended, and where few Blacks were enrolled. She was not looking forward to the change in positions. Meanwhile, Harold went ahead to find housing for the family. Eula and her children would follow in June after her chancel choir concert.

In the spring of 1966, Joseph received a phone call from Mayor Richard Daley apprising him of a new anti-slum program he was planning for Chicago. (No doubt Daley was attempting to counter Dr. Martin Luther King's decision to extend his civil rights movement to the North. On January 26, King and his family had moved into a dilapidated third-floor flat on South Hamlin Street in the West Side of Chicago, where he said he would live until his campaign was completed.[48] Daley's staff was outraged. What did King know about the North? Why didn't he stay where he was? These were some of the same questions being asked by the press. Would the tactics used in the southern campaign succeed in the North? Did King realize what a formidable foe Daley could be? Some of the Black leaders resented King's intrusion and felt they could better solve the problems in their own communities.) During Daley's phone call, he invited Joseph to participate with other Chicago clergymen in a series of three meetings to discuss his anti-slum program and to offer suggestions. He said he had also extended an invitation to Dr. King.

King was unable to attend the first meeting, but on March 25 he was present along with forty other clergymen. This was the first time the Mayor and King had met since King had arrived in Chicago. Daley paraded a line of city officials in front of the ministers. First Police Superintendent O.W. Wilson reported that "more than 100,000 unauthorized firearms" were in Chicago, and he asked those present to have their parishioners turn into the police "any such weapons." Fire Commissioner Robert J. Quinn noted that "accumulated rubbish is the largest single cause of fires and asked the clergy to help by having their congregations avoid such hazards," as well as aiding in "fighting false fire alarms, which seriously hamper the fire department's operations." Building Commissioner Sidney D. Smith said that "1,000 city employees who check for building violations need[ed] the aid of persons in the communities who [could] help fight slums by reporting violations." On the subject of new low-income housing, Charles R. Swibel, chairman of the Chicago Housing Authority, said that six thousand more living units would be added in two years to the thirty-two thousand now run by the CHA.[49]

When the city officials had completed their talks, the mayor turned to King, who sat next to Joseph, quietly listening. King and Daley talked for over thirty minutes as if no one else were present. "King engaged the jowly mayor in a twenty-minute dialogue about riots, stressing the 'collective guilt' of all for the plight of Chicago's Negroes." The mayor countered by saying that many of the city's problems did not originate in Chicago but in the southern states from which the Negroes had migrated. King was disappointed that no one from the school board was present, especially since Chicago had one of the most segregated systems in the North. Daley replied that Frank Whiston, president of the school board, would be in attendance at the third meeting scheduled for the following Thursday. Unfortunately, King could not attend, because he would be in Europe appearing with Harry Belafonte, who was giving a series of concerts to raise money for the civil rights movement.[50]

When Daley asked Joseph for his thoughts concerning the meeting, Joseph said it was a beginning; however, he felt there had been too much emphasis on the effect of poverty and the slums rather than the causes. He hoped the mayor's anti-slum program would eradicate many of these causes and that there would be more progress in terms of school integration.

Joseph told his family and friends that King would have a difficult time with Daley, a shrewd politician who could anticipate King's moves before they could be put into operation. For instance, when King planned a protest march against the irregularity of garbage pickup, Daley had his city workers out the night before collecting garbage in the slums. Joseph was not sure that King really understood the devious, underhanded ways of segregation in the North as he did the overt racism in the South. On the other hand, King's being in Chicago, and his protests, would force the mayor to act positively in getting rid of at least the most obvious violations. In addition, Dr. King gave courage to the masses of Blacks who had to deal with segregation on a daily basis, despite the resistance of some Black leaders who felt they could handle the situation in Chicago without King. Daley had used the old method of divide and conquer, assuring these leaders that his anti-slum program would more efficiently eliminate the slums by 1967 if they would cooperate with the administration. Besides, he had the power to grant political plums as a reward for their support.

"By April, Daley had neutralized King politically, had the mass of Negro voters 'hogtied and hornswoggled' through his own antipoverty projects and promises. . . . He felt strong enough to suggest that King go home to Georgia, and seven Negro ward committeemen seconded him."[51] Only the passage of time would determine whether or not the mayor's meetings and anti-slum program had any effect.

On June 5, the Gomezes attended the Fourteenth Annual Twilight Concert, presented by the Chancel Choir of St. James, organized and directed by Eula. To become a member the singers had to be able to read music and audition; consequently the choir had gained the reputation of being one of the finest church choirs in the city.

The concert consisted of music by Bach and Tchaikovsky, and some spirituals. The guest soloist for the evening was Charles Turner, Jr., a gifted cellist who was a student of Donald White, cellist in the Cleveland Symphony and its only Black member. Charles was accompanied by fifteen-year-old Curtis Jefferson, Jr., who was studying to be a concert pianist at the Cleveland Institute of Music. They gave brilliant renditions of the Concerto in B-flat Major by Luigi Boccherini and the Concerto in D Minor by Eduard Lalo. The final number by the choir was a cantata entitled *Job*, narrated by Annetta.[52] Joseph and Hazel were thrilled with the entire evening. They had always supported their children and grandchildren's artistic efforts and would continue to do so through the years.

That same month, Joseph and Hazel attended the Wilberforce commencement and then returned to Chicago for the Bishops' Council, at which Sargent Shriver, director of the Office of Economic Opportunity, was scheduled to address the meeting about job openings for Blacks and the programs his office was launching. When Joseph returned to Cleveland he found a letter from Shriver, dated June 17. He spoke of the "great pleasure" it had been to be able to talk to the bishops and "to share the platform with [Joseph]." In his program to eliminate poverty he had from the beginning hoped "for the participation of all religious groups." He looked forward to continuing his "relationship with the African Methodist Episcopal Church, which has worked so long and hard for the poor of the world."[53]

Joseph had received a letter from Charles Spivey, Sr., who had been in Chicago during the Council meeting. After speaking of the difficulties he was having in his new job as head of the Sunday School Union because of indebtedness and internal politics, his letter became more personal, echoing Joseph's growing philosophy. Spivey wrote, "As I grow older, friendships become more and more meaningful. You and I have come a mighty long way. I went over the list the other day to find that only here and there is there one left."[54] Joseph too had begun to count the list of those who had departed this life—friends whose places could never be filled. Now more than ever he thought about Reverdy Cassius Ransom and what Ransom had meant in his life.

That June Joseph read how Dr. King had taken leave from his Chicago campaign to continue "the James Meredith March against Fear." During a Memphis, Tennessee, to Jackson, Mississippi, voter registration drive Meredith had been shot down by a sniper. King and several other civil rights groups had continued the march where Meredith left off. Before the group had reached its destination, it was obvious that the younger marchers were growing tired of non-violence and the fight for integration. Some were even reported to have guns. Throughout the ranks they murmured against continuing to follow the previous goals of the movement. On the way back from the Grenada Court House, in Greenwood, Mississippi, Stokely Carmichael—who had been jailed for trying to put up tents in a Negro schoolyard—joined the march. He told the group he was never going to jail again. "The only way we gonna stop them white men from whuppin' us is to take over. We been saying freedom for six years and we ain't got nothin'. What we gonna start saying now is Black Power!"[55] This marked the beginning of the end of the civil rights movement as it had been.

Joseph read with interest and some alarm the accounts of the march. He had always believed in Black Power, but not the kind that was based on hatred and violence. Black Power to him meant pride in one's race, culture, and heritage, he told his daughters. It meant spiritual, economic, educational, and political strength, control of one's community, but also freedom of choice in all arenas of life. Black Power was not anti-White, but very definitely pro-Black. Richard Allen had understood the concept of Black Power and had used it as the basis for founding the African Methodist Episcopal Church. Carmichael's use of the word sounded anti-all-whites. Joseph wondered where the movement was headed. Was King losing ground?

Black Power and impatience with gradualism was growing among Black youth in Cleveland as well. On Wednesday, June 22, two Blacks were attacked by a white mob; Blacks "gathered at superior and 90th street" demanding that the police find and arrest the attackers. The police made no move to investigate the situation, saying there was crime all over the city and they were understaffed. This only angered the community further. The following Thursday a young Black was shot, reportedly by "two white men in a blue Corvair." One of the men resembled the owner of a supermarket on Superior. Again the police did nothing; in retaliation Blacks set fire to the supermarket and harassed other white businesses in the area. When the mayor promised to look into the matter, things quieted down for a short period.[56]

July 18, 1966, marked the beginning of the Hough riots. Addison Junior High, where Annetta had once taught, was in Hough. Even then she had been able to see the neighborhood was decaying, crying out for attention, so the events that followed were no surprise. On that evening in July someone put up a sign on a bar on 79th Street that said, "No Water for Niggers." Black people began to congregate in front of the bar, and the white manager and a friend came out with a shotgun and a pistol. The police arrived and "in their attempt to 'disperse the crowd,' began to push and shove individuals from the vicinity of the bar. Nearby stores became the targets of rocks. The crowd began to spread" and go out of control.[57]

The riot lasted for a week, during which four Blacks were killed, many others were wounded, and stores and buildings were burned to the ground. Hough resembled a battlefield. Over 2,200 National Guardsmen patrolled the neighborhood, and people who did not live in the area were warned to stay out. The Cuyahoga County grand jury later conducted an investigation; it concluded the riot had been started by a few well trained militants who were influenced by the communists. "Mayor Locher congratulated the grand jury for having 'guts to fix the approximate cause which had been hinted at for a long time, that subversive and Communist elements in our community were behind the rioting.'"[58]

Most Blacks, including Hazel and Joseph and their family, found the conclusions of the grand jury ludicrous. First of all, there were no representatives from Hough on the panel; how then could the members accurately assess the causes of the mayhem? Secondly, as Joseph had been preaching all his life, when people are powerless to control their own destinies, when they lack the bare necessities of existence, they explode! Hough had simply exploded, and there was no need for any communist matches to start the fire. The flames had sprung from human frustration and deprivation. Joseph believed the Church Universal had to play a major role in addressing the causes of riots in large cities throughout the country, rather than merely the effects.

In August, Joseph and Hazel left Cleveland to attend the World Methodist Council in London. In London the bishops decided that the next council meeting would be held in Washington, D.C., at which time they hoped to meet with President Lyndon Johnson.[59]

As planned, promptly at 11:20 A.M., September 27, 1966, a motorcade of cars furnished by the A.M.E. ministers of Washington pulled up to the West Gate of the White House. The bishops were met by Secret Service agents, who took them to the Cabinet Room, where they were to wait for the president.[60]

Johnson did not arrive until 11:55 A.M., because he was in conference with Chancellor Ludwig Erhard of Germany. When he entered the room, he walked around the table and shook hands with everyone. Bishop Baber introduced the bishops and told the president which districts they represented. After that Bishop Hatcher, now president of the Council of Bishops, read the Council's statement, which had been prepared by Bishops Baber, Blakely, Bright, Gomez, and Hatcher.

It began by commending the president for the accomplishments of the Great Society and the hope that this was the prelude to the elimination of all traces of segregation in America. Johnson, in turn, asked the bishops "to use the Church's 7,000 pulpits to drown out the ugly sounds of racial unrest [because Blacks] may lose more than they gain." He said he believed the violence that was occurring in the inner cities would keep people from listening to reason, consequently undoing all the progress of the civil rights movement to date. "You must help me," the president pleaded. "And we are not getting at it any too soon. I think we can head it off. I'm depending upon you for help." Johnson reminded the group that he had only one pulpit, while they had seven thousand; nevertheless he promised "that as long as he was President he would use the White House to bring his Great Society program to the nation."

He hoped the bishops would spread optimism to the people and assured them "a better day is dawning, a more secure society is on the horizon. We are getting in sight of that promised land," he said. He would not, he assured them, tell the 1.3 million members of the A.M.E. Church how to vote, "but would ask them to vote in a show of responsibility of freedom Negroes are gaining." He warned that the Church could not afford to stand aside from today's problems "but must take a part in politics and social change. Civil rights, better housing, better health, better food, the war against poverty, and all the Great Society programs are matters for the pulpit."

The meeting ended with a prayer given by Bishop R. R. Wright, who was in his eighty-eighth year. He prayed that "the judgment of history, as well as the judgment of God [would] write [Johnson's] name among other . . . great presidents as Washington, Lincoln, Roosevelt and Kennedy." Before they left Johnson told Joseph that Sam Rayburn had often spoken highly of him and his many accomplishments in Texas. He hoped Joseph would continue to fight in his district and in Cleveland. Joseph promised he would, thanked him, shook the president's hand, and followed the other bishops out to the waiting cars.

Although Joseph was opposed to the conflict in Vietnam, a war that would be the undoing of Johnson, he felt that history would record that Johnson had done more for civil rights than either Roosevelt or Kennedy. In Joseph's opinion, he was a man who had grown into the responsibility and integrity demanded by the office and the age. As a bishop in Texas Joseph had not been much impressed with Johnson, but he now sensed a moral passion in Johnson to do the right and fair thing. He had heard the president was overbearing, dictatorial, and stubborn; even if this were true, it did not detract from his record in terms of civil rights. Joseph was glad that he and the other bishops had been able to meet him personally. A few years before, when some of them had met with Kennedy, they had admired his intelligence and the obvious class he brought to the White House, but they had found him aloof and controlled. This was not true of Johnson, who exuded a great deal of warmth.

As had been the case throughout the '60s, the 1966 Annual Conferences were again largely dominated not only by church matters but also by public events. The Michigan Conference voted to join the Equal Opportunity Project sponsored by the dioceses of the Catholic Church, the Metropolitan Council of Churches, the Council of Jewish Synagogues, and the Greek Orthodox churches in their campaign to persuade companies with whom they did business to hire Blacks, and to boycott those who did not comply.[61]

During the Wednesday evening session of the Chicago Conference, Mayor Lloyd L. Turner presented Joseph a plaque "in recognition of [his] Christian statesmanship and outstanding service." Next the conference endorsed Archibald Carey for a judgeship on the Circuit Court of Cook County in the upcoming November elections. Before the conference adjourned, Joseph appointed two committees, one composed of involved citizens who pledged to work "in conjunction with Al Raby and Dr. Martin Luther King in their effort for civil rights on the southwest side of Chicago, the other to investigate the feasibility of getting scholarships from the Federal Government for students to attend Wilberforce University and Payne Theological Seminary."[62]

Hazel was pleasantly surprised at the Indiana Conference on September 30, when a minister's wife presented her with a portrait of Joseph painted by an inmate at Michigan State Prison from a snapshot.[63] The portrait was a good likeness and an appropriate finish to a highly successful series of conferences.

Just before Christmas Joseph attended the Triennial Session of the National Council of Churches in Miami, Florida, where he was elected vice president along with Bishop Bertran W. Doyle (C.M.E.) from Nashville and Mrs. Jesse Jai McNeil (Baptist) from Dallas. Dr. Arthur S. Fleming (Methodist), president of the University of Oregon, was elected the new president of the Council.[64]

Christmas 1966 brought the entire family together again. As they had every Christmas, they gathered around the large dining room table on Wade Park and gave thanks for each other and for the fact that Joseph had almost completely recovered from his 1965 heart attack. They also prayed that the racial climate in Cleveland would greatly improve.

After Annabelle Hicks, the housekeeper and an important part of the family, had cleared away the remains of Hazel's traditional Christmas chocolate cake, they retired to the front room to open presents, receive the numerous friends who always came to call on Christmas Day, and be entertained by the grandchildren. Curtis Jr. played the piano, Marvin the violin, Joseph the trumpet, and Sissy, Gerald, and Toni Jo (Jane's daughter) danced and participated in a skit they had put together on the spur of the moment. For the day at least the violence and hatred outside seemed far away. Hazel and Joseph felt a sense of well-being, as they always did when the family was together.

To everyone's surprise, the summer of 1967 was a relatively quiet one in Cleveland. Many attributed the truce to the fact that Carl B. Stokes was again challenging Locher for mayor, as he had done in 1965, when he had run as an independent. This time he was running as a Democrat, and many felt he had a good chance of becoming the first Black mayor of a major city. In the primary election on October 4 he defeated Locher by eighteen thousand votes, mainly because of the large turnout of Black voters. Now he would have to beat Seth Taft in the general election.[65] He would certainly have the votes of the Gomezes and Jeffersons. Carl was well known by them, and he and his brother Louis had been good friends of Eula and Harold and had worked with Harold in the NAACP.

Nine months before the 1968 General Conference, Joseph started his last round of Annual Conferences as prelate of the 4th Episcopal District with the words, "We go to Philadelphia! The God of our fathers, who has brought us through some difficult days, will be with us there. Remember this then, whatever befalls, God will be leading us on."[66]

Beginning with the Canadian Conference in Toronto in August, Joseph strongly urged the Church to take a stand on Black Power and "stress [the Church's] opposition to violence." Although he acknowledged that the natural outcome of continued racism is violence, he reasoned that the Watts riot of 1965 and the riots in Chicago and Hough in 1966 had resulted in Black people being killed and their own property destroyed. In July the rioting in Detroit had resulted in forty deaths, four thousand injuries, over four thousand arrests, and property damage in the millions.[67] It was suicide to believe that a minority could succeed by violent means when the opposition had all the weapons and control of the military. Like Martin Luther King, Jr., he believed that love was the strongest, most positive force in the universe. Love became his theme for 1967.

On Sunday afternoon, September 17, at the Chicago Annual Conference, Joseph and Hazel marched with other A.M.E.'s to the auditorium of Du Sable High School at 49th and State streets where Joseph addressed the audience on the subject, "The Preaching of the Cross." He told them that the "foolishness of God is wiser than the wisdom of men—Christ not only preached love, but lived love. . . . We are all mixed up about freedom, for freedom does not give us the right to burn, loot and destroy. . . . Freedom makes a man love, even his enemy."[68] And yet the summer of 1967 had been one of violence in Newark, Detroit, and Chicago, if not in Cleveland.

At the Illinois Conference (September 26–October 1) the Committee on the State of the Country argued that the politicians were using the riots to justify their slowness in passing civil rights legislation. One of the biggest setbacks to Blacks was the defeat in the Senate of "a Civil Rights Bill which would have outlawed Jim Crow juries, given the Attorney General of the U.S. more authority to bring suits against segregated school and public facilities and would provide protection for Negroes and civil rights workers exercising their rights." King had remarked after the bill failed that a lot of people had lost faith in America; Roy Wilkins had said, "This defeat was a kick in the teeth to the civil rights effort."[69]

Another setback occurred when "the Congress of the United States showed that it was as guilty of double-standards and double-dealings as the local white community." It had stripped Adam Clayton Powell of his office and seniority, whereas when Senator Thomas Dodd of Connecticut committed the same offense, he was not given the same harsh punishment. The only positive news reported by the committee was Johnson's appointment of Solicitor General Thurgood Marshall to the Supreme Court, and the possibility of several Blacks being elected mayors of large northern cities. As it turned out, Johnson appointed Walter E. Washington mayor of Washington, D.C., Carl Stokes was elected mayor of Cleveland, Floyd McCree mayor of Flint, Michigan, and Richard B. Hatcher mayor of Gary, Indiana.[70]

At all of the conferences it was difficult for Joseph to preach love to the ministers and laity, who were angry, frustrated by America's refusal to respond to Blacks' just demands for equal participation in the democratic process. But he had to speak his convictions, even though he too had known some dark days when his faith had wavered momentarily. Sometimes when listening to the younger ministers he wondered if he had lived too long—if he were out of tune with reality. In the 1920s, in his fight for immediate integration, he had been considered a "flaming radical." To a growing number of Blacks now, however, integration was viewed as a conservative goal. Some of the Black Power advocates in Newark were now calling for a partitioning of the U.S. into two independent nations, one White, and one Black.

Since 1967 was the year before the thirty-eighth session of the General Conference, the concerns of the Annual Conferences were not all centered on civil rights. The District as a united body endorsed the candidacies of Rev. S. S. Morris of Chicago for the bishopric; Rev. Harvey Walden as chairman of the powerful Episcopal Committee; Russell Brown as Church general secretary; Ralph Jackson as director of the Department of Minimum Salary; and Charles S. Spivey, Sr., as secretary-treasurer of the Sunday School Union. The district also sent a resolution to the Episcopal Committee that Bishop Joseph Gomez be returned to the 4th for four more years, even though the members knew that his time was up and the likelihood of the Church reassigning him was slim.

At the closing Sunday afternoon service the congregation sang prophetically, "God Be with You Till We Meet Again," the same hymn the members of St. James, Cleveland, had sung in 1948 when Joseph departed to assume his new responsibilities as bishop of Texas. It seemed fitting that he should preach from John 14:27, "My peace I leave with you, my peace I give unto you."[71]

On November 26, Joseph quietly celebrated his seventy-seventh birthday with his family on Wade Park, after which he composed his Christmas greeting. The message reflected his consciousness of how many friends had died over the past few years, and of the problems facing those who, like him, still remained.

We feel overwhelmed and well-nigh spent against the frustration so potent in the Viet-Nam struggle, the Mid-East conflict, United Nations ineffectiveness, internecine strife, particularly among new nations, born of despair, yet withal a yearning for freedom. And what of our racial riots and of our disturbed and disturbing national temper? What of the alarming growth of crime, the youth rebellion, and the general collapse of personal and social morality? Have we devised an approximately sure method to combat the curse of poverty, disease and ignorance? Is our faith "sufficient unto the day"?[72]

He reiterated the meaning of the season—the realities that abide in the Christmas story: "For here Hope grows stronger as we enter the sacred presence of Bethlehem. Never such love and service in fulfillment!" He hoped that the vision of Christmas might "illuminate new altars of peace and brotherhood, and thus create more enduring bridges of understanding for generations to come."[73]

◈ ◈ ◈

CHAPTER FOURTEEN

Africa at Last

The Polity & Zambia, 1968–1972

> It would not be too far afield to say that a new heaven and a new
> earth are aborning before our very eyes. . . . Whether in anger
> and hate or in love and service, we are destroying the old and re-
> making the face of the earth. And who are we to say, even those
> of us who abhor violence and destruction, that some divine will
> and purpose is not seen in the creating of a new heaven and earth
> wherein righteousness shall dwell? Out of the shambles of the
> past we resurrect the New Jerusalem.
> —Bishop Joseph Gomez, "The New Society of God,"
> General Conference, Philadelphia, 1968

February 9, 1968, Joseph held his Mid-Year Convocation at Coppin
A.M.E. Church in Chicago. That evening, at the new Youth Center built
under the leadership of Rev. S. S. Morris, Hazel was awarded the distinguished Layman's Award "for her contributions, leadership, meritorious
service and Christian precept and example over the past four years."[1] She
had been a favorite with the ministers and lay persons of the 4th, and they
would miss her when she left.

Letters written by Joseph in March indicate his preoccupation with the
General Conference. He had heard that a group of ministers were determined to retire Bishops Bonner, Gibbs, and himself; in a letter to Dr. J. L.
Leach he said he was "fairly well convinced now that generally the men
[were] in no mood for retiring." A redistricting plan, which would mean
the creation of more episcopal districts, would satisfy those men who
were determined to retire the older bishops so two new bishops could be
elected.[2]

National crisis took precedence over Church matters when on April 4, at 6 P.M., Martin Luther King, who was in Memphis to march with sanitation workers, was shot—allegedly by James Earl Ray—while standing on the balcony of the Lorraine Hotel. Hazel and Joseph watched with horror as the story unfolded on national television. When it was confirmed that King had been assassinated, the nation entered a state of shock, particularly the Black community. Shock was replaced by unrestrained anger: riots broke out all over the country, including Washington, D.C. Stokely Carmichael said, "When White America killed Dr. King last night she declared war on us. It would have been better if she had killed Rap Brown . . . or Stokely Carmichael. But when she killed Dr. King, she lost it. . . . Dr. Martin Luther King was the last prince of nonviolence."[3]

Realizing that many Blacks would interpret Carmichael's words as a summons to violence, Joseph called his leading pastors in the larger urban centers and instructed them to get out into the streets and counsel the people. Joseph seemed to be on automatic pilot in a world gone mad. Only a month earlier he had been in Memphis helping to dedicate the new Minimum Salary Building of the A.M.E. Church. The mayor of Memphis had reassured the gathering that racial matters there were getting better.[4] Now "The King" was dead, and so, Joseph suspected, was the civil rights movement in its present form. God only knew what direction the struggle would take next. The innocent faith manifested in "We Shall Overcome" had been silenced in Memphis. Only rapid, positive action by a reluctant federal government could hold back the tide of retaliation.

In the wake of civil and spiritual unrest, the thirty-eighth session of the General Conference opened May 1 at Mother Bethel, Philadelphia, the church founded by Richard Allen. After opening services, the delegates assembled at the tomb of Richard Allen for prayer and then moved to the Spectrum, on Broad and Patterson streets, for the regular morning session. Bishop Wilkes read the names of the bishops who had died during the past four years: Sherman L. Greene Sr., on July 26, 1967; R. R. Wright, December 12, 1967; Francis H. Gow of South Africa, March 29, 1968, just two months before the General Conference convened. Following the reading, Bishop Eugene Hatcher delivered the Quadrennial Sermon, and the conference was officially ready for business.[5]

That the frustrations of the times had spilled over into the conference became obvious at the afternoon session, when there was a lengthy, heated debate about seating arrangements. A short recess to resolve the problems did not help. When the conference reconvened, added to the dissatisfaction with the seating was the problem of malfunctioning microphones on the floor. Somehow the conference struggled through the first few days; delegates were finally seated, and the planned program began.[6]

On Thursday morning, May 2, it was Joseph's turn to preside. He closed the regular business session at 11 A.M. at the request of the Secret Service, who wanted to ready the building for the visit of Vice President Hubert Humphrey.[7]

That afternoon the delegates sang "My Country, Tis of Thee" as the vice president came down the aisle to the rostrum, escorted by the bishops, and stepped up to the microphone to thunderous applause. He first recalled two earlier conventions held in Philadelphia. One was the first convention of the A.M.E. Church in 1816. "Your heritage is from men and women who stood up for freedom back before most people ever knew what it meant—and from those who sustained it through the century and a half of its loneliness."[8]

The second convention took place "a hundred and thirty years later." This time it was a convention of the Democratic party. "A group of us," Humphrey said, "small at first, demanded at that convention that humanity be placed above politics." The group could not claim the same courage as that shown by Richard Allen; "It was more than a century too late for that." Nevertheless, its convictions matched Allen's. "I was privileged to lead that fight," he said, "to protest before that convention this nation's too-small 'faith in the brotherhood of man under the fatherhood of God'—to answer when they said we were 'rushing the issue of civil rights' that 'we were already 172 years late.'"

The small group had won that fight. "Those who disagreed left the convention," and the Democrats won the election that year. It was, he said, the turning point of civil rights. Humphrey had sat in the pews of Ebenezer Baptist Church in Atlanta at Dr. King's funeral. One of the ministers standing behind the coffin had asked in his prayer, "Do we face, O Lord, community or chaos?" As if to answer that question, Humphrey now noted that the President's Commission on Civil Disorders had reported that America was moving "toward two societies, one black, one, white, separate and unequal."

Humphrey said, "I did not mention idly either your history or mine— what the African Methodist Episcopal Church stands for. I think you know what I stand for." He believed that he and this body of A.M.E. delegates could say to each other what might elsewhere be misunderstood by both whites and blacks: "The vast majority of people in this country who are white are not racists; the overwhelming majority of people in this country who are black are not rioters; and most of us, black and white, are praying today and working today for the same things for our children." He recognized that whites had often been in the wrong, but he also knew that "there [had] been more gains in the last five years than in the hundred years before them. And the eye hath not seen nor the ear heard what things we can do together, united, determined and unafraid." At his conclusion "the conference, greatly inspired, applauded wildly and spontaneously, and in one accord rose to sing 'We Shall Overcome.'" Humphrey shook the hands of all the bishops on the platform as cameras flashed throughout the auditorium.

Joseph never forgot Humphrey's speech. It came at a time when he sorely needed his hope renewed. Despite Humphrey's optimism, and his naive assertion that most whites in America were not bigots, Joseph was sure that the vice president was a principled man who still dared to dream in a world which killed dreamers. Surely there must be more whites like him, if only a few. Maybe that was all that was needed to change things— just a few.

Joseph was scheduled to deliver the morning sermon on the following Sunday. Before he preached, Eula, who had flown in from Washington, D.C., sang "Sometimes I Feel Like a Motherless Child" with such richness that there were few dry eyes in the auditorium. Her lament echoed the feelings of most Blacks in 1968. Joseph then introduced his text, "The New Society of God," from Revelations 21:1–2: "And I saw a new heaven and a new earth; for the first heaven and the first earth were passed away. And I saw the Holy City, New Jerusalem, coming down from God out of heaven."

He began by speaking of John the Revelator, who had been banished to the Isle of Patmos. There God gave him visions of the future. Comparing John's vision of a new heaven and earth with the 1960s, he spoke of the riots; he believed they too would pass, "and that young and old [would] come to realize that every act of violence is a negation of the spirit and philosophy of the martyr whose immortality was sealed with the bullet of the assassin." Martin Luther King had been ready to give his life, if necessary, as a sacrifice for freedom. Joseph recalled the momentous speech at the March on Washington. "'I have a dream,' [King] cried again and again, a dream of a new America, where his children and all disinherited people shall find liberty and justice.'" This did not mean that a new day was inevitable. It did not mean that "the vision is fulfilled completely; but we are definitely on the way. I have come to tell you not to be dismayed by the awesome spectacles that greet your eyes. 'The vision is for an appointed time. Though it tarry, it will come. It will surely come.'"[10]

He ended by pledging that whatever disappointments the General Conference may bring, we have exaulted, singly and together; we have cheered and shouted; we have shaken hands and embraced, as the joy of reunion so dear to African Methodists warmed our hearts and brought tears to our eyes. And through these mists, and the noise of our dialogues, the heat and passion of debates, we saw a new Church, ultimately responsive to the needs of the new day, to the new generation of people.[11]

The "amens" that followed what many referred to as this "eloquent, prophetic message" continued well into the invitational hymn, "Life Is Like a Mountain Railroad." It was clear that the seventy-eight-year-old bishop had lost none of his passion or his ability to move an audience.[12]

At the Monday evening session, Roy Wilkins, executive secretary of the NAACP, spoke about his life as the son of an A.M.E. minister and about the vice president's visit to the conference. Wilkins blamed the riots on the prejudiced white group, who had done nothing to bring about equality. "In his opinion, the whole mission of the Church must be to change attitudes, to change the souls and the hearts of people. This, he said, would remake the face of the earth." That evening the delegates gave a generous contribution for the work of the NAACP, even though many of the young people thought of it as passé.[13]

During the Wednesday session, the Episcopal Committee reported that all members had passed on the character, physical well-being, and deportment of the bishops. Since all seventeen bishops were able to travel and a resolution to create no new districts had been passed the day before, it was their determination that only one new bishop should be elected. This did not please many of the ministers who were running for the bishopric; they would have to create some alternate plan so that at least two, and maybe three, bishops could be elected. Meanwhile, the conference proceeded as scheduled.[14]

That afternoon, Dr. Arthur Bonhomme, ambassador of the Republic of Haiti, brought greetings from the president of Haiti, Dr. François "Papa Doc" Duvalier, who wanted A.M.E.'s to know that "the Republic of Haiti would remain the sacred bulwark . . . of Negroes the world over." Joseph knew well the history of Haiti's struggle for independence but felt that Duvalier had betrayed that history and was more interested in his own personal gain than he was in the welfare of his people.[15]

Following this greeting the young people presented a resolution on behalf of supporters of the Rebirth of African Methodism. They asked the Church to organize a metropolitan ministry, an A.M.E. campus ministry, and an A.M.E. special youth ministry, and to take a definite position on the crisis in the nation. Joseph and Andrew White, secretary of the Division of

Christian Education, strongly supported their resolution, and the Church went on record as "favoring that adequate provisions be made for youth activities." Adequate provision was hardly the response the youth were looking for. Many felt that other denominations had left the A.M.E. Church far behind in their involvement in civil rights and social programs. They departed from the session frustrated but determined.[16]

On May 6, the Episcopal Committee announced that it was the unanimous vote of the committee that Bishop D. Ward Nichols be expelled from the episcopacy. After much discussion, the conference went into Executive Session. On the strength of Nichols's statement that he would never again take the Church to court, the General Conference voted to reinstate him.[17]

At the same session, Rev. U. A. Hughey read a resolution recommending that Bishops Gomez, Bonner, and Gibbs be assigned to writing the Church Polity as opposed to being given districts. Bishop John Bright ruled that the resolution was not in order, since "a prior resolution had established the desire of the General Conference to permit the Episcopal Committee the right to assign Bishops."[18]

On Friday afternoon, May 10, Hughey read another resolution, that "special assignments be given to coordinate the ecumenical activities of the A.M.E. Church and the completion of the polity and history of the A.M.E. Church." Those who opposed the resolution said the call for special assignments was purely political, an attempt to make way for the election of two more bishops, which the church could ill afford. Nevertheless, when Bishop Blakely called for a standing vote, the resolution was passed. Joseph saw immediately what the strategy would be. Since two bishops would be called upon to head these departments, this would leave two districts vacant. More than likely, Fred Jordan, who was already heavily involved in ecumenical affairs, would be asked to head the Department of Urban Ministry and Ecumenical Relations, and Joseph would be asked to write the polity. There was no doubt in Joseph's mind that the resolution was politically inspired, and he was deeply hurt. He became even more distressed when some of his friends urged him to accept the assignment. He tried to erase from his mind the thought that they too might have helped to plan the strategy.[19]

At the May 11 session, Bishop Frederick D. Jordan asked to make a brief statement. Several bishops and others had told him he could render the Church a great service if he would agree to head an office dealing with urban ministry and ecumenical relations. Jordan felt that to do so would be a real challenge, but he made it clear that if he were assigned to the work, he would want his status "as a fully active Bishop unchallenged . . . and that either the church not create such an office, or adequately fund it."[20]

At the same session Joseph proposed a resolution asking for "immediate and more effective cooperative efforts on the part of the Council of Bishops and the Department of Social Action to join in or initiate such civic and moral efforts as possible so as to give to all the people the urgent and decisive leadership so desperately needed in these critical days." In an earlier resolution, he had asked that the conference establish a "freedom budget" to be used for social action to:

Provide full employment for all who are willing to work.

Assure decent and adequate wages.

Insure a decent living standard for those who cannot work or should not work.

Wipe out slum ghettos, and provide decent homes for all Americans.

Provide medical care and adequate educational opportunities to all Americans at a cost they can afford.

Purify air and water, and develop transportation facilities.

Unite sustained full employment with sustained full production and high economic growth.

Both resolutions were seconded and passed.[21]

The Episcopal Committee passed on the character of Bishop Nichols and agreed to assign active bishops to the urban communities and to the writing of the polity of the Church. The report was adopted by the conference.[22] Joseph was not surprised, nor did he believe that the assignment to the polity lacked importance. But he had never been without a church or district, and he was not sure how well he would function without them.

The elections of the general officers and the bishops took place on May 11. Several general officers were elected on the first ballot, but no bishop received a majority. When the elections were completed, almost all of the general officers endorsed by the 4th Episcopal District had been elected. Rev. G. Dewey Robinson, a former chaplain and resident of Washington, D.C., and Rev. Henry Murph of Los Angeles, California, were elected bishops. The 4th District's endorsed candidate for the bishopric, Rev. S. S. Morris, had been defeated.[23]

The assignment of bishops was read by the Episcopal Committee on the final day of the conference. As expected, Joseph was made head of the Bureau of Polity, and Bishop Frederick Jordan was given the Office of Urban Ministries and Ecumenical Relations. All others, including Bishop Nichols, were assigned districts. Bishop H. Thomas Primm had been sent to the 4th District, and Bishop H. N. Robinson to the 9th district (Alabama).[24]

Joseph and Hazel left the conference with mixed feelings. They were convinced that many innovative and progressive programs had been created, including the Bureau of Church Polity, regardless of the reason it had come into existence. They were also pleased with the renewed interest and strong urgings of the young people. The visits of the vice president and Roy Wilkins had been invigorating. As Joseph said in a letter to Judge Sidney Jones of Chicago dated May 22,

> I confess that there were times in that General Conference when I too was somewhat discouraged; but one has to pick out the dross from the fine gold always.
>
> I believe that on the whole we have done many things to our credit, and the Fourth District had many gains. Our greatest loss was in not electing S. S. Morris to the Bishopric. I find for him tremendous respect and in many quarters affection for what he has been and done in the Church.[25]

In another letter, dated May 23, to Dr. J. L. Leach of Flint, Michigan, Joseph wrote that there had been a great deal of support for Bishop Hubert Robinson to replace him as prelate of the 4th District, and although Robinson had received the largest amount of votes from the Episcopal Committee, Robinson and Joseph "decided with some other friends that it might be best for him not to come to the fourth at this time."[26]

Joseph also wrote to Rev. and Mrs. Morris on the same day expressing encouragement and friendship. He hoped they had recovered from the General Conference. It had been difficult. "Trying to evaluate that whole experience, the conclusion is evident that we were face to face with forces that were beyond our powers to cope, particularly in the way the game was played," he wrote. But, he reminded Morris, "No man is defeated until his spirit is conquered." Joseph equated this election of the bishops to the one in Philadelphia in 1944 when votes had been stolen from him. "I had a vision of my election as I had of yours, but it was not to be." The morning after, God had come to Joseph with a message that strengthened him. He saw then that actually "what had happened was that God gave [him] the election, but that man decreed it otherwise," and he had to wait four more years. "Those four years of waiting were among the richest of my life," he recalled. He begged Morris not to give up but to begin then to work toward the next General Conference. Joseph regretted that his health was not as good as it had been in previous years. But the optimist as always, he ended the letter by saying, "Perhaps in this new position I shall have more time, in the Connectional sense, to give even greater service than I have before."[27]

As Joseph prepared for his new assignment, he reviewed the work done previously by Bishop Sherman L. Greene and planned to read the book on polity written years earlier by Bishop H. M. Turner. Rev. Hanley A. Hickey, dean of Payne Seminary now, was kind enough to send him the Turner polity, but Mrs. Greene was reluctant to let her husband's manuscript be used. Meanwhile, Joseph and Hazel had to go to Washington, D.C., to their granddaughter's (Sissy's) "Coming Out" debut. While there Joseph would have an opportunity to visit the Library of Congress and see what material he could find.

Joseph had been invited to visit Humphrey when he came to Washington. During their conversation he was further convinced that Humphrey was the most qualified candidate for the presidency and that his sensitivity toward the problems of minorities would enable him to promote the cause of civil and human rights. Joseph became a strong advocate for Humphrey's election in the fall, and his support did not go unnoticed. Near the end of the year (December 13, 1968), he received a letter expressing the vice president's "personal thanks for all of [Joseph's] efforts in behalf of the Humphrey-Muskie ticket." Although the ticket did not win, it "did the country's spirit some good even in defeat."[28]

After returning from Washington, Joseph set about defining the direction he wanted to take with the A.M.E. Polity. He was able to do this formally in the July–September issue of the *A.M.E. Church Review*, on the cover of which his and Bishop Jordan's pictures appeared. Inside, along with a copy of the sermon Joseph had preached at the General Conference, was a statement concerning his new assignment. He said that at first he had been somewhat reluctant to accept it, because he had never really liked desk jobs. At Philadelphia, however, "a situation had developed that was deeply disturbing. . . . The tension needed lessening, and [he] saw though dimly then, the need for such a contribution as the writing of a new polity." He promised to give full "dedication as [he had] all these years to a task assigned." He would put in "readable form" the beliefs, dogmas, way of life of the Church and related organizations, with interpretations that recognized not only the historical content of Methodist heritage but would "interpret those traditional and basic positions of doctrines and policies, to the end that [the polity] may bear relevance to the demands of our generation."[29] It would seem that Joseph was adjusting to not having a district. Only time would determine whether he could maintain his enthusiasm for the task.

The summer of 1968 proved disastrous for Clevelanders. In the Glenville area there occurred a shoot-out between a group of Blacks and the police. Reportedly the Blacks had been led by Fred Evans, who advocated separation from whites, control of the Black community, and violence in retaliation for injustices done to Blacks throughout their history in America. He dressed in African garb, took the name Ahmed, and ran the African Culture Shop and Bookstore, which became the hangout for his followers. The shop had been funded by "Cleveland Now" money granted to further the arts and crafts of the Black community.[30]

Annetta had resigned from Glenville, had taught one year in the master of arts in training program at John Carroll, and had written textbooks for a year at the Educational Research Council of America. Now a writer/producer for WVIZ, an educational television station, she had interviewed Ahmed on one of her talk shows. She recalled how he had frightened the people in the studio by arriving with armed body guards, who stood in the doors while he was being interviewed. Nevertheless, she had found him to be cooperative and informative on what was happening in the Black community, and she was surprised later at the tragic events involving him that summer.

The shoot-out took place on July 22, when a tow truck attempted to remove a 1958 Cadillac that had been abandoned on Buelah Avenue in the Glenville area. Before they could hitch the car to the truck, one of the workers was hit in the back by a sniper. It was later revealed that Ahmed Evans, the alleged gunman, had thought the tow truck driver was a policeman, because of the similarity of the uniforms, and that the police were removing cars from the neighborhood. Soon shots were being exchanged between several Blacks and the police. From 8:30 to 9:30 P.M. "at least 20 people were killed or injured in the raging gun battle by police and snipers."[31] A crowd began to gather on Superior Avenue and throw rocks at passing cars and the police. Twenty-eight Blacks were arrested for looting, "one [charged] with malicious destruction of property, and one with armed robbery."[32]

The newly elected Carl Stokes's first thought was that the National Guard should be called in and that the citizens of Cleveland needed to be told by him, through the media, what had happened so they could stay away from the area. In the end Stokes decided to send only black policemen into Glenville and to allow the militants, with whom he had been meeting, to go back into the community and restore peace, as they had asked to do. This greatly angered the white policemen, but the plan saved lives.[33]

When the damage was assessed five days later, losses exceeded $2.6 million. Sixty-three businesses had been burned or looted. The city was more divided between Black and white than ever before.[34] Joseph wondered what could be done to alleviate the smoldering ugliness that had so furiously erupted. He had admired Stokes's bold new strategy; what was needed in Cleveland was creative leadership, and Stokes seemed to be providing that.

Joseph and Hazel now faced a major personal adjustment, which was revealed in a letter written to Bishop Carey A. Gibbs. He was unable to attend some of the Annual Conferences that fall because he and Hazel had decided to move from their house on Wade Park to an apartment, and he could not "leave home" when Hazel was "surrounded with so much disorder, attendant on moving."[35] He also did not want to leave Hazel when the city was in such turmoil. In addition, he worried about Annetta, whose job took her through the Hough and Glenville areas filming documentaries for her series *Black Peoplehood*. Most of the station's cameramen were white, and they were not always welcomed in the Black communities.

The Gomezes moved into a three-bedroom apartment at 13855 Superior Road, in the Forest Park Tower, number 803. Although Rev. Alvia Shaw, now the pastor of St. James, had given Joseph office space on the third floor of the church building, as well as the services of Wilhelmena Lawrence, the church secretary, Joseph planned to use one of the bedrooms as an office and library.

Giving up the only home they had ever owned was extremely painful for the Gomezes. They were relieved when Annetta and Curtis Sr. agreed to buy the house; Joseph only required that they pay a token fee of a hundred dollars a month. The transaction was beneficial to everyone. The house would remain in the family, which meant that Thanksgiving and Christmas could be celebrated there. Items which could not fit in the new apartment could be stored in the basement on Wade Park. Curtis (now teaching at Cuyahoga Community College) and Annetta could save a good deal of money for the boys' education. Curtis Jr. welcomed the move, because he had always loved the family home, but little Joseph was reluctant to leave all his friends and neighbors and the house he had come to love. The boys, however, would still be able to go to Lutheran East High School, and Shane, the family collie, Joe's constant companion, would be moving to Wade Park with them.

After the Gomezes were settled into the apartment, Joseph found it difficult to get started writing. The hours seemed long, tedious, and uneventful, and he was grateful when invitations to speak pulled him away from his desk and the confining apartment.

He delivered the keynote address on Sunday, January 3, 1969, at Coppin Chapel in Indianapolis, and then addressed the students at Adrian College in Adrian, Michigan, on Wednesday, April 16. He spoke of the threats to small educational institutions—some would have to close because of the high cost of operating. He acknowledged the "whirlpool of change" colleges found themselves a part of, but observed, "Tomorrow we may discover many areas that in our zeal and dedication we have overlooked, or at best we have superficially touched. The so-called radicals of today may be looked upon as the conservatives of tomorrow, as in the past."[36] No doubt he was thinking of himself.

Howard C. Emrick sent Joseph a letter on April 16 in which he not only expressed his thanks but those of Jim Cone, who he said was "delighted that [Joseph] could stay with him and renew [their] friendship."[37] Cone, the author of *Black Theology and Black Power* (1969), had had many friendly debates with Joseph over the concept of Black Power when Joseph presided over the 4th District. Cone criticized the contemporary Black church as "a place of retreat from the dehumanizing forces of white power" and for its failure to respond favorably to the concept of Black Power, which demanded an all-out attack against the oppressor.[38] Joseph was more inclined to agree with his brother, Cecil Wayne Cone, who would in his *Identity Crisis in Black Theology* (1975) conclude there could be no Black theology "which does not see as its primary focus of starting point the black religion it purports to represent." Because Jim Cone had "used Black Power as the point of departure for his theological analysis of Black religion, he was unable to grasp its essence. Jim wrongly perceived Black religion to be primarily political activity as found in Stokely Carmichael and Rap Brown."[39] Despite their differences of opinion, however, Joseph had enjoyed his evenings with Jim Cone in Adrian. He always looked forward to a good intellectual battle, and Jim was a worthy opponent.

To Joseph there was no such thing as a white or Black religion; there was merely religion—the human search for the spiritual in oneself and the universe. "Although we speak of God as He, God is neither he nor she, neither black nor white," he often affirmed. "God is spirit—God is love. God is!" He believed that each group finds its own way of worshipping that spirit—a method which emerges from its culture and heritage. For Afro-Americans, the manner of worship had its roots in both African religions and American Christianity. Perhaps, Joseph thought, the way Blacks worshiped and the way they made the Bible live for them was what was meant by Black religion. That too was simplistic; Blacks do not all worship the same way, he reasoned. Joseph could, however, define the A.M.E. Church without hesitation: "African Methodism came into being promoting no new doctrine or tenet of faith, but as an advocate of religious freedom and as a champion of a free society of Christian Brotherhood. This then is the genius of our church. Wherever men suffer from discrimination, from social, economic or religious bigotry, there is, and will be need, for the operation of the African Methodist Episcopal Church with its central philosophy of liberty and equality."[40]

The following month Joseph read with interest the *Black Manifesto,* presented by James Forman, the executive director of SNCC, and adopted by the National Black Economic Conference in Detroit on April 26. Forman had earlier interrupted a service at Riverside Church in New York City and read the Manifesto to a startled group of ministers and laity. The document demanded reparations of five hundred million dollars, to be spent for the establishment of a Southern Land Bank for Blacks who had been forced to leave their land because of racism; "the establishment of four major publishing and printing industries, the establishment of four of the most advanced scientific and futuristic audio-visual networks to be located in Detroit, Chicago and Washington, D.C.; the establishment of a training center, a National Black Labor Strike and Defense Fund, a United Black Appeal, a Black University located in the South." The Manifesto also called "for the total disruption of selected church sponsored agencies operating in the U.S. and the world." May 4, or some day soon after "depending on local conditions," was to be the day for the disruption of the racist churches and synagogues through the United States. It accused white churches of being tools of the government of America "to exploit the people of Latin America, Asia and Africa." The demands on the white churches amounted to about fifteen dollars per Black person in the United States. Blacks would demand much "more from the United States Government."[41]

Many whites and some Blacks found Forman's Manifesto ludicrous as well as naive; it was another "pie in the sky," like "forty acres and a mule" had been after the Civil War. Nevertheless, Joseph could not help but admire Forman's audacity in pointing out the obligations of religious institutions to amend the damage done by the enslavement of Blacks, often committed in the name of Christianity. Joseph told his family that the Manifesto would cause much discussion, many pledges of good faith (mostly from guilt), and a few commitments made and carried out; then the entire matter, like so many dreams during the '60s, would be deferred indefinitely. Time would prove him right.

In May 1969 Hazel and Joseph visited Bermuda for the Men's Day celebration at Bethel in Shelly Bay. It had been fifty years since Joseph had
pastored there. Speaking of the critical time Blacks were going through, he
said, "The Black Power movement emerging in various parts of the world
has values of merit in that it creates an awareness of being Black." He
recalled the time when Negroes had been offended when they were called
"Black," and how they now found the term a badge of pride. He said
he could see that Bermuda had gone through some changes. "People
seem[ed] to have graduated from an almost rural attitude to a more sophisticated approach to community life." Racial policies were much improved since he had first come to Bermuda in 1914. He recalled how he
had almost been arrested because the government thought he was telling
Black men on the island not to join the army. He then talked about the
anti-Christ movements in the world, "along with militant groups bent on
bringing about changes in racial policies with open violence." The church
must become involved more in the current problems and be a "moving
spiritual force" in the depths of community life if the community was to
continue to function, he affirmed. When Joseph had finished, Rev. Joseph
Whalen, the pastor, said he understood that during Joseph's pastorate in
Bermuda Bethel had always been packed.[42]

On May 29, Hazel was guest speaker at the celebration of the sixth anniversary of the Matilda Smith Williams Home for the Aged in Hamilton,
Bermuda. The meeting was held in the auditorium of St. Paul's Church.[43]
She praised the work being done by the home and emphasized the importance of the establishment of more places for the aged the world over. So
often, she said, older citizens were cast aside rather than given the opportunity to share their experience and wisdom.

The Gomezes spent the entire month of May in Bermuda. They
thought the rest would surely equip them for the tasks ahead when they
went back home.

When Joseph returned to Cleveland, the confusion of the times, the
tension in the city, the loss of a district, the giving up of a home, problems
Annetta was beginning to have with her marriage, and the attempt to carry
out an assignment which every day seemed to be more devoid of luster,
preyed on Joseph's mind in curious ways. At first he got up every morning
and traveled to his office at St. James, where he would stare at the blank
pages of paper, thumb listlessly through the meager amount of material he
had been able to acquire, wander downstairs for a chat with Rev. Shaw, and
then leave for home to eat lunch. In the afternoons, he would convince
himself that there was too much to do at home to return to the office. He

would try to read, but lately his eyes had begun to bother him, so he would put down the book and nap. After a while, he stopped going to St. James altogether. Instead he sat in his rocking chair looking out on the balcony, keeping to himself his own confused thoughts. Hazel became alarmed.

One day Hazel found him rocking and holding a conversation with Rebecca, his deceased mother. Another time he complained of rats running across the floor. During those episodes he seemed neither to know Hazel nor to be aware of her presence. She called Annetta, who immediately contacted Joseph Brown, the family doctor. He, in consultation with Dr. Lewis, the heart specialist from the Cleveland Clinic, attempted to find the root of the problem. It was possible that Joseph had had a slight stroke or that his blood sugar needed adjusting. This would explain, in part, his disorientation and the deterioration of his sight.

Hazel and her daughters surmised that Joseph had lost interest in living, and they felt anger toward those who had persuaded him to write the polity. They wondered if he were subconsciously using his strong will to create a condition which would enable him to avoid writing without being accused of negligence. At times he seemed perfectly lucid; at other times he retreated into his own dark world, where not even Hazel could enter. He seldom spoke. His main activity was rocking back and forth, as though he received some kind of consolation from the monotony of the motion and sound.

Finally, Hazel sent for Hubie Robinson, with the hope that he could snap Joseph out of his lethargy. When he arrived on Superior Road, Joseph acknowledged his presence and seemed glad to see him. They talked for a while, then Joseph went into the bedroom to lie down.

Hubie agreed with the rest of the family: Joseph was finding the writing of the polity overburdening, since the process did not depend on human contact. He felt lonely, useless, and abandoned. The family and Hubie decided they would work with Joseph on the polity and ask friends to contribute articles on various aspects of African Methodism. For instance, Annetta would write a chapter on the history of the Church, Harold on housing and education, Hubie on forgiveness of sins, Hanley Hickey on the truths of Methodism, Bishop Fred Jordan on the witness of the Spirit, Alvia Shaw on the life everlasting, J. W. Yancy on public relations, James Webb on the youth revolution, and Andrew White on interdenominational cooperation and ecumenical relationships. This would leave Joseph to deal with the doctrinal and structural aspects of the Church. The trick would be to lead Joseph to think this had been his idea from the first.

With Robinson's subtle prodding, Joseph gradually began to regain his equilibrium. He started talking about the polity—asking for pen and paper—and finally writing enthusiastically. Whatever goblins there had been seemed to be leaving one by one. The doctors were uncertain as to the exact cause of the initial breakdown, or of the recovery. Within a month, except for the trouble with his eyes, no one would have ever believed Joseph had been ill. To compensate for his eyes he dictated his letters and other material to Annetta.

In the introduction to the polity, which was published in 1971, Joseph spoke of this period and apologized for the delay in completing the book. Circumstances had prevented him from traveling, researching, collecting data, and lecturing, he said.[44] Most of all was the serious illness he had suffered:

> At the very peak of the crisis my family and some friends—God bless them!—Called a council and decided to carry on. . . . The project was headed in love by my dear friend, Bishop Hubert N. Robinson . . . cooperating with my dear wife, Hazel, who was and has been everything a man could ask for—nurse, secretary helpmate, comforter, inspiration, hope; my two daughters, Eula, capable; and Annetta versatile, who in childhood hovered over me in gracious tender ways; and in other ministries of love joined by their families.

He gave thanks to Rev. Shaw, his pastor; Wilhelmina Lawrence and Joan Stokes, for their friendship and secretarial assistance; doctors Joseph Brown and R. C. Lewis; and to Myrtle Teal Ransom, "widow of [his] spiritual father and earliest benefactor, who had given him access to Bishop Ransom's library and valuable papers."

In the final paragraph, Joseph mentioned that he had always been an admirer of Harry Emerson Fosdick, renowned writer and preacher. Following his illness, Joseph had read Fosdick's autobiographical *Living of These Days*. To his surprise he had come across Fosdick's description of his own "almost fatal illness experienced prior to the assumption of his full ministry—'his nervous breakdown,' 'the pit of utter despair.'" Fosdick wrote of "'being finished,' 'obsessive anxieties,' 'the darkness,' then the 'lifting of the clouds'—all of which I understand now," Joseph concluded. He was "proud to keep company with him and such spirits as Tolstoi, Mark Twain, William James and others."

The finished A.M.E. Polity was different from the one Joseph had envisioned. Although a lucid and pleasant book to read, it is more a collection of well-written essays than a polity, nor does the part Joseph wrote reflect the scholarship or the depth one would have expected from him. But as it had with Reverdy Ransom when he was made historiographer, the A.M.E.

Church had once again waited too late. Either of these men, who were among the Church's best writers and scholars, could have in their prime contributed richly to the archives of African Methodism. When the polity was finished Joseph was eighty years old. (The Church has since changed its policy; persons who now hold the office of historiographer are scholars and historians in their peak years.)

On Saturday, December 26, 1970, Bishop George Wilbur Baber of the 2nd Episcopal District died after an illness of three months. There were to be two funeral services, one at Metropolitan A.M.E. Church in Washington, D.C., on December 31 at 11 A.M., and the other January 2, 1971, at Ebenezer in Detroit.[45] Elvira Baber asked Joseph to deliver the eulogy in Washington. This eulogy, of which no copy has been found, was thought by many to be Joseph's finest. Rev. Joseph Brockington and some of the younger ministers of the 4th spoke later of the difficulty they had in getting Joseph from the rostrum to the outside door after he finished, so great was the press of people who wanted to shake his hand.

Following the funeral, a special meeting of the Bishops' Council was called for the purpose of filling the vacancy in the 2nd. Bishop Murph of the 17th and 18th districts was assigned to the 2nd, and since Joseph had nearly completed all arrangements for the printing of the polity, he was sent to Central Africa (17th) in place of Bishop Murph.[46]

A letter to his sister Amanda gives some insight as to Joseph's reaction to the appointment. He told her he had completed the polity and that the church had offered him the supervision of Rhodesia and Central Africa, despite his poor health. He said he had "accepted it because [he] felt it was better for [him] to be busy and to be back in the line of duty. There are those who feel I made a mistake accepting the offer, but I believe that God has something in store for me that I am to discover only in Africa, and so I shall go gladly and willingly."[47]

In a letter to Rev. Jesse W. Cotton, Joseph wrote: "I pray God for the strength to stand upon the soil of Africa, and to feel the thrill I always knew would come to me when that happened. I am sure it will be an experience which I will never forget."[48] Nevertheless, he did have many reservations about going. First of all, since Annetta and Curtis had finally separated, and Curtis Jr. had won a piano scholarship to Curtiss Institute in Philadelphia, Annetta and Joseph would be alone in the house on Wade Park. (Curtis Jr., who eventually changed his name to his grandfather's, Curtis Antonio Gomez, had been chosen for the piano scholarship by Rudolph Serkin.) Secondly there was the matter of Joseph, who was completing his senior year at Lutheran East and would be entering college in the fall. When he left, Annetta would be by herself. Thirdly, he hated to be that far away from Eula, Harold, and her children. Fourthly, there was the matter of Hazel's health and his own. Hazel would have to have extensive dental work done before they could go. In addition they could not leave until July, when as acting president of the Missionary Society, due to the illness of Anne Heath, Hazel would be in charge of the Connectional Missionary Convention to be held in Los Angeles.

The first thing Joseph wanted to do was find out more about the 17th District which included Zambia, Southern Rhodesia (now Zimbabwe), Malawi, Zaire (now the Congo), and Tanzania. Prior to 1964, Zambia (then called Northern Rhodesia), Southern Rhodesia, and Nyasaland had been a part of the Federation of Central African Countries.[49] Nyasaland had seceded, and in the elections that year the United Federal party had been defeated by the United National Independence party. Zambia declared its independence October 24, 1964, and elected Kenneth Kaunda president.[50]

Joseph learned that the A.M.E. Church had been established in Africa in 1821, when Rev. Daniel Coker set up a church in Sierra Leone. It had spread to South Africa in 1896, at a time when native congregations were reacting against white missionaries and their practices of segregation. At its 1896 conference, the native Ethiopian Church had decided to unite with the A.M.E. Church. In 1898, "Bishop Turner visited South Africa to establish the church firmly there. . . . In a whirlwind tour, Turner boosted the church organization by ordaining 31 elders and 29 deacons."[51]

The A.M.E. Church had been established in Rhodesia in 1900 by Rev. S. J. Mabote, Presiding Elder from Transvaal in South Africa, just three years after the first Annual Conference was held in South Africa. In 1927, Bishop Gregg came to Southern Rhodesia, where he was able to get the government officials to grant the A.M.E. Church recognition. The church had expanded greatly between 1934 and 1945, "mainly along the line of rail and in the major towns." After that it began to diminish due to the lack of schools to provide a trained ministry, and the lack of health clinics. Nevertheless, it played an important role in the liberation of Zambia, in that it was one of the strongest advocates of nationalism and therefore was a church with which the natives readily identified. All the churches were run by African ministers, and the districts by African presiding elders. The Church's Afro-American heritage, rooted in the belief of self-rule and the dignity of humankind regardless of race or creed, coincided with the Zambians' own spiritual and political doctrines. "The very existence of a large, internationally organized Church run entirely by Black people was a symbol of African Independence."[52]

Most of the influential African leaders involved in the liberation movement had belonged to the A.M.E. Church at one time or another: Kenneth

Kaunda, Hastings Banda, John L. Dube, Justin Chimba, and W. K. Sika-lumbi. Banda had been brought to America by Bishop John Gregg "and received his first degree from Wilberforce University." His uncle had founded the A.M.E. Church in Malawi.[53]

For five years, Kaunda had been "an active member of Ebenezer Church in Lusaka. . . . He was a member of the Official Board, sang in the church choir, and had some of his children baptized in the church. He left the church in 1957 'after an argument on the conservatism of the church.' The presiding elder apparently said people were using the A.M.E. Church as a platform for political purposes." Kaunda believed the church should be involved in liberation politics. Justin Chimba, "an active and vociferous African National Congress leader in the anti-Federation campaign, Orga-nizing Secretary of the Northern Rhodesia General Workers' Trade Union and later an executive member of the Northern Rhodesia African Trade Union Congress," a coeditor of *Freedom Newsletter,* had once been a local preacher in the A.M.E. Church. W. K. Sikalumbi, former Trade Commis-sioner to Europe, Deputy General Secretary of the Zambia Africa Congress after it split with the ANC, and member of Kaunda's parliament, had also once been a minister in the church.[54]

As soon as the news of Joseph's appointment reached Central Africa, letters began to arrive petitioning the bishop for assistance. One of the more humorous letters was written by the members of Sims Chapel (named after Bishop Sims) in Salisbury, February 28, 1971. They reported that the church was in "big trouble." Rev. J. C. Chikulumeni had acted as a bishop, "giving pastors appointments without a conference and without a bishop's consent. He [had] expelled . . . all those who had complained about his wife's immorality." It seemed that Mrs. Chikulumeni had two husbands living in the Mission House—one legal, Rev. Chikulumeni, and the other illegal, Mr. A. Makwili. "Mr. Makwili takes Mrs. Chikulumeni for beer-drinking and are both found in beer-gardens, and around town in his car which also stays in the Parsonage," they wrote. Mrs. Chikulumeni had been caught in the parsonage with a young pastor by the Mission-ary Women, who had taken off her missionary uniform and reported her. As soon as Presiding Elder Rev. Waukunguma, left for Zambia, Rev. Chikulumeni had dismissed the Missionary Women, stating that since he was the "Bishop's representative, no one had the right to try [his] wife's case."[55]

Then there was the problem of Rev. S. J. N. T'ladi, who had bought books from the Matopo Book Concern in Bulawayo, sold them to the A.M.E. Schools, but never paid the Book Concern. The Concern had

"already started lawsuits against the Church through their lawyers."
Rev. T'ladi was also being charged with "using the Episcopal District property without authority from the Bishop or the Episcopal Residence Committee, which [meant he was] using the Bishop's car, changing even the
ownership, occupying the Episcopal Residence without permission.[56]

T'ladi claimed he had used the money to repair the Episcopal Residence
and had receipts for everything he bought. He also claimed he had permission from Bishop Murph to live in the residence until a bishop would need
the house.[57] Being so far away, it was difficult for Joseph to ascertain the
truth. He paid the Book Concern the money owed, and informed T'ladi
that he would soon have to move from the Episcopal Residence, because
he and Mrs. Gomez would be occupying it.

Since it would be impossible for Joseph to get to Africa in time to hold
his spring Annual Conferences, he wrote to Bishop Dewey Robinson of the
15th District (Cape, Cape Midlands, Organia, Natal, West Transvaal, East
Transvaal, and South West Africa) and asked him to hold his first series of
conferences. Bishop Robinson graciously agreed.[58]

Rev. Waukunguma, who was becoming Joseph's most valuable contact
in Central Africa, reported that the work in Malawi was going well except
for the schools, which were in deplorable condition. The same was true of
the schools in the Congo, in the presiding elder's province in Katanga;
however, the North Zambia Conference was "making unparalleled progress in all its aspects of work."[59]

Joseph hoped that one of the things he could do when he reached Africa
was to find a way to improve the A.M.E. schools and provide seminary
training for the ministers. Some few had studied in Epworth College in
Salisbury, Old Umtile Bible Institute in Umtile, Rhodesia Mansfield College in Oxford, England, and Wilberforce in America, but most had what
amounted to Standard III training (fourth grade) in the A.M.E. missionary
schools, unless their parents had been able to afford to pay tuition of thirty
dollars a year for further training.[60]

As it turned out, because of a Church controversy which threatened to
develop into a special session of the General Conference, involving Bishop
William F. Ball and Dr. Arthur Gaston, the Gomezes were not able to leave
for Africa until fall (though the special session was never held). In addition
they were having difficulty getting passports to get into Rhodesia.

During the Bishops' Council in May 1971 it was voted that Joseph should
preside over the trial of Bishop William F. Ball (7th Episcopal District,
Florida), president of the General Board, and Dr. Arthur G. Gaston, Treasurer of the Church, both charged with misconduct in office. Meanwhile,

Joseph C. McKinney was made acting treasurer.[61] The trial promised to be highly controversial, but the Council believed that the respect most A.M.E.'s had for the eighty-one-year-old Gomez would ensure an orderly session.

The Gomezes arrived in Los Angeles two days before the Missionary Convention was scheduled to begin. They had reserved a suite at the Hilton for themselves and a room for Annetta and Sissy, their granddaughter. Annetta was to direct a youth pageant during one of the night sessions.

The opening session was held at the Hollywood Bowl, in which more than eight thousand people attended an interfaith celebration. At the regular morning session, Hazel gave the Acting President's Address. After welcoming the bishops and all the delegates, she explained how in 1969 Bishop Harrison J. Bryant had called to inform her of the illness of Mrs. Heath and asked her to act as president until she recovered. Hazel then recalled all the missionary workers who had died during the past four years. She had felt "bewildered by the tremendous amount of responsibility placed on [her] as a result of these losses." She had asked her friends, what had she done to "inherit all this?" She had finally raised her head, "straightened [her] shoulders, stood erect and said, 'With God's help and the help of our dedicated members, we will have the best Quadrennial we have ever had.'" The rest of her speech was a plea for the society not to rest on its past laurels but to "create new, exciting programs that [would] more efficiently serve humanity in 1971 and in the years to come."[62]

That afternoon the Gomezes were introduced to the delegation from Zambia, which included Mrs. Waukunguma, Mrs. Ez Nhekaro, and Princess Nahatindi, whom Joseph described as "every bit a royal personage." They spoke of the work that needed to be done in the 17th and the potential for making it a strong district. In a letter to Rev. Waukunguma Joseph wrote, "I think I am safe in saying that all who met [the delegates] were also impressed by them, and I cannot think of persons whom you could have selected who would have better represented the Church than they did. . . . I trust that I shall get to know [the princess] personally, not only her family and the President of Zambia, but all the leaders of that section that go to make up the 17th Episcopal District."[63]

On the evening of July 19, Bob Hope was the toastmaster for a banquet welcoming the delegates and friends. The guest speaker was Mayor Charles Evers of Fayette, Mississippi, brother of Medgar Evers, assassinated NAACP field secretary. (Charles was also a candidate for governor of Mississippi.) At a luncheon given two days later, Rosa Parks was honored. She was then living in Detroit and serving as a deaconess at St. Matthew

A.M.E. Church. That evening the young people presented their program, which included a guest appearance of Gregg Morris, of the television series *Mission Impossible*.[64]

While the women were holding their workshops and presenting their programs, the trial of Bishop Ball and Dr. Gaston convened. Joseph presided with authority and dignity; the only outburst was firmly halted. "This is a Christian proceeding," Joseph said to the man in question, "and as such there will be no attempts to disrupt the proceedings. Either sit down, or leave the premises." To everyone's surprise, without further protest the man left. At the end of the trial, Ball was suspended from the bishopric and Gaston removed from his position as treasurer of the Church.[65]

Hazel was proud of Joseph's handling of the trial, and she was also rightfully proud of the job she had done with the Missionary Convention. Bishop Hickman told her that she had made her friends very proud of her. "If you were a few years younger, I would have been one who would have joined in drafting you for our new president. . . . I do not think I have attended a Quadrennial Session that was so well planned and carried out as planned," he added.[66] Many delegates had in fact tried to draft Hazel as the new president, but she had refused.

Hazel and Joseph left for a two-week stay in Woodland Park to complete the necessary paperwork for their trip to Africa. Waukunguma had written that he was expecting them before the end of September. Plans for the departure, however, were deferred due to a holdup of passports and refusal by the government of Southern Rhodesia to allow the bishop to enter the country. Although permission was not forthcoming from Rhodesia, Joseph decided to leave for Zambia, in early November. Waukunguma was delighted that they would be arriving in November and that they intended to stay until the General Conference in 1972. For almost six years no bishop had resided there.[67]

On Tuesday afternoon, November 9, Hazel and Joseph left Cleveland's Hopkins Airport for New York's Kennedy Airport and then for London. Arriving at Heathrow at 7:40 A.M., they were transported to the London Hilton Hotel, so exhausted that they never left their room until it was time to catch the plane for Lusaka. At 9:10 A.M., Friday, November 12, the Gomezes stepped on African soil for the first time. Though anxious to be shown their quarters, they took a few moments to say a prayer of thanks that God had allowed them to live long enough to experience this part of their heritage.

Zambia is a country of 290,000 square miles with a population of approximately three and a half million, who belong to seventy different tribes. The largest portion of the population lives in the "Copperbelt" and along "the line of rail." There are four large rivers: the Zambezi, Kafue, and Luangwa, which "drain the south and east," and the Luapula, which "rises in Lake Bangweulu and empties its flow into Lake Mweru in the northwest after forming a long boundary with the Congo." The red soil of the land is powdery and not particularly fertile; however, there are hundreds of miles of valuable woodlands, as in Barotseland, where there is an abundance of teak, mahogany, mopani, and the ugly baobabs from which cream of tartar is made. There had once been a large number of game in the country, but in 1971 it was confined to the reserves north and south (Luangwa Valley, North and South, and Sumbu) or sparsely peopled parts of the country.[68] Hazel hoped they would have an opportunity to visit the game reserves so she could take pictures of the animals.

Lusaka, the capitol, was surprisingly modern—much more than the Gomezes had been led to believe. They were impressed by the well-built highways, houses, business buildings (including the new Lusaka Trades Training Institute), and the supermarkets. Joseph was anxious to meet the progressive President Kaunda, who had led the Zambians to independence. He also wanted to see the A.M.E. churches and schools.

Rev. Waukunguma had met the Gomezes at the airport with a large delegation of A.M.E.s. Some were dressed in their brightly colored, native garb, which set off their glistening black faces. A few of the men were dressed in Western suits, white shirts, and ties, and a number of the women were in American-style summer dresses. All of them expressed their delight at meeting "My Lord, the Bishop," and "Mother Gomez," and hoped that they would enjoy their stay in the land of their ancestors.

The Gomezes were housed in the home of Rev. F. O. Bennett, dean of students at Evelyn Home College in Lusaka, a white man who had joined Ebenezer A.M.E. Church during the year. In September Bennett had been encouraged by Rev. Waukunguma to write Joseph for information concerning other Ebenezer Churches in the United States, such as the one in Detroit pastored by Fred Stephens, or Rev. Moses Hamlin's church in New York City, or possibly his namesake Rev. A. L. Bennett's Ebenezer in Tallahassee, Florida. He also asked Joseph to bring some copies of the A.M.E. hymnal, because "a lecturer in history of the University of Zambia [was] doing some research on the A.M.E. Church, including the use of hymns." Bennett said, "though born white, I am now a Zambian and owe so much to my fellow believers in Africa since I first came here to learn in 1948." Below his signature at the end of the letter he indicated that he was an assistant to Rev. M. K. Waukunguma, his pastor and presiding elder.[69] They later learned he was deeply in love with a Black African woman.

Living with Bennett was a pleasant experience. He went out of his way to make the Gomezes feel at home. All the household chores were done by hired workers, whose wages seemed to the Gomezes to be ridiculously low; Bennett explained, however, that this (less than sixteen dollars per month) was the going rate in the country. He would have been criticized if he had paid more. To make up for the poor pay, Hazel insisted on buying little gifts for the women who cleaned, from whom she learned a great deal about the country.

The Gomezes visited the A.M.E. churches in Lusaka, Mount Zion and Ebenezer, and learned that Zambia had over a hundred pastors and about nine thousand members. A few days later they were taken to the Copperbelt to visit the A.M.E. churches in Kitwe, Ndola, and Mufulira. During the long religious services they were fascinated by the singing of the old hymns, which the Zambians had transformed and now sounded decidedly African. Hazel watched with wonder as each person in the audience swayed down the aisle to put her or his coin in the collection plate. The singing, hand clapping, drum beating, and body movements of each person were sheer artistry—together they were hypnotic. Every aspect of the service was entered into totally. Hazel thought about some of the lukewarm worshippers she had encountered in America.

While in the Copperbelt the Gomezes had an opportunity to inspect the mines, and they were given souvenirs of mugs, trays, and a clock. The people also gave them such gifts as a handmade xylophone, drums of hide, shields, spears, canes, and African heads carved of wood.

Driving through the countryside, the Gomezes were better able to see the diversity of the people. While many in Lusaka were in business, educated, and making fairly good salaries, or were a part of that growing class who sought a livelihood in the mines (cooper, cobalt, zinc, manganese), in industry, commerce, or government, those in the rural areas lived in tribal units and were agrarians. Many were "dirt poor," were dependent upon growing corn, sweet potatoes, or tobacco for subsistence.

The following week Joseph was taken to meet Kenneth Kaunda. He was impressed by the president's strong presence and sensitivity. Kaunda reiterated to Joseph what he had said at Kitwe in October 1963 at the Mindola Ecumenical Center, concerning his disappointment with the Christian church. He still believed that the Church should play a vital role in Zambia. If it was to do so it could not remain static and orthodox but had to be creative enough to attract the young. The church could not separate itself from the social, economic, and political problems of the people, especially those that had to do with the independence and freedom of all Africa. His party, the United National Independence party, had accomplished much since coming to power. First, it had obtained independence, on October 24, 1964. Second, it had introduced the new cooperative approach to the economic development of the country. Third, it had in 1967 persuaded the National Council to adopt a philosophy of Humanism, which was finally accepted by the entire country in August of 1967 at the party's annual conference. Fourth, it had gotten the Council to accept the party's economic reforms.[70]

On November 2, 1968, Kaunda had dissolved the National Assembly and set December 19 as the date for Zambia's second general election. What had taken place in Zambia in less than four years was miraculous. Kaunda was quick to remind his fellow Zambians of the not-so-distant past: "the night passes, the bicycle licenses, the poll taxes, the stagnation in rural areas, the wastage of valuable manpower, the ambulance fees, the pigeon hole shopping system, indeed racial intolerance and hatred and many more" intolerable conditions, which the humaneness of the United National Independence Party had wiped out.[71]

Kaunda spoke to Joseph of "love in action"—that a leader's first responsibility was to the people who had put him in office.[72] At that moment Joseph felt like a young man again, full of enthusiasm. Kaunda's words further inspired Joseph to upgrade the A.M.E. Church in Zambia so it could help to effect change. What a way to end his ministry! He knew it would not be easy, because of the problems of tribalism and the divisions in the Church itself; but nothing in his life had been easy.

Kaunda expressed his desire that Joseph remain in the country, as so few of the bishops had done, and work with the people. The president's words brought Joseph back to reality. He explained that because of his age and failing health he probably would not be reassigned to the 17th after the General Conference in 1972, but that while he was there he would do everything he could. The two men shook hands amicably, and Joseph expressed the hope that Kaunda would again join the A.M.E. Church, which had in many ways helped to fight for Zambian independence.

During his stay in Africa Joseph tried repeatedly to gain entrance into Rhodesia, but even though the A.M.E. ministers in the country pleaded on his behalf, it was not to be. The white minority of fewer than 250,000, headed by Ian Smith, feared that the Afro-American bishop would encourage the natives in their struggle for majority rule. This meant that Joseph was prohibited from visiting the districts in the Rhodesia Annual Conference (Matebeland, Midlands, Wankie, Bulawayo, and Gokwe), nor was he ever able to occupy the Episcopal Residence in Bulawayo. In fact he remained in the home of Fred Bennett throughout his stay in Central

Africa, mainly inspecting churches and schools in the North and South Zambian conferences, and in Malawi.

Both he and Hazel learned to love the country and the people. For the first time they felt released from the burden of racism. Here Blacks and whites mingled freely as friends, business partners, husbands and wives, as classmates, and no one seemed to be concerned.

Six months was all too short a time even to begin the church program Joseph had in mind. He particularly wanted to upgrade the A.M.E. schools, which were in deplorable condition, poorly equipped and staffed, and whose teachers were severely underpaid. He planned to launch a financial campaign that would involve the various African governments and A.M.E. districts in the United States. Already he had a pledge from Kaunda that the Zambian government would provide a sizable sum to improve the A.M.E. schools there. Joseph also wanted to enroll ministers who had had no formal training in seminaries in Africa, England, or the United States. For this project, much money would be needed. With the assistance of Waukunguma he was able to persuade most of the ministers and presiding elders to endorse his innovations.

However, in May 1972, before he could do much more, he had to return to the United States to move back into the house on Wade Park before leaving for the Thirty-ninth General Conference. Annetta was not adjusting well to the divorce, and the family felt she needed Hazel and Joseph to be with her. The Gomezes would have liked to have ended their days in Zambia, but they knew that as they grew older and less able, it was best that they be near their daughters. At least Joseph had seen Africa, the home of his mother's people, even if in his twilight years. It was an experience they both would cherish for rest of their lives.

CHAPTER FIFTEEN

Sunset and Evening Star

Cleveland & Wooster, 1972–1979

We do not all see the rising sun. At midday this glowing, golden ball baffles and defies the scrutiny of eyes, but at sunset all the gathered beauty and brilliancy of a long march are poured out in blended tones, softened and hallowed by the touch of approaching night.

—Joseph Gomez, "Sunset," Bermuda, May 1917

The thirty-ninth Quadrennium of the A.M.E. Church convened in Dallas, June 21–July 3, 1972. The Gomezes had mixed feelings about returning to the state where Joseph had begun his episcopacy but where his successes had been accompanied by much pain. They were, however, delighted by the greetings they received from their Texas friends and the twenty-four delegates who had come all the way from Central Africa.

The opening worship services were interrupted by the arrival of Edward Nixon, brother of President Richard Nixon, who was to address the delegates. Immediately following his entrance, "a group of laymen and ministers rushed to the front of the pulpit protesting the change in the preliminaries of Worship Service, some saying that the motive was political." Order was not restored until Nixon and his personnel voluntarily left the auditorium. Several of the bishops, ministers, and especially, young people were incensed that anyone would have attempted to halt the worship to deliver to the assemblage what most certainly would have been a political message. Furthermore, Nixon was not a favorite among Blacks. Bishop Nichols tried to explain that Edward Nixon had been asked to speak at that time only because it was the sole opportunity to present "the honored guest; that it was not his intention to reflect irreverence toward the traditions and customs of [the] Church." When order had finally been restored, Bishop William F. Ball, who had been temporarily restored to the bishopric pending further action, delivered the Quadrennial Sermon, after which 1,800 people received the Holy Communion.[1]

On the following day, when it was Joseph's turn to preside, he introduced the delegates from the 17th District, who received a tremendous ovation. Joseph told the conference that "none had come as far and at a greater sacrifice than those delegates of the 17th Episcopal District." Many had had to pay their own air fare.[2]

On Monday morning Joseph read a communication from the Honorable Dr. Kenneth David Kaunda, president of the Republic of Zambia. In it Kaunda said he "valued the work of the Church in Zambia very much indeed. We believe that the teaching of Christ, that 'Man shall not live by bread alone,' is significant if we are to help lead our fellow human beings to enjoy a fuller life during their very short stay on this earth." All of the Christian churches were responding well in helping Zambia to develop; it was important that the A.M.E. Church participate. Kaunda stressed that the basic philosophy of Zambia was Humanism—and not the Humanism of Europeans. Zambians believed that man belonged to God, that he did not make himself. "Whatever he is in terms of race, colour, or ethnic grouping is God's work and is not something that should lead us, humble beings, to differ and to quarrel among ourselves."[3]

Joseph asked the conference to respond to Kaunda's letter. Among those who seconded the motion was the Honorable Rev. Frederick Talbot of the 16th District, and a permanent delegate to the United Nations from Guyana. Joseph informed the conference that the Zambian government was prepared to furnish at least three quarters of the money needed to support A.M.E. schools and hospitals in the area.[4]

Since before the conference had begun, Eula and Annetta had been trying to persuade Joseph to retire, write his memoirs, and do some of the other things he had always wanted to do. He was eighty-two, had had one heart attack, and had to inject himself every morning with insulin to control his blood sugar; also, his glaucoma was growing worse.

After over sixty-five years of an active ministry, it was difficult for Joseph even to consider retirement. He remembered what had happened to him when he had been relieved of a district in 1968; he also remembered what had happened to Bishop Ransom when he retired. Few people had come around, since he had had no more favors to give; he had often been restless and bored. On the other hand, Joseph knew his physical health was not what it should be. Perhaps it was best that he step down and give a younger person the opportunity that had been given him. Nonetheless, his family was taken by surprise when on June 27, he stepped behind the podium and asked them to join him on the platform. He faced the delegates with determination and some sadness:

> We are living in a new day. New things are pressing upon us. We who have borne the burden "in the heat of the day" must give way to stronger, if not wiser hands and hearts. I am asking for retirement in this Church of ours! We have made many friends, and thank God for this. In this, I have the concurrence of my beloved family, and I shall ever thank God for them, and for the host of friends throughout the Church and Connection; for the beloved friends from Africa, and for all the deepening experiences we had across the years. May God bless you, and bless the Church. Long live the African Methodist Episcopal Church.[5]

When he had finished, Bishop Robinson stepped up to the microphone. This, he said, was a painful moment for him. "Bishop Gomez has been like a second father who has contributed so much to my life. . . . But he has also contributed substantially to other 'Sons' . . . men and women . . . who have a fuller life because of his love and friendship. The A.M.E. Church has grown as a result of his leadership, his experience and judgment. His poise and gentleness have contributed to the respect and influence of the A.M.E. Church, in religious, civic and political circles. With a heavy heart, I move to accept the desire of Bishop Gomez to retire."[6]

Bishop Bright seconded the motion, expressing his great love and respect for Bishop Gomez. Others too rose to second the motion, that they might have an opportunity to express their admiration. The motion carried. "At this point Mrs. A. B. Williams, Director of Public Relations, moved that the conference extend to Mrs. Gomez a vote of thanks for her many years of service in the field of Missions." The motion was seconded many times and passed. "The General Conference gave Bishop and Mrs. Gomez, their daughters, Mrs. Eula Williams and Mrs. Annetta Jefferson, a rising vote of love and gratitude."[7]

Later, the 16th Episcopal District (West Indies) presented the Gomez family, along with Rev. Van Putten, who had attended General Conferences from 1928 to 1972, a special plaque of appreciation. Rev. Waukunguma of the 17th District presented a resolution to the conference on behalf of the district, thanking Joseph for his "excellent work, his fatherly love and guidance [in] Central Africa. "We further wish to express that his was a combination of superb performance of duty and sincere love for [those] whom he was serving." Because the bishop was a man of such rare "calibre and integrity," the district accepted his announcement with the hope that God would make his "retirement enjoyable" and that he would visit Central Africa as often as he could. The district expressed the hope that whoever followed Bishop Gomez would continue the "program of decentralization of the A.M.E. Church in Central Africa, a measure which is vital in independent and developing countries."[8]

When the announcement had been made and all the seconding speeches and words of thanks spoken, the family descended the platform, to be embraced by a throng of delegates at the bottom of the steps. Joseph said later that his stomach had begun to churn as it always did when he was feeling strong emotions. He and Hazel squeezed each other's hand as they tried unsuccessfully to keep back the tears. He turned to his family and said almost inaudibly, "Well, it's over." Eula and Annetta tried to assure him that it was just the beginning. He knew, however, that it was not true; this was the beginning only of the winding down—the placing of the final period at the end of a long sentence.

That afternoon the family returned to hear the Reverend Jesse Jackson address the conference. He "projected the image of Ezekiel's Valley of Dry Bones, and compared it to the present-day ghetto. He graphically described the situation of the Black people throughout the world and brilliantly portrayed their development, entreating God as the Power to invigorate action for the success of Black People." When he finished, he sang "Amazing Grace."[9] Few in the audience imagined he would be the first Black candidate to make a serious run for the presidency.

This conference seemed to be marked by retirements and other departures. When Reverend Charles S. Spivey, Jr., read his father's report for the Sunday School Union, he informed the conference that Charles Spivey, Sr., was also seeking retirement. He wished to leave ten thousand dollars to Payne Seminary, where he had been the dean for several years, and twenty thousand dollars to the A.M.E. Church, to be spent as needed. Additionally, Bishop G. Wayman Blakely asked for temporary location to regain his health, and the conference retired Bishop O. L. Sherman because of his age. Bishop William F. Ball was suspended again for four years. At the beginning of the year, Bishop Carey A. Gibbs of the 13th Episcopal District had died. To fill the vacancies the Episcopal Committee recommended that seven new bishops be elected.[10]

The election of bishops began Saturday afternoon, July 1. On the first ballot, John Hurst Adams (former president of Paul Quinn) received 806 votes and became the eighty-seventh bishop of the A.M.E. Church. The second ballot was completed at 11 A.M. Sunday morning, at which time it was announced that Richard A. Hildebrand, S. S. Morris, Jr., Fred Talbot,

H. H. Brookins, and Vinton R. Anderson had been elected. Joseph was overjoyed by the elections of Morris, who had just missed being elected four years ago; Frederick Talbot, the first bishop elected from Guyana; and Vinton Anderson, who had been one of his ministers when he was bishop of the 4th District. The American delegates joined with the overseas delegates to demonstrate their approval of the election of Talbot.[11]

The jubilation was short lived. Bishop Bright, having just pinned his own badge on the newly elected Bishop Hildebrand, slumped to the floor. The bishops on the platform rushed to his side and tried to revive him. Not long afterwards the emergency squad arrived, but its efforts were futile. Bright had suffered a massive heart attack. Eula and Annetta were on their way into the auditorium when they saw the medics carrying the stretcher to the ambulance. They did not know what was happening until they got inside the auditorium and saw the stunned crowd, some standing on chairs to watch, other slumped in their chairs weeping quietly. Reports soon came to the convention that Bishop Bright had been pronounced dead on arrival at the Dallas City Hospital.[12] Joseph was particularly saddened. Bright had been another young man whose career he had watched closely and nurtured. So many changes were happening, so rapidly, that Joseph's thoughts and feelings were muddled. He wondered how he would be able to get through the rest of the conference.

When the death was announced, the delegates paused for silent prayer, and the organ played "This Is My Story." They were too shocked to continue the meeting; Bishop Nichols declared the Conference in recess for an hour as a memorial tribute to Bishop Bright.[13]

Because of the death it was necessary for eight rather than seven bishops to be elected. This meant that two more were needed. On the third ballot, Fred C. James and Frank Madison Reid, Jr., became the ninety-third and ninety-fourth bishops. Joseph had known Frank, Jr., as a baby and had been a good friend of his father. Frank had been a classmate of Eula's at Wilberforce. As Bishop Murphy pointed out, Frank Madison Reid, Jr., was the second son of a bishop to be elected in the A.M.E. Church; Bishop Robert A. Grant, the son of Bishop Abraham Grant, had been the first, in 1889.[14]

In the evening, the eight bishops were consecrated and given Holy Communion and a Bible. When the assignments of the bishops had been read, Bishop H. H. Brookins had been sent to Central Africa, Bishop H. Thomas Primm to the 4th, and the new overseas bishop, Fred Talbot, to the West Indies. The departments of Polity and Urban Ministry were combined and were to be headed by Bishop Fred Jordan.[15]

In July, Hazel and Joseph flew to Georgetown, Guyana, to join the hundreds of people gathered at St. Peter's A.M.E. Church to hold their own service of thanksgiving for the election and consecration of Bishop Talbot as the ninetieth bishop of the A.M.E. Church. Included in the crowd were members of the diplomatic corps, government ministers, and the prime minister, Forbes Burham, who in "offering words of congratulations" described Talbot as "'a man of the people' and a man who had always demonstrated 'sincerity and humility' in the execution of his duties as pastor and Ambassador." Talbot's wife Sylvia was the former health minister of the country and was well respected by the citizens.[16] Joseph felt personal pride in being able to bring greetings to a fellow West Indian and a good friend, and to spend a few days in their spacious home.

1973 began with good news. Joseph received a report from Royston C. Lewis, the cardiologist at the Cleveland Clinic indicating that he was in fairly good health.[17] The couple settled once again at Wade Park, attended St. James Church regularly, visited friends, and tried to give support to Annetta, who was still working all hours of the night as a writer/producer for WVIZ. There she had completed twenty Black history and literature shows, produced and hosted several talk shows, written and produced four shows for the *Inside/Out* series for National Instructional Television, and had done a series funded by the Ford Foundation called *Black Peoplehood,* which included a documentary on Carl Stokes and his cabinet.

In February 1974, while serving as guest lecturer at The College of Wooster, in Wooster, Ohio, she was offered a position as assistant professor of English and drama beginning in September. She resigned her job at WVIZ and moved to Wooster. Not wanting to remain in the large house by themselves, because of the tremendous cost of upkeep, Hazel and Joseph moved from Wade Park for the last time, to a modern, three-bedroom apartment at 4400 Clarkwood Parkway, no. 307. They continued their activities in the city and at St. James, where Joseph was often asked to preach.

In November 1974, the Gomezes returned to Paul Quinn College in Texas, where Joseph, Bishops Primm, Ball, who had been reinstated, and Sherman were honored as former bishops of Texas. During one of the evening meetings the public was invited to greet the four bishops and their wives at the new Episcopal Residence, "a palatial ranch style mansion, situated on a sprawling 15 acre lawn, studded with pecan trees," a far cry from the dormitory made into an Episcopal Residence in which the Gomezes had lived on the campus.[18] They were delighted to see that the college was moving forward under the leadership of the bishop, John Adams.

On March 16, 1975, Joseph preached the seventeenth anniversary sermon at Gomez Temple A.M.E. Church in Fort Wayne, Indiana, where his good friend, Naomi L. Phillips, was pastor. In the afternoon, Hazel gave a lecture and slide demonstration about her stay in Africa.[19] On October 20 she was one of the honorees at a tribute banquet on the occasion of the thirtieth anniversary of the A.M.E. Ministers' Wives Organization of Cleveland and Vicinity.[20]

Early in 1976, Annetta began to have doubts about the advisability of her parents living alone. Joseph's health had deteriorated, and his eyes were bothering him so much that he had stopped driving altogether. Annetta knew that getting them to come to Wooster would be difficult, since they would view it as giving up some of their independence. Eventually, the matter was taken out of her hands. In the spring, they both had a bad bout with the flu and had to be nursed by May Phillips Smith, who had been a member at St. James when Joseph pastored there. She called Annetta and explained the situation. After consultation with Eula and Harold, Annetta rented a duplex in Wooster at 1582/84 Cedar Lane, drove to Cleveland, and brought her parents back. For a few days she left them on University Street in the care of Margaret Stevens, a neighbor and good friend, while she went back to Cleveland and, with the help of her nephew, Gerald, packed all her parents' belongings and had them moved to Wooster.

The then dean of the College (later president), Henry Copeland; the vice president, Fred Cropp; a chemistry professor, Ted Williams (one of the first Blacks hired by the college); and several other professors helped move the Gomezes into their side of the duplex. No one left until every book was in place and every appliance was installed.

The two apartments were identical: a long, rather oddly shaped living room, a half bath, combination kitchen/dining room, and a screened-in porch were on the ground floor. Upstairs were three bedrooms and two full baths. The master bedroom was huge; it had its own bath and looked out on a large back yard. The basement, which extended the entire length of the house, was large enough to accommodate all the boxes and extra books and papers that could not fit into the bedroom that Joseph made into a library.

It was not long before Wooster had fallen in love with the tiny couple. Regularly Hazel would drive them for lunch to the Ramada Inn or the Wooster Inn, where the waitresses would fight over who would serve them. Since there was no A.M.E. Church in Wooster, on Sundays they attended with Annetta Westminster Presbyterian Church on the campus; there the pastors, Barry Sheppard and Cindy Jarvis, fussed over them, as did the other members.

One of the young Black professors in political science, Mike Smith, adopted them as his parents. He called Joseph "Daddy" and was the only other person besides Joseph to call Hazel "Dear." He would drive them to Cleveland, or through the neighboring Amish country, or wherever else they wanted to go. Like Curtis Jr., Mike never tired of hearing their stories about the past—how they met and fell in love, their initial meeting with Reverdy Ransom, their first pastorate and honeymoon in Bermuda, the racial conflicts in Detroit, their trouble with Bishop Vernon, their trials in Texas, and their trips abroad.

A couple who lived on Cedar Lane took the Gomezes once a week out in the country to attend Methodist Church meetings. In the summer they would go to Woodland Park to be with Eula and Harold, who now owned the cottage in Michigan. When school started again Joseph often spoke in Mike's class on campus. He and Hazel attended Annetta's plays; they were especially fond of her original musical, written with Brian Dykstra, *Drown the Wind,* and of her production of Lorraine Hansberry's *A Raisin in the Sun.* At one point during the performance Beneatha was berating her brother, and Mama said, "I thought I taught you to love him. . . . If you ain't learned that, you ain't learned nothin.'" To everyone's amusement, Joseph said aloud "Amen!"

For a while the Gomezes seemed to be fairly happy in this small, picturesque college town. Downtown Wooster consisted of one long street, Liberty Avenue, which was lined with stores, the most popular being Freedlander's Department Store. Harold Freedlander usually met the Gomezes on the ground floor and made sure they were taken care of and that there were always chairs nearby when they became tired.

They loved to stroll the campus in all the seasons, but especially autumn, when the brightly colored leaves rustled beneath their feet, or spring, when the tiny pink and white flowers began to push up in search of the sun. Sometimes in spring or summer Annetta would drive them to Freedlander Park so they could watch the ducks paddle in the small man-made pond, or the children pump themselves as high as they could on the swings.

Perhaps the most enjoyable experience for the Gomezes in 1977 was when Eula and Annetta took them to Atlantic City to the Bishop's Council's summer session.[21] Although Joseph was pushed about in a wheelchair so he would not become overly tired, he was his old self again as he attended the private meetings of the Council. Bishop Robinson told the daughters that Joseph argued his convictions passionately, just as he had before he retired; although some of the meetings lasted into the early morning hours, Joseph stayed until they ended. At one of the worship services, when the congregation sang "O For a Thousand Tongues to Sing

My Great Redeemer's Praise," Joseph stood up, pushed aside his wheelchair, threw his head back, and sang loudly with the rest. During those few days he seemed to gain strength from the fellowship with the other bishops, ministers, and friends. He was among A.M.E.s again, and that was what counted most.

That same year Joseph, who wanted to leave Annetta a home before he died, put a sizeable down payment on a house at 2631 Tanglewood Drive, a brick split-level with large white columns in front, five bedrooms, and a large backyard. When the mover brought his boxes of books into the room that was to be a library, Joseph sat in the middle and would not budge until everything was placed where he wanted it. The Gomezes occupied the top floor, where the kitchen, master bedroom with bath, guest bedroom, living room, library, and dining room were located. They could also sit out back on the wooden sundeck and catch the breeze on summer evenings. Annetta slept on the bottom level, which had a large recreation room with a fireplace, two bedrooms, a utility room, and a bathroom

In July of 1978, Annetta left her parents with Kathy Thompson, a student and friend, who along with the housekeeper was to look after things while she went to London and Scotland on a one-quarter sabbatical leave. During her stay she was to attend the Edinburgh Festival and write a play. Letters and phone calls came frequently from 48 Egerton Gardens, Flat 4, London SW3, to Wooster. Joseph and Hazel missed her and did not adjust well to her being away. Her letters were full of talk concerning a man named Lionel whom she had met, and it sounded serious. If she were to marry and move to London, they wondered, what would happen to them? When she returned in November, they were greatly relieved. However, Lionel visited a few weeks later. Joseph decided he did not like the man, because, he said, he could not look Joseph in the eyes; both Joseph and Hazel were glad when he left. As it turned out, they did not have to worry. Before the following summer, the relationship ended rather abruptly.

For almost two years the Wooster police had followed Hazel around town, making sure she was safe. But when she started turning left from right-hand lanes and hitting the gas pedal instead of the brakes, they decided she should end her driving days. With the help of Annetta and Dr. James Robertson they were able to convince her to turn in her license. This proud, independent couple were suddenly dependent on their daughter for transportation, and since she was often busy at the college, the lunches and dinners at the Ramada and the Wooster Inn occurred less frequently. In addition, Mike Smith left the college to teach in New Orleans, so they were deprived of his companionship. They felt hemmed in. Hazel busied herself around the house, pulling out mementos and looking at them, but Joseph retreated more and more into himself. He seemed to have lost the will to live. Even through the Christmas holidays, which he shared with his family, he was preoccupied.

Joseph's last official act as a clergyman took place on March 3, 1979. He and Hazel flew to Washington, D.C., to attend the wedding of their grandson, Marvin Dewitt Williams to Febrieinne (Faye) Graves. The ceremony took place in Eula and Harold's town house at 621 4th Street, S.W., and Joseph officiated. The bride was elegant in her short, white, tailored suit as she stood beside Marvin, who wore a gray suit and pink shirt. Since Joseph could no longer see to read, he performed the ceremony by rote. Halfway through, he hesitated; his face became flushed as he found it difficult to remember the rite he had said for years without once having to glance at the words. Not missing a beat, members of the family helped him find his place, and he continued until the end without further problems. Afterwards the guests congratulated the couple and then enjoyed the refreshments, which had been catered by Sissy. Joseph and Hazel told Marvin and his bride how happy they were and hoped the couple would have as long a marriage as they had had themselves. Joseph excused himself and went upstairs to lie down. Suddenly he felt very tired. Although he would not have missed the wedding for anything, he was glad when he got back home and could sleep in his own bed.

April 28, 1979, was brisk and overcast, a typical Ohio Saturday preceding the end of the winter hibernation and the timid appearance of spring. At 6 A.M. Joseph injected himself with insulin, a ritual that was becoming more and more difficult with an eighty-nine-year-old body that was beginning to resemble a pincushion. (He jokingly referred to himself as the "Junkie Bishop," with diminishing humor—for as he so aptly put it, "the flesh was becoming a burden.") An hour later, he and "Dear" sat down to eat the usual breakfast—oatmeal, orange juice, coffee diluted with lots of milk, and toast—served by the usual hands. Joseph, however, only drank his coffee, while his wife and daughter discussed the Sunday service at Westminster Presbyterian Church and the homiletic skills of the Rev. Gordon Stewart, the minister who had replaced Barry Sheppard, and debated where they would eat dinner after church.

When the last of his coffee was gone, Joseph excused himself and returned to the bedroom, and then lay across the bed fully dressed. In the past month he had made a schedule for himself: breakfast and then back to bed—lunch and back to bed—light supper while listening to the news and trying to make out the fuzzy figures on the TV, and then back to bed. Since glaucoma was claiming his eyes and he could no longer read his books or watch television, more and more his bed became his reality. There he could dwell undisturbed in the darkness of his memories, contemplations, and half-realized dreams. Antigua, Trinidad, New York, Bermuda, Canada, and the 1920s in Detroit were more in focus than Wooster, Ohio, and the now of his life. A week before he had told Annetta that he really would not mind going home, except he hated to leave "Dear" behind. "You and Eula might not understand her the way I do. She has her peculiarities, but she's a wonderful woman." Annetta had laughed, assuring him that he would outlive her, but if he should not, she and Eula would take care of their mother and would never put her in a rest home. This had seemed to relieve his mind somewhat.

While Annetta was helping her mother get dressed, the phone rang. It was Kathy Thompson asking if she could have lunch with the family at the Ramada Inn, where they always ate on Saturdays. Annetta promised to pick her up at her dormitory at 11:30.

When it was time to leave for the Inn, Annetta roused her father, and then took him to the car first. As he reached the car door his legs slipped from under him, and Annetta grabbed him to prevent his falling on the driveway. She was concerned; two weeks earlier his legs had refused to function, while walking down the aisle of the church at her side. She suggested that perhaps it would be better if they stayed home that day, but Joseph shook his head. Once a routine had been established, he was reluctant to break it. He said he would be all right, and then pulled himself up into the back seat of the car. Annetta returned to the house for Hazel, who as usual had waited until she was bundled warmly in her coat, hat, and gloves before deciding she needed to go to the bathroom.

Shortly afterwards, Hazel was buckled into the front seat of the car. Annetta drove to the campus and picked up Kathy, who kept them laughing all the way to the Inn. At the Ramada the hostess and waitresses made their customary fuss over the tiny couple as they followed them to their special red booth. Over it hung pictures of ships, which were particularly appropriate for a couple who loved the sea. Both Joseph and Hazel ordered fried shrimp, their favorite luncheon dish; Annetta and Kathy ate steak.

The conversation was frivolous, with Joseph intermittently reprimanding the two younger women for smoking, although neither had ever smoked in front of him. This was his way of letting them know they were not putting anything over on him. "Ladies did not walk around with cigarette breaths, and if they didn't stop, he would have to get the hairbrush." The thought of the bishop with a hairbrush—a man would could never bring himself to spank his daughters and who took them riding if Hazel was going to spank them—sent them into fits of laughter. The waitress, who was also named Hazel, chided Joseph for picking at his food. To please her he made a strong show of trying to get it all down, but he was not really hungry.

When lunch was over, and to "Dear's" annoyance Joseph had left an overgenerous tip, as he always did, Annetta took her mother to the front of the lobby, where she was to sit by the picture window and wait for the car to be brought around. Then she went back into the restaurant to get her father, who sat joking with Kathy.

He stood. The women took his arms and led him from the restaurant, past the hostess counter, out into the hall. Once again his legs failed, and it was difficult to hold him up. "Don't pull me, Annetta," he said. "I'm not pulling you. I'm trying to keep you from falling," she answered. Suddenly a look of terror came over his face. He gasped, "Oh, my God," and fell to his knees. Annetta quickly laid him down, resting his head on the tile floor. He stared blankly up at the ceiling; his body convulsed violently as if it were trying to shake itself free, and strange noises came from his throat. Annetta wondered if this was the "death rattle" she had heard the old people speak of; she had always dismissed such tales as superstition. His dentures were loose in his mouth, and he seemed about to swallow them. She quickly removed the top plate and then looked up to ask Kathy for assistance. But Kathy was walking aimlessly back and forth, the tears streaming down her face, unable to function in any coherent way. By this time people had rushed out of the restaurant and Mitchell's barbershop across the lobby. They stood around wordlessly, shaking their heads.

Annetta phoned Dr. Robertson and told him what had happened. He told her to call the emergency squad and that he would meet her at the Wooster Hospital. Only a few minutes had passed, but it seemed as if Joseph had been convulsing for hours. Annetta sat on the floor beside him, talking to him and attempting to keep him warm. When the paramedics arrived they administered cardio-pulmonary resuscitation and then tried to restore his heartbeat by defibrillation, a series of electrical shocks. Finally, they lifted him onto the stretcher and carried him out the inn's front door. Only when they passed Hazel seated by the window did she become aware that something had happened to Daddy.

Annetta helped a stunned Hazel into the car and then went around to the driver's side. Before she could get in, one of the restaurant employees offered to drive; Annetta sat between her mother and the man, watching cars swerve in waves to the curb as they heard the approaching wail of the ambulance. In less than five minutes they pulled up at the emergency entrance of the hospital and were ushered into a private room, where they were told to wait. Annetta phoned Eula, who assured her that she would get there as soon as she could make airline reservations. This would take some doing, since most of the major airlines were on strike.

After thirty minutes Doctor Robertson came into the room to tell them what Annetta already suspected—that Joseph was dead, of a massive coronary infarction. He had probably been dead when he first fell in the inn's lobby. Hazel was too stunned to cry. She and Annetta just stood, holding each other. Annetta supposed her mother felt as she did, as if she were on the outside watching someone else move about.

It was unreal to leave Daddy in the hospital. Only once before had he ever been in one, in 1965 when he had his first heart attack, and he had asked to go home every day. It was unreal to put gas in the car before returning home from the hospital—unreal to find the friendly local undertaker waiting for them at the house—unreal to pick out clothes for Daddy to wear in the coffin (a dark suit, white shirt, black shoes and socks, underwear, a clerical robe for an unreal person who had nothing to do with Bishop Joseph Gomez, who laughed a lot and liked to eat fried shrimp)—unreal to talk to the doctor when he came to the house to leave tranquilizers for Hazel and sleeping pills for Annetta if she needed them.

Hazel took her pills and went immediately to sleep, only to wake late the next morning having to learn all over again what had happened the day before. "Where's Daddy?" she asked. When told again that Joseph had died, she became disoriented. From that time until her own death—except for the first time she saw Joseph's body in the coffin—she erased his death from her mind. Nature kindly intervened, shielding her from a pain which was insupportable. Annetta became "Daddy" to her, and she followed her daughter everywhere.

While Hazel slept on the Saturday of Joseph's death, Annetta called Rev. Gordon Stewart, who arrived immediately and helped her notify the family and church leaders. Through a series of chain calls the news was quickly carried throughout the Connection—"The Little Giant" was dead. The bishops and the family decided the funeral should be held at Bethel, Detroit, which had been his first charge in the United States and was in the last large district over which he had presided as bishop. Hubie Robinson, now bishop of the 4th District, arranged for Barksdale Funeral Home to pick up the body as soon as the embalming in Wooster was completed.

Annetta was later told that the body had arrived in Detroit naked, his clothes folded at the bottom of the coffin, and his shoes missing. Seemingly the funeral home in Wooster had been miffed because it would not be responsible for the funeral. This angered her until she thought of how her father would have laughed at the prospect of "the bishop" being transferred from Ohio to Michigan in the buff. Although he had not been naked when he first arrived in Detroit in 1919, he and Hazel had had very few possessions. In 1979, he was arriving with even fewer.

At Bishop Robinson's request, Annetta wrote an obituary, to be telephoned in as soon as it was completed. She also had to provide the names of favorite hymns and other selections the family wanted performed at the funeral. Meanwhile the phone was constantly ringing in Wooster. Calls came from the East and West coasts, the South and North, from Bermuda, Canada, Trinidad. Finally at 4 A.M. James Haden, one of Annetta's professor friends at the college, got her to take a sleeping pill and lie down on the couch for a few hours. Back in Washington, Eula was frantically trying to get a flight to Cleveland but managed only to book one to Detroit for the next afternoon.

When Annetta awoke, messengers flooded the house with cut flowers, plants, and telegrams. The phone never stopped ringing. Almost miraculously, Maggie Sawyer appeared from St. Louis and took care of Hazel. How Maggie had managed to get a plane to Cleveland was a mystery.

Hazel, Maggie, and Annetta arrived in Detroit on Monday morning, April 30, where they were met by Rev. Brockington, Eula, and Harold, and were transported to the Radisson Cadillac Hotel on Washington Boulevard. Here the family and friends were housed at the expense of the 4th District. That afternoon they went to the funeral home to select a coffin and complete the arrangements with Mrs. Barksdale, who took a special interest, since she had always admired Joseph. The family selected a black coffin, elegant in its simplicity, and they agreed with Mrs. Barksdale that the only flowers around the coffin should be two red rose arrangements at the head and foot. All other flowers were to be taken to the cemetery. In his hands Joseph would hold a single white orchid.

Annetta and Hazel shared a room in the hotel, but they were joined the night before the funeral by Michael Smith, who, having missed his flight, arrived at 2 A.M. Since he had made no reservations, he decided to sleep on the floor between the two beds. Maggie's room was conveniently located a few doors away.

Tuesday afternoon the family went to view the body at the funeral home. Hazel now saw Joseph for the first time since the luncheon. Out of respect for her privacy, everyone stepped back as she stood looking at her companion of over sixty-five years. She said very quietly, "He's so beautiful." Then she turned to Annetta and said, "I'm ready to go now." After that she once more pulled shut the protective curtain and retreated into fantasy.

Hazel was not able to attend the dinner given by Rev. Maurice and Marion Higgenbotham for the family and close friends, nor was she allowed to attend the wake which followed. None of the family members had wanted an open-casket wake, but knowing that at most A.M.E. funerals it was the custom, they acceded. At Bethel the family sat in the first two rows in front of the casket. Cousins Lorraine and Alfred Harper had come from New York. Curtis Sr. also joined the relatives to say farewell to his former father-in-law, for whom he had great admiration and respect. Several thousands of people passed in front of the casket, some barely glancing at the figure before them, others lingering for a while. One little old man dressed in soiled overalls stood weeping as if his tears could bring life to the bishop's powdered form.

The grandchildren, who were to serve as pallbearers, arrived in Detroit on May 2, the morning of the funeral. They were allowed to view their grandfather just before the casket was permanently closed for the funeral. The undertaker took the cross from around Joseph's neck and the ring from his finger and gave them to Annetta. (The ring had been presented to him when he pastored Bethel, Detroit, and he had never removed it.) She put it on her finger, and there it remains. Curtis Jr. kept the cross.

Pushed in her wheelchair by Annetta, Hazel led the procession into the church as the organ played "Holy Art Thou, Lord God Omnipotent." Her frightened faced was hidden from the congregation by a gray woolen scarf. The rest of the family and friends followed. After everyone was seated, Bishop Cummings lined the opening hymn, "God of Grace and God of Glory," and then Bishop S. S. Morris prayed for the deceased and especially for the loved ones left behind.[22]

A quarter of the way into the service, expressions were given by Richard Austin, president of the Detroit Memorial Association, who reminded the congregation that Joseph had been one of the founding members of the Association; Mamie Atkins from the Women's Missionary Society, speaking for Mary Frizzel, the president, who was ill; Ezra Johnson, representing the general officers of the Church, who referred to Joseph as a "Bishop non-parallel when the Church needed one . . . an effective author . . . a preacher *par excellence* . . . a prophet with a thundering voice when aroused . . . a tender, loving brother to the hurt, bewildered and outcast . . . a civil rights champion, even in the pre–civil rights era . . . kingly in bearing, immaculate in attire . . . . He was a Bishop who looked like a Bishop, spoke like one, presided like one and administered like one." When Johnson had concluded, Rev. John Hunter spoke for the Connectional clergy. He reminisced about his initial meeting with the bishop and his years as assistant pastor at St. James, Cleveland. He described Joseph as "a great Biblical preacher . . . a preacher every day of the week . . . a prince of pastors." Recalling Joseph's seminary lectures at Payne he said, "He had few scholastic equals in contemporary Christendom." Hunter concluded, "He developed leaders as he led. If you would see his living monument in leadership—look around, all around."

The choir now sang "Blessed Assurance." Rev. Joseph Brockington, representing the 4th District, then said in a voice filled with emotion that Joseph was "indeed one of God's anointed. . . . Bishop Gomez brought to us honor because of his ability to counsel with the greats of the nation and the world and to stand in the greatest pulpits of the country and abroad. And yet he could grace the pulpit of any of our storefront churches. He loved people—great people, small people." Brockington was followed by Labron Simmons, speaking for the laypersons; Rev. Alvia Shaw, speaking as the bishop's pastor at St. James; and Bishop Frank Madison Reid, Jr., speaking for the episcopacy in place of Bishop Fred Jordan, who could not be present.

The hymn "Crossing the Bar" (words by Alfred Lord Tennyson) was sung, acknowledgements were read by Maurice J. Higgenbotham, and the obituary was read silently, as the organist played Joseph's favorite hymn, "Amazing Grace."

Bishop Hubert N. Robinson rose to deliver the eulogy. His task, he began, was a difficult one, since Joseph had been like a father to him. He took as his theme, "Joseph Gomez, the man who stood in the darkness with God," alluding to Exodus 20:21: "The people stood afar off and Moses drew near unto the thick darkness where God was."

He related how Joseph first came to the United States from Trinidad, and how Bishop Reverdy Ransom took him under his wing and saw to it that he attended Wilberforce University, where he "wooed and won the hand of Hazel Thompson." He spoke of the "darkness of racism and segregation" when in his early twenties Joseph led his "people from Napoleon and Hastings Street and brought a lot of ground in a predominately foreign born area"; of his "standing firm during the Dr. Sweet trial in Detroit and thereby opening the question of restrictive covenants"; of his "courage and eventual victory in the darkness of his attempt to gain the Episcopacy despite the threat of some that no man from the West Indies would ever be elected to the Bishopric." After outlining other momentous events in the life of Joseph, he declared, "Never given to defeat by the fell circumstances of fate or opposition, neither by the barriers of time nor fortune, he was born with an indomitable spirit and an unconquerable passion for facing untried frontiers. . . . He was small in stature, but his compatriots had to look up to see him, for his heights of vision and his ideals made him lofty in stature." Joseph Gomez had Christianized "the Darkness of Death. He did not cross it over. He preferred not to cross it over. . . . [For] in the Darkness of Death is light. . . . God is there."

The eulogy, indeed the entire service, was not a mourning for the dead but the celebration of a life. Fittingly, when the choir of several hundred voices stood to sing Handel's "Hallelujah Chorus" the sun burst through the stained glass windows and continued to shine as the grandchildren carried the coffin to the waiting hearse for the long trip to Detroit Memorial Park Cemetery.

Hazel, mercifully, slept through the entire service. On the way to the cemetery she lightened the hour by waking up for a moment to ask, "Where is lunch?" When the limousine reached the graveyard she said, "You see there. I told you this driver didn't know where he was going. Not a restaurant in sight!"

After the brief burial service all the cars returned to Bethel, where the ladies of the 4th had prepared lunch for the visitors. This provided an opportunity for friends from all over the country to greet each other before they departed for home. Among those present was Cora Perry-Hoskins, Annetta's best girlfriend from high school, who had come from Flint to pay her last respects to "Pops."

White and Black newspapers across the country, from New York to California, carried the news of the death and funeral. Cards, flowers, and letters continued to pour in long afterwards. In a letter, Rev. Donald Jacobs of Cleveland noted that Joseph had "certainly loved his family . . . and one could never be in his company very long before he would start talking about his daughters and their beloved ones. . . . There was always the humorous sentence in the beginning of his conversations and a quiet peace about his daily life."[23]

Congressman Charles Diggs wired that Joseph "was a true pioneer in our community, seeking out and making opportunities for us to expand our religious, social and economic horizons."[24] Russell and Sally Brown reminded Hazel that as "school mates we were at your wedding in Wilberforce, and have been perpetual friends through all these years."[25] From Texas, Rev. and Mrs. C. C. Johnson wrote, "He leaves to us a beautiful and cherished memory of the very fruitful years he spent with us in Texas."[26]

On May 21, Bishop Talbot notified the family that the members of Fountain A.M.E. Church in Baratari, Trinidad, and Tobago, had voted to name a new building the Bishop Joseph Gomez Day Care Center.[27] Along with the Joseph Gomez Administration Building on the campus of Paul Quinn in Texas and several churches throughout the Connection, this building would be a monument to his contributions to his Church and his people. For instance, Gomez Chapel in Rockford, Illinois, sent a resolution that their church would "forever be a vivid reminder of the inspiration and dedication of one of the great spirits of African Methodism."[28] Rt. Rev. H. Coleman McGehee, Jr., bishop of the Roman Catholic diocese of Michigan, wrote: "He will be remembered not only for his ministry as pastor and bishop, but also for his many accomplishments in the liberation of Black people when such efforts were not as visible as they have been in recent years."[29] Annetta Williams, Joseph's only granddaughter, had written a poem for her grandfather (which was included in the funeral program) entitled "A Tribute to My Beloved Grandfather."[30]

Of all the reportage of the funeral itself, the *A.M.E. Report* (May 1979) summed it up best:

> This striving for excellence was seen in the elders who had to take their places on the platform and represent. Everybody seemed to know it was Joseph Gomez that they were burying. You could not just dig a hole and dump him in it. He had to be buried as he had lived with punctilious care. Every 'i' had to be dotted and every 't' crossed. No loose ends were permitted.[31]

Joseph had outlived most of his friends and all of the other bishops elected in the class of 1948. The last years had been lonely—except for a few faithful friends like Brockington and Robinson, his wife and family, he rarely had contact with A.M.E.s—but he was not bitter. He accepted the fact that when one retired, had little power to give or take, people quickly gravitated to someone else. That was a fact of life. However, at his funeral he had been reclaimed.

Hazel survived him by three years, never really regaining her perspective. Annetta, the new "Daddy," took her to play rehearsals, church, dinner, shopping—helped her put together jigsaw puzzles and fill in the coloring books she had come to love. During the summer months she went with Eula and Harold to Woodland Park, where she looked out at the lake for "someone who was missing." She was not sure who.

Early in 1981 she began to experience mini-strokes. By September she was bedridden. Annetta hired nurses around the clock so she could remain in her own home. At Christmas Annetta put a small tree in the bedroom and played carols on a tape deck. When Rev. Gordon Stewart came to give her communion, she seemed to know what he was doing. In addition, whenever Carol Hill, the day nurse, or Annetta came into the room, she would smile broadly, but she would never speak.

On Monday, January 17, her breathing became extremely labored, and Annetta had her taken by ambulance to the Wooster Community Hospital, where she was diagnosed with pneumonia. Annetta visited her twice a day. One morning she found her mother strapped to a wheelchair, slumped over. She angrily demanded to know who had given such an order; "the doctor," the nurse said. Annetta had Hazel put back into bed and tore up the paper which said her mother should sit up for a few hours every day; her mother was too weak even to hold up her head.

That Friday when Annetta stopped by the hospital on her way to a play rehearsal at the college, the nurse informed her that Hazel had not eaten that day. Annetta requested a bowl of broth and a basting dropper. When they arrived and Annetta started to feed her, Hazel smiled and began to swallow. She looked like a small, frightened bird. Her face was drawn, and she weighed only seventy-six pounds. When she had swallowed the last drop of soup, she gasped. Annetta saw the same look on her face that had been on Joseph's just before he died. She called the nurses, but Hazel was dead before they reached her bed. She was ninety-two years old.

Her body was taken to Boyd Funeral Home in Cleveland. At the funeral held Tuesday, January 25, at St. James, both Hubert Robinson and John Hunter paid tributes to Hazel. The congregation laughed as Hunter remembered how she could so often get her way with Joseph without his knowing it. Rev. Brockington, who had continued to send Hazel flowers on every special occasion just as he had done when Joseph was alive, delivered the eulogy, after Grace Mims had sung "Precious Lord." Prayer was offered by Rev. Gordon Stewart, who had traveled with the family from Wooster and would drive them to Detroit for a special wake and the interment.[32] Once again Mike Smith had flown in from Huntsville, to pay his last respects to "Dear" and to be with his adopted family in Cleveland and Detroit.

During the special evening wake held at Bethel, Detroit, several hundred people filed past the open casket. The next morning, January 22, 1982, Hazel was buried beside Joseph in Detroit Memorial Park on Thirteen-Mile Road. After an earthly separation of three short years, Hazel and Joseph could walk hand in hand out of the darkness, into the light with God.

◈ ◈ ◈

Appendix A

Organization of the African Methodist Episcopal Church (Based on the 1972 A.M.E. Discipline)

THE GENERAL CONFERENCE OR QUADRENNIUM

The General Conference is the supreme body. It makes all the laws and determines the doctrines and procedures of the Church. It is composed of the bishops, delegates (ministerial and lay, elected by the Annual Conferences and Electoral Colleges respectively). Other members are the general officers, college presidents, deans of theological seminaries, chaplains, and Connectional officers. The General Conference meets every four years but may have extra sessions with consent of the bishops and two-thirds of the Annual Conferences—or, if there is no bishop, of three elders with the consent of two-thirds of the Annual Conferences.

The General Conference Commission

It is composed of four bishops elected by the Council of Bishops, one lay and one ministerial representative from each Episcopal District, and six at-large representatives (three lay, three ministerial). The Commission selects the site for the General Conference eight years in advance, creating a subcommittee which, in conjunction with the Secretary of the Bishops' Council and the Secretary and Treasurer of the Church, perfect all arrangements for the General Conference.

The Board of Trustees

The Board of Trustees is the legal representative of the Church. "The right, power and authority to sell, donate, mortgage, convey, transfer,

{ 379 }

abandon, or encumber personal or real property, moveable or immovable or mixed, corporeal, or anything of value not held by or under the jurisdiction of an Annual Conference lies solely and exclusively under the jurisdiction and administration of the Board of Trustees/the Board of Incorporators of the A.M.E. Church." The Board is elected by each General Conference.

The Bishops Council

The Council of Bishops is the executive branch. Its members preside over General Conference and have the general oversight of the Church during the interim between General Conferences. It is made up of all of the bishops of the Church, who meet at least annually. The senior bishop is the president of the Council; next in seniority is the secretary.

General Officers

"Persons elected by the General Conference for administrative functions": Treasurer of the Church, Secretary of the Church, Secretary-Treasurer of Missions, Secretary-Treasurer of Church Extensions, Editor of the *A.M.E. Review,* Director of Worship and Evangelism, Secretary-Treasurer of the Department of Christian Education, Director of Salary Supplement, Secretary-Treasurer of Pensions, Editor of the *A.M.E. Christian Recorder,* Historiographer, Secretary-Treasurer of the Sunday School Union.

The General Board

The General Board is in many respects the administrative body. It is composed of the President, First Vice President, Second Vice President (all bishops), the General Secretary and the Treasurer of the A.M.E. Church, and the members of the various Commissions (Statistics and Finance, Pensions, Publications, Church Extension Worship and Evangelism, Lay Organization, Missions, Salary Supplement, Christian Education, Higher Education, Social Action, Ministry and Recruitment, Health, Women in Ministry) and a bishop as chairperson of each Commission.

The Judicial Council

The Judicial Council is the highest judicatory body. It is an appellate court, chosen by the General Conference and accountable to it. It is composed of nine members, five of whom are laypersons, three of them lawyers or judges who have full membership in the Church.

Episcopal Committee

The Episcopal Committee is composed of ministerial, lay, and youth delegates from each district. Its duty is to investigate, examine, and pass upon the moral, religious, and official conduct of each bishop, inquiring into their general physical and mental health. It suggests the number of bishops to be elected and makes assignments of bishops, subject to the approval of the General Conference.

Other Committees

Other Connectional-level committees are for the Report of the Treasurer, Annual Conference Boundaries, Credentials, Rules, Revisions, Worship and Liturgy, General Secretary, Salary Supplement, Pension, Evangelism, Christian Education, Sunday School Union, *A.M.E. Christian Recorder*, *A.M.E. Review*, Historiographer, Missions, Missionary Society, Educational Institutions, Theological Scholarships, Episcopal District Projects, Overseas Development, Social Action, Economic Development, Lay Organization, Richard Allen Youth Council, Health Commission, Public Relations, General Conference Commission, Christian Debutante–Masters, Memoirs, Reception of Fraternal Delegates, and the State of the Church.

THE DIOCESE OR DISTRICT

Bishops

The bishop is the "General Superintendent, chief executive, the administrative head of the A.M.E. Church, who is an Elder, elected and consecrated to the office of Bishop by the General Conference." Each Episcopal District is headed by a bishop.

There are nineteen Episcopal Districts in the A.M.E. Church. Each District is made up of a number of Annual Conferences, which are convened once a year by the bishop. During the Annual Conference worship services are conducted, the Episcopal District budget set, committee reports made, presiding elders' financial reports (evaluations and recommendations concerning the ministers under their supervision) given, and candidate ministers who have met all the qualifications are presented to the bishop for ordination. At the close of the conference, the bishop appoints ministers to the various churches.

Annual Conferences

1st District: Philadelphia, New Jersey, New York, New England, Delaware, Bermuda

2nd District: Baltimore, Washington, D.C., Virginia, North Carolina, Western North Carolina

3rd District: Ohio, Pittsburgh, North Ohio, South Ohio, West Virginia

4th District: Indiana, Chicago, Illinois, Michigan, Canadian

5th District: Missouri, Kansas-Nebraska, Colorado, Northwest Missouri, California, Southern California, Puget Sound

6th District: Georgia, Southwest Georgia, Atlanta–North Georgia, Macon, South Georgia, Augusta

7th District: Palmetto, South Carolina, Columbia, Piedmont, Northeast South Carolina, Central South Carolina.

8th District: Mississippi, East Mississippi, Northeast-West Mississippi, Central-North Mississippi, North Louisiana, Central Louisiana, Louisiana

9th District: Alabama, North Alabama, Central Alabama, East Alabama, South Alabama, West Alabama

10th District: Texas, Northeast Texas, North Texas, Northwest Texas, Central Texas, West Texas, Southwest Texas

11th District: Florida, West Florida, East Florida, Orlando Florida, Central Florida, Tampa Florida, South Florida, Bahamas

12th District: Oklahoma, Central Oklahoma, Arkansas, West Arkansas, Central Arkansas, East Northeast Arkansas, South Arkansas

13th District: Tennessee, East Tennessee, West Tennessee, Kentucky, West Kentucky

14th District: Liberia, Sierra Leone, Nigeria, Ghana, Ivory Coast

15th District: Cape, South West Africa (Nambia), Kalahari, Eastern Cape, Queenstown

16th District: Suriname-Guyana, Windward Islands, Virgin Islands, Dominican Republic, Haiti, Jamaica, Cuba, London

17th District: Southwest Zimbabwe, Northeast Zimbabwe, Malawi, Northeast Zambia, Northwest Zambia, Southeast Zambia, Southwest Zambia

18th District: Lesotho, Swaziland, Botswana, Mozambique, Northeast Lesotho

19th District: Orangia, East Transvaal, West Transvaal, Northern Transvaal, Natal.

Presiding Elder

Presiding elders are appointed by the bishop. They must keep a record of the Quarterly Conferences and give proper direction to all of the affairs of the Church. They have charge of the elders, deacons, preachers (itinerant and local), and evangelists in their particular district and give a report of each church and pastor to the bishop at the Annual Conferences. They travel and preach in the district, preside in the District Conferences, Sunday School, and A.C.E. Fellowship conventions, and at all Quarterly Conferences, and see that the business of the conference is in strict accord with the Discipline. In the absence of the bishop, they are in charge of all the ministers in their district and change, receive, or appoint preachers during the intervals between conferences, as the Discipline directs.

The District Conference

The District Conference is composed of all traveling ministers and local preachers, evangelists, presidents of missionary societies, and one steward from each Quarterly Conference within a presiding elder's district; and of presidents of lay organizations and a youth representative from each church, circuit, or station. The District Conference is held once a year, and the presiding elder is the presiding official. The District Conference makes provisions for obtaining the presiding elder's support, should the Annual Conference fail to do so. It examines, by committee, all applicants for admission into the traveling Connection. It appoints committees and submits reports on the local conditions of the charges and on progress of social services or mission programs.

The Quarterly Conference

The Quarterly Conference is held every three months in every circuit and in every station. The presiding elder is the presiding officer. It convenes to hear appeals, take applications for licenses to preach, to renew licenses, and to record membership in the churches including new members, the number of deaths, etc.

The Church Conference

A Church Conference is a meeting of a minister and the members of his church to consider and transact local church business. The minister is the presiding officer.

SUPERANNUATED PREACHERS: "A term applied to an ordained preacher who retires from active ministry because of age or disability."

SUPERNUMERARY: A minister or bishop for whom there is no appointment or who is allowed to be without appointment on request.

CONNECTION: "A structural organizational principle that all A.M.E. Church congregations are a connected network of unique compatible, interdependent relationships to accomplish the mission and purpose of the Church." Sometimes used to denote the entire A.M.E. Church.

DEACON: "The first of two ministerial orders of the A.M.E. Church; a preacher, satisfying the Disciplinary requirements, elected and ordained by the Annual Conference."

ELDER: "The second of two ministerial orders of the A.M.E. Church. A Deacon satisfying the Disciplinary requirements and elected and ordained to the order of Elder by the Annual Conference."

LAYMAN: Any member who is in good standing in the A.M.E. Church and is not a minister.

CHANCELLOR: The highest executive in a college or university. The bishop of a District where an A.M.E. college or university is located is often the chancellor of that school and president of its Board of Trustees.

EPISCOPACY: "A system of government or policy of the Church in which Bishops are the General superintendents, chief administrative and executive heads."

ECUMENICAL: A movement among Christian churches "furthering or intending to further the unity or unification of Christian Churches."

EX-OFFICIO: "By virtue or because of an office, e.g., the pastor is ex-officio president of all auxiliaries" of his church.

COLLEGES AND SEMINARIES

Wilberforce University, Wilberforce, Ohio 45384
Edward Waters College, Jacksonville, Florida 32203

*Paul Quinn College, Dallas, Texas 75241
Turner Theological Seminary, Atlanta, Georgia 30314
Jackson Theological Seminary, North Little Rock, Arkansas 72114
Allen University, Columbia, South Carolina 29204
Monrovia College, Monrovia, Liberia, West Africa
R. R. Wright School of Religion, P.O. Box 12, Residensia 1980, Republic
    of South Africa
Abington School of Religion, 3837 Simpson-Stuart Rd., Dallas, Texas 75241
Morris Brown College, Atlanta, Georgia 30314
Daniel Payne College, Birmingham, Alabama 35204
Payne Theological Seminary, Wilberforce, Ohio 45384
Shorter College, North Little Rock, Arkansas 72114
Dickerson Theological Seminary, Columbia, South Carolina 29204
Sizane School, P.O. Box 55, Mpopoma, Bulawayo, Zimbabwe

*Paul Quinn College has moved from Waco to Dallas, to the former campus
of Bishop College. The old P.Q.C. campus is up for sale at this writing
(1998).

PUBLICATIONS

The Christian Recorder. Published biweekly. Dr. Robert Henry Reid, Jr.,
    Editor, P.O. Box 24730, Nashville, Tenn. 37203
The A.M.E. Church Review. Published quarterly. Dr. Paulette Coleman,
    Editor, 500 8th Ave. S., Suite 211, Nashville, Tenn. 37203
The Missionary Magazine. Bertha O. Fordham, Editor. 800 Risley Ave.,
    Pleasantville, N.J. 08232
The Journal of Christian Education, 500 8th Ave. S., Nashville, Tenn.
    37203
The Voice of Missions, 475 Riverside Drive, #1926, New York, N.Y. 10027

❖ ❖ ❖

Appendix B

Historical Relationship between Wilberforce
University and the State of Ohio

Sept 21, 1844 to 1858	A.M.E. Church establishes Union Seminary twelve miles north of Columbus Ohio and two miles north of National Road. Education to be based on the manual plan, with emphasis on literature, science, agriculture, mechanical arts, theology. Closes for lack of funds in 1858.
Sept 28, 1856 to 1863	White Methodist Episcopal Church establishes Ohio African University, later changed to Wilberforce University, at Tawawa Springs, Ohio, Greene County, near Xenia.
March 10, 1863	Daniel Payne, A.M.E. minister, with the help of John G. Mitchell, principal of Eastern District Public School in Cincinnati, and James A. Shorter, pastor of A.M.E. Church in Zanesville, Ohio, contract to buy Wilberforce University for the A.M.E. Church.
July 10, 1863	Charter granted for Wilberforce University under the auspices of the A.M.E. Church. Payne becomes first president, J. A. Shorter treasurer, John G. Mitchell principal. A board of trustees appointed. School opens. Emphasis on liberal arts and religion. Articles of Association states "that this institution shall be and forever

remain under the management, direction and control of the African Methodist Episcopal Church."

1865	Main campus building burns. Funds needed for rebuilding.
1869–1870	Payne solicits funds from Salmon P. Chase, governor of Ohio, General O. O. Howard, Senator Charles Sumner, Garret Smith, Theron Baldwin. With support from the Ohio General Assembly and members of the state congressional delegation, Wilberforce gets appropriations from the Freedman's Bureau through the U.S. Congress.
1885	Rev. Benjamin Arnett, A.M.E., Republican, elected to Ohio State Legislature.
March 19, 1887	State of Ohio passes legislation setting up a Combined Normal and Industrial Department at Wilberforce University (two-year program), with a Board of Trustees composed of six members, three appointed by the governor of Ohio with approval of the Ohio Assembly and three from the Church with the approval of the University Board of Trustees. All subjects leading to a degree to be taught by the university. The state initially gives five thousand dollars per annum for its department, subject to review as needs increase.
1890	The university asks for federal aid for Combined Normal and Industrial Department under second Morrill Land Grant Act. Split results between Ohio State University and Wilberforce. Some Blacks oppose Wilberforce University's claims, believing the money would enable the state to set up a segregated school at Wilberforce, supported by federal funds, and delay the integration of Blacks into all universities. Outcome is compromise; Ohio State University receives federal funds, the state of Ohio allotts more funds for the Combined Normal and Industrial Department at Wilberforce.

June 1891	Payne Theological Seminary is established as a separate entity at Wilberforce University, with its own dean.
1896	Committee set up to examine relationship of state and church. Superintendent of Combined Normal and Industrial Department is separated from office of the president. State Board of Trustees changed to nine members: five appointed by governor, four by university.
1904	Controversy as to whether the Normal/Industrial part is a department of the university or a separate entity. Church calls it a department; state believes it to be separate. No consensus reached.
1910	Superintendent W. A. Joiner of the Combined Normal and Industrial Department pushes for less emphasis on industrial education and more on teacher training. University Board opposes the changes, calling them an infringement and duplication of its teacher education program.
1919	Combined Normal and Industrial Department tries to broaden its education program from two-year Normal track to a four-year program.
1923	State Board presents to Ohio legislature at its eighty-fifth assembly S.B. No. 233, which would establish Lincoln Normal Institute for Higher Education for Negro youth in the state of Ohio to preserve the rights and property of the Combined Normal and Industrial Department. University Board fights against the bill, which does not pass.
1929	To meet financial crisis of the university, courses in secondary education and the campus high school are turned over to Normal Department in exchange for the "clock-hour" plan: on a per-student, per-clock-hour basis, the state will pay the Liberal Arts College tuition for students who need general education

courses taught by the University to complete their high school teacher training work.

1932   With consent of University and State Boards, Bishop Reverdy Cassius Ransom asks Charles Wesley to become president of Wilberforce. Wesley serves one month and resigns.

1932–1936   R. R. Wright serves as president until elected bishop in 1936.

1935   University reviewed by North Central Association. Accreditation not given.

1936   D. O. Walker, former pastor of St. James. A.M.E. Church, Cleveland, elected president. Insists he is president of entire university.

1939   Walker gets university conditionally accredited by North Central Association, but has trouble with the State Board over politics. Gillespie Bill passed by Ohio legislature granting John Bricker, Republican governor, power to appoint six of the nine State Board members, leaving the Church only three.

1941   Walker dismissed as president as urged by the State Board, the governor, and finally the Church Board and Ransom. Combined Normal and Industrial Department becomes College of Education and Industrial Arts without consultation of University Board. Appointment of Joint Executive Board as suggested by the North Central Association, three members from University Board, three from State Board, "to consider and pass upon such matters as shall be referred to it by the respective boards." Joint Board largely in effective because of split decisions and lack of legal power.

1942   With consent of University and State Boards, Ransom again asks Wesley to become president. He agrees.

1945–1946	Wesley and University Board and Ransom differ over educational policies.
March 1947	Wilberforce loses accreditation from North Central Association.
1947	Bill 258 passed by Ohio legislature giving the State Board eight members and the University Board one member. Bill supported by Wesley, opposed by A.M.E. Church and university. Charles Wesley fired as president, Charles Leander Hill hired. Wesley sets up summer school on state side and becomes its president. State reclaims all its buildings and supplies. Wilberforce University continues as an A.M.E. school, utilizing its original buildings, eventually expanding across the highway.
1951	Wesley resigns. Former Normal/Industrial School officially becomes Central State University.

Two universities now reside on the same grounds: Wilberforce University, operated by the A.M.E. Church, and Central State, operated by Ohio. Both schools are attended largely by Black students.

❖ ❖ ❖

Notes

I. DAWNING: ANTIGUA, TRINIDAD, 1890–1908

1. *The Commemorative Magazine of the 150th Anniversary of Emancipation of Antigua and Barbuda,* Antigua, 1984, pp. 45–52.

For general information on the places and events of Chapter 1, see Morley Ayearst, *The British West Indies* (New York: New York University Press, 1960); Wendell Bell, ed., *The Democratic Revolution in the West Indies* (Cambridge, Mass.: Schenkman, 1967); Brian Dyde, *Antigua and Barbuda: The Heart of the Caribbean* (New York: Macmillan, 1967); Cyril Hamshere, *The British in the Caribbean* (Cambridge, Mass.: Harvard University Press, 1972); Eduardo C. N. Pereira, *Iehas de Zargo* (Funchal, Madeira: Adecio da Camra, 1989); and Ron Sanders, ed., *Antigua and Barbuda Independence* (St. John, Antigua: Department of Information, 1986).

2. See land distribution for this period. Colonial Office 239/77, enclosed in Fitzroy to Stanley, St. John, Antigua, May 12, 1845.

3. Dr. W. Farqhar, West Indian historian, interviews by Curtis Antonio Gomez, New York City (1988–1995).

4. Elizabeth Cornelius, interview by Curtis Antonio Gomez and Annetta Gomez-Jefferson, Willikies Village, Antigua (July 1988).

5. St. Phillips Parish baptismal records, Antigua, West Indies.

6. Bridget Harris, archivist, interview by Curtis Antonio Gomez, Antigua (1976).

7. Hewlett Richardson, interview by Curtis Antonio Gomez, Antigua (1976).

8. Baptismal records, archives, Funchal, Madeira.

9. *British Government Sessional Papers: 1847–48,* New York Public Library.

10. Lists of emigrants from Madeira to the West Indies, archives, Funchal, Madeira.

11. Daisy Pestano, interview by Curtis Antonio Gomez and Annetta Gomez-Jefferson, St. John, Antigua, (July 1988).

12. Charles Thwaites to John Beecham, Methodist Missionary Society archives; St. John, Antigua (February 28, 1838).

13. Bridget Harris, archivist, interview by Curtis Antonio Gomez, Antigua (1976).

14. Ibid.

15. Ibid.

16. Susan Loews Benjamin, *Decline of the West Indian Middle Class: 1834–1950,* 1994.

17. Mary Thomas, interview by Curtis Antonio Gomez and Annetta Gomez-Jefferson, Willikies Village (July 1988). (Ms. Thomas died in 1992).

18. Dan Mends, Portuguese historian, interview by Curtis Antonio Gomez, St. John, Antigua (1976).

19. Elsa Da Govia, *Slave Society in the British Leeward Islands,* (1965), chap. 2.

20. Records of baptisms, archives, Antigua, West Indies.

21. Records of births, archives, Antigua, West Indies.

22. Records of deaths, archives, Antigua, West Indies.

23. Records of births, archives, Antigua. West Indies.

24. Records of baptisms, archives, Antigua, West Indies.

25. Records of births, archives, Antigua, West Indies.

26. Records of marriages, archives, Antigua, West Indies.

27. Rebecca Gomez to Joseph Antonio Gomez (Author's file).

28. Records of births, archives, Antigua, West Indies.

29. Dr. W. Farqhar, West Indian historian, interviews by Curtis Antonio Gomez, New York City (1988–1995).

30. Ibid.

31. Arthur Bowers, interview by Curtis Antonio Gomez, New York City (1976).

32. Records of births, archives, Antigua, West Indies.

33. Daisy Pestano, interview by Curtis Antonio Gomez and Annetta Gomez-Jefferson, St. John, Antigua (July 1988).

34. Records of deaths, archives, Antigua, West Indies.

35. Ibid.

36. Dr. W. Farqhar, West Indian historian, interviews by Curtis Antonio Gomez and Annetta Gomez-Jefferson, New York City (1988–1995).

37. Records of births, archives, Port of Spain, Trinidad, West Indies.

38. Told to Curtis Antonio Gomez by his grandfather, Joseph Gomez.

39. Records of deaths, archives, Port of Spain, Trinidad, West Indies.

40. Told to Annetta Gomez-Jefferson by her father, Joseph Gomez.

41. Manifest of Alien Passengers for the United States Immigration Officer at Port of Arrival: The *Maraval,* arriving New York, August 3, 1908, Jas. M. Scott, Master.

42. Ibid.

2. THE INITIATION: NEW YORK CITY
AND REVERDY CASSIUS RANSOM, 1908–1911

1. Jervis Anderson, *This Was Harlem, 1900–1950,* p. 11.

2. Gilbert Osofsky, *Harlem: The Making of a Ghetto, Negro New York 1890–1939,* p. 3.

3. Anderson, *This Was Harlem,* p. 20.

4. Chart compiled by Tuskegee Institute of reported lynchings, 1882–1914, in Leslie H. Fishel and Benjamin Quarles, eds., *The Black American: A Documentary History* (New York: Scott Foresman, 1967), p. 376.

5. Lorraine Richardson Harper (James Richardson's daughter), interview by Curtis Gomez, New York City, (summer 1988).

6. *New York Age,* September 10, 1908.

7. Ibid.

8. Reverdy C. Ransom, *The Pilgrimage of Harriet Ransom's Son,* p. 15.

9. R. R. Wright, comp. *Encyclopaedia of African Methodism,* vol. I, pp. 184, 185.

10. W. E. B. Dubois, "The Word," in Reverdy C. Ransom, *The Negro: the Hope Or the Despair of Christianity.*

11. Anderson, *This Was Harlem,* p. 11.

12. *New York Age,* December 24, 1908.

13. *New York Age,* January 18, 1909.

14. Ransom, *Pilgrimage,* pp. 42, 203, 204.

15. *New York Age,* May 20, 1909.

16. *New York Age,* September 15, 1910.

17. *Encyclopaedia of African Methodism,* S.V. "One Hundred Years of African Methodism," p. 5.

18. Ransom, *Pilgrimage,* pp. 215, 216.

19. *Encyclopaedia of African Methodism.*

20. Ransom, *Pilgrimage,* p. 218.

21. Booker T. Washington, "Atlanta Exposition Speech," 1895, in *The Black American: A Documentary History,* eds. Leslie Fishel, Benjamin Quarles, p. 345.

22. Louis R. Harlan, *Booker T. Washington: The Wizard of Tuskegee, 1901–1915,* pp. 379–382.

23. *New York Age,* March 23, 1911.

24. Ransom, *Pilgrimage,* pp. 223–225.

25. *New York Age,* March 30, 1911.

26. Harlan, *Booker T. Washington,* p. 391.

27. Ransom, *Pilgrimage,* p. 225.

3. UPON THIS ROCK: WILBERFORCE AND HAZEL T., 1911–1914

1. Frederick A. McGinnis, *A History and an Interpretation of Wilberforce University,* p. 9.

2. Ibid., p. 33.

3. Ibid., pp. 37–39.

4. Ibid., pp. 41–42.

5. D. Ormande Walker, "The Struggle for Control of Wilberforce University," an address delivered at St. James Literary Forum, Cleveland, Ohio, Sunday, April 27, 1947. Transcript printed at Wilberforce and distributed, p. 4.

6. McGinnis, pp. 61–62.

7. *Wilberforce University Catalogue,* 1911.

8. *Encyclopaedia of African Methodism,* p. 344.

9. *Wilberforce University Catalogue,* 1911.

10. *Sodalian,* Wilberforce University year book, 1914.

11. McGinnis, pp. 145–146.

12. McGinnis, pp. 159–174.

13. *Wilberforce University Catalogue,* 1914; and *Tawawa Remembrancer,* 1914.

14. Cora Lockhart, interview by Curtis Gomez, Detroit, Michigan (April 1987).

15. Hazel T. Gomez, "Impressions of Wilberforce," personal notes 1958 (Author's file).

16. Hazel T. Gomez, notes, 1958.

17. Wilberforce faculty meeting minutes, December 1911, archives, Wilberforce University.

18. *Sodalian,* 1912.

19. *Sodalian,* Senior Issue, 1913.

20. *Tawawa Remembrancer,* 1914.

21. Wilberforce faculty meeting minutes, March 1913, archives, Wilberforce University.

22. Ibid., May 20, 1913.

23. Letter of certification for Hazel Thompson by president of Wilberforce University, W. S. Scarborough, April 19, 1913 (Author's file).

24. Letter of certification for Hazel Thompson by Instructor of Domestic Science, Wilberforce University, Bessie V. Morris, April 19, 1913 (Author's file).

25. Stationery of The Industrial-Agricultural College for Negroes, Selby, Miss. (Author's file).

26. *Sodalian,* Senior Issue, 1913.

27. Hazel T. Gomez, notes, 1958.

28. Bishop C. S. Smith, "The Noachian Curse," commencement address, Wilberforce University, June 1913.

29. Eileen Southern, *The Music of Black Americans,* pp. 44–45.

30. *Sodalian,* Senior Issue, 1914.

31. W. E. B. DuBois, *The Autobiography of W.E.B. DuBois,* p. 187.

32. J. M. Williamson, letter of introduction, (May 22, 1914) (Author's file).

33. *Sodalian,* Senior Issue, 1914.

34. Joseph Gomez, notes from an autobiographical sketch, n.d. (Author's file).

35. Ransom, *Pilgrimage,* pp. 228–234.

4. EARLY CHARGES: BERMUDA AND HAMILTON, ONTARIO, 1914–1919

1. *Encyclopaedia of African Methodism* (1948), pp. 336–38.

2. William Zuill, *Bermuda Journey,* p. 155.

3. *Encyclopaedia of African Methodism.*

4. Minutes of the Thirty-First Session of the Bermuda Annual Conference, 1914.

5. *Encyclopaedia of African Methodism,* vol. 1, pp. 122–23.

6. Lieutenant Colonel of Royal Engineer Office to Rev. Joseph Gomez. Bermuda (August 5, 1914) (Author's file).

7. Walter B. Hayward, *Bermuda Past and Present,* p. 230.

8. Ibid., p. 231.

9. Joseph Gomez, speech at Temperance Hall, December 1914 (Author's file).

10. Joseph Gomez, speech in Hamilton, Bermuda, 1957 (Author's file).

11. Hayward, p. 70.

12. Ibid.

13. Ibid., pp. 70–71.

14. Minutes of the Thirty-Second Session of the Bermuda Annual Conference, Shelly Bay. July 24–27, 1915.

15. Ibid.

16. Ibid.

17. Ibid., Allen Christian Endeavor Committee report.

18. Ibid., Temperance Committee report.

19. Ibid., Election of ministerial delegates to 1916 General Conference.

20. Ibid.

21. Ibid., Missionary sermon, Joseph Gomez.

22. Minutes Bermuda A.C., 1915.

23. Ibid., Presiding Elder's report.

24. Ibid.

25. Minutes District Conference, November 29, 30, 1916.

26. Joseph Gomez, speech at Citizens League and Ministerial Association. Bermuda, July 25, 1916 (Author's file).

27. Joseph Gomez, "Sunset," *Voice of Missions,* May 1917.

28. Joseph Gomez, speech at opening of the Bermuda Gymnastic Corps, 1917.

29. Joseph Gomez, "Christ in the Outdoors," Camp Baber, Michigan, August 4, 1965.

30. "Minutes Centennial General Conference, Philadelphia, May 1916," in Bishop C. S. Smith. *A History of the African Methodist Episcopal Church 1856–1922,* p. 291.

31. Ibid., pp. 291–292.

32. Ibid., p. 292.

33. Program notes, *The Star of Ethiopia,* Philadelphia, May 1916.

34. "Minutes Centennial General Conference. Philadelphia, 1916," pp. 299, 306–307.

35. *Encyclopaedia of African Methodism,* vol. 1, p. 205.

36. Bishop C. S. Smith to Walker, Minutes of the Thirty-third Bermuda Annual Conference, Hamilton, July 20–24, 1916.

37. Minutes Bermuda A.C. 1916, State of the Church Committee report.

38. Ibid., State of the Church Committee report.

39. Ibid.

40. Minutes Bermuda Sunday School Convention, September 1916.

41. Hayward, p. 231.

42. *Bermuda Colonist,* September 14, 1917.

43. George W. Williams, *History of the Negro Race in America, 1619–1880,* p. 71.

44. *Encyclopaedia of African Methodism* (1948), pp. 345–46.

45. Ibid.

46. Hazel Gomez, Notes on Ontario, 1917 (Author's file).

47. Ibid.

48. Charles A. Cottrill to Hazel Thompson Gomez (n.d.) (Author's file).

49. *Hamilton Press,* August 14, 1918.

5. BAPTISM OF FIRE: DETROIT, 1919–1928

1. C. S. Smith to Joseph Gomez (August 20, 1919) (Author's file).

2. Minutes of the Thirty-Third Session of the Michigan Annual Conference, Detroit, Michigan, September 1919, opening sermon.

3. Ibid., discussion of peace treaty.

4. Ibid., sermon by Joseph Gomez.

5. Ibid., final session, appointments.

6. "Short History of Bethel A.M.E. Church," *An Historical Sketch Eightieth Anniversary of Bethel A.M.E. Church, Detroit, Michigan.* (Detroit: Bethel Church, 1921).

7. C. S. Smith to Joseph Gomez, September 15, 1919 (Author's file).

8. Langston Hughes, *Fight for Freedom: The Story of the NAACP,* pp. 62–63.

9. David Allan Levine, *Internal Combustion: The Races in Detroit 1915–1926,* p. 137.

10. Levine, pp. 44, 47.

11. Research Bureau of Associated Charities, *Study of Housing Conditions of Negroes in Detroit,* 1919, Detroit Public Library.

12. Levine, p. 94.

13. Ibid.

14. Joseph Gomez, printed "Christmas Message, 1919" (Author's file).

15. Francis L. Broderick and August Meier, eds. *Negro Protest Thought in the Twentieth Century,* p. 67.

16. Chandler Owens to Joseph Gomez (February 15, 1920) (Author's file).

17. *Bethel Church Bulletin,* vol. 2, no. 8, Detroit, Michigan, November 21, 1920.

18. *Detroit Contender,* November 13, 1920.

19. Cora Lockhart, interview by Curtis Gomez, Detroit, Michigan, spring 1987.

20. Minutes of the Twenty-Sixth General Conference of the A.M.E. Church, St. Louis, May 1920, Quadrennial Sermon.

21. Ibid.

22. Ibid., Communion.

23. Ibid., Episcopal Address.

24. Ibid., Report Organic Union Committee.

25. Ransom, *Pilgrimage,* p. 262.

26. Minutes General Conference, 1920, Election of bishops.

27. *New York Age,* July 25, 1910.

28. Minutes General Conference, 1920, Consecration of bishops.

29. *Encyclopaedia of African Methodism.*

30. Joseph Gomez to ministers of Michigan Conference (July 2, 1920) (Author's file).

31. Cora Lockhart, interview by Curtis Gomez, Detroit, Michigan, spring 1987.

32. Minutes of the Thirty-Fourth Session of the Michigan Annual Conference, Fort Wayne, Indiana, September, 1920.

33. *Detroit Contender,* October 30, 1920.

34. Ibid.

35. Ibid.

36. David Levering Lewis, *When Harlem Was in Vogue,* pp. 16–17.

37. *Historical Sketch of Bethel A.M.E Church.*

38. Cora Lockhart, interview by Curtis Gomez, Detroit, Michigan, spring 1987.

39. Ibid.

40. Death Certificate of Walter Gomez, July 13, 1922, Detroit, Michigan.

41. Minutes of the Thirty-Sixth Session of the Michigan Annual Conference, Flint, Michigan, September, 1922, Recognitions.

42. Ibid., Bishop John Gregg's Address.

43. Joseph Gomez to James M. Conner, Detroit, Michigan (January 10, 1923) (Author's file).

44. Ibid.

45. Rev. Joseph Gomez to delegates to the 1924 General Conference (January 1923) (Author's file).

46. Program of Funeral Services for Bishop Charles S. Smith, Detroit, Michigan, February 5, 1923.

47. Autograph Book of Verses from the Gomez Family, Trinidad, April 18, 1923 (Author's file).

48. Joseph Gomez, Sermon on motherhood, Detroit, Michigan, 1923.

49. Joseph Gomez to James M. Conner (April 28, 1923) (Author's file).

50. Joseph Gomez to Croul (July 24, 1923) (Author's file).

51. Cora Lockhart, interview by Curtis Gomez, Detroit, Michigan, spring 1987.

52. Ibid.

53. Minutes of the Thirty-Seventh Session of the Michigan Annual Conference, Detroit, Michigan, September 1923, Election of Delegates to General Conference.

54. Levine, p. 137.

55. *Detroit Independence,* October 10, 1923.

56. Ibid.

57. Program of Groundbreaking Ceremony, Bethel A.M.E. Church, April 27, 1924.

58. Minutes of the Twenty-Seventh General Conference of the A.M.E. Church, Louisville, Kentucky, May 1924, Quadrennial Sermon.

59. Ibid., Missionary session.

60. Ibid., Bishop Conner's leave request.

61. Ransom, *Pilgrimage,* p. 263–264.

62. Minutes of the General Conference, 1924, Election of bishops.

63. Ibid., Assignment of bishops.

64. Minutes of the Thirty-Eighth Session of the Michigan Annual Conference, Grand Rapids, Michigan, September 1924, Bishop Vernon's address.

65. Ibid.

66. Ibid., Dr. Gilbert Jones's Address.

67. Frederick A. McGinnis, *A History and an Interpretation of Wilberforce University,* p. 85.

68. Minutes of Michigan A.C. 1924, Christian Endeavor League.

69. *Historical Sketch Eighty-Sixth Anniversary of Bethel A.M.E. Church.*

70. Articles of Incorporation of the Detroit Memorial Park Association, 1926.

71. Minutes of the Thirty-Ninth Annual Session of the Michigan Conference, Jackson, Michigan, September 1925, Presiding Elder's Report.

72. Ibid., Preface by bishop to appointments.

73. Ibid., Gomez's salary.

74. C. F. Green, M.D., to Rev. Joseph Gomez (February 21, 1926) (Author's file).

75. *The Independent,* February 1926 (?).

76. Cora Lockhart, interview by Curtis Gomez, Detroit, Michigan, spring 1987.

77. Joseph Gomez to *Detroit Free Press* (February 17, 1926).

78. Levine, p. 45.

79. Ibid., p. 152.

80. Ibid., pp. 152–155.

81. Cora Lockhart, interview by Curtis Gomez, Detroit, Michigan, spring 1987.

82. Richard W. Thomas, *Life for Us Is What We Make It: Building Black Community in Detroit, 1915–1945,* p. 138.

83. Levine, p. 169.

84. Ibid., p. 165.

85. Report, Mayor's Committee on Race Relations, 1926.

86. Cora Lockhart, interview by Curtis Gomez, Detroit, Michigan, spring 1987.

87. Rev. Joseph Gomez, Commencement Address, Kitrell College, May 23, 1926.

88. Souvenir and Official Program of the Annual Session of the Bishops' Council of the A.M.E., 1926.

89. Ibid.

90. Minutes of the Fortieth Annual Session of the Michigan Conference, South Bend, Indiana, September 1926.

91. Ibid., Presentation to Dean Woodson.

92. Minutes of the Forty-First Annual Session of the Michigan Conference, Detroit, Michigan, September 1927, Election of Delegates to General Conference.

93. Ibid., Reading of appointments.

94. Ibid.

95. *Detroit Independent,* September 30, 1927.

96. Ibid., October 7, 1927.

97. Ibid.

98. Ibid.

99. Ibid., October 14, 1927.

100. Ibid.

101. Joseph Gomez, Speech, Central Methodist Episcopal Church, Detroit, Michigan, January 30, 1928 (Author's file).

102. Ibid.

103. Ransom, *Pilgrimage,* p. 267.

104. Minutes of the Twenty-Eighth General Conference of the A.M.E. Church, Chicago, Illinois, 1928, Committee appointments..

105. Ibid., Organic Union.

106. Ibid., Gomez resolution.

107. Ibid.

108. Ibid., Election of bishops.

109. Ibid., Assignment of bishops.

110. Minutes of the Forty-Second Annual Conference of the Michigan Conference, Grand Rapids, Michigan, August–September 1928, Opening.

111. Ibid., Acknowledgements of Scarborough and Woodson.

112. Bishop John A. Gregg to Rev. Joseph Gomez (October 6, 1928) (Author's file).

6. A BROADENING VIEW: KANSAS CITY, MISSOURI, 1928–1932

1. Franklin D. Mitchell, *Embattled Democracy: Missouri Democratic Politics, 1919–1932,* pp. 63–64.

2. Henry C. Haskell and Richard B. Fowler, *City of the Future: A Narrative History of Kansas City, 1850–1950,* p. 118.

3. Ibid., pp. 124–126.

4. Benjamin Quarles, *The Negro in the Making of America,* pp. 207, 208.

5. *Kansas City Call,* September 28, 1928.

6. Ibid., October 19, 1928.

7. Ibid., November 9, 1928.

8. Ibid., November 16, 1928.

9. Ibid., November 9, 1928.

10. Ibid., November 16, 1928.

11. Bishop M. H. Davis to Rev. Joseph Gomez (January 14, 1930) (Author's file).

12. *Kansas City Call,* January 11, 1929.

13. Ibid., January 25, 1929.

14. Ibid., February 1, 1929.

15. Ibid., February 18, 1929.

16. Rev. Joseph Gomez, Abraham Lincoln speech, Jackson County Negro Republican Club, Kansas City, Missouri, February 12, 1929 (Author's file).

17. Frederick Douglass, "Oration in Memory of Abraham Lincoln," in Philip S. Foner, *The Voice of Black America,* pp. 465, 473.

18. Rev. Joseph Gomez, Abraham Lincoln speech.

19. *Kansas City Call,* July 21, 1929.

20. Minutes of the Nineteenth Annual Session of the Southwest Missouri Conference, Kansas City, Missouri, October 1929, Church and committee assignments.

21. Ibid., Presiding Elder's report.

22. Robert Weisbrot, *Father Divine and the Struggle for Racial Equality,* pp. 37–38.

23. *Kansas City Call,* February 7, 1930.

24. Ibid.

25. Ibid.

26. *Kansas City American,* February 6, 1930.

27. Dewitt Burton to Joseph Gomez, (February 25, 1930) (Author's file).

28. J. Edward Perry to Joseph Gomez (June 3, 1920) (Author's file).

29. Joseph Gomez, journal entry, July 10, 1930 (Author's file).

30. Ibid., July 11, 1930.

31. Hazel T. Gomez to Joseph Gomez (July 8, 1930) (Author's file).

32. Joseph Gomez, journal entry, July 13, 1930.

33. Ibid., July 18, 1930.

34. Ibid.

35. Ibid., July 19, 1930.

36. Ibid., July 20, 1930.

37. Ibid.

38. Ibid., July 25, 1930.

39. Joseph Gomez, "My Trip Abroad," part 4, *Kansas City Call,* August 1930.

40. Ibid.

41. Ibid.

42. Ibid.

43. Ibid.

44. Ibid.

45. Ibid.

46. J.A.S. Grenville, *A History of the World in the Twentieth Century,* pp. 133–138.

47. Joseph Gomez, journal entry, August 5, 1930.

48. S. S. Morris, "A Foreword," September 1, 1930 (printed with speech of Bishop John A. Gregg at World Christian Endeavor Convention, Berlin, Germany, August 8, 1930).

49. Bishop John A. Gregg, "The Call of Christ to Christian Brotherhood," address at the 8th World Christian Endeavor Convention, Berlin, Germany, August 8, 1930.

50. Ibid.

51. Joseph Gomez, "An Appreciation." October 30, 1930. (printed with speech of Bishop John A. Gregg at World Christian Endeavor Convention, Berlin, Germany, August 8, 1930).

52. Ibid.

53. Joseph Gomez, journal entry, August 10, 1930.

54. Ibid.

55. Minutes of the Twentieth Annual Session of the Southwest Missouri Conference, Sedalia, Gomez Resolution.

56. Ibid., Presiding Elder's report.

57. *Kansas City Call*, February 6, 1931.

58. *A.M.E. Review*, April 1931.

59. Ibid.

60. Ibid.

61. David Sims to Rev. Joseph Gomez (January 3, 1931) (Author's file).

62. Ibid.

63. Joseph Gomez to Hazel T. Gomez (February 20, 1932) (Author's file).

64. Joseph Gomez to Hazel T. Gomez (February 22, 1932) (Author's file).

65. Board of Managers, Paseo YWCA, Kansas City, Missouri, to Joseph Gomez (April 15, 1932) (Author's file).

66. Minutes of the Twenty-Ninth General Conference of the A.M.E. Church, Cleveland, Ohio, 1932, Quadrennial Sermon.

67. Ibid., Episcopal Committee.

68. Ibid.

69. Ibid., Fraternal Organizations' session.

70. *The Cleveland Press*, May 6, 1932.

71. Ibid., May 10, 1932.

72. Ibid.

73. Ibid.

74. *The Cleveland News*, May 12, 1932.

75. Minutes General Conference, 1932. Bishop Jones.

76. Ibid.

77. Ibid., Lay representation on Episcopal Committee.

78. Ibid., Election of bishops.

79. Ibid., Election of Secretary-Treasurer of Missions.

7. SCANDALIZIN' MY NAME: ST. LOUIS 1932–1936

1. *St. Louis Argus*, May 27, 1932.

2. Rev. Noah W. Williams, Seven and One-Half Years Report: St. Paul A.M.E. Church, 1932.

3. James Gomez to Rev. Joseph Gomez (September 15, 1932) (Author's file).

4. *Trinidad Guardian*, September 6, 1932.

5. Amanda Thomas to Joseph Gomez (October 1, 1932).

6. Ibid.

7. Mary Gomez, interview, Woodland Park, Michigan, summer 1986.

8. Ted Morgan, *FDR: A Biography*, p. 347.

9. Hughes, *Fight For Freedom*, p. 74.

10. Minutes of the Seventy-Eighth Missouri Annual Conference, November 1932, Western University.

11. *St. Louis Argus*, June 30, 1933.

12. Joseph Gomez, "Shakespeare's Faith," Sermonette, *Pittsburgh Courier*, n.d. (Gomez scrapbook. Date unknown, but belongs to St. Louis era 1932–36, celebration of Shakespeare's birthday.)

13. Joseph Gomez, "Thought for the Unsettled," Sermonette, *Pittsburgh Courier,* n.d. (Gomez scrapbook. Date unknown, but sometime in November 1932, after Roosevelt's election to the presidency.)

14. Eden Seminary Catalogue, 1932–33.

15. Ibid.

16. Joseph Gomez, transcript, Eden Seminary. 1934.

17. Joseph Gomez, "The Significance of the Negro Spiritual in a Program of Religious Education," master's thesis, 1934 (Author's file).

18. Ibid.

19. Ibid.

20. Joseph Gomez, "Aspects of Church Union," *Keryx,* December 1933.

21. Minutes of the Seventy-Ninth Missouri Annual Conference, Cape Girardeau, Missouri, November 1933, Gomez endorsement.

22. Ibid., Presiding Elder's Report.

23. Autograph Book, Signed by professors and members of Eden Seminary's graduating class during a breakfast given by the Gomezes, 1934 (Author's file).

24. Eden Seminary commencement program, June 7, 1934.

25. *St. Louis Argus,* June 15, 1934.

26. Ibid., July 20, 1934.

27. Program, Educational Chautauqua, Paul Quinn College, Waco, Texas, July 17–20, 1934.

28. Funeral Program, Rollin R. Dent, Grace Presbyterian Church, Chicago, Illinois, September 12, 1934.

29. David Sims to Joseph Gomez (October 19, 1934) (Author's file).

30. Davis Sims to Joseph Gomez (October 19, 1934).

31. *St. Louis Argus,* October 4, 1934.

32. Minutes of the Eightieth Session of the Missouri Annual Conference, St. Louis, Missouri, October, November 1934, Endorsements.

33. Hazel T. Gomez to Official Board of St. Paul A.M.E. Church (November 1934) (Author's file).

34. *St. Louis Argus,* December 14, 1934.

35. *Memphis World,* January 4, 1935.

36. Joseph Gomez, speech, Kappa Alpha Psi Fraternity, St. Paul A.M.E. Church, April 1935.

37. *St. Louis Argus,* August 23, 1935.

38. Ibid.

39. Ibid.

40. Ibid., August 25, 1935.

41. Maggie Sawyer, interview, St. Louis, Missouri, fall 1987.

42. Jewell Collier-Richie, telephone interview, Altadina, California, spring 1990.

43. Paseo Bible class, Kansas City, Missouri, to Joseph Gomez (May 8, 1935) (Author's file).

44. A. E. Berry to Joseph Gomez (August 23, 1935) (Author's file).

45. Minutes of the Eighty-First Session of the Missouri Annual Conference, St. Louis, Missouri, November 1935, Election of Delegates to General Conference.

46. Ibid., Presiding Elder's Report.

47. Joseph Gomez, "Unsafe Deliverance," Speech, Kappa Alpha Psi Fraternity's Silver Anniversary, St. Louis, Missouri, December 31, 1935, in J. Jerome Peters et al., *The Story of Kappa Alpha Psi Fraternity* (Philadelphia: Kappa Alpha Psi, 1932–1967), pp. 138–139.

48. Joseph Gomez, "The Menace of Cynicism," Speech, Fisk University, Nashville, Tenn., January 12, 1936.

49. Minutes of the Thirtieth General Conference of the A.M.E. Church, New York, New York, May 1936, Quadrennial Address.

50. Ibid., Election of Sec. of Sunday School Union.

51. Ibid., Episcopal Committee.

52. Ibid., letter from President Franklin D. Roosevelt to General Conference, 1936.

53. Ibid., Election of bishops.

54. *St. Louis Argus,* May 29, 1936.

55. Ibid., September 25, 1936.

56. Ibid.

8. INCENDIARY SPECTERS: CLEVELAND, 1936–1944

1. Minutes of the Fifty-Fifth Session of the North Ohio Annual Conference, Cleveland, Ohio, September–October, 1936, Joseph Gomez appointment.

2. Foster Armstrong et al. *A Guide to Cleveland's Sacred Landmarks,* pp. 134–135.

3. Ibid. p. 135.

4. Kenneth L. Kusmer, *A Ghetto Takes Shape: Black Cleveland, 1870–1930,* p. 207.

5. Ibid., pp. 182–183.

6. Ibid., pp. 183, 184.

7. Joseph Gomez to P. M. Watson (March 12, 1937) (Author's file).

8. Ibid.

9. Program and Inauguration Address of Dougal Ormonde B. Walker, president of Wilberforce University, March 18, 1937.

10. *Cleveland Call and Post,* March 18, 1937.

11. Joseph Gomez to Martin D. Davey (March 24, 1937) (Author's file).

12. Program, Noonday Holy Week Services, Cleveland Church Federation, Old Stone Church, Cleveland, Ohio, March 26, 1937; Rev. Joseph Gomez to Mr. Leo B. Marsh, Executive Secretary, Indiana Avenue Branch YMCA, Toledo, Ohio (March 24, 1937) (Author's file); and Program, Sesquicentennial Festival of Negro Methodism Celebrated by the A.M.E. Church, Memphis, Tenn., June 22–27, 1937.

13. Joseph Gomez to Charles S. Spivey, Sr. (September 3, 1937) (Author's file).

14. Minutes of the Fifty-Sixth Session of the North Ohio Annual Conference, Akron, Ohio, September–October, 1937, Ransom's appointment to Parole Board.

15. *Cleveland Call and Post,* November 4, 1937.

16. Reverdy C. Ransom, poem on the occasion of his and Emma Ransom's fiftieth wedding anniversary, Wilberforce, Ohio, November 4, 1937.

17. *Cleveland Plain Dealer,* January 3, 1938.

18. Ibid.

19. Joseph Gomez, handwritten notes, January 2, 1938 (Author's file).

20. *Cleveland Call and Post,* January 6, 1938.

21. Ibid., January 20, 1938.

22. *Cleveland Plain Dealer,* February 11, 1938.

23. *Cleveland News,* February 24, 1938.

24. Joseph Gomez, sermon, Old Stone Church, Cleveland, Ohio, April 15, 1938 (Author's file).

25. *Cleveland Call and Post,* June 16, 1938.

26. *Pittsburgh Courier,* July 16, 1938.

27. *Cleveland Plain Dealer,* July 4, 1938.

28. Ibid.

29. *Cleveland Call and Post,* July 14 and July 21, 1938.

30. Minutes of the Fifty-Seventh Session of the North Ohio Annual Conference, Piqua, Ohio, September–October 1938, Joseph Gomez sermon.

31. Ibid., Introduction of visitors.

32. Joseph Gomez to George Singleton (February 1, 1939) (Author's file).

33. *Cleveland Plain Dealer,* April 24, 1939.

34. *Chicago Defender,* June 10, 1939.

35. Joseph Gomez, baccalaureate sermon, Wilberforce University, Wilberforce, Ohio, June 4, 1939.

36. *Cleveland Call and Post,* June 22, 1939.

37. Allan H. Spear, *Black Chicago: The Making of a Negro Ghetto, 1890–1920,* chap. 3; and St. Clair Drake, *Black Metropolis: A Study of Negro Life in a Northern City,* passim.

38. Minutes of the Fifty-Eighth Session of the North Ohio Conference, Cleveland, Ohio, October, 1939, Ransom speech.

39. Ibid., Election of delegates to the General Conference.

40. Frank Steward, "A Stranger Goes to Church," *The Cleveland Press,* November 9, 1939.

41. Joseph Gomez to George Singleton (December 21, 1939) (Author's file).

42. Joseph Gomez, speech, Fifth Seminar on Judaism, Cleveland, Ohio, January 14, 1940 (Author's file).

43. Joseph Gomez to delegates to the A.M.E. General Conference, February 29, 1940 (Author's file).

44. Joseph Gomez to George Singleton (April 10, 1940) (Author's file).

45. Minutes of the Thirty-First General Conference of the A.M.E. Church, Detroit, Michigan, May 1940, Opening.

46. Ibid., New Episcopal District.

47. Ibid., Election of bishops.

48. Ibid., New legislature.

49. *Cleveland Call and Post,* May 16, 1940.

50. Ibid., October 19, 1940.

51. Morgan, *FDR,* p. 536.

52. *Cleveland Call and Post,* March 1, 1941.

53. *Christian Recorder,* May 15, 1941.

54. Ibid.

55. *Cleveland Plain Dealer,* May 5, 1941.

56. *Cleveland Call and Post,* May 15, 1941.

57. Morgan, pp. 593–595.

58. *Cleveland Call and Post,* July 5, 1941.

59. Ibid.

60. John A. Gregg to Joseph Gomez (July 8, 1941).

61. Morgan, pp. 614–616.

62. *Cleveland Call and Post,* January 11, 1942.

63. Ibid.

64. Thomas, *Life for Us Is What We Make It,* pp. 143–148.

65. *Cleveland Call and Post,* April 16, 1942.

66. Ibid., June 13, 1942.

67. Ibid.

68. Program, Wilberforce University Seventy-Ninth Commencement, Wilberforce, Ohio, June 11, 1942.

69. *Cleveland Call and Post,* October 17, 1942.

70. Joseph Gomez, speech, Oberlin Graduate School of Theology, Oberlin, Ohio, December 1, 1942 (Author's file).

71. Certificate, Award of Merit, Church Civic League of Greater Cleveland, to Rev. Joseph Gomez, January 27, 1943 (Author's file).

72. *Cleveland Plain Dealer,* January 27, 1943.

73. Ibid.

74. Joseph Gomez, sermon, Old Stone Church, Cleveland, Ohio, April 23, 1943.

75. Program of Ceremony of Appreciation for Rev. and Mrs. Joseph Gomez, St. James A.M.E. Church, Cleveland, Ohio, May 10, 1943.

76. Wm. H. Peck, to Rev. and Mrs. Joseph Gomez (May 6, 1943) (Author's file).

77. Ransom, *Pilgrimage,* p. 291.

78. Funeral Program, Emma Sarah Ransom, Wilberforce University, Wilberforce, Ohio, May 18, 1943.

79. Program of Eighty-First Commencement of Glenville High School, Cleveland, Ohio, June 10, 1943.

80. *Cleveland Call and Post,* June 26, 1943.

81. Ibid., October 7, 1943.

82. Ibid.

83. Minutes of the Sixty-Second North Ohio Annual Conference, Lima, Ohio, October 1943, Election of delegates to General Conference.

84. Arthur C. Spath to Rev. Joseph Gomez (February 29, 1944).

85. Joseph Gomez, radio address WGAR, Cleveland, Ohio, April 16, 1944.

9. ON MA' JOURNEY NOW: CLEVELAND, 1944–1948

1. Minutes of the Thirty-Second General Conference of the A.M.E. Church, Philadelphia, Pennsylvania, May 1944, Opening.

2. Ibid., Eleanor Roosevelt

3. Ibid., Legislation.

4. Ibid., Election of bishops.

5. Ibid.

6. Ibid.

7. *Cleveland Call and Post,* May 13, 1944.

8. Minutes of the Sixty-Third North Ohio Annual Conference, Cleveland, Ohio, September 1944, Introduction of Myrtle Teal Ransom.

9. Ransom, *Pilgrimage,* p. 323.

10. Ibid.

11. Minutes of North Ohio A.C., 1944, National elections.

12. Ibid., Bishops' election at last General Conference.

13. Joseph Gomez, Christmas Message, 1944 (Author's file).

14. *Cleveland Call and Post,* March 10, 1945.

15. *Cleveland Call and Post,* April 7, 1945.

16. Morgan, *FDR,* pp. 763–764.

17. *Cleveland Call and Post,* October 5, 1946.

18. Program, Vocal Recital, Irma Clark, Eula Gomez, Wilberforce University, Wilberforce, Ohio, May 24, 1946.

19. Program, 83rd Annual Commencement, Wilberforce University, Wilberforce, Ohio, June 13, 1946.

20. Minutes of the Special Session of the General Conference A.M.E. Church, November 1946, Opening.

21. Ibid., Charges.

22. Ibid., 1946. Decisions.

23. Ibid., 1946. Legislation.

24. *Cleveland Call and Post,* December 7, 1946.

25. *Cleveland Call and Post,* December 14, 1946.

26. *Cleveland Call and Post,* February 15, 1947.

27. Civic Committee of the Interdenominational Ministerial Alliance of Greater Cleveland to the City of Cleveland, February 11, 1947 (Author's file).

28. Ibid.

29. McGinnis, *Wilberforce University,* p. 57.

30. D. Ormond Walker, "The Struggle for Control of Wilberforce University," address, St. James Literary Forum, Cleveland, Ohio, April 27, 1947 (printed at Wilberforce and distributed).

31. Lathardus Goggins, *Central State University: The First One Hundred Years, 1887–1987,* pp. 5–6.

32. Walker, "The Struggle," p. 4.

33. Goggins, *Central State,* pp. 20, 22.

34. *Cleveland Call and Post,* May 21, 1974.

35. "The Wilberforce Dilemma," *Wilberforce University Bulletin,* January, 1948, pp. 17–28.

36. Goggins, *Central State,* p. 27.

37. "The Wilberforce Dilemma," pp. 5–6.

38. *Cleveland Call and Post,* April 26, 1947.

39. Ibid.

40. Ibid.

41. Ibid., May 3, 1947.

42. "The Wilberforce Dilemma," p. 6.

43. Printed Charges by Bishop R. C. Ransom against Dr. Charles Wesley, Wilberforce University, Wilberforce, Ohio, May 1947.

44. *Cleveland Call and Post,* May 31, 1947.

45. Ibid., August 16, 1947.

46. "The Wilberforce Dilemma," p. 32.

47. *Cleveland Call and Post,* June 21, 1947.

48. Joseph Gomez to Thomas J. Herbert (September 8, 1947) (Author's file).

49. *Cleveland Call and Post,* January 17, 1948.

50. Goggins, *Central State,* p. 32.

51. Minutes of the Sixty-Sixth North Ohio Annual Conference, Toledo, Ohio, October 1947, Ransom's speech.

52. Ibid., Loeb's speech.

53. Ibid., Prayer Day for Wilberforce University.

54. Ibid., Ransom's speech.

55. Ibid., Charles Leander Hill's speech.

56. Ibid., Closing sermon.

57. Minutes of the Thirty-Third General Conference of the A.M.E. Church, Kansas City, Missouri, May 1948, Opening session.

58. Ibid., Ransom prayer.

59. *Cleveland Call and Post,* May 21, 1948.

60. Minutes of General Conference, 1948, Gregg resolution.

61. Ibid., Seconding speeches.

62. Ibid., Paul Robeson.

63. Ibid., Episcopal Committee report.

64. *Southern Christian Recorder,* May 29, 1948.

65. Minutes of General Conference, 1948, Death of Fannie K. Smith.

66. Ibid., Election of bishops.

67. *Southern Christian Recorder,* May 29, 1948.

68. Minutes of General Conference, 1948, Election of bishops completed.

69. Ibid., Consecration of bishops, and Communion.

70. Ibid., Election of general officers.

71. Ibid., Assignment of bishops.

72. Ibid., Committee on Revision of the Discipline.

73. Ibid., Bishops' Council meeting.

74. Congratulatory messages: Attorney Sadie Alexander (May 21,1948), Frank J. Lausche (May 22, 1948), Rev. S. N. Tladi (May 18, 1948) (Author's file).

75. Program, Funeral Services of Bishop Henry Y. Tookes, Jacksonville, Florida, June 15, 1948.

76. Minutes of Emergency Session of the Bishops' Council Jacksonville, Florida, June 15, 1948.

77. Minutes of Bishops' Council, Atlantic City, New Jersey, June 23, 1948.

78. *Southern Christian Recorder,* July 10, 1948.

79. *Cleveland Plain Dealer,* June 12, 1948.

80. Ibid., August 2, 1948.

81. Ibid.

82. Ibid.

10. YELLOW ROSES AND THORNS: TEXAS, 1948–1951

1. *An Era of Construction* (pamphlet), Waco, Texas, 1954.

2. Paul Quinn College Catalogue, Waco, Texas, n.d.

3. Bishop John H. Clayborn, "Poor Bleeding Africa," *Christian Recorder,* July 1, 1948.

4. J. P. Wallace, "He Must Go!" *Christian Recorder,* July 10, 1948.

5. Bishop John H. Clayborn, "Haven't You Had Enough Broken Laws," *Christian Recorder,* July 20, 1948.

6. The A.M.E. Discipline. sec. 172, p. 195.

7. Bishop Joseph Gomez, handwritten article on the episcopacy, November 1948 (Author's file).

8. *Waco Messenger,* August 30, 1948.

9. Ibid.

10. Minutes of the Paul Quinn College Board of Trustees, August 28, 1948.

11. *Southern Christian Recorder,* September 11, 1948.

12. Minutes of the Mexico and Rio Grande Valley Annual Conference, Corpus Christi, Texas, September, October 1948, Opening.

13. Ibid., Bishop's speech.

14. Minutes of the Texas Annual Conference, Galveston, Texas, October 1948, Abington.

15. Minutes of the North Texas Annual Conference, Corsicana, Texas, November 1948, Reports.

16. *Waco Messenger,* November 28, 1948.

17. L. Nerissa Mance to Joseph Gomez (November 15, 1948) (Author's file).

18. Herbert L. Dudley to Joseph Gomez (November 28, 1948) Enclosure, letter from Bishop S.L. Green (November 24, 1948) (Author's file).

19. Joseph Gomez, eulogy delivered at the funeral of Bishop George B. Young, Waco, Texas, February 9, 1949.

20. George Singleton to Joseph Gomez (February 8, 1949) (Author's file).

21. Minutes of the Bishops' Council, Washington, D.C., February 1949.

22. *Waco News-Tribune,* April 27, 1949.

23. Joseph Gomez, speech, Second Yearly Meeting of the Waco Commission on Interracial Cooperation, April 28, 1949 (Author's file).

24. *Waco Messenger,* May 6, 1949.

25. Program, recital given by Eula Gomez-Butler, Waco, Texas, May 17, 1949.

26. Susan L. Pardon to Hazel and Joseph Gomez, Waco, Texas (May 23, 1949) (Author's file).

27. Doctor of Letters Degree from Paul Quinn College to Bishop Joseph Gomez, May 26, 1949.

28. Following quotations and information from Hazel Gomez, journal of trip to Trinidad, May–June, 1949 (Author's file).

29. *Trinidad Guardian,* June 8, 1949.

30. Minutes of the Paul Quinn Board of Trustees, Waco, Texas, July 1949.

31. Ibid.

32. *Pittsburgh Courier,* September 10, 1949.

33. *Informer,* September 3, 1949.

34. Ibid.

35. State Approval Agency to Nannie Belle Aycox, copy to Bishop Joseph Gomez (October 26, 1949).

36. John C. Horn to Joseph Gomez with enclosing to Nannie Belle Aycox (October 27, 1949).

37. Minutes of the West Texas Annual Conference, Smithville, Texas, November 1949, Brenham District report.

38. Joseph Gomez, speech, Baylor University, Waco, Texas, November 8, 1949 (Author's file).

39. *Christian Recorder,* November 10, 1949.

40. Minutes of the Northeast Texas Annual Conference, Denison, Texas, November 1949, Womack report.

41. Minutes of the North Texas Annual Conference, Fort Worth, Texas, November 1949, Bishop Ransom speech.

42. Reverdy C. Ransom to Bishop and Mrs. Gomez (December 5, 1949) (Author's file).

43. Ibid.

44. James Gomez to Joseph Gomez with enclosed letter from Cyril Gomez (February 13, 1950).

45. Ibid.

46. Ibid.

47. Ibid.

48. *Cleveland News,* March 16, 1950.

49. Program, Howard University, All University Religious Service, Washington, D.C., April 16, 1950.

50. Joseph Gomez, Eulogy, funeral of Rev. F. W. Grant, Dallas, Texas, April 27, 1950.

51. Reverdy C. Ransom to Joseph Gomez (May 1, 1950) (Author's file).

52. Ibid.

53. Joseph Gomez to all ministers of the 10th Episcopal District (April 3, 1950) (Author's file).

54. *Texas Layman,* vol. 1, Waco, Texas, August 1950.

55. *Southern Christian Recorder,* May 22, 1950.

56. *Waco News Tribune,* August 24, 1950.

57. *Southern Christian Recorder,* September 2, 1950.

58. *Waco News-Tribune,* August 24, 1950.

59. A.C. Upleger and Company, Audit Report of Paul Quinn College, Waco, Texas, August 31, 1950.

60. *Waco News-Tribune,* September 1950.

61. Minutes of the Mexico–Rio Grande Valley Annual Conference, Corpus Christi, Texas, September 1950, New accountant and auditor.

62. Ibid., Mrs. Aycox.

63. Minutes of the West Texas Annual Conference, Bellville, Texas, November 1950, Womack's endorsement.

64. Minutes of the North Texas Annual Conference, Fort Worth, Texas, November 1950, Bishop Joseph Gomez's sermon.

65. Joseph Gomez, printed Christmas message, December 1950 (Author's file).

66. John C. Horn to Nannie Belle Aycox, copy to Bishop Joseph Gomez (February 20, 1951).

67. Minutes of the Paul Quinn College Board of Trustees, Waco, Texas, June 1951.

68. Ibid.

69. Rev. Prince F. Jackson to Nannie Belle Aycox (May 26, 1951) (Author's file).

70. C. W. Cubia, "Aycox Dismissed from Paul Quinn," *Informer,* June 2, 1951.

71. Ibid.

72. Joseph Gomez, "Version of President Aycox's Ouster," *Informer,* June 2, 1951.

73. Ibid.

1. *Waco News-Tribune,* June 17, 1951.
2. L. P. Sturgeon to Sherman L. Greene (June 18, 1951).
3. Minutes of the Paul Quinn Board of Trustees, June 1951.
4. *Waco News-Tribune,* August 17, 1951.
5. Joseph Gomez, Journal on trip to Eighth Ecumenical Conference of Methodists. Oxford, England. August 22–September 24, 1951. All material on Oxford trip is drawn from this source.
6. Minutes of the North West Annual Conference, Brownwood, Texas, October 1951, Delegates to the General Conference.
7. *Houston Informer,* December 9, 1951.
8. Ibid., January 12, 1952.
9. P. E. Womack to Joseph Gomez (February 10, 1952) (Emphasis supplied).
10. Case No. 40748, Original Charge, *G. W. Brown et al. vs. Bishop Joseph Gomez,* District Court of McClennon County, Texas, 19th Judicial District, R. B. Stanford, District Judge, March 19, 1952.
11. Ibid.
12. Ibid., Original Amended Petition, G. W. Brown, et al., March 24, 1952.
13. Ibid., Original Answer, R. L. H. Rice, Hilton E. Howell, attorneys for the defendant, and Bishop Joseph Gomez, March 25, 1952.
14. Decision, District Judge R. B. Stanford, District Court of McClennon County, Texas, 19th Judicial District, March 18, 1952.
15. *Waco Tribune Herald,* May 3, 1952.
16. Minutes of the Thirty-Fourth General Conference of the A.M.E. Church, Chicago, Illinois, May 1952.
17. Ibid., Delegates assigned to Episcopal Committee.
18. Ibid., Texas delegates confirmed.
19. Ibid., Judicial Council created.
20. Ibid., 1952. Episcopal Committee report.
21. Ibid., Retirement of Ransom.
22. Ibid.
23. Ibid., 1952. Election of bishops.
24. Ibid., Reappointment of Gomez.
25. *Christian Recorder,* September 4, 1952.
26. *Southwestern Christian Recorder,* November 8, 1952. (The issue was dedicated to 10th Episcopal District.)
27. Rev. C. W. Abington, "The Whole Truth About African Methodism in Texas," *Waco Messenger,* January 16, 1953. All Abington material is taken from this source.
28. Waco Publication of Chamber of Commerce, January 1953.
29. Copy of charges of Revs. E. L. Burton, C. H. Sanders, and J. Bennett Brown to the A.M.E. Church against Revs. G. E. Browne, I. S. Aycox, E. A. Thomas, L. S. Godley, John D. Walker, U. S. Washington, S. E. Sims, M. C. Collins, January 6, 1953.
30. Report of Special Trial Committee of 10th Episcopal District, January 23, 1953.
31. *Houston Informer,* February 2, 1953.
32. Joseph Gomez, eulogy, funeral of Rev. Thomas R. Clemons, Waco, Texas, February 6, 1953 (Author's file).

33. Joseph Gomez, eulogy, funeral of Bishop John A. Gregg, Kansas City, Kansas, February 17, 1953, in *A.M.E. Review,* February 1953.

34. Ibid.

35. *Dallas Morning News,* May 5, 1953.

36. C. C. Davis to Joseph Gomez (May 5, 1953) (Author's file).

37. *Nashville Banner,* May 8, 1953.

38. Minutes of Paul Quinn College Board of Trustees, May 1953.

39. *Waco News-Tribune,* May 12, 1953.

40. Ibid., May 13, 1953.

41. Joseph Gomez, speech, WACO. May 15, 1953 (Author's file).

42. Reverdy C. Ransom to Joseph Gomez (June 16, 1953).

43. Mayor Edgar Dean, Proclamation, Fort Worth, Texas, Paul Quinn College Disaster Fund Day, June 16, 1953.

44. *Waco Messenger,* September 19, 1953.

45. Minutes of the Northwest Texas Annual Conference, Lubbock, Texas, October 1953, Judiciary Committee ruling.

46. Minutes of the Southwest Texas Annual Conference, San Antonio, Texas, October 1953, Judiciary Committee ruling.

47. Minutes of the West Texas Conference, Bastrop, Texas, October–November 1953, Illegal selling of Wyman Chapel, Temple, Texas.

48. Minutes of the Central Texas Conference, Waco, Texas, November 1953, Connectional property.

49. Ibid., Womack incident.

50. Minutes of the Northeast Texas Conference, Corsicana, Texas, November 1953, Gomez speech.

51. Ibid., A.S.B. Jones incident.

52. Ibid., Jones demotion.

53. *Houston Informer,* November 27, 1953; *Afro American,* November 28, 1953.

54. *Waco Tribune-Herald,* December 16, 1953.

55. Program, Annual Meeting Texas Council of Churches, Austin, Texas, January 6–8, 1954.

56. Joseph Gomez, Speech, Texas Council of Churches, January 6, 1954.

57. *Austin Statesman,* January 7, 1954.

58. Ibid.

59. Harold Kilpatrick to Joseph Gomez (January 28, 1954) (Author's file).

60. Reverdy C. Ransom to Joseph Gomez (January 8, 1954) (Author's file).

61. *Waco News-Tribune,* January 17, 1954.

62. *Waco Farm and Labor Journal,* March 26, 1954.

63. Ibid.

64. *Waco News-Tribune,* March 31, 1954.

65. *Courier,* April 24, 1954.

66. Joseph Gomez, speech, six universities in Atlanta, January 30, 1955 (Author's file).

67. *Christian Recorder,* February 17, 1955.

68. Program of the Bishops' and Connectional Council, Waco, Texas, February 23–25, 1955.

69. *Waco Times-Herald,* February 25, 1955.

70. Ibid.

71. Ibid., March 6, 1955.

72. Minutes of the Special Session of the Bishops' Council, Kansas City, Missouri, June 28, 1955.

73. Officers and members of the Second A.M.E. Church, Los Angeles, California, to Joseph Gomez (July 9, 1955).

74. *Cleveland Call and Post,* August 13, 1955.

75. Minutes of the Central Texas Conference, Austin, Texas, November 1955, Womack incident.

76. *Houston Informer,* March 17, 1956.

77. Minutes of the Judicial Council, Cleveland, Ohio, April 6–8, 1956.

78. Ibid.

79. Ibid.

80. Reid E. Jackson to Frank Veal (March 25, 1956) (Author's file).

81. Ibid.

82. Ibid.

83. *Georgia African Methodist,* vol. 21, no. 3, March 1956.

84. Resolution, Waco District of the Central Texas Conference, McGregor, Texas. April 12, 1956, in *Houston Informer,* April 7, 1955.

85. W.R. White to delegates to the General Conference, Miami, Florida, in *The Texas Record,* May 1955.

86. Harold Kilpatrick to delegates to the General Conference, Miami, Florida, in *The Texas Record,* May 1955.

87. Sidney Dobbins to Joseph Gomez, in *The Texas Record,* May 1955

88. Pamphlet, *The Texas Record,* published and distributed by the 10th Episcopal District of the A.M.E. Church, May 1955.

89. Minutes of the Thirty-Fifth General Conference of the A.M.E. Church, Miami, Florida, May 1956, Quadrennial Sermon.

90. Ibid., Passage of the budget.

91. Ibid., Episcopal Committee ruling.

92. Ibid., Gomez sermon.

93. Ibid., Civil rights.

94. Ibid., Election of bishops.

95. Ibid., Reinstatement of Sims.

96. Ibid., Assignment of bishops.

97. Joseph Gomez, speech WACO, n.d.

98. *Waco News-Tribune,* May 28, 1956.

12. BACK TO BETHEL: FROM TENNESSEE AND KENTUCKY TO MICHIGAN, 1956–1964

1. Reverdy C. Ransom to Joseph Gomez (January 20, 1956) (Author's file).

2. *Christian Recorder,* June 28, 1956.

3. Program, funeral Services for Bishop Alexander Joseph Allen, Cleveland, Ohio, November 27, 1956.

4. Minutes of the Special Session of the Bishops' Council, Cleveland, Ohio, November 27, 1956.

5. *Cleveland Call and Post,* January 19, 1957.

6. *Chicago Defender,* February 10, 1957.

7. Joseph Gomez, speech, Grant Memorial, Chicago, Illinois, February 10, 1957 (Author's file).

8. Program, welcome banquet, The Parkway, Chicago, Illinois, February 13, 1957.

9. Program, welcome reception, Bethel A.M.E. Church, Detroit, Michigan, March 1, 1957.

10. *Bermuda Royal Gazette,* May 11, 1957.

11. Minutes of the Chicago Annual Conference, Chicago, Illinois, September 1957, State of the Country Committee report.

12. *Cleveland News,* January 28, 1959

13. *Springfield (Ohio) Sun,* April 23, 1959.

14. *Journal Herald,* Dayton, Ohio, April 23, 1959; *Chicago Defender,* April 23, 1959.

15. Joseph Gomez, "Reverdy Cassius Ransom: Prevailer Extraordinary," eulogy, funeral of Bishop Reverdy Cassius Ransom, Wilberforce, Ohio, April 28, 1959.

16. Program, appreciation banquet for Bishop and Mrs. Joseph Gomez, Coppin Chapel, Chicago, Illinois, March 31, 1960.

17. Rev. Hubert and Mary Robinson to Bishop and Mrs. Joseph Gomez for Book of Tributes, n.d. (Author's file).

18. Minutes of the Thirty-Sixth General Conference, Los Angeles, California, May 1960, Report of Judicial Council.

19. Ibid., Opening services.

20. Ibid., Judicial Council and Nichols suspension.

21. Ibid., Episcopal address.

22. Ibid.

23. Ibid., Restoration of Sims.

24. Ibid., May 1960. Election of bishops.

25. Ibid., Assignment of bishops.

26. Minutes of the Chicago Annual Conference, Milwaukee, Wisconsin, September 1960, Presidential election.

27. Minutes of the Illinois Annual Conference, Champaign, Illinois, September–October 1960, Presidential election.

28. *San Francisco News,* December 5, 1960.

29. Joseph Gomez, typed Prayer, Public Session of the National Council of Churches of Christ in the United States of America, San Francisco, California, December 8, 1960 (Author's file).

30. *Michigan Chronicle,* January 7, 1961.

31. Ibid.

32. Sam Rayburn to Joseph Gomez (January 6, 1961) (Author's file).

33. Picture of bishops in front of the White House with President John F. Kennedy, January 21, 1961.

34. *Christian Recorder,* January 31, 1961.

35. Joseph Gomez, Handwritten statement to Bishops' Council, Louisville, Kentucky, February 15, 1961 (Author's file).

36. James Gomez to Joseph Gomez (May 8, 1961) (Author's file).

37. *Indianapolis Recorder,* June 14, 1961.

38. *Christian Recorder,* July 1961.

39. Archibald J. Carey, Jr., "The Negro Methodist Churches in America," 10th World Methodist Conference, Oslo, Norway, August 18, 1961.

40. Minutes of the Michigan Annual Conference, Detroit, Michigan, September 1961, Telegrams.

41. Minutes of the Chicago Annual Conference, Chicago, Illinois, October 1961, Committee on State of the Country report.

42. Anthony J. Celebreeze, open letter of introduction for Bishop and Mrs. Joseph Gomez (November 5, 1961) (Author's file).

43. Joseph Gomez, Handwritten log. "Special to the Cleveland Call and Post," New Delhi, India. November 30, 1961. passim (Author's file).

44. Joseph Gomez, Handwritten log, *"Special to the Cleveland Call and Post,"* Israel, December 6, 1961, passim.

45. *World Parish,* February 1962.

46. Itinerary, December 3–7, 1962.

47. *Cleveland Press,* March 15, 1962.

48. Itinerary, December 10, 1962.

49. *Cleveland Press,* March 15, 1962.

50. *Pittsburgh Courier,* February 24, 1962.

51. Program *Pittsburgh Courier "Appreciation Day,"* Soldiers and Sailors Memorial Hall, Pittsburgh, Pennsylvania, February 25, 1962.

52. *Christian Recorder,* August 28, 1962.

53. Minutes of the Michigan Annual Conference, Flint, Michigan, August–September, 1962, Condition of the Church Committee report.

54. Minutes of the Chicago Annual Conference, St. Paul, Minnesota, September 1962, Condition of the Church Committee report.

55. Minutes of the Indiana Annual Conference, Richmond, Indiana, September 1962, Condition of the Church Committee report.

56. Ibid., Civil Rights.

57. Minutes of the Illinois Annual Conference, East St. Louis, Illinois, 1962, Civil Rights.

58. Ibid., Committee on Condition of the Church.

59. Ibid., Telegram to Governor Otto Kerner.

60. Robert T. Fauth to Joseph Gomez (April 9, 1963) (Author's file).

61. Program Agricultural, Mechanical and Normal College baccalaureate services, Pine Bluff, Arkansas, May 26, 1963.

62. *Detroit Free Press,* June 19, 1963.

63. Civil Violence Research Center, Case Western Reserve University, *Report to the National Commission on the Causes and Prevention of Violence: Shoot-Out in Cleveland,* p. 7.

64. *Indianapolis Morning Tribune,* July 5, 1963.

65. Ibid.

66. Ibid.

67. Joseph Gomez, sermon, "Corporate Guilt and Responsibility in the Church," Connectional Laymen's Convention, August 5–10, 1963.

68. Minutes of the Canadian Annual Conference, Harrow, Ontario, August 1963, King's visit.

69. Minutes of the Michigan Annual Conference, Detroit, Michigan, August 1963, March on Washington.

70. Minutes of the Chicago Annual Conference, Chicago, Illinois, September 1963, Commendations.

71. Minutes of the Illinois Annual Conference, Des Moines, Iowa, September 1963, Resolution to Robert Kennedy.

72. Minutes of the Indiana Annual Conference, Indianapolis, Indiana, September 1963, Recommendations.

73. *Shoot-Out in Cleveland,* p. 7.

74. Ibid.

75. Ibid., p. 7, 8.

76. Ibid., pp. 7, 8, 9.

77. Ibid., pp. 8, 9, 10.

78. Joseph Gomez, manuscript, Episcopal Address, January 8, 1964 (Author's file).

79. Ibid.

80. *4th District Story,* December, 1956 to May 1964.

81. Ibid.

82. Minutes of the 37th General Conference of the A.M.E. Church, Cincinnati, Ohio, May 1964, Quadrennial Sermon.

83. Ibid., Missionary Night.

84. Ibid., Martin Luther King speech.

85. Ibid., Civil rights and other recognitions.

86. Ibid., Election of bishops and consecration.

87. Ibid., The Episcopal Committee recommendations and assignments of bishops.

88. Ibid., Resolutions.

89. Ibid., Closing.

13. THE GOLDEN YEARS: 1964–1967

1. Biographical sketch of Archbishop John Kodwo Amissah, 1964.

2. Bernard L. Strange to Joseph Gomez (April 20, 1964).

3. *Indianapolis News,* May 25, 1964.

4. Ibid. and May 30, 1964.

5. Program, Archbishop Amissah Day in Indianapolis, Sunday, May 24, 1964.

6. Honorary degree of Doctor of Divinity from Eden Theological Seminary of the United Church of Christ, to Bishop Joseph Gomez, June 5, 1964.

7. Joseph Gomez, sermon, "Dynamics of the Christian Ministry," Eden Seminary, Webster Grove, Missouri, June 5, 1964.

8. *Christian Recorder,* July 21, 1964.

9. Minutes of the Canadian Annual Conference, Chatham, Ontario, August 1964, Planning anniversary ceremony.

10. Minutes of the Illinois Annual Conference, Springfield, Illinois, September 1964, Committee on the State of the Country.

11. Minutes of the Indiana Annual Conference, East Chicago, Indiana, September 1964, Committee on the State of the Country.

12. *Cleveland Plain Dealer,* November 14, 1964.

13. *Christian Recorder,* December 29, 1964.

14. Ibid.

15. Ibid.

16. *Chicago Courier,* November 21, 1964.

17. Ibid.

18. *Trinidad News,* November 28, 1964.

19. *Christian Recorder,* December 29, 1964.

20. Ibid.

21. Ibid.

22. Ibid.

23. *Cleveland Plain Dealer,* November 14, 1964.

24. *A.M.E. Missionary Magazine,* December 1964.

25. Bishop and Mrs. Joseph Gomez, printed Christmas message, Cleveland, Ohio, 1964.

26. Peter Goldman, *The Death and Life of Malcolm X,* p. 303.

27. *Christian Index,* April 22, 1965.

28. Ibid.

29. Joseph Gomez, excerpts from "Conscience and the Cross," Old Stone Church, Cleveland, Ohio, April 5, 1965.

30. Joseph Gomez, sermon, "When Sight Becomes Vision," Old Stone Church, Cleveland, Ohio, April 6, 1965 (Author's file).

31. Ralph Locher to Edward C. Taylor (April 16, 1965).

32. *Daily Mirror* and *Port-of-Spain Trinidad Guardian,* both April 21, 1965.

33. *Atlanta World,* June 1, 1965.

34. Violet Glass to Joseph Gomez (June 21, 1965) (Author's file).

35. Funeral Program, Rev. A. Wayman Ward, Chicago, Illinois, July 2, 1965.

36. Joseph Gomez, sermonettes, Camp Baber, Cassapolis, Michigan, April 1–7, 1965 (Author's file).

37. Ibid.

38. Minutes of the Canadian Annual Conference, Windsor, Ontario, August 1965, Bishop Robinson presiding.

39. Minutes of the Michigan Annual conference, Detroit, Michigan, August, 1965, Commission on Expansion.

40. Ibid., Committee on the State of the Country.

41. Amanda Thomas to Joseph Gomez, 1965.

42. Ibid.

43. *Christian Recorder,* December 28, 1965.

44. Joseph Gomez, "The Ecumenical Outlook," *Pulpit,* vol. 27, no. 7, July–August 1966.

45. *Cleveland Plain Dealer,* March 2, 1966.

46. *Cleveland Press,* March 31, 1966.

47. *Cleveland Plain Dealer,* March 27, 1966.

48. Stephen B. Oates, *Let the Trumpet Sound,* p. 388.

49. *Chicago Tribune,* March 25, 1966.

50. Ibid.

51. Oates, *Let the Trumpet Sound,* p. 394.

52. Program, Fourteenth Annual Twilight Concert, Chancel Choir of St. James A.M.E. Church, Cleveland, Ohio, June 5, 1966.

53. Sargent Shriver to Joseph Gomez (June 17, 1966) (Author's file).

54. Charles S. Spivey, Sr., to Joseph Gomez (June 19, 1966).

55. Oates, *Let the Trumpet Sound,* pp. 11–12.

56. *Shoot-Out in Cleveland,* pp. 11–12.

57. Ibid., pp. 12–15.

58. Ibid.

59. Minutes of the Special Session of the Bishops' Council of the A.M.E. Church, London, England, August 22, 1966, Preparation for visit to President Johnson.

60. *Chicago Tribune,* September 28, 1966. The account of the visit is drawn from this source.

61. Minutes of the Michigan Annual Conference, Detroit, Michigan, September 1966, Equal Opportunity Project.

62. Minutes of the Chicago Annual Conference, Waterloo, Iowa, September 1966, Endorsements and appointments.

63. Minutes of the Indiana Annual Conference, Indianapolis, Indiana, September, 1966, Presentation of portrait of Bishop Gomez.

64. *New Courier,* December 24, 1966.

65. *Shoot-Out in Cleveland,* pp. 17–18.

66. Bishop Joseph Gomez, "The Bishop's Word," introduction to combined minutes of the 4th District's Annual Conferences, 1967.

67. Minutes of the Canadian Annual Conference, Toronto, Ontario, August 1967, Black power.

68. Minutes of the Chicago Annual Conference, Chicago, Illinois, September 1967, Bishop Joseph Gomez's sermon.

69. Minutes of the Illinois Annual Conference, East St. Louis, Illinois, September–October 1967, Committee on the State of the Country.

70. Ibid.

71. Ibid., Bishop Joseph Gomez's sermon.

72. Bishop and Mrs. Joseph Gomez, printed Christmas message, 1967.

73. Ibid.

14. AFRICA AT LAST: THE POLITY AND ZAMBIA, 1968–1972

1. *Chicago Defender,* February 3 and 9, 1968.

2. Joseph Gomez to Dr. J. L. Leach (March 20, 1968) (Author's file).

3. Flip Schulke, ed., *Martin Luther King, Jr.: A Documentary, Montgomery to Memphis,* p. 202.

4. *Christian Recorder,* March 12, 1968.

5. Minutes of the Thirty-Eighth A.M.E. General Conference, Philadelphia, Pennsylvania, May 1968. Opening Session.

6. Ibid., Seating of delegates.

7. Ibid., Gomez presides.

8. Ibid., Vice President Hubert Humphrey. The account of Humphrey's appearance is drawn from this source.

9. Ibid., Eula's solo.

10. Ibid., Sermon Bishop Joseph Gomez.

11. Ibid.

12. Ibid., Reaction to sermon.

13. Ibid., Speech Roy Wilkins, NAACP.

14. Ibid., Episcopal Committee.

15. Ibid., Greetings from Haiti.

16. Ibid., Young People's resolution.

17. Ibid., Bishop Nichols reinstated.

18. Ibid., Hughey resolution.

19. Ibid., Passage of 2nd Hughey resolution.

20. Ibid., Bishop Fred Jordan statement.

21. Ibid., Passage of two Gomez resolutions.

22. Ibid., Episcopal Committee.

23. Ibid., Election of bishops.

24. Ibid., Assignment of bishops.

25. Joseph Gomez to Sidney Jones (May 22, 1968) (Author's file).

26. Joseph Gomez to J. L. Leach (May 23, 1968) (Author's file).

27. Joseph Gomez to Rev. and Mrs. S. S. Morris (May 23, 1968) (Author's file).

28. Hubert Humphrey to Joseph Gomez (December 13, 1968) (Author's file).

29. *A.M.E. Review,* July–September 1968.

30. *Shoot-Out in Cleveland,* pp. 19–22.

31. Ibid., p. 38.

32. Ibid., pp. 57, 58.

33. Ibid., pp. 68–82.

34. Ibid., pp. 94, 95.

35. Joseph Gomez to Carey A. Gibbs (October 8, 1968) (Author's file).

36. Joseph Gomez, address, Adrian College, Adrian, Michigan, April 16, 1969 (Author's file).

37. Howard C. Emrick to Joseph Gomez (April 16, 1969) (Author's file).

38. James H. Cone, *Black Theology & Black Power,* chap. 2.

39. Cecily Wayne Cone, *The Identity Crisis in Black Theology,* p. 101.

40. Joseph Gomez, handwritten note, n.d. (Author's file).

41. James Forman. "Black Manifesto," April 26, 1969.

42. "Black Man at Critical Period—A.M.E. Bishop." n.p., May 10, 1969 (Author's file).

43. Program, celebration of the sixth anniversary of the Matilda Smith Williams Home for the Aged, Hamilton, Bermuda, May 29, 1969.

44. Joseph Gomez, Introduction, in *Polity of the A.M.E. Church,* pp. 10–11.

45. Funeral Program, Bishop George Wilbur Baber, Metropolitan A.M.E. Church, Washington, D.C., December 31, 1970.

46. Minutes of the Special Session of the Bishops' Council, Washington, D.C., December 31, 1970.

47. Joseph Gomez to Amanda Thomas (January 27, 1971) (Author's file).

48. Joseph Gomez to Rev. Jesse W. Cotton (January 27, 1971) (Author's file).

49. Vida M. Bright, "The 17th Episcopal District," November 1962, p. 1.

50. Kenneth Kaunda, *Zambia's Guideline for the Next Decade,* Address, National Council of UNIP, Mulungushi. November 9, 1968 (Lusaka: Zambia Information Services, September 1969).

51. Walton Johnson, *Worship and Freedom,* p. 5.

52. Ibid., p. 31.

53. Ibid., pp. 31–32.

54. Ibid.

55. Members of Sims Chapel to Joseph Gomez (February 28, 1971) (Author's file).

56. M. K. Waukunguma to Joseph Gomez (March 31, 1971) (Author's file).

57. S. J. N. T'ladi to Joseph Gomez (May 11, 1971) (Author's file).

58. Dewey Robinson to Joseph Gomez (May 19, 1971) (Author's file).

59. M. K. Waukunguma to Joseph Gomez (August 30, 1971) (Author's file).

60. Vida M. Bright, notebook, p. 5.

61. Minutes of the Bishops' Council, May 1971.

62. *Voice of Missions,* September 1971.

63. Joseph Gomez to Rev. M. K. Waukunguma (July 19, 1971) (Author's file).

64. Program, Missionary Society Convention, A.M.E. Church, Los Angeles, California, July 18–22, 1971.

65. Minutes, trial of Bishop W. F. Ball and A. G. Gaston, Los Angeles, California, July 19–22, 1971.

66. E. L. Hickman to Hazel T. Gomez (July 29, 1971) (Author's file).

67. M. K. Waukunguma to Joseph Gomez (October 5, 1971) (Author's file).

68. Richard Hall, *Zambia,* pp. 1–3.

69. F. O. Bennet to Joseph Gomez (September 1, 1971) (Author's file).

70. Kenneth Kaunda, speech, Mindola Ecumenical Center, October 1963.

71. Kenneth Kaunda "Zambia's Guideline for the Next Decade," address, National Council of UNIP, November 9, 1968.

72. Ibid.

15. SUNSET AND EVENING STAR: CLEVELAND AND WOOSTER, 1972–1979

1. Minutes of the Thirty-Ninth General Conference of the A.M.E. Church, Dallas, Texas, June–July 1972, Opening Service.

2. Ibid., Introduction of 17th District.

3. Ibid., Letter from Kenneth David Kaunda.

4. Ibid., Zambian support.

5. Ibid., Gomez retirement statement.

6. Ibid., Robinson's motion.

7. Ibid., Seconding speeches.

8. Ibid., Zambian resolution.

9. Ibid., Jesse Jackson speech.

10. Ibid., Other retirements.

11. Ibid., Elections of bishops.

12. Ibid., Death of Bishop Bryant.

13. Ibid., Memorial tribute.

14. Ibid., Election of bishops.

15. Ibid., Consecration of bishops.

16. *Guyana Daily Chronicle,* July 31, 1972.

17. Royston C. Lewis to Joseph Gomez (February 1, 1973) (Author's file).

18. *Christian Recorder,* November 11, 1974.

19. Program, 17th anniversary of Temple A.M.E. Church, Fort Wayne, Indiana, March 16, 1975.

20. Program, tribute banquet 30th anniversary of the A.M.E. ministers' wives of Cleveland, Cleveland, Ohio, October 30, 1975.

21. Program, Bishops' Council Summer Session, Atlantic City, New Jersey, June 1977.

22. Tape of funeral of Bishop Joseph Gomez, Bethel A.M.E. Church, Detroit, Michigan, May 2, 1979, Opening. The account of the funeral is drawn from this source. (Author's file).

23. Donald Jacobs to Gomez family (May 1, 1979) (Author's file).

24. Charles Diggs to Gomez family (May 1, 1979) (Author's file).

25. Russell and Sally Brown to Gomez family (May 1, 1979) (Author's file).

26. Rev. and Mrs. C. C. Johnson to Gomez family (April 30, 1979) (Author's file).

27. Frederick H. Talbot to Gomez family (May 21, 1979) (Author's file).

28. Resolution, Gomez Chapel, Rockford, Illinois, 1979 (Author's file).

29. Coleman McGehee, Jr., to Hubert Robinson for Gomez family (May 3, 1979) (Author's file).

30. Program, Memorial Service for Bishop Joseph Gomez, Bethel A.M.E. Church, Detroit, Michigan, May 2, 1979.

31. *A.M.E. Report*, May 1979.

32. Program, Memorial Services for Hazel T. Gomez, St. James A.M.E. Church, Cleveland, Ohio, January 25, 1983.

◈ ◈ ◈

Select Bibliography

The African Methodist Episcopal Church Discipline. Nashville: The A.M.E. Book Concern, 1972.

Anderson, Jervis. *This Was Harlem, 1900–1950*. New York: Farrar, Straus, Giroux, 1981.

Armstrong, Foster, et al. *A Guide to Cleveland's Sacred Landmarks*. Kent, Ohio: Kent State University Press, 1992.

Ayeast, Morley. *The British West Indies*. New York: New York University Press, 1960.

Bell, Wendell, ed. *The Democratic Revolution in the West Indies*. Cambridge, Mass.: Schenkman, 1967.

Benjamin, Susan Loewe. *The Decline of the West Indian Middle Class: 1834–1950*. Ph.D. dissertation. Columbia University, 1994.

Broderick, Francis L., and August Meier, eds. *Negro Protest Thought in the Twentieth Century*. Indianapolis: Bobbs Merrill, 1965.

Civil Violence Research Center, Case Western Reserve Unit. *Report to the National Commission on the Causes and Prevention of Violence: Shoot-out in Cleveland*. New York: New York Times Co., 1959.

Cone, Cecil Wayne. *The Identity Crisis in Black Theology*. Nashville: African Methodist Episcopal Church, 1975.

Cone, James H. *Black Theology and Black Power*. New York: Seabury, 1960.

Douglass, Frederick. "Oration in Memory of Abraham Lincoln." In Philip S. Foner, *The Voice of Black America*. Vol. 1. New York: Capricorn, 1972.

Drake, St. Claire. *Black Metropolis: a Study of Negro Life in a Northern City*. Vols. 1 & 2. New York: Harper and Row, 1945.

Du Bois, W. E. B. *The Autobiography of W. E. B. Du Bois*. New York: International Publishers, 1968.

Dyde, Brian. *Antigua and Barbuda: The Heart of the Caribbean*. New York: Macmillan, 1967.

Goggins, Lathardus. *Central State University: The First One Hundred Years, 1887–1987*. Wilberforce, Ohio: Central State University Press, 1988.

Goldman, Peter. *The Death and Life of Malcolm X*. Urbana: University of Illinois Press, 1973.

Gomez, Joseph. *The Polity of the African Methodist Episcopal Church*. Nashville: Division of Christian Education of the A.M.E. Church, 1971.

Gomez-Jefferson, Annetta L. *Through Love to Light: Excerpts from the Sermons, Addresses, and Prayers of Joseph Gomez, a Bishop in the A.M.E. Church*. Nashville: Christian Education Department of the A.M.E. Church, 1997.

Govia, Elsa Da. *Slave Society in the British Leward Islands*. New Haven: Yale University Press, 1965.

Grenville, J. A. S. *A History of the World in the Twentieth Century*. Cambridge: Belknap, 1994.

Hall, Richard. *Zambia*. New York: Frederick A. Praeger, 1965.

Hamshere, Cyril. *The British in the Caribbean*. Cambridge, Mass.: Harvard University Press, 1972.

Harlan, Louis R. *Booker T. Washington: The Wizard of Tuskegee, 1901–1915*. New York: Oxford University Press, 1983.

Haskell, Henry C., and Richard B. Fowler. *City of the Future: A Narrative History of Kansas City, 1850–1950*. Kansas City, Mo.: Frank Glenn, 1950.

Hayward, Walter B. *Bermuda Past and Present*. New York: Dodd, Mead, 1930.

Hughes, Langston. *Fight for Freedom: The Story of the NAACP*. New York: W. W. Norton, 1962.

Johnson, Walter. *Worship and Freedom*. New York: Africana, 1977.

Kusmer, Kenneth L. *A Ghetto Takes Shape: Black Cleveland, 1870–1930*. Chicago: University of Chicago Press, 1978.

Levine, David Allan. *Internal Combustion: The Races in Detroit, 1915–1926*. Westport, Conn.: Greenwood Press, 1976.

Lewis, David Levering. *When Harlem Was in Vogue*. Oxford: Oxford University Press, 1981.

McGinnis, Frederick A. *A History and an Interpretation of Wilberforce University*. Blanchester, Ohio: Brown, 1941.

Mitchell, Franklin D. *Embattled Democracy: Missouri Democratic Politics, 1919–1932*. Columbia: University of Missouri Press, 1968.

Morgan, Ted. *F.D.R.: A Biography*. New York: Simon and Schuster, 1985.

Oates, Stephen B. *Let the Trumpet Sound*. New York: Harper and Row, 1982.

Osofsky, Gilbert. *Harlem: The Making of a Ghetto, New York, 1890–1939*. 2d ed. New York: Harper and Row, 1970.

Pereira, Eduardo C. N. *Lehas de Zargo*. Funchal, Madeira: Adecio de Camra, 1889.

Peters, J. Jerome, et al. *The Story of the Kappa Alpha Psi Fraternity, 1932–1967*. Philadelphia: Kappa Alpha Psi, 1967.

Quarles, Benjamin. *The Negro in the Making of America*. 2d ed. New York: Macmillan, 1969.

Ransom, Reverdy Cassius. *The Negro: The Hope or the Despair of Christianity*. Boston: Ruth Hill Publishers, 1935.

———. *The Pilgrimage of Harriet Ransom's Son*. Nashville: A.M.E. Sunday School Union, 1950.

Sanders, Ron, ed. *Antigua and Barbuda Independence*. St. John, Antigua: Department of Information, 1986.

Schulke, Flip, ed. *Martin Luther King, Jr.: A Documentary, Montgomery to Memphis*. New York: W. W. Norton, 1976.

Southern, Eileen. *The Music of Black Americans*. New York: W. W. Norton, 1971.

Spear, Allan H. *Black Chicago: The Making of a Negro Ghetto, 1890–1920*. Chicago: University of Chicago Press, 1967.

Thomas, Richard W. *Life for Us Is What We Make It: Building Black Community in Detroit, 1915–1945*. Bloomington: Indiana University Press, 1992.

Washington, Booker T. "Atlanta Exposition Speech, 1895." In Leslie Fishel and Benjamin Quarles. *The Black American: A Documentary History*. New York: Scott, Foresman, 1967.

Weisbrot, Robert. *Father Divine and the Struggle for Racial Equality*. Urbana: University of Illinois Press, 1983.

Williams, George W. *History of the Negro Race in America, 1619–1880*. New York: G. P. Putnam Sons, 1882.

Wright, R. R., comp. *Encyclopaedia of African Methodism*. Vol. 1. Philadelphia: A.M.E. Book Concern, 1916.

———. *Encyclopaedia of African Methodism, 1948*. Philadelphia: A.M.E. Book Concern, 1947.

Zuill, William. *Bermuda Journey*. New York: Coward McCann, 1946.

Index

Abington, Dr. C. W., 210, 251–52
Adams, Bishop John Hurst, 363, 365
Africa, 350; A.M.E. Church in, 288, 306–7, 351–53
Africa (17th District), 350, 362–63
Aiken, Rev. James, 283
Alcohol: Joseph's fight against, 17, 86; problem on Bermuda, 56, 58; Ransom's struggle with, 23
Alexander, Sadie, 200
Allen, Betty Lou, 184
Allen, Bishop Alexander J., 161, 168, 169, 195
Allen, C. Emery, 80
Allen, Rev. Richard, 26, 66
Allen Anvil Awards, 299–300
Allen Chapel (Kansas City), 106–30
Allen Christian Endeavor League, Hazel's work in, 142
Alston, Isaiah H., 34
A.M.E. Church, 52, 66, 127, 168–69, 208, 211, 363; in Africa, 351–53, 357–58; and dissident ministers, 251, 254–55; historiographers of, 195–96, 249, 286; history of, 26, 62, 279–80, 349–50; and Independent A.M.E. Church, 254, 258–61; Joseph's continued love for, 182, 187; Joseph's decision to leave, 102, 104, 362; and Organic Union, 77, 105, 161, 288, 317; Polity of, 308, 339–42; and role of Black religion, 345–46; schools of, 353, 359, 361; sectionalism in, 126, 129; status of, 64, 296–98, 301–2; and trial of

Sims, 184–87; and Western university, 112, 135–36; and Wilberforce University, 32, 172, 188–94, 193; at World Christian Endeavor Convention, 115–22. *See also* Civil rights movement, A.M.E. in; General Conferences
A.M.E. Polity (Gomez), 349–50
A.M.E. Review, Ransom as editor of, 69, 75
A.M.E. Zion Church, and Organic Union proposal, 77, 105, 161, 288, 317
Amissah, Most Reverend John Kodwo, 310–11, 314
Anderson, Vinton R., 364
Annual Conferences: Africa, 353; California, 268; 4th District, 283, 290–91, 296–99, 319–20, 329–30, 344; Guyana, 318; Joseph supervising 4th District, 280–81, 302–3, 330–32; Joseph supervising Texas, 209–12, 222–23, 231, 269–70; Joseph visiting while running for bishop, 142; Michigan, 80, 83, 93, 99, 106; Missouri, 135, 139, 142, 146–49; North Ohio, 155, 160–161, 165, 178, 181–82, 193–94; representation of laymen at, 169; Southwest Missouri, 112, 122; split of Independent A.M.E. at Texas, 253–54, 258–61; Texas, 243, 251, 265, 269; wedding anniversary celebrations at 4th District, 312–16
Annual Ministerial Institute, Missionary, and Youth Congress, 208, 219–20, 229–30, 237

Bright, Bishop John Douglas, 178, 195, 286, 288, 328, 339, 362, 364

Bristol, V. A., 93

Britain, Joseph's criticism of policies on Bermuda, 54–57

Brockington, Rev. Joseph, 314, 350, 373, 375, 378

Brookins, Bishop H. H., 364

Brooks, Bishop W. Sampson, 77–78, 98, 141, 251

Brown, Doris, 163, 176

Brown, Dr. Joseph, 303, 319, 348, 349

Brown, Floy Smith, 48

Brown, Hallie Quinn, 35–36, 224

Brown, Julia Anne Dent (Hazel's mother). See Perkins, Julia Anne

Brown, Rev. J. Bennett, 254

Brown, Russell S., 34, 48, 279, 313, 332, 376

Browne, Rev. G. E., 245, 251, 254

Browning, H. G., 117

Browning, L. C., 245, 249–51, 259, 261

Brumbaugh, Governor Martin G., 63

Bryant, Bishop Harrison J., 308, 354

Bryant, Ira T., 148, 168

Bryant, Presiding Elder L. P., 112–13

Bureau of Polity, 340–42, 347–49, 348, 364

Burks, Paul, 222, 231–32, 237

Burnette, Presiding Elder William, 139, 147

Burton, Arlyn, 99

Burton, DeWitt, 76, 99, 114–15

Burton, Mayor Harold H., 158, 159 ·

Burton, Rev. E. L., 254

Butchart, Dr. Franklin D., 158

Butler, Tory (son-in-law), 194, 235

Butler, William, 92

Butler children. See under Williams

Caldwell, Mamie and Marybelle, 132

California, Joseph helping with Annual Conferences, 268

Camp Baber, 280, 307, 319–20

Canada: Joseph as bishop of Ontario, 279–34; Joseph transferred to Hamilton, 65–71

Carey, Bishop Archibald J., 77–78, 104, 106, 290, 329

Carmichael, Stokely, 326, 335

Carr, W. A., 248

Carter, Joseph N., 34

Casper, A. C., 34

Catholics, 4–5, 7, 10, 16

Caulfield, Henry S., 110

Central Africa, Joseph assigned to district of, 350

Chandler, Dr. Edgar H. S., 313

Chappelle, Bishop William A., 76–77, 91

Chicago, 323–25, 329

Chikulumeni, Rev. J. C., 352

Church Assembly on Civil Rights, Joseph speaking at, 311–12

Church Civic League of Greater Cleveland, award for Joseph from, 175

Civil rights movement, 283–84, 289, 318, 331, 336; A.M.E. Church in, 272, 274, 286, 290, 298, 302–3, 307–8; in Chicago, 300–301; in Cleveland, 300, 303–6; discussed at conferences, 286, 302, 308–9, 312–13, 320; nonviolence in, 293–94, 326; in Ohio, 281–82

Clayborn, Bishop John H., 179–80, 207–8, 213

Clemons, Thomas R., 204, 234, 245, 254–55

Cleveland, Fletcher and Pinkie, 111

Cleveland, Ohio, 300, 359: civil rights movement in, 303–6 family Christmases in, 295–96, 330; Gomez family home in, 250, 253, 277, 281, 344, 365; importance of St. James to, 158–60; Joseph's ministry in, 149–78, 203; race relations in, 177–78, 187–88, 322, 326–27, 330, 343–44

Cleveland Methodist Ministers' Union, 173

C.M.E. Church, and Organic Union, 77, 105, 161, 288, 317

Cockburn, Rev. M., 68

Coker, Rev. Daniel, 351

Collier, Jewell, 133, 140, 145

Collins, Bishop George Napolean, 286, 288

Collins, Rev. M. C., 254, 258–59

Colored Interdenominational Ministers Alliance of A.M.E. Preachers, 74

Colored Ministerial Alliance, 95

Committee of Management of the YWCA, 110

In Darkness with God

was designed by Will Underwood;
composed in 9.8/13 Galliard
on a Power Macintosh using QuarkXPress
by The Book Page, Inc.; printed
by sheet-fed offset lithography
on 50-pound Turin Book natural stock
(an acid-free, totally chlorine-free paper) with
halftones printed on 70-pound, acid-free enamel stock,
Smyth sewn and bound over binder's boards
in Kennett cloth, and wrapped with dust jackets
printed in three colors on 100-pound enamel
stock coated with polypropylene
matt film lamination
by Thomson-Shore, Inc.;
and published by
The Kent State University Press
KENT, OHIO 44242 USA